Advance and Destroy

ADVANCE
AND
DESTROY

Patton as Commander in the Bulge

JOHN NELSON RICKARD

THE UNIVERSITY PRESS OF KENTUCKY

Scholarly publisher for the Commonwealth,
serving Bellarmine University, Berea College, Centre College of Kentucky, Eastern
Kentucky University, The Filson Historical Society, Georgetown College, Kentucky
Historical Society, Kentucky State University, Morehead State University, Murray
State University, Northern Kentucky University, Transylvania University, University of
Kentucky, University of Louisville, and Western Kentucky University.

ISBN 978-0-8131-3455-0

Manufactured in the United States of America.

The only way you can win a war is to attack
and keep on attacking, and after you have done that,
keep attacking some more.
—Patton

Patton was your best.
—*Generalfeldmarschall* Gerd von Rundstedt

Contents

Appendixes

Illustrations

Photographs

Following page 170

Bradley, Eisenhower, and Patton in the ruins of Bastogne
Patton and Brigadier General Anthony C. McAuliffe in Bastogne
Bradley decorates Patton with the Distinguished Service Order,
    December 29, 1944
Major General Joseph Lawton Collins and Field Marshal Sir Bernard L.
    Montgomery
Lieutenant General Courtney Hicks Hodges
Major General John Millikin
Patton and Major General Manton S. Eddy
Major General Troy H. Middleton
Major General Willard S. Paul
Major General Paul W. Baade
Major General Stafford Leroy "Red" Irwin
Major General Hugh J. Gaffey
Major General Otto P. Weyland
Field Marshal Karl Rudolf Gerd von Rundstedt
Field Marshal Walter Model
General Erich Brandenberger
General Hasso von Manteuffel
General Heinrich Freiherr von Lüttwitz

Figures

Maps

Tables

Key to the Maps

U.S. map symbols were used to depict enemy formations on G-2 maps and situation maps. For battle maps in the current work, German map symbols are used. Numerical designation of regiments and combat commands are employed when space does not permit the full unit designator.

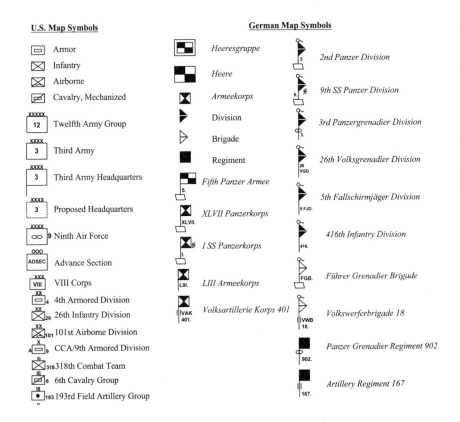

U.S. Map Symbols

Armor

Infantry

Airborne

Cavalry, Mechanized

12 Twelfth Army Group

3 Third Army

3 Third Army Headquarters

3 Proposed Headquarters

∞ 9 Ninth Air Force

ADSEC Advance Section

VIII VIII Corps

4 4th Armored Division

26 26th Infantry Division

101 101st Airborne Division

A 9 CCA/9th Armored Division

318 318th Combat Team

6 6th Cavalry Group

193 193rd Field Artillery Group

German Map Symbols

Heeresgruppe

Heere

Armeekorps

Division

Brigade

Regiment

Fifth Panzer Armee

XLVII Panzerkorps

I SS Panzerkorps

LIII Armeekorps

Volksartillerie Korps 401

2nd Panzer Division

9th SS Panzer Division

3rd Panzergrenadier Division

26th Volksgrenadier Division

5th Fallschirmjäger Division

416th Infantry Division

Führer Grenadier Brigade

Volkswerferbrigade 18

Panzer Grenadier Regiment 902

Artillery Regiment 167

8th Tank Battalion

818th Tank Destroyer Battalion

313th Field Artillery Battalion

22nd Armored Field Artillery Battalion

60th Armored Infantry Battalion

—xx— Unit/Formation Boundary

(-) Unit understrength

(+) Unit reinforced

318 318th Combat Team*

U.S. Symbols for G-2 Work Maps

Army Group G

First Army

XIII SS Corps

559th Volks Grenadier Division

25th Panzer Grenadier Division

17th SS Panzer Grenadier Division

5th Fallschirmjäger Division

21st Panzer Division

401st Artillery Brigade

Grey shading added for differentiation from U.S. formations.

Series Editor's Foreword

The study of military operations has been the staple of military academies and staff colleges for 200 years. Indeed, the analysis of operations is the basis for military doctrine, procedures, and attitudes and is rooted in past operations. Although famous captains have left their own accounts and theories, these relate to the past. The analysis of a battle or a campaign is different from a narrative of its events. Formerly, operational history was written for professional soldiers. In modern times, however, operational history has become little more than a scholarly recounting of details, emphasizing a narrative that is chronologically arranged and occasionally salted with assessments or conclusions. Many of these are unsupported by information given to the commanders or the participants, or they may in fact lack sufficient information for the reader to make a detailed military estimate and analyze the results. Official histories, which supposedly use all the records and are sometimes bolstered by interviews or a healthy national bias, offer details, but these should be viewed only as narratives and not a complete basis for judgment. Relying on after-action reports or operational summaries and personal diaries, most such accounts suffer from a lack of contemporary intelligence and terrain and weather analysis, and few, if any, note possible courses of action or excerpt details of operational directives or the commanders' own mission analyses.

Operational history should provide the information necessary to make a military estimate or "appreciation." To allow the reader to understand the situation as the commander saw it, the narrative should be based on the same elements that drove decisions, and it should account for the events that shaped additional decisions and actions. Ideally, this information is presented as the actors knew it, or some accounting of additional information is provided. The process of actions and orders—that is, the operation's decision points—should be followed to the action's completion. This type of history—staff college history—has fallen out of use. Today's digested narratives often fail to provide the details soldiers need to analyze an action, given that many academics or publishers find these narratives interesting, marketable, or understandable to themselves. Owing to the exclusion of topographic maps and terrain photography, light and weather data, and details of written orders (arguably due to production costs), the artistic process masks what might have been the decision makers' reality. This shading of the commander's view, whether intended or not, leaves the reader with the prejudiced view of the narrator, whose real function should be to provide a sustainable analysis, not channel the reader up the same worn path.

Moreover, the reality of action must come through. Thousands of factors influence results. The fighters at the bottom have no knowledge of the plan at the higher level; nor are they willing to commit suicide because some commander wants to be bold. Firepower generally trumps the willpower of any leader, and the reality of the field is that most plans are followed in concept but not in the specifics of the tasks laid out in orders or in terms of a desirable timetable. The battlefield determines the reality of movement and, ultimately, success. Knowledge of the enemy, though invaluable, does not grant capability if supplies, trained soldiers, or operating equipment is lacking. Soldiers know this, but narrators frequently view plans as an architect's blueprint rather than a concept the details of which are expected to be fluid and event driven. Most important, the perfect knowledge found in hindsight is never present on the field of battle, and overall commanders have more factors to consider than the results of a single decrypt or photograph, which commentators often refer to as "ignoring intelligence."

Advance and Destroy: Patton as Commander in the Bulge is a blend of old staff college history and the new narrative form. John Nelson Rickard has used his professional experience and education to assess the same military considerations that all the major players did and to describe and analyze the results. Using his own running estimate of the situation, as any commander would, he updates the common operational picture seen by the major players and assesses the effects of their decisions as the fighting units decide the results on the field of battle. Tied to a gripping narrative, this is operational history at its best. The result is not a rehash of legend or acrimony but rather a fresh vista from which to view operations and to permit readers to decide for themselves. A sustainable military analysis is the basis for good operational history, and Rickard has provided that in this study.

—Roger Cirillo

Acknowledgments

This book has been in the works for many years, and I cannot thank every person who assisted in its development. However, a few thanks are in order to the following people: Roger Beaumont, Ira Hunt Jr., Dan Crosswell, David O'Keefe, Harold Winton, Herb Pankratz, Richard Sommers, Timothy Nenninger, and Tim Frank. Special thanks go to my longtime friend and colleague Roger Cirillo at the Association of the United States Army. Roger made a significant contribution to this study, and his knowledge of the Ardennes campaign is profound. I peppered him with questions, and he patiently replied in detail to every one. Our correspondence alone would be a valuable collection for graduate students. His assistance was invaluable as I made my way through the pitfalls of writing operational history.

Thanks are also due to my current boss, Lieutenant Colonel Shaun Tymchuk in the Directorate of Army Training Professional Development section, for encouraging me in my studies and for providing me the opportunity to finish the book.

Finally, my darling wife Melissa Leigh remained steadfast during the writing of yet another book.

Any errors or omissions in the text and maps are mine alone.

Abbreviations

AAA	antiaircraft artillery
AAR	after-action report
Abn	Airborne
Abt	*Abteilung* (battalion)
ACC	armored column cover
ACSDB	Ardennes Campaign Simulation Data Base
AdSec	Advance Section
AIB	Armored Infantry Battalion
AIS	Army Information Service
AR	*Artillerie Regiment* (German)
ARCAS	Ardennes Campaign Simulation
ARCO	Aerial Reconnaissance Coordination Office
ARKO	*Artillerie Kommandeur*
Armd	Armored
Arty	Artillery
ASP	ammunition supply point
AW	automatic weapon
Bn	Battalion
Brig	Brigade
Bty	Battery
Cav	Cavalry
CC	Combat Command
CEV	combat effectiveness value
CIC	Counter Intelligence Corps
CIGS	Chief of the Imperial General Staff
C-in-C	commander in chief
ComZ	Communications Zone
Coy	Company
CP	Command Post
CT	Combat Team

Div	Division
D/S	direct support
DSA	Division Service Area
Ech	echelon
EEI	essential element of information
elms	elements
Engr	Engineer
ETO	European Theater of Operations
FA	Field Artillery
FBB	*Führer Begleit Brigade*
FDC	fire direction center
FEBA	forward edge of the battle area
FGB	*Führer Grenadier Brigade*
FJD	*Fallschirmjäger Division*
FJR	*Fallschirmjäger Regiment*
FM	Field Manual
FO	forward observer
FSR	force-to-space ratio
GC&CS	Government Code and Cypher School
GHQ	General Headquarters
GIR	Glider Infantry Regiment
Gp	Group
HARKO	*Higher Artillerie Kommandeur*
HE	high explosive
HHB	Headquarters and Headquarters Battery
HHC	Headquarters and Headquarters Company
How	howitzer
HQ	headquarters
Inf	Infantry
IP	initial point
IPW	interrogation of prisoners of war
ISUM	Intelligence Summary
JIC	Joint Intelligence Committee
KG	*Kampfgruppe*
LC	line of communications
LD	line of departure

LO	liaison officer
Mbl	Mobile
MLR	main line of resistance
MoE	measurement of effectiveness
MP	Military Police
MSR	main supply route
MT	motor transport
NTM	notice to move
OB West	*Oberbefelshaber West* (Commander in Chief West)
OKH	*Oberkommando des Heeres* (High Command of the German Army)
OKW	*Oberkommando des Wehrmacht*
OPLR	outpost line of resistance
OSS	Office of Strategic Services
Pcht	Parachute
PD	*Panzer Division*
PGD	*Panzergrenadier Division*
PGR	*Panzergrenadier Regiment*
PIR	Parachute Infantry Regiment
POW (or PW)	prisoner of war
QM	Quartermaster
RAF	Royal Air Force
Rcn	Reconnaissance
RCT	Regimental Combat Team
Regt	Regiment
s.	*Schwere* (heavy)
SHAEF	Supreme Headquarters Allied Expeditionary Force
SIAM	Signals Intelligence and Monitoring
Sigint	signals intelligence
Sigsec	signals security
SLU	Special Liaison Unit
SP	self-propelled
Sq	Squadron
SS	*Schutzstaffel*
StuG	*Sturmgeschütz* (assault gun)
TAC	Tactical Air Command

TAF	Tactical Air Force
TCP	traffic control point
TD	Tank Destroyer
TF	Task Force
Tk	Tank
TO&E	Table of Organization and Equipment
TOT	time on target
T/R	tactical reconnaissance
TUSA	Third U.S. Army
U/F	unit of fire
VAK	*Volksartillerie Korps*
VGD	*Volksgrenadier Division*
VGR	*Volksgrenadier Regiment*
VS	*Verbrauchssatze* (rate of fuel consumption)
VWB	*Volkswerferbrigade*
WFSt	*Wehrmachtführungsstab* (Armed Forces Command Staff)
zbV	*zur besonderen Werwendung* (for special purposes)

Studying Patton

Adolf Hitler launched his counteroffensive in the Ardennes forest, code-named *WACHT AM RHEIN* (Watch on the Rhine), on December 16, 1944, and proved that a tiger is at its most dangerous when cornered. The German army (*Heere*), *Waffen–Schutzstaffel* (SS; the guard echelon), and German air force (*Luftwaffe*) made a final, supreme effort against the U.S. Army during six weeks of bitter combat. Hitler committed the last of his carefully accumulated reserves in an attempt to wrest the strategic initiative from the Allies in the west. Even as the battle raged in the Ardennes, he launched a subsidiary operation, *NORDWIND* (North Wind), on January 1, 1945, to recapture Alsace-Lorraine and relieve some of the pressure on the southern flank of the "Bulge." *NORDWIND* dragged on until late January. It and *WACHT AM RHEIN* should be considered one and the same for the purposes of analysis.

For a brief moment at the end of the war, the German army profited from a massive injection of adrenaline and offered the Americans a fleeting but sobering glimpse of German offensive skill. The Supreme Allied Commander, General of the Army Dwight D. Eisenhower, committed almost 600,000 Americans to stem the German onslaught. The Americans clearly enjoyed important numerical and materiel advantages, but the Germans' achievement at the end of five years of war was remarkable. The Ardennes campaign represented the truest test of strength between the U.S. and German armies during the entire war.[1] Playing a conspicuous role in this marshaling of American power and its application against the counteroffensive was Lieutenant General George S. Patton Jr., commanding the Third United States Army.

On the eve of the Battle of the Bulge, Patton had barely seven months of combat experience in World War II. Nevertheless, he was the most seasoned of the four American army commanders in the European Theater of Operations (ETO). As commander of the Western Task Force during Operation TORCH (the invasion of French North Africa), II Corps in Tunisia, Seventh Army in Sicily, and Third Army in Normandy and Lorraine, Patton experienced combat in all its principal manifestations.

He planned and executed amphibious, airborne, and set-piece operations and fought defensive battles. He fought for numerous river crossings, battled the Germans in comprehensive urban fortifications and linear fortifications in depth, and blunted large panzer counterattacks. Patton's varied experience was gained in the most appalling conditions, from the sweltering daytime heat and frigid nighttime cold of the North African desert to the choking mud, floods, and snow of Lorraine.

Patton's diverse combat experience between late 1942 and the end of 1944 has not entirely mitigated criticism from military historians and others that he owed much of his success to ineffective opponents. The criticism has some validity. An objective portrayal of enemy effectiveness is necessary to arrive at an accurate analysis of one's own prowess, and the Germans were certainly not committed to holding fast in Sicily and Normandy in mid-August. Yet Patton's three-month battle of attrition with the German *First Armee* and *Fifth Panzer Armee* in Lorraine following the Normandy breakout softens the criticism that he always faced a disintegrating opponent.[2] The other Allied army commanders in the ETO— Courtney Hodges of First Army, Sir Miles Dempsey of Second British Army, Harry Crerar of First Canadian Army, William Simpson of Ninth Army, Alexander Patch of Seventh Army, and Jean de Lattre de Tassigny of First French Army—most certainly would have failed to replicate Patton's exploitation of enemy weakness in both the Sicilian and the Normandy campaigns. None of them possessed Patton's driving power, desire to maintain momentum, and willingness to engage in the "running fight." The Ardennes, however, was different from these campaigns, different even from Lorraine. In the Ardennes, Patton had to fight hard and maneuver extensively to gain positions of advantage over an opponent desperately trying to seize the initiative from him rather than merely defending. This fact, and the temporary rough parity of the opposing sides, makes the Battle of the Bulge the ultimate case study of Patton's generalship.

Studying Patton the army commander requires an understanding of that level of command and the scope and degree of his influence on the design of campaigns. Patton commanded Third Army in Twelfth Army Group, which was commanded by Lieutenant General Omar N. Bradley. Bradley had two other armies—the First, commanded by Hodges, and the Ninth, commanded by Simpson. Bradley was one of three army group commanders, along with Field Marshal Sir Bernard Law Montgomery commanding British Twenty-First Army Group and Lieutenant General Jacob L. Devers commanding U.S. Sixth Army Group. Montgomery had two armies—Crerar's First Canadian Army and Dempsey's Second British Army. Devers also had two armies—the U.S. Seventh Army commanded by Patch and the First French Army commanded by de Lattre de Tassigny. Theater strategy was the sole purview of Eisenhower, and his army groups directed military strategic operations below theater level. The army was the fundamental unit of strategic maneuver. The principal American canon, Field Manual (FM) 100–5, *Field Service Regulations, Operations*, declared that a *"group of armies* is primarily a tactical command." Important amplification was found in FM 100–15, *Larger Units*, which stated that army groups should "deal only with current operations."[3] Clearly, if Bradley was a tactical commander, so too was Patton, by definition; in practice, however, both planned beyond current operations.

This American doctrinal reality has influenced observers. In fact, Edward Luttwak argued that American ground warfare during World War II "was conducted almost exclusively at the tactical level, and then at the level of theater strategy above that, with almost no operational dimension in between." An understanding of Allied logistical practice heavily influenced Luttwak's perspective. He believed that beyond the tactical level the "important decisions were primarily of a logistical character. The overall supply dictated the rate of advance," and its distribution "set the vectors of the advancing front."[4] Luttwak's thesis was supported by the American official historian Roland G. Ruppenthal, who declared that logistical considerations "dominated the selection of the place for the Normandy invasion, determined the time when it could be launched, and clearly influenced the tactical decisions of September and October 1944." However, he also admitted that, from a logistical perspective, Eisenhower's decision to cross the Seine to continue the pursuit while simultaneously augmenting Bradley's drive south of the Ardennes "constituted a radical departure from earlier plans." The Allies "carried with them a supply task out of all proportion to planned capabilities."[5] Here, then, was a powerful example that logistical limitations did not *always* infringe on a commander's decisions above the tactical level.

One scholar has stated that if Allied commanders thought on the operational level, "they kept it to themselves. Their references to higher tactics, and at other times to generalship, may have meant something similar, but their way of war was not generally shaped by classical concepts of grand scale operational manoeuvre." This may have applied to most World War II army commanders, but Luttwak made a few intriguing exceptions, stating that "operational approaches remained the trade secrets and personal attributes of men such as Douglas MacArthur, Patton, and the British General O'Connor." It is true that Patton did not hold strategy in high regard during his early study of military history. The attrition of World War I soured him on the higher level of war, to the point where he declared in 1922 that "tactics should be placed above mere strategy. Without tactical success strategy could not be accomplished. Strategy which does not think of tactical success is condemned at the start to failure."[6] This suggests that Patton thought only in terms of tactics and strategy, but we can dismiss this idea immediately.

Although Helmuth von Moltke appears to have been the first to use the term *operativ*, or *operational*, as a way of linking the tactical and strategic levels,[7] the term *operational level* was not part of American doctrinal vocabulary during World War II. What was understood, if seldom expressed, was the concept of "grand tactics," attributable to Baron Antoine Henri de Jomini and defined by him as the "maneuvering of an army upon the battlefield, and the different formations of troops for attack."[8] Hugh M. Cole used the term *grand tactics* in the official history, and it is appropriate to use it here to avoid the propensity to judge Patton by the more modern and refined concepts of the operational level of war, even though he helped shaped those modern concepts.[9]

For my purposes, I define *grand tactics* as decisions concerning where, when, for what purpose, and with what formations the fighting is to occur. Decisions are conceptual only until they are actualized by physical maneuver. As an army commander, Patton possessed varying degrees of freedom to make these decisions. He gave his corps commanders missions and provided them with divisions and other army-level assets, such as heavy artillery, to accomplish their missions. Since he possessed much greater latitude to plan the conduct of a campaign than did a corps commander, who simply fought his corps, we can assert that grand tactics was first truly practiced at the army level.[10] Patton's freedom of decision at the grand tactical (army) level is what permits a critical analysis of grand tactical "art."[11] If one were to deny that this freedom of decision existed, elevating the first expression of grand tactics to the army group level, there would be no point in studying American army commanders of World War II at all. There would be no art, merely execution.

Patton practiced grand tactics in two ways. First, he made decisions and conducted maneuver to win the current campaign. Inherent in grand tactics is the sequencing of the application of force to achieve the goals of a given campaign.[12] Second, even while fighting the current campaign in the Bulge, he looked over the horizon to consider where his army should be employed next. His grand tactical vision was not stop-start sequential but sequential-simultaneous, meaning that he envisioned the start of the next campaign even before the Bulge was over. He clearly had more influence on the conduct of the present campaign than on the future one, but this differentiation permits a more compartmentalized and reality-based analysis of his decision making.

Questions that Need Answering

Despite the voluminous work devoted to Patton over the years, many aspects of his generalship have not received critical treatment. Several questions about his *command technique* and *operational technique* are important, but first these terms need to be clarified. FM 100–5 stated that command and leadership are "inseparable . . . the commander must be the controlling head; his must be the master mind."[13] Yet even as a grand tactical commander, certain factors were beyond Patton's control. One can subdivide command into a function-related element and an output-related element. The former consists of arranging and coordinating everything an army needs to exist, while the latter is expressed as an army's basic mission—that is, to inflict maximal destruction on the enemy in the shortest time while minimizing one's own losses.[14] The output-related element truly defines *command technique* because it pertains directly to how Patton communicated his intent to his subordinates for any given mission. The person-to-person interface is what makes command technique in large part an art. Based on this understanding of command technique, the following questions are appropriate: How effective was Patton as a leader? How effective was he at communicating his intent to his subordinates? How far did he trust his subordinates to achieve his intent? How tolerant was he of mistakes and, most important, how did he correct them? This question has particular relevance because it is a marginalized aspect of military history.[15] Finally, did he regularly accept the advice of his subordinates, and under what circumstances?

Patton's *operational technique*, his preferred method of reaching decisions on the battlefield, was a synthesis of accepted U.S. Army doctrine at the time and his own philosophy of battle developed over the years by private study and practical testing. His thoughts on many issues changed over time, but his operational technique by 1944 consisted of speed, mobility, and indirect means to destroy enemy forces. Although he displayed the bulldog tenacity of Ulysses S. Grant, he favored the indirect approach of Stonewall Jackson. He believed in enveloping maneuvers and continuous movement. Speed was essential not only in the execution of a plan but also in its conception. Patton believed that "a good plan violently executed *now* is better than a perfect plan next week." In comparing the grand tactical methods of Patton and Hodges, Bradley concluded that "whereas Patton could seldom be bothered with details, Hodges studied his problems with infinite care and was thus better qualified to execute the more intricate operations." Bradley felt that improvisation became Patton's modus operandi during the war, but this was not true, for Patton conducted detailed planning for the reduction of Metz in early November. He was, however, extremely reluctant to change plans once made.[16]

Patton's unique operational technique raises several questions. How much freedom of decision was he afforded by Eisenhower and Bradley? To what extent did terrain and weather affect his operations? How did Patton formulate his plans, and how much influence did his staff exercise over his concept of operations? How effective was he in consistently synchronizing the movements of his corps? How effective was he in concentrating his forces in space and unifying them in time? How did he react to changed circumstances? Was his ninety-degree turn of Third Army, from its positions facing east along the Saar River in Lorraine to attack positions in southern Luxembourg, as brilliant as has been claimed? Was his preferred line of action feasible logistically, and did it fit in with larger Twelfth Army Group and Supreme Headquarters Allied Expeditionary Force (SHAEF) strategy? Two final questions are worthy of consideration as well: To what extent did he absorb and apply the lessons of his previous experiences, particularly the recently concluded campaign in Lorraine, to his missions in the Ardennes? And finally, how important were Patton's operations to the ultimate defeat of the German counteroffensive? Answers to these questions will permit a more nuanced appreciation of Patton's skill sets as an army commander.

Methodology

My methodology for investigating the above questions consists of three elements: (1) differentiation between Patton's responsibilities and his means of influence; (2) an understanding of his decision-making process, based on the commander's *estimate of the situation*; and (3) a system to determine the *measurement of effectiveness* (MoE) for his operations. Patton's responsibilities as an army commander included the following: accept responsibility, anticipate future requirements, develop broad plans and concepts of operations, determine objectives and assign them to corps, establish priorities, advise corps commanders on schemes of maneuver, allocate divisions and other fighting assets to corps, support corps administratively and logistically, provide high-level intelligence, arrange tactical air support, coordinate the operations of two or more corps, and provide reports to higher headquarters. Patton's means of influence consisted of committing reserves; maneuvering artillery fire; employing tactical airpower and requesting strategic airpower; adjusting corps and divisional boundaries; shifting and regrouping formations; maneuvering formations; personally intervening; and delaying, halting, or expediting attacks.[17]

The estimate of the situation was a planning tool, driven primarily by intelligence, used by American commanders at all levels during the war to logically "work" a military problem and reach a decision. Because the estimate was intelligence driven, I have exploited ULTRA in ways previous historians have not. The commander's estimate was "based on the mission, the means available to him and to the enemy, the conditions in his area of operations including terrain and weather and the probable effects of various lines of action on future operations." Based on these factors, the commander had to consider "the lines of action open to him which, if successful, will accomplish the mission and the lines of action of which the enemy is physically capable. . . . He analyzes the opposing lines of action, one against the other, to arrive at conclusions as to the probability of success for each of his own lines of action. On the basis of this analysis he then considers the relative advantages and disadvantages of his own lines of action, and selects that line of action which most promises success regardless of what the enemy may do."[18] An enemy's capabilities *suggested* a commander's possible lines of action but did not always dictate his mission or the *most likely* line of action. Doctrinally, and when time allowed, it was preferable to take several days to prepare a written estimate based on the specialized estimates of the principal staff officers. This permitted a greater degree of analysis and ensured that due consideration was given to all the factors bearing on a given situation.[19] However, when time was short and decisions had to be made quickly, American commanders conducted the estimate process mentally.[20]

The advantage of the estimate methodology is that it accurately reflects a commander's decision-making process, which was designed to produce decisions practically expressed as line actions. The authors of many academic and nonspecialist accounts are not aware of, or do not understand, the estimate process and therefore naturally impose their own sense of order on past military decision making. Of course, much good history has been written by nonmilitary specialists, but studying Patton's generalship based on the estimate process mitigates the propensity to infuse subjective artificiality into the analysis.

To judge the efficacy of Patton's decisions and ultimately his generalship and to avoid broad-brush, uninformed pronouncements about his leadership in the Ardennes, I employ a three-tiered MoE borrowed from Colonel Trevor N. Dupuy. First, some elaboration on what I mean by *effectiveness* is required. I use the term *army combat effectiveness* and define it as the ability of an army to achieve its assigned missions with the least expenditure of lives in the shortest amount of time.[21] This is very similar to the definition of *combat power:* the physical elements of a military force, including weapons systems, troops, equipment, and logistical structures. *Combat power,* or what the Germans called *Kampfkraft,* is the "ability to inflict damage upon the enemy while limiting the damage that he can inflict in return."[22] This definition implies that combat power alone is the engine of an army's combat effectiveness, but German *Kampfkraft* heavily emphasized the moral plane of warfare and was built on the "caliber of a leader and the men." This is closer to the concept of *fighting power,* defined by Martin van Creveld as "the sum total of mental qualities that make armies fight" and manifested by discipline and cohesion, morale and initiative, courage and toughness, the willingness to fight and the readiness to die.[23]

For purposes of the present study, I differentiate *combat power* and *fighting power* as follows: the former equates to physical elements of military systems, and the latter equates to moral elements. The fusion of these two critical elements can be seen in the German classification system to judge the *Kampfwert* (combat value) of their divisions: *Kampfwert I,* suitable for offensive operations; *Kampfwert II,* suitable for limited offensive operations; *Kampfwert III,* suitable for defensive operations; *Kampfwert IV,* suitable for limited defensive operations; and *Kampfwert V,* not suitable for operations. The U.S. Army had no such rating system. Instead, division commanders expressed their combat effectiveness, based primarily on actual rifle strength in the case of infantry divisions, as a percentage in G-3 reports.[24]

The expected result of the combined application of *combat power* and *fighting power* against an opponent is *combat effectiveness*, but because of the inherent uncertainty of military operations, it is critical to speak in terms of *probability of success*.[25] The first MoE is the most basic: *mission accomplishment*. This entails asking the simple question, did Patton achieve the missions assigned to him by Eisenhower and Bradley in the Ardennes? The second MoE is *spatial effectiveness*, meaning Patton's ability to take and hold ground. The third measurement, *casualty effectiveness*, is a logical derivative of the first and entails evaluating his effectiveness in inflicting casualties on the Germans while limiting his own. Patton's operations came with heavy costs, and it is important to fully appreciate the cost-benefit relationship. Establishing the above criteria for evaluating Patton's overall effectiveness necessitates doing the same for his principal opponents, the *Fifth Panzer Armee* and *Seventh Armee*. Conclusions about effectiveness have no meaning unless judged relative to the opponent.

The literature on Patton's generalship in the Bulge is substantial but often thin. Most accounts overwhelmingly focus on Third Army's linkup with the 101st Airborne Division at Bastogne the day after Christmas, a span of time lasting a mere eight days. Cole's official history took the story only up to the end of December 1944, while Charles B. MacDonald cursorily covered the January battles in *The Last Offensive*. Patton directed multiple corps operations for a full month after punching through to Bastogne, but they have not consistently caught the attention of historians. Beyond the relief of Bastogne lay the vicious battles to secure that road junction, the collision of large forces intent on driving each other back, considerable disagreement on how best to defeat the Germans, and missed opportunities. The official histories represent a solid start but do not definitively account for Patton's strengths and weaknesses throughout the entire course of the Ardennes campaign. *Advance and Destroy: Patton as Commander in the Bulge* goes beyond the usual idolatry and antipathy so characteristic of Patton scholarship and advances new perspectives about his generalship in the Battle of the Bulge.

PART I

The Road to the Bulge

1

Origin of the Ardennes Counteroffensive

If we can deliver a few more heavy blows, then at any moment this artificially bolstered common front may collapse with a mighty clap of thunder.

—Hitler, December 12, 1944

On the morning of July 25, 1944, more than 2,400 American bombers and fighter-bombers launched an aerial assault on a narrow sector of the German front in western Normandy. The aircraft, approaching at an altitude of 12,000 feet, flew directly over the heads of awed American infantry below. Four thousand tons of explosives tumbled out of the bomb bays in great rectangular carpet patterns, and most of the bombs found their way to *Generalleutnant* Fritz Bayerlein's *Panzer Lehr Division*, dug in awaiting another American ground onslaught. The carnage on the ground was awful, and Bayerlein compared his front line to the face of the moon.[1] In an instant, 1,000 of his men died. The day before, the division had confidently shaken off the first American attempt to crush the line with airpower, but not today. As the stunned Germans tried to recover from the shattering effects of the new bombardment, American ground forces under the command of Major General J. Lawton Collins slowly began to exploit the breach. This was Operation COBRA, the long-awaited American breakout from the hedgerows of Normandy.

By August 1 Lieutenant General Omar N. Bradley, commander of the American Twelfth Army Group, finally deployed Patton's Third Army. Seizing on the opportunity presented by the hard work of Collins's men, Patton, who had taken command of VIII Corps, rapidly pushed two armored divisions south through a bottleneck at Avranches at the base of the Cotentin Peninsula and began to pour into Brittany to execute the pre-OVERLORD plan. This southward thrust of American armor startled *Generalfeldmarschall* Günther von Kluge, who declared, "If the Americans get through at Avranches they will be out of the woods and they'll be able to do what they want."[2] Kluge, however, had already conceded that his left flank had collapsed. Even as Patton began to fully deploy Third Army, Hitler conceived a bold stroke to regain the initiative in Normandy.

In a snap decision on August 2, Hitler ordered Kluge to concentrate a strong panzer force in the American sector, regardless of the repercussions in the British sector, to attack Third Army's lines of communications (LC) between Avranches and Mortain. Kluge, utterly shocked at the implications, tried to lecture Hitler on the fact that tanks were the backbone of the German defense in Normandy. If they were committed to such an operation, which looked from all angles to be a perfect trap, Kluge exclaimed, "catastrophe was inevitable." Hitler scoffed at Kluge's realistic assessment and considered the operation a "unique, never recurring opportunity for a complete reversal of the situation."[3]

In the early-morning hours of August 7, *General der Panzertruppen* Hans von Funck's *XLVII Panzerkorps*, consisting of the *1st* and *2nd SS Panzer Divisions* (PDs) and *2nd* and *116th PDs*, with some 300 combined panzers and assault guns, launched Operation *LÜTTICH* and achieved tactical surprise. ULTRA intelligence, however, provided sufficient information from German communications to permit the timely redeployment of American units. In his frustration, Hitler stated, "How does the enemy learn our thoughts from us?"[4] The panzers made some progress in the direction of Avranches and overran several American positions, but stout resistance by the American 30th Infantry Division at Hill 317 east of Mortain, the intervention of intrepid American dive-bombers, and the effectiveness of bazooka teams eventually crippled the attack. The failure of what the Americans called the "Mortain counteroffensive" quickly complicated Hitler's strategic dilemma. As Kluge had predicted, its failure led to catastrophe. Within two weeks of the operation, the entire German front in Normandy had given way, and a large part of the *Seventh Armee* was compressed and mostly destroyed in the "Falaise Pocket" as it desperately tried to fight its way east.

It is a commonly held assumption that the German collapse in Normandy represented a turning point, in that Germany simply played out the rest of the war like a football team watching the game clock tick down in a losing effort. In reality, Hitler continued to calculate strategically and never abandoned the spirit of *LÜTTICH*. He was bent on regaining the initiative somewhere in the west.[5] Hitler was not overly concerned that the Allies had crossed the Seine River in pursuit or that the disaster of the Falaise Pocket was only hours old when he conceived another large counterstroke. On August 19 *Generaloberst* Alfred Jodl, chief of the *Wehrmachtführungsstab* (WFSt) at the *Oberkommando der Wehrmacht* (OKW), noted in his diary: "Prepare to take the offensive in November when the enemy air forces can't operate."[6]

In early September Jodl told Hitler that for an offensive in the west to have a chance of success, Allied airpower had to be negated by a lengthy period of bad weather, and an operational reserve of twenty-five divisions had to be raised. Hitler quickly authorized the latter and on September 13 ordered the creation of the *Sixth Panzer Armee* to oversee the rehabilitation of the specific army and SS panzer divisions that would be pulled out of the line.[7] November 1 was considered the earliest date that any sort of operation could be launched. The idea of striking the Allies in the Ardennes finally crystallized in Hitler's mind during a routine briefing on September 16 at the *Wolfschanze* (Wolf's Lair), the Führer's field headquarters at Rastenberg in East Prussia. Jodl, *Generalfeldmarschall* Wilhelm Keitel, and *Generaloberst* Heinz Guderian, inspector-general of panzer forces, were all present. While outlining the situation on the Western Front, Jodl mentioned the Ardennes in passing. Hitler cut him off and after some tense seconds said, "I have made a momentous decision. I shall go over to the offensive . . . here, out of the Ardennes, with the objective Antwerp."[8] This vital port supplied the bulk of Allied logistical needs on the Continent. Guderian, no stranger to deep, strategic-level operations, was dumbfounded. The Germans were actually doing a decent job of holding the Allied advance in the west, but he pointed out the critical situation in the east. In Guderian's opinion, taking desperately needed resources away from the Russian Front was grossly irresponsible.

Irrevocably set on the counteroffensive idea, Hitler turned his attention to holding sufficient ground in front of the West Wall, a belt of concrete fortifications running along the German frontier, to permit the preparation and concentration of the necessary forces. By the time he had settled on an offensive in the west, Patton's Third Army was threatening the West Wall in Lorraine. Hitler, however, had identified Third Army as a threat much earlier, issuing orders on September 3 for an attack against Patton's southern flank to shield the withdrawal of *Nineteenth Armee* and

LXIV Armeekorps from southern France, as well as to protect the construction work in progress on the western defenses.[9] *General der Panzertruppen* Hasso Eccard von Manteuffel's *Fifth Panzer Armee* struck Third Army's armored spearhead on September 18. At the cost of hundreds of factory-new Panther tanks, Manteuffel blunted Patton's hard charge to the frontier fortifications in a week of heavy fighting.

By early November Hitler identified three danger areas on the Western Front: Metz (where Third Army was), Aachen, and Venlo. On November 9 he ordered no retreat in these areas, and even if Fortress Metz was encircled, the Nied River line (extending southeast of Metz) was to be held at all costs. However, the Germans were unsuccessful in holding any of these positions up to the beginning of the offensive. By December 7 Hitler signaled all commanders that holding the West Wall was critical because it was "superior as a fortification to all other possible natural obstacles," and penetrations had to be prevented "at all costs."[10]

Hitler never doubted that any counteroffensive aimed at gaining a breather for Germany would have to be launched in the west. Options in late 1944 were extremely limited. As Jodl reflected, "We had to attack in the West because the Russians had so many troops that even if we succeeded in destroying 30 divisions, it would not make any difference. On the other hand, if we destroyed 30 divisions in the West, it would account for more than one-third of the whole Invasion Army. . . . Italy offered more hope . . . but the railhead connections were much worse than in the West. . . . The West was the only place in Europe where we had a chance of success."[11]

Cultural considerations also motivated Hitler's decision to strike the Americans first. It is clear that he understood and feared American industrial might well before 1939, and a considerable argument can be made that his entire geopolitical strategy, including invading the Soviet Union, was designed to prepare Germany for an ultimate showdown with the American economic juggernaut.[12] When Hitler declared war on the United States on December 11, 1941, in response to the request of the Japanese ambassador, Baron Hiroshi Oshima, the German High Command was shocked by the addition of such a powerful foe to Germany's list of enemies. The declaration seemed all the more fantastic because the Tripartite Pact, which bound Germany, Japan, and Italy in a loose alliance, did not specifically state that Germany had to give aid to Japan in the event of war with the United States. After declaring war on the world's greatest economic power, Hitler publicly hurled abuse at President Franklin

Roosevelt and arrogantly announced that America's entry into the war would make little difference in the long run.

Hitler was even less fearful of American martial prowess. After three and a half gruesome years of battling the hated Bolsheviks, Hitler grudgingly admitted their toughness in unimaginable conditions. Their astounding capacity for punishment led him to conclude that they were far tougher opponents than the British, Canadians, and Americans. His contempt for the Americans in particular was evident in March 1943 when he declared, "There is no doubt that of all the Anglo-Saxons the English are the best."[13] Hitler's disregard for American fighting power coincided with the fact that the Americans were thinly deployed in the Ardennes, and when his almost slavish obedience to history is considered, his decision to attack through the forest (next to the Vosges mountains to the south, the most difficult terrain on the Western Front) seems almost inevitable.

Throughout September and October, Jodl and the General Staff developed Hitler's concept under conditions of extreme secrecy while pushing forward their own alternatives to match the actual resources of the Reich. They even proposed two operations to address the threat posed by Patton's Third Army in Lorraine: Operation LUXEMBOURG, a double envelopment from central Luxembourg and Metz to seize Longwy, and Operation LORRAINE, a double envelopment from Metz and Baccarat to converge on Nancy.[14] Neither *Generalfeldmarschall* Karl Rudolf Gerd von Rundstedt, *Oberbefelshaber* (commander in chief) *West* (*OB West*), nor *Generalfeldmarschall* Walter Model, commander of *Heeresgruppe* (Army Group) B, were brought into the picture until late October. The chosen army commanders—Manteuffel of *Fifth Panzer Armee*, SS-*Obergruppenführer und Panzergeneral* Josef "Sepp" Dietrich of the *Sixth Panzer Armee* (not officially designated SS yet), and *General der Panzertruppen* Erich Brandenberger of *Seventh Armee*—were not enlightened until October 27. Rundstedt exclaimed that the choice of the Ardennes was a "stroke of genius," but he was nonetheless "staggered" by the scope. "All," he lamented, "absolutely all conditions for the possible success of such an offensive were lacking." The fiery Model's first reaction was outright condemnation. "This plan," he stated, "hasn't got a damned leg to stand on."[15] Rundstedt and Model differed on how best to employ Hitler's new strategic reserves but agreed that Antwerp was an impossible objective.

On October 21 Aachen, a large urban metropolis with a prewar population of 165,000, was the first German city to fall to the Allies, and the heavy concentration of American forces there worried both Rundstedt and Model. From late October to mid-December they tried to limit the counteroffensive to outflanking and destroying a portion of First United States Army, perhaps two or three corps, east of the Meuse River in the Aachen area to preempt what they saw as the biggest threat to the important Ruhr industrial area to the north.[16] Hitler ridiculed the idea, declaring it a half measure with no real prospect of success. Moreover, he had no intention of attacking straight into the heart of American strength. He fended off every effort by his senior commanders to scale down the operation, and in the end, the scope and objective laid out in the final operations order on December 9 were unchanged from Rundstedt and Model's first briefing in October. To silence all further argument, Hitler emphatically scribbled the words "Not to be altered" on the final order for the attack.

Hitler's strategic intent was to split the Allies both physically and psychologically. He took great comfort from the fact that during the Seven Years' War his hero, Frederick the Great of Prussia, had managed to hang on against what appeared to be an overwhelming coalition of France, Austria, Russia, the Holy Roman Empire, and Sweden until fractures in the alliance undermined its strength. By retaining the initiative and inflicting decisive tactical defeats such as Rossbach and Leuthen in late 1757, Frederick had been able to withstand setbacks long enough to get him to the Treaty of Hubertusburg, which restored the prewar balance of power and recognized Prussia as a great power.[17]

The Western Front was divided among four army groups: *Heeresgruppe H* in the north held the *Twenty-Fifth* and *First Fallschirmjäger Armees*; Model's *Heeresgruppe B* contained the *Fifteenth Armee*, *Sixth* and *Fifth Panzer Armees*, and *Seventh Armee*; *Heeresgruppe G* contained only one army, the *First*; and *Heeresgruppe Oberrhein* (commanded by *Reichsführer-SS* Heinrich Himmler since November 30) contained the *Nineteenth Armee*. *Heeresgruppe B* was to execute the counteroffensive. The final objective was to reach Antwerp and thereby set the conditions for the destruction of a significant portion of First Army, all of the Ninth United States Army to the north, and the entire Twenty-First Army Group, consisting of the First Canadian and Second British Armies, north of the Antwerp–Brussels–Bastogne line. Such a feat would "set the stage for the annihilation of the bulk of twenty to thirty divisions," declared Hitler. "It will be another Dunkirk."[18]

As a strategic objective, Antwerp looked tantalizing, but the terrain of

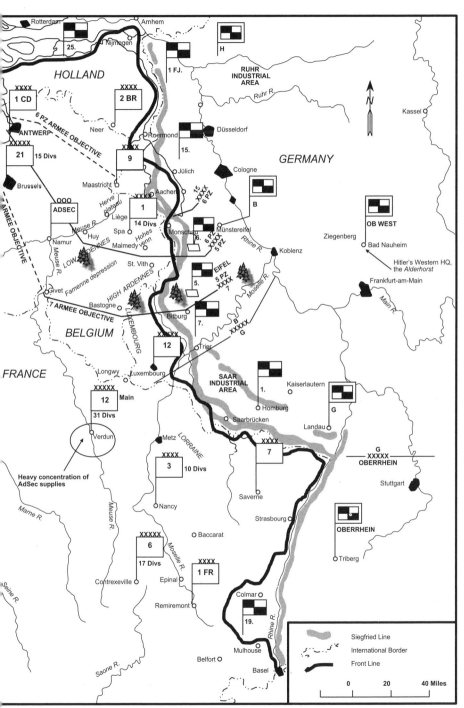

Map 1.1. German Attack Plan and Strategic Situation, December 16, 1944

this line of action presented a formidable military obstacle. The Ardennes was a wedge-shaped region covering areas of Luxembourg, Belgium, and northern France, bounded on the west by the Meuse River, on the north by the Hürtgen Forest, on the south by the French Ardennes (*Forêt des Ardennes*) and the Semois River, and on the east by the Our and Sauer Rivers. The Ardennes was subdivided into three distinguishable terrain areas. The Low Ardennes in the north was restricted on the west by the Meuse River and on the north by the Hürtgen Forest. The area consisted of low, rolling hills and two generally open areas suitable for movement—the Herve Plateau near Viviers, and the Condroz Plateau between the Ourthe and Meuse Rivers. This northern sector of the Ardennes also contained the Hohes Venn, a high plateau of lakes and marshes running southwest from Monschau toward Stavelot, as well as more marshland between Laroche and Vielsalm and, to the southwest, the great forest of St. Hubert. The Hohes Venn plateau was a terrain feature larger than the Schnee Eifel (Snow Mountains), a high, tree-covered ridge running southwest to northeast on the east side of the Our River and on which stood significant portions of the West Wall fortifications. In the gap between the Laroche–Vielsalm marshland and the St. Hubert forest ran the Ourthe River, a twisting, winding gorge.

The High Ardennes in the south is often referred to as the "true Ardennes." It consisted of a wide plateau from which rose generally unrelated ridges or higher plateaus. This basic fact, combined with patchwork sections of heavy forest, had a direct impact on tactics because possession of one hill did not necessarily ensure domination of another.[19] The High Ardennes was divided into the Hautes Fagnes (High Heaths) around Bastogne and Neufchâteau in the north and the Forêt des Ardennes, which extended to the Semois River, in the south. The average altitude in the Ardennes region was 1,600 feet. Cutting through the middle section of the Ardennes was the third distinguishable terrain feature, the Famenne Depression, a long, narrow, nearly treeless "trench" extending from the upper Ourthe River near the Belgium–Luxembourg border westward through Houffalize–Marche–Rochefort to the Meuse River near Dinant and Givet. In the northern part of Luxembourg the Wiltz, Clerf, and Sûre Rivers followed long, deep, narrow, and tortuous valleys.

The road net in the Ardennes was relatively good because the Belgians and Luxembourgers had invested heavily in auto tourism just prior to the outbreak of war. All the main roads were hard-surfaced macadam, and ten all-weather roads crossed the German frontier into Belgium and

Luxembourg between Monschau and Wasserbillig. However, there was not a single main road that traversed the Ardennes in a straight east-west direction.[20] In 1914 and 1940 the French High Command had placed great faith in the forest's ability to block German penetrations. The German *Third* and *Fourth Armees* had successfully penetrated the forest on their way to meet the French at the pivotal Battle of the Marne in 1914, and the bold march of the bulk of the panzer forces through the area in May 1940 had been the key to German victory over the larger combined British and French armies. In both 1914 and 1940 the Germans had essentially conducted route marches through the area in excellent weather conditions, but winter conditions posed major problems for German planners as they assigned troops to tasks and considered logistical requirements.

Heeresgruppe B was to assemble east of the Our and Sauer Rivers in the Eifel, a complex of heavily forested hills that stretched all the way to the Rhine. The road and rail net in the region was adequate for a large military concentration.[21] The success of both the marshaling of necessary forces and their advance through the Ardennes was heavily dependent on a guaranteed period of bad weather to blind and degrade Allied airpower's striking effectiveness beyond the cover afforded by the forest. Model was to execute a frontal penetration attack (*Durchbruchsangriff*) rather than an envelopment to smash through Twelfth Army Group, destroy the continuity of its front, and advance rapidly west and northwest while simultaneously enveloping the shoulders of the breakthrough.

Model estimated that there were five divisions with 300 tanks opposite *Sixth Panzer Armee*, three divisions with 150 tanks opposite *Fifth Panzer Armee*, and two divisions with 100 tanks opposite *Seventh Armee*. In the north he estimated fifteen divisions with 1,450 tanks opposite *Fifteenth Armee*.[22] His *schwerpunkt* (center of gravity) was estimated to be the weakest point of First Army, VIII Corps, holding a sixty-mile front from Monschau to Echternach. From north to south, VIII Corps consisted of the 106th Infantry Division, 14th Cavalry Group, 28th Infantry Division, Combat Command A (CCA)/9th Armored Division, and 4th Infantry Division. *Sixth Panzer Armee* in the north, built around a heavy concentration of SS panzer divisions, was Model's main effort oriented on the boundary separating V and VIII Corps. Dietrich's army frontage was some twenty-three miles, but his actual attack frontage was less than half that, a fact that would have an immediate negative impact on operations. Dietrich was expected to have his leading panzer elements at the Meuse astride Liège within twenty-four hours, followed by a second panzer wave.

The establishment of strong, north-facing defensive positions along the Albert Canal was critical to facilitate the final advance on Antwerp.[23]

To facilitate Dietrich's penetration to the Meuse, a small airborne operation code-named *STÖSSER* (Auk) was to be led by *Oberst* Friedrich August Baron von der Heydte. His small *Kampfgruppe* (*KG*) of around 800 men would drop in advance of the panzers onto the Hautes Fagnes to seize key road junctions and block reinforcements from the north. Simultaneously, *SS-Obersturmbannführer* Otto Skorzeny's makeshift *Panzer Brigade 150* would try to cause havoc in the American rear areas on Dietrich's line of action by disrupting communications and redirecting traffic. Skorzeny had rescued Mussolini from Gran Sasso in the Abruzzi mountains in September 1943 in a daring glider-borne operation, and Hitler placed considerable faith in his ability to function as a force multiplier.

In the center Manteuffel's *Fifth Panzer Armee* was to protect Dietrich's southern flank. *Fifth Panzer Armee* would attack the 106th Infantry Division and part of the 28th Infantry Division, cross the Meuse between Amay and Namur, and then turn northwest alongside *Sixth Panzer Armee* to prevent Allied forces from attacking Dietrich's rear from west of the Antwerp–Brussels–Dinant line. In the south Brandenberger's *Seventh Armee* was to attack the remainder of the 28th Infantry Division and the 4th Infantry Division and act as flank protection for Manteuffel, all the way to the Meuse and Semois Rivers, in the event that Patton's Third Army in Lorraine was redeployed against the counteroffensive.

Hitler added *Generaloberst* Gustav Adolf von Zangen's *Fifteenth Armee* to the order of battle on November 10, with the intent of having it open a secondary offensive code-named *SPÄTLESE* (Late Harvest) north of Aachen on December 18. However, Hitler had no stomach for directly attacking American strength around Aachen, and *SPÄTLESE* was restricted until the American positions east of that city had been severely weakened. *Generaloberst* Kurt Student, commander in chief of *Heeresgruppe H*, pressed for a complementary operation by his army group but was denied.[24] Hitler rationalized that withholding simultaneous supporting attacks elsewhere along the front was low risk because he anticipated a quick penetration to the Meuse, thereby presenting a wider range of options for employment of the flanking armies. His belief in the ability to carry out that quick penetration was built on his faith in the SS and the deception measures he had stringently enforced. Surprise was to be another key force multiplier.

Although Hitler canceled *SPÄTLESE*, he would authorize a subsidiary offensive code-named *NORDWIND* in Alsace, which would commence on January 1, 1945. *NORDWIND* represented the last large-scale German offensive of the war. Hitler would vainly try to orchestrate a counteroffensive against Marshal Polkovnik Tolbukhin's 3rd Ukrainian Front west of the Danube in early March 1945 with the remnants of *Sixth SS Panzer Armee*, but the depleted panzer force was destined for a precipitous retreat to the Austrian border.[25]

The Germans must be given considerable credit for their preparations in the fall of 1944. Assembling the necessary combat power entailed considerable risk in withdrawing forces from the line, holding critical ground forward of the assembly areas, rehabilitating the assigned forces, and assembling the requisite classes of supply. This was all done under cover of a sophisticated deception plan. The deceptive code name for the Ardennes operation, *WACHT AM RHEIN* (Watch on the Rhine), did not appear in the ULTRA signals because Hitler forbade its use over the telephone or wireless telegraph. However, the code name *ABWEHRSCHLACHT IM WESTEN* (Defensive Battle in the West) was purposely disseminated through German radio traffic to reinforce the defensive nature of the fighting around Aachen and the intention to employ *Sixth Panzer Armee* in a counterattack role west of the Rhine. Tracking the various armies was also problematic because each had a cover name, and the Germans made it a complex game of hide-and-seek. *Sixth Panzer Armee* was *Rest and Refit Staff 16*, *Fifth Panzer Armee* was *Jagerkommando zur besonderen Werwendung* (*zbV*, "for special purposes"), and *Fifteenth Armee* was *Gruppe von Manteuffel*.[26]

The success of the operation depended on many things going right. The probability of everything aligning for a rapid advance to the Meuse and beyond was low. If the original plan faltered, it would be imperative to have anticipated where and when problems might occur and to be ready with contingency plans. Main efforts might have to be shifted once other opportunities presented themselves. Hitler and his commanders needed to have true situational understanding to identify points at which new decisions had to be made. Although the main plan was well articulated, contingency planning was unrefined, perhaps because Hitler placed so much faith in *Sixth Panzer Armee*'s ability to accomplish its task. *WACHT AM RHEIN* had strong points and weak points in its grand tactical scheme of maneuver and main effort, and those weak points reduced the probability of achieving the goal of reaching Antwerp. It must be remembered that it had been almost two years since the last successful German strategic counteroffensive, back during *Generalfeldmarschall* Erich von Manstein's brilliant victory at Kharkov following Stalingrad. Much had changed since then to degrade the German war-fighting system.

2

The Opposing Armies in December 1944

It was not that his [Hitler's] soldiers now lacked determination or drive:
what they lacked was weapons and equipment of every sort.
— Hasso von Manteuffel

German ground forces in World War II were finally defeated in May 1945 because they fought a multifront war against the world's three greatest industrial powers. They were simply outnumbered in manpower and materiel. Eisenhower's G-3, Major General Harold R. Bull, calculated that Allied numerical superiority in Normandy on July 1, 1944, was between 2.5:1 and 3:1. At the end of the Normandy campaign the Joint Intelligence Committee (JIC) concluded that the "process of final military defeat . . . has begun. . . . Whatever action Hitler may now take, it will be too late to affect the issue in the West, where organized German resistance will gradually disintegrate under our attack, although it is impossible to predict the rate at which this will take place." The JIC assessment was deterministic and declared that German defeat would occur before 1945. The 200,000 casualties sustained by the U.S. Army from January to May 1945 ruined this estimate.[1] Yet the fundamental truth was inescapable: the Allies' numerical and material superiority, the major components of their war-fighting system, simply overmatched that of the *Wehrmacht*.

At the strategic level the Allies possessed the necessary margin of superiority to seize and retain the initiative in northwestern Europe and to conduct operations at a significantly higher tempo than their opponent. From D-Day until the beginning of the Bulge the Allies conducted large operations at a rate of almost six to the Germans' one. The Allied operational interval was just over three days, versus twenty-one days for the Germans.[2] Their sustained defensive posture was a clear indication of the Germans' numerical and material inferiority. Well before the first Allied soldier stepped ashore in Normandy, the *Wehrmacht* lost the strategic initiative in Russia, never had it in Italy, and did not have it in northwest Europe until the Ardennes counteroffensive. Mustering sufficient combat power to temporarily seize the initiative in the west in late 1944 was achieved by economy of force and the acceptance of considerable risk. Despite the drastic measures taken to assemble the necessary combat power, *Heeresgruppe B* suffered from major deficiencies.

The German Army in Late 1944

Hitler's combat power rested on twenty divisions for the main strike force and another nine division equivalents in reserve. At Kursk eighteen months earlier he had massed fifty divisions in a far greater display of German might. Yet his violation of that almost sacred rule in German military thinking—to avoid multifront wars—had significantly eroded German combat power in the west. Rundstedt and Model were hardly surprised at the totals for the Ardennes. They recognized that Hitler's November 10 order of battle listing thirty-eight divisions was pure fantasy. Patton's own actions had ensured that the stated requirements could not be met. His renewed offensive in Lorraine in early November drew in the *36th, 347th,* and *719th Infantry Divisions* and the *256th Volksgrenadier Division* (VGD). Most important, Third Army fixed the *11th* and *21st PDs* and the *17th SS Panzergrenadier Division* (PGD) plus *Panzer Lehr* for an extended period of time.[3]

The most potent of the three armies was Dietrich's *Sixth Panzer Armee*; it was nine divisions strong, with the greatest concentration of SS divisions since Normandy. *SS-Gruppenführer* Hermann Priess's *I SS Panzerkorps* contained *SS-Oberführer* Wilhelm Mohnke's *1st SS PD "Leibstandarte Adolf Hitler"* and *SS-Standartenführer* Hugo Kraas's *12th SS PD "Hitler Jugend."* The *Leibstandarte* had reorganized two months before the Ardennes and received about 3,500 new troops, bringing it to a strength of 17,988. It was the least diluted of the regenerated SS divisions, and its panzer regiment contained 100 *Panzerkampfwagen* (Panzer) IVs and Vs (Panthers) and was further augmented by thirty Panzer VI *Königstiger* (King Tiger) IIs of *Schwere* (Heavy) *SS-Panzer Abteilung* (Battalion) *1*, of which perhaps fifteen were operational.[4] Each of its two panzer grenadier regiments contained two battalions. This was the same for all the SS panzer divisions.

The *12th SS PD* had fought savage battles in Normandy against the Canadians in early June and suffered grievously. At the sharp end the division had sustained more than 9,000 casualties up to December 1944, but with the augmentation of some 2,000 *Luftwaffe* replacements, it was overstrength at 18,548. However, the new soldiers were not sufficiently trained as infantrymen. The *1st* and *2nd SS PDs* received the fewest *Luftwaffe* replacements. The *12th SS* had only thirty-seven Panzer IVs, forty-one Panthers, and twenty-two *Panzerjäger* IVs in *Schwere Panzerjäger Battalion 560.*[5] It had sixty-six *Flugzeugabwehrkanone* (Flak) guns, including eighteen of the deadly Flak 88mm. The major weakness was in armored personnel carriers. The division possessed only 118 when it should have had 522. On the eve of the offensive Kraas reported that the division was only "conditionally suited for the attack."[6] By December 1944 the *12th SS* was hardly the same powerful, fanatical division that had fought so hard with some effectiveness in Normandy. Priess also had *Generalmajor* Walther Wadehn's *3rd Fallschirmjäger Division* (FJD), *Oberst* Wilhelm Viebig's *277th VGD*, and *Generalmajor* Gerhard Engel's *12th VGD* in *I SS Panzerkorps.* The *3rd FJD* had been virtually destroyed in Normandy and rebuilt with rear-echelon *Luftwaffe* ground personnel. When it entered the Bulge it was still 25 percent understrength, with just under 12,500 personnel. Each of its three regiments had three battalions, but the division did not have a *Sturmgeschütz* (StuG; assault gun) brigade.

The *277th VGD* was one of sixteen such divisions that fought in the Ardennes. The *VGD's* Table of Organization and Equipment (TO&E) strength of 10,072 was a direct reflection of the serious manpower crisis the Germans faced in the fall of 1944, a result of the *Wehrmacht's* 6 million dead, missing, and permanently disabled between September 1939 and the beginning of December 1944.[7] By early 1944 Hitler ordered the reduction of infantry division strength from approximately 17,000 to 12,500. The *VGDs* represented a further weakening, equaling a 40 percent reduction from the pre-1944 infantry divisions. Each *VGD* had three regiments, but each regiment contained only two battalions, and all its artillery—fifty-four guns—was horse drawn. Indeed, the division's mobility was dependent on some 5,000 horses. The formations were authorized a significant increase in automatic weapons, but this augmentation never compensated for their overall degraded combat power in comparison to previous infantry divisions. The *277th VGD* was considered a weak division, containing only one strong battalion and five medium-strength battalions. The division had perhaps no more than 1,000 veterans; the remainder were ethnic Germans, totaling just over 7,000. The *12th VGD*, with just over 9,500 personnel, was considered the best of the infantry divisions, having earned the honorific *volksgrenadier* during the hard fighting around Aachen.[8]

Protecting the left flank of the panzer corps was *General der Infanterie* Otto Hitzfeld's *LXVII Armeekorps* with the *272nd* and *326th VGDs*. Both had been destroyed in Normandy and subsequently rebuilt to a poor standard. The *272nd VGD* had just under 9,000 personnel; the *326th VGD* had just over 9,000 and appears to have retained most of its equipment. A shortage of 400 horses impeded mobility, and there had been no opportunity to conduct combined arms training beyond the battalion level. Both divisions had a few of the *Jagdpanzer* 38t, known as the *Hetzer* (Baiter), an excellent purpose-built tank destroyer mounting a 75mm gun.[9]

Dietrich's second panzer wave was to be *SS-Obergruppenführer* Wilhelm Bittrich's *II SS Panzerkorps* with *SS-Brigadeführer* Heinz Lammerding's *2nd SS PD "Das Reich"* and *SS-Oberstführer* Sylvester Stadler's *9th SS PD "Hohenstaufen."* *Das Reich* was infamous for committing atrocities against French civilians as it struggled to reach the Normandy battlefront. *Hohenstaufen* also fought in Normandy and took part in repulsing the British 1st Airborne Division at Arnhem. *Hohenstaufen* contained 17,000 personnel on December 17 but possessed only some sixty-five Panzer IVs and Vs, with twenty-five more Panthers en route. *Generalmajor* Fritz Kraemer, Dietrich's chief of staff, reflected that the "weakest of our panzer divisions was 9 SS Pz Div. This Division was insufficiently equipped with vehicles, a condition which often required the units to move on foot. It had lost many of its artillery prime movers; also, it had many Volksdeutsch and not enough old cadremen."[10]

Patton would end up fighting several of Dietrich's divisions as they were eventually drawn south into the Bastogne fight, but Third Army chiefly fought against Manteuffel's *Fifth Panzer Armee* and Brandenberger's *Seventh Armee*. Manteuffel had three corps. *General der Panzertruppen* Heinrich Freiherr von Lüttwitz's *XLVII Panzerkorps* consisted of two veteran divisions—*Generalleutnant* Fritz Bayerlein's *Panzer Lehr Division* and *Oberst* Meinrad von Lauchert's *2nd PD "Vienna."* Heinz Kokott's *26th VGD* rounded out the corps.

Panzer Lehr had originally been an elite demonstration unit and had been one of the most powerful divisions in Normandy, but it had suffered heavily during COBRA and in Lorraine. Now its losses could no longer be made good. *Lehr* limped into the assembly area behind *Fifth Panzer Armee* at barely 50 percent strength after a seven-night march from the Saar area, where it had fought against the 4th Armored Division. A November 27 *First Armee* report decoded by Bletchley Park on December 3 indicated that the division had seven Panzer IVs and six Panther tanks, eight heavy *Panzerjägers*, and seventeen *StuGs*; 60 percent mobility; and a *Kampfwert III* rating. Its strength in personnel, at 12,672,[11] was still higher than that of an American armored division.

Oberst Helmut Ritgen, an officer in the division, stated that, superficially, the division's sixty-three Panzer IVs and Vs and fifteen *Panzerjäger* IVs "appeared to be favourable when compared to other divisions." German panzer divisions had one panzer regiment of two battalions and two panzer grenadier regiments of three battalions each, but *Lehr's* panzer regiment had no more than one mixed panzer battalion instead of two. To compensate for the Panther Battalion's continued absence in Hungary, *Lehr* was to receive *Schwere Panzerjäger Abteilung 559*, equipped with *Jagdpanthers*, but it did not arrive until after Christmas. *StuG Brigade 243*, which was also promised to the division, never arrived. Ritgen concluded that the panzer grenadiers "lacked their earlier fire-power, because they possessed neither gun APCs [armored personnel carriers] nor heavy infantry guns. Moreover, the considerable lack of training also could not be overlooked." It has been suggested that *Panzer Lehr* received some Panthers with the revolutionary infrared commander's sight,[12] but there is no proof of this.

The *2nd PD* was at 80 percent strength, with 12,680 personnel. The panzer regiment had twenty-seven Panzer IVs, fifty-eight Panthers, and forty-eight assault guns, but repair shop facilities were a major deficiency. The infantry component of the corps, Kokott's *26th VGD*, was close to its TO&E strength. ULTRA indicated that it had eight battalions, rather than the usual six of a *VGD*. Seven of the battalions were considered strong, and one was considered medium. The division possessed forty-two 75mm towed *Panzerjägers*. Overall, the division was rated *Kampfwert III*.[13] It had seasoned senior commanders, but they had no experience in offensive fighting, and to a large extent, the subordinate commanders and men had little combat experience.

General der Panzertruppen Walter Krüger's *LVIII Panzerkorps* consisted of *Generalmajor* Siegfried von Waldenburg's *116th PD "Greyhound"* and *Oberst* Rudolf Langhauser's *560th VGD*. Waldenburg was as happy as he could be with the artillery, personnel, and infantry weapons, which were nearly complete. Personnel strength was 15,500, but the division's continuous preceding commitment had "caused the loss of irreplaceable experienced officers and EM [enlisted men]." The *Pionier Abteilung* had personnel for only two companies. Most of the motor vehicles required major reconditioning, but spare parts were nonexistent. The division had only about 60 percent of the full complement of vehicles, and as a result, it was rated as 75 percent mobile. According to *Oberstleutnant* Heinz Günther Guderian, the division's Ia (first General Staff officer), the panzer regiment had forty-three Panthers and twenty-six Panzer IVs.[14] The *560th VGD* had been formed from occupation troops in Norway and had made its way to the Ardennes via Denmark minus an entire infantry regiment. Its strength, when the third regiment arrived, was close to TO&E. Its organic motor transport company was missing, and it possessed only two artillery battalions. *Oberst* Rudolf Bäder, who took command in late December, rated it *Kampfwert III* because it had no offensive training and far too few antitank weapons.[15]

Manteuffel also had *General* Walter Lucht's weak *LXVI Armeekorps* with *Generalmajor* Günther Hoffmann-Schönborn's *18th VGD* and *Oberst* Freidrich Kittel's *62nd VGD*. The *18th VGD* had just been formed in September in Denmark with 5,500 *Kriegsmarine* and *Luftwaffe* fillers and another 5,000 men from German industry. The *62nd VGD* had been destroyed in Russia and now contained Poles and Czechs who spoke no English; its strength was just over 11,000.[16] Neither division had many experienced leaders or men, and each probably had a dozen or so *Hetzers*.

Of the three army commanders, *General der Panzertruppen* Erich Brandenberger drew the toughest assignment and was forced to attempt to do the most with the least resources. He had to protect Manteuffel's left flank by blocking Third Army should it advance north. To accomplish this mission, Brandenberger realized he needed significant forces. "As I estimated my needs," he recalled, "one motorized unit was needed for the right wing if I was to keep pace with the more mobile units of the 5 Panzer Army. For the defensive front to the South, with the right wing in the vicinity of Givet, six divisions were requested. In addition, two to three more divisions were asked for as army reserve which would be drawn up behind the Army and available at the proper moment against the expected counterattacks. These claims were not fulfilled by Army Group!" He suggested that the difference between what he requested and what he received was due to Model's assessment of how counterattacks from the south would develop. "I was of the opinion," he stated, "that the enemy counterattacks would be directed in full strength against the rupture-point of the German operation, that is, along the line Bastogne–Echternach. Army Group believed that the pressure against this front would be less than that against the point of the panzer spearhead."[17] Brandenberger was given only four infantry divisions: the *212th* and *276th VGDs* of *General der Infanterie* Franz Beyer's *LXXX Armeekorps* and the *352nd VGD* and *5th FJD* of *General der Infanterie* Baptist Kniess's *LXXXV Armeekorps*. Brandenberger was also given *General der Kavallerie* Graf von Rothkirch und Trach's *LIII Armeekorps* headquarters to command reserve divisions once they were released.

The weakest division in *Seventh Armee* was apparently *Oberst* Ludwig Heilmann's re-formed *5th FJD*. It had suffered heavy casualties in Normandy and had been rebuilt around *Kriegsmarine* and *Luftwaffe* ground personnel and field units. On December 1, 1944, the rebuilding process was still incomplete. Its weak rear services ensured great difficulties in bringing up supplies. Heilmann stated that the TO&E strength was just under 16,000, but only 11,000 combat-effective soldiers were on hand. Some of the infantry remained in assembly areas for further training and would be sent forward as replacements during the fight for Bastogne. The division may also have had upwards of twenty self-propelled guns in its assault battalion. *Oberst* Freiherr von Gersdorff, Brandenberger's chief of staff, considered Heilmann to be excellent, but the subordinate commanders "had no qualifications whatever, because their training was defective, and they had no experience." Although Heilmann rated his division *Kampfwert IV*, its performance in the Bulge would prove otherwise.[18]

Gersdorff stated that the 10,595-man *352nd VGD* had a "small cadre of veteran lower officers and men." He thought the commanders were generally good, but the junior leaders and noncommissioned officers were lacking. The division suffered from the shortages plaguing all German divisions in the fifth year of the war. The division commander, Erich Otto Schmidt, reported that the average age of the men was twenty-two to thirty, but they were "too briefly trained" and had "no experience with terrain or combat." The artillery was weak and was "tactically and technically not dependable in directing and adjusting fire and observation." However, six of the battalions were considered strong and one medium.[19]

The last of *Seventh Armee*'s divisions was *Generalmajor* Franz Sensfuss's *212th VGD*. It was at TO&E strength, and Sensfuss stated that it possessed "good manpower, good old stock," and "proved, old commanders."

This assessment was seconded by Gersdorff. The division's training, Sensfuss added, "was indeed short, but enough." Although newly established, it had gained some limited fighting experience in the previous weeks. The division had two strong battalions and four medium battalions, possessed its full number of weapons, and was the only one of the three *VGDs* in *Seventh Armee* that had assault guns.[20]

There were several more divisions with significant material weaknesses held in reserve. Model had direct control over only one division, the *79th VGD*, which was still in Sudetenland. OKW reserves consisted of nine formations: *3rd PGD*; *9th, 167th,* and *257th VGDs*; *Führer Begleit Brigade* (FBB); *Führer Grenadier Brigade* (FGB); *6th SS-Gebirgs* (Mountain) *Division*; *10th SS PD*; and *11th PD*. The last three divisions would not fight in the Ardennes. The *3rd PGD* had twenty-five *Panzerjägers* and forty-one *StuGs*. The *FBB* and *FGB* combined contained thirty-four Panzer IVs, thirty-seven Panthers, and eighty-two *StuGs*. As the battle developed, the *15th PGD* and *340th VGD* would also be shifted from *Fifteenth Armee*. The *15th PGD* contained fourteen Panzer IVs, twenty *Panzerjägers*, and thirty *StuGs*.[21]

A total of thirty formations actually fought in the Ardennes. Considering the tremendous losses suffered during the last two years, Hitler's achievement in mustering this number was impressive. However, the *FBB* and *FGB* combined were the equivalent of one division, reducing the final total to twenty-nine divisions. The German total must be furthered qualified because of the diminished combat power of the *VGDs*, which represented 53 percent of the total divisional strength in the Ardennes. The deficiency of the *VGDs* was significant: forty-eight battalions, the equivalent of five infantry divisions. This reduced the actual divisional equivalent for the offensive to twenty-four. The breakdown of the other types of formations as a percentage of the total actually committed was as follows: two *PGDs* (6.5 percent), two *FJDs* (6.5 percent), eight *PDs* (27 percent), and two separate brigades (6.6 percent). According to the Ardennes Campaign Simulation Data Base (ACSDB), the total start strength of the thirty formations of Model's three attacking armies was 336,421. Nondivisional units brought the total to over 416,000, while *Heeresgruppe B*'s *verpflegungsstärke* (ration strength), including *Fifteenth Armee*, was 501,755 on December 15.[22] Its *Kampfstaerke* (combat-effective) strength cannot be determined with certainty.

The massing of heavy weapons did not meet expectations, with the possible exception of artillery. Model received General Headquarters

Table 2.1. Initial Strength of German Divisions that Fought in the Ardennes

Formation	Start Strength	Panzer Allocation Priority (%)	*Kampfwert* Rating (if known)
9 VGD	8,730		
12 VGD	9,517		
18 VGD	10,390		
26 VGD	9,951		III
62 VGD	11,050		
79 VGD	10,132		
167 VGD	11,050		
212 VGD	10,490		
246 VGD	8,9589		
272 VGD	8,771		
276 VGD	9,320		III
277 VGD	7,249		
326 VGD	9,083		
340 VGD	7,613		
352 VGD	10,595		
560 VGD	11,197		III
3 FJD	12,474		
5 FJD	13,543		IV
3 PGD	11,442		III (Nov 1)
15 PGD	10,988		II (Nov 1)
1 SS PD	17,988	100	III (Nov 4)
2 SS PD	17,000	100	III (Nov 1)
9 SS PD	13,363	100	IV (Nov 1)
12 SS PD	18,548	100	II (was IV on Nov 1)
2 PD	12,680	80	III (Nov 1)
Panzer Lehr	12,672	70	III
9 PD	12,889	60–70	II (Nov 1)
116 PD	15,468	?	II (Nov 8)
FBB	7,000		
FGB	6,270		
Total*	336.421		

*Total does not include *Panzer Brigade 150* (3,000) and von der Heydte's *Fallschirmjägers* (800).
Source: ACSDB, p. II-G-4–9; MS #A-862 (Schramm), pp. 197-98.

(GHQ) pooled artillery units equal to seven newly created and independent *Volksartilleriekorps* (*VAKs*) redesignated from GHQ artillery brigades. Each had sixty to ninety guns. Although the *VAKs* were supposed to possess *Zugstaffeln* (prime movers), many did not; some were detached to improve the mobility of the divisions. Model was also given seven *Volkswerferbrigaden* (*VWBs*). The *VWBs* possessed four battalions of three batteries each with between two and six *Werfers* (rocket projectors) that had a maximum range of 8,200 yards.[23] Each contained *Nebelwerfers* (smoke-throwers)—towed, multibarreled rocket launchers capable of unleashing a ton of high explosives in seconds. Allied troops had first experienced the *Nebelwerfers* in Normandy and called them "screaming meemies" because of the unique sound they made when fired. Army artillery consisted of heavy *Mörser* (mortar) batteries with two to six tubes per battery. *Vergeltungswaffe I* (Revenge Weapon No. 1), known to the Allies as V1 and V2 (supersonic) rockets, was assigned for deep fire.

According to *Generalleutnant* Karl Thoholte, Model's artillery adviser, *Heeresgruppe B* massed approximately 1,900 gun barrels, including *Mörsers*, for the offensive, a total considered sufficient for the mission.[24] However, independent calculation reveals that there were approximately 1,549 nondivisional pieces alone, including 552 guns in the *VAKs*, 912 *Werfers*, and 78 *Mörsers*. The breakdown of nondivisional gun assets equated to approximately 580 guns for *Sixth Panzer Armee*, 530 for *Fifth Panzer Armee*, and 420 for *Seventh Armee*. When the 1,504 guns from the divisions were added, *Heeresgruppe B* had an artillery strength of just over 3,000, not including Flak guns.[25] If this figure is correct, it represented 56 percent of the 5,422 guns *OB West* calculated were in the west, including coastal and antiaircraft guns on December 12.[26]

There are wide discrepancies in the exact number of German tanks deployed in the Ardennes. The official historian of the campaign, Hugh Cole, suggested upwards of 1,800, but this was the figure Percy Schramm gave for all of *Heeresgruppe B*, including *Fifteenth Armee*. Cole admitted that "a considerable number" were tied down in the Aachen sector.[27] A collation of various sources suggests a total panzer strength, including Panzers, *Panzerjägers*, and *StuGs*, of 1,428 in the divisions and *Heerestruppen* (army troops) units. Of these, 21 percent were Panzer IVs, 25 percent were Panthers, 22 percent were *Panzerjägers*, and 27 percent were *StuGs*. This figure is very close to Trevor Dupuy's 1,400. Schramm argued that only 80 percent of the panzers committed were operational. Using this as a baseline, *Heeresgruppe B* probably deployed no more than

Table 2.2. Estimated Total German Artillery in the Ardennes

Type of Formation	No. of Formations	No. of Tubes/ Formations	Total
Nondivisional			
VAK 388	1	87	87
VAK 401	1	72	72
VAK 402	1	90	90
VAK 405	1	60	60
VAK 406	1	72	72
VAK 408	1	90	90
VAK 766	1	81	81
Subtotal	7		552
Werfers			
VWB 4	1	108	108
VWB 7	1	124	124
VWB 8	1	124	124
VWB 9	1	124	124
VWB 15	1	108	108
VWB 16	1	108	108
VWB 17	1	108	108
VWB 18	1	108	108
Subtotal	8		912
Mörsers (Mortars)			
Army heavy batteries	18	1–6	78
Railway guns	1	66	6
Nondivisional subtotal			1,548
Divisional			
VGDs	16	54	864
PGDs	2	54	108
FJDs	2	36	72
PDs	4	54	216
SS PDs	4	52	208
Separate brigades	2	18	36
Divisional subtotal	30		1,504
Total			3,052

Source: Modified from Danny S. Parker, *Battle of the Bulge* (Conshohocken Pa.: Combined Books, 1991), 249.

Table 2.3. Estimate of the Effectiveness of Artillery Staff and Units in *Fifth Panzer Armee*

Formation	Arty Unit	Effectiveness (%)	Comments
LXVI Armeekorps			
18 VGD	AR 1818	75	Vehicles, horses almost complete
62 VGD	AR 162	75	Few shortages of essential equipment
LVIII Panzerkorps			
116 PD	Armd AR 160	Not indicated	War tested, efficient
560 VGD	AR 1560	70	Little combat experience
LXVII			
2 PD	AR 74	80	Not entirely equipped
Lehr	Armd AR 130	80	Combat experienced; lack of prime movers
26 VGD	AR 26	75	Combat experienced; small defects in equipment
VAK 401		65	Tired; personnel and equipment shortages
VAK 766		70	Tired; losses not replaced

Source: MS #B-393 (Metz), "The use of Artillery in the Ardennes-Offensive 1944 by the 5 Armored Army," pp. 55–58; MS #B-311 (Thoholte), "The Ardennes," p. 2.

1,134 operational panzers, and even this estimate is likely too high. Dietrich and Manteuffel probably had around 450 and 350 Panzers and *Panzerjägers/StuGs*, respectively.[28]

It is important to remember that despite the reconditioning achieved during the fall, the panzer divisions were "full strength" based solely on the late 1944 reduced TO&E established to address diminished production and expansion in the number of divisions. Compared with earlier in the war, they were woefully understrength and experienced a drastic reduction in their combat power. Moreover, maintaining a state of high operational readiness would prove difficult. *General der Panzertruppen* Horst Stumpff, the chief panzer officer at *OB West* under Guderian, was responsible for bringing all available repair shops forward into the Eifel area for the rapid servicing of damaged tanks. He began to do this on December 14 but had only six repair companies to perform third- and fourth-line repair work and one evacuation company for perhaps 1,000 armored vehicles. The repair shops avoided setting up near towns and road junctions and thus stayed relatively hidden from American airpower.[29]

Table 2.4. Estimated German Armored Strength, December 16, 1944

Division	Panzer IV	Panzer V	Panzer VI	Panzerjäger*	StuG
Sixth Panzer Armee					
1 SS PD	34	37	—	20	—
2 SS PD	28	58	—	20	28
9 SS PD	39	35	—	21	28
12 SS PD	37	39	—	47	
12 VGD	—	—	—	—	6
272 VGD	—	—	—	8	—
277 VGD	—	—	—	6	—
Subtotal	138	169	0	122	62
Fifth Panzer Armee					
130 Panzer Lehr	30	23	—	19	18
2 PD	27	49	—	—	24
116 PD	26	45	—	19	25
18 VGD	—	—	—	14	—
26 VGD	—	—	—	14	—
62 VGD	—	—	—	14	—
560 VGD	—	—	—	—	—
Subtotal	83	117	0	80	67
Seventh Armee					
352 VGD	—	—	—	6	—
276 VGD	—	—	—	?	—
212 VGD	—	—	—	5	—
5 FJD	—	—	—	—	20
Subtotal	0	0	0	11	20
Heeresgruppe B/OKW Reserves					
9 PD (Fifteenth Armee)	28	37	—	10	—
3 PGD	—	—	—	25	41
15 PGD	14	—	—	20	30
FGB	11	37	—	—	34
FBB	23	—	—	—	48
9 VGD	—	—	—	12	—
79 VGD	—	—	—	?	—
167 VGD	—	—	—	12	—
340 VGD (Fifteenth Armee)	—	—	—	—	—
Subtotal	76	74	0	79	153
Heerestruppen (GHQ)					
s. SS-Panzer Abt 501	—	—	15	—	—
s. SS-Panzer Abt 506[1]	—	—	30	—	—
s. Funklenk Abt 301	—	—	31	—	—
StuG Brig 244	—	—	—	—	14
StuG Brig 394	—	—	—	—	3
StuG Brig 667	—	—	—	—	5
StuG Brig 902	—	—	—	—	20
s. Panzerjäger Abt 519	—	—	—	10	11
s. Panzerjäger Abt 657	—	—	—	16	17
s. Panzerjäger Abt 668	—	—	—	?	—
s. Panzerjäger Abt 501 (Festung)	—	—	—	?	—
Panzer Brig 150	—	—	—	—	5
Subtotal	0	0	76	26	75
Total	297	360	76	318	377

Note: Does not include *Fifteenth Armee*. * Principally *Jagdpanzer* 38t. [1] Still in *Fifteenth Armee* on December 16.
Sources: Foreign Military Studies manuscripts; Danny S. Parker, *Battle of the Bulge* (Conshohocken, Pa.: Combined Books, 1991), 309–10; Jean Paul Pallud, *Battle of the Bulge* (London: After the Battle, 1999), 34–55.

Model's panzer and artillery strength was significant, but an uninterrupted flow of fuel and ammunition was critical to complete the combat power equation. The German planning factor was 260,000 gallons per day for all three armies. A *Verbrauchssatze* (VS) was the basic German supply ration, equal to the volume of fuel necessary to move any given formation sixty miles under normal conditions. A Panther tank consumed seventy U.S. gallons of fuel on the road and 175 gallons cross-country every sixty miles. By December 16 the German supply system had amassed 4.68 million gallons for OB *West*, but the fuel was not concentrated well forward. Perhaps as much as half of it was stuck in dumps along the Rhine.[30]

In summer conditions the German stockpile should have facilitated operations for eighteen days. However, Model's staff calculated that four times that ration would be required in the Ardennes terrain and weather. This meant that the 4.68 million gallons would last a mere four and a half days. Despite the impressive stockpiling of fuel, the German formations were issued only one and a half VS for the start of the campaign. In the Ardennes terrain, that equated to an operational radius of forty-five miles. Some accounts have suggested that using captured American gas was a key planning assumption, but Lüttwitz, commander of *XLVII Panzerkorps*, declared, "I never heard of a plan to count upon captured supplies."[31]

As for ammunition, Hitler allocated 100 trains from the special "Führer Reserve" to feed the attack. By December 13 Model had more than 15,000 tons stockpiled in dumps, but a severe shortage of artillery ammunition still existed. Thoholte stated that it was possible to issue only about 1,000 rounds for each battery of four guns.[32] Transportation capacity was clearly insufficient even in the assembly stage of the operation. As Cole observed, "When it is remembered that some of the German divisions in the Ardennes had more horses than the German infantry division in 1918 one has a clearer picture of the supply problem." *Generalmajor* Richard Metz, *Fifth Panzer Armee*'s senior artillery commander, stated that the harsh weather and mountainous terrain resulted in a "considerably increased expenditure of physical strength of man and horse, of fuel for all motorized vehicles and great technical wear and tear of all driven weapons and vehicles. The horses that had for many years been under-fed, lacked the necessary strength for such exertions, and in the first days of the attack and still within range of their own front many a horse perished."[33]

Brandenberger was under no illusions as to the state of his army. After the war he lamented:

The ammunition supply had been only a little improved, the transportation situation was just as bad! Army artillery trucks had to be released for other uses, many were out of service, the repair shops were over-burdened, and there was the danger that the motorized artillery units would lose their mobility before the attack began. There were still no bridging columns, and in addition it was announced that only material without the engineers would be made available. In the whole of 7 Army there were no specialized engineers for directing the use of the bridging material of the bridge columns. Pontoons were still lacking. These last minute attachments did not help the soldiers, they needed time for practice.[34]

An inadequate substitute for engineers were the volunteers of Organization Todt, a paramilitary construction organization set up by the former Reich's armaments minister Fritz Todt. It had been responsible for building the West Wall and Atlantic Wall defenses and many other military construction projects. However, according to Manteuffel, this group was a poor substitute for skilled engineers in an offensive. "At the start of the offensive," he stated, "units of the Organization Todt were only present in fragmentary numbers compared with their strength as authorized for the Army. They consisted further of over-age personnel, not really sufficiently mobile and were unfit for combat so far as equipment and physical fitness were concerned."[35]

Even if the fuel and ammunition had been sufficient and the supply system had been robust enough to get them forward, the reality was that the bad weather would not last forever. At some point in the race to the Meuse, the German columns would be subjected to the power of the Allied air forces. To compensate, *III Fliegerabwehrkannonen* (Flak) *Korps*, consisting of sixty-six heavy and seventy-four medium and light batteries, was issued seven basic loads of ammunition. *Luftwaffencommando West* had assembled a powerful force under *Generalmajor* Dietrich Peltz's *Jadgkorps II* to support the offensive, but the number of operational aircraft, including a few of the revolutionary *Messerschmitt* ME-262 jet-engine fighters, likely did not exceed 1,400. Total German operational aircraft at the time numbered 5,317, but the *Luftwaffe* suffered from a serious shortage of both fuel and trained pilots.[36]

Hitler massed an impressive number of troops in *Heeresgruppe B*, but sustaining the combat troops with sizable and timely replacements was beyond the power of the German army in late 1944. The German *Ersatzheer* (Replacement Army) was incapable of keeping the field force up to strength, although it did succeed in introducing replacements into combat units over time through *Feldersatz* (field replacement) battalions. The Germans found some relief from the contraction of occupation areas, which permitted an infusion of line of communications personnel to the field formations. However, the Germans' divisional slice—that is, the division plus the service and support troops required to keep it in the field—was 26,500, compared with the Americans' slice of between 40,000 and 43,000, meaning that there was less fat in the rear areas to leverage.[37] Another expedient was to transfer men from the *Luftwaffe* and *Kriegsmarine* as those services' roles in the war declined. By late 1944 the German army was also filled with *Hilfswillige*, Russian prisoners of war. Hitler's policy of fielding a very large number of divisions at the expense of keeping a smaller number up to full strength had its weaknesses, but the German army was still able to rotate divisions late in the war.[38]

Divisional rotation was critical to maintaining combat effectiveness, but the expedients did little to improve the quality of the replacements. Manteuffel felt that the *volksgrenadiers* were of varying quality; some were good, and others were below average. "Most of them," he observed, "were insufficiently trained for coordinated action; had no combat experienced non-commissioned officers; had not had time nor ammunition for training in firing of weapons; and were not conditioned to marching and fighting to the degree that modern warfare demands, unless they had been trained in a quiet front-line sector." Manteuffel had serious concerns about the infantry in general, not just the VGDs. He argued with Hitler to forgo a long preliminary artillery bombardment on his front for the valid reason that it would simply alert the Americans. Yet he also wanted to attack in darkness because "our infantry were not of the same caliber as those that had invaded France, and . . . they did not meet the required standards to achieve a breakthrough in daylight."[39]

The *Wehrmacht*'s diminishing combat power inevitably undermined its fighting power. In June and July 1944 only 40 percent of German POWs thought they could drive the Allies out of France. By August the German High Command finally announced that it would "henceforth often be no longer able to meet demands, however urgent and justifiable, for air, armour, and artillery support, even when enemy superiority is overwhelming." Shortages of weapons would be "made good" by "strengthening the morale of the troops."[40] Expectations of success deteriorated in the fall

and reached almost utter defeatism in October, but the *Heer* held nevertheless. Many reasons have been put forward to explain this.

For a long time the German soldier had been called on to compensate
for waning combat power with his own internal reserves of resilience. The
Heer has been described as possessing "extraordinary tenacity" despite its
defeats, primarily because of "the steady satisfaction of certain primary
personality demands afforded by the social organization of the army." It is
possible that units' sustained cohesion in combat resulted from their basic military skill and efficiency. Harsh discipline, however, clearly played
a major part. At least 15,000 German soldiers were executed by the *Heer*
during the war. It was not possible to opt out of combat. There was certainly an element of fatalism in the *Heer*, and Omer Bartov was correct in
observing that it demonstrated a "grim, determined and increasingly hope-
less commitment to professional and national duty." Juxtaposed with this
sense of fatalism was a continued belief in the availability of war-winning
secret weapons in the near future. Perhaps most important, however, was
the fact that at least 50 percent of the *Heer* still had faith in Hitler by the
time of the Ardennes.[41]

The fighting power of the German formations in the Ardennes was un-
even. Manteuffel's chief of staff, Carl Wagener, suggested that the soldiers
were merely fulfilling their duty according to their oath "and did nothing
more. The complete readiness to fight and combat moral[e] were lacking; most men avoided close combat. They slackened easily in difficult
missions, and lost their spirit soon after reverses."[42] Ritgen declared that
the large gaps in the ranks of *Panzer Lehr*'s panzer grenadiers were filled
numerically with replacements, whom he described as "some splendid,
but retrained cavalrymen from Mechlenburg and very young recruits, still
capable of enthusiasm, as well as older, discontented Luftwaffe soldiers."
The influx of equipment and the confidence gained by witnessing the
marshaling of substantial combat power in the Eifel most certainly had
an effect on the psyche of the German soldiers, and it has been argued
that the armies refitting for the Bulge possessed better morale than other
armies elsewhere along the Western Front. According to Manteuffel, the
morale of the *26th VGD* was excellent, and Erich Schmidt, commander
of the *352nd VGD*, considered the fighting spirit of his infantry, mostly
former *Kriegsmarine* personnel, to be good. Brandenberger said that the
5th FJD's men had good enthusiasm and morale, but "its fighting power
was no more than that." Overall, Rundstedt observed that the morale of
the troops taking part in the Ardennes was "astonishingly high at the start

of the offensive. They really believed victory was possible."[43] The sustainment of this morale was directly related to success and to the German soldiers' appreciation of the *Wehrmacht*'s combat power in relation to that of the enemy.

The U.S. Army in Late 1944

On the eve of the German counteroffensive there were seventy Allied divisions on the Continent, including forty-five U.S. divisions. Thirty-eight U.S. divisions, twenty-eight infantry divisions, and ten armored divisions were deployed at the front. Eisenhower's theater reserve, XVIII Airborne Corps, consisted of the U.S. 82nd and 101st Airborne Divisions; these two lightly armed divisions were resting and refitting near Reims after suffering heavy losses in Operation MARKET GARDEN and subsequent fighting under Montgomery's command. Eisenhower also had the U.S. 94th Infantry Division southeast of Paris deployed between Quimper and Auxerre and the newly arrived U.S. 75th Infantry Division around Ocquier, Belgium. The U.S. 42nd, 63rd, and 70th Infantry Divisions were at Marseilles, minus their normal divisional service support.[44] Three more U.S. divisions—the 11th Armored, 17th Airborne, and 66th Infantry— were in England. The British 6th Airborne Division was also in England, as was the headquarters of the First Allied Airborne Army. U.S. divisions amounted to 64 percent of Eisenhower's total strength.

A week before the counteroffensive, SHAEF calculated that the *Wehrmacht* deployed 286 divisions in all theaters. Twenty-six divisions (9 percent) were in Italy, twenty-one divisions (7 percent) were in the Balkans, nineteen divisions (6.4 percent) were in Scandinavia, and eleven divisions

Table 2.5. Distribution of U.S. Divisions Worldwide, December 16, 1944

Division Type	Mobilized	Europe (including Italy)	Pacific	Available
Armored	16	16	0	11
Infantry	67	48	19	31
Airborne	5	4	1	3
Cavalry*	2	0	1	0
Total	90	68	21	45

*One cavalry division was not sent overseas.
Sources: Compiled from Shelby L. Stanton, *World War II Order of Battle* (New York: Galahad, 1991); Ronald G. Ruppenthal, *U.S. Army in World War II: Logistical Support of the Armies* (Washington, D.C.: Center of Military History, 1987), 2:282–83.

Table 2.6. SHAEF Order of Battle, December 16, 1944

Army Group	Inf Divs	Armd Divs	Abn Divs	Total
Twenty-First Army Group (Montgomery)				
First Canadian Army	4	2		6
Second British Army	5	3		8
British 50th Inf Div at Ypres	1			1
Subtotal	10	5	0	15
U.S. Twelfth Army Group (Bradley)				
Ninth U.S. Army	4	2		6
First U.S. Army	11	3		14
Third U.S. Army	7	3		10
Subtotal	22	8	0	30
U.S. Sixth Army Group (Devers)				
Seventh U.S. Army	6	2		8
First French Army	7	3		10
Subtotal	13	5	0	18
Theater reserve			2	2
Unassigned at this time*	2			2
Other†	3			3
Total	50	18	2	70

* U.S. 75 and 94 Inf Divs.
† U.S. 42, 63, and 70 Inf Divs at Marseilles.

(4 percent) were in Germany. Seventy-one divisions were deployed on the Western Front (25 percent), and 134 divisions were deployed on the Eastern Front (47 percent). Thirty-two percent of the panzer divisions were in the west, increasing to 40.4 percent if those in Italy were included. The seventy-one divisions in the west were assessed by SHAEF as possessing an actual combat strength of only thirty-five and a half divisions.

Twelfth Army Group's thirty divisions compared favorably with *Heeresgruppe B*'s twenty-nine nominal divisions (twenty-four, based on the VGD battalion deficiencies, and even less according to SHAEF's calculations). The twenty-two infantry divisions and eight armored divisions in Twelfth Army Group had TO&E strengths of 313,566 and 98,433, respectively, for a total of 411,999. However, three days before the Germans attacked in the Ardennes, Twelfth Army Group was understrength by 32,047. Although it would be reasonable to assume that 78 percent of this deficiency was the result of infantry casualties, Twelfth Army Group's infantry shortage on December 15 was 17,581. Third Army's infantry shortage was

Table 2.7. SHAEF G-2 Estimate of German Divisions in All Theaters, December 16, 1944

Front	Total Divs	PDs/PGDs	Total (%)	PD/PGD Total (%)
West	71	15	24	32
Italy	26	4	9	8.5
Balkans	21	0	7	0
Scandinavia	19	0	6.4	0
Germany	11	0	4	0
East	134	28	45	60
Unlocated	4	0	0	0
Total	286	47	16	

Source: SHAEF G-2 Weekly Intelligence Summary No. 39, December 17, 1944, p. 949.

8,213 on December 1.[45] Subtracting 17,581 from 411,999 leaves 394,418. One can also subtract 5 percent, or 1,602, from the 32,047 figure for losses sustained by the armored divisions. This leaves Twelfth Army Group with a total divisional strength of 392,816. Given *Heeresgruppe B*'s start strength of 336,421, Twelfth Army Group possessed 56,395 more men in

Table 2.8. SHAEF Appreciation of German Strength in the West, December 10, 1944

Army Group	Panzer/Panzergrenadier		Infantry	
	Nominal	Actual	Nominal	Actual
Heeresgruppe H				
Fifteenth Armee	—	—	5	2 2/3
First Parachute Armee	—	—	5	2 2/3
Heeresgruppe B				
Fifth Panzer Armee	5	2	7	2 2/3
Sixth SS Panzer Armee	4	3	—	—
Seventh Armee	—	—	10	5 1/3
Heeresgruppe G				
First Armee	5	2	8	4
Nineteenth Armee	—	—	8	2 1/3
Total in line or immediate reserve	14	7	43	19 2/3
Transferring and unlocated	1	1/2	7	4 1/3
Defense works and LCs	—	—	5	2
Fortresses	—	—	1	2
Total	14	7 1/2	56	28

Source: SHAEF Weekly Intelligence Summary No. 38, December 10, 1944, p. 913.

Table 2.9. Twelfth Army Group Estimate of German Strength Opposite Allied Armies in the West, December 9, 1944

Allied Army Group	German Personnel (%)	German Tanks/ Assault Guns (%)	German Arty Bns (%)
Twenty-First Army Group	78,000 (20)	25 (4)	49 (22)
Sixth Army Group	37,500 (13)	55 (8)	37 (16)
Twelfth Army Group			
First Army	78,500 (27)	65 (9)	62 (28)
Ninth Army	26,500 (9)	90 (13)	29 (13)
Reserves on First/Ninth	32,000 (11)	320 (47)	16 (7)
Army fronts			
Third Army	37,000 (13)	130 (19)	32 (14)
Total	289,500	685	225

*Percent of theater total.

Source: Twelfth Army Group G-2 Weekly Intelligence Summary No. 18, December 9, 1944, pp. 5–8.

divisions than did *Heeresgruppe B*—a 14 percent superiority.[46] If in fact *Heeresgruppe B*'s divisional start strength is correct, it was significantly higher than the 289,500 figure cited by Twelfth Army Group intelligence prior to the offensive.

When the offensive started, Twelfth Army Group possessed a TO&E strength of 1,488 medium tanks in its eight armored divisions. Even allowing for an 11 percent replacement rate in effect at the time,[47] the armored divisions possessed somewhere in the neighborhood of 1,324 medium tanks, compared to *Heeresgruppe B*'s 733 Panzer IVs, Vs, and VIs—a superiority of 45 percent. Twelfth Army Group also contained eighteen separate tank battalions, each with a TO&E of 53 medium tanks, for a total of 954. Applying the 11 percent replacement rate leaves 850. Twelfth Army Group therefore had approximately 2,174 medium tanks, or a superiority of 66 percent. Its total superiority in armor skyrocketed when its sixteen self-propelled tank destroyer battalions were added.[48]

In terms of artillery, Twelfth Army Group possessed 1,488 divisional guns in its thirty divisions, and the field artillery battalions pooled at the army level swelled this figure significantly. By December 23 it would bring 4,155 guns into action. The Germans, for the most part, held American artillery in high regard throughout the war.[49] It excelled in all aspects, including close and continuous support for attacking formations, long-range interdiction of enemy movements, and counterbattery fire. It had powerful prime movers to transport the guns, observation planes,

Table 2.10. U.S. and German Artillery Ranges

Weapon	Caliber	Range (yards)	Range (miles)
Standard divisional			
U.S. howitzer (M2)	105mm	12,150	6.9
German le FH 18	10.5cm	11,675	6.6
German le FH 18M	10.5cm	13,478	7.7
Medium/heavy artillery			
U.S. howitzer (M1918)	155mm	12,400	7
U.S. howitzer (M1)	155mm	16,350	9.3
U.S. howitzer (M1)	8 inch	18,510	10.5
U.S. gun (M2)	155mm	20,100	11.4
U.S. gun	4.5 inch	20,500	11.6
U.S. gun (M1)	155mm	25,715	14.6
German SFH 18	17cm	14,572	8.3
Heavy artillery			
German K18	17cm	32,370	18.4
German M18	21cm	18,263	10.4
U.S. howitzer M1	240mm	25,255	14.3

Sources: Major Gregory V. Morton, "Field Artillery Support for III Corps Attack, 18–26 December 1944" (master's thesis, Fort Leavenworth, 1985), 10–11; W. J. K. Davies, *German Army Handbook, 1939–1945* (London: Ian Allan, 1973), 114.

and an excellent communications system with frequency-modulating radio-equipped forward observers and fire directions centers (FDCs). It possessed great mobility and flexibility and could quickly achieve time-on-target (TOT) concentrations, which consisted of hitting a target simultaneously from several different guns dispersed over the battlefield. The destructive effect of such coordination was awesome. Artillery would prove to be critical in the Ardennes, but the trump card in the U.S. arsenal was airpower. It guaranteed overmatch. Not counting aircraft in Italy, the Allies had 17,500 first-line combat aircraft, including 6,881 U.S. bombers and 5,000 U.S. fighters. It was doubtful whether the United States could have succeeded on the ground with only ninety divisions had it not produced such an effective and powerful air force.[50]

Twelfth Army Group clearly possessed a significant superiority over *Heeresgruppe B* when the offensive started. It has even been argued that by January 3, Eisenhower had a theater superiority of 2:1 in terms of "real" divisions. In actual fact, his overall numerical advantage was more than 2.5:1 in artillery, 10:1 in tanks, 3:1 in aircraft, and 2.5:1 in troops.[51]

Despite the U.S. superiority in manpower and the major platforms (tanks, artillery, and combat aircraft), two factors had degraded combat effectiveness throughout the fall, and these problems had not been fully resolved by the time the Germans struck. One factor was the strain on the logistical apparatus, and the other was the manpower replacement policy.

The Allied logistical system was superior to the Germans', but sustaining the armies still proved problematic during the fall. Eisenhower accepted considerable risk when he ordered the armies across the Seine in pursuit of the Germans at the end of the Normandy campaign. By early September American forces were already at Aachen on the German border, 200 miles beyond Paris. OVERLORD planners had anticipated being there only on D+330, or May 1945, and the logistical support plan did not envision this situation. The famous "Red Ball Express," an expanding circuit of supply trucks moving from the beaches to the front and back, could not keep the army supplied with enough fuel after Normandy. It was a temporary solution to a serious problem.[52]

Despite the fact that the great port of Antwerp had not been secured, Eisenhower decided to press toward the Rhine until logistical preparations allowed for a final all-out offensive into Germany in January 1945. As he candidly admitted in his memoirs, he was employing every means to "continue the offensive to the *extreme limit* of our ability."[53] The repercussions were felt immediately at the army level in the form of fuel and ammunition rationing. General Brehon B. Somervell, head of the Army Service Forces, declared on December 1, 1944, that emergency measures had been instituted to keep the armies supplied and that "this is the last rabbit we can pull out of the hat . . . what we are doing represents an all-out effort." The all-out effort yielded results because the Twelfth Army Group's after-action report noted, "The period from 8 November to 16 December was marked by continuous improvement in the G-4 picture. This was due to greater tonnage imports, increased rail facilities and improved distribution methods. . . . The ability of the armies to cope successfully with the serious enemy threat was largely a result of the improvement made in the logistical situation in the period just prior to the German attack."[54] Certain deficiencies remained, but fuel and ammunition would not be a problem in the Ardennes.

A greater threat to U.S. combat effectiveness was the limited number of divisions available. Army Chief of Staff General George C. Marshall ultimately capped the army at ninety divisions—sixty-seven infantry, two cavalry, sixteen armored, and five airborne—in June 1944.[55] A shortage of shipping almost certainly influenced the divisional cap, but Marshall was building the army to fight the Japanese army and the small portion of the *Wehrmacht* not engaged by the Red Army. Anywhere from 75 to 84 percent of total German casualties were sustained on the Eastern Front.[56] Marshall's ninety-division "gamble" caused great concern in Washington, but he told Secretary of War Henry L. Stimson before D-Day that the army was staking its success "on our air superiority, on Soviet numerical preponderance, and on the high quality of our ground combat units." Marshall's philosophy was that "our equipment, high standard of training, and freshness should give us a superiority which the enemy cannot meet and which we could not achieve by resorting to a matching of numerical strength."[57]

Marshall took this ninety-division gamble on the assumption that a steady flow of replacements would be available to sustain the divisions at or near their TO&E strengths, so they could stay in combat longer. The flow was absolutely critical for two reasons. First, the limited number of divisions available throughout the campaign in northwest Europe meant that many of them could not be rotated out of the line for rest and refitting. Second, as the official historian observed, "every ounce of fat" had been cut during the 1943 reorganization of the divisions, leaving the formations with degraded endurance.[58] By 1944 the U.S. infantry and armored divisions were triangular and "light" compared with their British and Canadian counterparts. The triangular concept was Lieutenant General Leslie J. McNair's idea to conserve manpower. Many assets, such as independent tank and tank destroyer battalions, were centralized at the army level based on the assumption that not every division needed them all the time. Such assets were organic to British and Canadian divisions, resulting in a larger Table of Equipment. For example, a British armored division had 3,414 organic vehicles, compared with 2,653 for a U.S. division—a difference of 761 vehicles, or 22 percent. Likewise, a British infantry division had 3,347 vehicles, compared with 2,012 for the United States—a difference of 1,335 vehicles, or 40 percent.[59]

The U.S. infantry division had a TO&E strength of 14,253, but the cutting edge, contained in the twenty-seven rifle companies, equaled only 5,184, or 36 percent of the divisional strength. If one evaluated the cutting edge based on the eighty-one platoons in the division, each consisting of forty men, the number fell to 3,240. Fortunately, even this thinning out of the U.S. infantry division left it with more infantry than a VGD, which possessed only eighteen companies of approximately 140 men each, for a total of 2,520. In terms of artillery, the U.S. infantry division had four field artillery battalions, three 105mm and one 155mm; each battalion contained twelve guns, for a divisional total of forty-eight. This was twenty-four less than a Canadian infantry division. For this reason, after the war the General Board called for greater artillery firepower in the infantry division.[60] The U.S. armored division had three 105mm armored field artillery battalions with eighteen guns each, for a divisional total of fifty-four, the same as a VGD. The realities of combat quickly disproved McNair's fundamental assumption, and American commanders habitually assigned separate tank and tank destroyer battalions to infantry divisions on a virtually permanent basis. Tank destroyer doctrine may have been problematic, but their presence beefed up the divisions.[61]

Well before D-Day, sustained combat also brought into question the basic philosophy behind the replacement policy. In early February 1944 the senior U.S. commander in the North African theater, Lieutenant General Jacob L. Devers, told McNair that divisions should not be left in the line for more than thirty to forty days because feeding replacements into a machine "is like throwing good money after bad." Army Ground Forces agreed and complained to the War Department in November that the philosophy of continuous divisional commitment fed by replacements "has created a vicious cycle with respect to battle fatigue."[62] As far back as April 1944 the War Department had encouraged the army to look within the theater to resolve its manpower shortage. With the start of major combat operations in northwest Europe, the replacement problem grew significantly. Between D-Day and the end of November the U.S. Army in the ETO sustained 364,785 casualties, including 134,589 nonbattle casualties. During the Lorraine campaign Patton sustained 55,182 battle and 42,088 nonbattle casualties. Up to December 7 the ETO was sustaining 3,000 battle casualties per day, or 90,000 per month, but was receiving only 53,000 replacements.

Conversion training within the ETO was stressed and reemphasized on November 8, the day Patton resumed his offensive in Lorraine. Patton twice drafted 5 percent of the army's headquarters and rear services, on December 6 and December 15, to retrain as riflemen in an attempt to keep one division in each corps at full strength. He selected the 5th and 87th Infantry Divisions. The seriousness of the replacement situation was captured in his diary entry on the day the Germans attacked in the Ardennes: "What a bunch of fools we have at home. The critical point of the war and after three years, no trained men." Indeed, the three-month fight in Lorraine had taken a heavy toll of Patton's divisions, a fact that would

Table 2.11. Status of Third Army Divisions Prior to the Ardennes

Division	CED*	Days in Combat	Battle Casualties	Combat Effectiveness (%)	Total War Casualties† (%)	Comments
5 Inf Div	July 16	160	1,337 (Nov)	94	167	Training
26 Inf Div	Oct 12	60	2,978 (Nov)	Low	120	Assimilating 3,000 converted replacements
35 Inf Div	July 11	160	2,013 (Nov)	Low	181	Attacking
80 Inf Div	Aug 8	102	1,105		181	Rehabilitating
87 Inf Div	Dec 13	2	0	100	82	Fresh
90 Inf Div	June 10	188	1,603 (Dec)	43	196	In line
95 Inf Div	Oct 20	58	?	61	72	In line
4 Armd Div	July 28	135	?	Medium	?	Resting
6 Armd Div	July 28	141	934 (Nov)	?	?	Reorganizing
10 Armd Div	Nov 2	43	?	?	78.5	Training

*Combat entry date, 1944.
† Total battle and nonbattle casualties, 1944–1945.
Sources: Peter Mansoor, *The G.I. Offensive in Europe: The Triumph of American Infantry Divisions, 1944–1945* (Lawrence: University Press of Kansas, 1999), 252; Division G-1 records.

influence his decisions about which formations to send into the Bulge first. Moreover, a trench foot epidemic began in the U.S. Army around November 10. Third Army showed the highest incidence, and it suffered from a shortage of cold-weather clothing and footgear during the worst of the winter weather.[63]

Many replacements for the 4th Armored Division who arrived at the end of the Lorraine campaign were converted riflemen or headquarters personnel who had no practical experience with tanks. In the 26th Infantry Division, one officer in the 101st Infantry observed that the converted riflemen "were willing enough but had very little idea of the job of an infantryman." Familiarization with the firing of as many weapons as possible and squad tactics had been the only training possible for most of the men. Samuel Lyman Atwood Marshall's observation that the converted riflemen "acted as if they had been betrayed by their country" probably misrepresented the true state of affairs, but there was no doubt that conversion undermined combat effectiveness even while trying to improve it by filling up units.[64] Even before he initiated conversion training, Patton had expressed doubts about the aggressiveness of American troops as far back as Tunisia. Patton declared, "Our infantry is certainly not up to the rest of our troops."[65]

The inability to rotate divisions more quickly hollowed out veteran divisions. New divisions suffered from individual and collective training deficiencies as a result of the practice of taking soldiers from divisions not scheduled to deploy overseas for some time and shipping them off to fill up other divisions. That trend has led some scholars to argue that 1944 divisions were inferior in terms of combat effectiveness compared with divisions produced the year before. This is a logical observation, but to suggest that 1944–1945 U.S. divisions were, on average, inferior to their German counterparts goes too far.[66] A VGD was not more combat effective than a U.S. infantry division.

In 1940 the *Wehrmacht* had actually been outnumbered in divisions and tanks when it invaded France. By fielding a highly skilled combined arms and joint force with superior and aggressive leaders, the Germans disproved the notion that an attacker needs a significant margin of superiority to achieve success. They faced a similar scenario in late 1944. *Heeresgruppe B* was outnumbered in actual divisions, artillery, armor, and combat aircraft, but the U.S. Army was not the French army. By December 1944 the U.S. Army was very close to its peak, and British official historians were correct to observe that American military power, at first only potential, was available "at the time of culminating impact upon the enemy." It had a superior number of divisions that it could maintain at close to TO&E strength with considerable exertion, and sixteen more divisions would arrive after the Bulge started. It possessed powerful and flexible artillery and a supply organization described as "highly complex, technical and skilled."[67]

The U.S. Army possessed enormous combat power, which manifested itself in pure brute force and what has been properly described as an "overwhelming dominance" in its ability to protect and sustain its ground forces.[68] Combined, these attributes produced operational flexibility, limited perhaps only by the number of divisions. The Germans would prove capable of penetrating the U.S. Army's protection and inflicting considerable damage on its combat power, but they would never be able to generate the dynamic synergy so apparent in 1940 to completely fracture it. Moreover, they could not even achieve the force ratios necessary to overmatch the U.S. Army and achieve the mission assigned by Hitler. It is important for the present study to remember that *Heeresgruppe B* had already endured six days of attrition by the time Patton entered the battle on December 22.

PART II

Panzers in
the Ardennes

3

Onslaught

The Wehrmacht achieved a surprise every bit as staggering as the one
in the same area in May, 1940.

—F. W. von Mellenthin

On the eve of the Ardennes offensive the Allied armies were deployed
from the North Sea coast to Switzerland—some 500 miles—a frontage
described by the American official historians as "excessively broad." The
sixty-three Allied divisions actually in the line on December 16 therefore
held, on average, a frontage of 8 miles, double that prescribed by doctrine for divisions on the offensive. In his October 28 directive to his army
group commanders, Eisenhower directed Bradley to support Montgomery's drive toward the Ruhr industrial area. However, Bradley was also
ordered to direct Patton's Third Army south of the Ardennes toward Germany's second most important industrial region, the Saar. Bradley therefore pursued two independent lines of action along his 230-mile front.
Doing so meant a subsistence-level economy of force in the center of his
line in the Ardennes. The 68,822 troops of VIII Corps held an 89-mile
front, far in excess of what a corps could realistically defend. Moreover,
Bradley had no army group reserve. It was this obvious and persistent area
of weakness that continued to fix Hitler's attention. Eisenhower admitted
after the war that his line had been "badly stretched," but he accepted full
responsibility, arguing that "risks had to be taken somewhere."[1]

The only sizable German force close to the Ardennes that gave
Eisenhower any pause was *Sixth Panzer Armee*. Eisenhower claimed that
SHAEF lost track of it in early December, but in the November 26 Weekly Intelligence Summary his G-2, Major General Kenneth Strong, indicated that its formations were deployed west of the Rhine, with a potential

center of gravity southwest of Cologne, possibly behind *Seventh Armee*. Its order of battle was thought to consist of *I* and *II SS Panzerkorps* with *1st*, *2nd*, *9th*, and *12th SS PDs*. Strong estimated that as many as nine panzer and five infantry divisions were known to be at the front, but they were all missing, including such veteran formations as *Panzer Lehr, 116th* and *2nd PDs, 10th SS PD, 3rd FJD,* and *3rd PGD.*[2]

Several of Eisenhower's deductions were sound. He correctly deduced that the German army would be vulnerable if it left the relative protection of the West Wall to retake ground. The belief that any westward penetration would be contained on the flanks was also valid; Model had made the same argument to Hitler. It is also difficult to argue with Eisenhower's conclusion that no Allied strategic objective was threatened in the Ardennes. Most important, he concluded that the sheer scale of effort required for a counteroffensive in the Ardennes was beyond German resources after the massive losses in Normandy and on the Eastern Front in 1944. The discovery of German measures to conserve fuel may have been incorrectly interpreted as the result of scarcity rather than the intent to stockpile for an offensive, but Strong accurately calculated that the operational radius of a sizable German mechanized force was only 120 to 150 miles, based on known fuel stocks. He also declared in the Weekly Intelligence Summary of November 12 that although *Sixth Panzer Armee* was formidable, it could not stage a "true counter-offensive" because it lacked the necessary size and fuel reserves.[3] Eisenhower correctly appreciated that Rundstedt assessed German capabilities in a similar fashion and would remain on the strategic defensive.

Eisenhower's willingness to risk economy of force in the Ardennes was also based on his appreciation of the Ardennes terrain. FM 100–5 declared that terrain "often exercises a decisive influence" on a commander's decision, and "proper evaluation and utilization of the terrain reduces the disadvantage of incomplete information of the enemy."[4] An orthodox analysis based on the staff manual in use at the time would have led any commander to conclude that the Ardennes, though permitting administrative mechanized road movement, was a poor choice for the full deployment of mechanized forces to conduct combat operations. Circumstances were different from those in May 1940, when the Germans had executed a route march through the region in good weather before coming to grips with the French army. In December 1944 the weather was abysmal, and American forces, though thin, were in place and had great combat power within supporting range.

In the Weekly Intelligence Summary of December 10 Strong declared, "There can be no option for the enemy but to fight hard for the SAAR without, however, prejudicing his position further NORTH. In the COLOGNE–DUSSELDORF sector, Sixth SS Panzer Army has been cleverly husbanded and remains uncommitted. And until this army is committed, we cannot really feel satisfied . . . we cannot expect anything else but continued reinforcement: hard and bloody fighting; every sort of defense. . . . It will be a bitter and hard struggle to reach the RHINE." Eisenhower therefore extrapolated that the enemy's *most likely* intent, or line of action, would be to launch a *tactical* counterattack with *Sixth Panzer Armee* (not a *strategic* counteroffensive) once Ninth and First Armies crossed the Roer River.[5] The possible lines of action for such a counterattack included northwest and north staged from the Eifel area. There was considerable evidence to reinforce Strong's logic. Ninth and First Armies had been hit hard by several heavy counterattacks as they probed toward the Roer River, and between November 16 and December 16 they suffered 31,000 combined casualties.

Strong did not identify a counteroffensive as a possible line of action in his *Weekly Intelligence Summary*, but he claimed in a postwar interview with Forrest C. Pogue that in early December he had informed Eisenhower and Lieutenant General Walter Bedell Smith, SHAEF chief of staff, that the re-forming panzer divisions could be used to "stage a relieving attack through the Ardennes," most likely when six days of bad weather grounded Allied airpower.[6] Montgomery had voiced his concern about Hodges's weakness in the Ardennes to Eisenhower on December 2, but the Supreme Commander made no mention of any anxiety about possible German activity in the Ardennes in his December 3 report to the Combined Chiefs of Staff. That day, however, Bradley wrote to Montgomery that the idea of moving some of Patton's divisions north into the Ardennes had been "given careful consideration" but was rejected. Eisenhower questioned Bradley about Hodges's vulnerability in the area four days later at Maastricht.[7] Bradley must have made a compelling case for his present dispositions, because Eisenhower ordered no regrouping.

Strong's postwar statement to Pogue is supported by his December 13 exchange of ideas with London, when he declared that "some relieving attack" was possible in the Ardennes if the numerous *VGDs* identified there did not soon begin to move off to active fronts. The next day Strong distributed a top-secret *Intelligence Digest* indicating that one possible German line of action was a "relieving attack" in the Ardennes.[8] The term *relieving attack* has a far different meaning in the military lexicon than *counteroffensive*. A relieving attack seeks to take pressure off a portion of one's own front by attacking the enemy elsewhere. In contrast, a spoiling attack seeks to preempt an enemy attack at the point of execution. The key is that both relieving and spoiling attacks are limited in scale, duration, and depth of penetration and are characterized by a limited mission and limited objectives.

Although Eisenhower was inclined to accept the likelihood of some type of limited attack in the Ardennes, he claimed that his only option was to pass over to the defense to "make our lines absolutely secure from attack while we awaited reinforcements."[9] This all-or-nothing argument misrepresents the way his divisions were employed at the time. Clearly, the lack of a larger theater reserve was a problem; he had no reserve comparable to *Sixth Panzer Armee*.[10] However, it is apparent that a greater reserve could have been accumulated. Bradley could not fully deploy all his combat power assembled on the left flank of his army group because of the realities of the ground. Indeed, on December 13 Eisenhower told Marshall that Bradley's advance would be held up owing to the flooded conditions of the Roer River rather than any lack of strength. Only ten of the seventeen divisions available could be deployed at one time.[11] The deduction from this admission is that Eisenhower did not have to suspend all offensive operations to reinforce the Ardennes. A few divisions stacked up in the Aachen corridor could have been repositioned to reinforce VIII Corps without significantly eroding the depth and power of the main effort on Hodges's left flank.

Eisenhower and Bradley were clearly affected by the Germans' deception operations for the counteroffensive. They both believed that the German army was virtually crippled. Although Eisenhower made some sound deductions, there were problems with his mental estimate: he had a gut feeling that something *could* happen in the Ardennes, allowed the weakness in the Ardennes to persist throughout the fall, and thus invited something *to* happen, and never forced Bradley to produce an army group contingency plan (built on Hodges's plan) for the rapid deployment of a mix of formations from the flanks in case something *did* happen.

Bradley, like Eisenhower, was gravely concerned about the shortage of ammunition and infantrymen, but he still believed that his forces overmatched the German forces opposite him. Brigadier General Edwin L. Sibert's last Weekly Intelligence Summary before the attack, issued on December 12, stated that "attrition is steadily sapping the strength of

German forces on the Western Front and . . . the crust of defense is thinner, more brittle and more vulnerable than it appears on our G-2 maps. . . . The enemy's primary capabilities continue to relate to the employment of the Sixth SS Panzer Army. . . . All of the enemy's major capabilities . . . depend on the balance between the rate of attrition imposed by the Allied offensives and the rate of [German] infantry reinforcements. The balance at present is in favour of the Allies." Bradley did in fact believe that German capabilities had greatly diminished after six months of continuous fighting, but Sibert's language was far different from that used by Strong. Indeed, Bradley mimicked Strong's estimate when he told Major General LeRoy Lutes of the Army Service Forces the very next day that "it is entirely possible for the Germans to fight bitter delaying actions until 1 January 1946."[12]

Sibert highlighted "considerable movement" west and southwest of Prüm (about ten miles east of the Our River) on December 7, indicating a "possible regrouping" opposite Major General Troy H. Middleton, commander of VIII Corps. ULTRA messages revealing such movement were corroborated by aerial reconnaissance conducted by the 67th Tactical Reconnaissance Group of IX Tactical Air Force. Although the weather was bad in the Ardennes and Eifel in the six weeks leading up to the counteroffensive, Bradley received important intelligence from this source. The official air force historian declared that the reconnaissance missions consistently reported "a noticeable shift" in the enemy's activity in the Eifel.[13]

Sibert's December 12 order of battle map listed only six *VGDs* opposite VIII Corps' three and a half divisions between Losheim and Trier, while Middleton's G-2, Colonel Andrew Reeves, estimated four infantry divisions and 24,000 men opposite the corps. Bradley later admitted that he had greatly underestimated the enemy's offensive capabilities, and only when a wider view was taken did a larger potential threat appear. Between Trier and Monschau, an area closely corresponding to the frontage of the actual attack on December 16, Sibert's map showed twelve divisions, including two SS *PDs*.[14]

Bradley's faith in VIII Corps' ability to hold six German divisions was bolstered by the obvious defensive value of the terrain, but significant gaps would invariably be created as VIII Corps formations attempted to execute a delay. As they withdrew, commanders would seek the best tactical positions available. Good defensive ground retains its value only if troops can exploit it from behind obstacles, natural or man-made, that are covered by fire, backed up by mobile reserves proportional to the frontage held, and screened by defensive counterreconnaissance. FM 100–5 declared that "reliance for protection against mechanized attack cannot be placed on terrain alone."[15]

Bradley also appeared to minimize the potential of surprise, even though Sibert observed prior to the attack that the Germans were capable of massing large forces "in an assembly area close to our lines without any of our sources being aware of it." The Germans collected their assault formations in dispersed assembly areas well out of contact before an offensive.[16] Dispersed assembly areas allowed the Germans to maintain operational flexibility to meet contingencies and then surge forward out of staging areas to attack their chosen *schwerpunkt*—in this case, VIII Corps—in distinct waves. Hitler had decreed that no assault divisions would be positioned closer than six miles from the Our and Sauer Rivers. This prevented them being identified by foot patrols from VIII Corps. American doctrine classified reconnaissance as "close" and "distant," but VIII Corps did not have the capability to conduct long-range or distant reconnaissance. Sibert's observation should have played a key role in Bradley's estimate of the situation, but he was looking for an obvious concentration of German forces to trigger a new decision regarding his dispositions in the Ardennes.

Bradley observed that the indicators of Rundstedt's "apparent intent" to counterattack at the Roer were "conspicuous," particularly with Sibert telling him that the Germans were building additional trenches along the Roer River line. Every commander is responsible for his own security, and Bradley certainly felt secure in the U.S. Army's overall mechanized mobility. "In accepting the risk of enemy penetration into the Ardennes," he reflected, "we had counted heavily on the speed with which we could fling this mechanized strength against his flanks."[17] There is no reason to doubt the sincerity of his claim, and in certain ways, it made sense. In the end, however, the essence of Bradley's "plan" to mitigate the risk of a severely overstretched corps in the Ardennes was captured in his offhand comment to Strong in early December: "let them come."

Heeresgruppe B Attacks

In the early-morning hours of Saturday, December 16, 0-TAG (Zero Day), the Ardennes was shrouded in fog and drizzle, and temperatures were freezing—the very conditions German planners had identified as an operational requirement. VIII Corps had some indications from patrols and outposts of unusual activity, but the pieces were never assembled and processed in time to convince anyone that the Ardennes was anything other than what the GIs had nicknamed it: the Ghost Front. That all changed at 0530 when German artillery erupted along the front, signaling the start of *Heeresgruppe B*'s offensive, code-named Operation *HERBSTNEBEL* (Autumn Fog). The fire plan had three distinctive "depths": direct tactical support of the infantry, counterbattery fire, and longer-range destructive fire on villages. Monstrous 280mm and 310mm railway guns bombarded positions near St. Vith and sought what were thought to be strong American artillery positions in the Elsenborn area. Some American soldiers even witnessed V-1 "buzz bombs" streaking overhead bound for Liège.

Despite the number of guns committed to the initial phase of the fire plan (roughly twenty tubes per mile), German artillery was not as effective as it might have been. German artillery underwent significant reorganization for the offensive, and armored forward observers and artillery information centers were introduced.[18] However, it is apparent that it had yet to overcome significant training and equipment shortfalls. Moreover, high-level command and control centralization was not on a par with that of the Western Allies. German artillery coordination was good at the divisional level but was less effective at the corps and army levels. Doctrinal issues were real, but ultimately, the enormous attack frontage, the inability to conduct trial fire to register the guns, and ammunition shortfalls were the primary reasons why greater damage was not inflicted on well dug-in American forces in the forward-most positions.[19]

What German artillery did accomplish was the intentional and systematic destruction of pole-mounted communications wires at crossroads, command posts, and elsewhere. Radio relays by way of artillery radio nets were employed as an inefficient substitute, but the mountainous terrain degraded their effectiveness, and many American units quickly lost the ability to communicate with one another or their next higher headquarters. The Americans relied overwhelmingly on line or wire communications because the tactical VHF radios had limited range and were highly vulnerable to jamming. Communications were degraded to such an extent by the opening barrage that when the Twelfth Army Group's morning briefing commenced at 0915, almost four hours after the opening barrage, VIII Corps' front was still reported as quiet.[20] Unfortunately for the Germans, they could not fully exploit the degraded state of American communications. Even worse, the German attacks on both flanks of the great counteroffensive experienced considerable difficulty.

Dietrich expected *Generalleutnant* Otto Hitzfeld's *LXVII Armee-korps* to envelop Monschau and press west to set the anchor for the *SS PDs*. Model would not permit a direct assault, allegedly because he feared damaging the historic town. Hitzfeld's corps, however, bogged down immediately in the face of V Corps' ongoing attack toward the Roer dams.[21] The *246th VGD* never arrived in time to take part because it was fixed in the Jülich area northeast of Aachen by American pressure. Similarly, the *272nd VGD* was fixed by the U.S. 78th Infantry Division in the Simmerath area a few miles northeast of Monschau. As a result, the *326th VGD* attacked alone (perhaps with only three battalions), it-self weakened by the need to help the *277th VGD* defend against American pressure.

Despite being supported by perhaps ten artillery battalions and one or two *VWBs*, the *326th VGD* failed to dislodge the single battalion of the 395th Combat Team (CT)[22] of the 99th Infantry Division and the 38th Cavalry Reconnaissance Squadron deployed in the Monschau–Hofen sector. The cavalry lines were well organized in an all-around defense with barbed wire, minefields, and trip-flares and boasted fifty dismounted machine guns. By noon the *326th VGD* had lost one-fifth of its attack-ing elements.[23] The push to establish blocking positions for Dietrich's SS panzer phalanx on the high Hautes Fagnes moorland to the north and northwest therefore collapsed ignominiously, with heavy casualties.

Down in the *Seventh Armee* area, Brandenberger still held out hope that despite the material deficiencies and planning limitations, a prelim-inary success could be achieved, but Franz Beyer's *LXXX Armeekorps*, charged with anchoring the counteroffensive's southern front, encoun-tered significant difficulty as soon as it crossed the line of departure (LD) at 0430.[24] After a short artillery preparation on known American positions and key villages, *volksgrenadiers* of *Generalmajor* Franz Sens-fuss's *212th VGD* made their way across the Sauer River in rubber assault boats, with the mission of eliminating American artillery positions in the Alttrier–Mompach–Herborn area and cutting the only good highway in the 4th Infantry Division's sector running from Echternach to Luxem-bourg. *Volksgrenadier Regiment* (VGR) 423 crossed northwest of Ech-ternach and advanced on the village of Berdorf, situated atop the first considerable high ground. VGR 320 initially attempted to cross directly at Echternach, but the strong current forced it to cross three miles to the south. *LXXX Armeekorps* reported that this initial crossing had been ac-complished "with almost no Allied opposition."[25] However, by 0600 all

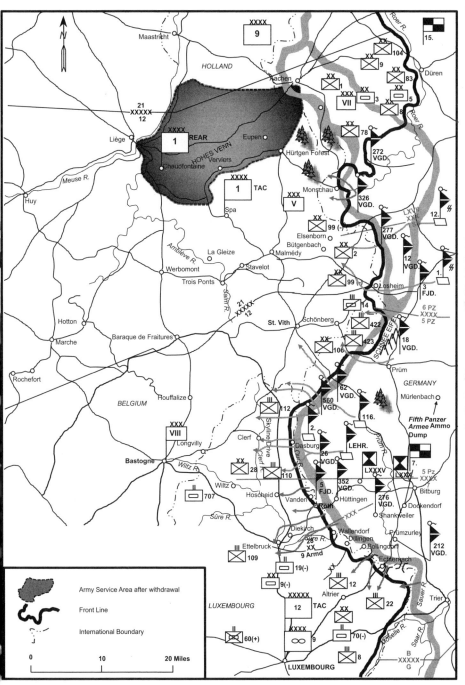

Map 3.1. *Heeresgruppe B* Attacks, December 16, 1944

three regiments of Major General Raymond O. Barton's 4th Infantry Division reported some form of contact with the *212th VGD*.

Just after 0900 the *volksgrenadiers* began penetrating Barton's overextended front with strong reconnaissance forces assisted by searchlights. Barton put his division on alert at 0929, but the 12th CT, with only the 42nd Field Artillery (FA) Battalion in position to support it, took the brunt of the attack. It was "easy to cross [the Sauer] and reach the highland," Sensfuss reflected, "but violent battles took place for the villages of Berdorf, Dickweiler, [and] Osweiler which blocked the roads." To his credit, Barton had kept a considerable portion of his division in reserve to defend against a German drive on Luxembourg. He also had eleven operational Shermans from the weary 70th Tank Battalion, a unit that had taken severe punishment in the Hürtgen Forest. Sensfuss quickly faced a cyclical situation. The failure to penetrate further meant that Barton's artillery could not be pushed beyond range of the crossing sites. This meant that no bridges could be constructed, and heavy weapons (the division possessed only five assault guns) could not be ferried across to help turn the tide in each of the small village battles.[26] The villages were the key to any further penetration and accomplishment of the larger mission.

Literally squeezed in between Major General Norman D. Cota's 28th Infantry Division to the north and Barton's division were elements of Major General John W. Leonard's 9th Armored Division. Holding three miles from Wallendorf to just south of Dillingen was the 60th Armored Infantry Battalion (AIB) with the 3rd Armored FA Battalion in direct support. Across from the armored infantry was the *276th VGD*. Although the artillery barrage here was not as heavy as elsewhere along the front, frontline communications were knocked out almost immediately. The *volksgrenadiers* started to probe the draws around 0800, and by 1130 they had succeeded in overrunning an individual platoon. However, counterattacks were launched by the battalion's reserve company, and the artillery kept up a steady fire against the crossing sites on the Sûre River.[27]

While Beyer's corps struggled to anchor the south flank, Baptist Kneiss's *LXXXV Armeekorps* to the north had the more ambitious task of trying to keep relative pace with the left flank of *Fifth Panzer Armee*. Kneiss's two divisions, the *352nd VGD* and the *5th FJD*, faced the 109th CT and elements of the 110th CT of Cota's 28th Infantry Division. The 109th CT was commanded by Lieutenant Colonel James E. Rudder, former commander of the Ranger battalion that had stormed the Pointe du Hoc in Normandy on D-Day. Rudder could not immediately count on much support—just a few tanks from the 707th Tank Battalion—but his regiment was well deployed on favorable terrain.

Both German divisions infiltrated numerous large patrols of between thirty and sixty men and seized crossings over the Our during the artillery barrage. On the corps' right flank, *Oberst* Ludwig Heilmann, the *5th FJD* commander, ordered his men to avoid pitched battles and to push rapidly through the American outpost line of resistance (OPLR). *Fallschirmjäger Regiment (FJR) 14* worked its way along the seam between the 109th and 110th CTs, which corresponded to the Stolzembourg–Hoscheid line. *FJR 15* crossed at Roth, the main divisional crossing site. Within a short time it had pushed its leading battalion the two miles to Walsdorf unopposed.[28] Vianden was secured when the *5th FJD* engineers quickly destroyed the 2nd Battalion/109th CT's outpost there. By noon *VGR 915* of *Oberst* Erich Schmidt's *352nd VGD* held Langsdorf and Tandel, some two miles west of the Our, but two miles represented the furthest extent of the penetrations for either Heilmann or Schmidt on December 16. Heilmann was supposed to be closing in on Wiltz, some ten miles west of the Our River, by the end of the day. At Hosdorf, *VGR 916* was pinned at the river by the 107th and 108th FA Battalions and never moved forward all day.

While the German assaults on the extreme flanks faltered, the interior effort made marginally better progress. SS-*Gruppenführer* Hermann Priess's powerful *I SS Panzerkorps* (*12th* and *277th VGDs, 3rd FJD, 1st* and *12th SS PDs*) was deployed to the south of the *LXVII Armeekorps* between Monschau and Manderfeld. The bulk of its combat power was concentrated against the Losheim Gap and the 393rd and 394th CTs of Major General Walter E. Lauer's 99th Infantry Division. The boundary between the *Sixth* and *Fifth Panzer Armees* ran just south of Krewinkel and Manderfeld through the Losheim Gap. *I SS Panzerkorps* was divided into two echelons because Model demanded that the infantry divisions make the initial breakthrough, followed by the armor. The echeloned deployment was sound in theory, but it rapidly broke down in the difficult terrain.

From north to south the *277th VGD, 12th VGD*, and *3rd FJD* attacked while the *12th SS* and *1st SS PDs* waited in a rear echelon that covered miles, hoping to exploit a breach and deploy onto the five *Rollbahnen* (march routes) designated A through E, leading to the Meuse. Route A started in Hollerath and proceeded through Krinkelt and Elsenborn and then passed through the Hohes Venn, with its end point at Liège. Route B started in Udenbreth and passed through Butgenbach,

Malmédy, and Spa. Route C ran from Losheim to Losheimergraben and Bullingen, then west to Butgenbach, Waimes, and Malmédy. Route C was to be the principal route for the *Hitler Jugend*. Route D ran through Losheim to Honsfeld then venturing off hard roads to move cross country before linking up at Moderscheid and Schoppen through Ligneuville and Wanne. This difficult route was the principal one for the *Leibstandarte*. Route E ran through Manderfeld, Andler, Born, and Recht before crossing the Salm River at Vielsalm.

Throughout the day the *277th* and *12th VGDs* brought increasing pressure to bear against the 393rd and 394th CTs, respectively. Colonel Mark A. Devine Jr.'s 14th Cavalry Group was hopelessly overmatched in the Losheim Gap, and although the *3rd FJD* initially stalled west of Ormont in front of a German minefield laid during the fall, it nevertheless penetrated the cavalry positions.[29] The Germans had infiltrated the cavalry in the fog, and those cavalry elements up close, near Roth and Kobscheid, quickly faced the prospect of encirclement. Devine's predicament was increased because immediately to the south, *General der Artillerie* Walter Lucht's *LXVI Armeekorps* (*18th* and *62nd VGDs*) of *Fifth Panzer Armee* was executing the encirclement of the Schnee Eifel in an attempt to isolate and destroy the 106th Infantry Division.

The Germans punched through between the 394th CT of Lauer's division and the north flank of Major General Alan Jones's 106th Infantry Division. The division after-action report declared that the German attack "increased in fury, generally along the whole sector, during the day."[30] Even though by noon the *VGDs* had failed to open any of the five principal routes for the panzer divisions, the attack in the Losheim Gap had generally gone according to plan. Penetration of the 14th Cavalry Group's lines directly threatened the 99th and 106th Infantry Divisions, as well as Major General Walter M. Robertson's 2nd Infantry Division, situated north of Lauer with precarious lines of communication (LCs) running down a single road perpendicular to *I SS Panzerkorps'* axis of advance. The 14th Cavalry Group was pushed back across the Our River and quickly found itself vulnerable on the Manderfeld Ridge. By 1700 the last cavalry troopers left Manderfeld, after Devine decided to pull back to ridges running along the Andler–Holzheim line.[31] Jones's left flank was thus turned by the *3rd FJD*, and his south flank was turned by the *18th VGD*, which had also succeeded in overrunning artillery positions at Auw.

While Dietrich chose to launch his infantry formations across the LD following the opening artillery barrage at 0530, Manteuffel decided on different tactics. *Fifth Panzer Armee* executed an opening barrage at the same time, but hours before, Manteuffel had sent his infantry forward in small bodies, and in most places they succeeded in infiltrating the front while bypassing many strongpoints in the Eifel.[32] Perhaps more important, he chose to deploy his combat power abreast, along a wide front, to achieve several simultaneous penetrations.

As *LXVI Armeekorps* maneuvered around the seven-mile-long Schnee Eifel, Walter Krüger's *LVIII Panzerkorps* (*560th VGD* and *116th PD*) and Heinrich von Lüttwitz's *XLVII Panzerkorps* (*26th VGD*, *2nd PD*, and *Panzer Lehr*) to the south represented the armored hammer. Krüger's corps straddled portions of the 110th and 112th CTs of the 28th Infantry Division. The *560th VGD* made little headway, and *Generalmajor* Siegfried von Waldenburg, commander of the *116th PD*, admitted that the Americans "fought very bravely and fiercely." Moreover, the Dragon's Teeth of the West Wall now worked against the Germans to prevent the panzer division from deploying on the intended axis. Waldenburg declared that his early operations were "decisively influenced" by the Dragon's Teeth because it was "impossible to commit and deploy the tanks in the direction which had been ordered." The "Greyhound" division had not even made it to the Our by sundown. In an attempt to get through Lützkampen, *II Abteilung/Panzer Regiment 16* lost six tanks in a matter of minutes, possibly from a single three-inch gun of the 820th Tank Destroyer Battalion situated on Jones's south flank.[33] The *XLVII Panzerkorps* failed to attain its objectives for the day, but it did put in two bridges over the Our. By sundown the first tanks of *Oberst* Meinrad von Lauchert's *2nd PD* were crossing at Dasburg, but *Panzer Lehr* was delayed by two enormous trenches blocking either side of Eisenbach. *Panzergrenadier Regiment* (*PGR*) *156* of the *116th PD* had greater success and moved to exploit a crossing of the Our at Ouren.[34]

At 1600 *SS-Obersturmbannführer* Joachim Peiper, commander of SS-*Panzer Regiment 1*, finally received orders from *I SS Panzerkorps* (which had lifted wireless silence at 1230) to move up to Losheim and begin to conduct a reconnaissance toward Losheimergraben. Thirty minutes later *KG Peiper* began its advance; however, its column of tanks and half-tracks, fifteen miles long, moved painfully slow on roads clogged with troops from the *12th VGD* and horse-drawn supply trains. Filtering in among the *Leibstandarte* were small detachments of Otto Skorzeny's *Panzer Brigade 150*, executing Operation *GREIF*. The brigade was a hodgepodge of units with different training that had been thrown together too quickly to mount effective harassing operations, but one team actually reached the Meuse on December 16.[35]

As darkness began to creep over the Ardennes late on Saturday afternoon, the American line did not look too bad. The left and right regiments of the 28th Infantry Division were holding, but Lüttwitz's entire corps was concentrated against the overstretched 110th CT in the center. This regiment was hit hard by the *26th VGD*. The 110th CT held the critical high ground known as Skyline Drive, a long, north-south ridge-line three to four miles west of the Our River. Atop Skyline Drive ran the St. Vith–Diekirch road, and Lüttwitz's corps had to bisect it in order to drive on Bastogne.

By 2000 the lines of Jones's 106th Infantry Division were still generally intact, even though he had committed his last infantry reserve, the 2nd Battalion/423rd CT, three hours earlier. The 14th Cavalry Group had been pushed back on his left flank, but Middleton had attached Combat Command B (CCB)/9th Armored Division to Jones at 1120, and it was moving up. However, the situation deteriorated rapidly. Jones and Middleton spoke over the phone twice that evening. During the first call Middleton stressed the importance of holding in place. When Jones called back later, indicating that he might have to withdraw, Middleton apparently did not give him a definitive verbal order either way; he seems to have left it to Jones's discretion as the commander on the spot. Jones believed he was to hold in place, perhaps because Middleton had not given him an unequivocal order to the contrary, although an VIII Corps order received later stated that positions were to be held at all costs on the west bank of the Our. That was fine, but all three of Jones's CTs were *east* of the Our. Middleton therefore expected the 106th to pull back at least to the west bank of the Our, but Jones never moved, perhaps confident that CCB/9th Armored Division and 7th Armored Division would help.[36]

Hodges first received word of attacks along VIII Corps' front sometime around 0700. His tactical headquarters was located at the Hôtel Britannique in Spa, an old resort town seventeen miles southeast of Liège. According to his aide, Major William C. Sylvan, Hodges initially considered the commotion at the front "spoiling attacks" to take pressure off Major General Leonard T. Gerow's V Corps drive against the Roer dams, reflecting the common view of German intentions held by SHAEF and army group. Sylvan added that by 1100 "it became more evident that the enemy was staking all on this drive." In fact, at that hour Gerow called and requested permission to halt the 2nd Infantry Division's drive on the

Roer dams in order to deal with the changed circumstances. Hodges re-fused. Though unwilling to suspend his offensive toward the dams, he did issue orders for a number of formations to go on alert, including 1st Infan-try Division and CCB/3rd Armored Division. His tentative response was partly attributable to the severely degraded communications. Robertson, however, had seen enough. Unlike German commanders, who feared death for violating orders, he halted his division on his own without tell-ing Gerow.[37]

Two hundred miles from the front line, Eisenhower first heard word of the German offensive at SHAEF headquarters located in the Trianon Palace Hotel in Versailles, just southwest of Paris. He reminded Mont-gomery about the bet they had made back in October 1943, with Eisen-hower wagering that the war would be over by Christmas 1944. "I still have nine days," he wrote, and "you must admit we have gone a long ways toward the defeat of Germany since we made our bet."[38] Eisenhower also had more pressing matters to attend to. Bradley was coming in to dis-cuss replacement shortages. Bradley skipped the 0915 situation briefing at Twelfth Army Group's tactical headquarters in Luxembourg City in order to get on the road to SHAEF, accompanied by his aide, Lieutenant Colo-nel Chester Hansen. There was not much to learn, however, because his G-3, Brigadier General A. Franklin Kibler, gave no hint of the German offensive during the briefing. VIII Corps' sector was deemed quiet; the irony was that the 4th Infantry Division had already been fighting for sev-eral hours just twenty miles northeast of Bradley's headquarters.

Eisenhower and Bradley met in the SHAEF Map Room around dusk, joined by Bedell Smith, Eisenhower's chief of staff; Air Chief Marshal Sir Arthur Tedder, Eisenhower's deputy commander; Lieutenant Gen-eral Carl A. "Tooey" Spaatz, commander of U.S. Strategic Air Forces in Europe; Major General Harold Bull, SHAEF G-3; and Strong.[39] Bedell Smith was in the process of asking Bradley what the chances were of cap-turing the Roer River dams when Strong was urgently called to the door by his deputy, Brigadier General Thomas J. Betts. Strong quickly read Betts's message aloud to Eisenhower and the others: "This morning the enemy counterattacked at five separate points across the First Army sec-tor." Strong did not appear to be overly surprised by this news, nor should he have been; he had known about German activity in the Ardennes at least seven hours earlier. He later admitted that he had received frag-mentary reports before breakfast of an attack during the night and early morning and that "several enemy divisions had already been identified in action." This coincided with Sylvan's claim that the first indications of trouble were reported by VIII Corps to First Army shortly before 0700.[40]

Strong further stated that these early reports had been "discussed very briefly," but it is unclear with whom he discussed them. He habitually withheld negative intelligence estimates and reports from Eisenhower and may have done so in this case.[41] Although it is possible that Eisenhower had some inkling of trouble prior to Betts's arrival, there is no indication that Bradley had any foreknowledge. He probably checked in by telephone with his chief of staff, Major General Leven C. Allen, back in Luxembourg when he arrived at Versailles, but in his memoirs, he never acknowledged receiving any report on the fighting at this stage.[42] It remains a mystery how SHAEF received reports from First Army but Twelfth Army Group did not; however, the communications disruption appears to be a plausible explanation.

Betts's report certainly must have deflated Eisenhower's good mood that day. Earlier he had been informed that the president had nominated him for general of the army, five stars, and the equivalent rank of field marshal. The postwar accounts of those present when Betts arrived offer little detail, but at the very least, his report must have caused raised eyebrows and turned heads among most of them. In his memoirs Eisenhower described the German attacks as "slight penetrations," but he was "immediately convinced that this was no local attack." Bedell Smith apparently turned immediately to Bradley and told him that he had been warned about the possibility of a German attack in the Ardennes.[43] At this stage, however, Bradley was clearly unconvinced that VIII Corps was facing a major threat.

Eisenhower reacted with more decisiveness than did Bradley, suggesting a greater appreciation for the truth at that moment. Eisenhower told Bradley he had better send Middleton some help and identified two formations, the 7th and 10th Armored Divisions, for the immediate task.[44] Both divisions were uncommitted at the time. The 7th Armored Division was in XIII Corps reserve near Heerlen in Holland and belonged to Ninth Army. It had been withdrawn for recuperation after fighting in the Peel Marshes but was available to the corps commander, Major General Alvan C. Gillem Jr., to exploit a crossing of the Roer near Linnich. The 10th Armored Division was out of the line in XX Corps, part of Third Army and south of VIII Corps.

A close look at the first day's fighting reveals three developments that would directly affect Patton and Third Army. Jodl's prediction that the only chance of success "was in a fluid advance over the Meuse" had not come true. Model and Rundstedt had hoped to penetrate cleanly on December 16, but the American soldier had his say. Model had committed seventeen divisions on the first day, including five panzer divisions. Indeed, by 2400 that day, Strong had identified sixteen divisions. Behind this was an additional seven infantry and three panzer divisions and two reinforced panzer brigades. This would be sufficient to satisfy one of the conditions considered essential for a *Durchbruchsangriff*: destroying the continuity of the enemy's front. The second condition, enveloping the shoulders of the breakthrough point, would prove beyond the powers of *Heeresgruppe B*.[45]

In the north *Sixth Panzer Armee* had attacked against the grain of the land, and the unavoidable terrain complexities were already thwarting Dietrich's advance west. *LXVII Armeeekorps* failed to capture Monschau and push northwest to establish blocking positions. Flank security for Dietrich's panzers should have been augmented by the rapid insertion of the seventy-ton *Jagdtigers* of *Schwere Panzerjäger Abteilung 653*, but they never got forward in the prevailing traffic jams. Operation *STÖESSER*, the airborne drop, was canceled due to fuel shortages.[46] That night *OKW* released the *3rd PGD* to assist *LXVII Armeekorps* in establishing the northern blocking position.

Another important development on the first day was the superior performance of Manteuffel's *Fifth Panzer Armee* compared with Dietrich's *Sixth Panzer Armee*. Because of better tactics and a superior operational plan, Manteuffel had set the conditions for greater success than Dietrich. Whereas *Sixth Panzer Armee* had succeeded in making only a single penetration in the Losheim Gap, *Fifth Panzer Armee* had attacked more broadly and achieved multiple small penetrations; it was only a matter of time before it exploited one or more into a major breach. The easier terrain in Manteuffel's sector increased the probability of success. As December 16 waned, Rundstedt observed that the swift advance of the panzer formations had not yet materialized, but he believed that penetrations in certain areas "had created the essential prerequisites for the successful continuation of the operation."[47]

The final development of the day was *Seventh Armee*'s failure to push its blocking positions further forward. The inability to overrun U.S. artillery positions was particularly costly. Considering his force-to-space ratio (FSR), Brandenberger could realistically maintain only a weak anchor a few miles forward of Echternach. Indeed, the *212th VGD* attacked the

4th Infantry Division at a ratio of barely more than 1:1.[48] Gersdorff had sent a staff officer to Model on December 15, pleading for additional divisions to accomplish *Seventh Armee*'s mission, but he had been refused. Manteuffel later praised Brandenberger for preparing his portion of the offensive "thoroughly and competently," but he understood *Seventh Armee*'s crippling limitations. Dietrich's lack of success in the north, Manteuffel's limited success in the center, and Brandenberger's weakness in the south would eventually become military factors impossible for Hitler to ignore.

Long before the fabled defense of Bastogne, the Germans' timetable had already been compromised, but that did not rule out their recovery from the slow start. On May 10, 1940, the Germans had been thrown off schedule with virtually no serious resistance simply trying to conduct an administrative approach march through the Ardennes. Undefended demolitions and traffic congestion had conspired to thwart the efforts of Herman Hoth's *XV Panzerkorps* and Heinz Guderian's *XIX Panzerkorps* to achieve their first-day objectives.[49] Yet they eventually got back on track, with devastating results. The effect of the performance of the three armies on 0-TAG was that the *schwerpunkt* of *Heeresgruppe B* would soon begin to shift south to chase the mirage offered by Manteuffel's success in the center. Looking into the future, it also meant that *Seventh Armee* would have to be heavily reinforced to protect *Fifth Panzer Armee*'s southern flank as it made its desperate bid for the Meuse. Though Brandenberger's FSR was low at the beginning of the offensive, it would increase significantly in the ensuing days, and Patton would have to assemble enough combat power to overmatch it.

4

Enter Patton

I called General Bradley and called his attention to the fact that the Third Army had paid a very heavy price in blood in the hope of a break-through at Saarlautern and Saarbruecken. . . . Bradley admitted my logic but took counsel of his fears and ordered the 10th [Armored Division] to move. I wish he were less timid.

—Patton, December 16, 1944

On December 16 Patton's energy was focused on breaking through the West Wall. After his rapid advance across France during August, his momentum was stopped cold at the Moselle River on the last day of the month. He had no gas for his tanks. On September 2 he, Hodges, and Bradley met Eisenhower at Chartres to discuss future operations. Eisenhower was prepared to reproach Patton for stretching the Allied line too thin and exacerbating logistical difficulties. However, by the end of the meeting Bradley and Patton had coaxed permission to keep attacking east. Indeed, Eisenhower permitted Bradley to attack toward Mannheim, Koblenz, and Frankfurt, but he made it clear that First Army's support for Montgomery's airborne-ground operation to gain a bridgehead over the Rhine in mid-September, MARKET GARDEN, had priority when it came to supplies.[1] Bradley allocated 1.5 million gallons of fuel to Third Army by September 7, and Patton thought he could charge through Lorraine. However, he quickly ran into difficulty at the Moselle River. The extensive fortifications of Metz, about which he knew precious little, proved especially challenging.

There is little doubt that had Patton been given sufficient fuel at the beginning of September, he could have advanced through Lorraine—thirty miles from the Moselle to the Saar River at its widest point—virtually unopposed and punched through the heaviest structural sections of the unmanned West Wall fortifications.[2] A Third Army deployed east of the West Wall in the secondary but still important Saar industrial region would have seriously compromised the German concept of operations for defending the Western Front. It would have furthered Eisenhower's broad-front strategy by forcing the Germans to sell out in an effort to contain Third Army, thus opening opportunities elsewhere along the Allied line. SHAEF planners admitted that a deep Third Army penetration was logistically feasible, but only to the Rhine and not beyond. Moreover, the probability of Third Army achieving a decisive strategic result on its own was highly unlikely. The terrain beyond the Saar River was difficult, and a deep penetration would mean little if Third Army advanced alone on a nondecisive axis that did not ultimately converge on the Ruhr industrial area or directly support its capture by other armies.[3] This did not mean, however, that Patton's operations in Lorraine were pointless.

When the window of opportunity to race through Lorraine closed, Patton fought his way by yards to the West Wall plagued by fuel, ammunition, and manpower shortages. He was up against *First Armee*, the strongest German army in the west. The weather quickly deteriorated, curtailing the effectiveness of Brigadier General Otto P. Weyland's XIX Tactical Air Command (TAC), Patton's great aerial ally throughout August. When Third Army got moving again in mid-September and threatened to penetrate *First Armee's* front, Manteuffel's *Fifth Panzer Armee* counterattacked. Major General John S. Wood's 4th Armored Division inflicted heavy damage on Manteuffel's hastily assembled panzer force and came out the winner in the great tank battle of Arracourt. Eisenhower then shut Third Army down again for six weeks at the end of the month. Patton refused to give up the initiative and persisted in correcting his line in limited attacks throughout October. For the most part, his policy of staying active proved beneficial to his later operations, but he suffered a particularly nasty setback while attacking Fort Driant, part of the defensive system surrounding Metz. Fort Driant defied all assaults, and as he watched his infantry waste away in futile attempts to take the fort, Patton, to his great credit, backed off and decided to tackle Metz a different way.

On November 8 Eisenhower and Bradley gave Patton the green light once again. With plenty of logistical support and men, Patton enjoyed good initial success. He bypassed Fort Driant and other tough defensive positions, encircled Metz, and inflicted terrific punishment on the German divisions in his path. As November turned into December, however, his combat power waned. The troops were exhausted, and sufficient and timely reinforcements were lacking. The mud, rain, and snow frustrated his attempts to break loose of the German defenders at every turn, but he clawed his way to the West Wall by the beginning of December.

Patton planned to finish the Lorraine campaign by blasting through the West Wall, supported by what he called "probably the most ambitious air blitz ever conceived." On December 5 Weyland attended a conference at SHAEF on how best to employ the Allies' vast superiority in airpower against the West Wall, and he managed to convince Eisenhower that Third Army deserved the air support. Spaatz was directed to assist Patton, and the next day he; Major General Hoyt S. Vandenberg, commander of the Ninth Air Force; and General Jimmy Doolittle, commander of the Eighth Air Force (and leader of the famous Doolittle Raid against Japan in the aftermath of Pearl Harbor), visited Patton to work out the details.[4] Operation TINK (Weyland's nickname for his wife) was to consist of three successive days of bombing by the Eighth Air Force and Royal Air Force (RAF) Bomber Command in the vicinity of Zweibrücken to assist Major General Manton S. Eddy's XII Corps in penetrating the West Wall. The initial date for TINK was December 19, but Patton postponed it for two days because enemy resistance was considerable and the assault divisions were still moving into position.

The Lorraine campaign frustrated Patton like no other since he had landed in North Africa in November 1942. He called Lorraine "nasty country" and a "hell hole" and wrote to his write Beatrice, "There is about four inches of liquid mud over everything."[5] The three-month battle of attrition had worn on his patience, and he eagerly anticipated Third Army's final all-out assault against the West Wall assisted by the air forces. It is little wonder that Patton's anger boiled over when Leven Allen telephoned Third Army headquarters in Nancy on the night of December 16 to have the 10th Armored Division moved north to help Middleton's VIII Corps.

Bradley did not hesitate in taking the 7th Armored Division from Ninth Army, but he was clearly reluctant to take the 10th Armored Division from Patton. When Bradley expressed this to Eisenhower, the latter responded: "Tell him that Ike is running this damn war."[6] Although Patton thought he should be the main effort, he was not. After Allen's call, Patton quickly phoned Bradley at SHAEF and made his argument, with an occasional curse or two, for keeping the 10th Armored Division. "That's no major threat up there," Patton declared. "Hell, it's probably nothing more than a spoiling attack to throw us off balance down here and make us stop this offensive." Patton's hubris was evident, but Bletchley Park had in fact sent a low-priority ULTRA message at 1618 that *Heeresgruppe G* was anxious about the situation in the Saarlautern bridgehead and feared that the situation "will become increasingly acute." Indeed, the Germans fired upward of 6,000 artillery rounds in the Saarlautern–Roden, Frau-lautern, and Ensdorf bridgeheads the day before.[7] Patton also told Brad-ley that Middleton, who had served in Third Army during the Normandy breakout, could handle the situation, and if the Germans extended their attack into Third Army's area, he would need the division. Patton's great-est concern was that Third Army had paid a very high price in blood to get to the West Wall, and he desperately wanted a shot at piercing it. The 10th Armored Division was at that moment conducting intensive combined arms training in night attacks on fortified positions.[8] What Patton wanted personally, however, was now operationally irrelevant.

Bradley was probably quite sincere when he replied, "I hate like hell to do it, George, but I've got to have that division. Even if it's only a spoil-ing attack as you say, Middleton must have help." Patton vented against what he perceived as Bradley's timidity, but he was fair enough to admit that Bradley probably knew "more of the situation than he can say over the telephone."[9] How much more Bradley actually knew at this stage is questionable, but it seems that Bradley was taking the division *only* be-cause Eisenhower had virtually ordered him to.

This was not the first time Bradley had taken divisions from Patton on the eve of a Third Army offensive. In early November Bradley had with-drawn the 83rd Infantry Division from Third Army to reinforce Hodges. The loss seriously upset Patton's plans for encircling Metz and gaining bridgeheads over the Saar River. Patton might have cleared the important Saar–Moselle triangle on his northern flank and taken Trier, thereby sig-nificantly affecting Hitler's assembly and staging areas and security for the Ardennes offensive. Full of righteous indignation over the loss of the 83rd Infantry Division, Patton blamed Bradley's "natural timidity" and hoped that "history will record his moral cowardice."[10]

Bradley's hesitancy reinforces two things. First, he probably would have deferred moving either armored division into the Ardennes if Eisen-hower had left the decision to him. In this sense, Eisenhower's reaction was truly fortuitous. The consequences of a delay of even a single day— perhaps even hours—could have assisted the Germans' scheme of ma-neuver and hurt American efforts at staging a counteroffensive.[11] Second, Bradley's "plan" for dealing with a large German attack in the Ardennes was a myth, even though he claimed in his 1951 memoir, *A Soldier's Sto-ry*, that he had identified certain divisions in different armies as reserves that could be used only with his consent. There was no contingency planning with Patton to employ the 10th Armored Division or follow-on Third Army formations in VIII Corps' zone; it was certainly news to Patton when he heard of it. According to Eisenhower's deputy, Air Chief Marshal Sir Arthur Tedder, Bradley declared on December 8 that if anything happened in the Ardennes, he simply planned to draw on undesignated formations in Third Army.[12]

Patton knew it was no use arguing further with Bradley. Within a few minutes of hanging up, Bradley issued an order by phone for Major General William H. H. Morris Jr.'s 10th Armored Division to move north into Luxembourg. Rapidly, Morris issued warning orders to his combat commands for a daylight move the next day and put them on ten minutes' notice to move (NTM). CCA, with the 90th Cavalry Reconnaissance Squadron out in front, began the march north at 0600 the next morning. CCB was on the move at 1320 and arrived complete in its assembly area at Merl just before 2000 that night.[13] Although still focused on TINK, Patton directed contingency planning through a simple warning order to the staff for Third Army to react if called on to do so.

Patton's Intelligence Philosophy

Despite his obvious anger at losing the division on the eve of a major operation, Patton had an intuitive understanding that VIII Corps' inactivity in the Ardennes, other than patrolling across the Our River, might come back to haunt First Army. His intuition was bolstered by his respect for ULTRA and Third Army's own intelligence-gathering capabilities. Patton had an intense desire for all types of intelligence—so much so that it has been suggested that he anticipated modern information operations.[14] His trusted G-2, Colonel Oscar W. Koch, reflected, "In Patton's command intelligence was always viewed as big business and treated accordingly." Patton demanded that friendly and enemy information move through the chain of command faster than normal because the process could be slow, and intelligence gathered at low levels might get diluted as it made its way up the chain. Each American army had a Signals Information and Monitoring (SIAM) unit, but Patton converted two squadrons of 6th Cavalry Group, commanded by Colonel Edward "Joe" Fickett, to function as an Army Information Service (AIS), similar to Montgomery's Phantom system of liaison officers first established in North Africa. The task of the AIS was to bypass normal communications channels and report observations "direct to the Army Commander with a minimum of delay."[15]

Patton derived enormous benefit from the quality of the intelligence officers around him. Koch had been with Patton since August 1940, when the latter commanded the 2nd Armored Division, and stayed with him throughout Tunisia, Sicily, and Normandy. By December 1944 Koch had been Patton's G-2 for well over two years. Patton trusted Koch and called him "the best damned intelligence officer in any United States Command." Koch was cautious and served as a good foil to Patton's aggressiveness. Third Army intelligence analyses contained none of the hyperbole found in Sibert's reports at Twelfth Army Group (intended to get people to read them), and Koch possessed the moral courage to speak his mind.[16]

Third Army's ULTRA representative, Lieutenant Colonel Melvin C. Helfers, was the only Regular U.S. Army officer selected for ULTRA duty, which meant that he gained the confidence of Patton and Koch more quickly than civilians who manned similar posts in the other American commands. Helfers declared that Bradley's G-2 section was "overrun with a bunch of civilian lawyer flunkies." Helfers's primary responsibility was to "evaluate" the ULTRA messages and present them in usable form to Patton and authorized staff recipients. This clearly meant a synthesizing process, because Koch did not have time to read the large number of daily messages.

Bletchley dispatched ULTRA messages prioritized by importance. A single Z at the top was the lowest-priority designation, and ZZZZZ was the highest. ZZZZ and ZZZZZ messages were sent to the ULTRA representatives as soon as they were received and deciphered.[17] When a ZZZZ or ZZZZZ message arrived at Third Army, Helfers and Koch briefed Patton immediately. Helfers also assisted Koch in "fusing" ULTRA with other intelligence sources, including "open" intelligence, and identifying and "killing" (as far as possible) intelligence errors proved by ULTRA. Major Warrack Wallace had assisted Helfers for a short time in the early fall and observed that after it had proved itself at Mortain in August, "the position of Ultra in Third Army intelligence could hardly be improved."[18]

The intelligence priority in Third Army, logically, was on the army's current area of operations, but Patton wanted an accurate, theater-wide intelligence overview because he was sensitive to other areas that might influence his own. He personally expressed what he considered his essential elements of information (EEIs) to Koch only once, while they were still in England, directing his G-2 to focus all intelligence planning on Metz. Koch recalled, "Anything which might affect the Third Army

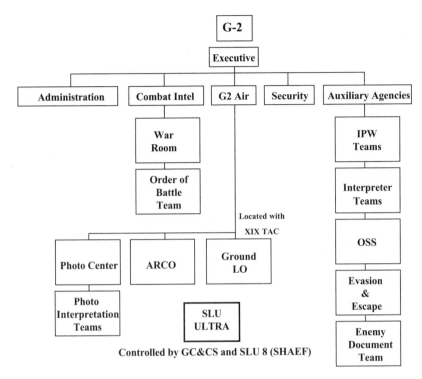

Figure 4.1. Third Army's G-2 Section

mission, from the coast of France all the way to Metz . . . was now of critical importance." Patton's nephew, Fred Ayer Jr., was assigned to the Counter Intelligence Corps (CIC) and visited Third Army in the fall of 1944. He recalled that in the war room, "mounted on sliding panels along the walls were detailed small-scale maps of all territory, Allied as well as enemy, held of immediate or future tactical and strategic interest. Each map was covered with an acetate overlay on which was marked, as it was received, every new piece of intelligence relative to troop, armor, transport, supply depot, rail, artillery and air dispositions likewise both Allied and enemy."[19] Patton was not unique in seeking such lateral situational awareness, but he was perhaps more attuned to its benefits than his peers were. It fundamentally set the conditions that allowed him to partially penetrate the German deception plan for the counteroffensive. He deserves credit for working the problem where others saw no problem, even while fully engaged in preparing for TINK.

In the world of intelligence gathering there were limits on what an army could do. Koch declared that Third Army was perfectly within its rights to overlap First and Seventh Armies "to protect our flanks," but it had "no right, implied or expressed, to roam the enemy rear areas indiscriminately to see what was going on. That was not a tactical headquarters responsibility." In November Patton received permission for XIX TAC to fly reconnaissance missions deeper into the Eifel, but according to Koch, it could do so only directly in front of First Army. Despite ten totally nonoperational flying days between November 17 and December 16, the 10th Photo Reconnaissance Group confirmed significant movement in the Eifel, identifying heavy rail traffic near Fulda, Trier, and particularly Merzig just north of XX Corps, Third Army's northernmost corps. Stacks of lumber, searchlights, and numerous vehicles were also spotted from November 18 onward.[20]

Patton's broad situational awareness in early December was the product of a variety of intelligence sources, including ULTRA. Third Army even had an Office of Strategic Services (OSS) detachment located within First Army lines at Ettelbruck, northwest of Trier. Koch stated that the detachments had "wide versatility and great value," but what intelligence they provided him is unknown.[21] Overall, Patton's situational awareness was probably better than Hodges's, although neither seems to have been privy to Twelfth Army Group's information about Allied dispositions known to the enemy and revealed in enemy estimates of Allied intentions.[22] Koch penetrated the German deception plan in more concrete ways than did Colonel Benjamin "Monk" Dickson, First Army's G-2. Koch's analysis did not parrot Dickson's assessment that the Germans were simply shuttling divisions in and out of the Eifel. Instead, Koch stressed the net increase of formations in the Eifel and focused on the degree of initiative possible as a result of the increased capability.[23] He also refused to build his order of battle data exclusively from ULTRA. Indeed, it has been argued that Koch demonstrated a greater maturity than other G-2s when it came to using ULTRA. As Captain George Church noted, Koch stressed the need to compile the profile of enemy formations "exclusively from open sources."[24] In this way Koch was able to more precisely differentiate between *complete identification* (echelon, type of unit, and numerical designation) and *partial identification* (lacking numerical designation).[25]

Based on his exploitation of the multisource intelligence at his disposal, Koch had built up a general estimate of German capability by late

November. He avoided confusing capability with enemy intentions when briefing Patton. Koch functioned under the intelligence concept that "no matter what the intentions of the enemy might be he must have the capability to execute them; the converse is not true."[26] His Periodic Report No. 165 for November 23 stated:

> The five re-formed Panzer divisions (1 SS, 2 SS, 9 SS, 12 SS, 130 Panzer) of 6 SS Panzer Army, though not as yet contacted on any Front, appear to have moved from their Westphalia concentration area. This powerful striking force, with an estimated 500 tanks, is still an untouched strategic reserve held for future employment. These five reconstituted Panzer divisions of 6 SS Panzer Army and the six re-formed Para divisions of 1 Para Army constitute a formidable strategic reserve for coordinated counteroffensive employment. Also, the constantly expanding crop of Volksgrenadier divisions in Germany gives the enemy another eight Infantry divisions capable of commitment in the West by December 1.[27]

Patton had this information in hand when he told a reporter the next day that the Germans were incapable of counteroffensives. However, he noted in his diary that same day that "First Army is making a terrible mistake in leaving the VIII Corps static, as it is highly probable that the Germans are building up east of them." This statement does not prove that Patton anticipated an attack, but he consistently preached that the Germans would attack given the slightest opportunity. Patton and Hodges came to opposite conclusions, for as Sylvan noted in his diary only a week later, "reports of considerable troop movement . . . in the lower V Corps and VIII Corps sectors, are not being considered as a serious threat."[28] First Army had assessed the Ardennes sector as a rest and rehabilitation area, just like the Germans did, but Patton had his doubts, based on Koch's superior intelligence analysis.

On December 2 XIX TAC spotted many vehicles north of Trier, close to Echternach. The next day Third Army radio intelligence agencies lost contact with *Panzer Lehr* but assumed it was moving north.[29] On December 6 ULTRA confirmed that *Heeresgruppe B* had requested fighter cover for trains bringing up troops and supplies to assembly areas behind the front in the Aachen sector, Bitburg, and Trier.[30] Three days later Koch briefed Patton on the German strategic reserve west of the Rhine, which was now estimated at thirteen divisions. Koch declared that the situation north of the Moselle, specifically the boundary between VIII and XX Corps, required "special attention" based on the continual heavy movement toward Third Army's zone. He declared that the Germans had the capability to launch significant spoiling attacks against First Army and possibly even Third Army because they had nine nominal divisions (the combat equivalent of seven and a half divisions) opposite VIII Corps. This was two and a half more divisions in equivalent strength than currently deployed against the entire Third Army. Koch made an even more emphatic statement in his Periodic Report the next day. The "massive Armored force" the Germans had assembled gave them "the definite capability to launching [sic] a spoiling (diversionary) offensive."[31]

Koch did not go so far as to tell Patton that the Germans would attack at location X at time Y, but he had identified a legitimate, quantifiable enemy capability to the northeast that could impact TINK. Patton instructed his chief of staff, Brigadier General Hobart R. Gay, to begin outlining lines of action to meet the threat from the north. One of Gay's responsibilities was to continuously study the situation, with input from the staff, in order to prepare for "future contingencies." In Koch's words, Patton wanted Third Army to be "in a position to meet whatever happens."[32]

Lieutenant Colonel Charles R. Codman, Patton's aide, recalled that Helfers briefed Patton at 0630 on December 16, telling him that they had intercepted radio messages indicating that previously identified troop concentrations near Trier were on the move. Lieutenant Colonel Paul D. Harkins, deputy chief of staff (operations), indicated that Colonel Robert S. Allen briefed Patton at the same meeting, telling the general that the Germans had gone on radio silence. When Patton asked what that meant, Allen apparently replied that it indicated an imminent attack.[33] Codman claimed that Koch said it was an attack, but there is no mention of any attack against VIII Corps in Koch's G-2 Intelligence Summary (ISUM) No. 411 released at 0900, and Allen recorded that he first heard of the attack at 1330.[34] Nor did Koch's work map as of 0300 depict any movement near Trier. This suggests either that the ISUM was already in production and could not be amended or that Codman and Harkins lied to make Patton look more prescient. Indeed, Patton claimed that his phone conversation with Bradley that night was "the first official notice we had of the, to us, anticipated German assault."[35] Clearly, Patton was aware of significant activity in Middleton's zone for several hours.

By 1800 on December 16 Koch's ISUM No. 412 identified heavy

vehicle movement and rail traffic heading south, twelve miles northeast of Trier; heavy artillery preparation along the entire front of VIII Corps; and six divisions, including the *116th* and *2nd PDs*.[36] Though confident that he understood the Germans' capabilities based on Koch's analysis over the last few weeks, Patton was not sure of their intentions. One reason was that XIX TAC's reconnaissance missions had also reported heavy rail traffic at Saarbrücken and Zweibrücken as far back as November 18.[37] This traffic was directly in front of his main axes of advance in Lorraine, not in the seam between VIII and XX Corps. Perhaps Patton did not want to believe it because he instinctively understood the repercussions: TINK would be canceled. However, he could not help but recall that *Fifth Panzer Armee* had struck the 4th Armored Division back in September, so the idea that the Germans could do so again, somewhere, was not lost on him. He may very well have anticipated some type of spoiling offensive in the Ardennes, but not a major counteroffensive. Whether he got it exactly right is irrelevant; what matters most is how he reacted.

Preliminary Moves

Patton started gathering additional information soon after Bradley ordered him to give up the 10th Armored Division. Patton phoned Major General Walton H. Walker the night of December 16 and asked him to call Middleton and gauge the seriousness of the situation. Middleton told Walker that it was "even worse" than Bradley had suggested. Walker then reported this to Patton. However, this does not entirely square with Koch's ISUM No. 413, issued at 2400 on December 16, which stated that although there were "numerous" attacks along VIII Corps' center, they were all company size and had limited objectives. Koch's assistant, Allen, had enough information to claim that the first objective was St. Vith.[38] Since Third Army's ISUMs were distributed to army group, this one might have influenced Sibert's interpretation of events.

Much has been made of Patton's December 17 instructions to Eddy to immediately commit the 4th Armored Division to operations that day. The claim is that this indicated Patton's underestimation of the scale of the German attack in the Ardennes. Bradley called sometime during the day to inform Patton that he might have to take two more divisions from Third Army.[39] The truth is that while elements of the division, including the 25th Cavalry Reconnaissance Squadron, 704th Tank Destroyer Battalion, and A Company/37th Tank Battalion, continued to support the

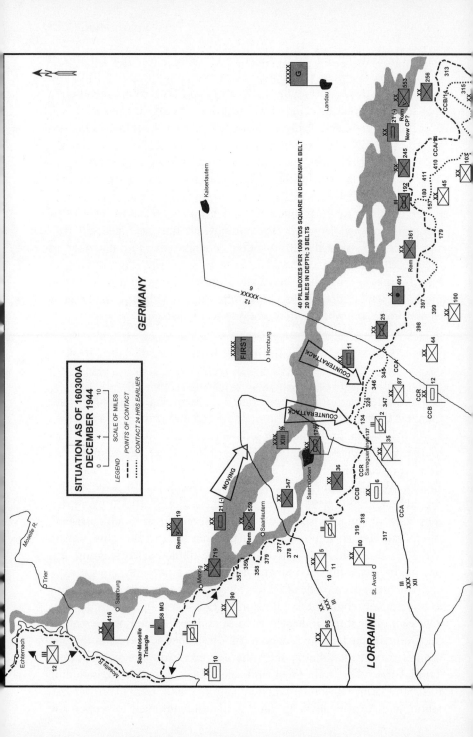

SITUATION AS OF 160300A
DECEMBER 1944

SCALE OF MILES
0   4   10

LEGEND
········· POINTS OF CONTACT
— — — CONTACT 24 HRS EARLIER

GERMANY

LORRAINE

Moselle R.
Trier
Saarburg
Saar-Moselle
Triangle
Merzig
Saarlautem
Saarbrücken
Sarreguemines
St. Avold
Echternach
Kaiserlautern
Homburg
Landau

FIRST

MOVING
COUNTERATTACK
COUNTERATTACK

40 PILLBOXES PER 1000 YDS SQUARE IN DEFENSIVE BELT
20 MILES IN DEPTH; 3 BELTS

58 MG

G

44th and 87th Infantry Divisions, the bulk of the division never moved throughout the day. It took care of much-needed maintenance and refits, and the entire 8th Tank Battalion conducted ranges until 1800. CCB was also ordered to organize patrols to hunt down suspected German paratroopers near Nancy until 1045 the next day. At 1100 on December 18 CCB was put on one-hour NTM to move up and support the 35th Infantry Division, but this never happened. If Patton actually ordered the entire division to get engaged—indeed, he reflected that "the fact that I did this shows how little I appreciated the seriousness of the enemy attack on that date"—it seems that neither Eddy nor Major General Hugh J. Gaffey, the division commander, executed it.[40] It did not mean that Patton did not appreciate the scale of the attack. It meant that he did not want to lose control of another armored division in case he was called on to respond.

Patton definitely appreciated the scale of the German offensive on December 17. He wrote to Major General Fox Connor that day that the attack "reminds me very much of March 25, 1918" and noted in his diary that the German attack "is on a wide front and moving fast. . . . Last night there was considerable road and rail movement into my area. This may be a feint, or the attack on the front of VIII Corps may be, although at the moment it looks like the real thing." Although Koch's 0300 work map now depicted seven new divisional identifications north of Trier, Patton said "feint" because the same map also depicted two specific concentrations along the Saar, one based on *21st PD* and one based on *11th PD*, as well as heavy movement converging behind Saarbrücken. XIX TAC's tactical reconnaissance was picking up numerous trains "headed generally S and W" in Third Army's zone of advance. Patton felt confident that he could hold an attack on his front, "as we are very well placed," but he was concerned about his northern flank, held at that time by Colonel Jimmy Polk's 6th Cavalry Group. Polk was reporting increased shelling in his zone north of XX Corps during the morning. After comparing the two threats, Patton concluded, "My guess is that our offensive will be called off and we will have to go up there and save their hides."[41]

Patton's interpretation that the threat north of Trier was the real thing can only be attributed to ULTRA. Relatively quiet throughout the preceding weeks, the high-grade signals intelligence (Sigint) now started to yield greater dividends, but it seems that some highly important messages

Opposite: Map 4.1. Third Army G-2 Work Map, Situation as of 0300 December 16, 1944

were not sent to Third Army. One such ZZZZ message, sent out in the early-morning hours of December 17, revealed that *Jagdkorps II*'s reconnaissance priorities were to identify crossings of the Meuse between Liège and Namur and to determine whether reserves were being diverted from the Aachen area. In the early afternoon Third Army received an ULTRA message revealing that *I SS Panzerkorps* had requested reconnaissance in a thirty-mile radius west and north of Krinkelt. *Jagdkorps II* promised that fighters would protect the attacking spearheads of the corps continuously, as far as weather permitted. The absence of Third Army's "ZE" prefix code in the address box of certain ULTRA messages cannot be explained. Ultimately, it appears that enough intelligence was reaching Third Army because during the XIX TAC briefing at 2000, Weyland referred to the "grand attack by 16 German divisions." According to Allen, during the 0800 General Staff meeting Patton declared that "what has occurred [is] no occasion for excitement" and cautioned everyone to "keep calm because alarm communicates itself very quickly from top downward."[42]

In anticipation of having to conduct a contingency operation in Luxembourg, Patton visited Walker on December 17 to inform him that XX Corps might be used to intervene in the north. Walker wrote to his wife that day that Patton had come by to "warn me of a big job ahead. It looks as if I am to be given another great opportunity." In *War as I Knew It* Patton noted that he had brought in Major General John Millikin, commander of III Corps, to discuss "the possible use of the III Corps in an attack to the north in case the Germans continued the attack on the VIII Corps."[43] However, the III Corps after-action report made no mention of this and indicated that Millikin first heard of the German attack from Third Army on December 18.[44] Whatever the truth, it is certain that Patton was setting the conditions for some sort of action. What he apparently did not do was phone Hodges to see how he was doing or offer additional help beyond the 10th Armored Division.

Hodges's situation was deteriorating fast. His communications with forward units were a shambles, and with the exception of some engineer units, First Army had few significant reserves. That morning he received word that German armor had broken through the Losheim Gap between V and VIII Corps, and at 0700 he reluctantly gave Gerow permission to halt V Corps and redeploy if he deemed it essential to do so. Lieutenant General William H. Simpson of Ninth Army offered Hodges the 30th Infantry Division.[45] Hodges had a difficult time reaching Bradley on December 16, and throughout the morning of December 17 First Army headquarters made frequent calls to Bradley's headquarters, seeking the release of the 82nd and 101st Airborne Divisions of the XVIII Airborne Corps.

During the night before the attack Hodges showed signs of illness. Members of his staff recorded conflicting views of his physical and mental condition. Sylvan made no mention of it in his diary, offering only that Hodges appeared to be "neither optimistic nor pessimistic" on December 16. His chief of staff, Major General William B. Kean, claimed Hodges was bed-ridden, suffering from viral pneumonia, while Kean's aide declared that throughout the morning of December 17 Hodges was leaning on his desk with his head in his arms. It seems that he was incapacitated in some way for at least two days, that his grip on the situation faltered, and that Kean effectively stepped in to minimize the temporary command vacuum.[46]

Bradley has been properly criticized for not departing Versailles until early on the morning of December 17. Hansen observed that he "did not look worried but he was tired . . . he had not slept well. He lay awake, thinking of the problem posed by the German attack." Bradley returned to Eagle TAC, Twelfth Army Group's tactical headquarters in Luxembourg City, in the late afternoon, and upon scanning the updated situation map showing fourteen German divisions, he remarked to Leven Allen, "Pardon my French, Lev—I think the situation justifies it—just where in hell has this sonuvabitch gotten all his strength?" According to Hansen, Bradley called it "Rundstedt's all-out attack" but thought it might actually be a good thing because "he might break his back on it." Most likely reflecting Bradley's attitude, Hansen also recorded: "This fellow aims to lighten the pressure in our pushes of the First and Third Armies. He is getting worried about the Third which is now up against the Wall and threatening to break through."[47]

Sibert, Bradley's G-2, was not convinced it was an all-out attack—an inevitable psychological condition, given his previous estimates. To be fair, however, based on how Twelfth Army Group was receiving information from the front, the situation looked like piecemeal efforts to kick-start small-scale attacks. His interpretation of the initial reports on December 16 dismissed long-range objectives, so he therefore concluded that the threat was limited, even though the long frontage on which the limited attacks were taking place suggested something greater. Just before 2300 on December 16, however, ULTRA decrypted a signal from *Jagdkorps II* indicating the intention to support the attack of "5 and 6 Armies."[48]

Bradley could hardly have misinterpreted the scale as the evidence mounted, but for some reason he, like Patton, was hoping he could deal with it with the forces in hand. As Hansen observed, "Brad has indicated the situation demands careful watching for the perfect timing that will be needed for a direct and strong counterattack if we are able to stop the German without too significant a redeployment of our strength here."[49] While Bradley was en route from Versailles, the SHAEF deputy G-3, Major General John F. M. Whiteley, a British officer, called Leven Allen and offered Major General Matthew B. Ridgway's XVIII Airborne Corps to Twelfth Army Group. Such augmentation, combined with the already committed 7th and 10th Armored Divisions, might have imbued Bradley with a false and temporary sense of security. In fact, he displayed considerable anxiety about halting preparations for TINK. At 1900 Bradley released the XVIII Airborne Corps to Hodges.[50] Though certainly a help, Ridgway's two light airborne divisions were not going to be enough, and Bradley slowly came to this realization by the next day.

Bradley was tired on the morning of December 18, having gotten little sleep during the night. German aircraft roared overhead, and the wail of sirens announcing new raids frustrated his attempt to rest. In a touch of irony, Gay called Eddy that morning at 0930 and told him the situation in the north "is under control."[51] An hour later, however, Bradley phoned Patton and asked him to come to Luxembourg with his principal staff officers as soon as possible. Within ten minutes of Bradley's call, Patton, Koch, Colonel Halley G. Maddox (G-3), and Colonel Walter J. Muller (G-4) left Nancy. Bradley had implied that Patton would not like what he was going to propose.

Patton arrived at Eagle TAC after 1330, and Hansen described the meeting as "charged with mystery." Sibert briefed the participants on the enormity of the German penetration, indicating that perhaps as many as seven panzer divisions had been committed. Bradley thought that some divisions must have come from the Russian Front. ULTRA had already revealed that the *Sixth Panzer Armee* was the main effort and that *Jagdkorps II* was exerting a maximum effort to "materially delay" the arrival of American reinforcements on the north flank. Moreover, German bridgeheads west of the Wiltz River were being "continually reinforced."[52] *Panzer Lehr* was closing in on Bastogne. Early on the morning of December 18 two highest-priority ZZZZZ messages were sent out and received by Third Army, revealing *Heeresgruppe B*'s intention to continue attacking to the west. *Sixth Panzer Armee's schwerpunkt* was in the St.

Vith–Manderfeld–Monschau sector, and the box Malmédy–St. Vith–Stavelot–Vielsalm appeared critical at the moment.[53] Two other ULTRA messages that morning revealed *Jagdkorps II*'s continuing main effort to interdict reinforcements heading south from the Aachen–Maastricht area for the north flank and identified fourteen divisions by name. It was also clearly understood that *Jagdkorps II* was searching for crossings of the Maas in the Liège–Huy–Namur–Givet area. However, neither of these messages (the second a ZZZZ priority) was sent to Third Army.[54]

Patton was impressed by Sibert's brief and admitted the seriousness of the situation in the Ardennes. However, despite looking harder at southern Luxembourg, Patton kept one eye on the Saar front. Koch's work maps were still Lorraine-centric because Patton had not been given a new mission yet. Third Army was opposed there by *First Armee*, consisting of the *416th, 719th, 347th,* and *36th Infantry Divisions*; remnants of the *19th* and *559th VGDs*; the *17th SS PGD*; and the *11th* and *21st PDs*. ULTRA had revealed that the Germans were maintaining a watchful eye on the Saarlautern bridgehead in Lorraine. In fact, there was considerable *Luftwaffe* activity over XX Corps on the morning of December 18. Third Army headquarters even issued an alert that morning about paratroopers dropping along the N74 Highway three miles south of Nancy.[55]

Bradley told Patton, "I feel you won't like what we are going to do, but I fear it is necessary." Third Army's ongoing offensive against the West Wall was to be halted immediately; TINK was dead. Patton, though clearly disappointed, resigned himself to the inevitable; he looked at Bradley, shrugged his shoulders, and said, "What the hell, we'll still be killing Krauts."[56] The standard version of their meeting is that Bradley asked Patton what he could do to ease the pressure on Middleton. This implies that Bradley had no definitive plan in mind before 1330, and in fact, he did not. The only plan being executed at that moment was Middleton's. The friendly reinforcement situation was as follows: The 422nd and 423rd CTs of the 106th Infantry Division were surrounded on the Schnee Eifel. CCB/9th Armored Division began arriving in the St. Vith area at 1030 on December 17. The 7th Armored Division had not been able to close on St. Vith to support Jones's 106th Infantry Division until late that day due to massive traffic jams, caused in part by American frontline units withdrawing in haste. By 1540 reconnaissance elements of CCB arrived, and by 1930 they had tied in with CCB/9th Armored Division to the southeast to block the Germans east of St. Vith. The bulk of the 7th Armored Division arrived by 2200. The 30th Infantry Division had moved toward

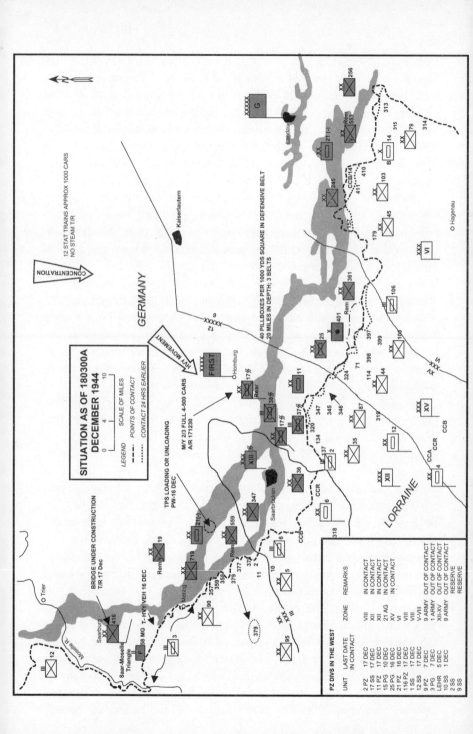

SITUATION AS OF 180300A
DECEMBER 1944

LEGEND
SCALE OF MILES
0   4   10
•••••• POINTS OF CONTACT
•••••• CONTACT 24 HRS EARLIER

CONCENTRATION

12 STAT TRAINS APPROX 1000 CARS
NO STEAM T/R

GERMANY

Kaiserlautern

IVY MOVEMENT

Landau

40 PILLBOXES PER 1000 YDS SQUARE IN DEFENSIVE BELT
20 MILES IN DEPTH; 3 BELTS

O Hagenau

FIRST
Homburg

M/Y 2/3 FULL 4-500 CARS
A/R 171230

TPS LOADING OR UNLOADING
PW-16 DEC

Saarbrücken

BRIDGE UNDER CONSTRUCTION
T/R 17 Dec

O Trier

Saar-Moselle
Triangle
Moselle R.

58 MG T- HVY VEH 16 DEC

LORRAINE

PZ DIVS IN THE WEST			
UNIT	LAST DATE IN CONTACT	ZONE	REMARKS
2 PZ	17 DEC	VIII	IN CONTACT
17 SS	17 DEC	XII	IN CONTACT
11 PZ	17 DEC	XII	IN CONTACT
15 PG	10 DEC	21 AG	IN CONTACT
25 PG	16 DEC	XV	IN CONTACT
21 PZ	16 DEC	VI	IN CONTACT
116 PZ	17 DEC	VIII	
1 SS	17 DEC	VIII	
12 SS	17 DEC	V-VIII	
9 PZ	7 DEC	9 ARMY	OUT OF CONTACT
3 PG	7 DEC	1 ARMY	OUT OF CONTACT
LEHR	5 DEC	XII-XV	OUT OF CONTACT
10 SS	1 DEC	9 ARMY	OUT OF CONTACT
2 SS			RESERVE
9 SS			RESERVE

the critical Stavelot area to prevent *1st SS PD* from capturing the massive fuel dump containing some 2 million gallons. The 82nd and 101st Airborne Divisions were on the move from Reims. To the south the 10th Armored Division had closed in behind Barton's 4th Infantry Division in good time. CCA had attacked in multiple columns north, northeast, and east at approximately 0815 on December 18 against an enemy front that was impossible to estimate because infiltration made the whole line fluid.[57]

Middleton's plan to deal with the threat had two distinct phases. In phase one he hoped to defend in place along the original corps front to effect maximum delay. In phase two the vital road nets would be denied to the enemy by erecting strong defenses in front of St. Vith, Houffalize, Bastogne, and Luxembourg City. The armored divisions converging from north and south would reinforce St. Vith and Luxembourg City, while the two airborne divisions en route to VIII Corps would be used to block Bastogne and Houffalize. This center section of the corps was critical, for as the corps after-action report stated, the 28th Infantry Division "weakened rapidly during the day under the savage pounding of enemy blows."[58] To reinforce Bastogne, Middleton also ordered CCB/10th Armored Division to redeploy there. It would begin arriving at 1600, approximately eight hours before the lead elements of the 101st Airborne Division began arriving.

Meanwhile, Bradley had already received instructions from Eisenhower that morning, although they were subject to modification "which may result from our discussions" intended to take place the next day at Verdun. Bradley's mission as of that morning was to check the enemy advance, secure the LC running from Namur to Liège and on to Aachen, relieve Twenty-First Army Group west of the Meuse, and then launch a counteroffensive north of the Moselle converging on the general Bonn–Cologne area.[59] Bradley appears to have conducted a quick mental estimate of the situation and needed Patton's feedback before he could confirm a new line of action.

Based on Bradley's broad intent that Third Army would be required to do something, Patton updated his own initial estimate of the situation. He had already given the problem some thought and quickly arrived at a decision about the action necessary to meet the situation described by

Opposite: Map 4.2. Third Army G-2 Work Map, Situation as of 0300 December 18, 1944

Bradley. Patton probably consulted the map brought along by Koch and told Bradley that he would halt the 4th Armored Division (most of it was already halted) and concentrate it near Longwy starting at midnight. He would move the 80th Infantry Division to Luxembourg in the morning and alert the 26th Infantry Division to move in twenty-four hours. With Bradley's approval, this initial concept was quickly communicated by phone to Gay in Nancy: "Stop Hugh [Gaffey] and McBride (80th ID) from whatever they are doing. Alert them for movement. They should make no retrograde movement at this time, but this is the real thing and they will undoubtedly move tomorrow. They will go under General M. (this means General Millikin). Arrange to have sufficient transportation on hand to move McBride. Hugh (this means the 4th AD) can move on his own power. I am going to leave here and stop to see Johnnie W. (General Walker). It will probably be late when I come home."[60] This brief phone message served as Patton's warning order to Third Army.

Understanding Bradley's concept for employing Third Army is important. When Patton left around 1530, Bradley walked him to his jeep. "We won't commit any more of your stuff than we have to," he told Patton. "I want to save it for a whale of a blow when we hit back—and we're going to hit this bastard hard." Patton grinned, pulled his parka tightly under his chin, and left.[61] Bradley's statement suggests that he envisioned deploying only minimal force to assist VIII Corps, followed by a much larger Third Army offensive. What is not clear is whether Bradley was talking about a follow-on offensive into the Bulge, some sort of modified TINK, or some other Third Army offensive along the front in Lorraine. The latter two possibilities seem reasonable because later in the day, although admitting that the situation was "worse than it was at noon," Bradley still hung his ultimate hope on Third Army in Lorraine. Indeed, one historian characterized Bradley's hope for Patton's success in Lorraine as an "obsession—it cannot be termed less."[62] Hansen recorded Bradley's thoughts as follows: "The German, according to Bradley, was desperately afraid [of] our strength there [in Lorraine] and has made this attack not only to divert us from the slugging match to the north but also to reduce the temper of our assault on the south where we have dealt the German a punishing blow and now threaten him with deeper penetrations. If we crack through at this point [Operation TINK], we will simply prove an old contention of Bradley's who once said the Frankfurt route of advance was the logical one for us to take into Germany."[63]

While Patton was on the road back to Nancy, Bradley called Gay, described the seriousness of the situation, and asked him if a combat command of 4th Armored Division could move at once. Gay replied that it could and quickly issued a warning order to Gaffey. At around 2000 Patton phoned Bradley and was told that "the situation up there is much worse than it was when I talked to you. Move Hugh and McBride at once, one combat command of Hugh's to move tonight, if possible. Destination, LONGWY. Have General Millikin report to General Allen at my CP at 1100A tomorrow. You and a staff officer meet me for a conference with General Eisenhower at VERDUN at approximately 1100A. I understand from General Eisenhower that you are to take over the VIII Corps as well as the offensive to be launched by the new troops coming in the area."[64]

Bradley's "much worse" perspective does not square with Bedell Smith's observation at the SHAEF Chiefs of Staff and Air Staff Conference at 0900 on December 19: "Last night General Bradley was inclined to take a fairly optimistic view of the situation. The German armored forces which had made the breakthrough were relatively small and the disorganization of the U.S. divisions who had taken the force of this thrust was less than he had feared earlier." Bradley said the same thing to Hansen after Patton left at 1530. "I don't take too serious a view of it," he declared, "although the others will not agree with me."[65] This seems an impossible deduction if Bradley was actually looking at ULTRA, which clearly revealed the size of the armored force being committed.

Nevertheless, Bradley had updated his estimate and issued specific orders to Patton. Patton now had to update his own estimate and make several supplementary decisions. He and his staff were already in the planning stage for the move north and for future offensive operations. In preparation for the move north, Millikin was called to Nancy and met with Patton at 2015 on December 18 to discuss the plan, "insofar as it was known."[66] At 2200 that night Millikin phoned his chief of staff, Colonel James H. Phillips, and told him to move the corps forward echelon to Longwy the following morning. Third Army was now in motion.

5

The Verdun Conference

Bradley, whose army group had been attacked, mostly observed
throughout the two hour conference, "saying little, offering nothing."
Even he realized that the only principal players were Eisenhower and
Patton.

—Carlo D'Este

Early on December 19 Major General Manton S. Eddy, commander of
XII Corps, was at Third Army headquarters in Nancy. At 0700 Maddox
briefed him on the situation. At that time, Eddy recalled, "They showed
me the plans rather sketchedly as all the plans were tentative." An hour
later he sat in on the General Staff meeting in Maddox's office. Weyland
and his staff were there as well. Patton told the assembled officers that
"the reputation of the 3rd Army and the XIX Tactical Air Command for
speed and effectiveness resulted from the efficiency of the officers present, and that I counted upon them for even greater successes."[1]

Colonel Brenton G. Wallace, Third Army's chief liaison officer, was
present and recorded the following:

General Patton told us that the situation with the First Army was
serious but not alarming. The Germans had made a major breakthrough to a depth of 15 to 20 miles in the north sector of the VIII
Corps and the south sector of the V Corps. . . . One whole U.S.
Division—the 106th—had been decimated, the 28th Division
had been badly battered and one Combat Command of the 9th
Armored had been practically destroyed. The VIII Corps Headquarters had been forced to flee and no one knew exactly where
it was at that time. Enemy armor and infantry had penetrated to
within a half mile of the First Army command post, forcing its
withdrawal. General Patton said that the preceding day he had
met at Luxembourg with General Bradley and had talked with

General Eisenhower by telephone. The whole situation was very fluid, but in general, the Third Army had been ordered to be prepared to turn on its axis and attack to the north. . . . General Patton . . . desired the staff to know as much of the plan as possible so they could be thinking along new lines and working out details while he was gone [to the Verdun meeting].[2]

Patton then made a "rough plan" for operations, based on the assumption that he would use Millikin's III Corps and be given command of VIII Corps.

Apparently, Patton did not know where Middleton was at the moment, because after this meeting Maddox asked Wallace to send a liaison officer out to look for VIII Corps headquarters. Middleton, under orders from Hodges, had withdrawn during the night to Neufchâteau. Eddy confirmed that his corps was not initially involved in Patton's scheme of maneuver: "I will stay generally in my present location and my sector will be much larger."[3] Patton did not devise the army's broad outline plan for offensive operations at the 0800 meeting. He had already done so beforehand, but the actual assignment of divisions had probably not been confirmed. Throughout the night of December 18 Patton would have considered his mission from Bradley, the means available to him and to the enemy, and any new intelligence. The most pressing need was an understanding of the conditions in his new area of operations in the Ardennes, including weather and terrain.

Planning Factors

Koch issued his preliminary study of the terrain in the new area of interest on December 19 and focused heavily on routes and avenues of approach. There were three first-class north-south routes but only one first-class east-west route. Many good secondary roads crossed the area in a northeasterly direction connecting the main north-south routes. The first principal north-south route was Arlon–Bastogne–Houffalize–Liège. This route followed the high ground and traversed wooded and boggy areas instead of following the river valleys where the towns were situated.[4] The second route was Luxembourg–St. Vith–Malmédy–Eupen (or Eupen–Monschau), and the third route was Luxembourg–Echternach–Prüm–Dahlem. The principal east-west route ran from Bastogne to Clerf and on to Lunebach–Prüm–Lissingen.

The terrain analysis led Koch to conclude that "the approaches to both the enemy's ECHTERNACH bridgehead and his St. Vith Salient are reasonably good. The LUXEMBOURG–ST VITH Road and a reasonably adequate secondary road net are available for entry into the bridgehead area. To the SAUER River the terrain is in general rolling and advantage may be taken of both primary roads leading from LUXEMBOURG, with a good secondary road net in the area, in approaching the enemy's penetration W of ECHTERNACH." The analysis of the ground farther west was important:

> In approaching the ST VITH area, use of the LUXEMBOURG–ST VITH road is limited by the enemy's ability to interdict this road N of ETTELBRUCK. The alternative main road ARLON–BASTOGNE–ST VITH allows access to both the ST VITH area and the area of the enemy's penetration Vic (P 6762). The secondary road net N of the ATTERT River is limited and cross country movement is restricted S of BASTOGNE by the hilly and forested nature of the terrain and the E-W streams in the area. The approaches to the E and NE from BASTOGNE are along the crest of the ARDENNE Plateau with relatively light forestation. . . . In the CLERF the rugged terrain and CLERF River will combine to create a substantial obstacle to an attack from the W. Nevertheless the road BASTOGNE–ST VITH *offers the best entry into the area.*[5]

The terrain was immensely challenging, and the main roads naturally factored heavily in Patton's potential lines of action.

Patton also had to determine which formations could move immediately and, more critically, which ones could follow. There was a limit to how much of Third Army he could pull out of Lorraine because Alexander Patch's Seventh Army to the south would have to sidestep north to compensate. Patch in turn was limited by the presence of the Colmar Pocket, another "bulge" in the Allied line fifty miles wide and twenty-five miles deep west of the Rhine, on the Alsatian Plain. This pocket was a serious thorn in the side of Lieutenant General Jacob L. Devers's Sixth Army Group.

In terms of threats, Patton knew that the *21st PD* had withdrawn in the area north of Saarlautern, replaced by the *719th Division*, and was now in reserve.[6] Patton also had to consider possible enemy attacks against XX

Corps. He felt reasonably confident that he could withdraw XII Corps because of the damage he had inflicted on *First Armee* during the Lorraine
campaign. In Periodic Report No. 190 for December 18, Koch assessed
that there were only four division equivalents opposite Third Army. However, he also stated that the heavy movement into the Trier, Homburg,
and Kaiserlautern sectors suggested that more reserves were moving into
place opposite Third Army.[7] The lay of the ground on XX Corps' northern
flank posed different problems.

The strip of land between the Saar and Moselle Rivers at the point
where they converged was called the Saar–Moselle triangle. It was approximately nineteen miles long from base to apex and ten miles wide
at its base. The base rested on the Orscholz switch line, connecting the
West Wall fortifications to the Saar River fortifications. The triangle was
bisected by a north-south ridge. That high ground was dominated by the
Germans' *416th Division* and therefore allowed them to dominate Trier
to the northeast, which guarded the entrance to the Moselle corridor.[8]
During the latter part of November, Walker had attempted to penetrate
the triangle with the 3rd Cavalry Group and then CCA/10th Armored Division, but they were halted along the Orscholz switch line. The triangle
represented a real threat to a corps redeploying into southern Luxembourg because ULTRA revealed that the Germans were aware through
photo reconnaissance that the road bridge over the Saar at Saarburg was
undamaged.[9] Once a corps was established in southern Luxembourg,
the triangle would continue to be a dangerous salient between it and XX
Corps.

As Third Army redeployed into Luxembourg, left flank security also
had to be considered because there was no anchor to tie in to. VIII Corps
at this time was still oriented north-south, not east-west, and its center was
shredded. Operational security moving north was not easy to solve either.
Although *Jagdkorps II's* main reconnaissance effort during the first two
days had discovered reinforcements heading for the *Sixth Panzer Armee*
spearheads, preparations began on December 18 to start watching the
left flank of *Seventh Armee*, as opposed to screening forward of the spearheads. *Luftwaffenkommando West's* principal intelligence requirement
early on December 18 was to determine whether American formations
were moving up on both sides of Luxembourg City.[10] Patton, then, knew
the Germans were on the lookout for him.

Patton also had to anticipate conditions when he got into position.
The situation appeared stable in the northeast, where the 4th Infantry

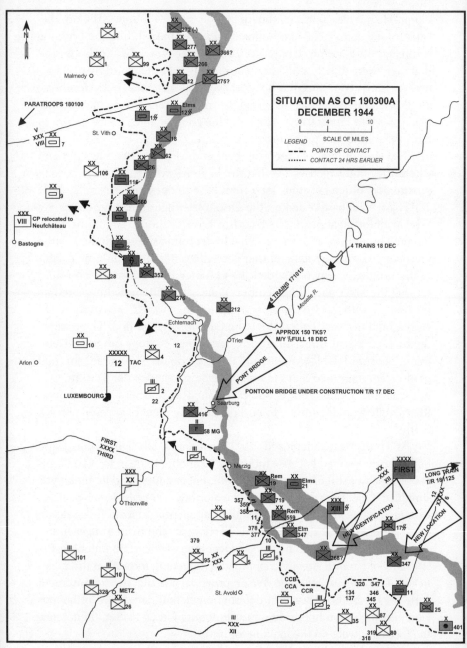

Map 5.1. Third Army G-2 Work Map, Situation as of 0300 December 19, 1944

Division was fighting against the *212th VGD*. ULTRA revealed on December 17 that *LXXX Armeekorps* anticipated "tough Allied resistance" in its sector. Seventh Armee considered the resistance in the Diekirch, Berdorf, Echternach, and Dickweiler areas strong, but progress was being made north of Waldbillig and Consdorf. However, the twenty-four-ton ferry at Bollendorf was out of commission, and *LXXX Armeekorps* seemed to be holding its ground rather than making significant efforts to drive forward.[11] The forward edge of the battle area (FEBA) was easy to distinguish in 4th Infantry Division's sector, but westward, Patton had to appreciate where he could safely stage from and establish assembly areas and where the new supply dumps would be.

Before he departed for Verdun, Patton identified three possible lines of action based on using III Corps and getting VIII Corps. The first line of action was from the general vicinity of Neufchâteau against what he considered the "left nose" of the salient. It is not known whether this implied a Neufchâteau–Bastogne axis or a Neufchâteau–St. Hubert axis. The second line of action was from the general vicinity of Arlon on Bastogne, and the third was due north from Diekirch up Skyline Drive west of the Our River. Curiously, Echternach was not mentioned as a staging point. The first option was based on using VIII Corps, but III Corps could have been deployed to execute all three. Patton assigned code names before he left so that, like a quarterback, he could call a play from Verdun once he received final orders from Eisenhower. According to Harkins, the code name for the Arlon–Bastogne line of action was NICKEL.[12]

Patton characterized this early-morning period of December 19 as follows: "When it is considered that Harkins, Codman and I left for Verdun at 0915 and that between 0800 and that hour we had had a Staff meeting, planned three possible lines of attack, and made a simple code in which I could telephone General Gay which two of the three lines we were to use, it is evident that war is not so difficult as people think."[13] Clearly, Patton was somewhat disingenuous. Selecting three possible lines of action by identifying the main highways was the easy part, but he had only started the planning process. Eddy was right to call the plans sketchy. No staff could properly evaluate three distinct lines of action in an hour. Maddox had certainly done some preliminary study as part of his future responsibility for planning, but there was still much work to be done by the staff. Maddox and Muller, the G-3 and G-4, worked closely together to produce the army's movement plan, and Maddox produced a tentative plan of attack. Gay coordinated everything produced by the staff sections to create a more mature plan to present to Patton, who would then amend it as required and sign off on it. The result of the collaborative staff effort was a consolidated field order from Maddox and a consolidated administrative order from Muller. Both were essential to realign the army.

Patton left Third Army headquarters in Nancy shortly after 0900, accompanied by Codman and Harkins. They rolled into Verdun in two armored jeeps mounting .30-caliber machine guns just after Devers arrived. Eisenhower and his deputy, Tedder, made their way to Verdun from Versailles in a heavily armored Packard. Security had increased greatly around the Supreme Commander since captured members of Skorzeny's *Panzer Brigade 150* confessed to trying to assassinate Eisenhower. He did not take the threat seriously, but the CIC did and persuaded him to move out of his villa at St. Germain-en-Laye and closer to SHAEF headquarters at Versailles.[14] Even with an escort of machine gun–mounted military police (MP) jeeps, however, Eisenhower was stopped several times on the road to Verdun by other anxious MPs.

The meeting took place in an unimpressive room on the second floor of an old French stone barracks, heated by a potbellied stove. There was an easel for Strong's maps, and the generals—Eisenhower, Bedell Smith, Tedder, Bradley, Patton, and Devers—all sat around a long table. Numerous staff officers from SHAEF, Twelfth Army Group, and Third Army stood by to help their respective bosses when necessary. Notably absent from this gathering were Hodges and Montgomery. Hodges remained consumed by a desperate defensive battle and had fallen back in a hurry to his rear echelon headquarters at Chaudfontaine, some eleven miles to the northwest of Spa, the day before. According to Robert Allen, Hodges called Bradley frequently during the conference seeking guidance and authorization for various actions.[15]

Eisenhower never invited Montgomery. In fact, Montgomery noted that day, "I have myself received no orders or requests of any sort." Apparently, no one from Twenty-First Army Group was present, unless one of Montgomery's liaison officers was there. Montgomery's chief of staff, Major General Sir Francis de Guingand, has often been cited as present, and Strong recalled having an exchange with him during the meeting, but at the time, "Freddie" was still making his way back from England.[16] Eisenhower, Patton, Bradley, Tedder, and Devers made no mention of de Guingand in their memoirs or diaries.

Montgomery's absence is best explained by the fact that Eisenhower considered the German offensive a Twelfth Army Group problem at this stage. As he declared in his memoirs, "I had already determined that it was not essential for our counterattack to begin on both flanks simultaneously. In the north, where the weight of the German attack was falling, we would be on the defensive for some days. But on the south we could help the situation by beginning a northward advance at the earliest possible moment. My immediate purpose at the Verdun meeting on the nineteenth was to make arrangements for the beginning of the southern assault."[17]

Choosing to exclude Montgomery from the earliest planning probably delayed the eventual closing of the Bulge and limited the Allies' options. However, Montgomery had already expressed his feelings on December 17, making "very strong representations" to SHAEF that the southern flank should provide the troops to deal with the offensive. The next day he argued that "the whole southern front should close down . . . and that Third U.S. Army under Patton should be moved north to help deal with the German offensive."[18] Montgomery spoke to Whiteley several times on December 19 and began to assemble Lieutenant General Sir Brian Horrocks's XXX Corps near Louvain–St. Trond. Eisenhower, however, pressed Montgomery to supply formations to assist First and Ninth Armies in attacking from the north.

The Eisenhower-Patton Relationship

The two most important people at the Verdun meeting were Eisenhower and Patton. Their relationship before the invasion of French North Africa was strong and personal. They shared the West Point experience, and both were early advocates of tanks. Despite often heated arguments, they respected each other's strengths—Eisenhower's quiet professionalism and Patton's dash and reckless courage. Eisenhower wrote to Patton in July 1942, "As you well know, there is no one else whose good wishes mean more to me than do yours." Eisenhower had tremendous respect for Patton's soldierly qualities and expressed some discomfort about "requesting the services of a man so much senior and so much more able than myself. As I have often told you, you are my idea of a battle commander, and if the fates decree that battles by big formations are to come either wholly or partially within my sphere of influence, I would certainly want you as the lead horse in the team."[19]

Eisenhower was delighted that Marshall selected Patton to lead TORCH. In February 1943 Eisenhower told Patton, "I know that I have no more loyal and devoted friend and subordinate in this whole theater than yourself." He bragged Patton up to everyone who would listen, citing his performance with II Corps in Tunisia and Seventh Army in Sicily. He told Marshall that Patton's job of rehabilitating II Corps was "quickly and magnificently done" and that the success in Sicily "must be attributed directly to [Patton's] . . . energy, determination and unflagging aggressiveness. . . . He never once chose a line on which he said 'we will rest here and recuperate and bring up more strength.'" Eisenhower may not have stated it publicly, for purposes of Allied solidarity, but he was happy the American army had beaten Montgomery's Eighth Army to Messina.[20]

Despite their close relationship and Eisenhower's recognition of Patton's skills, Eisenhower had little choice but to continually offer his old friend and difficult subordinate personal advice about his indiscretions. In Tunisia he had advised Patton to "count to ten before you speak" and warned, "Keep silent and appear stupid; open your mouth and remove all doubt." After the slapping episodes in Sicily, Eisenhower gave Patton a good scare, telling him, "I must so seriously question your good judgement and your self-discipline, as to raise serious doubts in my mind as to your future usefulness."[21] Yet Eisenhower defended Patton to everyone, including irate parents of GIs.

Eisenhower exhibited personal loyalty to Patton, but he also had a practical reason for defending him. Eisenhower told Marshall that Patton "has qualities that we cannot afford to lose unless he ruins himself." Eisenhower initially sought to keep the whole Sicily affair quiet, fearing that Patton would be sent home if the slappings were made public. "I simply cannot let that happen," Eisenhower told Brigadier General Frederick Blesse, the surgeon general, because "Patton is *indispensable* to the war effort—one of the guarantors of our victory." Eisenhower even told reporters at the time that he needed to save Patton for the great battles in Europe still to come, and incredibly, they agreed to sit on the story. In deciding to keep Patton, Eisenhower was strongly supported by Secretary of War Henry L. Stimson.[22]

Eisenhower saw a specific purpose for Patton. As he told Marshall in September 1943, "Many generals constantly think of battle in terms of, first, concentration, supply, maintenance, replacement, and second, after all the above is arranged, a *conservative* advance. This type of person is necessary because he prevents one from courting disaster. But occasions arise when one has to remember that under particular conditions, boldness is ten times as important as numbers. Patton's great strength is that he thinks only in terms of attack as long as there is a single bat-talion that can keep advancing." Eisenhower considered Bradley better balanced than Patton, but Omar lacked the "extraordinary and ruthless driving power that Patton can exert at critical moments." To Eisenhower, Patton remained "preeminently a combat commander" who was "never affected" by doubt, fatigue, or caution; consequently, "his troops are not affected." He was a "truly aggressive commander" and had more drive on the battlefield than "any other man I know."[23] As a result of these senti-ments, Eisenhower told Marshall in December that he wanted Patton as one of his army commanders for the invasion.[24]

Patton clearly owed Eisenhower a great deal professionally. Yet as ear-ly as December 1942, Patton recorded scathing criticisms of Eisenhower in his diary. By the end of the Tunisian campaign, Patton characterized Eisenhower as a "stuff doll" because the British "are running the show." Patton's personal physician, Colonel Charles B. Odom, reflected that Pat-ton tried to maintain his respect for Eisenhower at all times, but his inner-most thoughts revealed themselves in private conversations. Before taking command of Third Army in Normandy, Patton lamented, "We actually have no Supreme Commander—no one who can take hold and say that this shall be done and that shall not be done."[25] Patton never fully appre-ciated the great burden Eisenhower carried as the Supreme Allied Com-mander, but there was still an element of truth in his caustic comments.

According to Strong, the Verdun meeting was "crowded and the at-mosphere tense." Codman offered, "I have seldom seen longer faces." The meeting officially came to order when Eisenhower set the tone for the discussions: "The present situation is to be regarded as one of oppor-tunity for us and not of disaster. There will be only cheerful faces at this conference table." This was not staged for effect. Eisenhower truly be-lieved it, having written to Somervell two days previously, "If things go well we should not only stop the thrust but should be able to profit from it."[26] Strong then gave an update of the situation, declaring that the all-out German offensive was aimed at Brussels with the purpose of splitting the Allied armies.

By the time of the meeting, Eisenhower and Strong had seen enough ULTRA to convince them of the intent and main effort of the offensive. Moreover, at 0257 on December 19 Bletchley Park sent a ZZZZZ mes-sage revealing that *II SS Panzerkorps* was moving south from the Roermond area.[27] Prior to December 16, identifying the forward movement of *II SS Panzerkorps* had been one of Strong's EEIs. With it now satisfied, he could conclude that *Sixth Panzer Armee* had been fully committed. Bradley and Patton appreciated that *II SS Panzerkorps* was committed, but during the meeting both displayed doubt about the direction of the attack. Bradley even reiterated this belief in the air effects study he chaired after the war.[28]

This disagreement between Eisenhower and Strong on one side and Bradley and Patton on the other should have been resolved by the common picture created by ULTRA; however, they interpreted the intelligence differently, most likely because Strong, Sibert, and Koch were provided with different levels of ULTRA intelligence. Specifically, Signal Security Detachment D at Twelfth Army Group, a field element of the Signal Intelligence Division, ETO, sent Sibert material detailing the movements of German panzer and infantry formations in relation to Allied positions.[29] Perhaps this is why Sibert's situation map for December 19 did not match Koch's. Sibert's map depicted *II SS Panzerkorps* and *3rd PGD* moving south with a question mark and *10th SS PD* moving in behind *Fifth Panzer Armee* with a question mark, whereas Koch's work map showed neither activity.

Patton suggested that the offensive might eventually wheel southwest in an attempt to encircle Third Army in the Saar. He most likely got this idea from Koch, who stated that although *II SS Panzerkorps* was estimated to be moving into the southern portion of First Army, it could also conceivably intervene in Third Army's current zone. Koch's perspective was shaped in this particular aspect by Sibert. Bradley and Patton were clearly hedging their bets at this stage and might have been clinging to recent estimates. In fact, Strong's own Weekly Intelligence Summary for December 17 echoed his estimate of the situation four days earlier and claimed that Hitler's main objective, "without doubt," was to relieve pressure in the Cologne–Dusseldorf and Saar sectors, and Sibert's Weekly Intelligence Summary No. 18 stated that Rundstedt "must also realize" that a penetration in the Saar–Strasbourg sector would "have the gravest consequences."[30]

Third Army was on the verge of penetrating in strength to the Saar industrial area, so it was logical to assume that the Germans would ultimately maneuver against Third Army; they had before. Bradley's focus on Patton's operations in Lorraine, circumstantially proved by the closer proximity of Eagle TAC to Third Army's secondary effort than to First Army's main effort north of the Ardennes, only reinforced the perception. Perhaps *Jagdkorps II*'s preparations to watch the southern flank of *Seventh Armee*, *LXXXV Armeekorps*' intention to thrust forward to Harlange, and continuous rumblings in the Saarbrücken area painted such a clear picture of Third Army as a target that Patton could not let go of it. If these factors were not enough evidence to give him pause, Koch was also telling him that "strong evidence exists" that *11th PD* was coming up into the Trier area. This would prompt Eisenhower to inform his commanders the next day that a further German thrust "is likely in the Trier area."[31]

When Eisenhower finished his opening remarks, Patton announced with a big smile that they should have the guts to let the Germans "go all the way to Paris. Then we can really cut 'em off and chew 'em up." From all accounts, Patton's sudden outburst lightened the atmosphere and evoked some smiles, even from the Supreme Commander, but Eisenhower quickly defined his overall intent. He and his staff had already determined that the no-retreat line would run north of Luxembourg west to the Meuse, following the river north and then east along a point south of Liège. Yet he never passed on any instructions to Montgomery, who, on his own initiative, transferred XXX Corps from First Canadian Army to Second British Army at 1700 on December 19 to defend the Meuse.[32]

Patton's predilection for allowing the Germans to create their own trap spoke to his operational technique. As a cavalryman, he was definitely more comfortable than either Eisenhower or Bradley engaging in a running, mobile fight. He was certainly willing to be more aggressive and accept greater risk than Bradley, Eisenhower, and most if not all of the other senior American commanders. Whether Patton was actually serious is another matter, but Gay said much the same thing the day before. He noted, "It is thought that if we had the nerve" to let the Germans penetrate forty to fifty miles, "it would be possible by a bold move to cut them off from the rear"; he was probably reflecting Patton's initial gut reaction to the whole "problem" expressed in the confines of Third Army headquarters.[33] Consciously luring *Heeresgruppe B* across the Meuse, however, would have had predictable consequences because of the supply footprint of the theater.

The theater was divided into a *combat zone*, the forward area required for active operations and the immediate administration of combat forces, and a *communications zone* (ComZ), containing the area required for the administration of the theater as a whole. The combat zone extended from the rear boundary of the corps to the FEBA, and the *army service area* extended from the corps rear boundary to the forward edge of ComZ. ComZ was divided into an Advance Section (AdSec), an Intermediate Section, and a Base Section. ComZ headquarters was located in Paris, and AdSec headquarters was in Namur. The Base Section was subdivided into the Channel, Brittany, Seine, and Oise base sections. Patton knew that if *Heeresgruppe B* crossed the Meuse, it would overrun First Army's service area and pose a dire threat to ComZ's densest concentration of dumps, stockpiles, and logistical centers west of the Meuse in the Oise base section, entailing significant losses of friendly troops and equipment.[34] Yet Eisenhower's no-retreat line at the Meuse was sound for two reasons. First, it did in fact facilitate Patton's concept of stretching the Germans; fifty miles was deep enough. Second, and more important, it immediately set the conditions for considerable maneuver space for American counteraction. The ability to maneuver widely offered options and operational flexibility.

Eisenhower's intent was first to hold the shoulders, then to hold the line of the Meuse, and finally to attack the penetration. He told Patton to move his headquarters to Luxembourg City to colocate with Bradley and prepare counterattack plans. Eisenhower wanted six divisions and asked Patton when he could mount such an attack. Patton set the room astir with his instant reply that he could attack in mere days, but with only three divisions. The actual date Patton gave Eisenhower is debated, but no historian has addressed the irregularities; historians simply choose one of the dates—December 21, 22, or even 23—as definitive. The principal primary sources used by many historians—Patton's memoir *War as I Knew It* and Blumenson's *The Patton Papers*—indicate December 22. Many subsequent historians have cited this date as well, including Hugh Cole, the official historian of the campaign.[35] However, the evidence supporting December 21 is significant.

Bradley recalled that "George estimated 48 hours" and observed, "any other commander would have held his breath and believed himself taking a chance on 98." Eisenhower, sensing that Patton had not grasped the magnitude of the problem, declared, "If you try to go that early, you won't have all three divisions ready and you'll go piecemeal. You will start on the twenty-second and I want your initial blow to be a strong one! I'd even settle for the twenty-third if it takes that long to get three full divisions." This seems to square with the handwritten notes on the SHAEF meeting minutes for December 20, where some staff officer (assumed) penciled in, "Meeting was at Verdun and S.A.C. issued orders for Bradley's counter-attack on Dec 22."[36] Eisenhower distrusted Patton's forty-eight-hour estimate; Third Army had to disengage two corps and travel more than 100 miles over treacherous roads in terrible winter weather.

Eisenhower therefore hedged his bets when he informed the Combined Chiefs of Staff after the meeting: "Patton moves north with six divisions and taking over VIII Corps temporarily will organize major counterblow with target date of 23rd or 24th."[37] The twenty-first is the most plausible date because it fits with the reactions of those present, the recollections of Bradley and Strong, and Eisenhower's subsequent statement.[38]

Codman indicated that Patton's quick and confident reply to Eisenhower's question caused "a shuffling of feet, as those present straightened up in their chairs." Skepticism clouded the faces of some, but a "current of excitement leaped like a flame" through the room. Patton later noted that his confidence "created quite a commotion—some people seemed surprised and others pleased—however I believe it can be done." Strong noted that some British officers openly laughed, but Bradley was visibly impressed, and so, it seems, was Eisenhower. His secretary, Kay Summersby, later declared that Eisenhower told her, "Patton's cocky, confident attitude was superb amidst all the apprehension." Patton had center stage and knew it. He lit a fresh cigar, turned to Bradley, and motioned to the German penetrations on the war map. "Brad, this time the Kraut's stuck his head in a meat-grinder"—Patton made a fist and turned it—"and this time I've got hold of the handle." Patton's quick pronouncement that he could intervene on December 21 stemmed directly from his extensive preparations throughout December 18. After telling Eisenhower what he could do, Patton turned to Harkins and said matter-of-factly, "We can do that." Harkins remembered replying, "Yes Sir. There wasn't much else I could say. We had it pretty well figured out."[39]

Eisenhower recalled that the group discussed the advisability of "attempting to organize a simultaneous attack somewhat farther to the east, against the southern shoulder of the salient." But it seems clear that he was not comfortable with such a plan, even though "future events might indicate a desirability of such a move." He was seeking to mitigate risk and was concerned "only with a methodical advance to the Bastogne area." He personally cautioned Patton against a piecemeal attack; his advance had to be methodical and sure. When Eisenhower sensed that Patton was taking his mission too lightly, he impressed on him the need for strength and cohesion and added, "I did not want him to start until he was in sufficient force so that, once committed, he could continue gradually to crush in the southern flank of the developing salient."[40] Eisenhower's statement of six divisions can be based on two different possibilities. Either he intended Patton to commit another corps from Third Army, or he thought

VIII Corps was still combat effective, meaning that the 4th and 28th Infantry Divisions and 9th Armored Division could be used offensively.

Eisenhower's options were dictated in large part by the presence of the Colmar Pocket, which, he noted, had a "definite and restrictive influence on the plans" made at Verdun. Bradley's contribution at Verdun appears to have been insignificant. According to Patton, he "mostly observed . . . saying little and offering nothing" except to suggest that Devers take over Patton's front. When Eisenhower asked Devers how much of Third Army's line he could cover, Patton recorded that Devers "made a long speech on strictly selfish grounds and said nothing." Devers was clearly not happy at the prospect of shutting down his own offensive against the West Wall to take over Third Army's front in the Saar. "The tragedy to my mind," he recorded in his diary, "has been that the higher command has not seen fit to reinforce success on this flank."[41] Yet Sixth Army Group, containing Seventh Army and the First French Army, was nowhere near the main effort of the Ruhr, and Devers, entirely lacking Eisenhower's confidence and perhaps even goodwill, would never be allowed to outshine Bradley and Patton. Devers would ultimately thin his line considerably to free up Third Army, but this was risky, and the Germans would take advantage of it as the fighting in the Ardennes progressed.

According to doctrine, SHAEF should have been in either the AdSec or the army service area. This would have facilitated greater face-to-face contact between Eisenhower and his principal subordinates. However, his political responsibilities imposed on his day-to-day command responsibilities. Revealingly, back on October 13 he had told Montgomery that no single commander could "stay so close to the day to day movement of divisions and corps that he can keep a 'battle grip' upon the *overall* situation and direct it intelligently." He added that his function was "adjusting the larger boundaries" to facilitate the tasks of the army groups.[42] This is essentially what he did at Verdun, but only between Twelfth and Sixth Army Groups. Montgomery's army group was not part of the equation at this time; therefore, Eisenhower's concept was not holistic. Although boundaries were shifted between Sixth Army Group and Third Army, the concept of operations and scheme of maneuver had not been finalized because Eisenhower wanted Bradley to submit an outline that included Patton's strength, direction, and timings.[43] Moreover, although Eisenhower deserves credit for acting with greater decisiveness than Bradley in the early stages of the offensive, the Verdun meeting should have taken place at least a day earlier.

At the conclusion of the Verdun conference the two old friends of thirty years, Eisenhower and Patton, shared a moment of levity. Their relationship had deteriorated since the war began, but Eisenhower managed a small grin and declared, "Funny thing, George, every time I get another star I get attacked." Soon after being promoted to general, Eisenhower had been defeated by Rommel at Kasserine Pass in February 1943, and he had brought Patton in to straighten things out. Patton grinned back and replied, "And every time you get attacked, Ike, I have to bail you out."[44] Patton had made big promises during the meeting, and now he had to fulfill them. Those who doubted his ability to reorient Third Army in forty-eight hours would soon be proved wrong. Foresight, preparation, and energy gave reality to the boast.

PART III

Descent on Bastogne

6

The Ninety-Degree Turn

I think the German High Command had a high regard for George, but even they erred in underestimating George's ability to move from Metz . . . so fast. For that matter, Ike himself didn't believe George could move that fast.

— Troy Middleton

On December 19 Third Army was deployed in Lorraine between Remich and Hottweiler on a fifty-five-mile front opposite the German *First Armee*. Walker's XX Corps consisted of the 5th, 90th, and 95th Infantry Divisions. The 10th Armored Division had already moved up to VIII Corps on December 17. The 5th Infantry Division was in the Saarlautern–Roden and Fraulautern bridgehead across the Saar River, engaged in tough street fighting. It had relieved the 95th Infantry Division in the bridgehead on December 17 and assumed command at 0600 the next morning. Two regiments of the 5th Infantry Division had attacked on December 18 and 19 to widen the breach of the West Wall bunkers. The 818th Tank Destroyer Battalion and 735th Tank Battalion, both supporting the 5th Infantry Division, each had two companies across the river. The 90th Infantry Division was completely across the Saar in the Pachten–Dillingen bridgehead, with all three regiments in line. The 95th Infantry Division on the corps' right flank had one regiment in the Ensdorf bridgehead and two others out of contact.

To the south was Manton Eddy's XII Corps, consisting of the 35th, 80th, and 87th Infantry Divisions and the 4th and 6th Armored Divisions. The 35th Infantry Division had two regiments across the Saar northeast of Sarreguemines and was also across the Blies River beyond the Saar. The division faced considerable resistance, and comparatively few prisoners were being taken. The 87th Infantry Division to the south of the 35th also had two regiments astride the Blies River. The 6th Armored Division was holding defensive positions between Forbach and Sarreguemines and was not across the Saar but was preparing for offensive operations to exploit any enemy withdrawal in its sector.[1]

Behind the 6th Armored Division and partly out of contact since December 7 was the 80th Infantry Division near St. Avold. The division was in the process of moving back into the line to take part in TINK. Elements of the 319th CT were already on the battle line near Rohrbach, having relieved the 25th Cavalry Reconnaissance Squadron. Colonel William N. Taylor, commanding officer of the 319th Infantry, took pains to declare, "It was typical of the so-called 'quiet periods' which were quiet for those not assigned to rifle companies. We still had casualties during this period. . . . My regiment was definitely not resting at St. Avold." Three of the division's field artillery battalions remained in position to support the 6th Armored Division. The 318th CT was at Bettweiler preparing to relieve the 12th Armored Division, but at 2100 on December 18 it received the warning order to prepare for the move north. Behind the 35th and 87th Infantry Divisions was the 4th Armored Division. The 12th Armored Division, on loan by agreement between Patton and Patch, relieved the 4th Armored Division on December 8. The next day the 4th Armored Division went into XII Corps' reserve in the area of Cutting and Loudrefing.[2] Some elements, such as the 37th Tank Battalion, were still deployed well forward in the Epping–Urbach area eleven miles east of Sarreguemines, supporting the 87th Infantry Division. The 25th Cavalry Squadron was operating with the 12th Armored Division.

Behind XX and XII Corps and out of contact was Major General John Millikin's III Corps headquarters located at Metz. It became operational on December 8, relieving XX Corps of responsibility for Metz and the perimeter forts that had not yet surrendered. Headquarters and Headquarters Battery of III Corps Artillery was at Merlebuch, eight miles southwest of Saarbrücken, having moved there on December 17. Millikin was planning at that moment to take command of the 6th Armored Division and assume command of a portion of the front between XX and XII Corps, between Wadgassen and Sarreguemines, as a prelude to TINK. Millikin's only division, the 26th Infantry Division at Metz, had been relieved by the 87th Infantry Division on December 9.[3] Protecting the north flank of Walker's XX Corps and maintaining contact with VIII Corps was Task Force (TF) Polk, built around Colonel Jimmy Polk's 3rd Cavalry Group. TF Fickett, consisting of Colonel Edward M. Fickett's 6th Cavalry Group and the 5th Ranger Battalion, covered the five-mile gap between XX and

XII Corps. Patton thus had the bulk of two divisions—the 4th Armored and 26th Infantry Divisions—out of contact and another—the 80th Infantry Division—out of contact but on the verge of a new operation when he began his estimate process for the move north.

The routes to be used for the movement north were selected and confirmed by Third Army staff as early as December 18. After Bradley called Patton that night, a Third Army G-3 staff officer called Millikin and passed on routes for the 4th Armored and 80th Infantry Divisions.[4] Four principal routes, designated A through D, were selected. Route D, on the inner track, was the shortest; route A was the outermost track; and route C was the longest. Third Army's two MP battalions, the 503rd and 512th, were warned by special officer couriers of the four troop movement routes and their traffic control responsibilities. All possible personnel were concentrated on traffic duty thereafter. With the routes established, the basic movement concept was given to Millikin, Eddy, Walker, and Weyland before the Verdun meeting in the form of a warning order. When the Verdun meeting ended at roughly 1200 on December 19, Patton grabbed a phone, called Gay in Nancy, and gave him the following instructions: "26th Infantry Division to be moved December 20 to the vicinity of Arlon, advanced detachments to move at once. The XII Corps to disengage, and Corps Headquarters and artillery to move to vicinity of LUXEMBOURG 21st of December, leaving a working headquarters at old location until such time as it could be relieved by XV Corps, 7th Army. 35th Infantry

Table 6.1. Third Army Routes for the Turn North

Route	Route Description	Approximate Length (miles)
A	Moyenvic–Nancy–Pont-à-Mousson–Thiacourt–Vigneulles–Thillot–Harville–Conflans–Landres–Pierrepont–Longwy	110
B	Frenetrange–Cutting–Morhange–Luppy–Pont-à-Mousson–Arnaville–Chambley–Briey–Audun–Aumetz–Longwy–Arlon	100
C	Bining–Rahling–Sarre-Union–Sarralbe–Puttelange–St. Avold–Courcelles–Chaussy–Metz–Maizières–Uckange–Aumetz–Esch–Luxembourg City	120
D	Saarlautern–Bouzonville–Thionville–Luxembourg City	55

Sources: Major Peter S. Kindsvatter, "An Appreciation for Moving the Heavy Corps: The First Step in Learning the Art of Operational Maneuver" (School of Advanced Military Studies, U.S. Army Command and General Staff College, Fort Leavenworth, Kans., 1986), 39; 37th Tank Battalion AAR, December 1944.

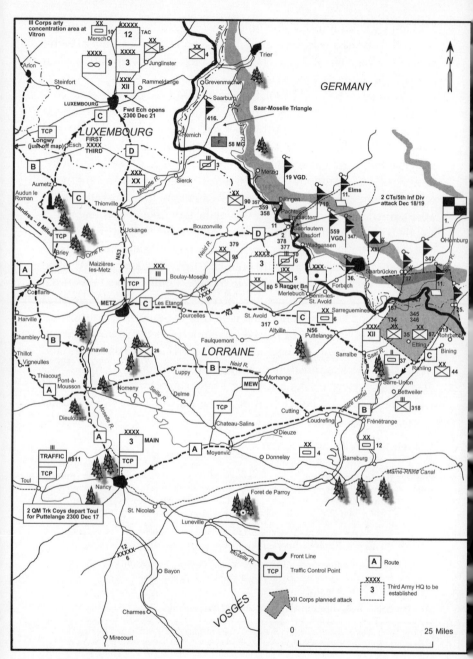

Map 6.1. Third Army Moves North, December 18–21, 1944

Division to be withdrawn from line and assembled at METZ. Tactical Echelon 3rd Army Headquarters to move on LUXEMBOURG 20th of December. Forward Echelon III Corps to move in vicinity of Arlon at once." This warning order was confirmed by a written operational directive for the record, issued on December 20.[5]

Despite being with Bradley when the above instructions were sent, Patton clearly had a different view of the destination and mission of III Corps. At 2200 on December 18 Millikin phoned Phillips and told him to move the corps' forward echelon north to Longwy, approximately thirty-five miles south of Bastogne, the following morning. The next morning Millikin, Phillips, and the III Corps G-2 and G-3 left Metz and traveled to Luxembourg City, where they met with Leven Allen at Twelfth Army Group at 1100, per Bradley's instructions the night before.[6] As the corps' forward echelon was arriving at Longwy, it learned it was to take command of the 9th and 10th Armored Divisions and the 4th Infantry Division and deploy north of Luxembourg City. How and when this order was disseminated are not known. At 1100, just as the Verdun meeting was beginning, the corps' forward echelon began to move toward Luxembourg City, twenty miles to the northeast. By 1600 the echelon was setting up in a schoolhouse. No sooner had this begun when Allen directed Millikin to revert to his original mission, as directed by Patton; III Corps headquarters was to set up at Arlon, not Longwy.[7]

The forward echelon's move toward Longwy, diversion to Luxembourg, and diversion again to Arlon wasted at least six hours and hindered a corps staff involved in its first fight. The fault was certainly Bradley's, not Patton's. Bradley's penchant for bypassing Patton was indicative of his anxiety over the situation, and it would not be the last time Bradley tinkered with the movement of corps and divisions. Bradley's intention seems to have been to launch an attack with III Corps from somewhere north of Luxembourg City.[8] However, it is more likely that he was trying to protect his tactical headquarters.

III Corps Assembles

As III Corps headquarters sorted itself out, the formations it was to command were already on the move. The 4th Armored Division was the farthest south of the initial divisions Patton would commit. Earlier in the day Gaffey had informed Eddy that he was "fairly sure" he would be leaving XII Corps, so they decided to concentrate the division somewhere centrally and moved the CP to Sarralbe. A general regrouping of the entire division was necessary to avoid confusion during the move. The 4th Armored Division was used to moving rapidly based on verbal orders, but Gaffey seems to have been the only division commander who issued a formal march order, albeit a brief one. The division trains, consisting of the maintenance, supply, and medical battalions as well as the headquarters and headquarters company, all had to be reoriented. In a retrograde movement such as that now planned, it was essential that the trains move rapidly into bivouac to avoid interfering with the rearward movement of the combat elements.[9]

Gaffey's division staged from Frenetrange. It crossed the initial point (IP) at 0300 on December 19 in three convoys—CCB, divisional headquarters, and CCA on route B, and the division trains on route A. Doctrine dictated that trains should always move as far as practicable from an exposed flank, but 4th Armored Division's trains were not exposed to a flank threat until they entered Luxembourg, at the earliest. There were so many vehicles that CCA did not clear the IP until 1300 on December 19, some eleven hours after CCB pulled out. After crossing the Moselle, the division, led by twenty-seven-year-old Major Albin Irzyk's 8th Tank Battalion, had to rely on Brigadier General Holmes E. Dager, commander of CCB, for directions. As Irzyk recalled, "After daylight came, the general was very visible weaving up and down the column, giving . . . the thumbs up. . . . He radioed instructions from his jeep, rode alongside to shout directions . . . and at tricky intersections, he dismounted to personally point the way." As CCB arrived in the assembly area south of Arlon, CCA was just clearing the IP. CCA closed at 0230 on December 20, twenty-six and a half hours after the march began. CCR did not move until 0730 on December 20 because it was waiting for the separate 704th Tank Destroyer Battalion and 37th Tank Battalion to join up upon their release from the 87th Infantry Division.[10]

Major General Horace L. McBride's 80th Infantry Division moved by regiments. The 318th Infantry was the first to move, crossing the IP at Bettweiler at 1400. It arrived in Helmdange at 1000 on December 20.[11] Eighty-two 2.5-ton quartermaster (QM) trucks were assigned to the regiment for the move. One of these trucks could carry a maximum of twenty-five soldiers, but for distances of more than seventy-five miles, this number was reduced to eighteen because it was "important that the soldiers arrive at their destination ready for action, not exhausted and cramped."[12] Thus, the eighty-two QM trucks would have carried between 1,476 and 2,050 troops. The 317th Infantry crossed the IP at 1420, shortly after the 318th, from Altville, just south of St. Avold, and it arrived in Gonderange in Luxembourg at 0400 on December 20. The last regiment to move, the 319th Infantry, had relieved the 25th Cavalry Squadron during the night of December 18–19, then handed the area over to the 12th Armored Division shortly thereafter.[13] The 319th crossed the IP at Hoelling at 1830 and arrived at Weimersck at 1500 the next day. The 702nd Tank Battalion, which would support McBride's division, crossed the IP at Sarre-Union at 1305 on December 19 on route C; it conducted a forty-five-minute halt just east of St. Avold, and the head of the column reached Esch at 2358.[14] The division CP opened at 0200 on December 20 in Luxembourg City, long before the division moved.

In total, McBride's division moved approximately 2,265 vehicles on routes C and D. This was accomplished by employing 278 QM trucks with a lift capacity of some 6,950 troops. The 26th Infantry Division would have moved approximately the same number of vehicles as the 80th Infantry Division. According to James Peale Jr., the 3rd Battalion/101st Infantry began moving north from Metz at 0750 on December 20 and assembled near Steinfort twelve hours later. Data in the after-action report are scarce, but the division closed in its assembly area by 2310 on December 20.[15] The CP opened at Eischen just east of Arlon.

The road conditions were satisfactory for the move. The roads on route C were in excellent condition, and flat tires caused the most trouble. Wyatt E. Barnes of F Company, 2nd Battalion/318th Infantry, recalled, "During the trip my truck had a flat. We unloaded and loitered at the roadside, answering bodily needs and shivering constantly. In a half-hour or so a repair truck arrived and changed the tire. I realized much later that this was remarkable given the circumstances; I have waited longer for a tow truck at home. After repairs were made we climbed back aboard. . . . Ten minutes later we had another flat. . . . We had barely dismounted when the repair truck returned and made the necessary change, sending us on our way again." Most of the Third Army's march north was conducted at night, but headlights were employed to increase the speed of movement. Contact with the enemy was not deemed imminent, so tactical considerations gave way to administrative marches until the formations neared Luxembourg.[16]

Prior to the start of the move, III Corps had only the 696th Armored and 177th FA Battalions assigned. They and the newly arrived 288th FA Observation Battalion, attached from Third Army, moved north from

Table 6.2. Trucking the 80th Infantry Division North

	Units							
Truck Company	317	318	319	Field Hospital	MP	Signal	Div HQ	Total
3597 QM			16	24	3	3	1	47
4051 QM			47					47
3805 QM		38	18					56
3905 QM	38		2					40
3327 QM		46						46
443 QM	43							43
Total	81	84	83	24	3	3	1	279

Source: 80th Infantry Division AAR, December 1944, G–4.

III Corps' sector with approximately 325 vehicles. On December 19 III Corps received nine additional field artillery battalions. The 193rd and 203rd FA Group Headquarters, along with the 274th Armored and 949th, 176th, 177th, and 731st FA Battalions, came from XX Corps. The 253rd Armored and 179th FA Battalions, on the southern boundary of XII Corps and supporting the 87th Infantry Division fifteen miles south of Saarbrücken, executed a 150-mile road march. The 404th FA Group with the 512th and 752nd FA Battalions, totaling some 466 vehicles, moved from XII Corps' sector.[17] All this artillery converged in the vicinity of Vitron, northeast of Longwy.

As the various formations and units that would make up III Corps converged in southern Luxembourg on December 19, Patton left Verdun and drove to XX Corps headquarters in Thionville. He explained the situation to Walker and sent Codman and Harkins back to Nancy to move Third Army TAC to Luxembourg City. At 1730 Gay oversaw a Third Army staff meeting to pass on the results of the Verdun conference and set the planning in high gear. Maddox recorded the results: "The tentative plan of attack and order of battle are as follows: XII Corps—4th Inf Div, 35th Inf Div, and 10th Armd Div will attack from LUXEMBOURG to the northeast. III Corps—80 Inf Div, 26th Inf Div and 4th Armd Div, on axis ARLON–CONSTHON [*sic*], making the main effort. VIII Corps—5th Inf Div, 28th Inf Div, 9th Armd Div and 101st A/B Div will attack on an axis BASTOGNE–ESELBORN [*sic*]. The XX Corps will hold."[18]

Patton's tentative plan bore no resemblance to what actually unfolded. On December 19 Patton was thinking in terms of a ten-division offensive. His intention to use the 35th Infantry Division was demonstrated by the hold and consolidate order issued to Major General Paul W. Baade that day.[19] Patton still assumed that VIII Corps could act offensively. Koch's work map for 0300 December 19 probably reinforced this belief because it depicted the 28th Infantry Division's front generally intact east of Bastogne. Twelfth Army Group's situation map, however, depicted the German spearhead at the gates of Bastogne. Moreover, there was no axis of advance on Bastogne because it had not yet been surrounded. III Corps' axis of advance was northeast, clearly paralleling XII Corps. Maddox most certainly misspelled Consthum, which was fifteen miles east of Bastogne.

It is clear that it took several hours for Patton's concept for employing XII Corps to crystallize and for Eddy to be informed. As late as 1600 on December 19 Eddy was lamenting, "I don't think anybody is very enthused about this new change"—meaning XII Corps' static mission. However, as he noted later that evening, Patton phoned, "informing me that all previous plans had been changed and that I was to move to the north, picking up the 4th Infantry and the 10th Armored Divisions. The XII Corps was to be one of the attacking Corps under the new plans. This, needless to say, suited everybody." Until Eddy could come up, Patton established a provisional corps consisting of Morris's 10th Armored Division and the 4th Infantry Division and put Morris in command. The 9th and 10th Armored Divisions were badly scrambled after the first days, so he ordered Major General John W. Leonard, commander of the 9th Armored Division, to Bastogne to take command of two of his own combat commands and CCB/10th Armored Division, which Middleton had redirected there on December 18. [20]

On the morning of December 20 Patton departed Walker's headquarters in Thionville and drove back up to Luxembourg City at 0900 to confer with Bradley. It was most likely at this point that Bradley and Patton discussed whether to hold Bastogne. This was important because Patton's tentative plan of the night before had no defensive aspect at all. In Bradley's presence, Patton asked Koch if it was a sound course of action to hold Bastogne, and the G-2 replied that from an intelligence perspective, it made sense. "General Patton, looking toward Bradley," Koch recalled, "nodded affirmation." The 101st Airborne Division had finally arrived complete—all four regiments—at Bastogne only two hours before the Verdun meeting commenced.[21] Establishing this timeline is important because after talking with Bradley, Patton headed out to inspect his formations, visiting III Corps at Arlon; the 4th, 9th, and 10th Armored Divisions; the 4th and 26th Infantry Divisions; and advance elements of the 80th Infantry Division.

Patton had Middleton meet him at Arlon because operational control of VIII Corps passed to Third Army at 1200 that day. When Middleton arrived, Patton apparently declared, "Troy, of all the goddamn crazy things I ever heard of, leaving the 101st Airborne to be surrounded in Bastogne is the worst!" This was Patton bombast, but it did suggest that if he had complete freedom of decision, he might have redeployed the 101st Airborne Division to ensure that he could use it offensively. Again, Koch's work map for 0300 that morning depicted a generally intact 28th Infantry Division front from Bastogne to the south. Perhaps Patton saw no reason at that precise moment to commit the 101st Airborne Division so definitely. He told Middleton to give ground and blow up bridges "so that we can get the enemy further extended before we hit him in flank." But ultimately he deferred to Bradley's suggestion, "in which Middleton strongly concurred," to retain control of Bastogne because it was "a very important road net." Middleton defended his action for that very reason. As he reflected in 1956, "One did not have to be smart to see this. . . . In war some people must die in order that other people and things survive." Patton would write him a letter in late April 1945, declaring his decision to hold Bastogne "a stroke of genius." Middleton, however, certainly had his own reservations about leaving the 101st Airborne Division in Bastogne to be surrounded when he withdrew his corps CP to Neufchâteau.[22]

During the discussion at Arlon, Patton also asked Middleton where he would attack from. Middleton apparently suggested sending the 4th Armored Division up the Neufchâteau–Bastogne highway far on the left and the 26th and 80th Infantry Divisions far to the right. Sensibly, Patton ignored this formula, with its excessive dispersion, and selected a different course of action. The personal discussion with Middleton was critical because it dissuaded Patton from his belief that VIII Corps could attack. VIII Corps "is fighting very well," he observed, "but at the moment consisting of nothing but remnants." Patton's willingness to visit virtually every commander taking part in the offensive was important. As Gay observed, he "might not . . . agree with you but he would always listen."[23] After visiting the divisions and talking with Millikin and Middleton, Patton decided that III Corps would attack on December 22, not December 21.

XII Corps Redeploys

Redeploying Eddy's corps required considerable coordination with Seventh Army. On December 20 Gay called the Seventh Army G-3 seeking a quicker handover of XII Corps' zone so that Eddy could shake "loose from the line." At 1750 Patton phoned Eddy and ordered him to move XII Corps headquarters and the 5th Infantry Division up to Luxembourg City the next morning. XII Corps' front was taken over by XV Corps at midnight on December 20, but Eddy's heavy artillery remained in place.[24] Eddy and his chief of staff, Colonel Ralph Canine, moved north on December 21. They arrived at Eagle TAC in Luxembourg City at 1000, and the Corps Advance Group CP arrived in Luxembourg City five hours later. The Forward CP of XII Corps opened in Luxembourg City at 2300.

Canine recorded, "It was cold as hell riding up there. . . . We got there . . . and went right to Gen Bradley's Headquarters. We were there for awhile and then took off and went over to Third Army Hq, three or four blocks away. Gen Patton was there, and a whole gob of other guys: Gen McBride, Gen Irwin, Gen Walker, Gen Morris, Gen Barton. 'Georgie' told us what he wanted us to do." The author of the XII Corps history declared that Patton's leadership was in full effect: his "courage and exuberance never appeared to better advantage during these gloomy conferences in the early days of the Bulge . . . he accompanied his instructions with a rip-snorting fight-talk which gave renewed confidence to everyone present."[25]

Eddy's new XII Corps composition was based on the 4th Infantry Division and 10th Armored Division (minus CCB in Bastogne) and the 5th Infantry Division coming up from XX Corps. Walker had informed Major General Stafford Leroy Irwin, the division commander, on December 19 that something was up, and the 10th CT, training for assault on fortified positions, was put on one-hour NTM. XX Corps began to withdraw elements of the division back across the Saar but retained a small bridgehead. The withdrawal was conducted by ferry in full daylight and completed by 1700 on December 20. At the same time, the 10th CT crossed the IP and was joined by its organic 46th FA Battalion. The 10th CT traveled sixty-nine miles and rolled into an assembly area at Rammeldange, despite some hiccups with guides, at 0145 on December 21. Fifteen minutes later the 11th CT, which Irwin had also withdrawn across the Saar, crossed the IP and closed in its assembly area at 1800. As it came up to cover the deployment of XII Corps between Ernzen and Reuland, the

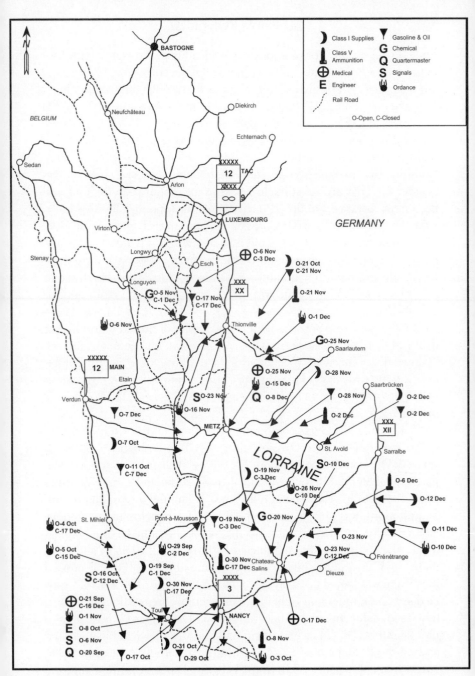

Map 6.2. Third Army's Logistical Footprint, December 1–17, 1944

11th CT was forced to halt when McBride gave the commander a direct order to keep off the road net for the 80th Infantry Division, which was shifting west to get into attack position. This created a large traffic jam. Despite the delay, Irwin had two combat teams and his entire divisional artillery in place by 2000 on December 21.[26]

As the bulk of Third Army's fighting elements moved north, so did the logistical infrastructure, including all the different types of supply, to support them. Classes of supply were broken down as follows: Class I, rations; Class III, QM gasoline, oil, and lubricants; Classes II and IV, broken down into QM, medical, signals, engineer, ordnance, and chemical warfare; and Class V, ammunition. Classes I and III were considered automatic supply items, whereas Classes II and IV were mainly equipment. Muller's G-4 Section faced a complex problem. It had to do three things simultaneously: maintain logistics to support XX Corps in place, rebuild VIII Corps, and position enough material to fully support the impending attack by III and XII Corps. Third Army exhausted many reserves of many classes of supply to rebuild VIII Corps, most notably 105mm artillery ammunition.[27] Moreover, by December 20 Muller also had to prepare for the aerial resupply of the 101st Airborne Division. Procedures had to be approved by army group. Requests from the division had to be compiled and transmitted to ComZ and SHAEF. The Third Army G-3 (Air) Section would then be notified of all air shipments so that coordination for fighter cover could be effected with XIX TAC. This aspect of the campaign, the need to suddenly assume responsibility for the supply of another corps in the midst of a major engagement, has perhaps been underappreciated.

Muller's section issued special administrative orders on December 19 detailing the logistical realignment. Patton benefited enormously from three key factors. First, basic conditions existed within Third Army for a quick realignment because Muller had already placed many installations on a semimobile status, and they were well dispersed.[28] Second, Third Army's basic supply installations were not threatened. The AdSec in the south, which fed Third Army, was centered on Verdun. Third, once Seventh Army took over XII Corps' zone of operations in Lorraine, Third Army's zone of operations became coterminous with Twelfth Army Group's zone of operations. The size of Patton's army service area therefore gave him "a vast rail and road net without which the shifting of from east to north would have been greatly handicapped." Third Army's area was divided into northern and southern railway districts controlled by the

6811th Traffic Regulatory Group. Its headquarters shifted from Toul to Conflans on December 21. The rail net in southern Luxembourg was also excellent. This was critical, because establishing a supply point also meant a new railhead.

The realignment of troops and supplies during the last two weeks of December was made possible in part by employing thirty-seven Third Army QM truck companies, each containing fifty 2.5-ton trucks with trailers, totaling 1,850 trucks.[29] Despite this number, Muller had to request additional lift capacity from Twelfth Army Group, and Brigadier General Raymond G. Moses, the G-4, collected several truck companies from ComZ and sent them forward to help Third Army move. These trucks were instrumental in finishing the realignment of supply points.[30] By December 20 six new supply points had been established in the vicinity of Longwy. The 4th Armored Division continued to draw on the supply dump at Verdun, but a new one was established at Fauvillers.[31] Supply points were established at Longwy for Class I and III supplies to support the 4th Armored and 80th Infantry Divisions. A total of 235,000 rations and 300,000 gallons of gas were stockpiled.[32] The ammunition supply point (ASP) for the 4th Armored and 80th Infantry Divisions was established at Audun le Roman. ASPs were to be outside enemy artillery range but as close as possible to the combat troops. Each division was supposed to have two ASPs.[33]

When the move started, Brigadier General Edward T. Williams, Third Army's chief artillery officer, informed Patton it would be very difficult to transport enough ammunition north because they were moving away from the army's stocks. Ammunition and ordnance dumps were located near Nancy and in the Sarre-Union area. One ammunition dump positioned for TINK was located just east of Thionville to support XX Corps. All possible ammunition shipments were diverted to the north flank of the army, and "every conceivable means of transportation was used to rebuild stocks in the depot nearest the northern front." Only the day before the German attack, Edwards had demonstrated the brand new and highly lethal proximity fuse east of the Moselle, in anticipation of its general use by January 1, 1945. He told Patton there was a plentiful stock of proximity fused ammunition, and if he could obtain its release at once, it would solve many of their problems. Patton called Bradley and quickly received authority to employ the new ammunition. Gas shells, another lethal munition, were also moved north in the thousands, a fact that drew a brief observation from Allen: "Very SINISTER."[34]

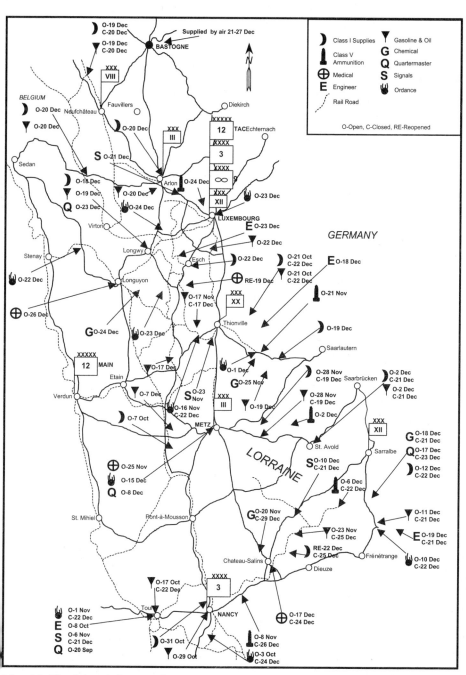

Map 6.3. Third Army's Logistical Footprint, December 18–31, 1944

Two other aspects of Patton's turn north need to be appreciated. One was the changes necessary in the signals footprint of the army. The key enabler that made an army the fundamental unit of strategic maneuver in the American way of war was communications. Third Army's chief signals officer, Colonel Elton F. Hammond, would have prepared a signals estimate of the situation to ensure he had considered all factors influencing Third Army's new mission. Wire networks and CP systems had been installed at St. Avold, Third Army's new headquarters to support TINK. Third Army's wire system was the primary means of signal communication and consisted of wire lines; telephone, manual telegraph, and teletypewriter operating equipment; and apparatus for facsimile transmission. It had to be uninstalled in St. Avold and reinstalled in Luxembourg City.[35]

Another aspect of the turn north was XIX TAC. Weyland noted in his diary, "If this goes through, [TINK] will be off since 3rd Army will not have the punch to exploit the Air Forces effort." Gay phoned Weyland at 1610 on December 19 to tell him that TINK was scrubbed. He has been criticized for failing to appreciate the gravity of the situation quickly enough, but the new mission forced him to rethink his support of Third Army. XIX TAC's 100th Fighter Wing consisted of the 354th, 362nd, 405th, and 406th Fighter Groups and the 10th Photo Reconnaissance Group. At 2020 he requested three additional fighter groups and one additional reconnaissance group from Ninth Air Force. Weyland was ordered to "expand" his efforts and destroy bridges at Trier on the Moselle River and at Saarburg and Merzig on the Saar River and to "keep aggressive reconnaissance on reaction of enemy to our present front."[36] The *Luftwaffe* was far more aggressive than it had been in Lorraine, conducting several raids. On December 21 Third Army installations were hit by thirty-nine aircraft, and at least sixty-five were sighted over the army.[37]

To carry out his new tasks, Weyland had his small mobile CP (called X-Ray), commanded by his chief of staff, Colonel Roger Browne, move up to join Third Army TAC in Luxembourg City on December 21. The close proximity to Ninth Air Force's advance CP in Luxembourg City would facilitate speedy coordination. XIX TAC's rear headquarters remained in Chalon. Weyland stayed at his advance headquarters in Nancy with his combat operations officer, Colonel James Ferguson. The Metz airfield, which would soon be operational, needed landlines extended to X-Ray and other XIX TAC airfields. This realignment of XIX TAC was completed by December 22. Plans were also made to disassemble the

Table 6.3. Breakdown of Third Army Vehicle Movement, December 19–21, 1944

Formation/Unit	Number of Units	TO&E (Vehicles)*	Total
Corps HHC	2	40	80
4 Armd Div	1	2,653[†]	2,653
26 Inf Div	1	2,012[†]	2,012
80 Inf Div	1	2,012[†]	2,012
CTs/5 Inf Div	2	232	464
FA Gp HHB	9	24	216
Separate FA Bns[‡]	25	84	2,100
Separate Tk Bns	3	167	501
TD Gp HHC	1	16	16
Separate TD Bns	3	158	474
Engr C Gp HHC	1	15	15
Engr C Bns	5	91	455
AAA Gp HHB	2	10	20
AAA Bns	4	131	524
Signals Bns (Corps)	2	200	400
Total			11,942

* Wheeled and tracked.
† Includes division artillery.
‡ Average of the different calibers.
Sources: FM 101–10, 1944; Major Peter S. Kindsvatter, "An Appreciation for Moving the Heavy Corps: The First Step in Learning the Art of Operational Maneuver" (School of Advanced Military Studies, U.S. Army Command and General Staff College, Fort Leavenworth, Kans., 1986).

microwave early-warning radar system, located at Morhange, and move it north to protect the army's front in southern Luxembourg.

By the end of December 21 Patton controlled four corps, twelve divisions, and three cavalry groups. Middleton's VIII Corps was oriented generally east, still absorbing the German blows. Millikin's III Corps and Eddy's XII Corps were abreast of each other, oriented due north. Walker's XX Corps remained in position along the Saar facing east, thus giving Third Army's line the look of a step. Third Army moved 11,942 vehicles north in forty-eight hours. III Corps moved some 9,400 vehicles north, meaning that XII Corps' share of the total was 2,400.[38] As Patton roamed throughout Third Army on December 20, he noted that although he had no staff officers with him, he managed to make numerous arrangements, conducting "the whole thing by telephone through Gay and a fine staff at Nancy." Patton described the army's realignment as "a most wonderful

Table 6.4. Third Army Order of Battle, End of December 21, 1944

VII Corps	III Corps	XII Corps	XX Corps
101 Abn Div	4 Armd Div	4 Inf Div	6 Armd Div
9 Armd Div (–CCB)	26 Inf Div	5 Inf Div	90 Inf Div
28 Inf Div (–109 Inf)	80 Inf Div	35 Inf Div	95 Inf Div
CCB/10 Armd Div	702 Tk Bn	87 Inf Div	712 Tk Bn
	735 Tk Bn	109th Inf	773 TD Bn (SP)
	610 TD Bn (SP)	10 Armd Div (–CCB)	5 Ranger Bn
	818 TD Bn (SP)	CCA/9 Armd Div	
	704 TD Bn (SP)	707 Tk Bn (SP)	
		70 Tk Bn	
		808 TD Bn	

Note: The 42 Inf Div was relieved of assignment to Third Army on December 24.

move." The "highly complicated road and supply movements were only made possible by the old and very experienced General Staff of the 3rd Army." Colonel William Whipple, chief logistical planner at SHAEF, agreed and characterized the move as "one of the most professional performances of the entire war."[39]

It has been argued that, based on the routes, the time available, and the number of vehicles to be moved, there was "nothing particularly extraordinary about this move." First Army had undertaken a similar redeployment of troops and supplies. By midnight December 17–18, First Army had arranged for the movement of 60,000 troops and 10,000 vehicles, and between December 18 and 22 it moved perhaps as much as 3 million gallons of MT80 gasoline away from the battle area.[40] However, it is important to remember that Patton had to move more troops over a greater distance, and his calculation of being able to intervene in the battle on December 21 with the forces described at Verdun was correct. Moreover, as a result of Third Army's rapid realignment, the opportunity existed to materially impact the course of the battle on the southern flank even earlier, but Patton allowed it to pass.

Task Force Ezell

Although Patton would later write that Bradley never injected himself into the operations of Third Army during the Bulge, it was not true.

Bradley had already made plans to use III Corps without consulting Patton, and on December 20 Eisenhower made a decision that left Bradley with little to do other than closely supervise Patton's conduct of the battle. Based on the recommendation of Bedell Smith, Eisenhower divided the Ardennes battlefield and gave Montgomery command of First Army, minus VIII Corps, which was now under Third Army. The boundary between First and Third Armies became Givet–St. Vith–Cologne. The issue was communications, and the fact that Bradley had apparently not contacted Hodges for two days made the decision, according to Bedell Smith, an "open and shut case."[41] Communications always ran vertically from higher headquarters to lower and then horizontally to various commands. The poor state of communications within the theater meant that even SHAEF had a difficult time exercising its full communications function. Communications for Ninth Air Force were also problematic. Eisenhower should have given Bradley a direct order to relocate to Namur so that he could effectively communicate with both his armies. Not doing so was a command failure. Bradley was incensed at the decision, and his conduct thereafter indicates a desire to regain contact with First Army as quickly as possible and a tendency to interfere in Patton's rightful prerogatives as an army commander.

As Gaffey's 4th Armored Division moved north, CCA and CCR halted well south of the Sûre River to prepare for the III Corps attack. Yet Dager's CCB kept going. During the night of December 18 Bradley had ordered Gay to send a combat command north immediately, and he informed Middleton that this reinforcement was coming up. This was why Dager stated that CCB moved "independently" from the rest of the division. Patton was certainly not happy that Bradley was playing with individual combat commands without at least informing him. "I said nothing," Patton recorded in his diary on December 20. Middleton apparently telephoned Hodges at noon on December 19, before CCB was attached to VIII Corps, and asked Hodges if he could use CCB to bolster the defense of Bastogne. Hodges was uncertain and referred the request to Bradley. Bradley then informed Middleton directly that he could use CCB, but only if it was required to hold his position. The VIII Corps after-action report accurately captured this aspect of the story. The corps was given operational control "only" over CCB, with the limitation that it could be used only in an emergency and with Third Army's approval.[42] Patton informed Middleton on the night of December 19 that a combat command from Gaffey's division was on its way to Bastogne to be attached to the 101st Airborne Division, but there is no evidence in either the Third Army G-3 operations diary or periodic situation reports of any operational transfer of CCB to VIII Corps.[43]

Irzyk recalled that as his 8th Tank Battalion reached Longwy on December 19, Dager, who was in the center of the town, waved him through vigorously. CCB continued on and stopped briefly at Arlon. According to Dager, Lieutenant Colonel Clay Olbon went looking for VIII Corps headquarters in Arlon, "under whose command they [CCB?] were serving at the time, to find where they were to move."[44] However, the VIII Corps CP had withdrawn from Bastogne to Neufchâteau, not Arlon, by the early morning of December 19. One source stated that while CCB loitered at Arlon, III Corps ordered Dager to continue to Fauvillers and from there to send a task force into Bastogne. CCB then went to Neufchâteau and beyond, finally halting and bivouacking at Vaux-les-Rosières, a mere nine miles southwest of Bastogne, sometime between 2000 and 2300 on December 19. While in the assembly area at Vaux-les-Rosières, Dager reported to VIII Corps by phone. It is unknown what instructions he received, but the fact that he was reporting to VIII Corps proved that Middleton believed he had the use of CCB.

At approximately 0500 on December 20 an unknown member of the VIII Corps G-3 staff contacted Dager and ordered him to send a tank company, an armored infantry company, and a self-propelled artillery battery into Bastogne. Dager argued against this piecemeal commitment, but he lost the argument; shortly thereafter he radioed Irzyk to send in a task force. Irzyk recalled that "General Dager called me on his radio and, without any preliminaries, ordered me to send a task force into Bastogne. I was stunned. I protested vehemently, reminding him that the situation up ahead was unclear, terribly confused, and that this was no time for a piecemeal commitment of my forces. To my great surprise, Dager agreed with me."[45] According to Dager, Middleton wanted to commit all of CCB but agreed to a task force. Dager was trying to keep his command together at least until Gaffey arrived.

Irzyk chose A Company of the 8th Tank Battalion, C Company of the 10th AIB, and C Battery of the 22nd Armored FA Battalion and placed Captain Bert Ezell, the executive officer, in command. By 1030 TF Ezell was on its way. Irzyk told Ezell simply to aid CCB/10th Armored Division. Ezell never encountered any enemy on the way up to Bastogne, and his column drove right past the CP of 28th Infantry Division at Sibret, on the left-hand side of the Neufchâteau–Bastogne highway. The CP had pulled back to that location early in the morning of December 19. TF Ezell arrived in Bastogne at approximately noon, just as Third Army assumed control of VIII Corps. Rumors abounded that the Germans had already cut the road, but American reconnaissance in the area south of Bastogne was woefully lacking.[46] Any reconnaissance patrols were probably from the 327th Glider Infantry Regiment (GIR) of the 101st Airborne Division.

There are two versions of what happened when TF Ezell entered Bastogne. According to one, Ezell reported to the 101st Airborne Division's chief of staff, who passed him off to the division G-3, Lieutenant Colonel Harry W. O. Kinnard, who passed him along to the assistant division commander, Brigadier General Anthony C. McAuliffe. McAuliffe assigned Ezell to Colonel William Roberts's CCB/10th Armored Division. Roberts's own force was divided into teams: Team Desobry was at Noville, Team Cherry was in Longvilly, and Team O'Hara, the farthest south, was near Wardin. Roberts instructed Ezell to take up a position at Villeroux, two and a half miles southwest of Bastogne and just northeast of Sibret. The second version was provided by Captain Abe Baum, an intelligence officer in the 10th AIB. He stated that when they arrived, Ezell remained in his tank to keep in touch with CCA while Baum went looking for Kinnard. When he found Kinnard, Baum announced, "We're here. What do you want us to do?" Kinnard sent him to see Roberts, and Baum asked him the same question. "He had no idea," reflected Baum, "of why we were there or what to do with us."[47]

When Dager finally established communications with Gaffey, the TF Ezell story was clarified, for better or worse. Gaffey responded immediately to Dager's concern about the dispersion of his command by ordering him to pull Ezell out of Bastogne and withdraw to the division assembly area northwest of Arlon in the Léglise–Habay-La-Neuve area. At 1400 CCB radioed Ezell to return to the 8th Tank Battalion's bivouac at Nives. Irzyk recalled that shortly after Ezell arrived in Bastogne, "I was astonished to receive an order from divisional headquarters to recall the Task Force to Nives at once." Ezell apparently had a hard time explaining to Roberts why he was leaving. Since the combat command had not been engaged, Patton ordered Gaffey to withdraw it to Arlon. On the way back south, Ezell discovered a U.S. 2.5-ton truck in the ditch on the right side of the road. The driver was still inside, but the top of his head had been blown off, perhaps by an armor-piercing shell. Ezell also discovered wide tracks across the road, which might have indicated the presence of tanks.

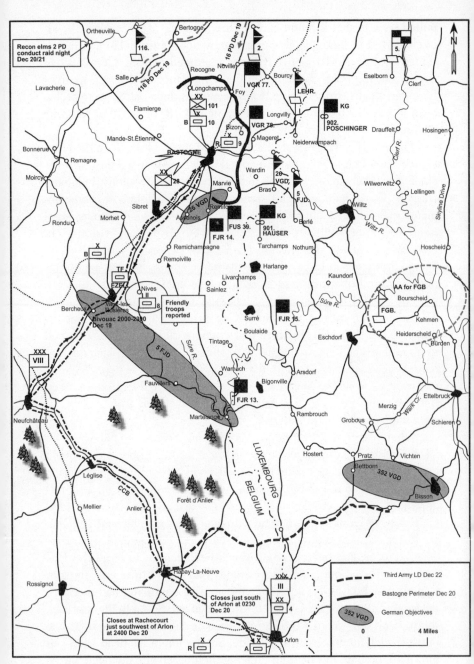

Map 6.4. Task Force Ezell, December 20, 1944

Farther down the road they encountered two batteries of intact American artillery, but no one was around. Some of the vehicles were still idling. He hauled back as much of the artillery and vehicles as possible.[48]

TF Ezell was absent from CCB for seven hours. Clearly, by the time darkness fell over the area at 1630, the Neufchâteau–Bastogne highway was still open. McAuliffe had actually driven down from Bastogne to Middleton's new headquarters at Neufchâteau that afternoon and drove back the same way after dark. There is no indication that McAuliffe and Ezell passed each other, but the irony would have been profound if they had. The accessibility of the Neufchâteau–Bastogne highway at this point has led to the consensus opinion that CCB should have been fully committed, as Middleton wanted, to bolster his barrier line. The further consensus is that this would have prevented the eventual encirclement of Bastogne.[49] Baum agreed, arguing that there was "no chance" TF Ezell could have kept the road open, but if all of CCB, "4,000 men and armor, had been sent to hold the way in, the Germans might not have been able to shut off Bastogne. And there wouldn't have been the need to fight through the woods to relieve the 101st."[50]

The Germans were very close to cutting the highway on December 20. Throughout the day, *PGR 901* of *Panzer Lehr* was still east of the Neufchâteau–Bastogne highway.[51] The *5th FJD* was already at Clochimont and Hollange, west of the Arlon–Bastogne highway. The tracks Ezell had discovered were likely those of reconnaissance patrols from *Panzer Lehr* or *5th FJD*. These patrols apparently did not reach the Bastogne–Neufchâteau highway near Sibret until late that night. Elements of the *5th FJD* did not attack Sibret until 0300 on December 21, with tanks and infantry forcing the 28th Infantry Division CP to withdraw south to Vaux-les-Rosières.[52] Only at this point was the Neufchâteau–Bastogne highway effectively cut, completing the encirclement of Bastogne. There had been a window of opportunity to alter the complexion of the battle, but Middleton's barrier plan and Patton's mission were not harmonized.

Patton could have committed the entire 4th Armored Division on December 20, but Eisenhower had cautioned him to avoid the piecemeal commitment of his forces. This limited flexibility and the ability to exploit opportunities. Patton could have executed a building attack, whereby he got progressively stronger on a specific line of action. Under the conditions of Patton's tentative plan of December 19, committing CCB made sense because it would have facilitated contact between VIII Corps and the rest of Third Army until the rest of the 4th Armored Division came up.

CCB could have tied in with the Bastogne garrison, with Team O'Hara at Wardin, or with elements of the 28th Infantry Division at Sibret, only three miles from the southern main line of resistance at Bastogne—not an unreasonable frontage for a full combat command. However, the plan changed on December 20.

Patton sent CCB north to VIII Corps under Bradley's orders, but when VIII Corps came under Third Army control, Patton withdrew it. Whether he informed Bradley is not known. Only at this point was Patton able to start harmonizing the concept of operations for VIII and III Corps. The decision to withdraw TF Ezell out of a somewhat chaotic situation was lamentable but understandable. Withdrawing CCB all the way back to division assembly areas northwest of Arlon was unfortunate. Gaffey's LD could have been established much farther north, but that would have entailed the simultaneous move north of the LDs of the 26th and 80th Infantry Divisions to stay in rough alignment. Patton was frustratingly silent on this critical aspect of the battle. In fact, it is not known whether he had full discretion in selecting the army's LD. Bradley's influence cannot be discounted. Patton could not have missed the fact that withdrawing CCB would mean paying for the same real estate twice. It was out of character for him to allow the opportunity to pass, but he was functioning under a tightly scripted concept of operations from above. Third Army would spend five long days trying to get back to Bastogne.

7

Third Army Attacks,
December 22–23

The amazing Patton said he would be there on time — and he was.
— Major General Kenneth Strong

The speed with which Patton pulled Third Army out of Lorraine and moved it north unsettled Eisenhower and his staff. Patton noted on December 21, "I received quite a few telephone calls from various higher echelons, expressing solicitude as to my ability to attack successfully with only three divisions." He declared, "As usual on the verge of action, everyone felt full of doubt except myself. It has always been my unfortunate role to be the ray of sunshine and the backslapper before action, both for those under me and also those over me."[1] At the 1000 SHAEF meeting, Tedder and others questioned whether Patton's swiftly mounted assault might not turn out to be a piecemeal action, similar to German counterattacks in Normandy. The recorder of the SHAEF meeting, Air Marshal James M. Robb, noted that Eisenhower wanted Bradley to understand that a counterattack for the purpose of holding Bastogne "was to be held in check and not to spread, and that, in fact, it was for the purpose of establishing a firm stepping off point for the main counter offensive. The Supreme Commander mentioned that what he was afraid of was that the impetuous Patton would talk Bradley into allowing him to attack at once with the object of going right through and not awaiting the fully co-ordinated counter offensive."[2]

It is clear from Robb's notes that Patton's mission was limited in scope and scale and was merely the first phase of Eisenhower's larger concept of operations. Eisenhower further restricted not only Patton's freedom of decision but also Bradley's, by his instructions to the latter. Bradley had to "make absolutely certain of the safety of his right flank in the Trier region from which a new offensive by the German 7th Army still threatened," and his attack "must" be by phase line, "with all forces held carefully together as to avoid dispersion and waste in strength before Montgomery can join the attack from the north."[3] According to Hansen, Bradley was planning to "conserve strength enough for [a] terrific counter-attack when the German momentum halted."[4]

As of 1200 on December 20, Twelfth Army Group's situation map showed the German *242nd Infantry Division* with a question mark immediately behind the *276th* and *352nd VGDs*, but twenty-four hours later the division and the question mark had disappeared, and no additional divisions were indentified in *LXXX Armeekorps*. The only panzer division in range according to Twelfth Army Group's situation maps was the *21st PD*, but it was shown moving southeast, away from Walker's XX Corps.[5] This did not match up with Koch's work map for 0300 December 20, which had the *21st PD* stationary behind the *719th* and *559th VGDs*.[6] Moreover, by 0300 on December 21 Koch's work map was showing the *57th Infantry Division* as possibly being in the Saar-Moselle triangle, along with the *416th Infantry Division*. This was a new identification, and the question mark remained beside it until December 26. Bletchley Park also sent a message on December 20 reporting that *11th PD* had been sent to *Fifth Panzer Armee*. It would turn out to be inaccurate, but SHAEF and Twenty-First Army Group believed it.[7]

American doctrine in 1944 identified two types of attack: envelopment and penetration. Both had main efforts, with the greatest possible offensive power concentrated to bring about a decision. Main efforts were conducted on narrow zones with a deep echelon of reserves to secure terrain objectives that facilitated the enemy's destruction. The objective of a penetration was the "complete rupture of the enemy's dispositions."[8] Despite Eisenhower's direction to keep "carefully together," the reality of the situation meant that Patton could not concentrate his combat power to attack on a narrow front with deep echelons. His new front in Luxembourg was approximately fifty miles; his left flank was entirely open, and he had to anchor his right flank in the Trier sector. Dispersion was inevitable. Indeed, Bastogne may have been designated the main effort in principle, but in reality, Gaffey hardly had more combat power than either Major General Willard S. Paul or McBride, and Allen logically questioned whether Third Army had enough "punch to power-drive them." Patton might not have concentrated his combat power even if Eisenhower and Bradley had given him full license to maneuver as he saw fit. In Lorraine, with only one notable exception, Patton chose to forgo concentration in favor of a broad advance.[9]

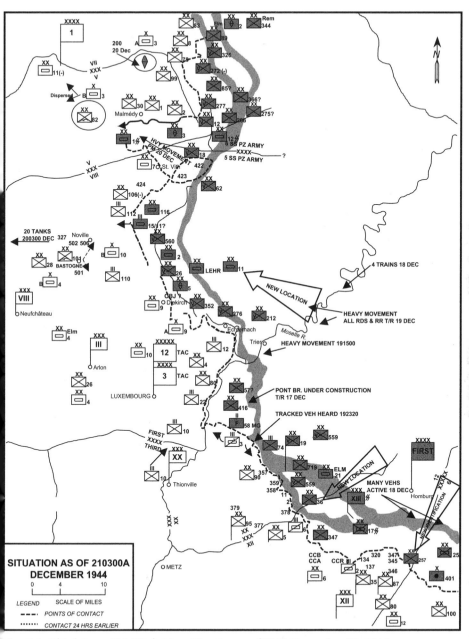

Map 7.1. Third Army G-2 Work Map, Situation as of 0300 December 21, 1944

Within the strict maneuver parameters dictated by Eisenhower and supervised by Bradley, Patton's concept of operations was further shaped by Koch's ongoing analysis of enemy capabilities. The Third Army intelligence section had been split since December 18 between Nancy and Luxembourg City. Koch, now located with Third Army TAC in the latter location, recalled, "Hasty blackboard sketches supplanted the customary maps in telling the story and in determining enemy capabilities. The chalk diagrams on the board were copied from sketch maps roughly drawn and kept current on the sheets of scratch paper." The sketch for 0600 December 20 listed seven enemy capabilities, which were outlined in G-2 Estimate No. 11, issued that day:

1. To continue the direction of the main effort to the west.
2. To broaden the shoulders, particularly to the south.
3. As the main effort lost momentum, to push through with armor to exploit in depth to the west.
4. Reserve armor to be committed to turn back the shoulders, particularly on the south with a frontal attack in the Echternach area.
5. If momentum to the west were lost, to launch another main effort to the west or southwest, along or astride the Moselle.
6. To launch additional small-scale diversionary attacks along Third Army's old front.
7. To continue small-scale paratroop attacks.

Koch considered capabilities 1 and 2, augmented by 3, as most likely, but he also believed that capability 5 could become significant "at any time from the 20th onward." Capabilities 1 and 3 were being executed at that moment, but Koch could not confirm whether II SS *Panzerkorps* was actually moving south.[10]

In such instances of uncertainty, FM 100–5 recommended caution when assessing enemy capabilities, declaring that the commander "must guard against the unwarranted belief that he has discovered the enemy's intentions, and against ignoring other lines of action open to the enemy. Even when the weight of evidence warrants the belief that the enemy is committed to a definite line of action, the commander must bear in mind that a change in the enemy's plans may occur at any time."[11] As an uncommitted armor reserve, II SS *Panzerkorps* represented a threat to Third Army. Yet once it was committed, its tanks would start to consume precious fuel. From an operational perspective, that would represent a positive development for U.S. forces. Without question, Patton avoided tunnel vision when it came to what the enemy might do; he was continually sensitive to new enemy lines of action, however unlikely.

On December 21 Patton issued the army's mission. XX Corps was to defend the Saarlautern bridgehead and assemble the 6th Armored Division to counterattack in any direction in the Third and Seventh Army zones. The rest of Third Army would "change direction and will attack to the north from the area LUXEMBOURG–ARLON to destroy the enemy on its front and be prepared to change direction to the northeast and seize crossings of the RHINE RIVER."[12] The last part was a standard refrain in virtually all Third Army operational directives, but as Colonel James Polk reflected, Patton "almost without exception . . . gave you an impossible objective. It was just standard treatment. If you got half there . . . in the time allowed, General Patton was really pretty happy about it." Patton always pushed the interpretation of his orders as far as possible. His desire to "cheat" right was apparent when he directed Eddy to "push aggressive patrols to east and northeast to determine location of crossings of SAUER RIVER and OUR RIVER and strength of enemy in ECHTERNACH area. Be prepared on Army order to change direction of attack to the northeast to force crossings and penetrate SIEGFRIED Line in zone and advance in direction of BITBURG."[13]

Since this new plan was distinctly different from what Patton had envisioned on December 19, it is safe to say that his planning cycle for the new plan was compressed. Normally, a commander tries to give his subordinates two-thirds of the time available before the execution of the plan to make their own preparations. Millikin had been planning on a northeast line of action. On December 19 Maddox had directed him to consider the road nets in his zone "so that subsequent elements of the 4th Armd Div and 80th Inf Div can be engaged east of the initial attack." Now, however, Millikin was told to execute a new line of action in the direction of St. Vith. American doctrine declared that a corps attack "ordinarily is a matter of days and not of hours." Planning required "weeks, even months ahead of contemplated, probable or possible operations."[14] Only sixty-seven hours had passed from 2000 on December 18, when Millikin received his initial warning order to move north, to the issuance of III Corps Field Order No. 1 at 1500 on December 21 for the attack toward St. Vith. Although he was probably cheated somewhat on the two-thirds rule, Millikin had enough time to prepare for his mission.

Millikin's Background

Millikin, born in 1888, was three years younger than Patton. He graduated from West Point in 1910 without distinction and took his first posting with the 5th Cavalry at Schofield Barracks, Hawaii. He married well; his wife was the daughter of Army Chief of Staff Peyton C. March. Millikin missed combat in World War I, serving instead as executive officer of the new General Staff School at Langres, France. After the war he returned to Hawaii as G-4 and later G-2 and finally gained entrance to the Cavalry Officer's Advanced Course at Fort Riley, Kansas. Based on his efficiency reports, Millikin appears to have been a capable and confident officer. His star rose in 1925–1926 when he gained distinction at the Combined and General Staff School at Fort Leavenworth. He subsequently spent four years on the faculty there. By the time he graduated from the Army War College in 1931, he was considered fit to command a division in combat. Jonathan M. Wainright, who was destined to be left behind in the Philippines by MacArthur to face Japanese captivity, noted that Millikin possessed "a brilliant mind, with perhaps a leaning to theoretical work rather than practical execution."[15] When Millikin was promoted to colonel in the summer of 1939, he received a congratulatory letter from Patton.

By April 1940 Millikin had taken command of an experimental outfit called the 6th Cavalry Regiment, which combined horses and motor vehicles. He won praise for his handling of the unit and was soon promoted to brigadier and given command of the 1st Cavalry Brigade at Fort Bliss, Texas. In April 1941 he took command of the newly formed 2nd Cavalry Division and was promoted to major general in July. In August 1942 he was given the 33rd Infantry Division, and by September 1943 he assumed command of III Corps at Fort McPherson, Georgia. At this point Leslie J. McNair judged him to be "well balanced, physically and mentally, active and aggressive."[16]

As corps commander, Millikin now had to direct the largest formation that fought tactical battles. He was the commander farthest to the rear who directed fire on the enemy and had to give purpose and direction to his divisions. A corps commander might handle upward of 80,000 troops and therefore required special skill sets, such as the ability to judge the relative capabilities of different types of divisions and to anticipate operations days in advance. Matthew B. Ridgway, commander of XVIII Airborne Corps, observed that a corps commander had to be "a man of

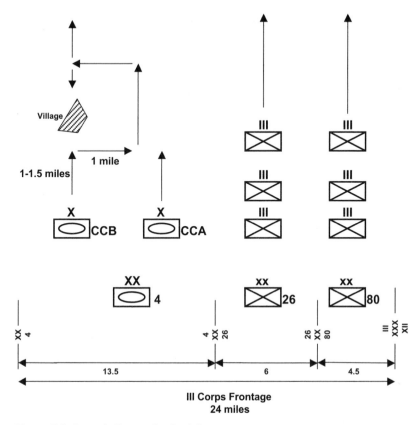

Figure 7.1. Patton's Tactics for the Advance

great flexibility of mind, for he may be fighting six divisions one day and one division the next as his higher commanders transfer divisions to and from his corps." Moreover, he had to anticipate where the hardest fighting was going to occur and be there in person, "ready to help his division commanders in any way he can."[17]

Millikin's inexperience seems to be a reasonable explanation of why Patton considered it necessary to dictate tactics for the attack. Army commanders did not normally do such things; indeed, Patton once said that no officer above the rank of colonel needed to know any tactics at all. Still, he directed Millikin to "attack in multiple columns, all columns to contain tanks and infantry. On contact put down base of fire and execute a turning movement, direction of envelopment always initially to the east." Patton also expected Millikin to attack in a column of regiments, "or in any case lots of depth."[18] Such detailed advice was not inappropriate in the context of a written letter of instruction. In Letter of Instruction No. 3, dated May 20, 1944, Patton presented many tactical points but declared, "I am not laying down inflexible rules. I am simply giving you my ideas. I must and do trust to your military experience, courage, and loyalty to make these ideas tangible. There are many ways of fighting, all of which are good if they are successful." Sometimes Patton did not give enough direction. Major General Ernest N. Harmon recalled that when Patton ordered him to Maknassy to relieve Major General Orlando Ward, he asked, "Do you want me to attack or defend?" to which Patton replied, "What have you come here for, asking me a lot of goddamned stupid questions?" Harmon considered the distinction fundamental, but Patton told him, "Get the hell out of here."[19]

Millikin passed on Patton's direction to Gaffey, Paul, and McBride in the form of a suggestion, not an order. Patton's tactics were not applicable in all circumstances, especially considering the likelihood of German infiltration between the multiple columns.[20] Infantry units would try to maintain contact with one another, assisted by regimental Intelligence and Reconnaissance Platoons maintaining contact with the various regimental CPs. Had Patton directed Millikin to attack with his regiments in a column of battalions, he would have been closer to standard American practice throughout 1944–1945.[21] The corps' twenty-four-mile front was not excessive. Doctrinally, an infantry battalion executing a main attack had a frontage of no more than 1,000 yards. This meant that an infantry division deploying two regiments, each with two battalions, would have a frontage of 4,000 yards. By this rationale, Paul and McBride, located side by side, would have had a combined frontage of 8,000 yards, or four and a half miles. However, frontages were ultimately dictated by mobility, type of armament, combat power, terrain, available fire support, and the mission. The broken terrain was the overriding factor. A *compartment* is characterized by an enclosed area, and the terrain features delineating it prevent direct fire and ground observation from outside the area. A *corridor* is a compartment whose longer axis "extends in the direction of movement of a force or leads toward or into a position." A compartment extending across or oblique to the direction of movement of a force or its front is referred to as a *cross-corridor* or an *oblique corridor*.[22]

Patton knew perfectly well that compartmentalized terrain swallowed up forces and undermined mutual support, so his instructions to Millikin can only be interpreted as a desire to strike deeply into the southern flank in wedges, each wedge possessing the ability to perpetuate its momentum by advancing regiments through one another. This is precisely what Brigadier General Bruce C. Clarke, commander of CCA/4th Armored Division in Lorraine, meant when he observed after the war that "breaking through and out of an enemy defensive zone in a column of combat commands gives as much or even more effective power in the break-through, and at the same time saves an uncommitted tactical command to handle contingencies and to push on promptly in exploitation."[23] It was the narrow *armor* wedge, vulnerable on both sides, that proved successful in penetrating the German front along the Moselle in September, but it was highly terrain dependent.

Millikin's hesitation in accepting Patton's instructions was based in part on the enemy. Millikin believed that the *5th FJD* and the *212th, 276th*, and *352nd VGDs* were in his immediate sector, but as the corps after-action report observed, "Information concerning the extent and strength of the enemy penetration was incomplete, and the situation of friendly units was uncertain."[24] Millikin's EEIs, therefore, logically included whether the enemy was going to continue to attack; if so, in what direction and strength; and whether there were uncommitted reserves capable of intervening against Third Army. There was no indication from VIII Corps' ISUM No. 302 for December 20 of an enemy FEBA south

Table 7.1. Estimated Enemy Strength in III Corps' Zone of Advance, December 21, 1944

Division	Men	Tanks
18 VGD	6,000	
62 Inf Div	8,000	
116 PD	6,000	50
2 PD	7,000	60
560 Inf Div	10,000	
5 Pcht Div	8,000	
352 Inf Div	7,000	
276 Inf Div	8,000	
212 Inf Div	6,000	
130 Panzer Lehr Div	4,000	25
11 PD (15 Panzer Regt)	1,000	25
Total	71,000	160

Source: III Corps Field Order No. 1, Annex No. 2, Intelligence Annex, 1100A, December 21, 1944.

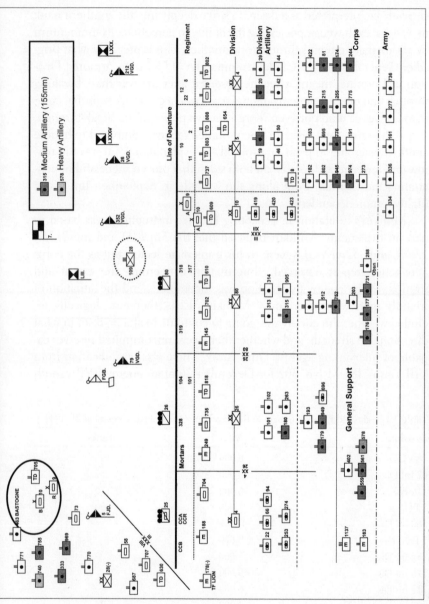

Figure 7.2. Third Army Arrayed for Battle, December 22, 1944

of Sibret–Wardin, but the III Corps after-action report identified roaming elements as far south as five miles north of Arlon. Millikin most certainly would have been sensitive to the intelligence indicating that the 2nd, 11th, and Panzer Lehr PDs were all in the Bastogne sector with a combined force of 110 tanks. Indeed, Gaffey reported on December 21 that tanks were approaching Arlon from the northeast, and Third Army Sigint regained contact with Panzer Lehr, whose reconnaissance patrols were overheard discussing the sector west of Bastogne. In fact, the Arlon–Bastogne road was reported as definitely cut at 1345.[25]

Millikin's left flank was another cause for concern. It was wide open, with no American units present except for ComZ troops on the Meuse. VIII Corps elements were somewhere to the northwest in the Neufchâteau area. The 6th Cavalry Group had not yet arrived, so he organized TF Lion, built around the 178th Engineer C Battalion, with the mission of protecting the left flank by erecting barriers and watching threats from Neufchâteau.[26] Millikin kept one infantry battalion from each of the 26th and 80th Infantry Divisions as corps reserve. After Millikin had convinced Patton that he needed two more hours, III Corps began to advance at 0600 on December 22, with the succinct mission to advance north toward St. Vith and destroy "any enemy encountered."[27] The corps' LD was essentially the Attert River. The 80th Infantry Division's LD was a bit farther south, along the Mersch–Arlon road between Mersch and Brouch. Mechanized cavalry squadrons were out front, trying to locate the Germans, while the three divisions attacked abreast—the 4th Armored Division on the left, the 26th Infantry Division in the center, and the 80th Infantry Division on the right.

The foul weather meant that there was no third phase, or close-in cooperation with the ground forces by Weyland's XIX TAC directly over III Corps' battlefield. Air doctrine established three priorities: gain air superiority, interdict movement within the theater, and "participate with ground forces to gain objectives on the immediate front of the ground forces." However, in the emergency that was the Ardennes, the third priority took precedence over the second.[28] Vandenberg still had not met Weyland's request for additional fighter groups, and even as Third Army ground forces began the advance north, Bradley, Patton, Vandenberg, and Weyland met at Eagle TAC to discuss the distribution of tactical air assets. Weyland argued that since Third Army was the main effort, he needed more groups. When Eisenhower divided the battlefield on December 20, the XXIX TAC supporting Ninth Army and the IX TAC supporting First

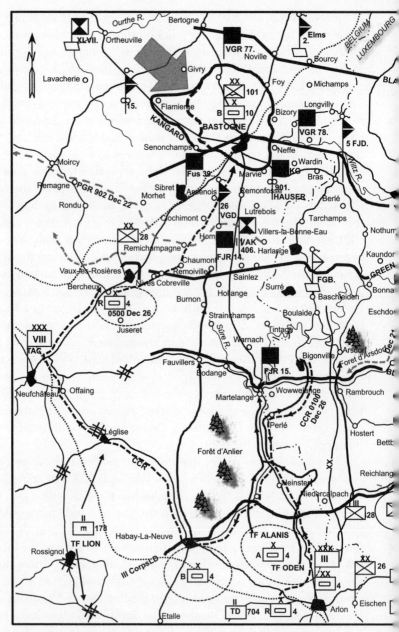

Map 7.2. Third Army Operations, December 22–26, 1944

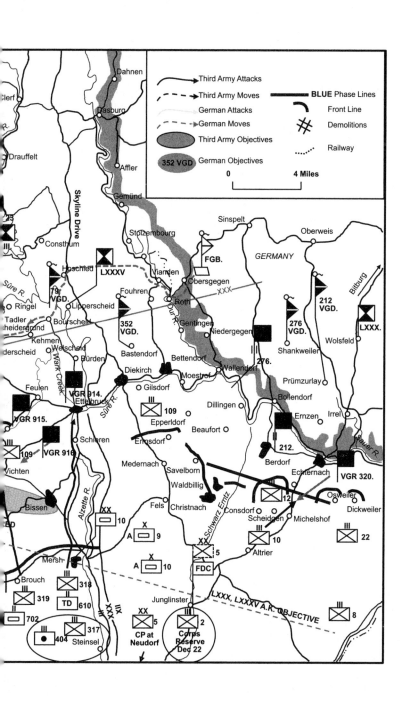

Third Army Attacks
Third Army Moves
German Attacks
German Moves
Third Army Objectives
352 VGD German Objectives

BLUE Phase Lines
Front Line
Demolitions
Railway

0   4 Miles

Dahnen
Clerf
Dasburg
R.
Drauffelt
Affler
Gemünd
Skyline Drive
Sinspelt
Oberweis
Stolzembourg
GERMANY
Consthum
FGB.
Hoschied
LXXXV
Vianden
Obersgegen
Bitburg
Süre R.
Fouhren
Roth
212 VGD.
Ringel
79 VGD.
Lipperscheid
Gentingen
276 VGD.
LXXX.
Tadler
scheidergrund
Bourscheid
352 VGD.
Niedergegen
Wolsfeld
derscheid
Kehmen
Welscheid
Shankweiler
Wark Creek.
Bürden
Bastendorf
Bettendorf
276.
Feulen
Diekirch
Moestrof
Wallendorf
Prümzurlay
VGR 914.
Gilsdorf
Bollendorf
Ettelbruck
Süre R.
109
Dillingen
Ernzen
Irrel
VGR 915.
Epperldorf
Beaufort
Schieren
Ernsdorf
212.
Berdorf
Sauer R.
109
VGR 916.
Medernach
Savelborn
Echternach
VGR 320.
Vichten
Waldbillig
Schwarz Erntz
Osweiler
Bissen
Fels
Christnach
Consdorf
12
Dickweiler
Alzette R.
Scheidgen
Michelshof
10
22
BD
10
A 9
10
Altrier
Mersh
5
A 10
FDC
Brouch
318
Junglinster
LXXX, LXXXV A.K. OBJECTIVE
8
319
TD 610
702
317
5
2
404 Steinsel
CP at
Neudorf
Corps
Reserve
Dec 22

Army passed to operational control of the British 2nd Tactical Air Force (TAF). Despite the protests of Major General Elwood R. "Pete" Quesada, commander of IX TAC, and Air Marshal Sir Arthur Coningham, commander of 2nd TAF, three groups—the 365th, 367th, and 368th—were transferred to XIX TAC the next day. The *Luftwaffe* was unusually aggressive, however. Throughout the day Third Army counted seventy-eight raids in its area; one successful raid struck a supply point at Mancieulles, destroying 100,000 gallons of gasoline.[29]

Despite possessing twenty-five battalions of corps and divisional field artillery—some 300 guns—Millikin did not precede the advance with artillery preparation.[30] This was most likely because III Corps was uncertain where the Germans' main line of resistance (MLR) was. Moreover, despite the tremendous number of guns available, their range was limited by design and doctrine. The 105mm principal gun was used in a D/S role to the divisions in contact with the enemy. In offensive operations, artillery locations were established well forward to exploit the guns' range as much as possible, but artillery was typically placed far behind the FEBA, as much as one-third of its range.[31] Therefore, a 105mm divisional gun with a maximum range of almost seven miles could, in reality, cover the advancing units to a depth of only about four and a half miles before it had to displace forward. Larger guns, such as the medium 155mm howitzers, had a much longer range but were typically used in the interdiction role, not the D/S role. Therefore, since intelligence indicated that first contact with the Germans might come five miles north of Arlon, it actually made sense to withhold an artillery preparation and conserve ammunition.

The 4th Armored Division's frontage was roughly fifteen miles from Bigonville to Neufchâteau, but the actual LD was eight miles, from Habay-La-Neuve on the left to Niedercalpach. Of the two main routes— the Arlon–Bastogne and Neufchâteau–Bastogne highways—Millikin preferred the former as his main effort. So did Patton. It was the most direct route. Moreover, it would block a German drive to the west and facilitate contact with the 26th Infantry Division on the right. Middleton agreed but suggested that if more troops were available, "another attack be made along the Neufchâteau–Bastogne highway. Troops were not available."[32] In fact, this route was open until just before Bastogne, as the encirclement had been completed only the day before.

Gaffey attacked with Brigadier General Herbert L. Earnest's CCA on the right, up the Arlon–Bastogne highway, while Dager's CCB on the left advanced on secondary roads west of the Arlon–Bastogne highway.

Brigadier General Wendell Blanchard's CCR was in reserve. Gaffey also had the 704th Tank Destroyer Battalion as reinforcement. Gaffey intended CCB to spearhead the division advance and instructed Dager: "you will drive in, relieve the force, and proceed from Bastogne to the NE." Irzyk recalled, "Our objective was clear and simple—Bastogne. Our Mission—get there as fast as we could." Both combat commands, however, were slowed considerably by the VIII Corps engineer demolitions. Indeed, 4th Armored Division was held up most of the day more by friendly demolitions than by the enemy. CCB advanced twelve miles to Burnon in two and a half hours but outposted the area, waiting for CCA to catch up. Here Dager violated Patton's tactical tenet that one "must never halt because some other unit is stuck. If you push on, you will release the pressure on the adjacent unit."[33]

Earnest had split CCA into TF Alanis and TF Oden, but TF Oden on the right was almost immediately diverted off its axis by a blown bridge at Niedercalpach. It then merged back with TF Alanis, and CCA proceeded on the main Arlon–Bastogne highway in a single column, only to be shortly halted by a crater at a road junction in Perlé. Engineers quickly put in a treadway bridge, but two miles north CCA was again brought to a halt, this time by a company of *FJR 15* at Martelange. The strength of the enemy was difficult to establish, but III Corps was under the impression, based on reports, that a single machine gun and six enemy soldiers held up CCA's advance through Martelange. TF Oden moved to Wolwelange to block any enemy reinforcements from the east while the 25th Cavalry Reconnaissance Squadron moved north to investigate Bigonville. TF Alanis fought its way into Martelange, but by 1720, when darkness covered the Ardennes, it was only halfway through the village and was still receiving small-arms and *Panzerfaust* fire from west of the town.[34]

Martelange was a good example of why Patton's tactical views could not always be followed to the letter. He believed that tanks "should never enter villages," and even when exceptional circumstances demanded it, entry should be from the rear.[35] Although this tenet had been promulgated back in May, Patton clearly believed it remained applicable in the more difficult snow and ice conditions of the Ardennes, dotted with numerous close villages and towns. Had CCA backed off a mile after coming in contact with the enemy at Martelange and attempted an envelopment by driving straight east for a mile, it would have come upon Perlé, which it might have had to fight through. Advancing north from Perlé, CCA would have had to enter Wolwelange and probably Grumelange in order to maneuver against Martelange from the rear. Maneuver was a good idea only if it furthered the main objective. Possibly fighting through three villages to clear one was not a good idea.

While Gaffey's division made its way north against the westernmost portion of *Seventh Armee*'s blocking position, Paul's 26th Infantry Division and McBride's 80th Infantry Division assaulted the middle portion. Paul had a frontage of roughly six miles and moved off on the general Arlon–Wiltz axis, straight into the forests and ravines without the benefit of a main north-south road. The 26th Cavalry Reconnaissance Troop was out front several miles beyond the LD. The 328th CT was on the left, the 104th CT was on the right, and the 101st CT was in reserve at Reichlange. The two leading regiments moved off in a column of battalions, with two field artillery and one armored field artillery battalions of the 193rd FA Group in direct support, augmenting the divisional guns. Paul also had the 818th Tank Destroyer Battalion and the 735th Tank Battalion. Patton told Paul to go night and day with his division, cross the Sûre River, and cut the supply road to Bastogne. Paul reflected that the division jumped off "in the only advance guard meeting engagement we had during the War."[36]

The 104th Infantry advance guard (the forwardmost element capable of fighting, but not the main body) did not contact the enemy until three miles north of the LD, near Pratz, where it met the advance guard of *VGR 915* of *Generalmajor* Erich Schmidt's *352nd VGD*. Schmidt's entire division was marching west to get into blocking positions between Bissen and Bettborn. The division was advancing with two regiments up — *VGR 916* moving along a ridge south of the Diekirch–Ettelbruck highway, and *VGR 915* on the highway itself. *VGR 914* and the artillery were following. North of Pratz the Germans counterattacked the 104th Infantry shortly after noon with some 400 infantry and drove back the leading company almost 1,200 yards. Artillery was called in, and the Germans withdrew over Hill 370 to Grosbous, two miles north, and defended the main road to Ettelbruck, Eschdorf, and Wiltz.

On the division's left the 328th CT covered six miles to the Forêt d'Arsdorf by noon. There was no contact, but the cavalry soon reported a strong enemy presence in Rambrouch, which turned out to be advance elements of *Oberst* Hans-Joachim Kahler's *FGB*, committed by Brandenberger on December 20 or 21. The *FGB* moved into position by way of Bourscheid–Eschdorf–Arsdorf. Concern for his left flank led Paul to form TF A, an infantry company reinforced with a company of tanks and a platoon of tank destroyers from the 101st CT, with the mission of securing the Hostert les Folchette–Rambrouch line. Paul reported a generally favorable situation throughout the day; opposition was stronger on the right, and on the left he faced "principally road trouble."[37]

McBride's division had a front of four and a half miles. The 319th CT was on the left, and the 318th CT was on the right. Both were deployed with two battalions up and one in reserve. The 317th CT was in reserve at Steinsel. In addition to the divisional guns, McBride had two field artillery battalions from the 404th FA Group and the 702nd Tank and 610th Tank Destroyer Battalions. McBride did not advance in a column of regiments as Patton had directed, the reason being the ground. The 318th CT faced canalizing ground, with steep banks on one side and the Alzette River on the other. This effectively separated it from the 319th CT on the left. It is interesting to note that Eddy had criticized McBride's habit in Lorraine of fighting individual regiments rather than the division as a whole. In fact, this was only one element of Eddy's dissatisfaction. After the Arracourt battle in late September, Eddy considered McBride emotionally spent and resentful of the 4th Armored Division's success: "They got there [to Arracourt] riding over our broken backs." This bellyaching and a higher incidence of combat exhaustion than battle casualties, which Eddy blamed on McBride's marginal leadership, led to Eddy's conviction that McBride had to go.[38]

By 0800 the 319th CT closed on the 109th Infantry's CP at Vichten and began relieving this unit of the 28th Infantry Division, which began to make its way into the 26th Infantry Division's lines farther west in the early afternoon. McBride's advance struck at right angles to the rear of the 352nd VGD. VGR 914 had just reached Ettelbruck when the 318th CT engaged it. The 318th CT essentially fixed the division on Ettelbruck, an important road junction leading in four directions, but the Germans defended it tenaciously; American reports told of taking "severe" small-arms fire in Ettelbruck.[39]

There is some evidence from captured enemy documents that *Seventh Armee* knew of the presence of the 80th Infantry Division in the Luxembourg area on December 21, but the *352nd VGD* did not advance west as if it were aware. Brandenberger stated that the attack on the *352nd VGD* had been unexpected and that the lack of air reconnaissance "meant that the advance of the American formations remained hidden to our eyes until their forward elements clashed with our own ground forces."[40] From a larger campaign perspective, *Fremde Heere*

West (Foreign Armies West) declared in an appreciation of December 21 that there was "no discernable systematic formation of major groups of offensive forces against flank German offensive salient." To the contrary, the Allies were "endeavouring on whole front to contain German attacks and halt them east of Meuse."[41]

Seventh Armee had serious reconnaissance deficiencies, but U.S. Army signals security (Sigsec) overall was an immediate and persistent problem in the Ardennes. It was so bad that Eisenhower told Bradley and Devers on December 20 that POW intelligence "clearly indicates that the enemy is getting precise information about the moves of our divisions due to lack of security in the use of radio." Model's intelligence officer, *Oberst* Roger Michael, later testified, "As far as troop movements were concerned, we were not at all surprised." The Germans rated Third Army's Sigsec the poorest.[42] This fact should have been addressed by Twelfth Army Group's Signals Security Detachment D, which was responsible for coordinating all Sigint activities within the army group.

Less than six hours after the general attack commenced, Patton phoned Phillips, the III Corps chief of staff, declaring that the attack had achieved surprise and that the Germans were unaware of the 26th Infantry Division's presence in the area or the whereabouts of the 4th Armored and 80th Infantry Divisions. Phillips recorded: "He directed that we drive like hell. That we keep on attacking tonight. That he feels this is their last struggle and we have an opportunity of winning the war." This jolt from the army commander may have been the reason why someone at III Corps signaled VIII Corps at 1500 to expect a linkup with the paratroopers during the evening.[43]

As it was nearing 1600 and growing dark, Patton went to see Millikin and Gaffey in Arlon to dictate further tank tactics. Patton wanted the limited-supply up-armored Shermans (called "Jumbos") to be used as much as possible at the point of contact. He again prohibited short envelopments in the face of stiff resistance, directing that wider envelopments, starting from a mile to a mile and a half back, be made at right angles. He told Millikin and Gaffey that they had to be ruthless and ensure that all tanks fired. He also ordered Millikin to "go up and hear them [the shells and bullets] whistle" and concluded, "I think he will."[44] There was probably some Patton "posing" here, but his direction to Millikin also indicated mentoring to prevent "headquarters-itis" from affecting the rookie corps commander's judgment.

One aspect of the story that has not been revealed is Patton's attempt to keep Gaffey on the ULTRA list. As Patton's chief of staff, Gaffey had been privy to ULTRA, but once he assumed command of the 4th Armored Division, he was removed from the list. On December 20 Patton sent a message to Bletchley Park through the Special Liaison Unit (SLU) at SHAEF, asking that Gaffey be reinstated. This was an extraordinary request, given the existing security protocols. The lowest formation commander in the Allied armies aware of and authorized to utilize ULTRA was Lieutenant General Guy Simonds, commander of II Canadian Corps. Patton received a negative reply the next day through Sibert. Bletchley Park called "such a step without precedent," and it informed Sibert that it would be "grateful if you bring . . . to the General's attention [the] importance of not relaxing security measures."[45] Despite the mild rebuke, it is not outside the realm of possibility that Patton passed on ULTRA messages to Gaffey during their frequent meetings in Arlon. Though certainly risky, given the higher probability of Gaffey's capture, the request demonstrated Patton's willingness to push the limits of the rules to gain an edge.

To protect Millikin's right flank, Patton also ordered Eddy to attack on December 22. Eddy, however, had to be pushed to do so. He told Patton he could not attack in full strength on December 22 because the 4th Infantry and 10th Armored Divisions were too weak. Patton clearly believed that Barton might not be up to attacking, but Eddy felt differently: "I talked to the Assistant Division Commander and the Chief of Staff of the 4th about Tubby's physical condition and stamina as the Army Commander thought he should go to London for a rest. They told me he was allright and was taking good care of himself. I thought Tubby looked allright too."[46] As for the 10th Armored Division, CCA had just attacked the day before with good results, taking Consdorf against an enemy considered to possess "excellent" morale.[47] Only Irwin's 5th Infantry Division was deemed capable of offensive action. The 10th CT had moved into an assembly area at Rammeldange on December 21 and was available immediately; on December 22 the 11th CT was in position in northern Luxembourg, and the 2nd CT was in an assembly area around Junglinster in corps reserve.

Although Patton had doubts about Millikin the rookie, he also had reservations about Eddy the veteran. Eddy had commanded the 9th Infantry Division in Tunisia. Bradley knew Eddy from Tunisia and considered him balanced and cooperative but not bold. He "liked to count his steps carefully before he took them," noted Bradley. Eddy was not fast and had demonstrated stickiness in Lorraine. Patton had been furious when Eddy ordered a withdrawal from the Gremercy Forest in September. Eddy "worries too much," Patton noted. "I would get rid of him but I do not know of any other better, except possibly Harmon, now commanding the 2nd Armored Division." Patton brought Eddy to Third Army headquarters on the nights of December 13 and 14, "as he is tired and nervous and should relax." The very day the Ardennes offensive started, Patton was "seriously contemplating making Eddy take a short rest" and giving the corps to Gaffey.[48]

"Red" Irwin had commanded the 9th Infantry Division artillery under Eddy at Kasserine Pass. He has been described as a quiet and cultured man who issued mission-type orders and gave his commanders considerable leeway. On December 21 Irwin stated that the situation on the "whole front from east of us to north varies from fluid to no front at all. Information is very scanty and the situation changes hourly." He declared, "I anticipate too much piecemeal action for a while to get any tangible results."[49] Eddy was unsure of enemy intentions and capabilities and could not have known that LXXX *Armeekorps* transitioned to the defense during the night of December 21. That day the *212th VGD* had pushed back the 12th CT, holding the left sector of the 4th Infantry Division, almost to Scheidgen. Eddy's plan, therefore, was simply to attach the 10th CT to Barton, who intended to pass it through the 12th CT and attack toward Echternach. Morris's 10th Armored Division, with CCA/9th Armored Division attached, was prepared to attach a task force to the 10th Infantry.[50] XII Corps had four field artillery groups with a total of fourteen field artillery battalions in place or on the way. The FDC was located at Junglinster. Each division was allotted greater artillery support than were the divisions in III Corps.

Eddy and Irwin both visited the CP of the 10th CT. The combat team was astride the Michelshof–Echternach road. At 1330, five and a half hours after III Corps began its attack, the 10th CT started to move through elements of the 12th and 22nd CTs, securing the LD at the Scheidgen–Michelshof crossroad. At that time about 400 infantry from *212th VGD* renewed the push toward Scheidgen. As the 4th Infantry Division's after-action report stated, "Furious fighting continued all afternoon in the vicinity of the line of departure." Eddy recorded, "The regiment had jumped off on time but had met a German attack just on the line of departure. From all reports they had killed a lot of Germans." Only thirty minutes before the 10th CT crossed the LD, an ULTRA message revealed that *LXXX* and *LXXXV Armeekorps* were to continue attacking toward the Redingen–Mersch–Grevenmacher line.[51] Clearly, knowledge of this at Third Army headquarters could never have made its way to Eddy in time for him to alter the planning for his opening battle. Eddy's regimental-sized attack did not gain any ground on December 22, but his corps was growing stronger by the hour.

By the end of December 22 Third Army had advanced an average of eight miles against light resistance. The 4th Armored Division had reached the first phase line, Blue, but was not completely beyond it. Patton could have attacked a day earlier, as he had claimed at Verdun, but it would have been with less force and on a shorter frontage. He admitted that an attack a day earlier "would have been a little ragged" but reflected, "It is better to attack with a small force at once, and attain surprise, than it is to wait and lose it. At that time I was sure that by the twenty-third or twenty-fourth, I could get up General Eddy's Corps and have him attack with the 5th Infantry and 10th Armored Divisions, and possibly the 4th Infantry Division, although the latter was very short of men and battle-weary."[52] Patton's eagerness to get XII Corps going was based on his legitimate fear that the Germans might renew their attacks against Barton's weakened division.

In III Corps' zone of action the German MLR had not yet been engaged across its breadth. The *352nd VGD* had been essentially cut in half, with the eastern half bottled up in Ettelbruck. Brandenberger had no choice but to withdraw the division to a bridgehead there. The 4th Armored and 26th Infantry Divisions had engaged the overstretched *5th FJD*, and Feulen, an important east-west crossroad, was in Third Army's possession. XII Corps had stabilized the southern shoulder and blocked the *212th* and *276th VGDs*. Patton had hoped for more but conceded that the weather conditions and demolitions were real problems. "I am satisfied but not particularly happy over the results of today," he noted. "It is always hard to get an attack rolling. I doubt if the enemy can make a serious reaction for another 36 hours. I hope by that time we will be moving. The men are in good spirits and full of confidence." Perhaps most important, he was satisfied with Millikin's work, noting that he "is doing better than I feared."[53]

Had Patton waited until December 23 to launch Third Army, *Seventh Armee* would have had time to overcome its initial slow start caused by a lack of bridging material, and it would have been much better situated to repel the advance of the 26th and 80th Infantry Divisions. As

Brandenberger stated, had it not been for this delay, the *LXXXV Armeekorps* "would doubtless have reached the envisaged defense line with time enough to prepare for mobile defense against the expected enemy attack against the . . . southern flank (by erecting barriers, by building field fortifications, by organizing itself for defense)."[54] This might have been asking too much by December 23, but an extra day probably would have allowed the *352nd VGD* to get into its blocking positions between Bettborn and Bissen and would have given the artillery more time to catch up. A significant gap in artillery coverage from Martelange to Ettelbruck already existed on December 22. Kniess reflected that the engagement of the *352nd VGD* was "surprisingly early."[55] In addition, another day might have altered the way the *FGB* was employed. Third Army's attack, therefore, struck an enemy force that was still moving to its assigned positions. It is in this context that one must appreciate the risk Patton was willing to take in attacking as soon as possible. It had everything to do with seizure and retention of the initiative, and he was willing to sacrifice extra reconnaissance at the outset to get the army moving.

To retain the initiative gained on the first day, Patton directed attacks to continue through the night. This was not surprising. In April 1944 he had declared that tanks "can and must attack at night," but they "must be preceded by meticulous day reconnaissance."[56] That had not taken place on December 22. Other than the Americans' poor situational awareness of the enemy, one of the biggest risks of continuing the advance at night was that it stretched the endurance of the tired and cold troops, who were already starting to suffer from frostbite. As Irzyk observed, the order "staggered all hands." Just as the troops were settling in for the night, "they were slapped hard in the head. . . . Move all night!" He admitted that his unit was habitually fatigued and added, "We became even more fatigued after we moved all night" during December 22–23. However, as far as he was concerned, "there was never any visible evidence that fatigue adversely affected our operations. Somehow, the guys always rose to the occasion." Patton's insistence on continuous attack was reflected in Millikin's direction to McBride. Although the 80th Infantry Division controlled Feulen, Millikin ordered McBride to "keep pushing through the night" to get to phase line Yellow (the Wiltz River) and secure a crossing.[57] The decision to fight through the night demonstrated Patton's willingness to accept increasing battlefield uncertainty for the opportunities it might provide. December 23 would reveal whether Patton was justified in his decision.

The Battle of Chaumont

On December 23 Brandenberger faced the daunting task of closing a significant gap between the LXXX *Armeekorps* anchored at Echternach and Kniess's *LXXXV Armeekorps* overstretched to the west, attempting to protect *Fifth Panzer Armee*'s southern flank. Kniess had failed to achieve his objectives, except at Martelange. Brandenberger faced the same fundamental problem as Patton: too little combat power along a long front. Brandenberger's MLR was supposed to be Gedinne–Libramont–Wasserbillig. Long-range planning foresaw the construction of an MLR along the Luxembourg City–Arlon–Neufchâteau line.[58] Heilmann's *5th FJD* protected the rear of Kokott's *26th VGD* facing Bastogne. Elements of the *5th FJD* had reached Vaux-les-Rosières on December 22, and motorized patrols pushed on to Libramont, Neufchâteau, and beyond. Kniess declared that Heilmann's division had moved too far west; Brandenberger believed it should have pushed even farther west but had been prevented from doing so by heavy losses of men and material on December 22. *FJR 14* was in the Hompré–Hollange area, while *FJR 13* was in the Martelange area on both sides of the Sûre. *FJR 15* was still moving west through Wiltz, and *Fallschirmjäger Pionier Abteilung 5* was defending along the Sûre south of Harlange. *Seventh's Armee*'s MLR was supposed to be protected by intensive mining, but the resources simply did not exist to do so.[59]

On December 20 Brandenberger had convinced Model to release *Heeresgruppe B*'s only reserve formation, the *79th VGD*. The *FGB* from OKW reserve situated in the Bitburg–Wittlich area was also released, and its advance elements were already south of the Sûre, opposite the 26th Infantry Division. The *79th VGD* was not expected to arrive until December 23 or 24. *LXXXV Armeekorps* would move to Lipperscheid just west of Skyline Drive, but Brandenberger felt that *Seventh Armee*'s front was too wide to handle with two corps headquarters, so he brought forward *General der Kavallerie* Edwin von Rothkirch's *LIII Armeekorps* headquarters for better control. Rothkirch established his headquarters at Dahl, two and a half miles south of Wiltz, and assumed command of the *5th FJD* and the *FGB*.[60] The *FGB* was originally going to be used as a mobile flank guard in the Gedinne–Libramont zone, but it was committed to the gap between *LXXX* and *LXXXV Armeekorps*. Brandenberger expected Rothkirch to create a bastion with the right wing of Heilmann's division by giving it assault guns, *Panzerjägers*, and bolstered artillery support. To provide such support, Brandenberger transferred VAK elements fighting under *LXXXV Armeekorps* to Rothkirch.[61]

Despite Brandenberger's claim that aerial reconnaissance was poor, *Jagdkorps II*, whose main effort over *Seventh Armee* was the Libramont–Neufchâteau–Mersch area, reported the 4th Armored Division coming up into the Marche–Libramont area at 2030 on December 22. It also warned of strong forces moving up from the Longwy–Luxembourg area. In fact, CCA was spotted on the Longwy–Arlon road just south of Martelange at 0020 on December 23. While CCA was held up at Martelange, waiting for the engineers to complete a bridge over the Sûre, CCB advanced through the night, per Patton's orders. Irzyk's battalion regrouped on the road at 2300 and began to advance once more at midnight; a cavalry platoon was in the lead, followed by a company of Shermans and then a company of armored infantry in half-tracks from Lieutenant Colonel Harold Cohen's 10th AIB. Less than 200 yards up the road the column was hit by *Panzerfaust* and small-arms fire, and sometime around 0300 on December 23 it was counterattacked.[62]

The 25th Cavalry Reconnaissance Squadron had moved beyond Burnon during the fighting there and had reached the high ground just south of Chaumont by 0800. At approximately 0900 the cavalry was hit from the northwest by a battalion from *FJR 14* with four or five tanks and artillery. The cavalry patrol withdrew back on the main body. Sergeant Nat Frankel, a member of the patrol, stated that moving toward Chaumont was a tactical error. The sunshine on the morning of December 23 had turned the snow and mud to mush, and the cavalry's progress was "excruciatingly" slow. Frankel reflected, "I felt like I had been thrown into a fathomless quicksand." He noted, "This was the first withdrawal I had experienced since Rennes," and he described it as a "rout."[63]

CCB continued to advance toward Chaumont against sporadic fire, and by 1200 it had reached the high ground immediately south of the village. An hour earlier Patton had telephoned Phillips at III Corps headquarters and declared, "The going wasn't so good yesterday. I am unhappy about it. I want to emphasize that this is a ground battle and they must move forward. Get them to bypass towns and get forward. I want a definite report at 1315 today on the situation. I want bastogne [sic] by 1350. Get those boys going. Tell Millikin to get them going if he has to go down to the front line platoon[s?]. . . . There is too much piddling around. Clear them up later."[64]

The village of Chaumont was to the left of the Arlon–Bastogne highway. Its roughly fifty small farms, spotted with large, conical manure piles, lay in a bowl formed by hills and connecting ridges. It was a key crossroad for four secondary roads. Chaumont was defended by a company of *FJR 14*, but an entire battalion was in the immediate vicinity. There is some evidence that portions of *FJR 14* had retreated to Kokott's CP at Hompré, a development that alarmed him. Taking matters into his own hands, he ordered *FJR 14* back to Chaumont and provided it with some of his own officers. Indeed, Kokott later indicated that because he believed the *5th FJD* to be a "very poor" formation, he had already decided to build a line of resistance near Chaumont. Kokott said the only good thing about Heilmann's division was that it was "heavily equipped with weapons."[65]

It appears that during the night of December 22–23 a liaison officer carrying CCB's orders, including missions, checklists, attack orders, composition of troops, and timings, was captured near Bodange, and either Kokott or Heilmann, or both, acted on the information with alacrity. Captain Abraham Baum, S-3 of the 10th AIB, believed the Germans were prepared for CCB's advance into Chaumont because of the captured orders. Heilmann sent forward *StuG Brigade 11*, consisting of perhaps fifteen *StuGs*. Simultaneously, Kokott exploited a new resource. He recalled that "an unknown major in command of four Tiger tanks came into Hompré. I don't know where he came from, or where he was going, but I ordered him south to aid 5 FS Div at Remichampagne and Chaumont." These seem to have been Ferdinand *Panzerjägers*, mounting 88mm guns.[66]

CCB was to execute a deliberate attack on Chaumont to occupy it, not skirt it, as Patton had directed. As the 8th Tank Battalion prepared to move into Chaumont, it had seventeen tanks, and Ezell declared that they were "so few in number that they were used to support the infantry."[67] Those academic historians who have criticized Patton for not conducting enough reconnaissance prior to launching his offensive should consider the opinion of Bruce C. Clarke. Clarke did not like reconnaissance leading the combat commands. He had tried it in Lorraine "but soon abandoned it because my reconnaissance and covering detachments were soon buried [i.e., destroyed]. I found it better to lead with my medium tanks which could stand the fire of machine guns and burp guns rather than jeeps that could stand the fire of nothing."[68] Clarke employed his reconnaissance assets for flank and rear area security.

The value of reconnaissance was clearly something the tankers debated. Irzyk declared, "Never once was I able to be on ground to take a look before we seized it. To me such an opportunity is highly unlikely." Irzyk did in fact conduct a visual reconnaissance of Chaumont from his turret, but the poor visibility obscured distant objectives. He confirmed his visual reconnaissance with a quick study on his 1:100,000 map and concluded that he had no alternative but to attack and take the town because he could not leave the roads. He admitted, "The enemy had graphically demonstrated that he was present, accounted for, and prepared to fight," and he also understood quite clearly that once his tanks were down in the town, they would be "totally committed and super vulnerable." Baum declared that before the attack, "foot patrols had drawn tank fire south of town indicating that the town was held in force."[69]

Irzyk's plan of attack was as follows: A Company of the 8th Tank Battalion and two platoons of B Company/10th AIB were to secure the high ground immediately south of the village. C Company/10th AIB and C Company/8th Tank Battalion (seven tanks) were to flank the village along the ridge to the west and take the high ground to the northwest. One platoon each from A Company/10th AIB and B Company/8th Tank Battalion (six tanks) were to provide a fire base into the village from Hill 480, a little more than half a mile southeast of the town. The assault force consisted of two platoons of A Company and one from B Company/10th AIB, along with two platoons of B Company/8th Tank Battalion. The artillery fire plan was simple. Irzyk recalled, "As for Artillery, the forward observers could get that in a moment. If I needed him, the battalion commander was always physically handy, and could confer with me on a moment's notice. He would be the one who could quickly get the support from other battalions if we needed heavier and broader concentrations. . . . So this [coordination] was not a special step. It was constantly ongoing."[70] The divisional guns began to drop shells on Chaumont for several minutes prior to H-hour.

Irzyk's force crossed the LD at 1330. When the assault force began to move, the artillery shelling switched from Chaumont to areas northeast and northwest of the town, but the planned envelopment never happened. Shortly after the main assault started, Irzyk received word that C Company was stuck in the ground to the west and could not maneuver north to protect the assault force's left flank.[71] Similarly, four of the six tanks that were supposed to unleash direct fire from Hill 480 never got into position because of the soft ground. Covered by limited tank fire from the southern high ground, the tanks, with six or seven men riding on each, drove into town and took scattered artillery, antitank, and small-arms fire from the high ground northwest of the village. Around 1430 more infantry were called in. Ninety minutes later another request for reinforcement came, and a platoon from C Company/10th AIB went in dismounted. *FJR 14* had to be rooted out of the buildings, but by 1700 CCB had taken perhaps 100 prisoners. Baum reflected, "It looked as though the fight was over."[72] Irzyk began to implement plans to outpost the town and push north, but the Germans still controlled three hills and key terrain north of the town and used them to devastating effect.

At approximately 1700 the Germans launched their counterattack, possibly with the entire *I* and *II Abteilungs/FJR 14*. Baum recalled, "From this direction [north of town] the enemy with 21 tanks and over 500 infantry counterattacked across the ridge northwest of the town, through GRANDURE [*sic*] at 1700. . . . The en[emy] coordinated tanks, infantry, and artillery. Supporting fires [from three hills north of Chaumont] were placed by the en[emy] on the Americans in the town. Employing smoke to cover movement, the tanks with mounted en[emy] infantrymen swept into town. The infantrymen dismounted. The tanks apparently withdrew after placing close-range fire against our tanks and infantry."[73]

Aligning battle details as remembered by different participants is always difficult. Contrary to Baum, Cohen later stated that the counterattack came from the north and northeast, not the northwest or down from Grandrue. His interviewer, Captain L. B. Clark, noted that this was a "very important point" and said that he believed Cohen's account. Clark added: "This means that it made no difference what happened to the force that was to envelop the town on the west since, even if it had accomplished its mission and reached the high ground northwest of the town, it would not have been in a position to deal with the German tank counterattack." Irzyk confirmed that "powerful" fire came from the northeast and offered a compelling commentary on the psychology of being ambushed: "It was the frightening, demoralizing, intimidating, unreal sounds, screeches, and screams of high velocity tank gun rounds hitting, crashing, exploding, and ricocheting all around them. It shook, staggered, numbed, alarmed and unnerved the men. It had happened so suddenly, so unexpectedly, that for a brief instant, there was panic."[74]

The reporting of tanks is also interesting. Ezell declared that "twenty-two enemy tanks appeared on the ridge to the north of town." American soldiers frequently mistook *Panzerjägers* for tanks. Irzyk later believed these were the tanks of the *FGB*, but on December 23 it was deployed well to the east around Eschdorf.[75] Another possible source of armor on December 23 was *KG von Hauser* (*PGR 901*) from *Panzer Lehr*, which had been attached to Kokott's division the day before. When he received reports from the *5th FJD* to the south that Americans had captured Chaumont, he grabbed four tanks, most likely Panthers, from the II *Abteilung* of *Lehr's Panzer Regiment 130* and formed a *Kampfgruppe* with elements of his own division, including some assault guns. Additionally, 4th Armored Division had reported the presence of perhaps ten tanks in the vicinity of the Forêt d'Arsdorf at 2145 on December 22. This report appeared to be valid because a prisoner captured by the 26th Infantry Division declared that the *SS Grossdeutschland Division* was near Arsdorf and had forty to fifty Tiger tanks.[76] Therefore, at the very least, Gaffey knew German tanks were within striking range of his combat commands.

As Irzyk retreated out of the "bowl" of Chaumont, his tank was hit and he was wounded—not seriously, but badly enough to shake him. He might have called in artillery to support his force in the town, but the artillery forward observer (FO) tank had been knocked out. According to Baum, the infantry withdrew without supporting artillery fire because "our men were in town and their exact locations unknown and because the artillery FO had been killed. Most of the men who got out did so by acting with initiative and good luck." CCB lost four tanks destroyed, four mired, and three hit and abandoned but recoverable. A Company's six tanks remained concealed south of Chaumont, and another three were all that was left of CCB's armored power that day. A Company/10th AIB lost all its officers and sixty-five men in and around the town. Getting a feel for the intensity is difficult, but apparently a single company of Irzyk's 8th Tank Battalion fired off three basic loads of .30-caliber ammunition, equaling 180,000 rounds, during the day.[77] CCB withdrew at 2000 to high ground south of Chaumont. Tanks withdrew while infantry continued to hold the town. The Germans made no effort to exploit this success and push CCB even farther back.

Strikingly absent from the battle was XIX TAC. The weather broke on December 23 when a high-pressure system rolled in from Russia, and conditions remained excellent for the next five days. The Germans put up 800 sorties that day; half were defensive.[78] There is no mention of American fighter-bombers flying over CCB, despite the fact that the 362nd Fighter Group flew six missions for III Corps during the day. During the battle, however, the 8th Tank Battalion shot down two *Fock-Wulf-190s*. XIX TAC was definitely busy, escorting C-47 Dakotas into Bastogne, flying armed reconnaissance over the Bulge and Eifel, and carefully watching the weakened Saar sector and the potential buildup of German forces in the Trier–Merzig area.[79]

Baum summed up CCB's battle at Chaumont as follows: "It should be noted that throughout the entire operation CCB was out by itself with not only both flanks exposed, but also the rear. Furthermore since the order to push forward to establish contact . . . at Bastogne had been pressing, pockets of en[emy] resistance had been purposely bypassed to speed the drive. Thus, there was the constant threat of counterattack from these small en[emy] concentrations to the south, east, and west."[80]

Patton did not order Chaumont to be taken. On the contrary, he gave directions to avoid towns. But the reality of the ground meant that 4th Armored Division had to attack and clear towns not only to make progress but also to ensure a secure LC. Third Army's axis of advance was based primarily on the road net, where it existed. Such extensive damage had been inflicted on an already understrength CCB during the battle of Chaumont that Dager and Gaffey rested it throughout December 24. While Irzyk rehabilitated his force after the setback at Chaumont, the 101st Airborne Division sent a message to the 4th Armored Division at midnight, suggesting that there was only one shopping day left before Christmas. Christmas would come and go before Patton could punch through.

8

A Rendezvous with Eagles, December 24–26

At the outside, we thought we could hold off 4 Armd Div until
25 Dec 44.

—Gersdorff, chief of staff, *Fifth Panzer Armee*

December 23 was not a productive day for Third Army. While CCB re-
coiled from the counterattack at Chaumont, the tanks of CCA sat virtually idle the whole day on the south bank of the Sûre River, after having
cleared Martelange by 0300 that morning. Corps engineers, assisted by
the 24th Engineer C Battalion, could not complete a ninety-foot-long
Bailey bridge until approximately 1400.[1] Meanwhile, Earnest ordered a
company to take the high ground immediately across the river, and the infantry made its way across the blown bridge without opposition. Had the
Fallschirmjäger vigorously defended the heights beyond, it is likely that
CCA's advance would have been delayed even longer.

With the Bailey bridge finished, TF Oden (35th Tank Battalion)
passed through the bridgehead and took the lead. After rapidly overrunning dug-in infantry and antitank gun positions about one mile up the
road, CCA was hit again, this time by automatic weapons and antitank
fire from Warnach, to the right of the Arlon–Bastogne highway. Warnach
was defended by *II Abteilung/FJR 15*. With the aid of artillery, CCA destroyed four German guns and drove the *Fallschirmjäger* into the woods,
but the Germans infiltrated back into Warnach in the dark. Lieutenant
Colonel Hal C. Pattison, CCA's executive officer, later reflected, "The
general impression was that we could just cut our way through" to Bastogne. That impression had proved false on December 23, when CCA
and CCB were effectively stalled for the entire day. Prematurely elated by
the completion of the bridge at Martelange, Millikin apparently radioed

Middleton that 4th Armored Division would contact the 101st Airborne Division that night.[2]

Paul's 26th Infantry Division attacked throughout the night but had made no progress by daylight on December 23. The 104th CT held Grosbous, but the commanding officer of the 735th Tank Battalion stated that the infantry "would not go into town ahead of the tanks. Troops of the 104th CT appear very timid and it is necessary for the tanks to do most of the work." It is not unreasonable to assume that the infantry units of the 26th Infantry Division contained many "empty" uniforms. Although Cole suggested that all the replacements "were steeled, according to the capacity of the individual, to meet a ruthless enemy," the quick conversion training at Metz could have done little to elevate the fighting power of the division. Perhaps this was why the 328th Infantry apparently told its replacements that "no SS troops or paratroopers will be taken prisoners, but will be shot on sight." Paul said the same thing: "Under no circumstances will these groups [infiltrating paratroopers] be allowed to return to their lines alive." Clearly, this order came from Patton and worked its way down. According to Allen, at the 0800 General Staff meeting on December 19, Patton declared that no SS prisoners were to be taken.[3]

Paul's other attacking CT, the 328th, was checked on the left at Grevels–Brésil by small elements of the FGB and made little progress during the day. At 1645 Millikin was at the 26th Infantry Division CP telling Paul that his division was lagging behind the others and to push patrols up to the Sûre. Perhaps the report of numerous Tigers, the large number of replacements, and the absence of the 101st CT in corps reserve had made Paul cautious, but Millikin's direction to hold back the main strength of the 104th and 328th CTs until the situation was better developed ensured a slow advance.[4] Patton's views on holding back one-third of the division are not known, but his general principle was that everyone should attack.

On Paul's right the 318th CT attacked Ettelbruck during the morning of December 23. Ettelbruck was now reinforced by VWB 18 and VAK 406, and the enemy exploited the heights around it with good fields of fire. Elements of the 2nd Battalion/319th CT ran into trouble at Heiderscheid when elements of the FGB drove it back. The Germans quickly withdrew but launched an uncoordinated attack shortly afterward, which the 319th CT destroyed in an hour. While the 318th CT continued to contain Ettelbruck, McBride brought up the 317th CT and passed it through the 318th. The 317th CT then proceeded to advance through the night in a column of battalions for a distance of approximately four miles, under

harassing artillery fire, and attacked north toward Bourscheid.[5] The farthest advance of December 23 was by the 319th CT, which pushed a patrol across the Sûre at Tadler.

In XII Corps the two battalions of the 10th CT continued to attack
into the woods northeast of Michelshof on December 23, supported by
six field artillery battalions. However, this assault was repelled and driven
back to its original positions while the reserve battalion sat uncommitted.
For the second straight day Eddy managed to orchestrate an attack by
only two battalions. That morning he had his three division commanders
in to discuss the plan to eliminate the Sauer River bridgeheads beginning
the next day. When Patton was briefed, Eddy noted, "He seemed satisfied
with the plan that we have, but according to Allen, Patton later "stalked"
into the situation room with Eddy and demanded to see the nature of
German activity opposite XII Corps.[6]

After forty-eight hours there was no discernible sign that Patton was
attempting to maneuver his formations to gain positional or numerical
advantage over *Seventh Armee*. Millikin conducted a straight-ahead advance to gain ground and destroy any enemy encountered, and Eddy was
cautiously preparing an orthodox corps advance for December 24. Despite his famous disregard for his flanks, Patton was very sensitive to the
German capability of attacking from Echternach to strike the east flank
of Third Army's counterattack. Bradley's situation map was now showing
the *21st PD* moving north from Lorraine with a question mark.[7] Patton
also knew from ULTRA that *LIII Armeekorps* was coming up to take over
the *5th FJD* and the *FGB*, with the mission of blocking the roads from
Bastogne south and southwest to prevent the Bastogne force from breaking out or Patton's forces from breaking in. *PGR 901* was maintaining the
ring around Bastogne, but *Panzer Lehr* spearheads were somewhere near
St. Hubert.[8] As Patton continued to evaluate the situation, he could hardly have avoided the theoretical possibility that he could be attacked from
both flanks. *Panzer Lehr* and *2nd PD* were both in a position to menace
the army's left flank in different circumstances, and he had to envision his
right flank not just in terms of Eddy's front but also in terms of a XII–XX
Corps front with points of varying vulnerability. Allen declared that an
envelopment of the left flank was "a very serious capability."[9] XIX TAC
continued to fly armed reconnaissance missions in the Trier area to cover
Third Army's right flank.

While Dager's CCB reorganized, CCA withdrew to a protected assembly area southwest of Warnach at 0600 on December 24 and reorganized

for a renewed assault. At 0915 CCA went in again, supported by artillery, and finally cleared the village by 1300.[10] Forward elements had bypassed Warnach and made it to Strainchamps. CCA's axis of advance on the main highway had made it impossible to broaden the advance to cover a greater frontage, and Gaffey was now faced with a new threat to his right flank. Advance elements of the FGB had been identified north of Bigonville. To address the threat, Gaffey committed his reserve, ordering CCR, consisting of the 37th Tank Battalion, 53rd AIB, and 94th FA Battalion, into the area.[11]

CCR moved from the area around Meix-le-Tige, drove through Arlon to Perlé, and then headed toward Flatzbourhof, where it bivouacked for the night. Getting to Bigonville required CCR to fight through a hastily laid minefield, a hail of small-arms fire, and probably snipers, for many tank commanders in one company were hit. Captain James Leach, commanding B Company, was hit by a sniper's bullet that penetrated his helmet and grazed his skull.[12] CCR attacked Bigonville at 0800 on December 24, preceded by a TOT. Conversely, FJR 13 could call on little defensive artillery fire; the division was now rationed to seven rounds per gun per day. By noon the town and some 328 POWs were in American hands.

The 5th FJD had given a good account of itself over the first week of the battle, but Third Army intercepted a message from Heilmann on December 24 declaring that he could not hold out much longer without help. Like 4th Armored Division, 5th FJD continually transmitted in plain language.[13] Frankel recalled: "They were raw, to be sure, but if you don't respect them, you can't possibly respect us, either. Simple amateurs couldn't have given us such hell. There was nothing simple about their amateurism. They were a remarkably valiant band of Germans, maybe the best we saw." As far as Frankel was concerned, at Burnon they "fought like the vanguard of the whole Wehrmacht!" Irzyk felt the same way: "I have a favorable impression of the fighting qualities of the 5th FJ. It seems to me that of all the German divisions committed to the Ardennes the 5th FJ was the only one that could claim that they had done what they had been asked to do."[14]

By dawn on December 24, Paul's lead elements were still three and a half miles from the Sûre. To achieve his objective of Wiltz, Paul focused on seizing Eschdorf south of the river by pushing TF Hamilton (2nd Battalion, 328th Infantry) through the 104th CT. Eschdorf was critical to the integrity of Brandenberger's MLR because it controlled lateral routes south of the Sûre. It was also important for the resumption of offensive operations south of the river. The fact that Brandenberger was still expected to gain his original objectives was betrayed to Patton by ULTRA early on the morning of December 24.[15]

At 0800 on December 24 TF Hamilton attacked the FGB on approaches to Eschdorf but was immediately pinned down at Hierheck and received only minor relief from the 362nd Fighter Group. Paul countermanded Hamilton's order to dig in for the night, and the task force subsequently launched attacks at 0045 and 0400 on December 25, to no effect. To the left at Arsdorf, a battalion of the 328th CT was involved in a pitched battle; another battalion of the CT reached Bonnal on the Sûre on Christmas morning, just as the Germans blew the bridge. Millikin repeatedly reminded Paul of his main mission to cross the Sûre River. By Christmas Eve both the 104th and 328th CTs could see the river, but neither could cross it.[16]

The first three days of fighting had taken a heavy toll of III Corps. On December 24 Millikin issued new directions to his formations: "All units are authorized to stabilize lines with all-around defense and active patrolling tonight (24–25 Dec). Troops will be rested as much as possible. . . . Attack will be resumed just before daylight 25 December."[17] While III Corps reorganized, Gaffey initiated the first attempt at maneuver outside the straight-ahead, line-abreast advance by requesting III Corps to shift the division boundary west to allow the 26th Infantry Division to assume responsibility for Bigonville, thereby freeing up CCR for employment elsewhere.[18] At 2100 on December 24 he ordered CCR to withdraw from the Bigonville area and move to the division's left flank. In *War as I Knew It* Patton declared that this was his idea, but the evidence supports Gaffey as the originator, supported by Millikin's sound decision with respect to boundaries.[19]

As Patton recalled, moving CCR opened a "huge gap" between Paul and Gaffey, but Millikin attached the 249th Engineer C Battalion to help. Moreover, the 6th Cavalry Group (TF Fickett) had arrived in III Corps' area late on the evening of December 24. Millikin assigned the 6th Cavalry Reconnaissance Squadron (Mechanized) to maintain contact with Gaffey and Paul, while the remainder of the group—the 28th Cavalry Reconnaissance Squadron (Mechanized), C Company/602nd Tank Destroyer Battalion, and B Company/293rd Engineer C Battalion—was given the mission of guarding the corps' left flank and assisting Gaffey. Millikin also attached two battalions of the 318th Infantry and a field

Bradley, Eisenhower, and Patton in the ruins of Bastogne. (West Point Library)

Patton and Brigadier General Anthony C. McAuliffe in Bastogne. (West Point Library)

Bradley decorates Patton with the Distinguished Service Order, December 29, 1944, at Third Army headquarters in Luxembourg. (National Archives)

Major General Joseph Lawton Collins, commanding general of VII Corps, and Field Marshal Sir Bernard L. Montgomery, commander in chief of Twenty-First Army Group. (National Archives)

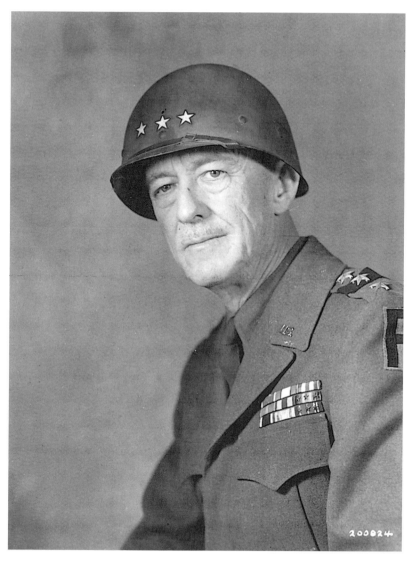

Lieutenant General Courtney Hicks Hodges, commanding general of First United States Army. (National Archives)

Major General John Millikin, commanding general of III Corps. The Ardennes was his baptism of fire. (National Archives)

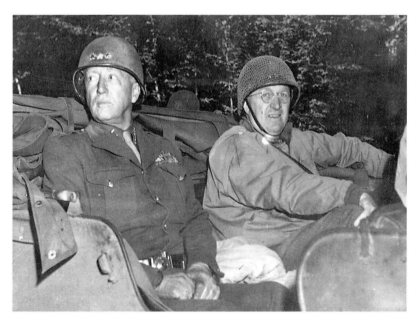

Patton and Major General Manton S. Eddy, commanding general of XII Corps. Patton considered relieving Eddy in Lorraine. (National Archives)

Major General Troy H. Middleton, commanding general of VIII Corps.
(National Archives)

Major General Willard S. Paul, commanding general of the 26th Infantry Division, here shown as a lieutenant general. (National Archives)

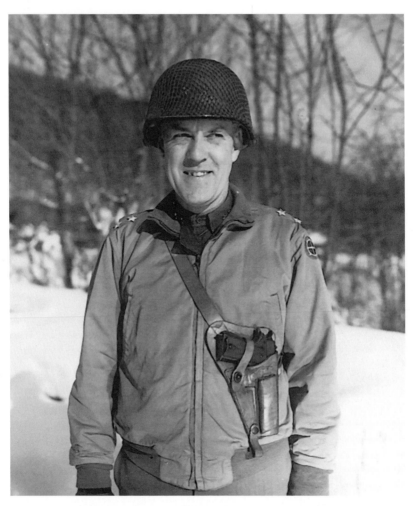

Major General Paul W. Baade, commanding general of the 35th Infantry Division. (National Archives)

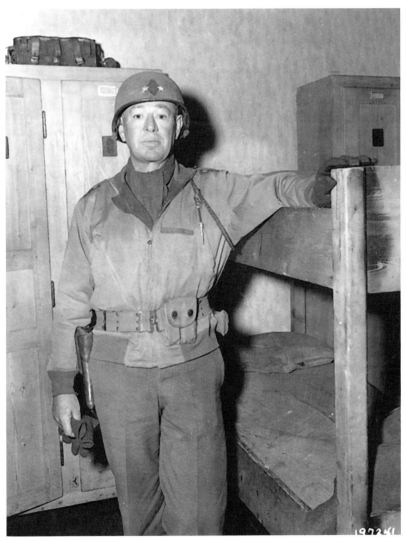

Major General Stafford Leroy "Red" Irwin, commanding general of the 5th
Infantry Division. (National Archives)

Major General Hugh J. Gaffey, commanding general of the 4th Armored Division. (National Archives)

Brigadier General Otto P. Weyland, commanding general of XIX Tactical Air Command, here shown as a major general. (National Archives)

Field Marshal Karl Rudolf Gerd von Rundstedt, *Oberbefelshaber West.* (National Archives)

Generalfeldmarschall Walter Model, commander in chief, *Heeresgruppe B.* (National Archives)

General der Panzertruppen Erich Brandenberger, commanding general of *Seventh Armee.* (National Archives)

General der Panzertruppen Hasso von Manteuffel, commanding general of *Fifth Panzer Armee*. (National Archives)

Generalleutnant Heinrich Freiherr von Lüttwitz, commanding general of *XLVII Panzerkorps*. (National Archives)

artillery battalion to 4th Armored Division at 1530. The 4th Armored Division simply did not possess sufficient organic infantry to fight through villages and woods, a point made by several armored officers.[20] Following a six-hour, fifty-five-mile road move, one infantry battalion was assigned to CCA and the other to CCB.

In XII Corps Eddy was finally ready to attack on December 24. Had he waited another day, the entire Third Army counterattack would have stood idle that day. Barton's 4th Infantry Division stayed in place, while the 5th Infantry and 10th Armored Divisions made the main effort, their mission being to seize and hold the line of the Sauer River. Colonel Charles H. Reed's 2nd Cavalry Group (reinforced), which had just deployed, protected Eddy's right flank all the way to XX Corps. The 90th Reconnaissance Squadron protected the corps' left flank. There was considerable combat power available for this attack, supported by two separate tank battalions, five tank destroyer battalions, and fifteen battalions of corps artillery.

The XII Corps attack got under way at 1100 in temperatures below twenty degrees Fahrenheit. CCA/10th Armored Division attacked to the northeast from the Diekirch–Medernach road. Morris attacked with two task forces. TF Standish, consisting of the armor of CCB, rapidly advanced northwest of Eppeldorf against little resistance. TF Rudder, consisting of two half-strength battalions of Rudder's 109th Infantry/28th Infantry Division, secured the south bank of the Sûre River between Gilsdorf and near Moestroff.[21] CCA/9th Armored Division was redesignated CCX to avoid confusion, and it reinforced TF Standish. CCX came up on the right and advanced toward Eppeldorf.

To the east Irwin attacked with all three regiments up: the 10th CT on the left, the 2nd CT in the middle, and the 11th CT on the right. XIX TAC's effort was directed at targets along the river rather than direct support of the infantry. Eddy went out to see his division commanders as the battle progressed and noted, "The 5th [Infantry Division] seems to be coming along pretty well and are making progress. . . . Arrived at the 10th Armored CP at Mersch and talked with Bill Morris. Things look rather bright. The Germans are not too strongly emplaced and I think they [10th Armored] will be able to go on to the river." Eddy, however, was not willing to push too hard. He was trying to preserve the combat power of his formations and told Irwin that if he thought the attack was proving too costly, he could shut it down.[22] Eddy also worried about the weakness between himself and Walker. During the day and night XII Corps fired 21,173 rounds of artillery.

The *276th* and *212th VGDs* were split by the deep Schwarz Erntz, which made mutual support virtually impossible. Indeed, by the end of December 24, tactical connection was nonexistent, and both divisions had been driven back to their original bridgehead areas. Sensfuss reflected, "My right flank, now exposed, was permanently menaced."[23] He withdrew to new positions from Berdorf to the hills in front of Echternach. He now had a perimeter around the town only 2,500 yards deep. By the end of the day XII Corps had achieved limited gains, and Irwin had successfully relieved Barton's tired division. At 1100 Koch and Allen briefed Patton and Bradley and discussed the potential threat from Trier. At 1700 Patton went to look at the G-2 situation map. According to Allen, he appeared anxious and, in a moment of frustration, declared that if he had only two more divisions he could effectively drive the Germans back.[24]

On Christmas Eve Patton and Codman went to a candlelight communion at the Episcopal church in Luxembourg City and sat in Kaiser Wilhelm II's box. Patton was not happy with his overall rate of progress. Eisenhower recalled that during this period Patton phoned him daily to apologize: "This snow is God-awful. I'm sorry." Eisenhower's reply to his old friend was simply to keep fighting. Patton noted on December 24, "This has been a very bad Christmas Eve. All along our line we have received violent counterattacks, one of which forced Dager of the 4th Armored back some miles with the loss of 10 tanks. This was probably my fault, because I had been insisting on day and night attacks. This is all right on the first or second day of the battle and when we had the enemy surprised but after that the men get too tired. Furthermore, in this bad weather, it is very difficult for armored outfits to operate at night." Patton was referring to Chaumont on December 23. Not only did he admit a possible error to himself, he actually continued this short self-analysis by concluding, "It takes a long time to learn war. Every once in a while I am impressed with how long it takes to really learn how to fight."[25]

Across the lines Rundstedt, Model, Manteuffel, Brandenberger, and Lüttwitz all felt that their ability to cross the Meuse and reach Antwerp had been lost by Christmas Eve. Rundstedt even told interrogators that by December 19 "it became obvious that the goal could no longer be pursued." Nevertheless, *OB West* held the broad view that eight days of fighting had at least neutralized the Allied threat to the Cologne and Ruhr fronts for some time to come. Rundstedt, Model, and Manteuffel all believed it was still possible to inflict significant damage on the Allies east of the Meuse by shifting the main effort and limiting expectations.[26]

Throughout December 24 Manteuffel and his chief of staff, Wagener, discussed with the *WFSt* which line of action—Marche or Bastogne—had priority. Manteuffel possessed enough combat power for one but not both.[27]

Manteuffel was already under orders to attack Bastogne on December 25, but in the early hours of Christmas morning he received word that Hitler had also ordered the attack on the high ground of Marche to continue with all available forces. Hitler assured Rundstedt and Model that a new offensive in Alsace, to be launched in a matter of days, would "compel Patton to withdraw the mass of his forces, now seeking to relieve Bastogne." Measures had already been taken to reinforce the shift in the *schwerpunkt.* Hitler released the *3rd* and *15th PGDs,* the *9th PD,* and the *167th VGD* to *Fifth Panzer Armee* on December 23. Model decided to send them to the left flank of *Fifth Panzer Armee,* but Manteuffel would give Lüttwitz only one regiment of the *15th PGD* for Bastogne to begin with.[28]

At 0300 on Christmas Day *Fifth Panzer Armee* renewed its attack on Bastogne with the *26th VGD, KG von Hauser, PGR 115/15th PGD,* and elements of *9th PD* in the Mande–St. Étienne sector. *XLVII Panzerkorps* did not have the weight of artillery or ammunition to subdue Bastogne. The only artillery available consisted of the *II, III,* and *IV Abteilungs* of *Artillerie Regiment 26* of the *26th VGD* in the Givry area; the *II Abteilung* of *Artillerie Regiment 33* (two light field howitzer batteries) south of Frenet; and one *Mörser* battery from *XVLII Panzerkorps.* The artillery of the *15th PGD* did not arrive until late on December 25. *Generalmajor* Richard Metz, Manteuffel's chief artillery adviser, declared that as a result of the clear weather and the introduction of Allied airpower, "the available transport area was from now on measurably smaller." Indeed, he told Manteuffel they needed to bring up the artillery still at the LD on the Our River, but because of the fuel shortage, they would have to concentrate on resupplying the artillery battalions already in situ. Metz brought forward the light field howitzer batteries of a battalion of *VAK 766* that would be arriving battery by battery over the next few days. Fuel supplies dictated that light rather than heavy batteries should be brought forward. This also eased the ammunition weight burden. *Fifth Panzer Armee's* ammunition distribution point managed to move forward, which helped the supply situation at Bastogne, but it never moved forward far enough to help the spearheads. The attack failed because the artillery was "numerically too weak" and the battle area "too wide to everywhere overcome simultaneously appearing enemy resistance and the effects of their weapons."[29] Lüttwitz believed he still had a chance to take Bastogne, but only until the evening of December 25.

Gaffey issued instructions on December 25 to mitigate against the likelihood of one combat command reaching Bastogne before the rest of the division, and he declared that it was "considered particularly desirable that the division, or elements thereof, stay out of town and operate from favorable ground outside." He also advised all commanders to be prepared to repel German counterattacks, "which will probably occur shortly after arrival."[30] Koch's work map for 2400 December 24 depicted the 2nd PD only a few miles east of Bastogne, and twenty-four hours later he correctly identified the 15th PGD as a new arrival. The locations of the 11th PD, depicted southeast of Bastogne, and the 21st PD, depicted just to the northeast with a large question mark, were inaccurate, but the amount of armor perceived to be immediately within range of Bastogne must have made Gaffey, Millikin, and Patton very uneasy as the under-strength 4th Armored Division fought its way north.

CCA and CCB advanced on Christmas Day with the infantry leading—the 51st AIB on the left of the Arlon–Bastogne highway for CCB, and the 1st Battalion/318th Infantry to the right of the highway for CCA, with the 35th Tank Battalion in support. CCR began to move at 0100 on Christmas morning, retracing its steps through Flatzbourhof–Perlé, across the Arlon–Bastogne highway to Heinstert, and then on to Habay-La-Neuve–Léglise–Offaing and northwest to the Neufchâteau–Bastogne road. CCR lead elements began arriving at the new assembly area southwest of Bercheux at 0500, after a thirty-mile night march. Martelange–Fauvillers was the most direct route, but bridges were still out. CCR moved from Bercheux at 1200 on Christmas Day with a company from the 37th Tank battalion leading, supported by the 94th FA Battalion and a battery from the 177th FA Battalion emplaced at Juseret. The 6th Cavalry Group simultaneously screened the left flank and conducted a reconnaissance in force.[31] CCR advanced through Vaux-les-Rosières with no opposition and continued on through Nives and Cobreville with no contact. Lieutenant Colonel Creighton Abrams' 37th Tank Battalion was blocked south of Remoiville by a blown bridge. A bulldozer was brought forward, and it collapsed a stone wall into the crater. By 1515 Abrams was on his way once again and eventually engaged and defeated the III Abteilung/ FJR 14 in Remoiville, taking 400 POWs.

Patton's frustration was evident on December 25. "The 4th Armored is fighting hard," he noted, "but [is] making slow progress. I feel that all are doing their best." That morning Maddox called III Corps and reminded Phillips that Patton was "very much interested in your people's progress" and wanted a special report each morning at 0800. Patton left headquarters early in the morning to visit as many divisions as he could. Perhaps as a result of Maddox's call, Millikin released the 101st Infantry from reserve and told Paul to "get going" and get Wiltz.[32] The Sûre River was only ten to twenty yards wide, and the current was not swift. The deep gorge, however, dictated crossing sites. Getting across was not the problem; finding passage through the heights on the north side was. The average elevation was 1,200 feet. From the river to Kaundorf, the elevation increased 450 feet in one-third of a mile.

Paul had three possible crossing sites: Heiderscheidergrund, Esch sur la Sûre, and the area between Bonnal and Lultzhauzen. The first was the most desirable. The Germans blew a span of the Heiderscheidergrund bridge during the evening of December 25 and blew the bridge at Bonnal–Lultzhauzen that morning. Confusion was evident at the river. During the night Paul received a report that the 328th Infantry was across. Shortly before midnight, however, another report came in: "Situation at the river crossing north of Bonnal is very vague . . . we may or may not have the bridge."[33] On Paul's right McBride missed the two battalions sent to Gaffey. The 318th CT, with a single battalion, managed to get troops into Ettelbruck following heavy artillery fire and direct fire from the 610th Tank Destroyer and 702nd Tank Battalions. McBride ordered the 319th CT to clear the enemy on the south bank of the Sûre instead of establishing bridgeheads over it, and the combat team managed to seize Ringel from elements of the *79th VGD*.[34] He also pushed the 317th CT through the 318th CT with the mission of seizing Kehmen and Bourscheid, but the advance faltered.[35]

In XII Corps Morris reported that the 10th Armored Division sector was quiet, but the division sat idle the whole day. Moreover, the 5th Infantry Division captured two German runners who indicated that the Germans were going to withdraw; how far was unknown. Eddy's reluctance to follow up this withdrawal with greater pressure was unfortunate. He went over to see Patton, but the latter was out visiting. Eddy's impression from Maddox was that XII Corps' progress was satisfactory. Indeed, after visiting the 4th Infantry Division, Eddy was confident that it was "getting into pretty good shape," having received some badly needed replacements.[36] After returning to his CP Eddy received word from Third Army that he would be losing the 10th Armored Division, which was being sent to Metz for a rest. Major General Robert W. Grow's 6th Armored Division would replace Morris's division. At that moment, the head of Grow's division was just pulling into Metz. At 1045 Patton released the 35th Infantry Division to Millikin, to be effective the next day, and McBride's division was to move to Eddy's XII Corps. Patton had wanted to send Millikin a combat team from the division on December 24, but Gay had resisted. Colonel Maddrey A. Solomon, chief of staff of the division, stated it was "simply too badly mixed up to move . . . at this time; that while they had received hundreds of replacements, they actually didn't know what they had as they had moved the night before yesterday, were strafed en route, and had not yet had time to get their units collected."[37]

On December 26 Patton noted, "Today has been rather trying as, in spite of our best efforts, we have failed to make contact with the defenders of Bastogne." Eisenhower expressed disappointment during a staff meeting: "I have just been set back thoroughly on my heels by this failure of the attack from the south to join up with the 101st." Perhaps this was why Major General Harold R. Bull, Eisenhower's G-3, called Third Army and stressed action. Patton noted that Bull "had the nerve to call me up and say that Ike was very anxious that I put every effort on securing Bastogne. What the hell does he think I've been doing for the last week[?]"[38] During the morning the 94th FA Battalion deployed to Sûre from Juseret, a distance of less than three miles, and opened fire on Remichampagne at 0925. CCR secured it by 1200 and moved on to Clochimont against little resistance. This was fortunate, because CCR possessed only twenty tanks and was 230 men short in the 53rd AIB. Patton, Maddox, and Weyland met at 1230, and shortly thereafter Patton requested maximum air support in front of Gaffey's division.[39]

Kokott believed that CCB was the only threat; he had no idea as to the whereabouts of CCR. When the interrogator, surprised by this revelation, asked for confirmation, Kokott replied, "I really don't remember, the situation was so bad; however, if I knew, I didn't pay any attention to it. There was nothing I could do about it anyway. My only hope was to continue with the attack on Bastogne." Kokott reflected, "It is an uncomfortable feeling to have someone launching a drive toward your rear." During the night of December 24 he spoke to Manteuffel on the telephone. "I told him," he recalled, "that I could not watch two fronts, and that the southern situation was most dangerous. I did not think that 5 FS Div could hold, and I was in no position to prevent a breakthrough."

Manteuffel told him to forget about the 4th Armored Division and focus on attacking Bastogne from the northwest. Kokott passed this on to the commander of *Fusilier Regiment 39*, deployed in the Assenois, Salvacourt, and Sibret areas, ordering him to "continue facing Bastogne and not to form a front to the south."[40] Although he warned the commander to watch his rear and prepare an all-around defense, Kokott probably made Gaffey's penetration easier.

The decision to attempt a *coup de main* into Bastogne seems to have been made by Abrams and Lieutenant Colonel George Jacques, commander of the 53rd AIB. Abrams was an aggressive man. Hal Pattison reflected that he was "a brilliant tactician . . . he knew what had to be done . . . and his people were always prepared." Delk Oden put it another way: "God damn what a leader." According to Patton, Gaffey phoned at 1400, soliciting permission to authorize CCR to attempt a rapid breakthrough. "I told him to try it," declared Patton.[41] However, there is no evidence of this in the division's G-3 journal. Brigadier General Wendell Blanchard, commander of CCR, was clearly out of the loop because at 1640, while CCR tanks were literally driving through Assenois, he radioed division to say that he was ordering a breakthrough to Bastogne that night. According to Major Robert M. Parker Jr., commanding officer of the 94th FA Battalion, Blanchard was not involved and apparently never gave any orders for the attack. At Bercheux the battalion commanders "waited and waited" and eventually worked out attack plans on their own. Abrams said the same thing: Blanchard "had very little to do" with the direction of the battalions. Abrams made decisions without consulting him.[42]

At 1520 Abrams called his S-3 (equivalent to G-3 at the battalion level) and ordered him to move up the rest of CCR, saying, "This is it." Abrams's plan was simple. C Company/37th Tank Battalion and C Company/53rd AIB would strike through Assenois in an attempt to contact the Screaming Eagles. B Company/53rd AIB would follow and clean out Assenois. Abrams's force started its final run at 1610 with tanks leading. Forty minutes later, after running a gauntlet of small-arms and *Panzerfaust* fire and negotiating hasty minefields, Abrams's tanks made contact with KANGAROO, the code name for the 101st's barrier line.[43] After five days of heavy fighting, Abrams repeated what Ezell had done six days earlier.

When he related the moment of CCR's breakthrough to postwar interrogators, Kokott held his head in his hands and stated simply, "I knew it was all over." His frustration was no doubt exacerbated by the fact that it was impossible to bring up artillery to quickly deal with the penetration due to pressure west and north of Bastogne and fuel shortages. Guns would come up to assist only during the night of December 26–27.[44] The initial reports of the linkup were not to Patton's satisfaction. He sent a responsible officer to CCR to find out what "contact" meant, but once he was satisfied he noted, "It was a daring thing and well done. Of course they may be cut off, but I doubt it."[45]

Patton's penetration to Bastogne took five days, and III Corps fired more than 55,000 rounds of artillery—some 4,387,746 pounds, or 2,194 short tons—to get there.[46] He had initially engaged the *212th*, *276th*, and *352nd VGDs* and the *5th FJD*, but soon attracted the *79th VGD*, *FGB*, and *PGR 115* as well. Patton should have concentrated more combat power on the main effort to Bastogne, especially since Gaffey's division had not been at full strength for quite some time. The addition of two battalions from McBride's division highlighted the critical need for more infantry, something that should have been foreseen by Patton, Millikin, and Gaffey. However, balance across the front seemed to overrule the need for concentration. Patton's unwillingness to commit CCB on December 20 to prevent the encirclement of Bastogne was a lost opportunity, but he could have lessened the impact had he weighted Millikin's attack more to the left. Though five days had passed since Third Army crossed the LD, Patton had secured the relief of the 101st Airborne Division. Eisenhower and Bradley now turned their attention to the next phase of the southern counteroffensive. Patton had very definite views on what should be done.

PART IV

The Incomplete Victory

Patton's Alternative Lines of Action

> It remained for Patton, the diligent student of military history, to state in forthright terms the classic but venturesome solution . . . the Ardennes salient should be cut off and the German armies engulfed therein by a vise closing from north and south against the shoulders of the Bulge.
>
> —Hugh Cole

At this juncture it is important to examine Patton's estimate process. Through it, the historian can evaluate his favored lines of action and compare them with those favored by Eisenhower and Bradley. The estimate process was designed to guard against selecting lines of action that did not lead anywhere decisive. The estimate offers insights into Patton's ability to think and plan beyond the present problem faced by Third Army. He had accomplished his initial mission. He had reoriented Third Army, penetrated the German southern front, and relieved the 101st Airborne Division at Bastogne. Even as the 4th Armored Division made its final attempt to get into Bastogne, Patton was regrouping Third Army and updating his estimate based on directions from Bradley. Patton's post-Bastogne mission was to continue the counteroffensive toward St. Vith, along with two secondary tasks: containing the German advance east of the Meuse, and holding along the present line between Saarlautern and Echternach.[1]

Third Army Capability

On December 26, after five days of hard fighting, Third Army still possessed considerable combat power. Patton now had three armored divisions—the 4th, 6th, and 10th—and nine infantry divisions—the 4th,

Table 9.1. Third Army Order of Battle Following the Relief of Bastogne

VIII Corps	III Corps	XII Corps	XX Corps
101 Abn Div	4 Armd Div	80 Inf Div	90 Inf Div
CCB/10 Armd Div	26 Inf Div	5 Inf Div	95 Inf Div
CCR/9 Armd Div	35 Inf Div	4 Inf Div	10 Armd Div
28 Inf Div (–)	CCA/9 Armd Div	6 Armd Div	5 Ranger Bn
4 French Pcht Bn	6 Cav Gp	2 Cav Gp	3 Cav Gp
HQ/9 Armd Div	735 Tk Bn	702 Tk Bn	712 Tk Bn
609 TD Bn (elms)	654 TD Bn	70 Tk Bn	778 Tk Bn
	704 TD Bn	609 TD Bn (elms)	607 TD Bn
		610 TD Bn	
		803 TD Bn	

5th, 26th, 28th, 35th, 80th, 90th, and 95th and the 101st Airborne Division. The weakened condition of the 4th and 28th Infantry Divisions, however, reduced the total to the equivalent of seven or eight infantry divisions. Despite its ordeal in Bastogne, the 101st Airborne Division, according to Maxwell Taylor, was in excellent condition, had adequate supplies, and was ready for offensive combat.[2]

Patton's reorganization of Third Army at the time was as follows: At 1300 he assigned CCA/9th Armored Division, situated near Luxembourg City, to III Corps. Millikin was to attach it to Gaffey's division for an attack on the left flank to widen the relief corridor by opening up the Neufchâteau–Bastogne highway. The main weight of Gaffey's division was still held up at Hompré and farther southeast. CCA/9th Armored Division was relieved by CCA/6th Armored Division, now fully concentrated around Mersch after moving up from Lorraine.[3] The 10th Armored Division (less CCB, still in Bastogne) withdrew from XII Corps' front and began to move to Metz to refit; it would be replaced by the 6th Armored Division. At 2000 McBride's 80th Infantry Division was assigned to XII Corps.[4] To fill the gap between Paul and Gaffey, Patton ordered the 35th Infantry Division up from Metz and assigned it to III Corps.

This reorganization was intended to give Third Army "the strongest possible striking force into the enemy bulge." Patton's staff assessed the army's overall capability as follows:

All the known German striking power in the west is now concentrated in a well-defined area. . . . At present the Third Army composes seven (7) strong infantry divisions and three (3) armored divisions. These forces are supported by 108 battalions of artillery. In addition, four potential divisions exist (94th, 87th, 17th AB, and 11th Armored). . . . The Third Army service installations are exceptionally well situated at the present time to support continuation of the attack. Our stores in these installations are being improved daily. Our rail net in this area is excellent. The present supply situation within the Army is good. It has been geared to support the attack and if the Communications Zone can continue to put supplies within reach of [Third] Army, we can continue. Presently we have a strong Signal Communication Network, well placed and in operation. Third Army's continued attack is a constant threat to communications within the salient. A general [enemy] withdrawal permits the enemy to effect reconstruction of forces, later permitting him the initiative.[5]

One obvious flaw in this appreciation is the first sentence, which undervalued German striking power in Twenty-First and Sixth Army Group areas.

Despite Third Army's current level of combat power, Patton wanted more, particularly to accomplish his mission of containing the Germans east of the Meuse. He lost the 87th Infantry Division to SHAEF reserve on December 25, and it was now in the Reims area. He urged Bradley to press for redeployment of the 17th Airborne and 11th Armored Divisions from Reims to a switch position along the Semois River, "from which location they could cover the left flank of the Third Army and be just as well placed to protect the rest of the American forces as they were on the line of the Meuse."[6] Patton was frustrated with the delay in doing so, but Eisenhower was wary about committing the newly created SHAEF reserve prematurely and potentially in the wrong place.

German Capability

In the southern half of the salient the Germans were defending along a sixty-five-mile front from St. Hubert to Echternach. In the west Lüttwitz's *XLVII Panzerkorps* consisted of the *2nd* and *9th PDs* and *Panzer Lehr*, minus *KG von Hauser* (*PGR 901*), which had remained southeast of Bastogne. *KG von Poschinger* (*PGR 902*), centered on St. Hubert, was screening a twenty-one-mile front from Wanlin to Remagne for *2nd* and *9th PDs* at the tip of the *Fifth Panzer Armee* spear.[7] *PGR 115/15th PGD* was deployed between Flamierge and Mande–St. Étienne, southeast of *KG von Poschinger's* screen. Kokott's *26th VGD* was spread all over the Bastogne perimeter, covering sixteen miles of front. The reconnaissance battalion was in the Mande–St. Étienne–Senonchamps area, with *Fusilier Regiment 39* to the southwest in the Sibret–Villeroux area overlooking the Neufchâteau–Bastogne highway. *VGR 77* was to the northwest above *PGR 115*, while the *Pionier* company and *VGR 78* were deployed on the northeast face of the Bastogne salient between Noville and Mageret.

The *Fifth Panzer–Seventh Armee* boundary ran from Marvie to Wardin. South of the boundary *KG von Hauser*, attached to the *26th VGD*, was southeast of Bastogne between Marvie and Lutrebois.[8] The remainder of the *15th PGD* was between Lutrebois and Lutremange, while the weary *5th FJD* was west of Harlange, holding Brandenberger's extreme right or northwest flank as part of *LIII Armeekorps*. On December 27 Kokott's *Feldersatz* battalion and *KG von Hauser* would be transferred to Heilmann's command to bolster the weary *Fallschirmjägers*. The Germans probably possessed enough combat power around Bastogne to take the town by sheer weight, but all the attacks had been piecemeal, permitting the "light" 101st Airborne Division and key attachments to repeatedly react at critical sectors to prevent a significant breakthrough against a superior, armor-heavy force.[9]

The leftmost formation in *LIII Armeekorps* was the *FGB*, deployed north of the Sûre River between Kaundorf and Tadler. The *LXXXV Armeekorps* had the *79th VGD* in the Bourscheid area and the *352nd VGD* in the Ettelbruck–Diekirch area. The *LXXX Armeekorps* still had its original divisions, the *212th* and *276th VGDs*. The *416th Division* still occupied the Saar–Moselle triangle, and elements of four more divisions—the *36th* and *719th Divisions* and the *19th* and *559th VGDs*, described as "remnants" on Koch's work maps—maintained their positions opposite Walker's XX Corps. *Heeresgruppe B's* reserve, the *79th VGD*, had been committed. Of the *OKW* reserves, the *FBB*, *FGB*, and *3rd PGD* had been committed. The *9th VGD* was near Bitburg, and the *167th VGD* was at Berg–Ruland. Koch's work map for 2400 December 27 had the *10th SS PD* in reserve at the West Wall in *Sixth Panzer Armee's* sector, along with the *2nd* and *8th FJDs*. The *49th*, *275th*, and *348th Infantry Divisions* were listed as re-forming. Dietrich's second echelon—*II SS Panzerkorps*, with

Table 9.2. German Order of Battle versus Third Army Following the Relief of Bastogne

VIII Corps	III Corps	XII Corps	XX Corps
130 Panzer Lehr (–)	26 PGD	212 VGD	36 Inf Div (elms)
15 PGD	5 FJD	352 VGD	559 VGD (elms)
	FGB	276 VGD	719 Inf Div (elms)
	79 VGD		19 VGD (elms)
	PGR 901/Lehr		416 Inf Div

Note: Just south of the First Army–Third Army boundary were 2 PD (elms), 2 SS PD (elms), and 18 VGD. The table does not include 11 PD.

the *2nd* and *9th SS PDs* — had also been committed. Koch's work map for 2400 December 24 had the *2nd SS PD* in a new location, south of the army group boundary in the Manhay–Grandmenil sector, on Christmas Day.

Beyond Sibert's statement on December 26 that the enemy was "exhibiting a recklessness . . . that is unprecedented,"[10] an X-factor in the assessment of German capability at this time was the inability to positively identify the location of the *11th* and *21st PDs*. On December 21 Koch located the *11th PD* east of Vianden, a sudden change from its previous, consistent position in the Sarreguemines sector. On December 23 he placed it west of the Our, and on Christmas Day he located it northeast of the *5th FJD*. His work map for 2400 December 26 showed the division only a few miles north of Bastogne. As of December 24, Koch had consistently placed the *21st PD* opposite XX Corps, but on Christmas Day he placed it northeast of *11th PD*, with a question mark. The next day he had it only a few miles northeast of the *212th VGD* in the Bitburg area but designated it as unlocated.[11]

Sibert's maps were no more definitive. Bradley's situation map for 1200 December 26 located the *11th PD* north of the Ourthe River, and Sibert declared that "at least the tank elements" of the division had been identified in the fighting around Bastogne. This, however, was an inaccurate identification.[12] Sibert also located the *21st PD* far to the southeast in Lorraine, possibly moving in the direction of Kaiserlautern. Positive identification of the *21st PD* would prove elusive. Neither it nor the *11th PD* was ever west of the Our. Patton, of course, could never be sure, although he could be reasonably certain that both were somewhere opposite Third Army's right flank. The *11th PD*'s radio communications were

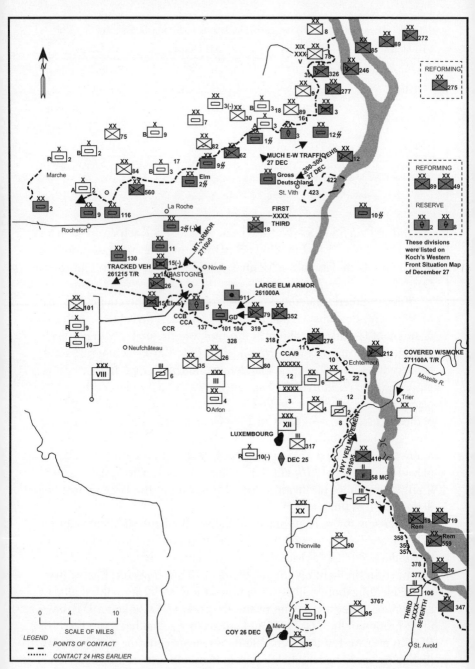

Map 9.1. Third Army G-2 Work Map, Situation as of 2400 December 27, 1944

"marked by exceptionally good security." Third Army lost radio contact with it in mid-December.[13] The ability of both *PDs* to intervene anywhere along the army's front had to be added to the overall German capability. This was important because it altered the perception of force ratios. On December 27 Koch's theater map listed fourteen division equivalents in Third Army's zone, compared with nine in First Army's zone and fourteen and a half combined in the zones of Twenty-First and Sixth Army Groups. Based on this assessment, Third Army, with only eleven division equivalents, faced 37 percent of identified, deployed German divisions in the west, whereas there were six other Allied armies to confront the rest. Six other German divisions were listed by Koch as re-forming or in reserve. Patton also had to consider the German capability to deploy additional combat power against Third Army from the north side of the salient. Montgomery had not yet transitioned to the offensive, so the possibility of a shift in the main effort could not be ignored.

The possible intervention of German combat power against Third Army from north of the army group boundary was dependent on Hitler's willingness to fully commit *Fifteenth Armee* and the continued defensive posture of First Army. Hitler's decision to hold back *Fifteenth Armee* was a serious error because it freed Ninth Army to send five divisions to First Army during the first week of the offensive.[14] In turn, Hodges, faced with no threat to his center, was able to freely redeploy and decisively engage *Sixth Panzer Armee*. Not committing *Fifteenth Armee* also meant that Montgomery had flexibility in using XXX Corps. Bradley met with Montgomery on December 25 at St. Trond, Belgium. According to Air Marshal Robb, Bradley was "very disturbed" because Montgomery was focused on defense for the foreseeable future. Although Montgomery suggested the next day that the time was approaching when he could pass over to the offensive—that is, after the Germans had reached their culminating point—he was intent on creating reserves. Indeed, only three days before, he had considered pulling V Corps off the Elsenborn ridge because that terrain feature formed a salient.[15]

Bradley and Patton discussed the former's unpleasant encounter at St. Trond on Christmas night. "Monty says that the First Army cannot attack for three months," noted Patton, "and that the only attack that can be made is by me, but that I am too weak; hence we should fall back to the Saar–Vosges line or even to the Moselle."[16] Montgomery in fact said no such thing. He signaled the Chief of the Imperial General Staff (CIGS), Field Marshal Sir Alan F. Brooke, that night and warned, "It must be

Table 9.3. Tracking the *11th* and *21st Panzer Divisions*

	11 PD Location	21 PD Location
Dec 16	Sarreguemines sector	Moving SE away from XX Corps
Dec 17	Sarreguemines sector	Still opposite XX Corps
Dec 18	Sarreguemines sector	Still opposite XX Corps
Dec 19	Sarreguemines sector	Still opposite XX Corps
Dec 20	Sarreguemines sector	Still opposite XX Corps
Dec 21	New location, E of Vianden	Still opposite XX Corps
Dec 22 0300	E of Vianden	Still opposite XX Corps
Dec 22 2400	W of Our River, Vianden sector	Still opposite XX Corps
Dec 23	No data available	No data available
Dec 24	W of Our River, Vianden sector	Still opposite XX Corps
Dec 25	NE of 5 FJD	NE of 11 PD with "?"
Dec 26	N of Bastogne	NE of 212 VGD (unlocated)
Dec 27	N of Bastogne	Unlocated
Dec 28	No data available	No data available
Dec 29	N of Bastogne	Unlocated
Dec 30	N of Bastogne	Unlocated (as well as 17 SS PGD)

Source: Third Army G–2 Work Maps.

clearly understood that we had not now got the troops for the offensive"; however, he anticipated having them in a matter of days, not three months. Though worried about the infantry strength in the American divisions under his command, Montgomery noted in his diary the next day: "The time was approaching when we could pass over to the offensive."[17] Clearly, Bradley had misunderstood Montgomery. Bradley wrote to Hodges on December 26 that he did not consider the situation to be as grave as Montgomery apparently did, and he wanted Hodges to study the problem from the perspective "of pushing the enemy back"; there was no hint of any envelopment in Bradley's suggestion. Patton could not readily counter increased German combat power shifted from the north; he had only two divisions left in XX Corps, and both had definite defensive missions. Extra combat power would therefore have to come from either Sixth Army Group or SHAEF reserves.[18] Montgomery had the advantage over Bradley, in that he controlled four armies. This allowed Montgomery to reorganize at will. Controlling only Patton's army, Bradley had to seek assistance from SHAEF.

In view of the German capability that remained opposite Third Army,

Patton's sense by December 26 that the enemy had "shot his wad" was somewhat premature. Although he could clearly count enemy divisions, the slow reaction to CCR's relief of Bastogne led to his misinterpretation of the German pause as a strategic culminating point, the point at which the attacker can no longer develop the situation to his advantage due to the natural diminishing strength of the initial attack and the inability to generate and sustain follow-on attacks. Even though the two main highways east and west of the corridor were still controlled by *Seventh Armee*, German dispositions were such that they prevented a rapid and concentrated reaction to CCR's penetration along the Assenois–Bastogne corridor. Direct fire artillery was the only immediate response to interdict CCR's slim corridor. An enemy armored column attacked from the Sibret–Morhet area at 2300 on December 26 but was repulsed.[19] Moreover, combat intelligence, POW interrogation reports, Sigint, and ULTRA were painting a picture of growing fuel and ammunition shortages and transportation difficulties.

The German culminating point on the southern flank actually occurred in both *Seventh* and *Fifth Panzer Armees*. Sibert declared in a periodic report on December 27 that German activity opposite Third Army "assumed a definitely defensive character." By sunset, ULTRA revealed *Seventh Armee*'s intentions to conduct a decisive defense on the north bank of the Sûre River because the situation was "especially critical on both wings."[20] This weakness was clearly perceived by Third Army on the ground. On December 26 Eddy learned that the Germans opposite Irwin's division were "swimming the river trying to get back and they were also feverishly trying to repair their bridges while our artillery was inflicting severe casualties on them."[21] Patton noted, "On our right the enemy in front of the 5th Division is clearly on the run. Last night we got a battalion of them with the proximity fuses and counted over 700 dead." By December 28 Irwin observed, the battle "appears to be virtually over except for minor cleaning up," having virtually destroyed the enemy "in front of us."[22]

ULTRA reinforced the perception in Third Army headquarters that the Germans had permanently transitioned to the defense across the entire front. Around Bastogne, ULTRA reported late on December 27 that the *15th PGD* was developing a defensive line from Magerotte to southeast of Sibret.[23] Koch therefore altered his EEIs to include indications of enemy withdrawal such as blown bridges, minefields, and the replacement of reconnaissance elements with engineers. His December 28 work map contained evidence of some demolitions at the western tip of the salient, but "who had performed them was not clear." Koch thought that one possible German line of action was a strong, limited-objective attack in the general area of Saarlautern.[24] How he came to the conclusion that the Germans possessed this capability is not readily apparent, particularly since he had the *11th* and *21st PDs* out of Lorraine at the moment; however, withdrawal of the 10th Armored Division back to Metz, diminished as it was, would mitigate the potential threat at Saarlautern.

Terrain Analysis

Once Patton understood where the potential threats were, he could study the ground to appreciate where to apply his combat power most effectively against German weakness. Twelfth Army Group's Weekly Intelligence Summary No. 20, issued on December 26, contained an appreciation of the terrain of the current Ardennes zone of action and the future zone of action in the Eifel. This permits a glimpse into Bradley's longer-term, next-campaign planning and its influence on Patton's shorter-term conduct of current operations.

Bradley's overall scheme of maneuver was to cross the Rhine at Cologne (Köln) with First Army and at Frankfurt with Third Army and link up the two armies east of the river.[25] Twelfth Army Group planners appreciated that a line running from Luxembourg to Cologne offered lines of action "parallel with the pattern of terrain corridors, ridges, compartments and major routes." Deductions from the terrain revealed four lines of action: lines A and B were west of the West Wall and converged on St. Vith, while lines C and D were "dependent on TRIER, the possession of which is almost essential to their exploitation" because it was the center of "a critical four-way confluence of difficult stream obstacles." Trier was a "strong natural pivot and anchor" that acted as the gateway to lines C and D, including the ridge routes via Bitburg. The Luxembourg Plain acted as the portal to lines A and B.[26]

Discernible from the analysis was the lack of corridors running from northwest to southeast. The only avenue of approach in the north was east of Monschau, but the Germans still held it. They also retained control of Schmidt. Neither Elsenborn nor Losheim were viable staging areas either. Planners at First Army and Twelfth Army Group argued that there was no major highway leading from Montgomery's side southeast into the Eifel area by which a pincer deep in the Eifel could be executed.[27] There

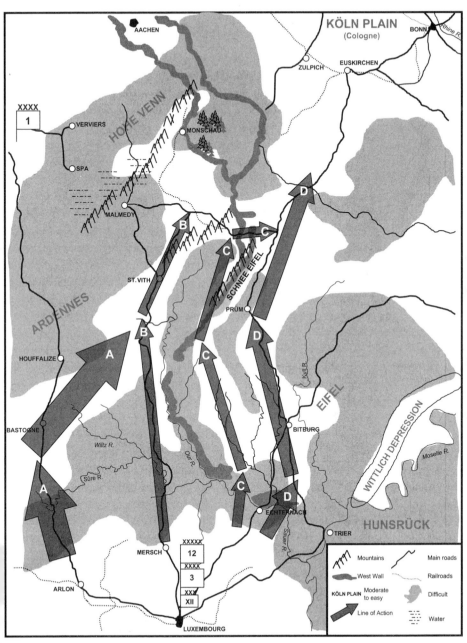

Map 9.2. Twelfth Army Group, Military Aspects of Terrain Area of the Eifel,
December 28, 1944

were roads that crossed the Schnee Eifel in a southeasterly direction. One went from Elsenborn to Bullange to Prüm, another went from St. Vith to Habscheid to Pronsfeld, and a third went from Schonberg to Bleialf to Prüm. However, weather conditions, including deep snow, were not conducive to a rapid advance in that direction.

Twelfth Army Group's estimate of the situation issued two days later was based on this terrain appreciation. The best corridor, "the one best suited for tank action," was line A, along the Bastogne–St. Vith ridge. The next best was the easternmost corridor, line D, following the Bitburg–Prüm ridgeline between the Prüm and Kyll Rivers. To enter this corridor, however, required an assault crossing of the Sauer River. The advance northward in this corridor then had to be protected on the right by deployments in the direction of Trier.

Enemy capabilities were intimately tied to Twelfth Army Group's lines of action and were identified as follows: (1) the availability of reserves to counterattack any offensive action by Twelfth Army Group, (2) the reinforcement of troops in the salient for further impetus, and (3) the ability to counterattack in another sector. The area north of the Aachen salient toward Maastricht was identified as the most likely area for such a counterattack, but Saarbrücken, just south of the XX Corps–Seventh Army boundary, was rated second. It was estimated that "we have available [a] sufficient margin of superiority to warrant the launching of a strong counter-attack [of] about Corps strength." The preferred line of action was to continue attacking in corridor A, while the balance of Third Army maintained defensive positions along the line of the Sauer and Saar Rivers (XII and XX Corps), "releasing maximum number of troops for the counter-attack." Bradley favored corridor A because it took advantage of the best terrain in the area and was the widest, thereby permitting the simultaneous deployment of more combat power; in addition, it was only twenty-two miles from the edge of the Bastogne salient to St. Vith.

The logic of corridor A was undeniable; it was the staff college solution. However, the corridor also worked for the Germans and, when wedded to the first capability described earlier, implied attrition. What is most illuminating is the army group's conclusion that "this line of action does not cut off enemy troops on the southern shoulder of the salient east of the LUXEMBOURG border, though a secondary attack up the ETTELBRUCK corridor [B] converging with the main attack on the southern shoulder would furnish additional protection for the east flank of the main attack." When Twelfth Army Group planners looked at Patton's Echternach–Bitburg line of action, they conceded that it had "the advantage that the attack leads directly to an objective; the STADTKYLL–BLANKENHEIM area from which further offensive action can be launched." However, they concluded that the assault crossing, fighting through the West Wall, and the possibility of delay in the rougher country north of Bitburg would make "the closing of the salient by this method a considerably longer operation than our other line of action." The stated objective of the counterattack was to "trap the maximum troops in the salient" and favorably position forces for further offensive operations.[28] Yet the preferred line of action in corridor A would only drive the Germans back, not trap them. It is logical to assume that a key element in Bradley's support for corridor A was the fact that it represented the shortest route to Houffalize, the point at which Eisenhower had determined First Army would return to Twelfth Army Group. Bradley claimed that on December 26 he demanded of Bedell Smith that First and Ninth Armies be returned to Twelfth Army Group.[29] Patton's less orthodox Bitburg line of action meant that Bradley would not get First and Ninth Armies back until much later, and this was probably more than he was willing to tolerate.

Comparing Lines of Action

Patton certainly recognized that, from his perspective in the south, St. Vith represented a legitimate objective. "I remember he looked at the map," said Brigadier Edgar T. Williams, Montgomery's General Staff officer 2 (intelligence), "and said 'That's where I'll go'—pointing to St. Vith."[30] It is unclear how Patton envisioned getting there. It seems certain that he favored corridor B (Skyline Drive), one of the three lines of action he had identified back on December 18 before going to Verdun. The Bitburg option was developed later. The southern entry point for corridor B was in the Ettelbruck–Diekirch area. The corridor had two appealing aspects: it merged at St. Vith with the larger corridor A, so it was not a dead end, and it had the legitimate objective of cutting main supply routes (MSRs) and interdicting crossings of the Our River. Patton, however, was influenced against it by Grow, who objected to the Skyline Drive attack because it offered no room for maneuver and because an advance north would be vulnerable to flank attack from the West Wall. On December 26 Patton noted, "I think I made a mistake in bringing the 6th Armored Division up so soon, it might have been better sent to the left. I can still do it but that requires two moves. The corridor on the right, that is, north of Diekirch, is rather narrow for an armored division."[31]

Patton also considered forcing the Sauer River near Echternach and attacking northeast to Bitburg. This was corridor D. Getting to Bitburg looked simple when studying a 1:1,000,000 map, but if one considered realistic lines of action, a 1:50,000 map suddenly revealed the complexity of the military problem: terrain dictated everything. To get to Bitburg, Patton would have to achieve the following sequential tasks: (1) execute a deliberate crossing of the Sauer River against enemy resistance, (2) penetrate the bunkers of the West Wall, (3) maintain contact with III Corps, (4) maintain left and right flank security for the assault crossing force, (5) cross the Prüem River, (6) cover the twelve miles to Bitburg, and (7) support himself, thereby protecting his LC. Though difficult, it was not impossible. The weather, a factor Patton simply could not overlook, also appeared favorable. Despite a minimum temperature of seventeen degrees Fahrenheit on December 27, Koch declared that the cold was aiding ground movement.[32]

When V Corps had hit the West Wall in September, Major General Lundsford E. Oliver's 5th Armored Division had attacked between Vianden and Echternach. There was high ground near Mettendorf, only five miles inside Germany, and it was twelve miles to Bitburg. Hill 407 was just southeast of Mettendorf. There were two corridors of approach to Bitburg in the area. The one that went northeast from the vicinity of Wallendorf was sharply compartmentalized and offered fewer good roads. The second corridor was due north from the eastward bend of the border east of Echternach. The right flank of this corridor hugged the Nussbaumer Hardt—a large forest barrier—but the avenue opened up a few miles inside Germany to allow for greater lateral deployment. The ground rose abruptly beyond Wallendorf. This corridor was approximately four miles wide from Wallendorf to Niedersgegen. The West Wall was very thin there, and the river near Wallendorf was only forty yards wide (in September). Gerow picked the first corridor for the 5th Armored Division, and CCR quickly punched through to the Prüem River six miles distant. Oliver was ordered to seize Bitburg, then swing north on main roads to Pronsfeld and Prüm, right through the Eifel. This involved a march of fifteen to thirty miles by two armored columns parallel to, but deep behind, the enemy facing the 4th and 28th Infantry Divisions.[33]

Patton's Eifel campaign following the Bulge proves that, from a terrain standpoint, it was possible to execute the Bitburg maneuver—the earlier in the Ardennes campaign the better, because contraction by *Heeresgruppe B* would only increase its FSR at the West Wall. On February 6 Eddy's XII Corps crossed the Sauer between Wallendorf and Echternach on a seven-and-a-half-mile front, with the objective of capturing Bitburg. Granted, it took Eddy several days to "carve a full-fledged bridgehead from the inhospitable terrain," but Gaffey's 4th Armored Division successfully maneuvered all the way to Bitburg and beyond.[34] This was facilitated, of course, by the heavy attrition of German armor by that point. Bitburg was a legitimate intermediate objective for the current campaign in the Ardennes and a transitional objective to the next campaign because it was the most important communications center east of the Our River. Units detraining along the Rhine as far north as Remagen swung south through Bitburg on their way to the Ardennes front.[35] Securing Bitburg would have aided the fulfillment of Bradley's larger concept of crossing the Rhine between Cologne and Bonn.

In considering the value of corridor D, Patton was heavily influenced by his subordinates. On December 26 Eddy went to Luxembourg to see Patton. Bradley was also present, and Eddy noted, "Omar thinks the Germans are trying to hold in our sector and launch an attack to the northwest. He was somewhat in favor of me holding rather than to attack with the 6th Armored and the Army Commander also seemed to be of this opinion." Eddy believed there would be "many advantages to attacking across the river and northeast to Bitburg. However, if we do this, that is, holding on the right and attacking with a flank division, we would have to widen the sector of the other divisions in order to protect our exposed flank."[36]

Patton and Eddy discussed corridor D again the next day, after Eddy had talked with Irwin and Grow. Both division commanders rejected an assault crossing. Irwin noted: "Consulted with staff and consensus of opinion is that we could get across, but could not hold out on other side due to insufficient backing and a not too good terrain setup. Although speed is essential, it would take quite a while to mount the operation, particularly from an Engineer standpoint. Certainly worth a thought as line in front of us is weak and we have destroyed most of the garrison." Eddy explained the rough terrain to Patton on December 27, and when he was asked to suggest an alternative line of action, Eddy replied: "I told him I would hold this corps [XII] and the three infantry divisions and send the 6th Armored around through the III Corps and attack over more favorable terrain [corridor A]. He said he would think about it and that I should

Table 9.4. XII Corps Strength, December 26–27, 1944

Formations	Corps Units	Artillery	Cavalry	Engineers
4 Inf Div	702 Tk Bn	512 FA Bn	2 Cav Gp	1135 Engr C Gp
5 Inf Div	610 TD Bn	752 FA Bn (155)		1103 Engr C Gp
80 Inf Div (–318 CT)	803 TD Bn	802 FA Bn		
6 Armd Div	808 TD Bn	945 FA Bn (155)		
		974 FA Bn (155)		
		273 FA Bn		
		81 FA Bn (155)		
		174 FA Bn (155)		
		244 FA Bn (155)		
		255 FA Bn		
		775 FA Bn		
		215 FA Bn (155)		
		107 FA Bn*		
		108 FA Bn*		
		695 FA Bn		
		191 FA Bn		
		276 FA Bn		

Note: Division reserve consisted of 609 TD Bn/10 Armd Div in the vicinity of Mersch, and 68 Tk Bn/6 Armd Div.
* Reverting to 28 Inf Div control at 1200 December 28.
Source: XII Corps Operational Directive No. 59, December 26, 1944.

prepare to hold here." Later that day Patton directed Eddy to hold.[37] So Eddy, Grow, and Irwin were all against corridor D, even though on December 26 XII Corps was ideally situated for the attempt after driving *LXXX Armeekorps* back across the Sauer River with relative ease. However, XII Corps was already transitioning to the defense with MLRs, intermediate delaying positions, demolitions, obstacles, and minefields. Eddy set up the corps for counterattack purposes, not offensive purposes.[38]

On December 28 Eddy was back at army headquarters to discuss crossing the river. Also present was Major General Samuel E. Anderson, deputy commander of the Eighth Air Force. Eddy declared, "If this plan has the success we hope for we will definitely put the Germans in a tight spot." Eddy told Irwin that day to "get prepared to defend a river line and make every effort to have his troops made as comfortable as possible." Indeed, XII Corps Operational Directive No. 60, issued at 1200, stated that the corps "continues to clear area S[outh] of SAUER R and regroups."

Patton noted, "During the night and after talking with Brad I am going to plan an attack over the Sauer River on Bonn, crossing near Echternach. General Anderson of the 8th Air Force is here and we are planning a combined operation with an air blitz. I will precede it with an attack on Saarburg by the XX Corps and so to—if possible—pull the troops in that direction."[39]

The Saarburg action was likely the result of Bradley's concern about German concentrations near Trier. Concern about right flank security for XII Corps as it crossed the Sauer River was lessened somewhat by the December 23 destruction of the Saarburg bridge by Allied airpower and the constant targeting of bridges in the Moselle Valley. Since that day, Allied airpower had been interdicting the battlefield in two belts: medium bombers of IX Bombardment Division/Ninth Air Force from west of the Rhine to south of Saarburg, and heavy bombers east of the Rhine beyond Frankfurt. Moreover, the deep trench of the Moselle River isolated German forces south of it in the Saar region—forces that might otherwise move north to strike Third Army in the southern flank. Patton concluded that the operation would be "very profitable if we can get the troops, but it should not be attempted with less than five divisions."[40]

The apparent dilemma about whether to launch the Sauer crossing is indicated in Canine's chief of staff journal entry at 1115 on December 27, where he noted that the 6th Armored Division, with the 10th CT from Irwin's division attached, would attempt "crossing of SAUER R early 29 Dec."[41] Planning proceeded apace that day, and Eddy recalled some of the details as follows:

> [Brigadier General Harold W.] Blakeley presented his ideas on the operation for crossing the river. He strongly recommends having at least two divisions and if possible three making a coordinated attack. I agree with him on this. The Air Corps will arrange for an almost continuous bombing as we cross. I am working on a plan by which we can load the infantry into trucks and DUKW's and after the bombing right along the river line lifts and rolls back we can rush the infantry who will make the initial crossing down to the bank and we hope in some cases to push them across in the DUKW's. There are a good many disadvantages of crossing the river right in the face of the Siegfried Line. However, I hope that the bombing will neutralize what troops are manning the line, and I don't think that it is strongly held.[42]

Patton's desire to exploit corridors B and D was ultimately based on his realization that corridor A was enticing for both sides. This illustrates where Patton clearly separated himself from his orthodox superiors. He believed that one should "never attack where the enemy expects you to come. It is much better to go over difficult ground where you are not expected than it is over good ground where you are expected. This remark applies to units to include the division. For corps and larger units an exception is necessary, in that such units must take ground where roads and railways permit the establishment of lines of supply. These roads and railways will probably be defended."[43]

The initial focus on Bastogne shaped the entire battle and left very little operational flexibility, primarily because it represented the entry point to corridor A. Moreover, Bradley wanted Patton to "inflict maximum damage" on the Germans.[44] This implied attrition, and corridor A guaranteed that outcome. The relief of Bastogne offered the perfect opportunity to transition to a new line of action farther east to keep the Germans off guard, but the risk inherent in corridors B, C, and D dissuaded Bradley. These corridors were risky because each was in fact a *turning movement,* an envelopment "which passes around the enemy's main forces, striking at some vital point deep in the hostile rear." Doctrine cautioned that a force executing such a maneuver "usually operates so far from the secondary attack that the principal tactical groupings are beyond mutual supporting distance." The force executing a turning movement had to be strong enough to avoid defeat in detail.[45] This was why Patton calculated that he needed five divisions.

This basic fact was not appreciated by Weyland when he observed that even if the Germans reached Antwerp, Third Army could have "cut up right behind them" to end the war.[46] Weyland's bombast was a gross underestimation of not only the disruption that would have ensued in First Army's rear area and the Oise base section but also the difficulties involved in the ground movement necessary to counteract it. Trevor Dupuy argued that "about fifteen German divisions . . . might have been cut off, and it is hard to see how, even in speculation, they could have avoided destruction" had Patton struck toward Bitburg.[47] However, the straight-line distance from Elsenborn ridge to Prüm was twenty miles. Had First and Third Armies somehow managed to reach Prüm and Bitburg simultaneously, there still would have been a gap of seventeen miles between those two points through which the Germans could withdraw. Trapping the Germans in the Eifel had a low probability of success based on the weather conditions.

Bradley and Patton could have mitigated the risk inherent in corridors B, C, and D by limiting their objectives. Third Army did not necessarily have to get to Bitburg, but the establishment of bridgeheads across the Sûre and Sauer Rivers at the entrances to corridors B and D might have had significant repercussions on how the Germans deployed their reserves. The threat of Third Army deployed at the entrances to these important corridors certainly would have drawn a strong reaction from the Germans, potentially altering the picture around Bastogne. They would have had no choice but to react strongly to patrols and fire cutting their LC. Even if a Sauer River bridgehead proved too risky, XII Corps should have immediately established a bridgehead over the Sûre. Indeed, this operation should have been started even as III Corps closed in on Bastogne.

With Patton, it was an article of faith that one should never halt on the near side of a river. Securing bridgeheads offered flexibility because "even if you do not intend to exploit the crossing, the possession of a bridgehead . . . cramps the enemy's style."[48] This was why he maintained the bridgehead at Saarlautern. Bridgehead operations were not simple, however, and any bridgehead across the Sauer at Echternach had to be sufficient to protect the crossings from long-range German artillery. That meant a bridgehead ten miles deep held by a full division. Nevertheless, the risk associated with establishing immediate bridgeheads at the entrance to either corridor B or D was justified. *Seventh Armee*'s left flank was given far too great a breather following the relief of Bastogne.

Patton did not articulate a double envelopment in the Eifel to trap the Germans. In fact, back in Normandy he told Allen that "traps should not be closed. [It was] a mistake to do that, contrary to popular belief. The wiser course is to leave an opening and then let the sons-of-bitches walk themselves to death."[49] Rather, Patton sought to maneuver the enemy out of the Ardennes and exploit opportunities thereby created. However, it was not meant to be. Restrained by Bradley from exploiting corridors B and D, Patton was forced to confront the remaining German combat power head-on in corridor A. As he began preparations for what Clausewitz referred to as pointless battles—those that cannot be fully exploited—he would try to keep his preferred lines of action alive.

10

Path to Attrition,
December 27–29

It is of decisive importance that the enemy attack wedge towards
Bastogne and in the Bastogne area be destroyed as soon as possible.
— Rundstedt to Model, December 28

Late on December 25 Manteuffel told Model that the window of opportunity to take Bastogne had vanished and that the attacks in the Marche sector had achieved only limited success. This estimate reached Model only
after he had sent his own estimate at 2000 to Hitler via telegram through
OB West, recommending that the bulk of the panzer armies should advance to the area of Ciney (approximately nine miles from the Meuse)
and wheel to the northeast to attack Allied forces opposite *Sixth Panzer
Armee*. Model had resurrected his "small solution" and clearly identified
Third Army as the main Allied effort, seeking a decision between Bastogne and Echternach. To protect the south flank of this wheel movement, Bastogne would have to be taken. He assumed that all the reserves
in his area, including OKW reserves, would "be available for deployment
to achieve these objectives," and he also expected the addition of three to
four panzer divisions from other theaters of war for the formation of an
operational reserve. Model's telegram was probably the latest available information Hitler had from the front, but it did not include Manteuffel's
pessimistic assessment.[1]

Model's telegram was most likely discussed at the Führer conference
early the next morning, at which point Hitler concluded that intermediate objectives were still possible, contingent on regaining equilibrium
along the Sûre River against Third Army and destroying American forces
between the Ourthe and Meuse Rivers north of the Marche–Dinant line.
Hitler completely rejected Guderian's Christmas Eve plea to halt the

offensive and shift the panzer divisions east, remarking that the Russian Front "must take care of itself." By Christmas Eve the Russians had encircled Budapest, but Hitler refused to believe the intelligence estimates of *Fremde Heere Ost* (Foreign Armies East).[2] Model's estimate was much more palatable, and OKW issued orders to continue operations according to *Heeresgruppe B*'s concept.

Hitler's simultaneous pursuit of the Marche plateau and Bastogne undermined Manteuffel's ability to concentrate his combat power in time and space. To achieve as much concentration as possible, he proceeded to reshape the battlefield, with Model's tacit approval. Manteuffel received permission to call off the attacks in the Marche area and withdraw *2nd PD* at 1500 on December 26. An hour later the orders were issued to *XLVII* and *LVIII Panzerkorps*. Under heavy pressure, *2nd PD* fought its way back to the Rochefort area, where the *9th PD* and *Panzer Lehr* had established new defensive positions. Hitler ordered the *FBB* to cease supporting the *116th PD* at 1500 and move to Bastogne to strike Patton's relief wedge from the direction of Hompré. Although the brigade had taken Hampteau, it began moving south via Halleux–Ronchamps to a road junction west of Champlon. Wagener viewed the decision to redeploy it with a "heavy heart" because it was the first action that had nothing to do with trying to reach the Meuse.[3] *Fifth Panzer Armee* had reached its culminating point in trying to get to the Meuse. With the retreat of the *2nd PD* and the withdrawal of the *FBB* from Hampteau, the left wing of Dietrich's army was the only sector conducting full-scale offensive operations by December 26.[4]

Manteuffel began to create a defensive front on the triangle Bastogne–Rochefort–Amonines. The Rochefort–Amonines line was sixteen miles, the Rochefort–Bastogne line was twenty miles, and the Amonines–Bastogne line was twenty-four miles. He reflected that he did so, "even at the price of giving up parts of the terrain which had just been won . . . in order to straighten out the situation in the Bastogne area first." He envisioned withdrawing the army line to Odeigne–Laroche–St. Hubert and ultimately establishing an MLR along the Vielsalm–Pt. Tailles–Houffalize–Noville line.[5] This certainly would have permitted a much greater concentration of force for the Bastogne operation.

Manteuffel's reaction to Patton's relief of Bastogne was a three-phase plan. First, the ring around Bastogne had to be reclosed. Second, Patton's forces had to be pushed south. Third, Bastogne would have to be taken in a final assault. Time was the critical element in the first phase; sufficient

Table 10.1. *Armee Gruppe Lüttwitz*

XXXIX Panzerkorps (attacking east to west)	XLVII Panzerkorps (attacking west to east)	Reinforcements on the Way (days away)
1 SS PD (elms)	FBB	12 SS PD (elms)
167 VGD	3 PGD (–)	9 SS PD (–)
PGR 901/Lehr	26 VGD (–)	340 VGD (full)
	15 PGD (–)	

force had to be assembled quickly to overwhelm Patton's ability to reinforce the corridor. Manteuffel believed he had a maximum window of only forty-eight hours to execute phase one, but he was already twenty-four hours behind his estimate.[6] Brandenberger's ability to continue to block Third Army was the critical element of the second phase.

Manteuffel brought forward *Generalleutnant* Karl Decker's *XXXIX Panzerkorps* headquarters from *OKW* reserve on December 27 to take over the battle on the east side of Bastogne; Lüttwitz's *XLVII Panzerkorps* would look after the fight on the west side. Decker was subordinated to Lüttwitz, and a provisional organization that was intermediate in status between corps and army level, called *Armee Gruppe Lüttwitz*, was established for a few days for the sole purpose of coordinating the Bastogne fight.[7] *XXXIX Panzerkorps*, with the diminished *1st SS PD* and the fresh *167th VGD* coming up from *OKW* reserve, was to attack the corridor from the east. *XLVII Panzerkorps*, with the *FBB*, elements of the *26th VGD*, and the *3rd* and *15th PGDs*, was to attack the corridor from the west. Of the formations envisioned for this pincer attack, only the *26th VGD, 15th PGD, FBB,* and *KG von Hauser* were in position on December 26. The *167th VGD* was twenty-two miles northeast of Bastogne at Burg-Reuland, Belgium, during the morning of December 26.[8] The *3rd PGD* was preparing for an assault on Elsenborn ridge and would be placed under Lüttwitz's command the next day. Model also promised Manteuffel the *9th* and *12th SS PDs* and the full-strength *340th VGD,* but they would not arrive in time for the attack on December 30.

Manteuffel's calculations and preparations were subject to the pressure of the ongoing battle throughout the salient. That battle quickly went against *Heeresgruppe B* as December 27 dawned. *OB West's* morning report announced that both panzer armies "are forced completely into the defense." *OB West* also "expected that the units of the Third Army under the energetic leadership of General Patton will make strong attacks against our southern flank."[9] Those attacks commenced at 0800, when III Corps renewed its advance north to widen and strengthen the corridor into Bastogne. Gaffey's forward elements were generally along the line Assenois–Hompré–Hollange–Honville. While CCR conducted convoy duty on the Assenois–Bastogne road, Gaffey's other combat commands proceeded to widen the corridor by securing roads to the east and west. CCB attacked from west of Hompré and engaged *PGR 15/15th PGD* in two patches of woods northeast of Assenois. The 10th AIB made contact with the 101st Airborne Division perimeter at 1900, and only a few minutes later the 2nd Battalion/318th CT, attached to CCB, also contacted the perimeter, opening up a second road into Bastogne. On the right, CCA, with tank destroyers watching avenues of approach to its tank lanes and aided by 1st Battalion/318th CT, advanced toward Sainlez.[10] By sundown Gaffey had cleared Sainlez, Hompré, Livarchamps, and Salvacourt defended by *FJR 14*.

Gaffey's tactical problem on the left was to widen the corridor and secure the left flank. CCA/9th Armored Division, attached to the 4th Armored Division at 1300 the previous day, attacked in a single column of three task forces screened by C Troop/89th Reconnaissance Squadron. CCA marched fifty-five miles to its assembly area eleven miles southwest of Bastogne in twenty-four hours. Shortly after crossing the LD, the reconnaissance troops discovered enemy in Sibret.[11] Mines laid by VIII Corps during the initial withdrawal held up one of the task forces north of Vauxles-Rosières, but only moderate resistance was encountered as elements of CCA advanced to the outskirts of Sibret by 1400 and quickly cleared it from rearguard elements of the *5th FJD* and *26th VGD*. By dark CCA captured the high ground just north of Sibret and Villeroux from elements of *PGR 104/15th PGD*, pushed to the edge of Chenogne, and temporarily occupied it. West of CCA/9th Armored Division, the 6th Cavalry Group reported minimal enemy contact but discerned that *Panzer Lehr* was screening along the line Hatrival–Vesqueville–Moircy–Remagne and had established strong outposts.[12]

As CCA/9th Armored Division advanced north, the first elements of Otto Remer's *FBB* began arriving west of Bastogne, following its twenty-mile move south from Hampteau. A severe fuel shortage prevented the brigade from arriving earlier; half the formation's vehicles had to tow the other half. Upon arrival, the brigade CP was set up in Tronle. Remer conducted a personal reconnaissance and quickly realized that Kokott's

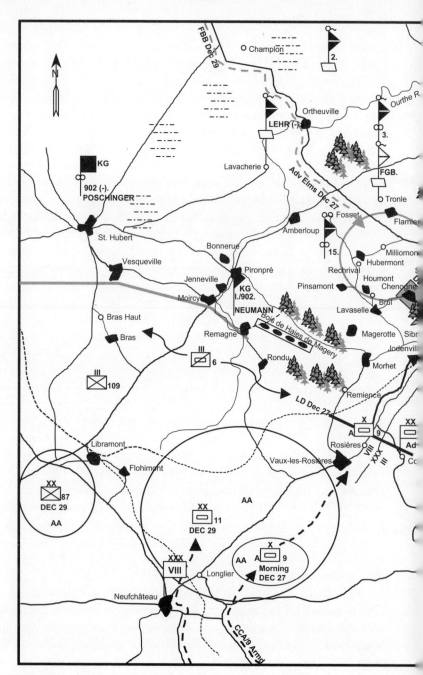

Map 10.1. Third Army Operations, December 27–29, 1944

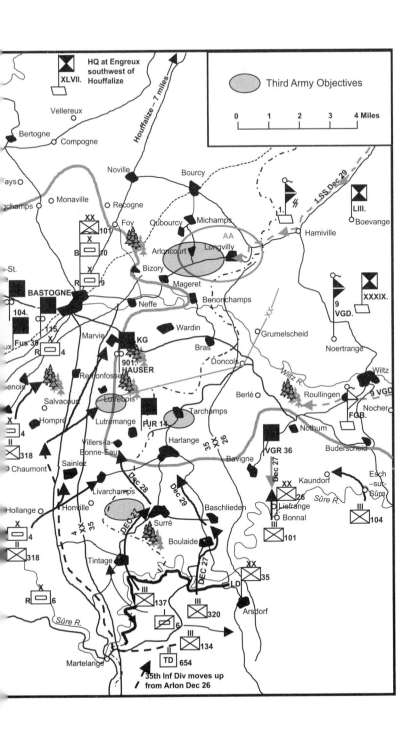

HQ at Engreux
southwest of
Houffalize

XLVII.

Third Army Objectives

0   1   2   3   4 Miles

Vellereux

Bertogne   Compogne

Houffalize – 7 miles

Noville   Bourcy

...ays

Monaville   Recogne

...champs

XX
101

X
B   10

X
R   9

Foy   Oubourcy   Michamps

Arloncourt   Longvilly

Bizory

Mageret

Neffe   Benonchamps

BASTOGNE

104.

115.

Fus 39   Marvie   KG

R   4   901.

HAUSER

Renfonfossey

Salvacourt   Lutrebois

Hompré

X
4

II
318

Chaumont   Sainlez

Livarchamps

Hollange   Honville

X
4

II
318

R   6

Sûre R.

Martelange

AA

1. SS   Dec 29

LIII.

Boevange   Hamiville

9
VGD.

XXXIX.

Grumelscheid

Noertrange

Wardin

Bras

Doncols

Berlé   Roullingen   9 VGD

Wiltz R.   Wiltz

Nocher

FGB.

Lutremange   FUR 14   Tarchamps

Nothum

Villers-la-
Bonne-Eau   Harlange

35   XX   26   Bavigne

VGR 36

Buderscheid

Esch
-sur-
Sûre

Dec 27

Kaundorf

XX   26   Sûre R.

Liefrange

III   104

Dec 28

Dec 29   Baschlieden

Bonnal

III
101

DEC 27   Surré

Boulaide

XX   35

Tintage   DEC 27   LD

XX   35

III
137   Arsdorf

III
320

6

III
134

TD   654

35th Inf Div moves up
from Arlon Dec 26

screen between Sibret and Morhet was too weak to offer proper protection to *FBB*'s Flamierge–Chenogne–Pinsamont assembly area. The high ground south of Chenogne needed to be held "under all circumstances if the conditions for an attack to the south were to remain favorable." Remer therefore positioned a battery of 105mm Flak guns and a light field howitzer battery in Chenogne to dominate the high ground west and south of the town.[13] During the night, elements of *Fusilier Regiment 39/26th* VGD reinforced Villeroux, but artillery and fighter-bombers shattered the village and the defense.[14]

Millikin's tactical problem on the right flank of the corridor was pushing Baade's newly arrived 35th Infantry Division north quickly enough to protect Gaffey's right. This required an advance of some seven to eight miles over difficult ground. At 0800 Baade attacked through the 6th Cavalry Squadron on a five-mile front between Tintage and Bavigne with the 137th CT on the left, the 320th CT on the right, and the 134th CT in reserve. The 137th CT quickly crossed the Sûre at Tintage, moving by truck into Gaffey's zone for a better approach, and it managed to clear Surré despite "bitter" resistance. The 320th CT also crossed the Sûre by dark and occupied Boulaide and Baschleiden. Crossing the Sûre, no more than twenty-five yards wide in places, was less of a problem than the steep ascent to the heights beyond. Despite being afforded no time for proper reconnaissance, the division made good initial progress in difficult terrain. To Baade's right, the 26th Infantry Division's 101st CT crossed the Sûre at Bonnal, while the 104th CT crossed at Esch-sur-Sûre and seized the high ground east of Kaundorf from the *FGB*, which had withdrawn to the north bank on December 26.[15]

Despite the favorable defensive terrain north of the Sûre River, *LIII Armeekorps* was the most vulnerable element in the entire southern flank. Brandenberger was aware of XII Corps' inactivity from December 26 onward, and he assumed the risk of transferring significant artillery assets from *LXXX Armeekorps* to *LXXXV Armeekorps*.[16] However, the transfer was slow, and little artillery could be brought forward to defend the line of the river and reinforce Rothkirch's weak formations. Heilmann's mission was to hold the Lutrebois–Villers-la-Bonne-Eau–Harlange salient under all circumstances as a prerequisite for *XXXIX Panzerkorps*' attack. His weary division was augmented by the attachment of *KG von Hauser* and the *FGB*, but as *Oberst* Werner Bodenstein, Rothkirch's chief of staff, reflected, despite the corps' best efforts, it was unable to properly support Heilmann. *Generalmajor* Hellmuth Mäder, who had come forward to replace the seriously wounded Kahler, quickly concluded that the combat power of the *FGB* had seriously deteriorated.[17]

During the afternoon of December 27, *LIII Armeekorps* informed *Seventh Armee* that it needed to establish a reserve defensive line to the rear to prevent the *5th FJD* from being cut off by the advance of the 26th Infantry Division. Brandenberger considered Paul's advance a "highly threatening" breakthrough in the rear of the *5th FJD* but rejected Rothkirch's request.[18] Instead, Brandenberger tried to reinforce *LIII Armeekorps* with the *9th VGD*, once it was released from the *OKW* reserve near Bitburg, but fuel and transport shortages limited movement to a single battalion at a time. About 60 to 70 percent of the *9th VGD* was "unfit for combat being war-injured," and it included many *Landesschuetzen* (Home Guard). According to the division commander, *Oberst* Werner Kolb, the first battalion to arrive, a bicycle battalion from *VGR 36*, was in a "completely exhausted condition" after a thirty-mile march; nevertheless, it was immediately committed at Liefrange against Paul's division four miles southwest of Wiltz, without either artillery or assault gun support. The result was predictable: the battalion was almost annihilated, suffering 40 percent casualties. Brandenberger declared that the "psychological effect of this fiasco later spread to the whole of the division." By the end of December 27, Paul had a secure bridgehead across the river, and Brandenberger believed the sacrifice of the battalion from the *9th VGD* had temporarily sealed the Harlange–Nothum–Duderscheid line.[19]

LXXX Armeekorps' task of holding the Sûre front to the east was helped by the Bourscheid bridgehead and the high ground west of Masseler. This high feature facilitated artillery coverage as far as Neiderfeulen and Heiderscheid.[20] Two hill masses at Ringel and near Bourscheid on the west bank of the Sûre, along with the heavily wooded areas around Kehmen and Welscheid, made the entire bridgehead position tough to penetrate. The *79th VGD* occupied the bridgehead, but Brandenberger could not gather enough combat power to do more than hold the ground. It was at only 80 percent of TO&E, and its *StuG* brigade never arrived. Only 10 percent were combat veterans, and the division commander, *Oberst* Kurt Hummel, who had replaced *Oberst* Alois Weber, reflected that the formation possessed "only a mediocre combat value." The *79th VGD* would spend December 27–29 launching small counterattacks against Ringel Hill, beyond the division's MLR, but it did not possess sufficient artillery to suppress American guns. Deeper interdictory fires were virtually impossible. Brandenberger could expect little additional assistance from

Heeresgruppe B because at 2200 on December 27 Rundstedt received a Führer order to take Bastogne under all circumstances by a concentric attack against the deep flanks of Patton's corridor.[21]

During the night Patton met with Middleton and Millikin to plan a new army offensive. With his preferred line of action shelved, Patton now revised his estimate to address the line dictated by Eisenhower and Bradley. That day Bradley discussed current and future operations with Eisenhower at Versailles. In the short term, Bradley pushed for an "immediate pincer attack against the waist" of the salient by a reinforced Third Army attacking out of Bastogne, northeast toward Houffalize and St. Vith, with two corps. Bradley hoped First Army would attack southeast toward Houffalize and St. Vith as well. Bradley's desire to strike quickly was based partly on his estimate. He had called Bedell Smith that morning, urging SHAEF to press Montgomery for action because the Germans had "reached the high water mark today" and would soon start to withdraw— "if not tonight, certainly tomorrow." Bradley apparently told Eisenhower he was prepared to move his headquarters to Dinant or Namur to coordinate the operations of First and Third Armies.[22] Although certainly leaning Bradley's way, Eisenhower deferred his decision until he talked to Montgomery the following day.

Patton envisioned meeting Bradley's tentative intent by attacking with one reinforced armored division and taking Houffalize "not later than the 30th," then attacking northeast on St. Vith with one armored division and two infantry divisions on December 31. VIII Corps, with the 101st Airborne Division, the combat commands of the 9th and 10th Armored Divisions, and the 6th Cavalry Group, would protect the left flank. At this point, Bastogne appeared secure. The only German action against the town was in the 327th GIR sector.[23] Gaffey was steadily widening the corridor; a convoy of seventy ambulances and forty supply trucks went into town at 0500, and the airlift continued during the day, despite effective German antiaircraft artillery.[24] Patton noted, however, that III Corps would keep control of VIII Corps units in Bastogne "until the situation is clarified." The III Corps after-action report observed that by the end of the day, the Germans seemed "content to fight a delaying action, evidencing stubborn resistance and little aggressiveness." The only indication of German reinforcement came from an ULTRA message received just after 2100, stating that an unspecified brigade had been transferred to Tronle to block the Bastogne garrison. This was a reference to the *FBB*.[25]

Patton's scheme of maneuver was not fully expressed. If he intended to have VIII Corps simply protect the left flank, it would be reasonable to deduce that III Corps was to conduct the attack toward both Houffalize and St. Vith. Patton's main attack was not immediately apparent either, but since the St. Vith axis had three divisions and the Houffalize axis had only one reinforced division, III Corps contained the main attack by definition. Patton boasted that if he could get just three more divisions, "I could win this war now."[26] He did not say where he would use them, but he most likely would have employed them in corridor D, where he felt he could achieve a decision.

As the Third Army staff continued preparing, resistance stiffened opposite VIII Corps on the morning of December 28, and the weather grounded XIX TAC. As Weyland noted, "No Ops 28 Dec *except* for 1 TAC R mission of 2 sorties." The *FBB* executed the attack for which it had been called south, but it failed to advance beyond the woods between Chenogne and Sibret. The woods changed hands several times during the day. Remer reflected that the flanking fire from Villeroux (CCA/9th Armored Division) had an "especially unpleasant effect." By nightfall he reported that his brigade was too weak to take Sibret alone and that concentrated artillery would be required to silence the American guns. Manteuffel and Lüttwitz both concluded that Remer had arrived at the end of the forty-eight-hour window and that Third Army's corridor was now too wide to close. No other formations were immediately at hand. As the *OB West* War Diary stated, Remer's brigade, the only reserve available, "has been committed." The *3rd PGD* was still closing in the Bastogne sector. *Generalmajor* Walter Denkert, the division commander, reflected that American air superiority "proved particularly detrimental," and it was "very difficult to move the Division forward."[27]

Late in the morning CCB/4th Armored Division finally linked up with the 101st Airborne Division's perimeter due south of Bastogne. The loss of the 1st Battalion/318th CT, which began moving back to the 80th Infantry Division, caused Earnest of CCA to become anxious about his open east flank. To compensate, he requested the 134th CT, Baade's reserve, to come up into the line on his right, with the task of taking Lutrebois east of the Arlon highway.[28] During the night the 3rd Battalion/134th CT relieved the 1st Battalion/318th CT and took up attack positions east of Hompré, with the mission of pushing the enemy to the right, away from the road. Baade's advance at 0600 on December 28 made little progress, and the absence of its usual supporting tank battalion, the 737th, might have had something to do with it. It was supporting the 5th Infantry Division. The 137th CT made only slight gains and was repulsed at Villers-la-Bonne-Eau, while the 320th CT advanced barely half a mile to Baschleiden. Leapfrogging the 134th CT to cover CCA's right flank was expedient and effective, but it altered the alignment of the 35th Infantry Division from north to northwest.[29] The 134th was now the farthest forward on the left, while the 137th and 320th CTs were echeloned to the right. The widely dispersed nature of the division, coupled with the good defensive terrain, aided the 5th FJD in sustaining its MLR at Harlange.

December 28 was a day of pessimism at OB West. The War Diary recorded that the first phase of the Ardennes battle was over. Antwerp was out of the question because the Allies had established a cohesive defense all around the Bulge. Model, however, still thought prospects were good for defeating the Allies in the Liège–Marche–Ciney area, provided Bastogne could be captured quickly and fuel and ammunition were assured. Rundstedt, under pressure from OKW, issued orders identical to those of the day before, despite the altered situation: it was "of decisive importance" to destroy Patton's attack wedge in the Bastogne area as soon as possible "and with sufficiently powerful forces and means." The attack "must take place no later than December 29."[30]

While Rundstedt was pressing for offensive action, so too was Eisenhower. December 28 was an important date for Patton's future operations. Eisenhower flew to Hasselt to meet with Montgomery at 1430 to ascertain when the field marshal could launch a general counterattack. Montgomery told his four army commanders that day that the offensive in the north was now "completely held," and "we would now get ready to pass over to the offensive."[31] He expected one more full-blooded German effort against First Army, an attack he intended to absorb before counterattacking with Houffalize as his objective. ULTRA convinced him that such a culminating effort was certain, but since he could not say when, he gave Eisenhower only a general time frame for the counterattack. It seems they both agreed that if the German attack failed to materialize in the next few days, Montgomery would transition to the offensive by January 1. Montgomery, however, was far less interested in a precise date than were Eisenhower and Bradley; he considered the current battle secondary. Montgomery was looking well beyond the Ardennes to VERITABLE, his main effort into the heart of the Ruhr to seek a decision in the west.[32]

After this meeting, Eisenhower cabled Bedell Smith at 1700: "There are great possibilities in the Bastogne to Houffalize thrust which should be reinforced promptly and in strength. . . . With the area BASTOGNE to HOUFFALIZE firmly in our possession profitable operations can later be developed. Make this clear to BRADLEY at once." Montgomery's influence on this decision is apparent. He informed Brooke that night that Eisenhower had agreed "and accepted my views on the correct action to be taken by 12 Army Group and he sent an order to BRADLEY to take that action. This was just in time as BRADLEY was about to embark on another and somewhat unsound line."[33] The only way to reinforce Bradley "promptly and in strength" was to give him the SHAEF reserve—the 87th Infantry and 11th Armored Divisions. Eisenhower did so later that night, but not before he took steps to create a new reserve. Four hours before meeting with Montgomery in Hasselt, he ordered Devers to "form a SHAEF reserve of a Corps of two Divisions, one armored and one infantry, and station it West of the Vosges available to SHAEF on call."[34] Devers complied the next day, selecting the 12th Armored and 36th Infantry Divisions, but he was not happy about it.

Bradley immediately released the SHAEF reserve to Third Army during the night. At 2030 Middleton's chief of staff, Colonel Cyrus H. Searcy, phoned Brigadier General Charles S. Kilburn and directed him, through coded message, to move his 11th Armored Division, currently near Charleville, to the Neufchâteau area.[35] CCA led off at 0145 the next morning, followed by other major units in the following order: CCB, Division Artillery, CCR, and Division Trains. A limited-capacity bridge over the Meuse at Sedan delayed the march for several hours, as did the misdirection of the column near Carignan, Belgium, a blinding snowstorm, and icy roads. After an eighty-five-mile march, CCA reached the new assembly area a couple of hours before receiving the corps attack order issued at 1800 on December 29. CCB and the remainder of the division were still on the road. The last combat element closed at 2400. As J. Ted Hartman recalled, "After nearly 18 hours of slow, tedious travel, we finally reached our campsite at Longlier, Belgium, long after dark. We performed first-echelon (basic) maintenance and then received orders to attack the enemy the following morning. Amid the sounds of the big guns in the distance, I ate my supper of cold C-rations, rolled my sleeping bag out on the snow, and had a restless, frigid sleep for the seventh straight night." The 87th Infantry Division, commanded by Brigadier General Frank L. Culin Jr., commenced its 100-mile move to VIII Corps from Reims on December 28. Additional lift from the Oise base section was not made available until 1100 on December 29, a delay that Gay took pains to note in his diary.[36] The 87th Infantry Division assembled between Bertrix and Libramont.

Patton welcomed the addition of the SHAEF reserve, but on explicit instructions from Eisenhower, Bradley told him they could be used only in VIII Corps. Whiteley certainly influenced this decision. As deputy G-3, Whiteley had a legitimate role in developing future plans for Eisenhower. In fact, Bedell Smith stated that he, Tedder, Strong, and Whiteley worked together on future plans. Whiteley reflected that "SHAEF would work out plans for all the Army Gps. . . . Our planners would let Army Gps know what they were doing and would get ideas from below. Ike would have the pattern of the SHAEF plan in mind when he talked with Bradley and Montgomery." Whiteley was keen to tell Pogue that it was "not true that SHAEF G3 worked *in vacuuo*." Yet the evidence suggests it might have been otherwise at the time. Colonel James Gault, Eisenhower's assistant, noted that during the Bulge, "Whiteley was the big man."[37]

During a meeting with Bedell Smith on December 26, Whiteley outlined plans he had prepared for employing a reinforced VIII Corps to counterattack northeast from the area of Givet. In fact, SHAEF files contain a handwritten note entitled "Copy of Instructions Handed to Comdr VIII Corps," dated December 26, instructing Middleton to prepare plans and conduct reconnaissance for two possible attacks using the SHAEF reserve. The attacks were from Givet on Rochefort and from Givet northward across the Lesse River between Furfoot and Glouye. The objective of both was to relieve pressure against First Army forces holding south of Namur. "Either of the attacks," the note declared, "may be ordered by SHAEF on short notice."[38] It is not known whether Whiteley was the drafter, but it seems highly probable.

When Bedell Smith indicated that the VIII Corps option would have to be discussed with Bradley, Whiteley objected that this would result in the loss of an entire day, and time was vital. That day Bradley's G-3, Brigadier General A. Franklin Kibler, informed Patton's G-3, Maddox, that Whiteley intended to give orders directly to the 11th Armored Division, bypassing Kibler, Maddox, and Middleton in the interest of saving time. Kibler told Maddox that it was "naturally an irregular channel. . . . It seems to me that General Middleton should know about this as soon as possible." Whiteley continued planning, and later in the day he briefed Eisenhower on another option: a thrust by VIII Corps north from Bastogne that would cut one of the two roads the Germans had for supply.[39]

Eisenhower's selection of corridor A as the principal line of action to exploit the Bastogne–Houffalize axis inhibited Bradley's use of the SHAEF reserve in any other corridor, and certainly in corridors C and D. III Corps, however, was a legitimate option because it also sat astride corridor A. Eisenhower was justified in dictating its use in this corridor, but he should have left the decision of how to employ it there to Bradley, who should have given Patton the freedom to decide how best to advance within the corridor.

Patton issued a new operational directive on December 28, after already disseminating his plan orally to the corps commanders and *before* the SHAEF reserve was released to him that night. Third Army's mission was to seize Houffalize, continue the attack northeast in the direction of St. Vith, cross the Sauer River in the vicinity of Echternach, and drive up the Prüm Valley in the direction of Bonn. VIII Corps was to seize the high ground in the vicinity of Houffalize in order to control the road net there; protect the left (northwest) flank of the army; and attack northeast, echeloned to the left rear of III Corps. III Corps was to attack northeast in the direction of St. Vith and, in conjunction with XII Corps, seize crossings of the Rhine in the vicinity of Bonn. XII Corps was to maintain contact with III Corps, continue to exert pressure along the present front of the 80th Infantry Division, cross the Sauer River in the vicinity of Echternach, and then drive up the Prüm Valley in the direction of Bonn on army order. XX Corps was to hold its present sector, including the Saarlautern bridgehead, with minimum force; advance north and clear the enemy from the area between the Moselle and Saar Rivers on army order; and be prepared to follow XII Corps to the northeast.[40]

Such distant objectives were typical of Patton. In Lorraine, he always spoke of crossing the Rhine even while the Saar had yet to be crossed and the West Wall had yet to be penetrated. Thinking days and even weeks ahead is an essential requirement for an army commander, but Patton had not even achieved the second objective (Houffalize) of Eisenhower's larger operational concept (the first objective being Bastogne). The absence of attack dates or the specific assignment of troops to tasks in Patton's directive reflected the uncertainty of the availability of the SHAEF reserve, but he phoned Middleton and Millikin that night and told them to go on December 30 and 31, respectively.[41] During the evening Harkins met with Middleton at Millikin's headquarters in Arlon. Grow and Gaffey were present as well. Harkins told Middleton that it was Patton's "urgent desire that this attack be pushed with all boldness and the objective be seized as quickly as possible."[42] This appeared to be the clear intent, and one must give Middleton the benefit of the doubt that he understood it.

Yet the absence of a detailed concept of operations and scheme of maneuver in Patton's directive soon caused problems.

Middleton expressed reservations about Patton's plan almost immediately. The next day he phoned Third Army, seeking permission to alter the scheme of maneuver. Gay said that Patton was sick and "could not go out on a long trip," so Middleton outlined his concerns over the phone. He had two issues: location and timing. First, he did not believe it was feasible for the 11th Armored and 87th Infantry Divisions to attack north out of the Bastogne Pocket; heavy congestion would ensue, and he requested permission to mount his attack outside the pocket to the southwest. Gay relayed Patton's reply that he "didn't care how" the attack was made, but Middleton "must make it, and he must take the objective." Patton was seemingly granting Middleton considerable flexibility to fight his corps—something that all commanders appreciate; however, commanders also require sufficient direction to fight their battles effectively and in harmony with the higher commander's intent. Patton's grip here may have been too loose due to his illness. A similar incident had occurred in Lorraine, when Patton should have expressed his intent with greater clarity to Eddy.[43]

Patton must have recognized that the twenty-five-square-mile pocket could not accommodate the formations and artillery already inside as well as the SHAEF reserve. Middleton and Millikin were already dealing with boundary and control issues, and during the afternoon they agreed that control of III Corps units in Bastogne would pass to VIII Corps at 1800. Until further notice, 4th Armored and 101st Airborne Division artillery in Bastogne would remain connected to III Corps' FDC. Indeed, the guns of both divisions were to support VIII Corps' attack on December 30.[44] Middleton's request to shift west to avoid congestion therefore made sense, based on using both divisions; apparently, using only one division was not considered.

Patton's scheme of maneuver for expanding the Bastogne Pocket is not clear. He seriously considered employing Taylor's division because it was "up to strength." However, he decided against it. Patton initially wanted the 4th Armored Division to spearhead the III Corps attack toward Houffalize, but Gaffey convinced him that the division's combat power was insufficient.[45] Patton assigned the 6th Armored Division to III Corps at 0230 on December 29. His intention to have that division go into Bastogne under cover of darkness to achieve surprise was sound, but the pocket would become too congested if Middleton pushed the SHAEF reserve into it as well. Grow's division was to advance through Gaffey's division and attack northeast. Once this maneuver was complete, the 4th Armored Division would pass to the control of VIII Corps.[46] What is important here is that Patton consistently sought to spearhead the breakout of the Bastogne Pocket with a single armored division.

The relevant issue is the significant difference in staging the VIII Corps attack from inside the Bastogne Pocket versus staging it from an LD west of the town. The shortest distance to Houffalize, Bradley's stated objective, was from the front lines of the 502nd and 506th Parachute Infantry Regiments (PIRs), only two miles south of Noville. It was less than five miles beyond to Houffalize. Conversely, it was more than seventeen miles from Middleton's proposed LD southwest of Bastogne to Houffalize. This scheme of maneuver represented a significant change in location of the main attack and made it much harder to get to Houffalize quickly. Why Bradley and Patton agreed to it requires further analysis.

At this stage, one can profit from tracing the dissemination of Eisenhower's intent for the south side of the salient down to Middleton. According to Air Marshal Robb, Eisenhower's intent on December 29 was as follows: "our one object must be to break through the enemy, get inside the salient and move East along the enemy's supply lines—lines he obviously could not demolish or obstruct as he had done [to] other roads." Based on his meeting with Montgomery and his earlier direction to Bradley, Eisenhower sought a decision at Houffalize by way of a double pincer attack. Houffalize therefore became Eisenhower's *decisive point*, defined by Jomini as "the possession of which, more than any other [point] helps to secure victory, by enabling its holder to make a proper application of the principles of war." The decisive point of vulnerability for any army has traditionally been its rear areas, but that vulnerability can be realized and exploited only after MLRs have been breached to the point where the attacker achieves a degree of freedom to move as he pleases. To break through the German MLRs shielding the LCs back to the West Wall required powerful *penetration* operations such as COBRA, which in turn demanded concentration of combat power. A penetration is a much different beast from the simple application of concentric pressure. It is a mathematical problem based on the depth of the penetration required and the nature of the enemy defense and terrain.[47] The fundamental difficulty of any penetration operation in the face of an enemy with unbroken capability is continuity, which was why FM 100–5 required "deep echelonment of reserves." At no point during the campaign in northwest Europe had such Allied operations yielded fast results.

Bradley seems to have favored a penetration attack because it was the quickest way to get to Houffalize. Beyond stating that the SHAEF reserve could be used only in VIII Corps, it is difficult to reconstruct his intent as transmitted to Patton. Bradley may very well have given Patton explicit directions regarding his intent and thoughts on the scheme of maneuver, but direct evidence is limited. William Simpson commented, "From Bradley . . . I never get any orders that make it clear to me what I have got to do,"[48] shedding some light on Bradley's command technique. Details concerning Patton's back brief of his plan to Bradley on December 29 are also frustratingly elusive, but Gay indicated that Bradley approved it in principle, including Eddy's assault crossing at Echternach. Bradley therefore accepted Patton's proposal to send VIII Corps to Houffalize and III Corps to St. Vith, even though those two objectives were eighteen miles apart. It was twenty-four miles from Bastogne to St. Vith.

Patton communicated his intent for a rapid advance to Houffalize to Middleton, but the latter's understanding was questionable. Martin Blumenson noted that in Normandy, Patton exhibited the command defect of sometimes ineffectively expressing his intent to Middleton. This may have been the case here, for Gay had "no conception" that Middleton planned to launch an attack "from the vicinity of Neufchâteau, several miles from the east-west line through Bastogne."[49] If Gay had no conception, it strongly suggests that Patton had no conception either, because they were supposed to be on the same page. This obvious disconnect over the critical issue of commander's intent makes one wonder exactly what Harkins had said to Middleton at Arlon.

One critical note recorded by Gay is that Patton apparently briefed Bradley that Millikin would attack only "after" Middleton had seized the high ground near Houffalize.[50] If Gay's notes are an accurate reflection of what Patton said, it meant one of two things: (1) since Millikin was scheduled to attack on December 31, Patton expected VIII Corps to cover the seventeen miles to Houffalize in a single day, or (2) Patton envisioned VIII Corps striking out of the Bastogne Pocket to cover the seven miles to Houffalize in a single day, December 30. It is inconceivable that Patton expected Middleton to cover seventeen miles in a single day when the average daily advances of Third Army were in the thousands of yards. A reasonable deduction, therefore, is that Patton briefed Bradley before Middleton called to request a change in the scheme of maneuver and the location of the main effort.

Middleton's second objection, conveyed during his phone call to

Third Army, was timing; he did not want to attack on December 30 with the two new divisions. His disagreement with Patton's timetable was evident in the VIII Corps after-action report:

> The order to initiate the attack so soon . . . imposed a heavy task on the divisions, since they were still involved in a long movement over snow-covered roads and could not close in their assembly areas before dark. Terrain selected for the attack was entirely strange to the commanders, and early darkness of mid-winter permitted only a few hours for reconnaissance. Moreover, the severe cold endured by the two divisions over the long movements as well as late arrival in assembly areas caused considerable fatigue among the men. An attack under these conditions would have been difficult for a veteran division. For an infantry division of limited combat experience and an armored division with no battle service, it was a severe test.[51]

Patton refused to change the timing of the attack, for two reasons. First, he believed in continuous attack and in the rapid application of new combat power, exclusive of any pressure from superior commanders to do so. Conceding preparation time to the enemy was anathema to Patton. His basic philosophy of continuous movement was summed up in France: "It is terrible to halt. . . . No one realizes the terrible value of the unforgiving minute except me." As the VIII Corps after-action report stated, the urgency to attack with the new divisions was to "achieve surprise . . . before they [Germans] could be reinforced from the north."[52] Second, Houffalize loomed large in Eisenhower's decision making, and especially in Bradley's, because getting there meant the return of First Army to Twelfth Army Group. Bradley enjoyed Patton's complete support in this: "If Ike will put Bradley back in command of the 1st and 9th Armies, we can bag the whole German army."[53] Patton's first reason for refusing Middleton's request for a delay, however, was more reasonable than the second.

Patton's approach to dealing with enemy capability was fundamentally different from Montgomery's. On December 28 Montgomery noted that intelligence indicated the Germans were "lining up for one more determined effort to break through to the LIEGE area." He felt he could not launch his own offensive "against that strength as the enemy was deployed for the attack opposite where we would want to attack ourselves." His solution: absorb the enemy attack, then "hit him a hard blow on the rebound."[54] Had Montgomery commanded Third Army, he would have launched the SHAEF reserve only *after* he had absorbed the German attack on the Bastogne corridor. This would have allowed the new divisions, particularly the 11th Armored Division, more time to prepare and conduct reconnaissance. However, neither Eisenhower nor Bradley nor Patton was built that way. Eisenhower signaled Montgomery that day that they must not allow the Germans to withdraw their mobile forces into a ready reserve. This would permit the enemy "to deal either with our attack against his salient or to deliver another blow at some other point. . . . *This is a very important point.* We must break him up while he is out in the open."[55] This was possible only by attacking, and Patton was relentless in the attack. Eisenhower considered that his greatest strength. Patton would continue to advance as long as he had a single battalion capable of doing so, but attacking the enemy's main strength was not smart.

With his second recommendation rejected, Middleton issued his field order at 1400, with the following scheme of maneuver: The 87th Infantry Division, with its left flank on the Remagne–St. Hubert road and its right flank in the Bois de Haies de Magery, would be on the left on a six-mile front. It was to advance to the Ourthe River, seize crossings, and peel off units to protect the left flank of the 11th Armored Division and hence the flank of the corps and Third Army. The 11th Armored Division had its right flank on Sibret and a frontage of five miles. It was to advance on a curve between the Ourthe and the positions held by CCA/9th Armored Division and the 101st Airborne Division. The latter formations were to be the anchor and pivot of the corps attack.[56]

Middleton did not identify a main attack (or decisive attack) in the field order, but the supporting role of the 87th Infantry Division implied that Kilburn was the main attack. Based on the ground, Middleton had placed the 11th Armored Division in the right place, or in a decisive direction. Although Culin had access to a main northeast road from St. Hubert to Laroche, it was a heavily wooded ridge route—rolling, hilly, and swampy. The ground between Moircy and Bertogne, however, was more open, dotted with small patches of woods and therefore better for tanks. Kilburn's main route, from Moircy to Bertogne, ran perpendicular to a series of small stream valleys and ridgelines, and numerous high points dominated certain areas. However, when one considers Kilburn's objections to Middleton's scheme of maneuver, the main attack becomes vague. Kilburn went to Neufchâteau to see Middleton on December 29, even as the 11th Armored Division marched to VIII Corps. Kilburn wanted to attack with both combat commands solidly abreast, but Middleton, apparently concerned by the prospect of the relatively untested 87th Infantry Division attacking without tank support, ordered Kilburn to divide his force on either side of the Bois de Haies de Magery so as to place one combat command close to Culin's infantry. Kilburn considered this dangerous and futile but was overruled by Middleton. However, Middleton's Field Order No. 12 clearly stated that Culin would have the 761st Tank Battalion in support. Moreover, the division had fought for a time under Third Army in Lorraine and was not totally raw. Middleton's decision undermined the very nature of a main attack, characterized by "narrow zones of action . . . and a deep echelonment of reserves," and it leaves one wondering who was actually executing the supporting attack. However, doctrine stated that in large commands, such as a corps, a penetration was often initiated by "launching simultaneously two or more powerful attacks (a *multiple penetration*) against weak localities on the hostile front."[57]

Between 2200 and 2230 Kilburn issued a verbal order to the assembled major unit commanders to attack at daylight the following morning. CCA received orders at 0130 and issued its own field order two hours later. By 2130 details for coordinating supporting artillery fires "were anything but clear and specific." Air-ground liaison groups from XIX TAC had not arrived. The division, with no combat experience, had no more than nine hours for troop-leading procedure (today called battle procedure),[58] and it was apparently expected to penetrate seventeen miles to Houffalize in a single day.

Patton's estimate at this stage is important because his ability to achieve his mission of getting to Houffalize and St. Vith required proper deductions of his own capability and that of the enemy. Patton had ten infantry divisions and the equivalent of four armored divisions. That day Eisenhower ordered CCR/9th Armored Division to withdraw from Bastogne and move to Reims to form a new SHAEF reserve; it began withdrawing at 0100 on December 29.[59] Five infantry divisions and one armored division were idle in XII and XX Corps, leaving Patton with four infantry divisions and three and a half armored divisions to achieve his mission. Due diligence had to be paid to the vulnerable flanks of the army, but one could reasonably argue that far too much combat power was sitting idle when the force ratios in corridor A were not heavily in Third Army's favor.

Over the years, a general rule of thumb has emerged that many

Table 10.2. Third Army Order of Battle, December 29, 1944

VIII Corps	III Corps	XII Corps	XX Corps
87 Inf Div	4 Armd Div	4 Inf Div	10 Armd Div (–CCB)
101 Abn Div	6 Armd Div	5 Inf Div	90 Inf Div
11 Armd Div	35 Inf Div	80 Inf Div	95 Inf Div
CCA/9 Armd Div	26 Inf Div	2 Cav Gp	5 Ranger Bn
CCB/10 Armd Div	Elms 6 Cav Gp		3 Cav Gp
28 Inf Div (–)			
6 Cav Gp			
4 French Pcht Bns			

military historians and defense analysts have perhaps given too much credit. This is the 3:1 rule, which holds that an attacker requires a 3:1 superiority to successfully execute a breakthrough of a main defensive area. Some historians even posit that a 4:1 superiority is the minimum force ratio required to achieve a break-in at the point of contact.[60] Yet the military historian is justified in seeking greater precision. Colonel Trevor N. Dupuy argued that the 3:1 rule is "so crude that it is practically useless as an analytical tool," and he logically questioned its basis of comparison. He is not alone in challenging the "rule."[61]

Clearly, the idea that an attacker requires some form of superiority is intuitive if one accepts the fact that it takes less force to defend a certain frontage than it does to overcome it.[62] Yet F. O. Miksche avoided numerical ratios in his discussion of how to break in against a main defense area; instead, he cited the requirements of surprise and speed (forming maneuver) and material superiority expressed in the form of firepower (or systems delivering it).[63] For purposes of the present study, it is important to remember that the World War II editions of FM 100–5 did not identify any force ratio rule with regard to penetration attacks. It merely called for the "greatest possible offensive power" to be "concentrated." The essential conditions for success included surprise, sufficient firepower, favorable terrain, and sufficient strength to carry the attack through. Clearly, some degree of numerical superiority was required to achieve what FM 100–5 referred to as the three "impulses" of the penetration—breakthrough, widening of the gap, and seizure of the objective.[64]

If the 3:1 rule were defined in terms of the number of divisions in corridor A, Patton would have required twenty-four to penetrate the MLR, defeat reserves, and get to Houffalize. But fitting twenty-four divisions into corridor A was not physically possible. In fact, the FSR in the corridor on both sides was nearing the limit as more divisions arrived. Patton appreciated this fact, but he also recognized that he still possessed an overall superiority in combat power. This overall superiority—the product of more infantry, tanks, tank destroyers, artillery, ammunition, and airpower and a more robust logistical system—translated into the ability to generate a higher offensive tempo. Even if Patton's overall combat power superiority did not necessarily provide a sufficient margin to penetrate the enemy's main defense area and defeat reserves, it was sufficient for the gradual pushing back of the German defenses, despite the terrain.

Patton's FSR problem in corridor A was highlighted by Strong's assessment that the Germans possessed the capability to "hold us round Bastogne" or "make his attack North against the First Army" or, "if he wants to, he can get out of the salient."[65] By December 29 Koch's ISUMs were no longer listing the German capability to advance to the west. The contraction of the *Fifth Panzer Armee* spearhead was clear; the *9th* and *116th PDs* of LVIII *Panzerkorps* were located digging in around Marche and were under heavy pressure from the air. That day, *Generalmajor* Frederick W. von Mellenthin made his way to the *9th PD* and reflected, "I witnessed the uninterrupted air attacks on our traffic routes and supply dumps."[66] According to Koch's assessment, the Germans were capable of operating only against Third Army's salient around Bastogne. There was no aggressive enemy action opposite VIII Corps; the enemy "continued improving his defensive [positions]."[67] The 6th Cavalry Group reported *Lehr*'s strong outpost line from St. Hubert–Moircy–Remagne–Lavaselle, with dug-in infantry supported by tanks and self-propelled guns.

Koch placed the *1st, 2nd, 9th*, and *12th SS PDs* north of the army group boundary, concentrated in the Marche–Hotton area. The *10th SS PD* was above the army group boundary and east of the West Wall. Koch's work map for 0300 December 29 still showed the *11th PD* north of Bastogne, just below the army group boundary; the Twelfth Army Group situation map had it south of the Ourthe River with a question mark. The *21st PD* was now placed east of Trier and designated "unlocated." However, ULTRA had reported at the end of December 28 that *2nd SS PD* had begun to assemble at Dochamps.[68]

Koch's ISUM for 0900 December 29 placed elements of the *3rd PGD* in the Houffalize area, seven miles northeast of its location the previous afternoon, but his work map for 0300 December 30 had it moving south from Elsenborn with a question mark. In fact, advance elements of the

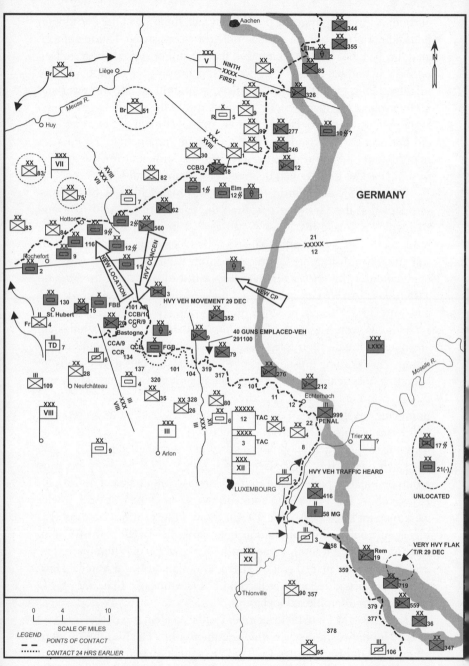

Map 10.2. Third Army G-2 Work Map, Situation as of 0300 December 30, 1944

division were moving into position north of the Bois de Fragotte. His work map displayed a new arrow labeled "h[ea]vy concentration" pointed directly at Bastogne from the north. He had not moved the *11th PD*, so it is logical to assume that he thought the *3rd PGD* was there. Koch therefore missed the deployment of the *3rd PGD* into the area opposite the 11th Armored Division and did not fully identify it from POW reports until 0900 on December 30.[69]

Armored reconnaissance observed a concentration of vehicles, including tanks and half-tracks, moving into the woods near Noville at 1130 on December 29. Heavy flak was reported there as well. These were advance elements of the depleted *1st SS PD*. It had been relieved from its defensive battle in the Amblève–Salm sector between Stavelot and Trois Ponts by *LXVI Armeekorps* during December 27–28. It assembled in the forest east of Vielsalm and departed its assembly area at 1625 for the Arloncourt–Harzy–Schimpach–Longvilly area, some twenty-five straight-line miles to the south.[70] During the night of December 29–30 the *Leibstandarte* negotiated a traffic jam in Houffalize and moved into its assembly area in the Tarchamps–Warrange–Harlange area. The key element of Koch's analysis was captured in ISUM No. 451, issued at 1800 on December 29: "Build-up of enemy forces continued NE Bastogne during day."[71]

Two hours later Gay was called to Twelfth Army Group headquarters, where Patton was meeting with Bradley and Sibert. Gay was informed that intelligence revealed a German intention to attack north of Bastogne in the morning, supported by heavy bombing of the woods immediately north of the town.[72] Patton noted in his diary that the "'Black Market' stated that there would be a bombing attack on Bastogne at 0400, December 30. It is also rumored there will be an attack on the same town by ground troops from Houffalize."[73] Bletchley Park sent out a message at 1741, indicating that *167th VGD* and *3rd PGD* would attack Bastogne, but neither Third Army's identification code (ZE) nor Twelfth Army Group's code (NX) was in the address block. This was a one-Z message, making it a low priority; this was odd, however, considering it introduced two new divisions in the Bastogne sector.[74] Therefore, Sibert may have received other ULTRA or intelligence from another source. If this was in fact ULTRA-based intelligence, Patton faced the dilemma of how to pass on the warning to III Corps without violating the ULTRA security protocols, which dictated that "when operational action is taken on the basis of Ultra intelligence, the utmost care must be taken, by means of proper cover, to insure that the action does not reveal or in any way suggest that this source of intelligence is at our disposal."[75] There is no indication of any special redeployment to meet the threat.

Patton's estimate of enemy capability should have led to an adjustment of his expectations regarding VIII Corps, but he interpreted the situation like Middleton did at this point. Only small groups of German tanks had operated against his front in the preceding days, the lack of artillery suggested the Germans were having trouble deploying it forward, and intelligence revealed chronic fuel shortages. Middleton's G-2, Colonel Andrew Reeves, concluded that the Germans were regrouping to contain Bastogne and observed that "no considerable movements or concentrations . . . have been noted along the south perimeter of the salient west of BASTOGNE." He estimated the Germans had 16,500 men and eighty tanks between St. Hubert and Bastogne, consisting of elements of *Panzer Lehr, 15th PGD, 26th VGD, FBB*, and 800 men of *FJR 13*, considered cut off and out of contact with the rest of the *5th FJD* to the east. Reeves concluded that the number-one enemy capability was defending their present positions with forces in situ. Based on their inability to take Bastogne and the use of mines and roadblocks on the southwest perimeter of the salient, he believed "that for the moment he has adopted a defensive attitude in this sector . . . it is very probable that his reaction to an advance by VIII Corps will initially be defensive, then quick movement of his reserves to stop such an advance and ultimately a counterattack to push back the advancing force." Reserves capable of intervening against the corps included the *10th SS* and *21st PDs* and several other infantry formations of marginal effectiveness.[76] Although the Germans were not exhibiting overt offensive intentions there, they had plenty of time to prepare the zone to receive Middleton's attack.

Third Army's failure to identify the *3rd PGD* was felt at Kilburn's level. The 41st Cavalry Reconnaissance Squadron conducted limited reconnaissance on December 29, but all Kilburn really knew was that somewhere to his front were the *15th PGD*, elements of *Panzer Lehr*, and the *FBB*. Kilburn considered the intelligence provided by the 6th Cavalry Group to be "of a hazy and indefinite nature." Culin was in the same position, and his first EEI was to identify enemy units, their dispositions, strength, and morale; "all organizations will exert every effort" to do so. This was a direct reflection of Middleton's own EEIs for the attack.[77]

Manteuffel's estimate of the situation on December 29 led him to conclude that the offensive should be stopped and the armies withdrawn from the salient. The Ardennes offensive, as originally conceived, was at an end. Indeed, *Sixth Panzer Armee's* final attack on the left wing at Erezee had failed, and the entire army was now on the defensive. However, Hitler was determined to fight it out, and during the day Manteuffel explained his concept of operations to his corps commanders. Bastogne had become the "central problem." Indeed, more combat power was massing for the final effort against Bastogne than had been devoted to *Fifth Panzer Armee* for its drive to the Meuse. By evening Manteuffel had eight divisions in the Bastogne sector, and despite the fact that the actual division equivalent was perhaps only five, he expressed the view of the German High Command that the forthcoming battle was an "opportunity" to win a striking victory or at least to chew up the enemy divisions that would be poured into the fight.[78]

It is impossible to determine whether Manteuffel truly believed he could reach a decision at Bastogne, but Patton certainly thought his new offensive, planned for the next day, "may well be decisive," if he could only get Eisenhower to "use reserves to attack and not to defend." This had become Patton's biggest battle. "I now have sixteen divisions," he noted, "but four have strings tied to them."[79] On December 29 Bradley pinned a second Oak Leaf Cluster to the Distinguished Service Medal on Patton's uniform for his rapid movement across France in August, but he was not moving rapidly now. Bastogne had clearly become the center of gravity for both Patton and Manteuffel. For Patton, it meant he was to face the bulk of the remaining combat power of the German armies in the salient.

11

Slugging Match, December 30–31

The 11th Armored and the 87th Infantry jumped off west of Bastogne as planned and ran right into the flank of a large German counterattack headed southeast.

—Patton, December 30, 1944

On the west side of the Bastogne corridor the *XLVII Panzerkorps* formations crossed the LD at approximately 0730—the *3rd PGD* advancing on Villeroux, and the *FBB* advancing on Sibret. Despite the fact that 4th Armored Division and III Corps artillery pounded Denkert's assembly area in the southern edge of the Bois de Fragotte, and *PGR 29* did not arrive and detruck until 0630, *3rd PGD*'s attack started off well. Yet it was brought to a halt by CCA/9th Armored Division, under command of VIII Corps as of 0600, short of Villeroux. Denkert did not possess sufficient artillery to properly secure his left flank and reflected, "It very soon became obvious that shortly after the begin[ning] of our attack an enemy attack had also started . . . with considerably stronger forces with all kinds of weapons." Denkert's division made repeated attacks throughout the morning, forcing back CCA/9th Armored Division's left flank, but VIII Corps reported the situation under control at 1245.[1] On Denkert's right the *FBB* spotted two tank groups heading toward Morhet and Jodenville when the fog lifted. Remer's tanks immediately opened fire and destroyed several tanks from CCB/11th Armored Division, initiating a two- to three-hour tank battle. Remer's brigade never made it to Chenogne, but he claimed a "complete defensive success" against Kilburn's armor, attributable in large measure to his men's will to fight.[2]

VIII Corps also crossed the LD at 0730. On the left the 87th Infantry Division passed through the 109th CT, the remnant of the 28th Infantry

Division holding the LD near Bras. Culin's infantry was trucked north from its assembly area around Bertrix in the early hours. The 346th CT on the left captured Bras Haut but was limited to screening the left flank. The 345th CT on the right advanced five miles before hitting *KG Neumann* of *Panzer Lehr* south of Moircy by 1400. *KG Neumann* consisted of *I Abteilung/PGR 902* and two Panther companies. Two companies of the 345th CT advance guard battalion were rapidly chewed up, and the remaining company suffered heavy casualties trying to maneuver toward Jenneville.[3] To protect the vital St. Hubert–Morhet supply route, *KG Neumann* counterattacked Moircy at 2100 and recaptured it, but possession of the town was contested during the night.[4]

Kilburn's LD was just south of the Bras–Remience line. He had little precise knowledge of what was in front of him. Elements of 6th Cavalry Group had been pushed out of Remagne at 0300, and dense ground fog inhibited visibility for both sides. Artillery was brought down on the woods to the front thirty minutes prior to H-hour, and at 0822 CCA made contact with elements of *KG Neumann* south of Remagne. At this point the commanding officer of the 42nd Tank Battalion (TF White) recalled that "all hell broke loose" just beyond the crest at Rondu, a mile and a half south of Remagne. The 63rd AIB suffered almost 100 casualties in thirty minutes.[5] The combat command was pinned down in place due to strong defensive terrain and excellent weapons siting. Streams and large wooded areas limited maneuver, and *KG Neumann* brought down a considerable volume of defensive artillery fire throughout Kilburn's zone.[6] CCA failed to advance any further during the day. CCB ran into elements of *PGR 104* of *15th PGD* at Jodenville at 0930, bypassed this resistance to the west, and advanced to Brul and Houmont but quickly ran into the *FBB*.[7]

On the east side of the corridor Decker's *XXXIX Panzerkorps* attacked earlier than *XLVII Panzerkorps*, between 0430 and 0625.[8] Hoecker's boundary with Moncke was Grumelscheid–Doncols–Lutrebois. The cloudy and misty conditions, and the apparent lack of an artillery preparation due to logistical difficulties, helped *XXXIX Panzerkorps* achieve an element of tactical surprise, but *Jagdkorps II* failed to provide the promised overwatch in the corps attack corridor. In the north *VGR 331/167th VGD*, with *KG von Hauser* attached, attacked from Wardin down the road to Bastogne. Hauser's panzer company had been badly mauled in the previous day's fighting.[9] Although the *167th VGD* had arrived at its full TO&E strength, it possessed no heavy mechanized weapons, and its worn-out transport consisted of Italian trucks with no spare parts. It had never conducted combined training above company level but seems to have had very good morale.[10] The *167th VGD* apparently bypassed Marvie, held by 1st Battalion/134th CT, and advanced to the edge of the woods southeast of Assenois by early morning. It was soon engaged by CCA/4th Armored Division (CCR was around Assenois), which had been ordered to turn east to assist Baade at 0635.[11] Hoecker reflected that his lead battalion was "cut to pieces" by fighter-bombers and artillery. Indeed, his *volksgrenadiers* were subjected to the gruesome effects of proximity fuse ammunition, but the MLR was retained due to the "excellent" support from his own divisional artillery.[12]

South of the *167th VGD* attack, the *1st SS PD* moved forward from its staging area in the low ground of Lutremange and crossed the LD at 0445 in two *Kampfgruppen—KG Poetschke* (remnants of SS *Panzer Regiment 1* from the La Gleize pocket) to the north and *KG Hansen* to the south. Preparatory fire was weak, but both *KGs* made good initial progress. *KG Poetschke* advanced northwest, engaged and defeated companies of the 134th CT at Lutrebois, and then infiltrated west. The *KG* advanced quickly to Remonfosse, immediately north of Hill 535 on the Martelange–Bastogne road. Panzer commander Manfred Thorn recalled, "I could drive my panzer at high speed" on the open and frozen ground between Lutrebois and Remonfosse.[13] *KG Poetschke* might have cut the road had it not been engaged by CCA/4th Armored Division. Earnest's command filled the armored deficiency stemming from the decision to remove Baade's attached tank battalion. CCA destroyed perhaps ten tanks as they emerged from Lutrebois. *KG Poetschke* also received heavy fire from the woods to the south. Thorn recalled that American observation planes were flying so low that he could have thrown rocks at them. From the Germans' perspective, the extremely accurate American artillery fire appeared to follow "every move we made," and effectively blocked the *Leibstandarte*. Indeed, Gaffey's guns were now simultaneously engaging the *1st SS PD* on the east and the *3rd PGD* on the west.[14] *KG Hansen* advanced to Villers-la-Bonne-Eau, surrounded two companies of the 3rd Battalion/137th CT, captured the Chateau Losange, and made it to the Bastogne–Arlon road, but it was brought to a halt by artillery and CCA/4th Armored Division.

The 35th Infantry Division's after-action report described the German operations in the north part of the division as "an extremely heavy counterattack," with "very heavy pressure" on the rest of the division. To the south the 320th CT attacked at 0800 but was quickly blocked at Harlange. At 1410 Maddox called Millikin seeking "full, detailed information" on the counterattack against Baade.[15] The 4th Armored Division phoned III Corps at 1515 and stated that things were under control, but the division had "had a pretty good scare so far."[16] *XXXIX Panzerkorps* had driven a two-square-mile salient into Baade's left flank and by the end of the day controlled Lutrebois and Villers-la-Bonne-Eau. Baade's division would have been in serious trouble had *LIII Armeekorps* executed a supporting attack to assist *XXXIX Panzerkorps* as planned, but Rothkirch's tenuous right wing could offer little weight by this stage. The *9th VGD* had been pushed back to the Wiltz–Schumann road, and the *FGB* was defending positions between Winseler and Berlé. *FJR 15* may have committed two companies to assist the *167th VGD*, but coordination and cohesion among the different German formations were lacking.

Patton's understanding of the battle developed throughout the day. By 0900 he knew that *3rd PGD* and *167th VGD* had definitely arrived in strength. His reaction to the identification of *3rd PGD* is unknown, but a raised eyebrow in Koch's direction was not improbable. By 1800 Koch had interpreted the attack on VIII Corps as "several small counterattacks" by infantry and a few tanks at Chenogne. The 35th Infantry Division had been hit at Lutrebois by 500 to 600 infantry, with a few tanks. By the end of the day Koch was reporting a heavy counterattack at Moircy, and prisoners stated that many tanks and infantry from the *1st* and *9th SS PDs* were in the area east of Bastogne.[17]

Patton described the fight between VIII Corps and *XLVII Panzerkorps* as a "lucky meeting" in his diary. It "stopped the Germans and probably corrected a bad situation. Every one of the generals involved urged me to postpone the attack . . . but I held to my plan."[18] What he meant by a "bad situation" is unclear. Perhaps he was referring to Middleton's scheme of maneuver. This seems probable, because Gay noted that "at present it indicates a complete misunderstanding of the problem involved" on Middleton's part. The purpose was to seize the high ground immediately south of Houffalize, but Middleton's attack "would drive the enemy back on this high ground rather than take it away from him."[19] The only way to accomplish what Gay envisioned was to envelop the Germans, but he did not explain how to bypass *Panzer Lehr, FBB, 3rd* and *15th PGDs*, and elements of *26th VGD*. Gay's perspective surely reflected Patton's to some degree, but unfortunately, the latter did not articulate his thoughts on the issue. Patton's claim that he did not know the German attack against VIII Corps was coming must be accepted, based on the evidence. Clearly, he anticipated a significant attack from the north, not from west and east of

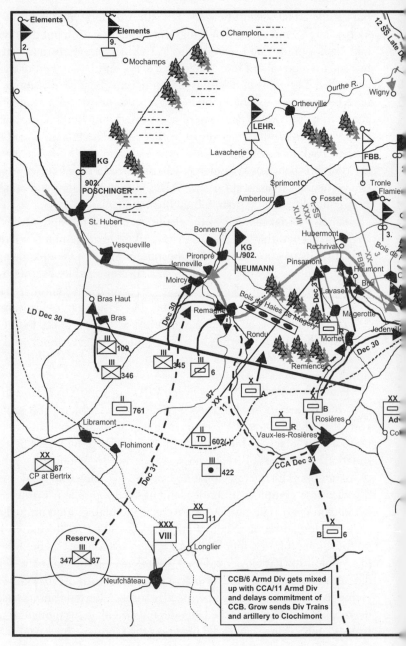

Map 11.1. *Fifth Panzer Armee's* Pincer Attack, December 30–31, 1944

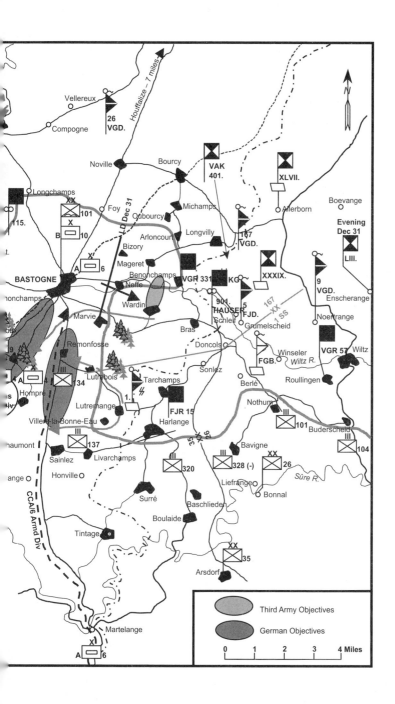

Vellereux

Compogne

26 VGD.

Houffalize – 7 miles

Noville

Bourcy

VAK 401.

XLVII.

Boevange

Longchamps

XX 101

X B 10

115.

Foy

Oubourcy

Michamps

Allerborn

Evening Dec 31

Longvilly

167 VGD.

LIII.

Arloncourt

X A 6

Bizory

Mageret

Benonchamps

BASTOGNE

onchamps

Neffe

VGR 331

KG

XXXIX.

9 VGD.

Enscherange

Wardin

901

5 FJD.

Noertrange

Marvie

HAUSER

Schlei

Grumelscheid

Bras

Doncols

167

XX 1 SS

Remonfosse

VGR 57 Wiltz

Winseler

FGB.

Wiltz R.

III A 34

Lutrebois

Sonlez

Berlé

Roullingen

1.

Tarchamps

Hompre

Lutremange

Nothum

III 101

Buderscheid

Villers-la-Bonne-Eau

FJR 15

Harlange

Bavigne

III 104

haumont

III 137

35

III 328 (-)

XX 26

Sainlez

Livarchamps

Sûre R.

ange

Honville

III 320

Liefrange

Bonnal

CCA/6 Armd Div

Surré

Baschlieden

Boulaide

Tintage

XX 35

Arsdorf

Martelange

XI A 6

Third Army Objectives

German Objectives

0   1   2   3   4 Miles

the corridor simultaneously. Patton justified his decision to insert Baade's 35th Infantry Division by pointing out that "things could have been critical" had it not been in place to absorb the German attack. Indeed, the Germans definitely would have cut the Arlon–Bastogne road. Patton stated, "We had an inkling that it was coming and were set for it."[20] Proving this is difficult, and Baade's division did not react as if it were aware of the threat.

Patton unquestionably considered December 30 "the critical day of the operation" because the Germans had employed "at least five divisions, to again isolate Bastogne."[21] He concluded that this was "probably the biggest co-ordinated counterattack that troops under my command have ever experienced," including Manteuffel's *Fifth Panzer Armee* counterattack back in late September with the new panzer brigades. Despite the new circumstances at Bastogne, Patton remained consistent in identifying success there as a prerequisite for his larger plan of maneuver. Eddy briefed McBride and Irwin on that larger plan on December 30, as he understood it from Patton: "Our attack is to be a part of the 4 phases of a coordinated attack. Ours is depending on the success of the attack up through Bastogne, also on the attack of the 1 Army and following the attack of the XX Corps." This clearly demonstrated that XII Corps was last in priority, even though Eddy told McBride and Irwin that "the line on our front is lightly held and that it would be easy to go through."[22] Bulldog Walker visited Third Army that day looking for an attack date but was told it depended on the progress of III and VIII Corps. He had to be content with limited-objective attacks in the Saarlautern bridgehead, and the 95th Infantry Division captured two city blocks on December 30.[23] Eddy and Walker, holding almost half the army's combat power, would sit idle until Patton solved the Houffalize problem with VIII and III Corps.

The Houffalize line of action had only gotten harder with the arrival of the German reinforcements. In his intelligence annex to the III Corps field order issued at 1100 on December 30, Millikin's G-2, Colonel Horner, estimated there were some 21,000 men and ninety-five tanks and assault guns opposite the corps.[24] This did not include *1st SS PD* or *167th VGD*, and one has to assume he had not had time to assimilate the latest identifications. Although he laid out the formations capable of intervening against the corps, he offered no estimate of enemy capability. EEIs regarding whether the enemy would renew the offensive or counterattack the corps, and whether he possessed reserves or would defend the salient, substituted for analysis. Some of these questions were answered at 1642 when Bletchley Park sent a ZZZZZ message indicating *1st SS PD*'s intention to attack the corridor again on December 31.[25] Patton concluded that the best line of action—the one most likely to be successful, despite what the enemy might do next—was to continue with the VIII Corps attack and launch III Corps on December 31. His decision boiled down to a desire to preempt the possible redeployment of enemy formations against Third Army in the corridor best suited for that very purpose.

As Middleton prepared to continue the attack, he faced the problem of how to concentrate his combat power. An implied task was to link up with British XXX Corps to help protect the Meuse crossings, and Patton could not ignore Eisenhower's concern here. French paratroopers were employed on the left for this purpose, but the 6th Cavalry Group could have been used to guard the left flank. Of Culin's nine infantry battalions, only three, those of the 345th CT, were committed to attacking. The 346th CT was securing the left, and the 347th CT was held in reserve. The 11th Armored Division after-action report noted at the end of December 30: "it became apparent that the infantry fight confronting CCA and the wide dispersal of forces was seriously crippling the attack."[26] Kilburn requested a boundary shift to exclude Remagne, and Middleton approved it at 1700. Kilburn's original complaint was thus justified, and Middleton conceded the fact by agreeing to a new scheme of maneuver after just ten hours of fighting. At 0100 on December 31 CCA/11th Armored Division handed over its frontage to the 41st Cavalry Reconnaissance Squadron and began moving to a new attack position near Morhet. Remer thought VIII Corps could have "saved a lot of blood" if they had continued attacking at night.[27]

At 1100 December 30 Millikin issued his field order for the next day. He faced a complex problem. Although his straight-line frontage from Bastogne to the Wiltz–Heiderscheid road was only ten miles, the Harlange Pocket made it longer by at least half. Coordination issues with VIII Corps regarding boundaries were real, the terrain was very difficult, and there was a significant salient in the very center of his front. Grow was instructed to "take maximum advantage of initial successes" and bypass all centers of resistance as he attacked northeast. Baade was to make his main attack on the left to support 6th Armored Division. Paul was to strike for the high ground north and northeast of Wiltz and be prepared to detach a combat team to Grow on order. It is apparent that Patton anticipated the 6th Armored Division would make considerable gains toward St. Vith, and the deduction is that Grow's would be the main attack, but that was

Table 11.1. Estimated Enemy Strength in III Corps' Zone of Advance, December 30, 1944

Formation	Men	Tanks/Assault Guns
5 FJD	3,000	0
26 VGD	3,000	0
79 VGD (elms)	2,500	0
9 VGD (elms)	2,500	0
15 PGD	2,500	25
130 Panzer Lehr	4,000	30
Miscellaneous	3,000	25
FGB	3,000	15
Total	21,300	95
Possible commitment piecemeal by daylight December 31		
11 PD	4,500	35
2 PD (on VIII Corps' front)	9,000	80
2 SS PD (on VIII Corps' front)	9,000	90
9 PD	7,000	60
Miscellaneous	1,500	20
9 VGD (balance of formation)	5,000	0
Total	36,000	285

Source: III Corps Field Order no. 2, Annex No. 2, Intelligence Annex, December 30, 1944.

not clear in Millikin's field order. In fact, as originally written, it suggested a disregard for the Harlange Pocket plaguing the 35th Infantry Division.

Millikin made several important verbal amendments to his field order at 1925. Whereas the 35th and 26th Infantry Divisions had originally been moving away from each other, Millikin now ordered Baade to attack northeast and Paul northwest.[28] This was a radical change in the scheme of maneuver, most likely driven by Patton's desire to eliminate the Harlange Pocket. Moreover, 4th Armored Division was given no tasks under the field order because Patton planned to attach it to VIII Corps. However, Middleton and Millikin agreed late that night that since Gaffey was already engaged, he should stay where he was until the situation developed the next day. At 2200 Millikin directed Gaffey to be prepared to assist Baade's advance on December 31 and to block any counterthrust from the north or northeast, commit some of his division to support CCA/9th Armored Division, and support Baade and Grow with artillery.[29]

The issuance of a field order by a corps commander is predicated on the assumption that the army commander has signed off on it. Millikin most likely back-briefed Patton on what he wanted to do, or, owing to Millikin's inexperience, Patton may have told him what he wanted for a scheme of maneuver. Something therefore triggered Patton to scrap the scheme of maneuver whereby III Corps would essentially picket the Harlange Pocket as Grow spearheaded the drive to Houffalize in favor of turning in to eliminate the problem. It is not clear whether this decision was a product of Patton's own estimate process or Bradley's influence. Grow had issues with the scheme of maneuver immediately. He understood the 11th Armored Division would support his left, but "much to everyone's amazement," he noted, Kilburn "was not making a punch north of Bastogne but had gone in southwest of 9th Armored Division. . . . I am the goat and will make a number two punch with no one on my left." He also apparently understood that Gaffey would advance on the left flank of the 6th Armored Division. Moreover, it seems that the 6th Armored Division was originally scheduled to attack through the 101st Airborne Division toward Houffalize.[30]

The redeployment within VIII Corps impacted III Corps' preparations for attack on December 31. CCA/11th Armored Division halted briefly at Vaux-les-Rosières and then continued on through Rosières to Morhet. The straight-line distance was only four miles, but CCA did not close until 1130 on December 31 because it ran into CCB/6th Armored Division, which had come onto the Neufchâteau–Bastogne highway at 0400 from its assembly area northwest of Arlon. CCB was marching to its assembly area east of Bastogne to spearhead III Corps' attack the next morning. Snow and ice on the highway did not help matters. Grow actually came across the congestion and called it "the worst traffic jam I ever saw."[31] Even the trains were having a difficult time getting forward, and the trains commander did not know the exact location of the front.[32] Grow set up his advance CP at Cobreville and ordered CCB and the divisional artillery into an assembly area at Clochimont. CCA closed at 0900 with little difficulty. Fortunately, 6th Armored Division's entanglement with CCA/11th Armored Division was not replicated with 4th Armored Division. Gaffey expressed concern about Grow passing through his area during the night of December 30 because he did not know which routes to keep open for 6th Armored Division. Millikin sent Grow the following message at 1640: "OLYMPIC is a little uneasy because they have not been contacted by your people re your movement tonight." Grow replied that he would contact Gaffey at once, but they already had an understanding that Grow planned to "use the two highways but that circumstances might force him to use secondary roads."[33]

The second day of Middleton's offensive, December 31, brought little progress. The 345th CT continued spearheading the 87th Infantry Division's advance alone. It repulsed a strong counterattack from KG *Neumann* at Moircy during the morning, but by afternoon the 345th CT had captured Remagne.[34] At this point Culin brought forward the 347th CT to relieve the 345th, the latter moving back into reserve. The 11th Armored Division, concentrated at the head of the Rechrival valley, launched CCB and CCR at 0845—the former along the east side of the Rechrival valley toward Chenogne, and the latter from the vicinity of Magerotte toward Pinsamont. Remer was no longer attacking. He assumed risk in the Gerimont–Rechrival sector to create two strong reserves for immediate counterattacks.[35] CCR reached Pinsamont by 1630 but withdrew to the high ground south of the town because of heavy mortar and artillery fire. CCB entered Chenogne but could not control it and withdrew south to high ground for the night. CCA was to advance down the center of the valley from Morhet to Rechrival and on to Hubermont and Flamierge, but because of the traffic jam with CCB/6th Armored Division, it did not advance until 1510. By 1600 CCA was south of Rechrival, but heavy antitank and mortar fire and a counterattack at 1630 forced it to consolidate for the night southeast of the town.[36] Middleton visited Kilburn at 1400, and at 2020 he ordered Kilburn to attack the next day at 0900.

In III Corps' sector Millikin did not have to face another large attack by XXXIX *Panzerkorps* on December 31. The author of the *1st SS PD* history claimed the division renewed its attacks with undiminished intensity that day. However, the 35th Infantry Division after-action report made no mention of it, and the III Corps after-action report stated that during the morning the enemy "showed no indication of resuming his attack" against Baade's division, probably because plans to do so "had been frustrated by the volume and accuracy of artillery fire which had been placed on his assembly areas during the night and morning." Though successful in preempting another German attack, III Corps struggled to kick-start its own advance. Baade's attempt to attack on December 31 "met with little success."[37] The 2nd Battalion/134th CT suffered ninety casualties trying to retake Lutrebois, and the 137th CT failed to relieve its two isolated companies in Villers-la-Bonne-Eau. *FJR 14*, "decimated though it was," was still fighting hard there.[38] South of Harlange the 320th CT made no headway against *FJR 15*.

The main pressure on III Corps during the day was on the right flank. The 26th Infantry Division was completely across the Sûre River, with its center combat team almost in sight of the Wiltz–Bastogne highway. At 0530 *VGR 57/9th VGD* struck the 101st CT northeast of Nothum. Just over three hours later Paul reported to III Corps that he was receiving a "severe" counterattack in his center by two battalions supported by tanks, but he thought he could take care of the situation if he committed his reserve. The 104th CT was engaged immediately north of Buderscheid by direct tank fire and *Nebelwerfer* fire. A "savage" attack drove the 1st Battalion off a commanding ridge and partly overran two companies. Paul brought up a battalion from the 328th CT to take over the 104th CT's flank duty. By the end of the day his division formed a salient across the Sûre; the 101st CT was at Nothum, the 104th CT was at Buderscheid, and the understrength 328th CT was at Bavigne. Both division flanks were exposed.[39]

The Harlange Pocket and XII Corps' enforced idleness were significantly impacting Millikin's flexibility. Ultimately, the geometry of the pocket worked to reduce III Corps' offensive toward St. Vith to the 6th Armored Division's attack, and despite planning and preparation, the offensive on December 31 was spearheaded by a single combat command of Grow's division. CCB/10th Armored Division, inside the Bastogne perimeter, could have been employed for added weight. On December 31 it possessed almost 2,200 personnel and 457 vehicles, including 32 tanks and 145 half-tracks. Although Grow could be mercurial, there was some truth in his observation, made on the night of December 30, that Patton was attempting "too much with too little and is getting in a hole by using his reserves piecemeal."[40]

Grow delayed his H-hour from 0900 to approximately noon to permit further reconnaissance, and he changed his orders to a limited-objective attack conducted by CCA alone.[41] CCA crossed the north-south LD, roughly from Bizory to Marvie, at 1230 to secure the high ground at Wardin. The delay was probably a good thing because the weather forecast called for poor visibility until 1200, but heavy shelling of the combat command's assembly area was probably the trigger. The division artillery fired some 3,300 rounds on Wardin, Mageret, Arloncourt, and Oubourcy during the day.[42] CCA gained a mile and a half, captured Neffe, and secured the high ground overlooking Wardin.

No sooner had CCA attacked than Phillips received a phone call from Patton stating that "he didn't care how much ground to the Northeast [*sic*] Bob [Grow] gained today—to fan out and kill Germans."[43] Fanning out was not what Grow had in mind. He was clearly worried about his exposed position and called Phillips at 2050 requesting that the 101st Airborne Division maintain its posture to protect his left flank.[44] Grow was in fact thinking of veering to the southeast to tackle the Harlange Pocket, but doing so would take him away from the 101st Airborne Division. At 2335 Millikin's G-3 sent the following message to Grow: "Our CG understands that you are studying and making plans to effect pinch off in the BRAS area in conjunction with the 26th and 35th Inf Divs. BRAS is out of your zone and the CG desires you to have plans for this, which will be effected on Corps order."[45]

VIII and III Corps' minimal advances during December 30–31 did not live up to Patton's expectations. As the III Corps after-action report stated, by nightfall on December 31, "neither the Germans nor our own forces could claim success." Some seventeen separate counterattacks identified on December 31 led Patton to note, "This has been a very long day for me." He further described the day as a "slugging match." He appears to have had second thoughts about continuing the VIII Corps advance, admitting that pushing Middleton to attack was "just mulishness on my part." He was confident, however, that since he now had Grow's division in line, things would be better. "Tomorrow will be the crucial test. I think, in fact know, we will stop them and attack at once."[46]

Patton may have been disappointed in the progress of the last two days, but Third Army was in good condition to continue the fight in corridor A. He lost some combat power when 9th Armored Division began moving to Sedan and CCR was withdrawn from Bastogne to become the SHAEF reserve on December 30.[47] Yet the army was in good logistical condition. It possessed 1,544,466 rations, and an additional 660,000 rations were held in reserve for the army at Verdun. The army depots contained 2,789,993 gallons of V-80 gasoline. To support the heavy fighting, two special trains carrying 260,000 operational rations and one train of V-80 gasoline totaling 206,000 gallons were sent forward from ComZ's AdSec depot at Verdun to Longwy on December 30. Another 194,000 gallons of gasoline was transferred from Third Army's mobile reserve at Valleroy to Longwy.[48] Because of a shortage of transport, III Corps suffered from a lack of heavy artillery ammunition, resulting in a noticeable slackening of III Corps' harassing and interdictory fires, but the corps was still sufficiently supplied to gain the upper hand in any artillery duels with *I SS* and *XXXIX Panzerkorps* and *LIII Armeekorps*. Most important, while the Germans were growing numerically weaker, Third Army was getting stronger; its strength on December 31 was 344,935, with some 925 separate units on its troop list, and this would increase to 353,655 the next day.[49]

In his G-2 Periodic Report No. 203, dated December 31, Koch perceived identifiable defensive positions opposite VIII Corps from Vesqueville to Hatrival, but "no regular lines" were discernible elsewhere on the corps' front. Middleton's advance faced booby-trapped roadblocks, abatis, and scattered minefields. The locations of the 3rd PGD and 1st SS PD "indicate[d] enemy determination to attempt to check increasing pressure" from Third Army and suggested a "drastic disruption" from the Liège line of action. Formations capable of intervening against VIII and III Corps were a cause for concern. The 2nd and 10th SS PDs, reported as out of contact with First Army, were "believed immediately available for commitment. No physical contact with 11 Pz Div has been established . . . this unit is considered unlocated and uncommitted, along with 21 Pz Div, 17 SS and 25 SS Pz Gren Divs." This appreciation again brings into question how much ULTRA Koch was able to digest, because Bletchley Park sent a message at 2214 on December 30 stating that 21st PD was moving to an area east of Pirmasens.[50] However, Koch's interpretation of 2nd SS PD's availability was spot on, because ULTRA revealed it was in the Amonines–Hampteau area, approximately fifteen miles from the northern Bastogne perimeter.[51] All the original panzer reserve in the west was committed or disposed close to the battlefront, and the enemy's infantry reinforcements were "far below his estimated capability of six to eight divisions a week."[52]

Koch concluded that there was no change in enemy capability, except that capability 3 from his Periodic Report No. 201 of December 29 — reinforcing against Bastogne with two panzer divisions and one infantry division — had expired because it had already taken place. The favored enemy capability was continuing to attack the shoulders and/or the base of the Bastogne corridor, primarily because Montgomery was still three days away from starting his own offensive. The second favored capability was to concentrate the equivalent of two panzer divisions and one infantry division in the Rochefort–La Roche–St. Hubert area and strike south to envelop VIII Corps' left flank. This was potentially a very dangerous line of action, because VIII Corps' flank was weakly held. It could not be completely ignored and would serve to keep Middleton's line stretched. This enemy capability on the northwest flank of the army was mirrored by enemy capability to disrupt the army's southeastern flank because intelligence indicated "additional build-up in progress SAARBRUCKEN area."[53]

Patton still had to be wary of both his flanks, even as he pushed hard in the middle. As far as Eisenhower was concerned, preventing the stabilization of the salient was the first priority, and he explicitly told Montgomery that day, "We must regain the initiative, and speed and energy are essential." The implication is that Eisenhower believed neither Montgomery nor Patton actually held the initiative, and the heavy battles south of Bastogne on December 30 and 31 proved him right as far as the latter was concerned. On December 31 Montgomery met with Hodges, Collins, and Ridgway and decided to launch VII Corps (2nd and 3rd Armored Divisions, 83rd and 84th Infantry Divisions) toward Houffalize while XVIII Airborne Corps protected Collins's left flank. As Sylvan noted, "D-Day and H-Hour not yet known."[54] As long as the Germans did not have to face a general counterattack from Montgomery's side, they could exploit interior lines and continue to seek a decision at Bastogne. Indeed, the Germans would now make their culminating offensive effort against Third Army over the next four days.

12

Culmination, January 1–4

III Corps reports that the heaviest fighting yet encountered on its front was met during the day of 4 January.
— Twelfth Army Group G-2 Periodic Report, January 5, 1945

On December 31 Eisenhower cabled Marshall that there were "several indications that the Germans may be preparing a counter offensive in the area of the upper Rhine."[1] As a precaution, Kibler sent a message to Third Army at 1730 to "initiate without delay" the necessary reconnaissance and organization to tie into Patch's reserve position west of Bitche.[2] Less than six hours later *Heeresgruppe G* launched Operation *NORDWIND*. Rundstedt had begun planning it on December 21 as a way of taking advantage of Patton's withdrawal from the Saar sector to deal with the southern flank of the Bulge. Hitler, however, expanded it on December 22 and turned it into a major offensive aimed at the Saverne Gap, twenty miles northwest of Strasbourg, to regain the Zabern rise, destroy Allied forces in northern Alsace, and regain contact with *Nineteenth Armee*.[3] It was also an attempt to deflect Third Army from *Fifth Panzer Armee* and restart the drive to the Meuse. It employed reserves that could not be effectively employed in the Ardennes due to road and logistical limitations. If *NORD-WIND* was successful, Hitler envisioned another series of operations, code-named *ZAHNARTZ* (Dentist), from the Saare valley–Saverne area toward Metz and the rear of Third Army. Indeed, Hitler had even considered the possibility of turning southward after the initial breakthrough during *WACHT AM RHEIN* to attack Patton's rear.[4]

As *NORDWIND* got under way, Model was already sending more combat power to Manteuffel. *Fifth Panzer Armee* had lost 324 panzers since December 16.[5] At 0005 December 30 *Heeresgruppe B* ordered *340th VGD* to be transferred as quickly as possible to a location southwest of Houffalize.

Table 12.1. German Order of Battle for NORDWIND

Army Group	Area	Divisions	Artillery
Heeresgruppe G First Armee			
XIII SS Korps	Saare River valley	17 SS PGD* 36 VGD*	VAK 404* VAK 410 VWB 20 × 2 Heer Arty Abt
XC Armeekorps	Bitche	559 VGD* 257 VGD*	
LXXXIX Armeekorps	Bitche	361 VGD* 256 VGD*	
Reserve			
XXXIX Panzerkorps		21 PD* 15 PGD*	
Other identified Reserves		6 SS-Gebirgs Div 10 SS PD 7 FJD	

* Formations engaged by Third Army during the Lorraine campaign.

All elements that could be made mobile by motor transport, along with the antitank battalion and artillery, were to be rushed forward. On December 31 *Fusilier Abteilung 340*, *Panzerjäger Abteilung 340*, and the main body of the *340th VGD* were near Dahlen and Kall.[6] That day Manteuffel ordered Hermann Priess, commander of *I SS Panzerkorps*, to take over part of Lüttwitz's *XLVII Panzerkorps'* northern sector and indicated that the *9th* and *12th SS PDs* would arrive soon.[7] *I SS Panzerkorps* assumed command of the sector held by *Panzer Lehr* and the *FBB* at 1300 on January 1, with the mission of holding the Remagne–Morhet line.[8] *Panzer Lehr* had sustained 2,465 casualties as of January 1; its artillery regiment still had twenty guns but had to borrow prime movers from *VWB 15*, and the supply situation was critical. *Werfer Regiment 55* from *VWB 15* was subordinated to *XLVII Panzerkorps* on January 1, but it could not get forward on time due to fuel shortages.[9] Remer's *FBB* was to be relieved by the *12th SS PD* and then go into *Fifth Panzer Armee* reserve.

The first elements of Hugo Kraas's *12th SS PD* departed Samrée at 1700 on January 1 and arrived at Wigny, seven miles northwest of Bastogne, at 2300. Kraas drove ahead to confer with Remer. Even as the *12th SS PD* was moving into position via various routes, Manteuffel made a significant change. At 1800 he briefed Priess at *Fifth Panzer Armee* headquarters at Wandebourcy that his corps would take over the *26th* VGD's positions in the northeastern sector of Bastogne as of 1200 on January 2. Priess's new mission was to push the 6th Armored Division back on Bastogne. The *12th SS PD* was then redirected from southwest to northeast of Bastogne, but significant elements of *SS PGR 26* had already been committed near Hubermont. An engagement with the 11th Armored Division at 1600 delayed the regiment's departure.[10]

While Manteuffel reorganized his combat power, VIII Corps renewed its offensive on New Year's Day. On the corps' far left the 4th French Parachute Battalion established contact with British XXX Corps. This must have given Middleton some satisfaction as he continued to push back German forces on his front. The 347th CT passed through the 345th CT during the night and captured Jenneville by 1200; it then advanced through a heavily mined and booby-trapped area to the Morhet–St. Hubert road. The 346th CT continued to contain St. Hubert–Vesqueville. In Kilburn's sector, CCB attacked at 0830 toward Chenogne and captured it by 1200, supported by what Denkert called an "extraordinarily strong artillery preparation." Thirteen field artillery battalions from the 4th, 9th, and 11th Armored Divisions and the 101st Airborne Division fired 6,000 rounds.[11] CCB defeated a heavy counterattack, cleared the Bois de Valets by 1700, and dug in for the night on terrain overlooking Mande–St. Étienne. CCA attacked at 1200 toward the heavily defended Hubermont–Millmont–Rechrival sector but was hit by a heavy counterattack from the northwestern tip of the Bois de Valets. It reached the edge of Hubermont just before dark but withdrew to consolidate on high ground east of Rechrival. On VIII Corps' right flank, CCA/9th Armored Division, which had yet to join the division in SHAEF reserve, attacked at 1100 toward Senonchamps, but icy roads, extreme cold, and difficult terrain prevented seizure of the objective.[12]

The 11th Armored Division lost forty-nine Shermans and seventeen light tanks during the day. The division after-action report noted that personnel and material losses "were mounting at a rapid rate." Middleton blamed Kilburn for this. When Middleton found Kilburn directing traffic at a crossroads, he told him, "a PFC could do that . . . I told him to move on. He was very nervous and kept most of those around him nervous. He wanted to do too much." Patton noted that the division "fought well but stupidly and lost too many tanks. Apparently they are very green and particularly inept at fighting in the woods." Since Bradley had told him that day he could move the 28th Infantry Division back into the

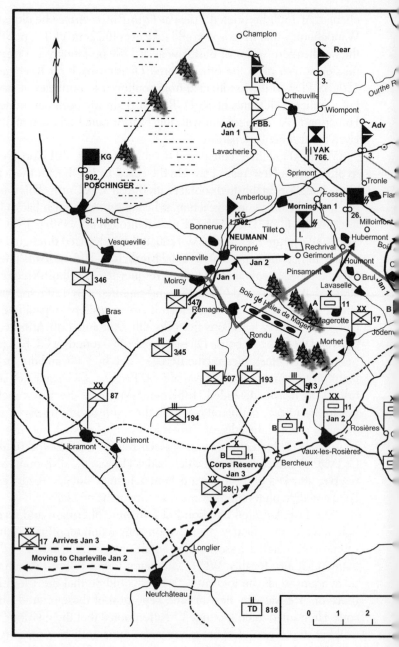

Map. 12.1. Third Army Operations at Bastogne, January 1–4, 1945

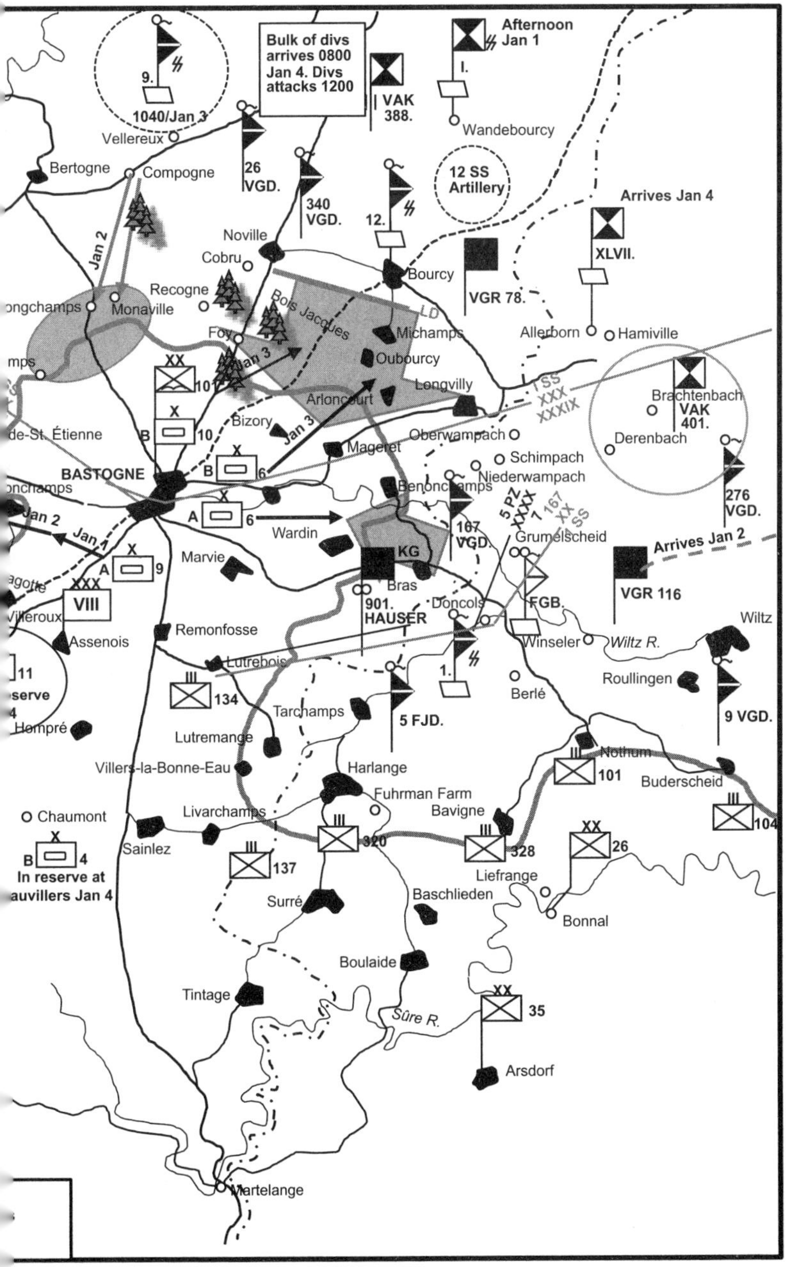

Bulk of divs arrives 0800 Jan 4. Divs attacks 1200
Afternoon Jan 1
9.
1040/Jan 3
VAK 388.
I.
Wandebourcy
Vellereux
Bertogne
Compogne
26 VGD.
340 VGD.
12.
12 SS Artillery
Arrives Jan 4
XLVII.
Jan 2
Noville
Cobru
Recogne
Bourcy
VGR 78.
Longchamps
Monaville
Bois Jacques
LD
Michamps
Allerborn
Hamiville
Foy
Jan 3
Oubourcy
101
Longvilly
Arloncourt
I SS
XXX
XXXIX
Brachtenbach
VAK 401.
Bizory
10
Jan 3
Oberwampach
Derenbach
de-St. Étienne
B
Mageret
Schimpach
BASTOGNE
6
Niederwampach
Benonchamps
276 VGD.
A
6
5 PZ
XXXX
7
167
XX
SS
Jan 2
Jan 1
Wardin
167 VGD.
Grumelscheid
Arrives Jan 2
KG
Marvie
9
VIII
Bras
VGR 116
901.
HAUSER
Doncols
FGB.
Wiltz
Villeroux
Assenois
Remonfosse
Winseler
Wiltz R.
Lutrebois
1.
Berlé
Roullingen
11
134
Tarchamps
5 FJD.
9 VGD.
Hompré
Lutremange
Nothum
101
Villers-la-Bonne-Eau
Harlange
Buderscheid
Fuhrman Farm
Chaumont
Livarchamps
Bavigne
104
320
328
26
B
4
In reserve at
auvillers Jan 4
Sainlez
137
Liefrange
Surré
Baschlieden
Bonnal
Boulaide
Tintage
Sûre R.
35
Arsdorf
Martelange

SHAEF reserve and bring up the 17th Airborne Division to an assembly area near Neufchâteau, Patton resolved to pull Kilburn back behind the 17th Airborne.[13]

In III Corps, CCB/6th Armored Division captured Mageret by midafternoon, and by nightfall the division had severed the important Longvilly–Mageret–Benonchamps MSR. Patton phoned Phillips at 1305 and told him "it was time for Bob [Grow] to turn a little to the right and assist in taking care of that [Harlange] pocket." He added, "Those bastards in there can't hold out much longer." Patton appreciated that a "definite pocket" had formed from which the Germans "seriously threaten our line of supply," making it necessary to "evict them." Phillips assured Patton that Millikin had already ordered Grow to start the maneuver.[14]

South of the 6th Armored Division the 35th Infantry Division had dug in, anticipating an attack that never came.[15] Baade's G-3, Colonel Walter J. Renfroe Jr., cabled III Corps at 0925: "The counterattack we expected did not materialize primarily, I think, because of the artillery concentration on enemy assembly areas. Around 10 o'clock Gen. Baade issued orders to dig in to meet the counterattack. He has now issued orders to continue the attack which should get under full headway by the middle of the day. Gen. Baade's plans include tying in with the 6 Armd on the North as per instructions from your headquarters last night." Three hours later, Millikin's G-3, Colonel Harry C. Mewshaw, cabled Renfroe to send in the division plan as soon as possible and asked, "Are you leaving any gaps that might be dangerous?" Renfroe replied that the only place the division was thin "was where they always had been, i.e., SW of HARLANGE." None of Baade's regiments gained much ground, and the division after-action report described the resistance as "fierce," "all-out," and "stonewall." The III Corps after-action report stated that although it was holding the Harlange salient successfully, it had been "temporarily stopped in its advance to the North" but expected 6th Armored Division's attack to "improve the situation."[16]

One can sense Patton's frustration with III Corps, for its daily gains were marginal. He visited Baade and Paul that day and noted that they were "doing well but going slowly." With the exception of the 6th Armored Division, "all other units made little to no progress." Patton was particularly frustrated because III Corps had so far been unable to clear out the Harlange Pocket. Hundreds of miles away, Eisenhower, too, was frustrated, describing Patton's progress to Marshall on January 1 as "slow and laborious."[17] After just two days of operations by III Corps in line with his December 28 directive, Patton reevaluated the army's scheme of maneuver.

Looking at the larger picture, Patton was not overly concerned about the new attacks against Seventh Army in Alsace because "all the [German] units identified . . . were those we had chased across the mud flats from the Moselle to the Saar." He was confident that all his troops were where they should be: defeat "will be due to better fighting on the part of the enemy . . . not to any mistakes which I may have made." Third Army radio intelligence identified *21st PD* opposite XV Corps on January 1.[18] The reappearance of the *Luftwaffe* with a vengeance did not negatively affect him either. The intent of Operation *BODEN-PLATTE* (Base Plate), a coordinated attack with perhaps as many as 1,000 aircraft, was to cripple Allied airpower in a single stroke by striking sixteen airfields in Belgium, Holland, and France. At 0945 Third Army phoned XIX TAC to report that Luxembourg had been strafed by approximately twenty-five FW-190s. Fifteen to twenty-five Bf-109s attacked the Metz airfield, the forwardmost of Weyland's bases, destroying twenty aircraft and damaging eleven others. The Metz air defense battery claimed twelve of the German aircraft. Gay called the *Luftwaffe* offensive on January 1 the "heaviest German air attacks" ever experienced by Third Army.[19]

Patton would not have been so confident, perhaps, had *NORDWIND* been launched in a more sensitive area. A powerful attack on either XX or XII Corps would have immediately deflected significant portions of Third Army's combat power from Bastogne. Indeed, Rundstedt appears to have contemplated an operation aimed at retaking Metz, but planning never matured.[20] Although *NORDWIND* was linked to the Ardennes strategically, in terms of grand tactics, it was launched in the wrong place and beyond the mutually supporting distance of *Seventh Armee* and *Fifth Panzer Armee*. The Germans, however, frequently selected strategic and grand tactical directions that actually nullified tactical success.[21]

Patton's calm reaction to *NORDWIND* was not mirrored by Eisenhower. The day before, Devers had informed him that he could not maintain the integrity of the northern half of his army group and simultaneously protect Bradley's right flank unless all forces east of the Moselle were under his command. Devers believed Walker's XX Corps should be turned over to him and a new interarmy group boundary established in the Thionville area, and he lobbied for the "earliest possible allocation" of infantry replacements.[22] Eisenhower replied to Devers's request for aid on

January 1: "There is no way in which we can help you . . . at the present time." Eisenhower also told Bedell Smith, "You must call up Devers and tell him that he is not doing what he is told, that is, to get 6 Corps back and to hold the Alsace Plain with recce and observational elements . . . tell him to obey his orders and shorten his lines." Eisenhower's intention to uncover Strasbourg in an effort to shorten his line and create reserves brought an outcry from General Charles de Gaulle and Alphonse Juin, the French army chief of staff. Later that night Eisenhower upbraided Devers personally for not doing as instructed and demanded that he form a SHAEF reserve. Bedell Smith declared, "It is a terrific struggle to keep a reserve."[23] Now that Eisenhower had two widely separated threats to deal with, it was possible that combat power for Third Army might be diverted to Sixth Army Group.

Patton discussed his updated army plan with Eddy in person on January 1. Eddy noted: "I am very strongly against the plan which calls for us to cross the Sauer river and then go through the Siegfried Line in the same location. I recommended that we attack to the north after we cross the river and General Patton said he would consider this."[24] Patton considered it, accepted it, and explained it within the army's larger scheme of maneuver to Middleton that day in a written memorandum:

> As I see the situation now, you will eventually use the 17th Airborne to augment your attack on Houffalize. When this starts, I believe that the further use of the 87th will terminate, and we can trade that for the 94th [Infantry Division]. Looking into the future, I propose to have you . . . attack on the axis Bastogne–St. Vith. In conjunction with an attack by the XII Corps from Diekirch north on St. Vith, the VII Corps will attack the day after tomorrow morning on the road Houffalize–Vaux–Chavanne. It is therefore my belief that, if the 101st feels it can do it, and the situation otherwise is satisfactory, you should move on Noville the day after tomorrow. For the big picture, with you and Eddy moving on St. Vith, the III Corps will hold defensively on any line obtained and successively break off divisions from the west to augment the attack of the XII Corps. This plan is subject to change without notice as all plans are. However, we must still bear in mind that the 4th Armored Division should eventually get to the XII Corps, so that the XII Corps can have one armored division and two infantry divisions. You will then have one armored

division and two or three infantry divisions, which should make a very powerful pair of scissor blades.[25]

This was a radical change from the December 28 directive, which called for III Corps to drive to St. Vith and for XII Corps to cross at Echternach and advance up the Prüm valley.

Terrain played a large part in Patton's estimate at this stage. III Corps' task during January was greatly increased by the complex ground, "which ranged from sweeping hills and deep valleys to precipitous heights. . . . The terrain alone would have presented tremendous obstacles to an attack in even a mild and temperate season. In the right of the Corps zone the mountainous country, aptly named the 'Luxembourg Alps,' was in itself a formidable natural obstacle and re-crossed by numerous icy streams, which, with the hills and ridges between them, formed compartments across which the Corps advanced. The road net, especially in the right of the Corps zone, was poor; and dense forests covered a large portion of the area."[26] Patton's new scheme of maneuver was designed to exploit the good ground in corridors A and B while neutralizing the enemy and avoiding the poor ground in between.

On January 2 VIII Corps continued to advance slowly. The 87th Infantry Division attacked at 0830, and the 347th CT captured Gerimont from the *FBB*. CCB/11th Armored Division attacked at 1500 with an artillery preparation described by Denkert as "heavier than that of the previous day." Regimental organization within his division had broken down, and he held the MLR with a series of strongpoints. The "irreparable" loss of signals communication facilities forced independent action by groups.[27] However, a *Kampfgruppe* from *3rd PGD* reached Hill 488 via Millmont and established defensive positions. CCB captured Mande–St. Étienne and defeated a counterattack at 2245, at which point Denkert ordered a withdrawal to a new MLR along the elevated terrain northeast of Renaumont. CCA/9th Armored Division captured Senonchamps but was then pinched out by the 11th Armored Division on the left.[28] As the fighting continued, advance elements of the fresh 17th Airborne Division relieved CCA/11th Armored Division by 1500, and the depleted 28th Infantry Division cleared Neufchâteau on its way to Charleville.

In the northwestern Bastogne sector, *I SS Panzerkorps* committed incoming elements piecemeal on January 2, although the main attack was scheduled for the next day. A reinforced regiment of the *9th SS PD* attacked from Compogne toward Monaville, Longchamps, and Champs at 0006, with the intent of establishing a line from there to Recogne.[29] On the other side of Bastogne, in the 6th Armored Division's sector, nine field artillery battalions massed to repel an attack between 0100 and 0200, probably by the advance guard of the *340th VGD*, which penetrated the outpost line of CCB/10th Armored Division and broke into Mageret.[30] Massed artillery was also fired on enemy forming-up areas near Wardin between 0300 and 0600. A TOT was fired on Arloncourt, and twelve battalions massed on Michamps.

Grow adjusted to Millikin's direction to broaden the division objective to include Bras by bringing up CCR from Cobreville and reorganizing the combat commands. All tank and infantry elements of the division were committed at 0925 on January 2. In the south, CCA attacked east toward Wardin against elements of the *167th VGD*; in the north, CCB, with two tank battalions, attacked northeast toward Arloncourt and Michamps. CCB captured Oubourcy at 1100 and pushed into Michamps at 1500 against *VGR 78*. CCA entered Wardin by the end of the day, but Grow withdrew his commands to high ground generally west of Michamps–Arloncourt–Wardin for the night. *KG von Ribbentrop* of the *12th SS PD* reoccupied Oubourcy during the night.[31]

Brandenberger considered 6th Armored Division's penetration of the *167th VGD*'s lines a "serious crisis." He correctly appreciated the attempt to cut off the Harlange Pocket, so he committed more elements of the *VAK* and *VWB* on the right wing of *Seventh Armee* and withdrew the *276th VGD*, described as "a mere combat team," and moved it to *LIII Armeekorps* northeast of Wiltz. He requested permission to attempt to rescue Heilmann's division from the pocket, but Model refused. In Brandenberger's opinion, higher command "was primarily concerned with fixing as many enemy forces here as possible." Brandenberger also feared for the center of his line, where reports stated that Third Army was firing 10,000 rounds of artillery per day in the Wiltz sector. He moved his CP from Dockendorf to Jucken, a few miles east of Dasburg, on January 1 to better control the center of his front. Through ULTRA, Patton appreciated on January 2 that Brandenberger felt confident of maintaining his MLR at the Sûre River but feared Third Army pressure in the Heiderscheidergrund sector.[32]

While *I SS Panzerkorps* made piecemeal efforts throughout the day, Priess briefed Kraas; *Oberst* Theodor Tolsdorff, commander of the *340th VGD*; and *SS-Oberführer* Sylvester Stadler at 1000 on the corps' attack plan for January 3. Priess's scheme of maneuver consisted of the three divisions attacking abreast. The 9th SS PD was to attack from the forest south of Compogne on the west side of the Noville–Bastogne highway toward Longchamps and Monaville. The 340th VGD was to attack east of the highway astride the Bourcy–Bastogne railroad, and the 12th SS PD was to attack from the Bois Jacques southwest to Michamps, Arloncourt, and Mageret. Stadler and Tolsdorff reported that the bulk of their units would not arrive until midnight. Stadler reported that his division had thirty tanks and 150 men per battalion. Since Priess could not predict with any accuracy when the 340th VGD, VAK 401, and SS-Artillerie Regiment 12 would arrive, he left H-hour undecided.

At 1430 on January 2 Model visited Manteuffel to inspect plans for the final effort against Bastogne. Model's desire to concentrate for this final attack north and northeast of Bastogne has been interpreted as a conscious decision to position the formations for an easier withdrawal from the salient instead of risking their isolation too far south. Yet the better tank terrain northeast of Bastogne was clearly a factor. Moreover, Decker's XXXIX Panzerkorps, which apparently still contained the 167th VGD, 1st SS PD, and KG von Hauser, simply prevented any greater concentration of force southeast of Bastogne. Manteuffel again appealed to Model to pull back to Houffalize and pressed him to delay Priess's attack to January 4, but Model set it for 1200 on January 3, most likely because the assigned divisions had not closed in their assembly areas.[33]

On January 2 Patton brought all his corps commanders to Third Army to discuss plans "so that now each one knows what all the others are doing." Eddy recalled, "He put the plan, as I had suggested, into effect and we will attack to the north." Irwin and McBride were particularly happy about the new plan because, in Eddy's words, they "opposed and dreaded the one outlined before." As Gay noted, it was "decided definitely" to launch Eddy north from Diekirch.[34] The result of this planning session was XII Corps Field Order No. 13, issued at 1900 the next day. D-day was not indicated, but the scheme of maneuver was as follows: The corps would attack with two infantry divisions and one armored division in the direction of St. Vith. Irwin's 5th Infantry Division would carve out a bridgehead across the Sûre River, supported by McBride's 80th Infantry Division. An unnamed infantry division would then pass through Irwin and seize the high ground northeast of Bettendorf, while the 4th Infantry Division cleared the remaining enemy from the south and west bank of the Sûre and established an advance OPLR. The 4th Armored Division, which would assemble in the area west of Luxembourg City, would prepare to attack through the Sûre River bridgehead in the direction of St. Vith.[35] Once again, Patton's favorite division was to be the spearhead.

Patton's attempt to shift some of his combat power out of corridor A made sense because he appreciated, as did Montgomery, that Eisenhower's scheme of maneuver would be slow and costly. Montgomery specifically warned Eisenhower on January 2 that "tactical victory within the salient is going to take some little time to achieve and that there will be heavy fighting." In his situation report to Brooke that night he added, "We may not have sufficient strength to push the Germans out of the penetration area and obtain what IKE calls 'tactical victory in the salient.' The Germans are in great strength . . . I foresee a very great deal of hard and bitter fighting in the penetration area and I doubt if the Americans have the reserves to keep it up."[36]

Sibert also appreciated the concentration of German combat power. In his Weekly Intelligence Summary issued on January 2, he stated that the Germans could not advance northwest while Bastogne overlooked their LC. As a result, "the first team" had gathered around Bastogne "in an array which clearly exposes the enemy's anxiety over this position." Sibert assessed the enemy's primary capability as follows: "When the enemy recognizes failure in the attempt to drive the Third Army from BASTOGNE, it is quite possible that he will withdraw to the strongest possible defensive positions he can and attempt a shallow hook in a north-westerly direction in an effort to drive the Allied forces out of the area East of AACHEN." A secondary capability included attacking southward from Trier to Luxembourg and from Saargemunde southward toward the Colmar bridgehead, but it was impossible to predict whether any of these operations were diversionary or main efforts. The *11th PD* and *10th SS PD* were unlocated but were "believed to be in reserve in the *Heeresgruppe B* area," and the *21st PD* was believed to be located opposite Sixth Army Group. Sibert also identified several divisions out of contact for some time, including the *16th*, *48th*, *91st*, and *275th Divisions*, and he anticipated the arrival of the *6th SS-Gebirgs Division* from Denmark "very shortly." He calculated that of the 339,000 troops on the Western Front, Patton was facing a nominal eighteen divisions (twelve equivalent), 93,500 men, and 285 tanks, while Hodges was facing 75,500 men with 345 tanks.[37]

Based on Sibert's estimates, Patton was facing 28 percent of the German combat power in the west in the Bulge, and most of that 28 percent was stacked up in corridor A around Bastogne. This is why Patton wanted

Table 12.2. Twelfth Army Group Estimate of German Strength Opposite Allied Armies
in the West, January 2, 1945

Allied Army	German Personnel	German Tanks/ Assault Guns	German Arty Bns
Ninth U.S.	44,000	40	50
First U.S.	75,500	345	77
Third U.S.	93,500	285	89
First Canadian and Second British	59,500	40	40
Sixth Army Group	66,500	80	63
Total for Western Front	339,000	790	323

Source: Twelfth Army Group Weekly Intelligence Summary No. 21, January 2, 1945, pp. 6–9.

to get Eddy moving. There was little prospect of VIII and III Corps advancing quickly without a large injection of combat power, especially considering the estimate of the threat. Patton noted on January 2: "The enemy may make one more effort on Bastogne from the north tonight, or he may try our left rear. I rather fancy he will try Bastogne. The 4th Armored is well set to stop anything that can happen."[38] The recognition of a possible threat to VIII Corps' left rear was a reflection of Koch's estimate of capability on December 31, and it was yet another reason why Middleton could not concentrate more.

At 0830 on January 3 VII Corps attacked across the high marshes of the Plateau des Tailles, with the 2nd and 3rd Armored Divisions leading and the 83rd and 84th Infantry Divisions behind. The 2nd Armored

Table 12.3. Estimated Enemy Strength in XII Corps' Zone of Advance, January 3, 1945

Formation	Strength	Combat Efficiency Rating	Morale
79 VGD	6,000	Fair	Poor
276 VGD	3,500	Poor	Poor
212 VGD	5,000	Fair	Not stated
23/999 Penal Regt	250–300	Little aggressiveness	Not stated
352 VGD in immediate reserve	4,000	Fair	Not stated
Total*	18,800		

* Total does not include artillery—estimated to be 16 battalions (66 batteries) with 77mm howitzers to 210mm multibarreled rocket launchers.
Source: XII Corps Field Order No. 13, Intelligence Annex, January 3, 1945.

Division ran into an "extremely heavy fight" with *2nd PD* (again), and losses on both sides were heavy.[39] Thirty minutes later Middleton phoned Patton, seeking to postpone the attack on January 4 due to enemy buildup near Bastogne. Koch's ISUM for 0900 stated that heavy enemy movement on the west flank of the Bastogne Pocket "may indicate" the arrival of new divisions.[40] Patton refused, citing his long-held conviction that once an attack was planned, it should proceed, and his mission was to destroy Germans. However, he seems to have had some concerns about VIII Corps. He sent Gay to see Bradley, who thought VIII Corps should be launched from Bastogne to Houffalize because it was the direct route. Gay suggested that this had been the original concept, but Middleton had changed it, and it was too late to alter it now. This strongly suggests that Patton's lack of specific direction to Middleton when he called Third Army on December 29 was now having a negative effect on operations. Patton insisted that the 101st Airborne Division attack generally astride the Bastogne–Houffalize road, and Gay passed this on to Bradley.[41]

Middleton rested the bulk of VIII Corps on January 3, launching no attacks of significance against the *FBB* and *3rd PGD*.[42] The 11th Armored Division had temporarily lost its effectiveness, and Middleton withdrew it into corps reserve. CCB moved back to an assembly area southwest of Bercheux, while CCA withdrew to supporting positions behind the right flank of the 17th Airborne Division at Sibret. CCR remained at Morhet. In five days of combat, Kilburn's formation had suffered 220 killed and 441 wounded, as well as losing forty-two Shermans and twelve light tanks.[43] The planned attack of the newly arrived 17th Airborne Division at 1200 had to be postponed a day. It had taken seven days to fly the division over from England. It had not arrived at Charleville until December 27, and even by January 3 it was still not ready. Patton blamed the slippery road conditions, but a lack of trucks compounded the problem. By daylight on January 3 only 50 percent of the division had closed on the Acul–Houmont line. The relief of the 11th Armored Division and CCA/9th Armored Division was finally completed at 1800 hours. The commander of the 17th Airborne Division, Major General William M. Miley, prepared to attack the next day to reach the line of the Ourthe River.

The only formation in VIII Corps that attacked on January 3 was the 101st Airborne Division. The 501st PIR attacked at 1200 to clear the Bois Jacques and struck elements of the *340th VGD* in their assembly areas. German troops in *I SS Panzerkorps'* sector spent the morning of January 3 awaiting the arrival of as much combat power as possible, and by noon the decision was made to attack. Between 1300 and 1400 a regiment of the *9th SS PD* attacked toward Monaville, Longchamps, and Noville with thirty to fifty tanks, but it stalled in front of the villages.[44] The *340th VGD* attacked with *VGR 694* on the right and *VGR 695* on the left and battled for strongpoints inside the Bois Jacques.

The *12th SS PD*'s LD was a mile and a half south of the Noville–Bourcy road, with the division artillery north of Bourcy. Kraas attacked with *SS PGR 26* on the right and *SS PGR 25* on the left, supported by *Schwere Panzerjäger Abteilung 560*. It struck the 6th Armored Division from Michamps southwest. The appearance of the *Hitler Jugend* must have come as a surprise to Koch and Patton, because at 1800 on January 2 the former had reported that the division was out of contact, and at 0900 on January 3 he placed it and the *9th SS PD* in the Houffalize area.[45] Grow inflicted heavy losses, but the Germans retained control of the town at 1100. Koch described the several counterattacks as the "strongest" received north of the Bastogne salient, and he called the fighting "fierce."[46] The *9th SS PD* arrived complete at 2000 on January 3, and Priess ordered Stadler to attack again at 0800 the next morning. By that time, the rest of the *340th VGD* had arrived, as well as the bulk of its artillery.

Even as *I SS Panzerkorps* executed its main attack on January 3, Manteuffel ordered *Fifth Panzer Armee* to start withdrawing from the Bastogne sector, and Decker's *XXXIX Panzerkorps* headquarters began its withdrawal in order to move to *Heeresgruppe G*. Hitler admitted failure that day and ordered Model to hold the ground gained and defeat the largest possible force. *Oberst* Wilhelm Meyer-Detring, chief of the *WFSt*, stated that Model's mission was now to fight the Bastogne battle "to its conclusion and then . . . stiffen the northern front [of the salient]. Model could expect no further reinforcements."[47] This meant that Grow's 6th Armored Division, facing a significant portion of *I SS Panzerkorps*' combat power, would be involved in further desperate fighting.

On January 4 VIII Corps returned to the attack. In the 87th Infantry Division's sector, 347th CT attacked at 0915 but made little progress toward Pironpré. A counterattack by *KG Neumann* at 1600 wiped out all gains. Middleton's main attack was executed by the 17th Airborne Division, supported by the 101st Airborne Division's secondary attack on the right. CCA/11th Armored Division was at Sibret on semialert status to aid either Miley or Maxwell Taylor's 101st Airborne Division. Even before Taylor's division attacked, it found itself under heavy artillery and mortar fire at 0400, followed two and a half hours later by a series of attacks by

PGR 104/15th PGD, supported by a company of tanks at Longchamps. At 0900 the *9th SS PD* attacked with a battalion and fifteen tanks from Noville but was repulsed by 1200. By 1830 the 101st Airborne Division reported that it had destroyed thirty-four tanks.[48]

Miley's paratroopers attacked at 0815 with the 194th GIR on the left, the 513th PIR on the right, and the 507th PIR in reserve behind the 194th, preceded by a ten-minute artillery preparation. The 194th GIR quickly moved through Rechrival, Hubermont, and Millmont but then hit *XLVII Panzerkorps'* MLR. *PGR 29/3rd PGD* reacted strongly with artillery and tanks and struck both leading airborne regiments. By 1300 the 194th had sustained "fairly high" casualties between Renaumont and Hill 480. An hour later its 2nd Battalion was counterattacked by infantry, supported by an estimated eleven tanks, and suffered severe casualties. On the right, long-range small-arms and sporadic artillery fire was received almost immediately by the 513th PIR. The 1st Battalion was counterattacked at around 1300 by a company of infantry supported by tanks, and it took severe casualties. C Company/22nd Tank Battalion (attached) lost six of ten Shermans near Monty around noon. The 513th PIR succeeded in taking the woods between Chenogne and Flamizoulle with a bayonet charge, but observation was minimal and artillery was ineffective. Moreover, Miley recalled that they could not get the artillery up close enough to properly support the troops. As a result, the 513th PIR was driven back almost to the LD. *PGR 29* somehow managed to converge on the 17th Airborne Division from three directions, capturing 200 paratroopers.[49]

Miley probably lost control during his division's baptism of fire. He admitted in a postwar statement that withdrawals were necessary because the units were "out on a limb—past supporting distance." That was his fault and the fault of the regimental commanders, but the light division needed to be reinforced with armor, antitank weapons, engineers, and artillery beyond its organic light 75mm guns to make it viable in the existing conditions. Following this grim introduction to combat, Miley stated, "I don't know what's the matter with my men. We're just not getting anywhere."[50] Miley later suggested that his mission was too large for a new division, but "the high command was insistent at this time that there was nothing in front of us. By high command, I mean that Third Army was presenting this view to VIII Corps. The latter didn't figure it would be that easy, they said in passing the estimate on to us, but even their calculations were an under-estimation of the enemy situation." Miley's recollection did not square with the intelligence produced by Third Army, which

Table 12.4. Estimated Enemy Strength Opposite Third Army, January 3, 1945

German Strength	VIII Corps	III Corps	XII Corps	XX Corps	Total
Combat-effective troops	27,000	34,500	16,500	15,000	93,000
Tanks/assault guns	170	95	10	15	290

Source: Third Army AAR, vol. 1, p. 207.

estimated there were 27,000 men and 170 tanks opposite VIII Corps at the time. Moreover, the 101st Airborne Division had reported heavy vehicle movement southwest from Houffalize, some of which was detrucking at Bertogne.[51]

The performance of the 17th Airborne Division quickly drew Patton's attention. He noted in his diary that Miley's division had "run into violent resistance" and "got a very bloody nose and reported the loss of 40% in some of its battalions. This is, of course, hysterical. A loss for any one day of over 8 to 10% can be put down to a damn lie, unless the people run or surrender. General Miley did not impress me when I met him at Bastogne. . . . He told me he did not know where his right regiment was, yet he was not out looking for it."[52] Perhaps because of the performance of the 17th Airborne and 11th Armored Divisions, Patton commented that day: "We can still lose this war . . . the Germans are colder and hungrier than we are, but they fight better. I can never get over the stupidity of our green troops." In his opinion, new units "are not worth a thing in their first fight." Yet elsewhere he noted that the individual fighting of the green paratroopers was "excellent."[53]

Despite Koch's description of the German attacks north of Bastogne on January 3 as the strongest yet received, *I SS Panzerkorps* made another major effort against III Corps on January 4. In the early-morning hours the *12th SS PD* and *340th VGD* struck the 6th Armored Division and drove it back through Mageret and Wardin. Grow called Phillips at 1315 and stated he would have to fall back 1,000 yards to better terrain and anchor his left flank on the 101st Airborne Division. Phillips recorded the following: "He stated that his men had been out four days now on an extended front and it was impossible for him to hold unless he got reinforcements. . . . General Grow brought up the question as to why the 4th Armored Division or the 11th Armored Division could not be used to assist him and I informed him that all of the troops under our command were committed." CCB/4th Armored Division was actually in reserve well south at

Fauvillers. Grow called back at 1745 and told Phillips he had been forced to give ground during the afternoon "under continuous pressure." Phillips recorded that "it was a melee with a great deal of confusion," but Grow "thought he had it stopped. He had employed all his reserves, and while he believed he could hold for the night, he would have no reserves in the morning." Grow requested additional infantry support, and Phillips noted that Grow "would be informed later as to what assistance, if any (which was doubtful) would be given him."[54] Grow could do no more than hold on because at 1900 a "fierce counterattack" came in around Wardin from *167th VGD* and attached armor of *1st SS PD*, which was finally repulsed at 2030 with artillery. The 6th Armored Division reported the day's fighting as "the stiffest resistance yet encountered."[55]

III Corps' principal offensive success during the day was the capture of Fuhrman Farm, "which the enemy had so bitterly defended," by the 320th CT with the aid of C Company/735th Tank Battalion. The 320th CT entered the outskirts of Harlange but was driven back by a heavy counterattack. On Baade's right the 26th Infantry Division had made only small advances since January 1. *VGR 36* and *VGR 57/9th VGD* had put up a good fight, and by January 2 *VGR 116* finally arrived and took up positions between the two others in the Nothum–Roullingen sector. On January 4 the 328th CT relieved the 101st CT, which then moved into an assembly area in the Kaundorf–Tannerie–Bavigne area. That night elements of the *79th VGD* began relieving *Fusilier Abteilung 9* and portions of *VGR 57*.[56]

By the end of January 4 Manteuffel and Brandenberger had expended their offensive potential, and Model told Rundstedt that the western tip of the salient had to withdraw. To conduct an orderly withdrawal, the Germans had to maintain key anchor positions. On the west of the Bastogne corridor, the *3rd PGD*, *Panzer Lehr*, and *FBB* were holding a narrow wedge, the tip of which pointed south between Tillet and Flamierge. The maximum width of this corridor was no more than four miles. On the east, Brandenberger had succeeded in blocking the 26th Infantry Division north of Nothum but had to maintain an MLR south of the Wiltz River line. The *FGB* was between Doncols and Winseler, holding the withdrawal routes for the *1st SS PD* and *5th FJD*.[57]

Despite the decision to withdraw, the Germans remained fully capable of conducting an aggressive defense, a fact that Sibert acknowledged in his periodic report at the end of the day: "Very determined opposition was encountered throughout the day on both the VIII and III Corps fronts, and the build-up of enemy forces around the Bastogne salient continued." Patton remained convinced that his original scheme of maneuver to avoid corridor A was correct. He noted, "I want to attack to the north from Diekirch but Bradley is all for putting new divisions in the Bastogne fight. In my opinion, this is throwing good money after bad. In this weather, on the defensive, the Germans can hold us well enough so that we can never trap them there, whereas if we attack close to the base, they will have to pull out and we will regain ground and probably catch just as many Germans as the other way."[58]

As the Germans grew more concerned about their withdrawal corridor through Houffalize, the spearheads would continue to contract east, inevitably increasing the combat power between First and Third Armies. That was already happening. On January 4 *General der Panzertruppen* Walter Krüger's *LVIII Panzerkorps* moved into the sector east of Bastogne. Krüger established his headquarters at Allerborn and assumed command of the *167th VGD* and the *1st SS PD*. The headquarters of *Artillerie Regiment 167* was established at Schleif, and the guns were concentrated in the Oberwampach–Niederwampach area. *VAK 401* concentrated in the Brachtenbach–Derenbach area.[59]

Middleton offered the following comment on the contraction of the *Fifth Panzer Armee* spearheads:

> When Patton gave me his first reserves after the relief of Bastogne I put the Eighty-Seventh Infantry, the Eleventh Armored, and the Seventeenth Airborne into action before there was ever a hint of action from the north side where Montgomery was in command. My men here ran into the Germans coming back from the west to join in the last effort to break into Bastogne. If I'd sat back and waited at the end of the year, instead of attacking on December 30, the Germans most likely would have got into Bastogne . . . we didn't find out until later how many Germans were coming back from the west and punching at us from the north.[60]

Patton could expect little further combat power from SHAEF because Eisenhower had decided the day before not to give Bradley the reserve Devers had created in Sixth Army Group. Brooke and Churchill flew to Paris on January 3 to speak with Eisenhower, and Brooke recorded that the Supreme Commander had decided "not to withdraw the 2 divisions that were to have moved up into Patton's reserve."[61]

Bradley can justifiably be criticized for a lack of boldness in the post-Bastogne relief operations, but the estimate process was partly to blame. The process was designed to reveal not the boldest option but the option that guaranteed success no matter what the enemy did. Bradley's decision to fight it out in corridor A did this because Montgomery's offensive increased the probability of ultimate success. Montgomery thought that by the morning of January 4 the Germans were regrouping to withdraw from the salient.[62] Bradley's was the orthodox, textbook solution that any commander lacking the confidence to maneuver aggressively and accept risk would have selected, and based on previous experience, he was not about to alter his modus operandi.

In Normandy, Bradley had demonstrated his unwillingness to risk closing the Falaise Pocket, preferring "a hard shoulder at Argentan to a broken neck at Falaise."[63] The pocket was thirty miles deep (from St. Paul, halfway between Tinchebray and Flers) and fifteen miles wide at the shoulders, consisting of Monteraux in the north and Argentan in the south. The base of the Bulge was forty-two miles from Elsenborn to Echternach, two and a half times wider than the Falaise Pocket on August 16. This simple fact meant there was no chance of Bradley going for the jugular. His line of action did not guarantee success *quickly*, and he admitted at his January 4 press conference that he anticipated a long fight to close the gap.[64] This only confirmed Montgomery's statement to Eisenhower two days earlier.

Patton could see the inevitable attrition in corridor A. Montgomery's operational technique—digging in and enticing the Germans to waste themselves against prepared defensive positions powerfully supported by massed artillery and airpower—would have saved the lives of American soldiers had it been applied by Patton. Yet it also would have left the Germans with more maneuver room and the initiative to exploit interior lines. Even if Patton had been psychologically inclined to do this (which he was not), Eisenhower had already demonstrated impatience with Montgomery's operational technique *and* Patton's rate of advance. Patton clearly understood that the defense had achieved a rough parity with the offense in corridor A, and his desire to exploit corridor B may have saved many American lives and retained the initiative. His attention, however, now turned away from larger grand tactics to an immediate problem.

13

The Harlange Pocket, January 5–8

My soldiers were battle weary. Nevertheless Regiment 13 bravely held out in the forests east of Harlange.

—Heilmann

The intense fighting around Bastogne since December 30 had taken its toll on Middleton. Gay visited him on January 5 and observed, "It was quite remarkable to note the difference in the attitude of the commanders." Middleton was "quite depressed and felt that he could not attack, and also questioned if he could hold against the enemy's attacks." On his own authority Gay advised Middleton to postpone his next attack in order to re-form his divisions and improve his attitude. The commanding officer of the 194th GIR/17th Airborne Division appeared more positive, telling Gay, "God, how green we are, but we are learning fast and the next time we will beat them."[1] On January 5 his regiment had been pushed back with significant losses near Renaumont once again. The 17th Airborne Division spent the day reorganizing. The 193rd GIR moved into positions north of Senonchamps, while the 507th PIR occupied the high ground north of Pinsamont.

On Miley's left the 347th CT defeated a counterattack near Bonnerue at 0730 and then cleared the woods east of Pironpré while the 346th CT moved up on the right to tie in with Miley's paratroopers. On the corps' right the 101st Airborne Division faced little pressure during the day. On January 5 the *9th SS PD* withdrew from the Bastogne front and began moving to *Sixth Panzer Armee*. Only small *Kampfgruppen* remained. The *26th VGD* once again assumed responsibility for the sector. Middleton's negativity was understandable, up to a point, because although January 5 was a quiet day on VIII Corps' front, prisoners had been captured from

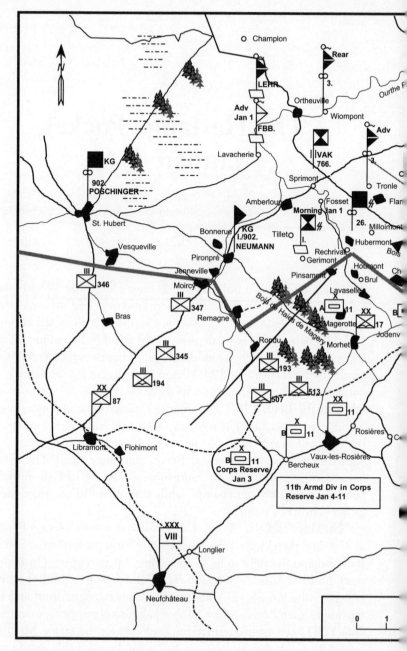

Map 13.1. Third Army Operations, January 5–8, 1945

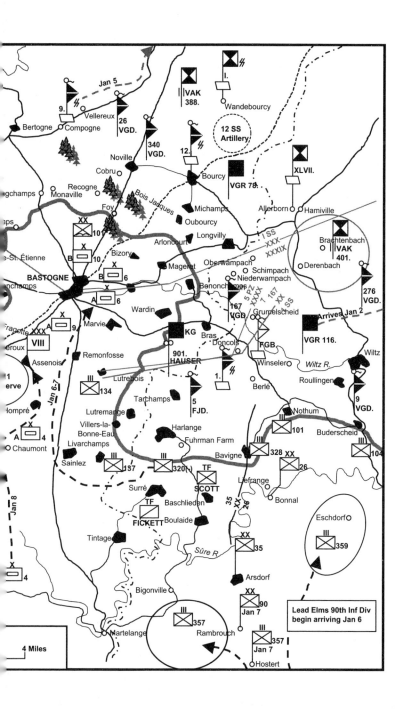

Jan 5

9. &&

Bertogne Compogne Vellereux

26 VGD.

340 VGD.

VAK 388.

I. &&

Wandebourcy

12 SS Artillery

Noville

Cobru

12. &&

Bourcy

VGR 78

XLVII.

Recogne
gchamps Monaville

Bois Jacques

Michamps

Allerborn Hamiville

Brachtenbach

Foy

Oubourcy

VAK 401.

ps

XX
101

Arloncourt

Longvilly

I SS
XXX
XXXIX

Derenbach

276 VGD.

-St. Étienne

X
B 10

Bizory

Mageret

Oberwampach

Schimpach
Niederwampach

BASTOGNE

X
B 6

Benonchamps

5 PZ
XXXX
7 167
XX
SS

nchamps

X
A 6

Wardin

167 VGD.

Grumelscheid

Arrives Jan 2

VGR 116.

ragotte XXX A
X
9

KG

Bras

Doncols

FGB

Wiltz

Marvie

Winseler

Wiltz R.

roux

VIII

Remonfosse

901. HAUSER

Roullingen

Assenois

Lutrebois

1. &&

Berlé

9 VGD.

erve

III
134

Tarchamps

5 FJD.

Nothum

ompré

Lutremange

Harlange

III
101

Buderscheid

A
X
4

Villers-la-
Bonne-Eau
Livarchamps

Fuhrman Farm

Bavigne

III
328 XX 26

III
104

Chaumont

Sainlez

III
137

III
320(-)

TF
SCOTT

Liefrange

Bonnal

Surré

Eschdorf

Jan 8

TF
FICKETT

Baschlieden
Boulaide

35
XX
26

III
359

Tintage

Sûre R

XX
35

Arsdorf

X
4

Bigonville

XX
90
Jan 7

III
357

Rambrouch

Lead Elms 90th Inf Div
begin arriving Jan 6

Martelange

III
357
Jan 7

Hostert

4 Miles

the *9th PD*, indicating that the spearhead was falling back on Bastogne.[2] This signaled harder fighting for VIII Corps in the days to come.

Millikin handled the pressure of his first two weeks of combat fairly well, but his division commanders were showing the strain. The 6th Armored Division used artillery to break up attacks that formed during the morning of January 5 in the Mageret–Wardin sector, but Grow called Phillips at 1215 to say that action was required by a higher commander to sort out the boundary issues: "He desired to point out that the 6th Armored Division has no reserves for counterattacks which is unsound. He stated that he believed there should be an adjustment on the entire front and that the situation should be presented to higher authority. He stated that he has been hit harder in the last four days than anytime during the SAAR campaign. He desires to know what the plans are for tomorrow."[3] Grow did have an "alert force" based on CCR headquarters north of Assenois, but it contained no tanks. The division was counterattacked again at 1900 by a battalion of infantry and eight tanks from Mageret and Wardin. Once again the Germans were repulsed by massed artillery and tank fire.[4]

The boundary issues between VIII and III Corps had lingered for several days. Phillips told Millikin that it was "impossible" to supply Grow's division "unless III Corps uses roads west of the ARLON–BASTOGNE highway because of mortar and artillery fire on that road." VIII Corps informed III Corps that due to the large number of troops in the Bastogne Pocket and on the west flank of the defenses of the town, "both the Neufchâteau–Bastogne Highway and the Remichampagne–Assenois–Bastogne Road are essential to the VIII Corps for supply and evacuation." Third Army intended to change the boundary, but VIII Corps deemed it undesirable "at this time." VIII Corps recommended that the present boundary remain in effect and that both corps use the Remichampagne–Assenois–Bastogne road. III Corps ultimately agreed to this.[5]

Two hours after Phillips spoke with Grow, Baade called and declared the battle on his south and southwest flank to be "pure attrition"; he was unable to make any progress there. Indeed, the 320th CT, with its 1st Battalion attached to the 134th CT, was making no headway around Harlange. Baade "firmly recommended" that he be allowed to dig in there while staying mobile elsewhere, "although, in fact, little progress could be made." Baade "hated to make such a recommendation but the conditions were such that they were not getting anyplace." Millikin approved Baade's request, but Patton's reaction was not recorded. What was recorded was his observation on German fighting power that day: "Those

Germans are vicious fighters. . . . Some times even I get skeptical about the end of this show."[6]

Baade was not getting anywhere because Patton and Millikin had thus far devoted insufficient combat power to break through, focusing instead on breaking out of the Bastogne Pocket to the northeast. Grow, however, was hard pressed to hold his position; breaking out on his own was improbable. On January 5 Patton discussed the situation with Bradley. Patton was keen on his plan to squeeze out III Corps by the simultaneous advance of VIII and XII Corps on the flanks to St. Vith. However, owing to Bradley's influence, it was decided that the pocket had to be eliminated before Third Army's general attack toward Houffalize could begin or, more important, before XII Corps could attack in corridor B. Unable to convince Bradley to accept the risk of picketing the Harlange Pocket, Patton resigned himself to planning its elimination. He wanted to send the 94th Infantry Division to XX Corps to relieve the 90th Infantry Division, which in turn would move up to III Corps and attack through the 26th Infantry Division to cut off the Germans in the pocket. He would then send the 94th Infantry Division to XII Corps to reinforce the attack north from Diekirch. He noted this was "the shortest way I know of cleaning out the [Harlange] pocket." Bradley convinced Eisenhower that Patton needed another division, and at 1730 the 94th Infantry Division (minus a CT) was assigned to Third Army.[7]

The 94th Infantry Division began moving to Thionville immediately, thereby freeing Patton to bring up his best remaining infantry formation still in Lorraine—Major General James A. Van Fleet's 90th Infantry Division. This further denuded XX Corps' strength, but Eisenhower and Bradley were willing to accept the risk despite the continued attacks in Alsace. Although NORDWIND had essentially failed, despite the commitment of the 6th SS-Gebirgs Division, Himmler's Heeresgruppe Oberrhein finally launched supporting attacks on January 5 with the XIV SS Korps against the southern flank of VI Corps.

By the time III Corps launched its assault on December 22, the 90th Infantry Division had withdrawn across the Saar, destroyed its ferry, and pounded Dillingen and Pachten with artillery for good measure. The after-action report of the 3rd Battalion/358th CT declared, "This was the first time this battalion ever gave ground, and even though it was a strategic retreat rather than tactical, it still hurt." Van Fleet was not happy either.[8] The "Tough Hombres" were situated defensively behind an obstacle barrier that included more than 14,000 antitank mines. Van Fleet was preparing for an assault on the Saar–Moselle triangle at its base through the Orscholz switch line. During the night of January 5 XX Corps phoned a cryptic message, "Be prepared for movement," but it offered no time, direction, or destination. The division began its fifty-mile march north in "most unfavorable" weather. The 357th CT cleared the division's area by 0430 the next morning, and that night the 712th Tank, 773rd Tank Destroyer, and 345th FA Battalions moved.

The relief of the 90th Infantry Division by the 94th Infantry Division was achieved with greater secrecy than the initial redeployment of divisions between December 19 and 21. III Corps was instructed to make no mention of the 90th Infantry Division in telephone conversations or official reports.[9] Van Fleet's division took over radio traffic, covered its unit markings, and moved in behind the 26th and 35th Infantry Divisions. It did not take over any frontage, but artillery was emplaced battery by battery. As each gun registered, a 26th Infantry Division gun stopped firing to avoid any increase in fire density. Prisoners captured by Paul's division were interrogated, 1:10,000 maps were distributed to platoon commanders, and the wooded areas on the division's 1:25,000 maps were corrected using photo interpretation.

Patton was confident that "we can wholly deceive the enemy" about the arrival of the 90th Infantry Division, but this was only one phase of his larger plan to eliminate the pocket.[10] The attack was tentatively set for January 9, the date of the larger army offensive including VIII Corps. In the meantime, continuous pressure had to be applied to the Germans in the Harlange Pocket, and on January 5 Millikin issued an operational directive to do just that. He set Grow's main effort on the right toward Bras. Paul's main effort was toward Doncols, and Baade's was on the left toward Hill 550 and Doncols. Millikin also ordered the 1st Battalion/101st Infantry to move into corps reserve at Tintage to support either Grow or Baade.[11]

Grow called Phillips at 0900 on January 6, stating that it was "imperative that he get an infantry battalion in support of his division. That his men have had no sleep for two nights and although he is not having heavy battle casualties, he feels that in the next 24 hours the battle fatigue casualties will be so excessive that his division will be severely affected." Indeed, Grow had withstood piecemeal tank and infantry assaults from dark the previous night to daylight that morning, and he considered Millikin's order to keep attacking the "most absurd thing I ever read." Millikin's response to Grow's request was to initiate relief of the 320th CT at

Harlange by the 101st CT/26th Infantry Division (TF Scott) for attachment to the 6th Armored Division. The 3rd Battalion/320th CT was attached to Grow's division at 1645.[12]

Redeploying the 320th CT was actually another preliminary phase of Patton's larger plan for reducing the pocket. Augmenting Grow's combat power for the northern pincer was a fundamental requirement. Another requirement was Paul's freedom of maneuver to properly protect Van Fleet's right flank, and this could be achieved only by distracting the left flank of LIII Armeekorps.[13] XII Corps was thus finally given a small offensive role to play. The objective was the high, L-shaped plateau north of the Sûre River in McBride's 80th Infantry Division zone. One leg of the plateau ran north-south through Nocher, Dahl, and Goesdorf. The other leg ran east from Dahl and Nocher. This plateau was surrounded by deep and thickly wooded ravines. Before daylight on January 6 the 166th Engineer C Battalion constructed a bridge near Heiderscheidergrund, and at 0400 the 319th CT/80th Infantry Division crossed over. While the 1st Battalion captured Goesdorf, the 3rd Battalion bypassed the town and seized Dahl under heavy artillery and mortar fire. This attack achieved complete surprise, catching the Germans in the process of relieving elements of the 9th VGD with elements of the 276th VGD.[14] Dahl was an appropriate objective because its seizure created a deep salient in LIII Armeekorps' left flank and deprived Seventh Armee of important high ground. Brandenberger ordered a counterattack to regain the Sûre front as far as Esch-sur-Sûre, and he attached the FGB and elements of the worn-out 276th VGD to LIII Armeekorps.[15]

While the threat to LIII Armeekorps' left flank was being developed, Millikin, Van Fleet, and Patton finalized preparations for the 90th Infantry Division's attack on January 6. It seems that Millikin initially wanted the 90th Infantry Division to attack through the 35th Infantry Division from the southwest, but Van Fleet asked for and received permission to attack from the southeast.[16] Patton wanted Van Fleet to attack through the 26th Infantry Division, along the ridge road, to cut the base of the salient while the 26th and 35th Infantry Divisions, 6th Armored Division, and 6th Cavalry Group Task Forces attacked concentrically along the perimeter. Paul was to send one CT on each side of the 90th Infantry Division, while the 6th Armored Division and a CT attached from Baade's division attacked southeast to link up with Van Fleet. Some 1,000 guns were scheduled to support this attack, "some firing in prolongation and others at right angles to the main effort to insure dispersion both ways."

This artillery fire plan and the use of smoke to blind the enemy's guns that were most likely emplaced on the ridge northeast of the Wiltz River were Patton's own ideas.[17]

Throughout January 7 and 8 the 26th and 35th Infantry Divisions regrouped and prepared for the attack. Neither division received major counterattacks during these two days. Instead, they reported a decrease in ground activity.[18] The reduced activity opposite Baade's division was no doubt a product of the weakened condition of the *5th FJD*, which had a total strength, including *Flak* and *StuG Brigade 11*, of 3,251 as of January 6. *FJR 13* had 412, *FJR 14* had 487, and *FJR 15* had 498 men.[19] At 1800 on January 6 Manteuffel ordered *12th SS PD* into reserve, and during the night of January 7–8 the *340th VGD* assumed Kraas's sector. *I SS Panzerkorps'* sector was relatively quiet on January 7. On January 8 the *12th SS* assembled in the Rachamps–Hardigny area, but panzer elements remained behind the *340th VGD* in the Michamps–Oubourcy sector.

The 6th Armored Division, however, was still being heavily engaged from the east by the *167th VGD*, with armored support from *KG von Hauser* and the *Leibstandarte* on both days. The *167th VGD* was now under Krüger's *LVIII Panzerkorps*. During the January 7 attack against Neffe, *Generalmajor* Gerhard Triepel, *Artillerie Kommandeur 458* in *LVIII Panzerkorps*, directed fire from all corps assets from the CP of *Artillerie Regiment 167* at Schleif. A task force from CCA was pushed out of a wooded area east of Neffe, and the entire division was under pressure throughout the day and into the night. Had it not been for superiority in artillery firepower, Grow's division, exposed in a vulnerable salient, might have suffered much greater damage. From January 1 to 7 more than 53,000 rounds of artillery had been brought down on the fronts of 6th Armored and 101st Airborne Divisions to halt, break up, and defeat German attacks.[20]

In *Seventh Armee* Brandenberger's attention was focused on the Dahl salient. On January 7 the 319th CT, supported by the 610th Tank Destroyer Battalion, was attacked from the north and northeast by the *FGB*, *Schwere Panzerjäger Abteilung 519*, and elements of the *276th VGD*, supported by *VAK 406*. Brandenberger managed to assemble 108 guns, and the 2,500 rounds fired helped the assault forces reach the northern and eastern outskirts of Dahl, but then the ammunition failed.[21] *LIII Armeekorps* renewed its attempt to close the Dahl salient early the next morning, with the *FGB* and a regiment of the *79th VGD* attacking from the east, but the 319th CT repulsed all assaults. Brandenberger declared, "There was nothing left for us to do now but to put up with the situation as best we could and go over to the defense along the re-entrant front." He conceded that his combat power "was now slight indeed." In fact, the 80th Infantry Division after-action report mentioned no large counterattack that day.[22]

On the other side of the Bastogne corridor, the *3rd PGD, FBB,* and *Panzer Lehr* received a breather on January 5 and 6. XLVII *Panzerkorps'* MLR on January 7 was Hatrival–Vesqueville–Tillet. The 87th Infantry Division battled elements of the *FBB* at Tillet and was counterattacked between 1820 and 2023 at Bonnerue, preceded by some artillery at 1630. The *FBB* continued to exploit key terrain features, towns, and important crossroads to cover natural lines of the division's approach. The division noted that the Germans were fighting skillfully.[23] Denkert called January 7 "particularly critical." The 17th Airborne Division did not attack on January 6 but did so at 0800 on January 7, with three regiments in line and the 507th positioned behind the left flank in case the 87th Infantry Division did not attack. Although the 194th GIR made little headway on the left, the 513th PIR, crossing the LD an hour later, penetrated some two miles and captured Flamierge, getting in behind Denkert's MLR. However, the 513th PIR became a victim of its own success. Having pushed so far ahead of the other regiments, it was vulnerable on three sides.

Denkert's first counterattack, executed by a *Kampfgruppe* from the *9th PD* that had just arrived from the northwest, failed to retake Flamierge. Denkert then prepared detailed plans for a concentric assault at daybreak on January 8. Although he claimed that he retook Flamierge the next morning without a fight because of the voluntary withdrawal of the paratroopers, the 17th Airborne Division's after-action report told a different story. The *3rd PGD* attacked the 513th PIR from both flanks, got behind it, and overran significant portions of the 1st and 2nd Battalions. Miley noted that on January 8 "our losses were terrible. Bns 1 and 2 on the high ground held until almost annihilated. They withdrew during the morning—the relatively few survivors—after having resisted until their ammunition was gone. They said that all of our men had fought to the last and that they had seen no prisoners taken."[24] By routing the 513th PIR, Denkert effectively resealed his MLR.

Patton was not happy with the performance of VIII Corps. He noted that Culin and Miley "got fairly well chopped up . . . due at least in part to Middleton's reluctance to use the 11th Armored in backing them up. He is still over-worried about his left flank and rear. Too much so." Despite Kilburn's January 6 report that his combat efficiency was at 92.5 percent and his tank strength was at 75 percent, Middleton was probably reluctant to commit the division based on its baptismal performance.[25] Kilburn had worked out contingency plans to come to Miley's aid if required, but they were never executed even as the 513th PIR was being wrecked.

Patton hoped to capture large numbers of Germans in the Harlange Pocket, but at 2200 on January 7 Bradley informed him that the Germans had withdrawn all their armor from the Bastogne Pocket area and possibly all their troops as well. Based on the lack of force behind the few counterattacks that day, Patton feared the Germans were withdrawing. Indeed, since the 101st Airborne Division patrols had pushed out 1,500 yards in all directions and contacted nothing, Patton told Middleton to keep pushing out until he bumped into the enemy.[26] However, according to Gay, prior to Bradley's call, Koch had solicited the opinions of all the G-2s in Third Army, and their consensus was that there was no evidence the Germans were withdrawing. This does not mesh with Allen's journal entry of January 6: "Germans beginning to back out of salient." Moreover, Sibert had reported the day before that most of the traffic observed by tactical reconnaissance "was moving out of the salient. . . . Only on the road north from HOUFFALIZE where 67 motorized enemy transport were reported strafed and destroyed, was there any sizable internal movement toward the front lines." He interpreted this development as a pause to regroup opposite Third Army.[27]

Patton also had to consider rumours of an impending attack against XII Corps from the area of Diekirch. Eddy was worried, and Patton noted, "Bradley fears the same thing. It could be but I doubt it." Still, Patton had Colonel John F. Conklin, the army engineer, inspect Eddy's barrier line, and he felt confident the Germans would be "well stopped" if they attacked there. ULTRA placed the *2nd SS PD* west of Dochamps and near Baraque de Fraiture, and the *21st PD* was in the Hagenau–Weissenburg area. Koch's work map for 0300 January 8 showed no build-up opposite XII Corps, but the *11th PD* and *10th SS PD* were listed as unlocated.[28] However, on January 7 *Nineteenth Armee* launched Operation *SONNENWENDE* (Winter Solstice) out of the north part of the Colmar Pocket against the northern flank of VI Corps; at the same time, Decker's *XXXIX Panzerkorps*, previously withdrawn from the Bastogne sector, attacked the center of VI Corps in the Hagenau Forest with the *21st PD* and *25th PGD*.

As *SONNENWENDE* unfolded on January 7, Millikin issued his field order for the Harlange Pocket operation and went to Luxembourg to

Table 13.1. Estimated Enemy Strength in III Corps' Zone of Advance, January 6, 1945

Unit	Strength	Tanks/Assault Guns
12 SS PD (elms)	2,500	25
26 VGD (elms)	2,000	
340 VGD	4,000	
167 VGD	6,500	
130 PD (Lehr) (elms)	1,000	
1 SS PD	5,500	40
FGB	1,500	15
9 VGD	6,000	
5 FJD	3,500	
Miscellaneous units	4,000	15
Total	36,500	95

Source: III Corps Field Order No. 3, Annex No. 2, Intelligence Annex, January 7, 1945.

brief Patton on the plan. Van Fleet would have the 357th CT on the left and the 359th CT on the right on a frontage of 3,500 yards. The 358th CT was in reserve south of Rambrouch. His main effort would be on the right along the road, with the objectives being to take the high ground near Bras and cut the only east-west highway remaining to the Germans in the Doncols area. A company from both the 712th Tank Battalion and 773rd Tank Destroyer Battalion was attached to each assaulting CT. The 357th CT would advance with two battalions abreast to peel off and contain the enemy on the left. The 359th CT would advance in a column of battalions to penetrate the German line and cut the MSR at Doncols. The 358th CT would then attack through the 359th CT to the final objective—the high ground northeast of Bras.[29] All of Van Fleet's guns, with the exception of the 345th FA Battalion at Bonnal, were north of the Sûre River. The division was to maintain radio silence until H-hour. On Van Fleet's right, Paul's objective was the high ground at Noertrange north of the Wiltz River. On Van Fleet's left, TF Scott (101st CT/26th Infantry Division) and TF Fickett were to advance toward Harlange and be prepared to mop up the pocket once it was cut off. Baade's objective was Hill 550. Grow's main effort was on his right toward the high ground at Bras; Grow also had two intermediate objectives. H-hour was set for 1000, and the attack was to be preceded by an artillery preparation assisted by the guns of VIII and XII Corps.

Patton issued his operational directive for the general army attack on January 8. VIII Corps, with the 4th Armored Division now assigned to it, was to make a determined effort toward the high ground around Houffalize, while Taylor's immediate objective was Noville. III Corps was to "attack aggressively" and cut off the pocket. Millikin was instructed to be prepared to assist VIII Corps in seizing Noville and Houffalize or continuing the attack northeast toward St. Vith.[30] On the verge of the new army offensive, Patton was confronted with pressure from above and below to alter the plan. At 0945 on January 8 Bradley called to ask whether Third Army could attack immediately that day. This was no doubt the result of his belief that the Germans were getting away. In fact, that day Hitler ordered a withdrawal to Donchamps–Longchamps and instructed *Sixth Panzer Armee* to assemble in the St. Vith–Wiltz area to counter anticipated attacks there. "I said I could," recorded Patton, "but felt it a mistake, as all plans were made for a general attack tomorrow morning." He believed Sibert had a hand in influencing Bradley, as well as suggesting that Third Army troops were not being employed judiciously. Patton lashed out: "He [Sibert] is the same genius who let the Germans attack without discovering their presence."[31] Patton must have made a good case, because Bradley did not push the issue, and planning continued for January 9.

Whereas Bradley wanted to push up the attack to January 8, Middleton wanted to delay it. Middleton issued his field order at 1200 on January 8. His mission was to reduce the Bulge in conjunction with III Corps, with divisions abreast. The 87th Infantry Division was to capture the high ground near Menil, capture or bypass and contain Tillet, and contain the enemy in the St. Hubert–Vesqueville area with no more than one infantry battalion. The 17th Airborne Division was to secure the Ourthe River line, and the 101st Airborne Division was to make a "strong demonstration" toward Recogne and attack northeast on orders to capture Noville. Kilburn was instructed to be prepared to give immediate assistance to either Miley or Culin, and Gaffey was in reserve.[32]

Despite issuing the field order, Middleton phoned Third Army around 1700 and told Gay the 87th Infantry and 17th Airborne Divisions could not attack, and the 101st Airborne and 4th Armored Divisions needed another day to prepare. This was after Patton had sent Maddox to explain the plan and his scheme of maneuver to Middleton sometime earlier that day. The 101st Airborne Division reported its combat efficiency on January 8 as excellent, and the 11th Armored Division had been resting for a few days.[33] Patton told Middleton that "everything would go on as ordered and that all units would attack on the 9th . . . with the understanding that the 87th and 17th Airborne would probably not be able to put on a very good show." This left little room for interpretation, but according to Gay, Patton told Middleton, "This was a *must*." VIII Corps had to attack the next day with the 101st Airborne Division and at least one combat command of the 4th Armored Division. "If the 17th Airborne Division was definitely not in shape to attack, . . . they could be used for regrouping in preparation for an attack the next day." The 87th Infantry Division had to attack. Gay phoned Middleton back and asked him if he understood the orders. Middleton said yes, but according to Gay, "He wished to invite attention to the fact that if disaster overtook them, in that they were cut off and another pocket was formed, that he had warned the Army Commander of this possibility." Clearly, Middleton was rattled. Gaffey had talked to Middleton, and that night he called Patton to relay his impression that Middleton had no faith in the corps' ability to attack. Gaffey never attempted to offer an excuse for why his division could not attack, adding, "I know I am going to," to which Patton responded, "You are right. Don't bother me with it. You will attack."[34]

Patton also had to deal with a jittery Eddy, who called on January 8 complaining that if the 4th Armored Division participated in the general attack the next day, it would not be able to support him if the Germans did in fact attack from the direction of Diekirch. When Eddy told Patton it would take nine hours for the 10th Armored Division to reach him from Metz, Patton replied, "In that event, he would certainly have to hold for nine hours. Again I earned my pay." Patton did not believe Eddy would be hit from the direction of Diekirch. Instead, he thought the Germans "will attack towards Metz. The Twelfth Army Group believes they will attack to the south and cut in behind the 7th Army."[35]

The III Corps after-action report put the problem of eliminating the Harlange Pocket in proper perspective: "During the first 8 days of the new year, neither Corps nor the enemy was able to muster sufficient force to break through the deadlock which had followed the German counterattack of December 30."[36] The necessary combat power was now in position, but it had taken three days to do it. Perhaps the delay was for the best, because it gave the 6th Armored and 35th Infantry Divisions time to absorb 200 and 581 replacements, respectively, on January 8. The planning of the Harlange Pocket operation was well done, and secrecy was maintained. Rest was needed, particularly by the 6th Armored Division, but the 90th Infantry Division could have attacked sooner. Patton, however, appears to have had enough of staggered attacks with his corps.

Patton's intent was for an eight-division attack on January 9, but he gave Middleton an "out" by telling him that only the 101st Airborne Division and a portion of the 4th Armored Division *had* to attack. This possibly left the impression in Middleton's mind that the other divisions did not *have* to attack. At this point, Patton faced the simultaneous and difficult tasks of addressing the psychological needs of his corps commanders and accepting risk to keep the January 9 offensive on schedule. Middleton's aggressiveness was low, and Eddy was as nervous as ever. However, despite persistent indications that the Germans might attack XII Corps and were building up in the Saarbrücken area opposite XX Corps, Patton never blinked; he stuck to his intended attack date. He ordered Walker to prepare all roads in XX Corps' sector for demolition as a precaution, but he was willing to accept the risk in order to maintain the initiative and finally reach a decision in III Corps' sector. Patton's willingness to attack while threatened elsewhere was one of the qualities that set him apart from his peers.

14

No Risk, No Reward, January 9–25

This is the second time I have been stopped in a successful attack due
to the Germans having more nerve than we have—that is, not me, but
some of the others.

—Patton, January 10, 1945

January 9 was a dull, cloudy day with heavy snowfall. XIX TAC flew only
twenty-four missions during the day. Third Army attacked at 1000, but
not with the number of divisions Patton expected. He spoke of the new offensive in terms of a "hell of a show which should really rock them," but
Middleton held back the 17th Airborne Division, ordering Miley to assume defensive positions and consolidate. Miley reflected that Middleton
ordered him to conduct active patrolling "so as to avoid an appearance of
the defensive." With Miley's paratroopers consolidating, it is difficult to
explain why Maddox's G-3 situation report at 1200 described a "coordinated attack" by VIII Corps, including the 17th Airborne Division.[1] Perhaps Patton's instructions to Middleton delivered through Gay had not
been passed on to Maddox, or perhaps Patton really did expect Miley to
make at least a limited attack.

Although Patton left no record of his thoughts about Middleton's decision to withhold the 17th Airborne Division on January 9, he was not
happy with Middleton's use of the 11th Armored Division the day before
when Miley had been driven back. At some point during January 9 Patton called Middleton to voice displeasure at his failure to properly support
Miley with the 11th Armored Division. Patton told him that "this would
not be allowed to happen again." Kilburn's formation "would be used,
and used vigorously and promptly." This was a *must* order," and "failure
to do so would not be tolerated."[2]

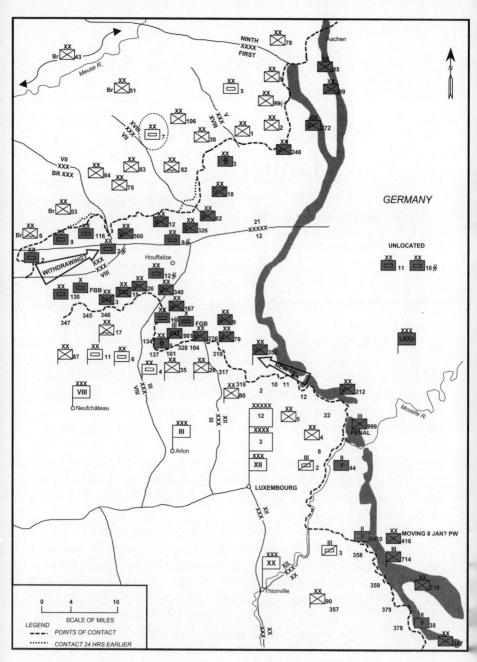

Map 14.1. Third Army G-2 Work Map, Situation as of 0300 January 9, 1945

Despite the planning and preparation, Patton's January 9 offensive did not "rock" the Germans. In VIII Corps Culin met strong opposition in the Bonnerue–Tillet area and could not advance through the Hais-de-Tillet woods due to "extremely heavy fire." *KG von Poschinger* counterattacked and drove elements back to the LD. The MSR through Bertogne to the east was a sensitive area for *XLVII Panzerkorps*, and it fought hard to retain it. It was now more important than taking Bastogne.[3] On Miley's right the 101st Airborne Division—with CCB/10th Armored Division, 705th Tank Destroyer Battalion, and a company from the 611th Tank Destroyer Battalion attached—attacked toward Noville at 1100. The 506th PIR advanced toward Noville against *II Abteilung/VGR 78* while the 502nd PIR protected the 506th's left flank. The 501st PIR attacked an hour later toward Recogne and captured it by 1700. CCB/4th Armored Division was attached to Taylor's division, but he never utilized it.[4]

In III Corps CCA/6th Armored Division attacked at 1000 toward Arloncourt. The *12th SS KG* repulsed this attack, but it and *SS-Aufklärüngs Abteilung 12* then withdrew toward Bochholz to be at the disposal of *Sixth Panzer Armee*. To Grow's right the 134th CT/35th Infantry Division attacked southeast in conjunction with the 2nd Battalion/320th CT (TF Hannum) attached to CCA/6th Armored Division and gained several hundred yards, while the 1st and 2nd Battalions held their positions. The 137th CT made no progress. On the corps' right the 26th Infantry Division attacked at 1030—the 104th CT with a single battalion, and the 328th CT in a column of battalions. The latter managed to advance only 500 yards during the day.[5] The outcome of the entire offensive essentially rested on what the 90th Infantry Division could accomplish.

As the 90th Infantry Division's after-action report noted, after a night of "disturbed, half-frozen" sleep, the infantry rose to action, facing the prospect of advancing through deep snowdrifts and dense forests. Rothkirch appreciated at 0023 that morning that Third Army would attempt a pincer-type breakthrough from Wardin, Nothum, and Berlé to the crossroads northeast of Doncols in order to cut off the Harlange salient. In anticipation, he moved all operationally serviceable elements of the *FGB* into the area southeast of Doncols. This was critical because, according to Brandenberger, the *5th FJD* was "completely exhausted and fantastically outnumbered" by this time. However, neither Rothkirch nor Brandenberger anticipated the 90th Infantry Division's attack in the Doncols area. Heilmann and Rothkirch were probably unaware of the division's whereabouts. Even as late as 2015 on January 10, *FJR 13* declared, "It is

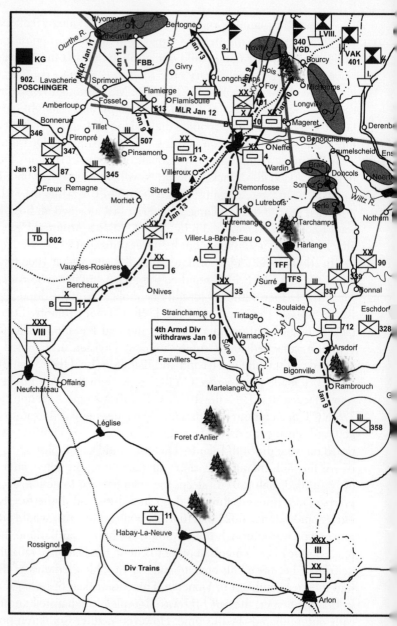

Map 14.2. Third Army's Offensive, January 9, 1945

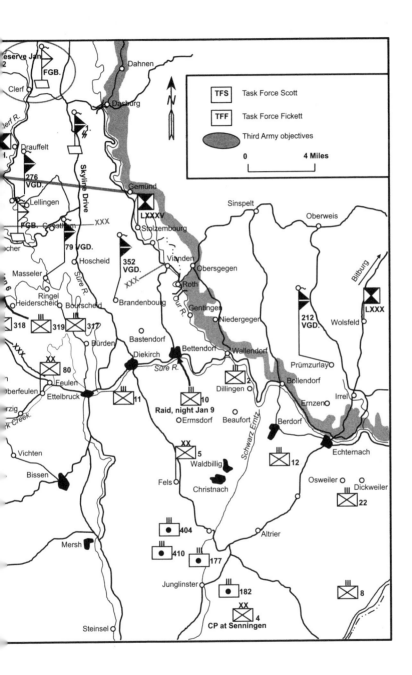

Reserve Jan 2
FGB.
Clerf
lerf R.
Drauffelt
276 VGD.
Lellingen
FGB. Crosthum XXX
cher
79 VGD.
Hoscheid
Masseler
Ringel
Heiderscheid
Bourscheid
Bürden
318 319 317
XXX
XX
80
oberfeulen Feulen
Ettelbruck
rzig
k Creek.
Vichten
Bissen
Mersh

Dahnen
Dasburg
Skyline Drive
Gemünd
LXXXV
Stolzembourg
Sinspelt
Oberweis
Sûre R.
352 VGD.
XXX
Vianden
Obersgegen
Roth
Tur R.
Brandenbourg
Gentingen
Niedergeger
212 VGD.
Bitburg
LXXX
Wolsfeld
Bastendorf
Bettendorf
Wallendorf
Prümzurlay
Diekirch
Sûre R.
11
2
Dillingen
Bollendorf
Irrel
10
Ernzen
Raid, night Jan 9
Ermsdorf
Beaufort
Berdorf
XX
5
Waldbillig
12
Echternach
Fels
Christnach
Osweiler
Dickweiler
22
404
Altrier
Vichten
410
177
Junglinster
182
8
Steinsel
XX
4
CP at Senningen

TFS   Task Force Scott

TFF   Task Force Fickett

        Third Army objectives

0   4 Miles

imperative that steps be taken to ascertain whether or not the . . . 90th Infantry Division has been committed."[6]

Van Fleet's attack was complicated by the dominating ground on his
right, northeast of the Wiltz River. The 357th CT attacked at 0950 toward
Berlé, just beyond the head of a ravine; it was defended by VGR 36/9th
VGD and subordinated elements of 5th FJD. The 1st Battalion/357th CT
captured Berlé by dark. As expected, the Germans' strength was on the
right, where VGR 116 and VGR 57 were deployed. They "fiercely contested" the advance of the 359th CT with artillery, tanks, mortars, Nebelwerfers, and small arms. The infantry sustained heavy casualties from this
fire, but the 3rd Battalion bypassed pockets of resistance and drove a mile-
deep wedge into the enemy's line. The trailing battalions, however, took
punishment from artillery and mortars.[7] Despite considerable mortar, artillery, and Nebelwerfer fire, LIII Armeekorps could not decisively block
the 90th Infantry Division's advance. The unique aspects of the terrain
permitted Van Fleet to attack in a column of battalions because the Germans could not quickly maneuver to strike the flanks. Attempts to eliminate the Berlé salient proved impossible because visibility was poor and
the hilly terrain prevented properly supported and integrated attacks. Van
Fleet called Millikin in the late afternoon to report that there was a "pretty firm crust" still to be penetrated, and Berlé had caused "considerable
trouble." Nevertheless, when Patton phoned III Corps at 1940, Millikin
announced, "I think old Van did pretty well." Millikin now wanted to give
Gaffey priority as he moved through Grow, and Patton agreed. Millikin
and Middleton established a temporary boundary during the night to facilitate 4th Armored Division's attack through 6th Armored Division the
following day.[8]

On January 10 Grow made little progress, but at 0900 the 4th Armored Division attacked through his front. Resistance was light at first,
but as the division emerged from the wooded areas northeast of Bastogne, heavy German artillery fire inflicted numerous casualties.[9] Gaffey
reached the outskirts of Mageret and captured more than 200 prisoners
of the 340th VGD. TF Fickett captured Bettlange and Harlange, and the
134th CT of the 35th Infantry Division finally captured Villers-la-Bonne-
Eau and the high ground to the northeast.[10] Van Fleet renewed his attack at 0720. The 357th CT pushed on through the snow and woods to
the high ground overlooking Doncols. Although the 357th's progress was
decent—a mile in an hour and a half—it was described as "tortuously
slow." The 359th CT made no headway against an enemy strongpoint

at Trentelhoff. At 0900 the 1st Battalion swung past the right of the 3rd Battalion to cut off the town, but it was deflected by heavy fire from the high ground northeast of the Wiltz River. At 1010 Gay phoned Millikin for an update. Gay asked, "How does it look to you?" Millikin replied, "Your guess is as good as mine. We are all optimistic." Gay noted, "I think Van is going to get through," and Millikin agreed. The confidence in Van Fleet was widespread. Collins called him "my idea of what a combat commander ought to be: he was a front-line soldier and a great fighter."[11] Anticipating a potential stalemate, Van Fleet prepared for a night assault to maintain momentum and deny the Germans the opportunity to consolidate their positions.

Just as Third Army was gaining some momentum on January 10, Bradley telephoned Patton at 1030, alerting him of a threat to Saarbrücken and instructing him to withdraw divisions out of contact to move to XX Corps. Patton noted, "This will mean the suspension of our attack on Houffalize."[12] Potential threats to Third Army's right flank, however, were not new. Rumors had been building over the last several days, but Patton's reaction to them is important because it speaks to his willingness to accept risk. He was in fact concerned about threats against XX Corps. His sensitivity was noted by Weyland during the special 0845 briefing at Third Army that morning. Weyland recorded that Patton "was concerned about Saarbrucken area as possible major German offensive." Only the day before, Gay had had Koch prepare a study of the probability of German attacks against VIII Corps and Saarbrücken, and the latter was deemed more likely. Based on this, Gay contacted Bradley and requested and received permission to move the 302nd CT/94th Infantry Division, guarding the Meuse River west of St. Hubert, to XX Corps at once. Patton had already taken steps to build up a strong defensive area between Saarbrücken and Metz. Koch's identification of Saarbrücken as the most likely place for a new German attack, however, was not supported by the German capability as assessed by Sibert, who had declared only the day before that there was "no satisfactory evidence" the Germans possessed enough capability to turn a threat there into a major attack. Twelfth Army Group's situation map for 1200 that day depicted no concentration opposite Saarbrücken. However, it did list six divisions (*7th FJD; 49th, 344th, and 711th Infantry Divisions; 11th PD; and 10th SS PD*) as unlocated.[13]

Patton told Bradley it was a mistake to stop Third Army's attack because it would be playing into enemy hands. Patton suggested withdrawing a combat command from either the 10th or 11th Armored Division, or both, but Bradley told him the order to withdraw the divisions in their entirety came from Eisenhower.[14] Patton thereupon asked Bradley to inspect the situation with him personally. As a result of their deliberations with Middleton and Millikin at Arlon, they decided to halt the entire VIII Corps, which transitioned to aggressive patrolling. This was not a difficult decision, because VIII Corps had accomplished little on January 10. The 101st Airborne Division had made little progress, and the 17th Airborne Division continued to consolidate.[15] The most productive advance was made by the 87th Infantry Division, which cleared almost all the Bois de Haies-de-Tillet and captured Tillet by 1450.

At approximately 1300 Patton phoned Gay and directed him to halt VIII Corps and select an assembly area for the 4th Armored Division to support either Eddy or Walker. Gaffey was ordered to break contact at 1350 and assemble around Assenois. Patton called Taylor directly and ordered him to halt, but instead of digging in, Taylor withdrew to his LD of the previous day, thus voluntarily surrendering the high ground around Foy. This could not have been Patton's intent, especially since Taylor had CCB/10th Armored Division to assist in holding the gains made up to that point.[16] Even as Patton was returning to Luxembourg from Bastogne, he discovered that elements of the 4th Armored Division were already moving to their new assembly areas southeast of Luxembourg. "The remarkable ability which Gaffey has of doing what he is told fast," noted Patton, "was well exemplified here."[17]

Sometime during the day Bradley's headquarters also warned of another possible enemy concentration on Third Army's right flank. Patton noted, "There is a new rumor, invented by Sibert I think, of an enemy concentration just north of Trier. To me it is patently impossible that the Germans can have concentrations all over the face of nature—I do not believe it. However, the position in which we have placed the 4th A.D. is such that it can operate against this threat too." When Eddy received a report indicating that the Germans were concentrating in the Wasserbillig area on the Moselle River, just west of Trier, he went over to Bradley's headquarters "to check this and make my own deductions." He talked with Sibert, who seemed "to give the source of this information the highest reliability." Gay, however, noted that, from Koch's perspective, Sibert's information came from "a very questionable source," and he described it as follows:

It appears that an unknown radio station called "Atlantic" announced that the Germans were assembling a large force north of

Trier for an attack. This is alleged to have been heard by someone
in the SHAEF Mission, who in turn told a Colonel of the SHAEF
Mission, who in turn told G-2 of the Twelfth Army Group. . . .
It is of interest to note that neither the reconnaissance planes of
the XIX Tactical Air Command nor the Cub planes of the Third
Army could find any evidence of a German concentration east of
the SAAR RIVER or east of the XII Corps and XX Corps. There is
some evidence of concentration in the SAARBRUCKEN area.[18]

Even as Patton and Eddy addressed the new threat from Trier, they
had to pay due diligence to the lingering threat from Diekirch. While at
Third Army headquarters on January 7, Eddy overheard a call from Bradley, who stated that the "Black Market" indicated the Germans "may try
something in my area." Bradley directed Patton to get cub planes up to
have a look that day. On January 9 Eddy noted, "We were getting information of considerable movement along the Corps front. . . . Had reports of
enemy tank columns and long vehicle columns, including some infantry.
I called Hap Gay and gave him this information and that we were plas-
tering these movements with plenty of artillery. One PW report said that
the enemy planned a general attack all along the line on either the 10th
or 11th." After talking to Irwin and McBride, however, Eddy concluded,
"Apparently these reports we have been getting were more the product of
somebody's imagination more than actual fact." Imagination was driving
the intelligence process at this point because Eddy was even alerted to the
threat of a German airborne drop in his area. XII Corps issued an operational directive at 1800, outlining Plan P to meet an airborne attack in the
corps zone, particularly south and west of Luxembourg City.[19]

Despite four different potential threats to his right flank (Saarbrück-
en, Trier, Diekirch, and Luxembourg City), Patton refused to relinquish
the offensive. He told Bradley he was "perfectly willing to gamble that
the Germans would not attack, in spite of reports of prisoners of war to
the contrary." Patton was utterly convinced that his successful attack had
been stopped "due to the Germans having more nerve than we have—
that is, not me, but some of the others." Withdrawing the 4th Armored
Division did not really bother him; it needed rest and rehabilitation, and
he believed he could still get to Houffalize without it. He considered the
new situation advantageous. If the threat to Saarbrücken or elsewhere
did not materialize, he speculated, "I can at once attack north with the
XII Corps, thus advancing the date for that attack." ULTRA received at

1734 on January 10 indicated traffic interruption at both bridges at Roth, which may have eased Patton's anxiety somewhat about an attack in the Diekirch sector. At 1933 ULTRA revealed Rothkirch's intent to withdraw Heilmann's line from the stream crossing just north of La Tannerie–Lutremange to the edge of the woods north of Harlange.[20] Patton was therefore justified in maintaining pressure with III Corps. Millikin adjusted boundaries and changed Grow's mission to assume Gaffey's positions and to hold on a line generally southwest of Mageret. The 320th CT was returned to Baade. Patton visited the 26th, 35th, and 90th Infantry Divisions during the day to check on progress and morale, and at 0100 on January 11 Van Fleet executed his night attack.

The 359th CT achieved complete surprise, advancing two battalions abreast in a column of files. It overran three positions and five 75mm guns and advanced to within 500 yards of the objective of the crossroads of Bohoey, just east of Doncols, while on the left the 357th CT captured and secured Doncols by dark. On January 11 alone, the 90th Infantry Division accounted for 1,265 prisoners. On Van Fleet's right the 328th CT made good progress to the high ground southwest of Winseler but was brought to a halt by "extremely heavy" artillery fire. One officer of the 26th Infantry Division recalled, "Every inch that we made forward cost us. The area was completely saturated with Shu-mines and Bouncing Bettys. . . . The ridge from Kaundorf to Mon Schuman was like a bowling alley. The Division was stretched so far and so thin that infiltrators had a field day. The men were dug in in the woods with the enemy only a few yards away in the same woods."[21]

The III Corps after-action report declared that the German MLR in the southwest portion of the Harlange Pocket "appeared to give way." By 0800 on January 11 ULTRA revealed that *Fifth Panzer Armee* was withdrawing, according to plan, to a new MLR from the Ourthe River bend northwest of Laroche–Beau Saint–Mierchamps–Champlon–Bois de Chabry–Amberloup–Tillet. *Seventh Armee* was withdrawing to a new MLR from the eastern edge of Lutrebois to the southern edge of Lutremange, the northern edge of Harlange, and the southern edge of Nocher, thence southeast to the Sûre River.[22]

Heeresgruppe B's day report noted that the 90th Infantry Division had made a wide and deep breakthrough north of Berlé, which necessitated commitment of the *1st SS PD* to seal the gap. Heilmann's infantry and the *FGB* were assessed as considerably mauled, and Model wanted to withdraw them from the line as soon as possible to incorporate replacements being brought up. By this time the strength of the *Leibstandarte* was 11,810, but its fighting strength was reported as 4,945. Since January 1 the division had lost 584 killed, 1,961 wounded, and 699 missing. It had also lost sixty tanks—eighteen Panzer IVs, twenty-nine Panthers, and thirteen Tigers—as well as six Panzer IV *Panzerjägers*.[23]

Van Fleet believed he had wiped out the *I* and *II Abteilungs* of VGR 36/9th VGD, almost all of the *FGB*, *Bicycle Abteilung 929*, *FJR 13*, and *Möser Abteilung 5* of the *5th FJD*. These heavy losses led Heilmann to order withdrawals on his own authority. He reflected, "For the first time in my military career I started to go my own way. I intended to save human lives." Based on his experience in Italy, Heilmann noted, "It was quite obvious to me that the 5 Parachute Division would not stand through tough defensive combat" in the Ardennes. Yet it persevered over a wide area and against a superior force, fighting major elements of the 4th and 11th Armored Divisions, CCA/9th Armored Division, and 35th and 90th Infantry Divisions for more than three weeks. Indeed, the performance of this division is worthy of independent study.[24]

By the end of January 11 Patton declared that the end of the Bastogne operation was "in sight"; it was now "simply a question of driving a defeated enemy." As the Harlange Pocket operation neared completion, however, he continued to pay attention to his right flank. Koch prepared a map showing the road nets and river lines in Walker's area, and Patton compared possible enemy intentions against XX Corps:

> The enemy can attack over the Saar at three places. First in the vicinity of Saarburg. It is known that he has quite a few pontoon sites constructed, and there is one road and one railway bridge not wholly destroyed between the junction of the Moselle and Saar and Saarburg. However, I doubt if this is where he will come, because it cramps his style of maneuver, although protecting his flanks, and the road net is not too good. The next place he can attack is through our present Saarlautern bridgehead, but in order to do this he would have to fight through that half of the town which is on the west bank of the river and now held by us. Also, he would have to construct a bridge, since the concrete bridge in existence is mined and will be blown up if we have to abandon our bridgehead east of the river. Speed is of such importance to him that he will not want to attack here where it will take at least three or four days to cut a road. Finally he can attack from the

bridgehead at Saarbrucken. This is the place, I believe, he will use if he comes at all . . . there are seven good bridges . . . and he has a bridgehead of seven to ten miles. The road net from there to Thionville, Metz, Nancy and to the south is excellent. However, St. Avold is a critical point, and as long as it is held by us, any operations he makes will be slowed down or stopped.[25]

Patton ordered Walker to prepare all crossings of the Nied River flowing southeast from Metz for demolition, "so we can canalize the enemy." On January 9 the 9th Armored Division began moving into XX Corps' area. Patton had barely completed this defensive estimate when ULTRA revealed at 2042 that the *11th PD* was moving to the Saarburg area, where he had not expected the Germans to go. This must have given Patton some pause, but ULTRA also revealed that the *10th SS PD*, so long uncommitted on Koch's maps, was to be employed against Seventh Army in the Hagenau Forest.[26]

While Patton waited for the Germans to attack his right flank, he directed Middleton to resume offensive operations on January 12 in horrible weather, which forced XIX TAC to cancel most missions. VIII Corps attacked with the 87th Infantry and 17th and 101st Airborne Divisions. The 11th Armored Division was still in reserve, but it began relieving elements of the 101st Airborne Division in the vicinity of Longchamps in anticipation of attacking as far as Bertogne the next morning. The division artillery moved into position southwest of Longchamps and registered all its guns by dark on January 12. The FDC was set up in Bastogne and tied in by wire with the FDCs of VIII Corps and 101st Airborne Division. Kilburn opened his CP at Sibert at 2000.[27] The day before Culin had occupied Bonnerue, Pironpré, Vesqueville, St. Hubert, and Hatrival without a fight, as *Panzer Lehr* and supporting elements withdrew during the night to the irregular Champlon–Ortheuville–Lavacherie–Sprimont line. The *FBB* withdrew across the Ourthe River at Wiompont at 0500 that morning and went into *Fifth Panzer Armee*'s reserve during the night. The rear guard was assumed by the *9th PD*, which had taken up blocking positions with its left flank on Noville–Bastogne and its right flank on Givry–Flamizoulle.[28]

The 87th Infantry Division advanced slowly through minefields, obstacles, and difficult terrain. The 345th CT occupied Fosset, Orreaux, and Sprimont, while the 347th CT occupied Amberloup and captured Lavacherie. The 17th Airborne Division attacked at 0830, advanced its positions north some 2,000 yards against "negligible resistance," and captured Flamierge. Miley was definitely anxious about the vulnerability of his paratroopers. When the advance reached the first phase line at 0931, the regiments paused for two and a half hours before pressing ahead in division order.[29] Either Miley became more cautious on his own or Middleton imposed greater control measures to help him. Either way, it seems probable that the early setbacks of the "Golden Talons" had a lingering psychological impact. On Miley's right the 101st Airborne Division reported no enemy withdrawal in its sector.

LIII Armeekorps had effectively shielded the critical MSRs and prevented a breakthrough from December 23 to January 11, but the Harlange Pocket was now being attacked from all sides, and German defenses began to crumble. On III Corps's right flank the 26th Infantry Division was still bogged down in heavy woods south of Wiltz and was making no headway.[30] However, Van Fleet finally committed the 358th CT. It moved forward from its assembly area at Arsdorf–Rambrouch to a forward assembly area at Bavigne behind the 357th CT on January 11. At 0730 on January 12 the 358th CT attacked in a column of battalions, captured Sonlez and entered Bras from the south, and captured half the town by midafternoon. The 35th Infantry Division, advancing through the woods toward Bras, contacted Van Fleet's infantry during the evening. TF Scott and TF Fickett advanced to the general line Tarchamps–Sonlez, and the 6th Armored Division finally captured Wardin. By the end of the day III Corps had finally closed the Harlange Pocket, capturing more than 1,000 prisoners on January 12 alone.

With the closure of the Harlange Pocket, III Corps began a much needed reorganization. Millikin began pulling back the 35th Infantry Division for rehabilitation throughout January 12–13, and Paul withdrew the 101st CT to Hierheck for reorganization on January 12. As III Corps reorganized, *Fifth Panzer Armee* continued its retrograde movements on January 12 to a new MLR: Laroche–Champlon–Amberloup–Noville–Wardin. At 0500 *I SS Panzerkorps* handed over to *LVIII Panzerkorps*; Krüger's CP was at Allerborn. He also assumed command of the *167th VGD* at this time. The next day *I SS Panzerkorps* moved to Emeschterhof just west of Asselborn. During the night *Seventh Armee* began an organized retreat behind the Wiltz River sector and reorganized. *LXXXV Armeekorps* withdrew and departed for *Heeresgruppe G*. *LIII Armeekorps* now had the *79th*, *276th*, and *9th VGDs* holding the MLR from west to east. As of 2030, *LIII Armeekorps* was supposed to withdraw into *Heeresgruppe B* reserve, but it stayed to compensate for the transfer of *LXXXV Armeekorps*. The *352nd VGD* went to *LXXX Armeekorps*.[31] The new boundary between the two corps was Biewels, two kilometers north of Vianden–Hoscheid, and west along the Sûre River. *Seventh Armee's* boundary with *Fifth Panzer Armee* was Dasburg–Draufelt–Grumelscheid–Doncols. The *FGB* was in reserve at Clerf.

The organized withdrawal of the *Fifth Panzer* and *Seventh Armees* must be factored into any analysis of Patton's effectiveness. So too must the wholesale withdrawal of German combat power from the Bulge precipitated by the eruption of the Russian Front on January 12. The First Ukrainian Front destroyed *XLVIII Panzerkorps'* three divisions and overran the divisions of *XXIV Panzerkorps* in their assembly areas, initiating an onslaught the Germans could not contain.[32] The *12th SS PD* had seen its last offensive action near Hill 510 on January 7. Thereafter it began withdrawing by *Kampfgruppen* early in the morning of January 10 to an assembly area east of St. Vith. All four *SS PDs* had withdrawn by January 10, but some elements of the *Leibstandarte* remained southeast of Bastogne.[33]

At this stage Bradley briefed Patton on his long-range plans for Twelfth Army Group, but the latter noted, "I think they are too long range." First Army would advance east on Cologne from Aachen, while Third Army protected its right flank. Patton recognized the logic of attacking where the West Wall had already been breached. "It is probably sound," he acknowledged, "but slow. . . . Personally I believe that an attack by the XX Corps, supported by another Corps (III or XII) straight east through Saarlautern would bring better results." Patton, and apparently Walker as well, wanted to attack the Saarbrücken bridgehead immediately. "We have sufficient troops to do it," Patton noted, but Bradley "believes in waiting to see what is going to happen." Walker had the 94th and 95th Infantry Divisions and the 10th Armored Division. The 8th and 9th Armored Divisions from SHAEF reserve had been released to Bradley on January 10. At 1400 lead elements of the 8th Armored Division reached Pont-à-Mousson, the 9th Armored Division closed at Thionville and Metz, and Gaffey's 4th Armored Division was between Luxembourg and Thionville in army reserve. "Wherever we attack," Patton concluded, "one thing is certain—we should attack, because if we don't the Germans will."[34]

The period from January 13 to 16 was characterized by slow progress and phased German withdrawals. Middleton grew increasingly unwilling to push his corps hard. Although he issued a field order at 1745 on January 12 directing a continuation of the offensive, he had sought a delay. Gay, who was visiting Middleton at the time, "definitely refused this request in the name of the Army Commander" and told him "that everything in the VIII Corps would be thrown into the attack."[35] The 87th Infantry Division cleared the area south of Bertogne–St. Hubert and reached the Ourthe River, where it contacted the British 6th Airborne Division. The 17th Airborne Division advanced against slight resistance, closed up to the Ourthe River, and captured Bertogne on January 14.

Middleton finally recommitted the 11th Armored Division on January 13 after seven days in reserve. At 1000 CCA attacked astride the Longchamps–Bertogne road, supported on the left rear by CCR, just as CCB closed in the vicinity of Villeroux after an all-night march from southwest of Bercheux. CCA defeated a tank counterattack from the east at 1100 with massed artillery fire adjusted by an air observation post. It then breached a minefield and cut the crossroads southwest of Bertogne three hours later. The division consolidated astride the German MSR between Gives and Compogne. Middleton visited Kilburn at 1420 to see whether CCB was ready for commitment. It had moved up to an assembly area astride the Bastogne–Noville highway one mile south of Foy. At 0930 on January 14 CCB attacked Recogne with a tank task force and Foy with an infantry task force. Both towns were taken, but at 1500 a tank counterattack came in from Vaux. That night the task forces withdrew to high ground south and west of Cobru and astride the highway south of Noville. On Kilburn's right the 506th PIR captured Foy, only to be driven out around 0600 the next morning. With the assistance of heavy artillery and elements of the 11th Armored Division, the 506th seized Foy and secured it three hours later.[36]

III Corps' advance on January 14 had little impact on *Seventh Armee*. It reported general quiet along the entire army front but expected an imminent attack on the right wing. III Corps was tired. The 90th Infantry Division made small gains against heavy resistance. As VIII and III Corps clawed closer to First Army, Patton began preparations for XII Corps' attack north in corridor B by transferring the 87th Infantry Division to Eddy. At 0800 the 346th CT departed VIII Corps, with the remainder of the division to follow the next day. Patton wanted the division to go into the line immediately, but Eddy requested that it be permitted to "stay out for a while to rest up, train, and get in good condition."[37] Patton agreed, but he was clearly eager to strike out on a different line of action. Corridor B was his best solution to the immediate problem of finishing off the Bulge, but his attention also turned at this point to operations beyond the Ardennes.

Down in XX Corps the 94th Infantry Division began a series of limited-objective attacks against the Orscholz switch line. The 376th CT seized Butzdorf and Tettingen two miles east of the Moselle River. The next day the regiment captured Nennig and Wies. The 95th Infantry Division attacked at the Saarlautern bridgehead and captured a few more city blocks. This was all part of Patton's post-Ardennes plan to resume the offensive on his old line of action in Lorraine. His concept of operations was simple: hold from St. Vith to Saarburg with minimal force and attack all-out through the Saarlautern bridgehead.[38] Although Bradley had held out great hope for Third Army's operations in Lorraine prior to the Bulge, he revised his concept of operations as a result of the attack. In contrast, Patton retained faith in the feasibility of the earlier concept.

Fifth Panzer Armee started withdrawing to another MLR—Nadrin–Bertogne–Noville–Harlange—on January 14–15. The *FBB* attacked at dawn from Michamps toward Oubourcy in an attempt to restore the MLR of the *167th VGD*. A *Kampfgruppe* of *9th PD* was to attack simultaneously from the Bourcy area toward Bastogne. The *FBB* attacked as planned, but the *9th PD* did not. The *FBB* then established a hedgehog position and repelled attacks during the day.[39] *LIII Armeekorps'* task at this point was to pull back the *9th* and *276th VGDs* from Third Army column by column. The right flank of the corps was to move through Grumelscheid north of Enscherange to Dasburg on the Our River. The corps' left was to move via Sure–Roscheid to north of Vianden.

As the Germans continued to withdraw in stages, Third Army maintained contact. On January 15 CCA/11th Armored Division closed in on Compogne, and the 506th PIR finally captured Noville. Patton recognized that Millikin was facing the hinge of the German switch position in the Bulge. III Corps faced bitter resistance, and Van Fleet's right was held up, but the 358th CT succeeded in capturing Niederwampach. The next day the 359th CT captured Oberwampach.[40] *Panzer Lehr* was ordered to hold Houffalize at all costs, and Bayerlein put *KG von Poschinger* with *Panzerjäger* units on the high ground to the south. However, by this date, Bayerlein had already left fifty-three tanks by the roadside for lack of fuel. His forward panzer repair shops had been at Lavacherie, his former CP, but they had to be vacated under threat from XIX TAC. The key moment came at 1140 on January 16 when the 41st Cavalry Reconnaissance Squadron of the 11th Armored Division contacted the 41st AIB of CCA/2nd Armored Division southwest of Houffalize. In the four days of combat since reentering the line, Kilburn's division had sustained an additional 575 casualties and lost forty-two vehicles, including twelve medium tanks. Patton called January 16 "a tidying up battle," so there was "not much to do."[41]

It had taken almost an entire month for First and Third Armies to regain contact, but it was anticlimactic. No German formations had been trapped; the lines of actions converging on Houffalize had been telegraphed, and the Germans had responded effectively; and no complementary operations were executed immediately to take advantage of the hard fighting. As a result, the Germans were able to execute what Sibert identified as the most favored capability—phased withdrawal. They could do so in part because an estimated 143,500 men and 375 tanks were still in the Bulge: 56,000 men and 130 tanks opposite First Army, and 87,500 men and 245 tanks opposite Third Army.[42]

Patton did not immediately and aggressively follow up the meeting at Houffalize. On January 17 he personally congratulated Middleton and Millikin for their efforts but told them to rest their corps and resume the attack on January 21.[43] Patton's decision to halt VIII and III Corps conformed with Bradley's concept of operations. At midnight First Army returned to Twelfth Army Group; Ninth Army (holding the Aachen approach with only two divisions) would stay with Montgomery, despite Bradley's protest. Bradley envisioned holding attacks by XVIII Airborne and VII, VIII, and III Corps while V and XII Corps attempted to converge along Skyline Drive. V Corps had started its attack on January 15. The linkup at Houffalize pinched out the 2nd Armored and 84th Infantry Divisions, but the 3rd Armored and 83rd Infantry Divisions swung east on January 17–18 to advance toward St. Vith. LXVI Armeekorps bitterly opposed this advance. VIII Corps was southeast of Houffalize with the 17th Airborne Division in the north, the 11th Armored Division in the center, and the 101st Airborne Division in the south, on the right flank of the corps. Middleton continued to face XLVII Panzerkorps. III Corps had, from left to right, the 6th Armored Division and the 35th, 90th, and 26th Infantry Divisions; it was still opposed by LVIII Panzerkorps.

Gay noted that Bradley called Patton on January 15 "to propose a new plan of attack. . . . In substance, the plan was to have a Corps of the First Army attack south astride the ST. VITH–DIEKIRCH road; the Third Army to continue pressure on the west by the VIII and III Corps; attack north astride the DIEKIRCH—ST. VITH road with the XII Corps."[44] Only on that day, with contact between the two armies imminent, did Bradley give Patton the green light for the XII Corps operation. The argument has been made that Patton recognized he could not launch XII Corps until VIII and III Corps had unhinged the German defenses.[45] Yet Bradley, not Patton, established the time and space relationship between operations around Bastogne and those farther east. It is entirely logical to assume that northward pressure applied by XII Corps so close to the Our crossings would have helped unhinge the German defenses around Bastogne more effectively than frontal attacks against German strength. Bradley's sequential approach to operations naturally won out over Patton's overlapping, simultaneous approach.

With the go-ahead from Bradley, Patton called Eddy on January 15 and told him to relieve the 4th Infantry Division with the 87th Infantry Division immediately; he also informed Eddy that the 4th Armored Division was released to him at once. A whole series of reliefs began across the army. On January 17 Bradley relieved Third Army of responsibility for defense of the Meuse River line below Givet, well beyond the point where the Germans posed a serious threat, but Patton lost the 10th Armored Division, which departed for Seventh Army. The next day the 35th Infantry Division began moving to Metz, and the 8th Armored Division, centered on Pont-à-Mousson, started rotating one combat command at a time up to the Orscholz line to gain combat experience with the 94th Infantry Division.

Despite the fact that XII Corps had been sitting idle for three weeks, Patton was unable to get it rolling once he received authorization. The 87th Infantry Division should have been sent in to replace the 4th Infantry Division immediately, as Patton wanted, so that Blakeley could get ready to attack. The 4th Armored Division's absence to the south should not have delayed the attack either. It could have come up and participated in a later phase; in fact, Eddy had told Gaffey he did not plan to use him in the initial attack. Patton set the attack date as January 18, but this certainly did not reflect his desire to get XII Corps going if the threat to Saarbrücken did not materialize.

Eddy was not the right man to command an operation designed to achieve a quick decision. He had proved that in Lorraine on more than one occasion. Thirteen divisions of *Seventh Armee* and *Fifth Panzer Armee* needed to withdraw across bridges in the southern part of the Bulge. This was an extraordinary opportunity because the Germans possessed only five tactical bridges across the Our, and three of them were close to Eddy's front line. He thought he "stood a good chance of cutting off a good part of the German 79th Division" if Irwin's division could move rapidly

Table 14.1. XII Corps' Schedule of Movement, January 15–18, 1945

	87 Inf Div	4 Inf Div	5 Inf Div
Day Jan 15	346 Inf 347 Inf move to 4 Inf Div area	Bn 8 Inf	Move to 10 Inf area
Night Jan 15–16	346 Inf relieve	8 Inf Bn 8 Inf	Relieve Bn 10 Inf
Day Jan 16		Bn 22 Inf 8 Inf (–)	Move to 11 Inf area Move to 10 Inf area
Night Jan 16–17	347 Inf relieve	22 Inf Bn 22 Inf	Relieve Bn 11 Inf
Day Jan 17	345 Inf arrive	4 Inf Div area 22 Inf (–)	Move to 11 Inf area
Night Jan 17–18	345 Inf relieve	12 Inf 22 Inf (–)	Relieve 11 Inf (–)
Day Jan 18		12 Inf	Move to reserve area

Source: XII Corps Operational Directive No. 67, 1830, January 15, 1945.

enough, but he also appreciated that the enemy movement north of the 5th Infantry Division was "natural as the Germans are pulling out of the salient and coming down this way." A rapid mounting of the attack in corridor B was therefore critical to achieving decisiveness, but on the eve of the attack, Eddy phoned Gay and requested permission to delay for a day because the weather forecast indicated air support would be unavailable. Gay cautioned Eddy about suggesting a delay to Patton, and Eddy rescinded the request.[46]

Eddy met with his division commanders at 1100 on January 17 at Irwin's CP. XII Corps now had five divisions: the 4th, 5th, 80th, and 87th Infantry and the 4th Armored. Blakeley's 4th Infantry Division was to attack across the Sûre River with one CT, seize the high ground northeast of Bettendorf and be prepared to extend to the left to relieve elements of the 5th Infantry Division, and clear the enemy from the area west of the Our River. Irwin was to attack across the Sûre and advance north along Skyline Drive. On the corps' left flank, McBride's 80th Infantry Division was to clear the area west of the Wiltz and Sûre Rivers. The 87th Infantry Division was to smoke off the Sauer at Steinheim and Bornport and simulate a crossing in the Wasserbillig area. Once a bridgehead had been

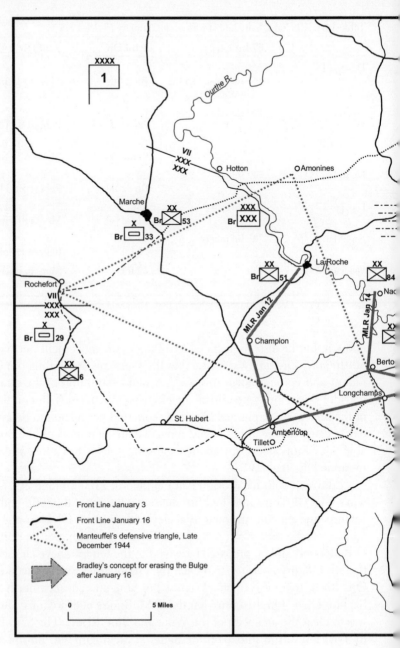

Map 14.3. Meeting at Houffalize, January 16, 1945

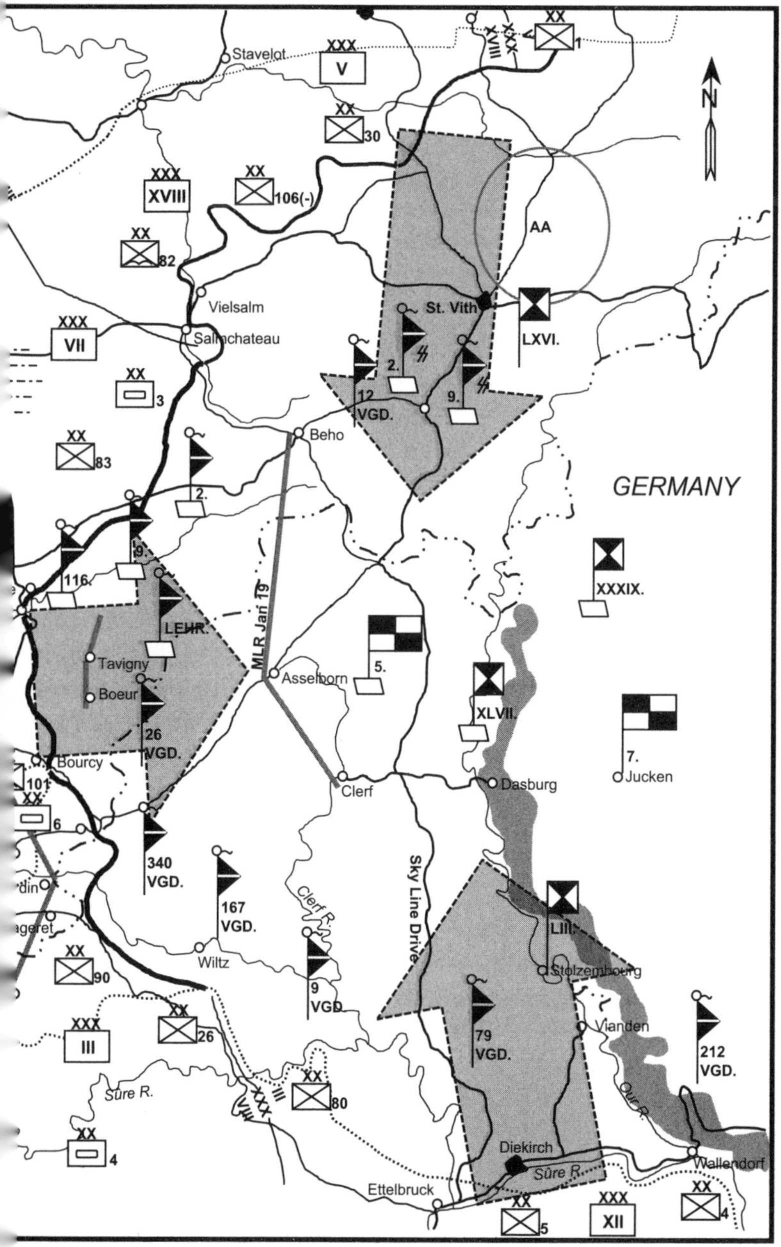
Stavelot
XXX V
XX 30
XXX XVIII
XX 106(-)
XX 82
Vielsalm
XXX VII
Salmchateau
XX 3
XX 83
Beho
St. Vith
AA
LXVI.
2.
9.
12 VGD.
GERMANY
116.
LEHR.
Tavigny
Boeur
26 VGD.
Bourcy
101
XX 6
MLR Jan 19
Asselborn
5.
XXXIX.
XLVII.
7.
Jucken
Clerf
Dasburg
340 VGD.
167 VGD.
Clerf R.
Sky Line Drive
LIII.
Stolzembourg
Wiltz
9 VGD.
79 VGD.
Vianden
212 VGD.
XX 90
XXX III
XX 26
Sûre R.
XX 80
XX 4
Our R.
Diekirch
Wallendorf
Sûre R.
Ettelbruck
XX 5
XXX XII
XX 4

established across the Sûre, Eddy had the option of committing Gaffey for a drive toward St. Vith.[47]

The corps fire plan consisted of a prearranged four-hour schedule to strike fourteen CPs, two observation posts, six supply dumps, twenty-four defiles, twenty-one towns, and nine heavy weapons locations. The air plan consisted of the Ninth Air Force attacking crossings of the Our at Roth, Vianden, and Dasburg and deeper targets to the east, such as Bitburg.[48] Even though this operation had been in development for many days, as late as January 16 Blakeley was still unclear about what was to take place, and Eddy told him, "We had better have a meeting of all artillery commanders tomorrow and have this plan ironed out and coordinated."[49] Although the XII Corps after-action report stated that the corps began an artillery preparation at 0230, the corps artillery did not actually fire until H-hour at 0300 January 18. Thereafter and for the remainder of the day it fired 13,716 rounds.

Visibility was poor due to snow, but the corps achieved surprise. On the left only the 319th CT of the 80th Infantry Division attacked. The 3rd Battalion seized Nocher despite heavy enemy resistance, but the 1st Battalion, attacking to the east, failed to capture Masseler by dark and fell back to positions around Dahl.[50] The 5th Infantry Division crossed the Sûre River with two regiments up on a 6,000-yard front between Reisdorf and Ettelbruck. The 2nd CT crossed with two battalions abreast. The 1st Battalion occupied Erpeldange, while the 2nd Battalion faced heavy resistance and captured Hill 350. The 3rd Battalion crossed and captured Ingeldorf and attacked the heavily mined and booby-trapped town of Diekirch; it succeeded in clearing one-third of it by dark. On the right the 10th CT crossed with two battalions abreast at Gilsdorf. By 1500 the 1135th Engineer C Group had constructed a class 40 Bailey bridge at Ettelbruck and a treadway bridge at Gilsdorf. By the end of the day Bettendorf was partially cleared.[51] On the corps' right flank the 8th CT/4th Infantry Division attacked with two battalions abreast. Despite the fact that the 4th Engineer C Battalion struggled with the terrain and weather and succeeded in completing only a single footbridge by dark, all the infantry crossed. The 1st Battalion crossed north and south of Moestroff and bypassed Bettendorf. The 3rd Battalion crossed immediately behind at the same locations, as did the 2nd Battalion, advancing toward Reisdorf despite a delay at the river due to heavy mortar and artillery fire.[52]

Patton was present as the long-awaited XII Corps attack unfolded. Eddy noted that he "seemed pleased with our progress." At 1300 Eddy

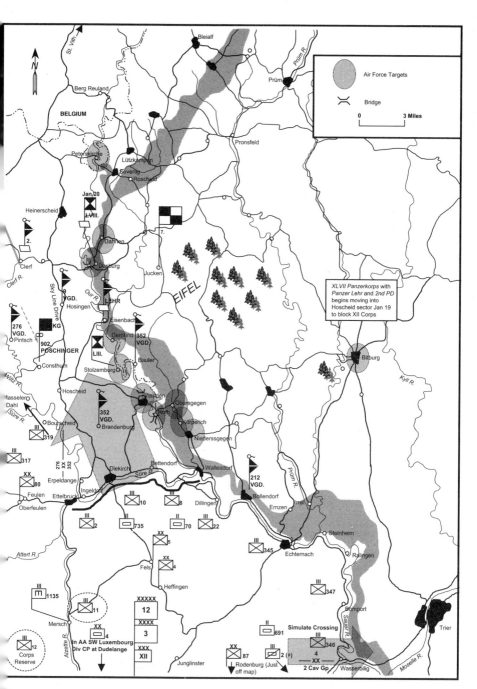

Map 14.4. XII Corps Operations, January 18–25, 1945

picked Patton up and drove to Irwin's CP, stopping on the way to visit Blakeley at the 4th Infantry Division CP. Trouble getting a bridge in for the 8th CT led Eddy to note, "I think Gen. Patton thought that Blakeley was a little too complacent about the situation and didn't have a very good opinion of him. He may be right."[53] Since Patton now believed that XII Corps' attack was the decisive line of action, he was in the right place—up front. He and Irwin went up in an air observation post to assess the situation.

The long inactivity of XII Corps may have lulled Brandenberger into a false sense of security. He believed there was little likelihood of a major attack in the Echternach area because of the absence of the 6th Armored Division, but the attack of the 5th Infantry Division "came as a great surprise." He did not anticipate a major crossing of the Sûre River sector around Diekirch, and his dispositions reflected his situational understanding. *Seventh Armee* was strongest west and northwest of Ettelbruck. *LIII Armeekorps* contained the 79th, 276th, and 9th VGDs from west to east, while the Sûre line between Ettelbruck and the frontier was defended by the 352nd VGD of *LXXX Armeekorps*. The only other division in this corps was the 212th VGD. Once Brandenberger appreciated that XII Corps' attack was a main effort, he quickly transferred the bulk of the artillery behind *LIII Armeekorps* to *LXXX Armeekorps* and shifted a regiment-sized *Kampfgruppe* to the right wing of *LXXX Armeekorps* to help block Skyline Drive. Model also took immediate action, ordering *Panzer Lehr, 2nd PD*, and *XLVII Panzerkorps* headquarters to *Seventh Armee* and directing that another bridge be constructed north of Vianden to avoid entrapment.

ULTRA intercepted the orders for *XLVII Panzerkorps* to move across Eddy's front, but Allen was damning in his criticism of Sibert's dissemination of the intelligence to Third Army: "A U message 24 hours old came in that 47 Panzer Corps [had] been ordered to take [a] certain position in XII Corps zone. Not only was message 24 hours late, but we had overrun position. Without stopping to check those facts, he burst out with a hot warning of danger of threat counterattack, and advised Bradley to order us to rush up an Armored Div. . . . Clear case [of] unfounded jumping to conclusion and outrageous example of incompetence."[54] Allen frequently made charges of incompetence, but his entry highlighted Sibert's oversensitivity to new threats and a corresponding overestimation of German capability at this stage of the campaign.

No sooner had XII Corps launched its long-delayed attack than *11th PD*, identified as a threat for some time, was finally committed. It had spent the first half of January reconditioning near Bitburg and eventually reached a strength of thirty Panzer IVs, fifty Panthers, and twenty-five *Panzerjägers*. On January 16 *LXXXII Armeekorps*, responsible for the Orscholz switch line, requested assistance due to XX Corps' attacks. During the evening of January 17 *Generalleutnant* Wend von Wietersheim was ordered to cross the Saar and attack on January 18 to regain the lost fortifications in the Orscholz line. Since the *416th Division* was "seriously battered," it was placed under Wietersheim's command. Although the infantry and a few tanks managed to cross into the triangle, the bulk of Wietersheim's panzers had to remain east of the Saar due to fuel shortages. Nevertheless, he succeeded in retaking Nenning and Butzdorf from the 376th CT.[55] This, however, was a last gasp, and it demonstrated Hitler's flaw of initiating low-probability lines of action and persisting in them, thereby wasting critical reserves. His persistence with SONNENWENDE in Alsace followed the same pattern. He committed his last major reserves—the *10th SS PD* and the *7th FJD*. They linked up with *XIV SS Korps* and inflicted considerable damage on the 12th Armored Division but could achieve little more. Had even one of these divisions, rebuilt to a respectable level, been sent to reinforce *Seventh Armee's* MLR, Patton's rate of advance most likely would have been reduced.

Heavy rain and slush slowed XII Corps on January 19. The Ninth Air Force failed to bomb Vianden, but XIX TAC managed to get off 149 sorties, several of which were flown in support of XII Corps. *KG von Poschinger*, reinforced by a panzer company and *II Abteilung/Armored Artillerie Regiment 130*, pushed through the heavy snow to take up positions southwest and south of Hoscheid, the key blocking position for the withdrawal. By the morning of January 20 it was in place, with the *9th VGD* on the right.[56] By the end of the day XII Corps had advanced four miles "with stiff fighting all the way." The estimated strength opposite Eddy was only 13,500, but the weather, deep snow, and terrain amplified German numbers. Patton showed up in Eddy's office right after breakfast and was, "as usual, impatient about the progress we had made." Eddy, however, felt that "we are doing as well as can be expected and have made a pretty good advance." *LIII Armeekorps* was now threatened with encirclement, but appalling snow on January 21–22 seriously impeded XII Corps. By this time the 5th Infantry Division was almost due west of Vianden. Eddy noted that Irwin "is doing very well in this operation and there seems to be no stopping him."[57] The 4th Infantry Division was well behind on the right.

The weather cleared on January 22, and the German columns were subjected to heavy attacks from XIX TAC around the crossing sites and roads in the Eisenbach, Hosingen, and Merscheid areas, destroying an estimated 600 vehicles. Medium bombers destroyed the bridge at Dasburg, creating an enormous traffic jam.[58] An air observation post spotted massed vehicles on the road northwest of Vianden, and the fires of the 273rd and 21st FA Battalions were adjusted for effect. That day elements of 2nd PD were identified on the corps' front, and during the next three days the 3rd PGD, Lehr, and 5th FJD would be identified, all indications of the Germans' complete withdrawal from the Bulge.

On January 23 Patton phoned Eddy and gave him the "what the hell's the matter" speech, stressing the importance of attacking aggressively. Yet Patton now recognized that XII Corps' rate of advance was insufficient to trap large numbers of enemy. Irwin could not penetrate KG von Poschinger's line south of Hoscheid. Corridor B could be fully exploited only while the Germans were at full stretch, reaching for the Meuse. That window of opportunity had closed while Patton and Eddy prepared XII Corps for operations. As the Fifth Panzer and Seventh Armees withdrew in phases and got closer to the Our River crossings, their combat power increased and proved sufficient to prevent Eddy from reaching a decision in corridor B. Patton therefore decided to send VIII and III Corps straight east across XII Corps' front to the Our River, just north of Vianden, while XX Corps began attacking in earnest. He phoned Walker shortly after voicing his displeasure to Eddy: "Johnny, what's going on down there? You're not going pacifist on me are you? Get those Divs of yours going. . . . It's vital we keep on attacking everywhere at this time. No let-up."[59]

The U.S. Army recognizes the end of the Ardennes campaign as January 25, but even on that day, the Germans successfully counterattacked the 80th Infantry Division bridgehead at Lellingen on the Clerf River and forced a withdrawal to the south bank.[60] The German capability to lash out in small-scale but effective counterattacks led to continued vigilance by Eddy. In his operational directive of January 23 he tasked portions of the 4th Armored and 5th Infantry Divisions to counterattack penetrations of the corps' zone.[61] Though cautious, Eddy was justified to a certain extent because, by this time, XII Corps had identified eight divisions on its front.

It was this concentration of remaining combat power that allowed the Germans to effectively withdraw in stages all the way to the West Wall without leaving a single formation trapped. Lüttwitz reflected that after the linkup at Houffalize, "the heavy pressure" on XLVII Panzerkorps "ceased for some days to come," and Bodenstein declared, "We succeeded time and again in staging a more or less effective defense along the ordered lines of resistance." Eisenhower admitted in a cable to the Combined Chiefs of Staff on January 18, the day XII Corps attacked, that despite suffering a tactical defeat and suffering heavy losses in men and material, the enemy "will probably manage to withdraw the bulk of his formations."[62] Eisenhower's overall concept for eliminating the Bulge, and Bradley's execution of that concept, gave the Germans the flexibility to maneuver out of what might have been a devastating trap. The Ardennes was an orthodox victory characterized by a head-on test of strength and, inevitably, heavy casualties. Patton played a major role in the victory, but he knew there was a better way.

15

Assessment

The Ardennes was not where Patton wanted to fight in late December 1944. Set to punch through the West Wall after a brutal campaign in Lorraine, he had to stop and realign Third Army for an entirely new operation. Although more than sixty-five years have passed, his conduct of the battle remains relevant for study by senior commanders today. Patton's *command technique* encompassed the "human" factor in war and therefore offers timeless instruction. Although the march of technology has been relentless since the end of World War II, Patton's *operational technique* can still serve the modern practitioner of maneuver warfare. The modern observe, orient, decide, and act (OODA) loop concept is sometimes characterized as an epiphany, but Patton's operational technique functioned on the same premise. Utilizing the estimate process, he continuously updated his situational awareness and consistently strove to disrupt German intentions. The estimate process, combined with the communication of his intent to subordinates, shaped the conduct of operations and the ultimate outcome of the missions assigned by Eisenhower and Bradley. The outcomes are the most important aspect of this study; therefore, his overall effectiveness as an army commander in the Bulge must be based on *mission accomplishment, spatial effectiveness,* and *casualty effectiveness.*

Patton's Command Technique

Fundamental to Patton's command technique was his philosophy of leadership. He wrote to his son on January 16: "I have it—but I'll be damned if I can define it. Probably it consists in knowing what you want to do and then doing it and getting mad if anyone stepps [sic] in the way."[1] It also involves being seen at the front. Patton consistently went forward to visit his commanders. Maxwell Taylor recalled that Patton left a fine impression on him because he frequently visited the 101st Airborne Division in

Bastogne, seeking to help in any way possible. Patton also arrived unexpectedly at the CP of the 26th Infantry Division, threw his arm around Paul's shoulder, and said, "How's my little fighting sonofabitch?" Paul later told Eddy, "I was so cheered for not getting relieved, there was nothing I wouldn't do for the man." Before the 90th Infantry Division attacked the Harlange Pocket, Patton gave Van Fleet considerable encouragement. He patted him on the back and told him, "Van Fleet, you've never failed me. I know you can do it. The 90th has always accomplished anything I give them to do." Van Fleet vividly remembered that moment, reflecting, "Now that's an element of command. When you praise somebody, damn it! You have to go out and succeed, and that's in football. That's in anything. You capture the art of leadership there, and that was one of Patton's prime qualities."[2]

Though it is impossible to quantify, Patton probably transferred some of his energy and enormous self-confidence to his subordinates. Hansen noted on December 24 that Patton was "boisterous and noisy, feeling good in the middle of a fight." Weyland reflected, "I loved the old guy" and "considered him the best field army commander that the world has ever seen." Patton's leadership also manifested itself at the lower levels. James Graff, a nineteen-year-old replacement, recalled that on his way north from Metz, Patton passed his convoy in an open jeep "and gave us the old hubba hubba." Patton's ability and willingness to satisfy the basic soldier's need for recognition explains why he was cheered by the soldiers of the 90th Infantry Division when he drove through their columns.[3]

Patton demonstrated leadership and developed trust by regularly accepting advice. Although he alone bore the ultimate responsibility for decision making, he was open to frank discussion and suggestions from his staff and subordinates before issuing orders. Gay and Harkins were his closest tactical advisers.[4] He deferred to Gay's judgment on the risk of sending the 35th Infantry Division into action prematurely and to Eddy's judgment on where to employ the 6th Armored Division, as well as delaying the 87th Infantry Division's commitment in XII Corps until it had rested. The psychology of seeking advice is important to both the commander and the subordinate, but sometimes Patton accepted advice against his better judgment, with consequences for his operational design. Diverting the 6th Armored Division from corridor B left XII Corps with no armored division and reduced options for offensive action in the Sûre–Sauer sector. The one area in which Patton ignored the recommendations

Table 15.1. Patton's Visits to Corps and Divisions during the Ardennes Campaign

	Formations	Circumstances
Dec 20	III, VIII Corps; 4, 26, 80 Inf Divs; 4, 9, 10 Armd Divs	
Dec 21		Conference at Third Army
Dec 22		
Dec 23		Eddy visits Patton
Dec 24		Eddy visits Patton
Dec 25	4 Armd Div; 5, 26, 80 Inf Divs	
Dec 26		
Dec 27	III, VIII Corps	
Dec 28	III Corps (visited by Harkins)	Patton meets with Eddy at Third Army
Dec 29		Patton stays in all day due to head cold
Dec 30	III Corps, 101 Abn Div	
Dec 31		Spaatz and Doolittle visit
Jan 1	III Corps; 26, 35 Inf Divs	
Jan 2	III, VIII Corps	
Jan 3		No visits
Jan 4	III, VIII Corps; 101 Abn Div	
Jan 5	VIII Corps; 17, 101 Abn Divs	
Jan 6		Bradley
Jan 7		No visits
Jan 8	III Corps, 4 Armd Div, 90 Inf Div	
Jan 9	26, 90 Inf Divs	
Jan 10	III, VIII Corps; 101 Abn Div; 4, 6 Armd Divs	
Jan 11	XX Corps	
Jan 12	III, VIII Corps	
Jan 13	III, VIII Corps; 101 Abn Div; 6 Armd Div	
Jan 14		Eddy and Walker visit Patton
Jan 15		Eddy visits Patton
Jan 16		
Jan 17	III, VIII Corps; 6 Armd Div, 26, 90 Inf Divs	
Jan 18	XII Corps, 4, 5 Inf Divs	

of his corps commanders almost without exception pertained to the time of attack. On four separate occasions Middleton recommended a delay to permit greater preparation. Only once, when the 17th Airborne Division could not close in time, did Patton acquiesce. Considering his almost pathological aversion to inactivity, this seemed inevitable.

Once Patton had considered all the feedback from his subordinates and staff, he issued orders—usually verbal orders followed by written confirmation. Face-to-face orders cannot be improved upon, and it is clear from the lack of elaboration of the commander's intent in his written orders that Patton preferred to explain his ideas in person. He did not have to justify his decisions to subordinates or seek their approval,[5] but he had to ensure that they understood his intent. Patton regularly brought all the corps commanders together to achieve the unifying effect of a common operating picture, but the frequent changes in plans required continual updating of his intent to them.

Even when Patton's intent was clearly expressed, the corps commanders sometimes resisted. Seeing to it that orders are carried out is indispensable to the very nature of command, and Patton frequently found it necessary to push the corps commanders. Middleton and Millikin became more cautious as the campaign progressed because they started to question the effectiveness of their operations in terms of lives expended for ground gained. One sees this particularly in Middleton's frequent requests to delay attacks and his unwillingness to expose the 11th Armored Division to extended combat for ten days after its initial setbacks. On January 6 Patton noted, "I had to use [the] whip on both Middleton and Millikin today. They are too cautious." Patton had little sympathy for this trait. His command technique vis-à-vis the corps commanders was simple: "I will do all the worrying necessary. The corps commanders must fight." Indeed, FM 100–15 defined a corps commander's task primarily as sensing opportunities to "take full advantage of enemy weaknesses, to exploit those weaknesses, and defeat decisively the hostile force."[6] Ultimately, Patton decided when the cost outweighed the gain. That was the burden of command, and he carried it alone.

Patton's belief that the corps commanders must fight and leave the worrying to him meant that they had to trust him. They had to know that when he ordered them to fight in a certain place at a certain time with certain resources for an unknown length of time, he had thought it through and it corresponded to a higher campaign objective. Patton's ability to develop good relationships with the corps commanders helped build such trust. Martin Blumenson asserted that there was a history between Patton and Millikin, but apparently it did not negatively impact operations. Indeed, Patton should be given credit for trusting the unproven Millikin with the difficult Bastogne operation, especially when the experienced and aggressive Bulldog Walker was available. Though they often frustrated him, he interacted effectively with Middleton, Millikin, and Eddy during the campaign. By way of comparison, Hodges seems to have created considerable and unnecessary tension with his corps commanders.[7]

The human element of command was something Patton consistently calculated. It was ever present and took on different tones with each operation. He appreciated human sensitivities, strengths, and limitations. Knowing the skills and limitations of each corps commander was essential to Patton's command technique. Short-term tactical success gained by driving a corps commander might actually be negated by that subordinate's loss of faith in the superior. In Lorraine he expected Eddy to attack on September 16—a critical moment when he could have decisively penetrated the German MLR. But Eddy told Patton he needed three more days, which, in the latter's estimation, would be "too late." However, instead of pushing Eddy to make it happen, he sent his chief of staff, Gaffey, to investigate. Patton's reason was based on simple psychology: "I have been going to the front so much and kicking so much about delay that I have the generals jittery."[8] He remained wary of this command effect in the Bulge. Still, there were times when he issued "thou shalt" direction, and Middleton was the recipient.

Patton was very tolerant and relieved only a small number of his corps and division commanders throughout the war; gross negligence or excessive fatigue (in the case of Barton, commander of the 4th Infantry Division) were the key factors he considered.[9] Patton was sufficiently dissatisfied with the leadership of Kilburn and Miley to consider relieving them both. However, he ultimately acted in accord with his long-standing philosophy: "one should not act too fast."[10] Instead of summarily relieving Kilburn and Miley, Patton properly delegated to Middleton the responsibility for coaching them in their baptism of fire. Whether Middleton did this effectively is open to debate. Indeed, Patton had to intervene and order Middleton to use the 11th Armored Division to support the 17th Airborne Division. The disaster that overtook the 17th Airborne Division in the first week of January must be blamed partly on Middleton. Nevertheless, by the end of the campaign, Patton concluded that Middleton and Millikin had done "exceptionally well. Of course, Millikin being a greenhorn, required considerable shoving, but I think he has done a good job."[11] The Patton command technique contained a good mix of push and praise to maximize the performance of his subordinates. That he was capable of commending and criticizing when required demonstrated his balanced command technique.

Table 15.2. Patton Pushes His Corps Commanders to Attack

Patton's Original Attack Date	Corps Commander's Recommendations	Recommendation Accepted?
Dec 22, 0400	0600 (Millikin)	Yes
Dec 30	Middleton (delay for more reconnaissance	No
Jan 3	Middleton (delay 17 Abn Div attack)	Yes
Jan 8	Middleton (delay for rest)	No
Jan 12	Middleton (delay for rest)	No
	Gaffey (delay for rest)	No
Jan 17	Eddy (delay due to weather)	No

Patton's Operational Technique

The evidence conclusively demonstrates that Third Army was more than just a tactical headquarters as defined by FM 100–5. Patton had no ability to shape ground operations at the theater level, the way Montgomery and Bradley did,[12] but Third Army was a grand tactical (operational) headquarters because it did more than simply fight the current battle. The function of his headquarters and his decision-making range equated to the operational level of war as it is understood today. He received, sought clarification on, and used the highest level of intelligence available. He received operational reserves from the highest level and influenced their use, and he possessed a great deal of control over his own logistics within the army service area and combat zone.

Nevertheless, at various points during the campaign, Patton's freedom of decision was severely restricted by Eisenhower and Bradley. Appreciating their influence is important because Patton has been heavily criticized for lacking a "single coherent design" for the battle up to Bastogne. It has been argued that only the "eventual weight of the intervention, not Patton's handling of it," turned the scales on the southern side of the Bulge.[13] Although this statement contains an element of truth, the censure entirely misses the fact that Patton had to tailor his grand tactics to fit the campaign design as conceived by Eisenhower and filtered by Bradley. Eisenhower identified the mission, established the geographic parameters, and committed Twelfth Army Group and Third Army to a main line of action in corridor A. Bradley's own estimate of the situation confirmed

Eisenhower's selection of corridor A as the main line of action. The fact that Houffalize was the key to getting First Army back made Bradley's decision easier. Doctrinally, the criterion by which Patton judged the efficacy of his own decisions was whether they furthered Bradley's and, ultimately, Eisenhower's intent. FM 100–5 put it simply: "any independence on the part of a subordinate commander must conform to the general plan for the unit as a whole."[14]

Harkins was essentially correct when he stated that Bradley and Patton "seemed to get along fine," but on the eve of the Bulge, Patton lamented that it might have been better to serve under Devers: "he interferes less and is not as timid as Bradley." Indeed, Bradley's headquarters contained a staff of more than 1,200, while Devers's headquarters contained half that. Even allowing for Twelfth Army Group's larger size, the imbalance said much about their command styles. As Charles B. MacDonald observed, Bradley employed his staff "in intricate, detailed planning."[15] Twelfth Army Group records bear this out.

An example of Bradley's interfering in Patton's design of the campaign was their apparent disagreement over where the 90th Infantry Division should be employed. *War as I Knew It* contains the following passage: Bradley "did not order, he did strongly suggest, that instead of attacking north of Diekirch . . . we should put in a new division southeast of Bastogne so as to insure the integrity of the corridor. I let myself be overpersuaded by him in this connection and assume full responsibility for the error of subsequently engaging the 90th Division too far west. Had I put the 90th Division in north of Diekirch, I am sure we would have bagged more Germans and just as cheaply."[16] Bradley was obsessed with the present fight longer than he should have been, whereas Patton attempted to transition to a different line of action to aid the Bastogne fight in an indirect way. Moreover, Bradley's refusal to even consider allowing Patton to attack in corridor B until physical contact had been established between First and Third Armies spoke volumes about the former's stop-start sequential approach to execution at the grand tactical level.

The problem was that Bradley's deduction from his estimate process was logical; corridor A permitted the maximal simultaneous deployment of combat power. Patton conceded that point but avoided tunnel vision by concluding that the best line of action was to strike somewhere close to the base, threatening to change the campaign from west of the Our River to east of it. Corridor B was closely connected with the present battle at Bastogne and represented a good transition to a new campaign. Corridor

D also represented a sound transition to the next campaign, but the lack of Allied reserves crippled flexibility and went back to Marshall's ninety-division "gamble."

Both corridor D and corridor B were risky because Patton had to defend his south flank (XX Corps along the Saar); a vulnerable pivot position on the right in XII Corps; and, as far as he was concerned, an open, vulnerable left flank. Since these two lines of action contained greater risk, it is impossible to determine whether Patton considered them to be the best course no matter what the enemy did. If he did not, which seems likely, it demonstrated his willingness to disregard the built-in safety mechanisms of the estimate process. Bradley's unwillingness to link corridors A and B much earlier conclusively proved that Patton could only influence, not author, the design of the campaign.

Eisenhower and Bradley were clearly much more risk-averse than Patton, and it is appropriate to consider the role of boldness in the campaign. A good place to start is with Michael D. Doubler's observation that senior American commanders faced the dilemma of maintaining the initiative while keeping casualties to a minimum. They followed more conservative lines of action because large flanking actions and mobile exploitation were "filled with risk, exposed U.S. forces to greater casualties, and had no certainty of returns commensurate with the risks involved. Boldness is an important trait in a general, but prudence also has a place in campaign planning."[17] In response, one can immediately challenge the assertion that bold operations produce greater casualties. To the contrary, orthodox operations typically lead to the massing of forces on both sides at the same point because of a common interpretation of avenues of approach. Deliberate caution produces strength-on-strength engagements, which most definitely expose both sides to the probability of greater casualties. That should be intuitive. It is ironic that the probability of a frontal assault is never characterized as a "risky" line of action. One could even argue that selecting line of action X, when the probability is high that the enemy will do the same, is the antithesis of superior grand tactics, or what is called maneuver warfare today.

Consider the words of Clausewitz: Boldness "must be granted a certain power over and above successful calculations involving space, time, and magnitude of forces" because it is "a genuinely creative force. . . . Whenever boldness encounters timidity, it is likely to be the winner, because timidity in itself implies a loss of equilibrium. Boldness will be at a disadvantage only in an encounter with deliberate caution, which may be considered bold in its own right."[18] Patton can justifiably be called a creative force, but Eisenhower and Bradley intentionally restrained him. Back in Normandy he declared, "If I were on my own, I would take bigger chances than I am now permitted to take. Three times I have suggested risks and been turned down and each time the risk was warranted." Patton expressed his frustration on December 27: "I wish Ike were more of a gambler but he is certainly a lion compared to Montgomery and Bradley is better than Ike as far as nerve is concerned." Yet he really had little use for Bradley's skills. He called Bradley "the tent maker" and a "good officer but utterly lacks 'it.' Too bad." Clausewitz's observation that boldness "grows *less common in the higher ranks*" was echoed by Bedell Smith, who declared, "We never do anything bold. There is at least seventeen people to be dealt with so [we] must compromise, and compromise is never bold."[19]

Although Patton was hamstrung by being ordered to weight his operations in corridor A, he is properly open to criticism about *how* he fought there. Even here, however, he was constrained by Middleton's initial decision to hold Bastogne. MacDonald concluded that Bastogne "in large measure" dictated the way the Allied command would go about eliminating the penetration. It was "conservative," but this was necessitated, "at least in the opening moves, by the surprise, early success, and persistent strength of the German assault."[20] Eisenhower's initial focus on Bastogne led to a focus on Houffalize—a study of the road net logically took one in that direction. At that point, it became an issue of time and space. Patton was then under considerable pressure from above to make progress toward Houffalize.

Patton began the campaign with a bold redeployment of Third Army. He had long since demonstrated his ability and desire to move fast, whether in prewar maneuvers, in Sicily, or in Normandy. Guderian, himself a master of movement, offered a simple postwar comment: Patton "was very quick."[21] Patton's redeployment of III and XII Corps north was impressive, not simply because of its achievement in terms of time and space and the number of vehicles moved in terrible weather, but also because of the opportunities it created. Ultimately, it was only the preliminary movement stage of Eisenhower's larger concept, but Patton's achievement produced various options. Indeed, he moved so fast that Eisenhower and Bradley did not fully grasp those options. One of them was a "building" reinforcement of Middleton's barrier position around Bastogne, which might have radically altered the entire battle on the southern flank.

Patton was not allowed to attempt an envelopment of *Heeresgruppe B* at the base of the Bulge; instead, he was afforded the opportunity to execute half of the pincer to cut off the spearheads. To do this he had to cover the seven miles from Bastogne to Houffalize before the Germans appreciated their culminating point and began withdrawing their spearheads. The opportunity looked good on paper, but the geospatial nature of the Ardennes salient and the Germans' FSR ensured a low probability of achieving decisiveness under the existing weather conditions. Still, at certain points Patton did utilize an important element of decisiveness: surprise. He clearly caught the 352nd VGD in the process of advancing west on December 22 and essentially fixed and divided it. In addition, the 90th Infantry Division was redeployed from the Saar in secrecy, resulting in surprise on January 9. This materially assisted in eliminating the Harlange Pocket. The 319th CT's attack on Dahl and XII Corps' attack on the Sûre River line on January 18 also achieved surprise, with good results.

One problem that plagued Third Army in Lorraine was the coordination of corps operations. After the capture of Metz, the campaign became disjointed in terms of grand tactics. Cooperation between corps and continuity from one operation to the next existed, but it could have been improved on.[22] This problem resurfaced in the Bulge. Patton frequently moved units and formations among corps to gain advantage, and the majority of these transfers were well executed. Yet the movement of 6th Armored Division into Bastogne to spearhead the drive out of the Bastogne Pocket was impeded when coordination at division, corps, and army levels broke down. A traffic jam involving the 11th and 6th Armored Divisions ensued, which negatively impacted the combat power of both VIII and III Corps on December 31. This was purely a staff issue.

In reality, Patton was permitted to coordinate only the activities of VIII and III Corps. Bradley would not allow XII Corps to take the offensive, and XX Corps had to protect the army's southern flank. VIII and III Corps therefore did the bulk of the fighting, and the intercorps boundary running through Bastogne did not help coordination. After the linkup at Houffalize, VIII and III Corps paused, which allowed the Germans to break contact and move east to block Eddy, who was not ready to go when Middleton and Millikin halted. This was grand tactical sequencing, but time was wasted. All three corps should have attacked simultaneously to stretch the remaining German capabilities to the limit. Bradley's concept of operations played a significant role in Patton's inability to achieve this, but in Lorraine he executed broad-front, sequenced corps assaults. With one exception, he demonstrated an unwillingness to concentrate for *penetration* attacks.[23] Patton did narrow III Corps' front to achieve greater concentration southeast of Bastogne, but the difficult terrain undermined the intent.

Patton believed in the simultaneous application of all his combat power and in the immediate commitment of reserves to apply constant pressure against the enemy. Moreover, there was a stubbornness to his operational technique. He firmly believed it was "desirable to inculcate in the German mind that when the Third Army attacks, it always succeeds." Even at the end of the campaign he noted that he, Bradley, and Hodges "are determined to carry on our attack no matter how much they deplete us. . . . To do otherwise at this moment would, in my opinion, be criminal." This was entirely consistent with his statement back in France: "It is terrible to halt . . . no one realizes the terrible value of the unforgiving minute except me." He felt this way for two reasons. First, more lives would be lost if the Germans were allowed to recover and reorganize. Second, pushing his commanders and soldiers beyond endurance was necessary to finish the war because they were "forced to fight it with inadequate means." By this, he meant there were insufficient divisions.[24] One suspects that if Patton had possessed more divisions, he would have committed them.

Impact of Patton's Operational Technique

Patton's philosophy of attack was shared by most, if not all, of his peers in the U.S. Army, and it may have owed its origins to Grant and Sherman. Middleton concluded that "Patton's principal worth was that he kept things moving. He kept everybody else moving—not only his juniors but his seniors. Otherwise, during the Battle of the Bulge, there would have been a tendency to play Montgomery—to dress up the lines instead of getting in there and hitting the Germans hard." Collins agreed, reflecting, "You can estimate the situation all you want," but it was drive that made things happen, and Patton "exemplified that to the top degree."[25] Patton equated drive with offensive spirit, and FM 100–5 preached that decisions could be reached only through offensive means. Yet Patton's faith in this doctrine came with a considerable cost. His operational technique was hard on his troops in the short term; its effectiveness must ultimately be judged based on his ability to inflict maximum damage on *Fifth Panzer* and *Seventh Armees* while limiting the damage to Third Army.

In terms of *mission accomplishment*, Patton was effective because he did what he had been ordered to do—disengage from the Saar front, launch a counteroffensive from the south, relieve Bastogne, and link up with First Army at Houffalize. In the format of modern orders, Bradley would have instructed him to "establish contact with First Army at Houffalize by such and such a time in order to" meet a higher objective, but since there was no time frame in Patton's mission (beyond "as quick as possible"), he cannot be faulted for how long it ultimately took to get there. On the other side, *Heeresgruppe B* did not succeed in reaching Antwerp or destroying Allied forces north of the Antwerp–Brussels–Bastogne line. However, it did succeed in stopping Allied attacks in the Roer and Saar areas, and it delayed Eisenhower's timetable by six weeks.[26] *Fifth Panzer Armee* failed to take Bastogne, and *Seventh Armee* failed to protect *Fifth Panzer Armee's* southern flank.

In terms of *spatial effectiveness*, it took Patton five days to cover the 17 miles from his LD along the Attert River to Bastogne, or 3.4 miles per day. He covered the 26 miles from his initial LD to Houffalize in twenty-six days, for an average daily advance of 1 mile. This hardly seems impressive, until one compares it with the median daily advance of 2,400 yards in northwestern Europe calculated by one study.[27] However, the Germans started significant withdrawals on January 11–12, leaving one to wonder what Third Army's average daily advance would have been had the Germans stood firm. After the linkup at Houffalize, it took another twelve days to drive the Germans back to the West Wall. German spatial effectiveness looks impressive at first glance. *Heeresgruppe B* penetrated the weakest part of Bradley's line to a depth of 60 miles and almost reached the Meuse River in eight days. Conversely, Twelfth Army Group penetrated only 22 miles in ninety-six days after crossing the German border on September 11.[28] The circumstances and factors were different, however. *Heeresgruppe B* could not hold the ground gained in the Bulge.

Perhaps the most telling measure is *casualty effectiveness*. Determining total casualties for both sides is not easy. Indeed, quantifying the damage inflicted on the enemy is fraught with difficulty, and there are many historical examples of gross overestimation in this regard. According to the American official history, the U.S. Army suffered 75,482 killed, missing, and wounded during the Ardennes campaign (excluding Alsace), including 39,947 casualties in First Army and 35,152 in Third Army. Yet according to Kibler's numbers, Twelfth Army Group sustained 81,810 battle casualties between December 22 and January 14 alone.[29]

Table 15.3. Third Army Division Casualities, December 22, 1944–January 16, 1945

Division	Killed	Wounded	Missing	Total
4 Inf Div	31	134	245	410
5 Inf Div	101	813	125	1,039
26 Inf Div	214	2,024	379	2,617
28 Inf Div*				
35 Inf Div	124	1,307	915	2,346
80 Inf Div	276	1,395	696	2,367
87 Inf Div	148	650	338	1,136
90 Inf Div	161	832	98	1,091
17 Abn Div	239	1,042	1,199	2,480
101 Abn Div	583	3,225	647	4,455
4 Armd Div	143	632	125	900
6 Armd Div	134	896	202	1,232
9 Armd Div	102	408	163	673
10 Armd Div	134	625	306	1,065
11 Armd Div	125	994	121	1,240
Total	2,515	14,977	5,559	23,051

*Not included in calculations due to the nature of its commitment in Third Army.
Source: ACSDB.

There is a major discrepancy between the official history and Third Army's calculations. Shortly after the linkup with First Army, Third Army calculated that its seventeen divisions had suffered 24,598 killed, missing, and wounded from December 22 to January 16.[30] Third Army later adjusted this figure upward to 25,145 in the after-action report for the same period. The 25,145 figure is very close to the ACSDB's estimate of 23,051 for Third Army's total divisional casualties (including attachments) from December 22 to January 16. In the remaining twelve days of the thirty-eight-day campaign, Third Army sustained an additional 6,094 casualties (698 killed, 4,683 wounded, and 713 missing). This means the Germans inflicted 20 percent of Third Army's total campaign casualties (31,239) in 32 percent of the total campaign days. In the Ardennes, Third Army sustained 824 battle casualties per day. By comparison, in 109 days of combat in Lorraine, Third Army sustained 55,182 casualties (6,657 killed, 36,406 wounded, and 12,119 missing), or 506 battle casualties per day.[31]

Determining German losses in the Bulge is even harder than determining American losses. The United States calculated 120,000 German casualties from December 16 to January 16, not including Alsace. Early postwar analysis conducted by Magna E. Bauer and Percy Schramm established a range of 81,582 to 98,024. Both the high of 120,000 and the low of 81,582 have been cited by historians.[32] However, subsequent research by German historians has revised the figures significantly downward to the 68,000 range. The German official history cites 10,749 killed and 34,225 wounded.[33]

What is certain is that Third Army grossly inflated enemy casualties; one can immediately dismiss its wild claim that it inflicted 103,800 casualties (24,200 killed, 63,200 wounded, and 16,400 POWs) on the twenty divisions it faced in the Ardennes.[34] The ACSDB calculated 30,871 German divisional losses against Third Army from December 22 to January 16. This figure would be slightly higher (perhaps by several hundred) if the 2nd and 9th PD casualties were added, but they played only a small role in the late stages of the battle. Comparing Third Army's casualties of 25,145 with the Seventh Armee–Fifth Panzer Armee figure of 30,875 for the period December 22 to January 16, one finds that Patton inflicted casualties at a rate of 1.23 for every casualty he received. This inverts Trevor Dupuy's claim that the Germans possessed a relative combat effectiveness value (CEV) and casualty inflicting capability of up to 1.5:1 versus the Allies.[35]

Third Army's slight advantage in inflicting casualties is not surprising when the terrain, weather, German capability, and Patton's operational technique are considered. Moreover, it suggests there was nothing brilliant about his performance in the Bulge. Yet Patton was forced to fight on the line of action chosen by Eisenhower and Bradley and consistently advised others to avoid the type of attrition that ensued in corridor A. After the war the General Board implied that units that did not act boldly and aggressively to close with the enemy suffered higher casualties. Patton was the highest-ranking consultant for that study. Patton's operational technique demanded bold and aggressive action, but his high casualties in the Ardennes suggest that Third Army's divisions could not sustain that philosophy indefinitely in the attrition environment of corridor A.[36] One must objectively consider the fact that his operational technique was sometimes part of the problem. Faster is not always better, and he may have exposed the 17th Airborne and 11th Armored Divisions to

Table 15.4. German Division Casualties versus Third Army, December 22, 1944–
January 16, 1945

Division	Killed	Wounded	Missing	Total
9 VGD	218	559	520	1,297
26 VGD	325	935	1,799	3,059
79 VGD	237	793	495	1,525
167 VGD	226	686	881	1,793
212 VGD	124	287	381	792
276 VGD	172	427	458	1,057
340 VGD	291	972	649	1,912
352 VGD	198	426	648	1,272
5 FJD	943	3,503	3,381	7,827
3 PGD	210	669	557	1,436
15 PGD	175	518	1,076	1,769
Lehr	266	941	559	1,766
1 SS PD	302	864	210	1,376
9 SS PD	86	260	87	433
12 SS PD	211	560	226	997
FBB	212	469	213	894
FGB	258	586	823	1,667
Total	4,454	13,455	12,963	30,872*

* Average damage inflicted on each division: 262 killed, 792 wounded, 762 missing. Casualties for
2 and 9 PDs are not included due to their limited contribution, but they would increase the total by
only a few hundred.
Source: ACSDB.

unnecessary damage by pushing these raw formations to attack so aggressively; the airborne divisions in particular were not designed for grinding
advances.[37]

Patton could persist in his operational technique because he possessed
air superiority, artillery superiority, and more replacements. Determining
exactly what damage XIX TAC inflicted on the Germans is problematic.
Between December 16 and January 16 the Allies flew 63,741 sorties, or
an average of 1,992 per day. The total cost was 647 aircraft, which speaks
in part to the effectiveness of German Flak units. XIX TAC flew 9,392
fighter and fighter-bomber sorties during the thirty-eight days of the campaign, but twelve days, or 32 percent, were nonoperational days. On the

Table 15.5. Third Army Artillery Expenditure, December 24, 1944–January 28, 1945

Week Ending	III Corps	VIII Corps	XII Corps	XX Corps
Dec 31	107,661	41,457	124,541	34,036
Jan 7	176,661	130,784	85,948	29,226
Jan 14	111,021	82,421	55,842	19,900
Jan 21	39,406	88,830	90,964	49,389
Jan 28	50,818	21,169	98,103	46,989
Total*	485,567	364,661	455,398	179,540

* Combined total – 1,485,166.
Source: Third Army AAR, vol. 2, Artillery.

days that Weyland's command flew, it put up an average of 361 sorties. The Allied air forces achieved air supremacy and denied the *Luftwaffe* the ability to significantly hinder a single Allied ground movement or operation.[38] Nevertheless, Allied airpower never completely isolated the battlefield west of the Our. XIX TAC never completely isolated Third Army's battlefield but did partially interdict the movement of German reinforcements from within the salient and from east of the Our.

Superiority in artillery greatly aided Patton's operational technique. III Corps claimed it inflicted casualties on the Germans at a ratio of 11:1, attributing the imbalance "in great part to a direct result of artillery fire." Thoholte claimed that although *Heeresgruppe B* was competitive in terms of numbers of gun barrels and caliber, U.S. artillery expenditure was "at least ten times as great."[39] Patton believed the infantry needed all the artillery it could get. Twelfth Army Group fired 1,255,000 rounds up to January 3, and Third Army fired a total of 1,485,166 rounds up to January 28. VIII, III, and XII Corps fired 1,305,626 rounds. This contradicts John Sloan Brown's argument that Trevor Dupuy's quantified judgment model overvalued the role of artillery.[40] The General Board concluded that there was "no substitute for massed artillery fires . . . these fires played a major role in the advance of our troops and in breaking up and disorganizing enemy counterattacks."[41]

Another reason why Patton could persist with his operational technique was that Third Army received enough replacements to match its losses up to January 16, plus 6,000 more.[42] Conversely, the best estimate of replacements in the German divisions opposite Patton up to December 31 was 1,796, with the largest reinforcement, 900, going to the *3rd PGD*.

Table 15.6. Reinforcements Received by XII Corps, December 22–31, 1944

	Corps Troops	6 Armd Div	10 Armd Div	4 Inf Div	5 Inf Div	80 Inf Div	Total
Dec 22	0	—	72	37	—	—	109
Dec 23	1	—	—	23	82	—	106
Dec 24	10	—	360	21	00	—	490
Dec 25	9	—	62	52	—	—	123
Dec 26	5	354	—	668	45	2	1,074
Dec 27	10	28	—	551	636	310	1,535
Dec 28	29	6	—	526	5	230	796
Dec 29	39	—	—	68	—	1,065	1,172
Dec 30	12	—	—	31	2	19	64
Dec 31	12	—	—	104	836	750	1,702
Total	127	388	494	2,081	1,705	2,376	7,171

Source: XII Corps AAR, December 1944, p. 42.

Kokott noted that replacements for the *26th VGD* in late December consisted of "lost clumps" of wandering infantry. The *FBB* received approximately 100 replacements during the night of December 30.[43] Hitler apparently promised 24,000 replacements, including 6,000 *panzergrenadiers*, for January, but this was impossible. Gay noted that the replacement situation was improving and estimated that within three or four days Third Army could bring many divisions up to strength.[44] Third Army actually grew numerically stronger as *Seventh* and *Fifth Panzer Armees* grew weaker. German combat power was insufficient to inflict decisive damage on Third Army and limit the damage it received in return.

Patton's effectiveness would have been reduced if Manteuffel and Brandenberger had not labored under significant deficiencies. If they had simply possessed sufficient fuel to redeploy formations to meet the tactical requirements and time estimates, the battle with Third Army might have unfolded differently. The fact that the *9th VGD* traveled to the battle area on bicycles for eight days was indicative of their diminished capacity.[45] In fact, the *9th*, *79th*, *167th*, and *340th VGDs*; *3rd PGD*; *1st SS* and *12th SS PDs*; and *FBB* all failed to get into position to execute attacks on time. Piecemeal attacks, *Einzelangriffe*, were the antithesis of German doctrine, but they quickly proved to be the norm in the Ardennes.

Manteuffel declared, "All our attacks on Bastogne were made by small groups, because of the gasoline shortage." Additionally, the use of horse transport impacted the operational radius of the more mechanized formations. Under Allied air superiority in the west, horse columns could move effectively only at night and over short distances. This created a fundamental inflexibility for infantry divisions trying to maneuver their artillery to support a *schwerpunkt* or a withdrawal from danger.[46]

Even if the German formations had arrived on time, they might have simply presented a massed target for Patton's artillery. Patton, too, suffered from such delays, but his were due to traffic conditions, not fuel shortages. The arrival of the 17th Airborne Division, CCA/11th Armored Division, and CCA/6th Armored Division are cases in point. Had Manteuffel and Brandenberger possessed enough transport to bring forward sufficient artillery ammunition to at least match Patton's expenditures, many tactical engagements would have turned out differently; German attacks would have possessed greater power and endurance.

The Germans certainly created many of their own problems. From Hitler downward they failed to properly assess Eisenhower's potential strength. Rational calculus of capability virtually evaporated. The German official history argues that even Rundstedt and Model failed in this regard; their small solutions were disconnected from reality.[47] This is an arguable point, but there are other areas in which German effectiveness can be called into question. One problem was the excessive number and movement of corps headquarters on the southern flank of the salient. While Patton effectively controlled the battle with three corps (VIII, III, and XII), the Germans used seven: *LIII, LXXX,* and *LXXXV Armeekorps* and *LVIII, XLVII, XXXIX,* and *I-SS Panzerkorps*. This suggests considerable inefficiency in command and control, not to mention consumption of fuel in the numerous moves.

Patton's contribution to victory in the Ardennes was considerable. David Belchem's comment that Montgomery's task in the north was "considerably more difficult" than Patton's is simply untrue.[48] Had Patton not intervened, First Army might have been thoroughly wrecked. He fought the entire *Seventh Armee,* half the *Fifth Panzer Armee,* and major elements of the *Sixth Panzer Armee*. He fought elements of twenty different formations, eight *volksgrenadier* divisions, two *panzergrenadier* divisions, seven panzer divisions, a *Fallschirmjäger* division, plus the *FGB* and *FBB*. Ten German formations (and a *Kampfgruppe*), or 40 percent of the combat power of *Heeresgruppe B* committed to the Bulge, were diverted to his

Table 15.7. Prisoners Processed by First and Third Armies, December 23, 1944–January 9, 1945

	First Army	Third Army
Dec 23	?	160
Dec 24	?	119
Dec 25	?	1,184
Dec 26	440	1,236
Dec 27	922	1,181
Dec 28	502	1,089
Dec 29	153	638
Dec 30	77	303
Dec 31	149	279
Jan 1	34	361
Jan 2	27	486
Jan 3	1,088	625
Jan 4	815	176
Jan 5	946	270
Jan 6	651	264
Jan 7	858	199
Jan 8	1,342	116
Jan 9	363	176
Total	8,367	8,862

Source: Twelfth Army Group G-2 Periodic Report Nos. 201–219, December 22, 1944–January 9, 1945.

front after he began his attack on December 22. A new German formation arrived opposite Third Army every 1.5 days between December 23 and January 7. He received three divisions from SHAEF reserve (11th Armored, 87th Infantry, and 17th Airborne Divisions), while Brandenberger and Manteuffel received six from OKW reserve. Patton was able to introduce three additional divisions from Third Army in Lorraine, while Manteuffel received three understrength SS PDs from *Sixth Panzer Armee.* The shift in German combat power was north to south to deal with Patton, not south to north to deal with Hodges and Montgomery, until close to the end. Prisoners of war, however, were about equal. The ultimate compliment to Patton's contribution was *NORDWIND,* designed to address his effectiveness in fixing, attriting, and threatening *Seventh Armee* and *Fifth Panzer Armee* by aggressive offensive action.[49]

Patton waged a campaign of attrition in the Ardennes. He crippled the *5th FJD* and *Panzer Lehr*, which made it to the Our River with a dozen tanks and 400 infantry. The *276th VGD* had been attrited to the point where it could field the equivalent of three reinforced battalions, and the other German divisions were heavily mauled. Yet sufficient combat power remained to hold the MLRs, and Patton never succeeded in penetrating them to interdict German MSRs with ground elements. The Germans were exposed in the Harlange Pocket and suffered accordingly, but they still managed to withdraw effectively, under contact, back along their MSRs.

Eisenhower's strategy was designed to push the Germans out of the Bulge, and although *Heeresgruppe B* suffered heavy attrition, all its divisions successfully withdrew with their basic structure intact—a situation very similar to the end of the Falaise Pocket. According to the Combined Intelligence Committee, the Germans still fielded a total of 289 divisions on January 23, 1945, the same number cited by SHAEF on December 10. Appreciating Eisenhower's campaign design is essential to an objective analysis of Patton's effectiveness in the Bulge. Eisenhower later admitted that his strategy produced "slow, laborious going, with a sudden breakthrough an impossibility."[50] Patton would not have designed it that way.

Bradley's and Eisenhower's Assessment of Patton

Bradley considered the following to be essential characteristics of a successful leader: knowledge of one's job (without being a specialist in every facet), mental and physical energy, understanding and consideration for others, stubbornness when required, imagination to foresee the consequences of decisions, high character, and luck. Patton possessed most of these attributes. On December 31 Bradley submitted an efficiency report in which he described Patton's performance as "superior" and recommended him for command of an army or even an army group. Most critically, he rated his one-time superior as the best army commander in combat in the ETO. On January 14 Eisenhower informed Marshall that Patton "has done a remarkable job," and a few weeks later Eisenhower rated Patton as the fourth greatest contributor to victory in Europe (behind Bradley, Spaatz, and Bedell Smith) and described him as "highly intelligent." This meant that Eisenhower considered Patton the most valuable of the seven Allied army commanders. Indeed, Gerow and Collins were ranked higher than Patch, Hodges, and Simpson.[51]

Patton is deserving of his number-one rank among the Allied army commanders. He possessed high energy and had an effective command technique. He could fight a static battle as well as Hodges and had no peer when it came to moving fast. He was fully in tune with the potential of the various intelligence assets available to him and exploited them to the limit in assuming risk. Eisenhower had saved Patton's career because the latter possessed unique talents, but it is not unreasonable to suggest that Patton did not maximize those talents during the Ardennes. Here it is important to recall Clausewitz's statement that the higher the level of command, "the greater is the need for boldness to be supported by a reflective mind, so that boldness does not degenerate into purposeless bursts of blind passion."[52] The evidence clearly indicates that Eisenhower and Bradley feared such degeneration by Patton. One cannot forget the slapping episodes that led Eisenhower to question Patton's judgment. That was, of course, Patton's own fault, and no excuse should be made for him. Neither Eisenhower nor Bradley fully trusted Patton the man. As a result, Patton the grand tactical commander—the highest card in Eisenhower's deck—was perhaps not used the way he could have been in the Bulge.

Appendixes

A. Eisenhower's Order of Battle, December 16, 1944

SHAEF: General of the Army Dwight D. Eisenhower
Chief of Staff: Lieutenant General Walter Bedell Smith
SHAEF Liaison HQ with Twelfth Army Group: Major J. E. Latham

British Twenty-First Army Group: Field Marshal Sir Bernard Law Montgomery
Chief of Staff: Major General Sir Francis de Guingand

First Canadian Army: Lieutenant General H. D. G. Crerar

British I Corps: Lieutenant General John T. Crocker
   1st Polish Armored Division
   4th Canadian Armored Division
   51st Infantry Division

II Canadian Corps: Lieutenant General Guy G. Simonds
   2nd Canadian Infantry Division
   3rd Canadian Infantry Division
   49th Infantry Division
   6th Guards Tank Brigade

Second British Army: Lieutenant General Sir Miles C. Dempsey

VIII Corps: Lieutenant General E. H. Barker
   3rd Infantry Division
   15th Infantry Division
   11th Armored Division

XII Corps: Lieutenant General Neil M. Ritchie
   43rd Infantry Division
   52nd Infantry Division
   53rd Infantry Division
   7th Armored Division
   Guards Armored Division
   33rd Armored Brigade
   34th Tank Brigade

Twenty-First Army Group Reserve

XXX Corps: Lieutenant General Sir Brian Horrocks
   79th Armored Division (Special)
   50th Infantry Division (at Ypres)

U.S. Twelfth Army Group: Lieutenant General Omar N. Bradley
Chief of Staff: Major General Leven C. Allen
Chief Combat Liaison Officer: Colonel Karl L. Bendetsen

Ninth Army: Lieutenant General William H. Simpson

XIII Corps: Major General Alvan C. Gillem (in Twenty-First Army Group's zone)
   84th Infantry Division
   102nd Infantry Division
   7th Armored Division

XIX Corps: Major General Raymond S. McLain
   2nd Armored Division: Major General Ernest N. Harmon
   66th Armored Regiment
   67th Armored Regiment
   41st Armored Infantry Regiment
   14th Armored FA Battalion
   78th Armored FA Battalion
   92nd Armored FA Battalion
   17th Armored Engineer Battalion
   18th Reconnaissance Battalion
   702nd TD Battalion
   195th AAA AW Battalion
XVI Corps (not operational)
   75th Infantry Division

Ninth Army Reserve:
30th Infantry Division

First Army: Lieutenant General Courtney H. Hodges
Chief of Staff: Major General William B. Kean Jr.

VII Corps: Major General J. Lawton Collins
   9th Infantry Division
   746th Tank Battalion
   83rd Infantry Division
   772nd Tank Battalion
   104th Infantry Division
   5th Armored Division

VII Corps Reserve:
1st Infantry Division: Brigadier General Clift Andrus
745th Tank Battalion
3rd Armored Division: Major General Maurice Rose
32nd Armored Regiment
33rd Armored Regiment
36th Armored Infantry Regiment
54th Armored FA Battalion
67th Armored FA Battalion
391st Armored FA Battalion
23rd Armored Engineer Battalion
83rd Reconnaissance Battalion
643rd TD Battalion
486th AAA AW Battalion

V Corps: Major General Leonard T. Gerow
    2nd Infantry Division: Major General Walter M. Robertson
    741st Tank Battalion
    8th Infantry Division
    78th Infantry Division: Major General Edwin P. Parker Jr.
    709th Tank Battalion
    99th Infantry Division: Major General Walter E. Lauer
    801st TD Battalion

V Corps Reserve:
CCB/9th Armored Division

VIII Corps: Major General Troy H. Middleton
Chief of Staff: Colonel Cyrus Searcy

14th Cavalry Group: Colonel Mark Devine
4th Infantry Division ("Ivy"): Major General Raymond O. Barton
    8th Infantry Regiment
    12th Infantry Regiment
    22nd Infantry Regiment
    20th FA Battalion
    29th FA Battalion
    42nd FA Battalion
    44th FA Battalion
    4th Engineer Combat Battalion
    70th Tank Battalion
    802nd TD Battalion
    803rd TD Battalion
    337th AAA AW Battalion
28th Infantry Division ("Keystone"): Major General Norman D. Cota

109th Infantry Regiment
110th Infantry Regiment
112th Infantry Regiment
107th FA Battalion
108th FA Battalion
109th FA Battalion
229th FA Battalion
103rd Engineer Combat Battalion
707th Tank Battalion
630th TD Battalion
447th AAA AW Battalion
106th Infantry Division ("Golden Lions"): Major General Alan W. Jones
422nd Infantry Regiment
423rd Infantry Regiment
424th Infantry Regiment
589th FA Battalion
590th FA Battalion
591st FA Battalion
592nd FA Battalion
81st Engineer Combat Battalion
309th Engineer Combat Battalion
820th TD Battalion
563rd AAA AW Battalion
634th AAA AW Battalion
9th Armored Division: Major General John W. Leonard
2nd Tank Battalion
14th Tank Battalion
19th Tank Battalion
27th Armored Infantry Battalion
52nd Armored Infantry Battalion
60th Armored Infantry Battalion
3rd Armored FA Battalion
16th Armored FA Battalion
73rd Armored FA Battalion
89th Cavalry Reconnaissance Squadron
506th CIC Detachment
482nd AAA AW Battalion
9th Armored Engineer Battalion
811th TD Battalion

VIII Corps Reserve:
CCR/9th Armored Division

Third Army: Lieutenant General George S. Patton Jr.
Chief of Staff: Brigadier General Hobart R. Gay

Army Troops:
631st TD Battalion
A and B/119th AAA Gun Battalion
120th AAA Gun Battalion (Mobile)
128th AAA Gun Battalion
217th AAA Gun Battalion
411th AAA Gun Battalion
456th AAA AW Battalion
465th AAA AW Battalion
546th AAA AW Battalion
550th AAA AW Battalion
565th AAA AW Battalion
567th AAA AW Battalion
120th AAA AW Battalion
776th AAA AW Battalion
778th AAA AW Battalion
795th AAA AW Battalion
2nd (French) Parachute Regiment
16th (French) Chasseur Battalion
30th (French) Chasseur Battalion
1301st Engineer General Service Regiment
1303rd Engineer General Service Regiment
1306th Engineer General Service Regiment
293rd Engineer Combat Battalion

XII Corps: Major General Manton S. Eddy
Chief of Staff: Colonel Ralph J. Canine

6th Armored Division ("Super Sixth"): Major General Robert W. Grow
    15th Tank Battalion
    68th Tank Battalion
    69th Tank Battalion
    9th Armored Infantry Battalion
    44th Armored Infantry Battalion
    50th Armored Infantry Battalion
    128th Armored FA Battalion
    212th Armored FA Battalion
    231st Armored FA Battalion
    86th Cavalry Reconnaissance Squadron
    506th CIC Detachment
    777th AAA AW Battalion
    25th Armored Engineer Battalion
    128th Armored Ordnance Maintenance Battalion
35th Infantry Division ("Santa Fe"): Major General Paul W. Baade
    134th Infantry Regiment
    137th Infantry Regiment

320th Infantry Regiment
127th FA Battalion
161st FA Battalion
216th FA Battalion
219th FA Battalion
60th Engineer Combat Battalion
448 AAA AW Battalion
735th Tank Battalion
654th TD Battalion
87th Infantry Division ("Golden Acorn"): Brigadier General Frank L. Culin Jr.
345th Infantry Regiment
346th Infantry Regiment
347th Infantry Regiment
334th FA Battalion
335th FA Battalion
336th FA Battalion
912th FA Battalion
312th Engineer Combat Battalion
761st Tank Battalion
549th AAA AW Battalion

XII Corps Reserve:
80th Infantry Division ("Blue Ridge"): Major General Horace L. McBride
317th Infantry Regiment
318th Infantry Regiment
319th Infantry Regiment
313th FA Battalion
314th FA Battalion
315th FA Battalion
905th FA Battalion
305th Engineer Combat Battalion
702nd Tank Battalion
610th TD Battalion
633rd AAA AW Battalion
2nd Cavalry Group: Colonel Charles H. Reed
6th Cavalry Group: Colonel Joe Fickett

XX Corps: Major General Walton H. Walker

3rd Cavalry Group: Colonel James Polk
5th Infantry Division ("Red Diamond"): Major General Stafford Leroy Irwin
2nd Infantry Regiment
10th Infantry Regiment
11th Infantry Regiment
19th FA Battalion
21st FA Battalion

46th FA Battalion
50th FA Battalion
7th Engineer Combat Battalion
737th Tank Battalion
818th TD Battalion
449th AAA AW Battalion
90th Infantry Division ("Tough Hombres"): Major General James A. Van Fleet
   357th Infantry Regiment
   358th Infantry Regiment
   359th Infantry Regiment
   343rd FA Battalion
   344th FA Battalion
   345th FA Battalion
   915th FA Battalion
   315th Engineer Combat Battalion
   712th Tank Battalion
   773rd TD Battalion
   537th AAA AW Battalion
95th Infantry Division: Major General Harry L. Twaddle
   377th Infantry Regiment
   378th Infantry Regiment
   379th Infantry Regiment
   358th FA Battalion
   359th FA Battalion
   360th FA Battalion
   920th FA Battalion
   320th Engineer Combat Battalion
   95th CIC Detachment
   95th Reconnaissance Troop
   547th AAA AW Battalion
XX Corps Reserve:
10th Armored Division ("Tiger"): Major General William H. H. Morris Jr.
   3rd Tank Battalion
   11th Tank Battalion
   21st Tank Battalion
   20th Armored Infantry Battalion
   54th Armored Infantry Battalion
   61st Armored Infantry Battalion
   419th Armored FA Battalion
   420th Armored FA Battalion
   423rd Armored FA Battalion
   90th Cavalry Reconnaissance Squadron (Mech)
   510th CIC Detachment
   796th AAA AW Battalion
   55th Armored Engineer Battalion
   132nd Armored Ordnance Maintenance Battalion

Third Army Reserve:
III Corps: Major General John Millikin
Chief of Staff: Colonel James H. Phillips

4th Armored Division: Major General Hugh J. Gaffey
  8th Tank Battalion
  35th Tank Battalion
  37th Tank Battalion
  10th Armored Infantry Battalion
  51st Armored Infantry Battalion
  53rd Armored Infantry Battalion
  22nd Armored FA Battalion
  66th Armored FA Battalion
  94th Armored FA Battalion
  25th Cavalry Reconnaissance Squadron (Mech)
  504th CIC Detachment
  24th Armored Engineer Battalion
  704th TD Battalion
  489th AAA AW Battalion
26th Infantry Division ("Yankee"): Major General Willard S. Paul
  101st Infantry Regiment
  104th Infantry Regiment
  328th Infantry Regiment
  101st FA Battalion
  102nd FA Battalion
  180th FA Battalion
  263rd FA Battalion
  101st Engineer Combat Battalion
  735th Tank Battalion
  309th AAA AW Battalion
5th Ranger Battalion

U.S. Sixth Army Group: Lieutenant General Jacob L. Devers
Seventh Army: Lieutenant General Alexander M. Patch

VI Corps: Major General Edward H. Brooks
  3rd Infantry Division
  45th Infantry Division
  79th Infantry Division
  103rd Infantry Division
  14th Armored Division

XV Corps: Major General Wade H. Haislip
  44th Infantry Division
  100th Infantry Division
  12th Armored Division

French First Army: General Jean de Lattre de Tassigny
I Corps: Lieutenant General Marie E. Bethouart
 1st French Amored Division
 2nd Moroccan Division
 9th Colonial Division
II Corps: Major General G. de Montsabert
 2nd French Armored Division
 3rd Algerian Division
 36th Infantry Division
SHAEF Theater Reserve (on the Continent)
XVIII Airborne Corps: Major General Matthew B. Ridgway
Chief of Staff: Colonel Ralph D. Eaton

82nd Airborne Division ("All American"): Major General James M. Gavin
 504th Parachute Infantry Regiment
 505th Parachute Infantry Regiment
 508th Parachute Infantry Regiment
 325th Glider Infantry Regiment
 551st Parachute Infantry Battalion (attached)
 376th Parachute FA Battalion
 456th Parachute FA Battalion
 307th Airborne Engineer Battalion
 80th AAA AW Battalion
101st Airborne Division ("Screaming Eagles"): Major General Maxwell D. Taylor
 501st Parachute Infantry Regiment
 502nd Parachute Infantry Regiment
 506th Parachute Infantry Regiment
 327th Glider Infantry Regiment
 1st Battalion/401st Glider Infantry Regiment
 321st Glider FA Battalions
 907th Glider FA Battalions
 377th Parachute FA Battalion
 326th Parachute Engineer Battalion
 705th TD Battalion
 377th Airborne AAA AW Battalion
Other:
94th Infantry Division (covering German forts in Brittany)
42nd Infantry Division (at Marseilles)
70th Infantry Division (at Marseilles)
75th Infantry Division (at Yvetot)

SHAEF Reserve (in England)

First Allied Airborne Army: Lieutenant General Lewis H. Brereton
6th British Airborne Division: Major General Eric L. Bols
17th Airborne Division ("Golden Talons") (Dec 31–): Major General William M. Miley

507th Parachute Infantry Regiment
513th Parachute Infantry Regiment
193rd Glider Infantry Regiment
194th Glider Infantry Regiment
680th Glider FA Battalion
681st Glider FA Battalion
466th Parachute FA Battalion
139th Airborne Engineer Battalion
155th Airborne AAA AW Battalion
66th Infantry Division: Major General Kramer
11th Armored Division ("Thunderbolt") (Dec 28–): Brigadier General Charles S. Kilburn
  2nd Tank Battalion
  14th Tank Battalion
  19th Tank Battalion
  27th Armored Infantry Battalion
  52nd Armored Infantry Battalion
  60th Armored Infantry Battalion
  3rd Armored FA Battalion
  16th Armored FA Battalion
  73rd Armored FA Battalion
  9th Armored Engineer Battalion
  89th Cavalry Reconnaissance Squadron
  811th TD Battalion
  482nd AAA AW Battalion
Divisions en Route to SHAEF from the United States
8th Armored Division
Communications Zone: Lieutenant General John C. H. Lee
IX (U.S.) Air Defense Command
Allied Air Forces
U.S. Strategic Air Forces, Europe: General Carl A. Spaatz
RAF Bomber Command: Air Chief Marshal Sir Arthur T. Harris
Eighth U.S. Air Force: Lieutenant General James H. Doolittle
Ninth U.S. Air Force: Lieutenant General Hoyt S. Vandenberg
IX Tactical Air Command: Major General E. R. Quesada (working with First Army)
XIX Tactical Air Command: Brigadier General Otto P. Weyland (working with
  Third Army)
XXIX Tactical Air Command: Major General R. E. Nugent (working with Ninth
  Army)
IX Bombardment Division: Brigadier General Samuel E. Anderson
2nd Tactical Air Force (working with British Second Army): Air Marshal Sir Arthur
  Coningham

B. German Order of Battle, December 16, 1944

Oberbefelshaber West: Generalfeldmarschall Karl Rudolf Gerd von Rundstedt
Chief of Staff: Generalmajor Siegfried Westphal

Heeresgruppe B: Generalfeldmarschall Walter Model
Chief of Staff: General der Infanterie Hans Krebs
HARKO: Generalleutnant Karl Thoholte
Eisenbahn-Artillerie Abt 725
Panzer Pionier Kompanie 813
Brüko 888
Brüko 921
Brüko 956
Brüko 969

Fifteenth Armee: General der Infanterie Gustav von Zangen
VAK 403
VAK 407
VAK 409
Festung Arty Bty 1076
Festung Arty Bty 1310
StuG Brig 341
Construction Pionier Abt 434

LXXIV Armeekorps: General der Infanterie Karl Püchler
85th Infanterie Division
89th Infanterie Division
344th Infanterie Division
353rd Infanterie Division

LXXXI Armeekorps
47th Infantrie Division
246th VGD
363rd Infanterie Division

Korps Felber
183rd Infanterie Division

340th VGD: Oberst Theodor Tolsdorff
VGR 694
VGR 695
VGR 696
AR 340
Panzerjäger Abt 340
Nachrichten Abt 340
Pionier Abt 340

XII SS Korps
59th Infanterie Division
176th Infanterie Division

15th PGD: Oberst Hans-Joachim Deckert
Panzer Abt 115
PGR 104
PGR 115
AR 15
Aufklärungs Abt 115
Panzerjäger Abt 33
Pionier Abt 33
Flak Abt 315

9th PD: Generalmajor Harald von Elverfeldt
VGR 352
VGR 404
VGR 689
AR 246
Panzerjäger Abt 246
Pionier Abt 246

Sixth Panzer Armee: SS-Obergruppenführer Josef Dietrich
Chief of Staff: Generalmajor Fritz Kraemer
HARKO: Generalleutnant der Waffen-SS Walter Staudinger
s. Panzerjäger Abt 519
StuG Brig 394
StuG Brig 667
Sturmpz Abt 217
Panzerjäger Abt 653
Panzerjäger Abt 683
s. Möser Bty 428
Pionier Abt 62
Pionier Abt 73
Pionier Abt 253
Baupionier Abt 59
Baupionier Abt 798
Pionier Brüko Abt 655
s. Panzer Abt 506
Brüko Abts 602, 967, 968, 403, 406, 895, 844, 851, 175

LXVII Armeekorps: General der Infanterie Otto Hitzfeld
VAK 405
VWB 17
Sturm Möser Kompanie 1000
Sturm Möser Kompanie 1001

Möser Bty 1110
StuG Brig 902
StuG Brig 394

326th VGD: Oberst Erwin Kaschner
VGR 751
VGR 752
VGR 753
AR 326
Panzerjäger Abt 326
Pionier Abt 326

272nd VGD: Generalleutnant Eugen König
VGR 980
VGR 981
VGR 982
AR 272
Panzerjäger Abt 272
Pionier Abt 272

I SS Panzerkorps: SS-Gruppenführer Hermann Priess
Chief of Staff: Oberst Rudolf Lehmann
SS-ARKO I
VAK 388
VAK 402
VWB 4
VWB 9
SS-Arty Abt 501
SS-Arty Abt 502
s. Möser Kompanie 1098
s. Möser Kompanie 1120
Festung Arty Abt 1123

12th VGD: Generalmajor Gerhard Engel
Fusilier Regt 27
VGR 48
VGR 49
AR 12
Panzerjäger Abt 12
Fusilier Abt 12
Pionier Abt 12

277th VGD: Oberst Wilhelm Viebig
VGR 989
VGR 990
VGR 991

AR 277
Panzerjäger Abt 277
Pionier Abt 277

1st SS PD—*Leibstandarte Adolf Hitler:* SS-Oberführer Wilhelm Mohnke
SS-Panzer Regt 1
SS-PGR 1 (3 Abts)
SS-PGR 2 (3 Abts)
SS-AR 1
SS-Aufklärungs Abt 1
SS-Panzerjäger Abt 1
SS-Pionier Abt 1
SS-Flak Abt 1
SS s. Panzer Abt 501

12th SS PD—*Hitler Jugend:* SS Standartenführer Hugo Kraas
SS-Panzer Regt 12
SS-PGR 25
SS-PGR 26
SS-Aufklärungs Abt 12
SS-Panzerjäger Abt 12
SS-Pionier Abt 12
SS-Flak Abt 12
Panzerjäger Abt 560

3rd FJD: Generalmajor Walther Wadehn
FJR 5
FJR 8
FJR 9
AR 3
Aufklärungs Abt 3
Panzerjäger Abt 3
Pionier Abt 3

Panzer Brig 150: SS-Obersturmbannführer Otto Skorzeny

II SS Panzerkorps: SS-Obergruppenführer Wilhelm Bittrich
SS-ARKO II
VAK 410
SS s. Arty Abt 502

2nd SS PD—*Das Reich:* SS-Brigadeführer Heinz Lammerding
SS-Panzer Regt 2
SS-PGR 3 (3 Abts)
SS-PGR 4 (3 Abts)
SS-AR 2

SS-Werfer Abt 508
SS-Aufklärungs Abt 2
SS-Pionier Abt 2
SS-Flak Abt 2

9th SS PD—*Hohenstaufen:* SS-Oberführer Sylvester Stadler
SS-Panzer Regt 9 (2 Abts)
SS-PGR 19 (3 Abts)
SS-PGR 20 (3 Abts)
SS-AR 9
SS-Aufklärungs Abt 9
SS-Panzerjäger Abt 9
SS-Pionier Abt 9
SS-Flak Abt 9
SS-Werfer Abt 9
SS-Nachrichten Abt 9
s. Möser Bty 1039
s. Möser Bty 1122
Penal Abt 999
Flak Regt 15
Todt Brig 1 (–)

Fifth Panzer Armee: General der Panzertruppen Hasso Eccard von Manteuffel
Chief of Staff: Generalmajor Carl Wagener
HARKO: Generalmajor Richard Metz
Flak Brig 19
Pionier Abts 207, 600
s. Panzerjäger Abt 653
Ost (East) Abt 669
s. Arty Btys 638, 1094, 1095
Festung Arty Bty 25/975
s. Möser Btys 1099, 1119, 1121
Todt Brig 3 (paramilitary engineers)

LXVI Armeekorps: General der Artillerie Walter Lucht
ARKO 466
VWB 16
Arty Bn 1099
StuG Brig 244
s. Arty Abt 460

18th VGD: Generalmajor Günther Hoffmann Schönborn
VGR 293 (2 Abts)
VGR 294 (2 Abts)
VGR 295 (2 Abts)
AR 1818

Panzerjäger Abt 1818
Pionier Abt 1818
StuG Brig 244 (attached)
Arty Abt 460
Leichte Flak Abt 74

62nd VGD: Oberst Friedrich Kittel
VGR 164
VGR 190
VGR 193
AR 162
Panzerjäger Abt 162
Pionier Abt 162

LVIII Panzerkorps: General der Panzertruppen Walter Krüger
ARKO 458: Generalmajor Gerhard Triepel
VAK 401
VWB 7
s. Möser Abt 1121
s. Möser Abt 1125
Flak Sturm Regt 1

116th PD—Greyhound: Generalmajor Siegfried von Waldenburg
Panzer Regt 16 (2 Abts)
PGR 60 (2 Abts)
PGR 156 (2 Abts)
Panzer AR 160
AR 146
Aufklarüngs Abt 146
StuG Abt 226
Pionier Abt 675
Flak Abt 281

560th VGD: Oberst Rudolf Bäder
VGR 1128
VGR 1129
VGR 1130
AR 1560
Pionier Abt 1560

XLVII Panzerkorps: General der Panzertruppen Heinrich von Lüttwitz
ARKO 447: Oberst Langenbeck
VAK 766
VWB 15
Flak Sturm Regt 182

s. Arty Abt 1124
s. Möser Abt 1119
Pionier Abt 600

2nd PD: Oberst Meinrad von Lauchert
Panzer Regt 3
PGR 2
PGR 304
Panzer AR 74
Aufklärungs Abt 2
Panzerjäger Abt 38 (StuG III)
Panzer Pionier Abt 38
Flak Abt 273

26th VGD: Oberst Heinz Kokott
Fusilier Regt 39
VGR 77
VGR 78
Arty Abt 26
Panzerjäger Abt 26
Pionier Abt 26
Aufklarüngs Abt 26

XLVII Panzerkorps Reserve
130th Panzer Lehr Div: Generalleutenant Fritz Bayerlein
Panzer Regt 130
PGR 901
PGR 902
Panzer AR 130
Aufklärungs Abt 130
Panzerjäger Abt 130 (Jagdpanzer IV/70)
Pionier Abt 130
Flak Abt 311
s. Panzerjäger Abt 559 (Jagdpanther—attached from Armee Reserve)
StuG Brig 243 (attached)

Seventh Armee: General der Panzertruppen Erich Brandenberger
Chief of Staff: Generalmajor Freiherr von Gersdorff
HARKO: Generalmajor Paul Riedel
VAK 406
VAK 408
VWB 8
VWB 18
Heeresartillerie-Batterie 1092 (six 12.8cm cannon)
Heeresartillerie-Batterie 1093 (six 12.8cm cannon)
Heeresartillerie-Batterie 1124 (six 12.8cm cannon)

Heeresartillerie-Batterie 1125 (six 12.8cm cannon)
Heeresartillerie-Batterie 1122 (one 28cm Mörser; one 22cm Mörser)
s. Arty Bty 660
s. Panzerjäger Abt 657
s. Panzerjäger Abt 668
Festung Panzerjäger Abt 501
Pionier Abt 47

LXXXV Armeekorps: General der Infanterie Baptist Kniess
Chief of Staff: Oberstleutnant Lassen
ARKO: Oberst Walter Beisswaenger
Panzerjäger Abt 668

5th FJD: Oberst Ludwig Heilmann
FJR 13 (2 Abts)
FJR 14 (2 Abts)
FJR 15 (2 Abts)
Fallschirm-AR 5 (3 Abts, partly mobile)
Aufklärungs Abt 5
Fallschirm-Pionier Abt 5
Fallschirm-Flak Abt 5
Fallschirm-StuG Brig 11

352nd VGD: Oberst Erich Schmidt
VGR 914
VGR 915
VGR 916
AR 352
Panzerjäger Abt 352
Pionier Abt 352

LXXX Armeekorps: General der Infanterie Franz Beyer
Chief of Staff: Oberst I. G. Koestin
ARKO: Oberst Schroeder
VAK 408
VWB 8

276th VGD: Generalmajor Kurt Möhring (–Dec 18); Oberst Hugo Dempwolff
(Dec 18–)
VGR 986
VGR 987
VGR 988
AR 276
Panzerjäger Abt 276
Pionier Abt 276

212th VGD: Generalleutnant Franz Sensfuss
VGR 316
VGR 320
VGR 420
AR 212
Panzerjäger Abt 212
Pionier Abt 212
Infanterie Abt 212 (+)

LIII Armeekorps: *General der Kavallerie* Edwin von Rothkirch Und Trach
Chief of Staff: Oberst Werner Bodenstein

Heeresgruppe B Reserve
79th VGD: Oberst Alois Weber
VGR 208
VGR 212
VGR 226
Fusilier-Kompanie 79
AR 179
Pionier Abt 179
Panzerjäger Abt 179
Nachrichten Abt 179
Feldersatz Abt 179
Versorgungseinheiten 179

OKW Reserve
XXXIX Panzerkorps: General der Panzertruppen Karl Decker
ARKO 439

10th SS PD—*Frundsberg:* SS-Brigadeführer Heinz Harmel
SS-Panzer Regt 10
SS-PGR 21
SS-PGR 22
SS-Panzer AR 10
SS-Flak Abt 10

6th SS-Gebirgs Div-*Nord:* SS-Gruppenführer Karl-Heinrich Brenner
SS-Gebirgs-Jäger Regt 11
SS-Gebirgs-Jäger Regt 12
SS-Polizei-Grenadier Abt 506
SS-Inf Regt 5
SS-Inf Regt 9 (removed from the division in 1943)
SS-Schützen Abt 6
SS-(Gebirgs) Panzerjäger Abt 6
SS-StuG Bty 6
SS-Gebirgs AR 6

SS-Flak Abt 6
SS-Gebirgs-Nachrichten Abt 6
SS-Gebirgs-Aufklärungs Abt 6
SS-Gebirgs-Pionier Abt 6

11th PD—*Gespenster:* Generalleutnant Wend von Wietersheim (in the process of being withdrawn from Heeresgruppe G)
Panzer Regt 15
PGR 110
PGR 111
Aufklärungs Abt 11

3rd PGD: Generalmajor Walter Denkert
PGR 8 (3 Abts)
PGR 29 (3 Abts)
Panzer Abt 103
Panzerjäger Abt 3
AR 3
Pionier Abt 3
Heers Flak Abt 272

FGB: Oberst Hans-Joachim Kahler (–Dec 22); Generalmajor Hellmuth Mäder (Dec 27–)
PGR 99
Panzer Abt 101
StuG Arty Brig 911
AR 124
Panzerjäger Abt 124
Aufklärungs Abt 124
Pionier Abt 124
Flak Abt 124
Grenadier Abt 929 zbV

FBB: Oberst Otto Remer
Panzer Abt 102
StuG Brig 200
PGR 100
AR 120
Aufklärungs Abt 120
Panzerjäger Abt 120
Pionier Abt 120
Grenadier Abt 828
Grenadier Abt 928 zbV
Flak Regt 673

9th VGD: *Oberst* Werner Kolb
VGR 36

VGR 57
VGR 116
AR 9
Fusilier Kompanie 9
Panzerjäger Abt 9
Pionier Abt 9
Nachrichten Abt 9

167th VGD: Generalleutnant Hans-Kurt Höcker
VGR 331
VGR 339
VGR 387
AR 167
Panzerjäger Abt 167
Pionier Abt 167
Nachrichten Abt 167

257th VGD: Oberst Erich Seidel

Luftwaffe

Luftwaffenkommando West: Generalleutnant Josef Schmidt
Jagdkorps II: Generalmajor Dietrich Peltz
Jagddivision 3: Generalmajor Walter Grabmann
III Flak Korps: Generalleutnant Wolfgang Pickert
Flak Div 2 (attached to Sixth Panzer Armee)
Flak Brig 1 (attached to Fifteenth Armee)
Flak Brig 19 (attached to Fifth Panzer Armee)
Flak Regt 15 (attached to Seventh Armee)

C. German Reinforcements versus Third Army, December 22, 1944–January 18, 1945

	Third Army	Location	German Unit	Location
Dec 22	4 Armd Div	Arlon	212 VGD	Echternach
(in place)	26 Inf Div	Arlon	276 VGD	Sauer Front
	80 Inf Div	Arlon	352 VGD	Ettelbruck
	10/5 Inf Div	Mersch	5 FJD	S Bastogne
	28 Inf Div (−)	Neufchâteau	FGB	Heiderscheid
	CCR/9 Armd Div	Bastogne	26 VGD	Bastogne
	CCA/9 Armd Div	Sauer Front	Panzer Lehr	SE Bastogne/St. Hubert
Dec 24			79 VGD[†]	Sauer Front
			15 PGD (elms)	Bastogne
Dec 26	35 Inf Div			
Dec 27	6 Armd Div	Mersch	FBB	SW Bastogne
			9 VGD[†]	Sauer Front
Dec 28			3 PGD	SE Bastogne
Dec 29	11 Armd Div	SW Bastogne	1 SS PD	SE Bastogne
	87 Inf Div	SW Bastogne	167 VGD[†]	SE Bastogne
Dec 31			12 SS PD	NE Bastogne
Jan 2	17 Abn Div	SW Bastogne	340 VGD[†]	NE Bastogne
Jan 3			9 SS PD	NW Bastogne
Jan 7			KG/9 PD	NW Bastogne
Jan 8	90 Inf Div	SE Bastogne		
	9 Armd Div	To SHAEF reserve		
Jan 9	28 Inf Div (−)	Departs TUSA		
Jan 10	4 Armd Div	Departs III Corps	1 SS PD	Withdraws
Jan 17	10 Armd Div	Departs TUSA		
Jan 18	101 Abn Div	Departs TUSA		
	35 Inf Div	Withdrawn from III Corps		
	76 Inf Div	Assigned to TUSA		

Note: dates reflect the moment divisions moved into the area of operations.
[†]Heeresgruppe B and OKW reserves.
Observations: The total number of German formations committed against Third Army after December 22 was ten; the reinforcement interval was 1.5 days.

D. Selected ULTRA Messages

In these messages, ZE represents Third Army, and NX represents Twelfth Army Group.

W. 902   M.I. 807

IMMEDIATE
TO: AT COL GORE-BROWNE
FROM: SLU SHAEF
((OLSU/SR 618 FOR GORE BROWNE))
74 REQUESTED TO YOUR INFORMATION AND NECESSARY ACTION:
"GENERAL GAFFEY NOW COMMANDING 4TH ARMOURED DIVISION
AND GENERAL GAY IS CHIEF OF STAFF HERE. GENERAL PATTON HAS
REQUESTED GAFFEY BE LEFT ON LIST"
LEONARD SITTING
T.O.O. 201640/12/44
10 COPIES HUT THREE
T.O.R. 202126/12/44

For S.C.U. ZETA
T.O.O. 211250Z/12/44
ZZ
F. NO. ....
TO BE ENCODED
PROC 320 WM SIBERT, repeated SH ZE 17 from GORE-BROWNE and
HILLES, reference ORB/ZE 73, 74, in 2 parts. Part 1.
General PATTON requests that his former Chief of Staff General GAFFEY, who
now commands 4th Armoured Division, remain on list. Regret we cannot comply
with request. Such a step without precedent. Regulations for maintaining security of
special intelligence severely restrict ULTRA to army level. Specifically they provide
that (a) Transfer of officers who have had intimate knowledge of ULTRA to posts
which might involve capture by enemy is highly undesirable and (b) An officer
relinquishing a post which entitles access to ULTRA automatically forfeits right to
see this material and will sign an undertaking to this effect. Grateful if you bring
this to the General's attention importance of not relaxing security measures.

REF. CX/MSS/T411/16   BT 479
ZZZZ
((BT 479 £ 479 ONA ON QX YKA YK ZE GU 94 £ 94 TGA TG 43 £ 43 WM 10 £
10 NX 43 £ 43 LF 96 £ 96 DL 25 £ 25 STA 22 £ 22 ST 11 £ 11 SH 55 £ 55 %
(FAIR INDICATIONS AOK £ AOK SEVEN NOUGHT ONE HOURS
TWENTYSEVENTH COLON ON ENTIRE)) WIDTH OF ARMY FRONT,
HEAVY DEFENSIVE FIGHTING AGAINST ALLIES WHO HAD MATERIAL
SUPERIORITY. INTENTIONS COLON DECISIVE DEFENCE ON NORTH
BANK SAUER £ SAUER WHERE SITUATION MIGHT MAKE IT POSSIBLE

TO GO OVER TO OFFENSIVE AGAIN. SITUATION ESPECIALLY
CRITICAL ON BOTH WINGS
GELC/WM   271656Z/12/44.
FB

REF: 949, CX/MSS/T412/20   BT 674

                                        Z
((BT 674 £ 674 CR FZ TG 92 £ 92 LF 45 £ 45 SH 21 £ 21 %
SUMIT (BAKER TARE FIVE SEVEN EIGHT) INTENTIONS
UNSPECIFIED)) AUTHORITY TWENTYSEVENTH INCLUDED COLON
ONE SIX SEVEN VG £ VG DIVISION AND THREE PANZER DIVISION
(COMMENT PRESUMABLY THREE PG £ PG) TO TAKE BASTOGNE £
BASTOGNE
RS/HYD/IFF   291741Z/12/44

REF: CX/MSS/T413/77   BT 708

                                     ZZZZZ
((BT 708 £ 708 ONA ON QX YKA YK ZE TG 15 £ 15 WM 78 £ 78 NX 9 £ 9 LF
68 £ 68 A.D. 26 £ 26 EFR 47 £ 47 SH 48 £ 48 %
ACCORDING JAGDKORPS TWO AT TWO ONE FOUR FIVE HOURS
TWENTYNINTH SECOND ATTACK)) ON BASTOGNE £ BASTOGNE
ORDERED AT NOUGHT SIX THREE NOUGHT HOURS. PANZER ARMY
FIVE TO REPORT BY NOUGHT FOUR HOURS WHETHER ATTACK CAN
STILL BE CARRIED OUT.
NH/RFB/
EVB   292318Z/12/44

REF. CX/MSS/T414/34   BT 752

                                     ZZZZZ
((BT 752 £ 752 ONA ON QX YKA YK ZE GU 92 £ 92 TGA TG 49 £ 49 WM 12 £
12 NX 41 £ 41 LF 3 £ 3 DL 49 £ 49 STA 78 £ 78 ST 67 £ 67 SH 85 85%
INTENTIONS ONE REPEAT ONE SUGAR SUGAR DIVISION
ACCORDING)) FLIVO ONE ONE THREE NOUGHT HOURS THIRTIETH
COLON THRUST SOUTH OF BASTOGNE £ BASTOGNE (PETER FIVE
FIVE) TO WEST WEST, AGAIN ENCIRCLED ALLIES IN BASTOGNE £
BASTOGNE
CAZ/HYD   301642Z/12/44

FB

REF. CX/MSS/T416/39   BT 923

ZZZZ
((BT 923 £ 923 ONA ON QX YKA YK ZE GU 58 £ 58 TGA TG 75 £ 75 WM 35 £
35 NX 61 £ 61 LF 27 £ 27 DL 38 £ 38 STA 85 £ 85 ST 74 £ 74 SH 27 £ 27 %

(FAIR INDICATIONS PANZER ARMY FIVE) TWO NOUGHT HOURS
THIRTYFIRST COLON ONE SUGAR SUGAR)) CORPS TO TAKE OVER
SECTOR OF PANZER LEHR DIVISION AND GRUPPE REMER £ REMER
FROM ONE ONE HOURS FIRST. NEW SECTOR BOUNDARY TO FOUR
SEVEN CORPS SPRIMONT £ SPRIMONT PETER FOUR SIX – MORHET
£ MORHET FOUR FIVE. GRUPPE REMER £ REMER TO BE RELIEVED
FROM FRONT BY JANUARY FIRST BY EMPLOYMENT ONE TWO
SUGAR SUGAR DIVISION, THEN TO BE AT DISPOSAL OF ARMY. ONE
SUGAR SUGAR CORPS WILL HOLD SECTOR AND PREPARE LOCAL
ATTACKS (COMMENT GERMAN TEILANGRIFFE) IN DIRECTION
REMAGNE £ REMAGNE THREE FIVE – MORHET £ MORHET FOUR
FIVE. COMMENT. FUEHRER £ FUEHRER ESCORT BRIGADE CALLED
BRIGADE REMER £ REMER ((ON TWENTIETH))

JB/NDD/DC   011714Z/1/45

REF. CX/MSS/T.424/62   BT 1800

ZZZZ
((BT 1800 £ 1800 YKA YK ZE 28 £ 28 FZ TGA TG 7 £ 7 WM 60 £ 60 NX 78 £ 78
LF 54 £ 54 DL 63 £ 63 STA 17 £ 17 ST 6 £ 6 SH 50 £ 50 %

(FAIR INDICATIONS SEVEN ARMY) TWO NOUGHT THREE NOUGHT
HOURS NINTH)) TO WITHDRAW MAIN DEFENCE LINE DURING NIGHT
TO LINE LUTREBOIS £ LUTREBOIS – LUTREMANGE £ LUTREMANGE
(BOTH PETER FIVE FIVE) – HARLANGE £ HARLANGE (PETER SIX FOUR)
NORTH £ NORTH. INTENTIONS, DEFENCE IN MAIN DEFENCE LINE

TNLB/PCP/JEM   092251Z/1/45

E. Weather Conditions in Third Army's Area, December 23, 1944–January 10, 1945

	Time	Temperature (°F)	Comments
Dec 23	0900		Clear. Mud and slush continue to hamper operations
Dec 23	2400		Clear and cold. Frozen ground . . . aided operations considerably.
Dec 25	2400		Operations facilitated by continued cold, clear weather.
Dec 27	0900	Min 20	Continued cold and clear weather facilitating operations.
Dec 28	0900	Min 13	Operations enhanced by continued cold.
Dec 29	0900	Min 18	Continued cold improved ground conditions.
Dec 30	0900	Min 20	Fog. Cold weather continued to improve ground conditions.
Dec 30	1800	Max 29	Poor visibility hampered operations somewhat.
Dec 30	2400	Min 27	Deteriorating weather conditions impeded ground/air operations.
Jan 1	0900	Min 21	Road and cross-country movement impaired by icing.
Jan 2	1800	Max 25	Cloudy to overcast. Icing conditions.
Jan 3	0900	Min 24	Scattered rain and snow showers, fog, and icing conditions.
Jan 4	0900	Min 32	Scattered rain and show showers, mud and slush, low overcast.
Jan 5	0900	Min 25	Overcast, light snow; snow and ice restrict ground operations.
Jan 6	2400	Avg 26	Visibility 1–2 miles. Icing impairs cross-country movement.
Jan 8	2400	Min 28	Overcast, light to moderate snow; visibility 1–2 miles.
Jan 10	1800	Max 29	Overcast; ice and snow continue to hinder ground operations.

Source: Third Army G-2 ISUM Nos. 432–487.

F. XIX TAC Daily Fighter and Fighter-Bomber Sorties, December 22, 1944–January 28, 1945

	Number of Sorties
Dec 22	No operations due to weather, except for 10 night fighter sorties
Dec 23	493
Dec 24	652
Dec 25	599
Dec 26	558
Dec 27	544
Dec 28	No operations due to weather, except for 4 unsuccessful T/R sorties
Dec 29	456
Dec 30	492
Dec 31	296
Jan 1	457
Jan 2	407
Jan 3	No operations due to weather
Jan 4	No operations due to weather, except for one 4-plane scramble mission
Jan 5	191
Jan 6	No operations due to weather
Jan 7	No operations due to weather
Jan 8	No operations due to weather
Jan 9	24
Jan 10	325
Jan 11	No operations due to weather, except for T/R missions
Jan 12	No operations due to weather, except for T/R missions
Jan 13	546
Jan 14	633
Jan 15	472
Jan 16	577
Jan 17	No operations due to weather
Jan 18	No operations due to weather
Jan 19	149
Jan 20	10
Jan 21	53
Jan 22	627
Jan 23	183
Jan 24	213
Jan 25	198
Jan 26	167
Jan 27	No operations due to weather, except for 7 night fighter sorties
Jan 28	70
Total	9,392

Note: For these 38 days, the average was 247 sorties per day. There were 12 nonoperational days, or 32 percent.
Source: Third Army AAR, vol. 1, Annex No. 3: XIX Tactical Air Command Report.

G. Third Army Reinforcements versus Casualties, December 22, 1944–January 28, 1945

	Casualties			
	Killed	Wounded	Missing	Total Reinforcements
Dec 22	158	1,121[*]	1,877[*]	1,117
Dec 23	29	512	285	609
Dec 24	75	801	328	2,150
Dec 25	53	824	181	576
Dec 26	124	682	312	2,603
Dec 27	82	500	311	2,521
Dec 28	44	385	218	1,282
Dec 29	79	420	179	1,430
Dec 30	50	509	102	302
Dec 31	85	750	355	2,323
Jan 1	105	582	122	1,986
Jan 2	102	531	102	583
Jan 3	89	482	140	793
Jan 4	190	1,081	458	675
Jan 5	136	649	258	864
Jan 6	56	363	57	541
Jan 7	234	922	340	614
Jan 8	52	544	663	1,305
Jan 9	100	658	127	768
Jan 10	103	682	172	1,069
Jan 11	45	623	127	992
Jan 12	70	393	101	890
Jan 13	72	423	66	640
Jan 14	115	504	111	1,883
Jan 15	58	618	50	1,346
Jan 16[†]	55	460	66	1,521
Totals Dec 22–Jan 16	1,946	16,019	7,180	31,388
Jan 17	49	438	43	2,717
Jan 18	81	310	122	1,237
Jan 19	51	465	74	1,410
Jan 20	64	353	47	689
Jan 21	61	440	76	1,991
Jan 22	74	350	39	1,849
Jan 23	60	313	50	3,357
Jan 24	96	494	50	1,602
Jan 25	47	375	121	2,918
Jan 26	33	373	18	1,883
Jan 27	52	479	46	3,368
Jan 28	30	293	27	1,095
Totals Jan 17–28	2,644	20,702	7,893	40,586
Daily averages	81	507	131	1,450

[*] Both figures appear to be far too high based on the daily average.
[†] ACSDB calculations end.
Note: Total casualties were 25,145 for December 22 through January 16 and 31,239 for January 17 through January 28.
Source: Third Army AAR, vol. 1, pp. 190–91, 238–39.

H. Patton's Staff

Commanding General: Lieutenant General George S. Patton Jr. (Lucky 6)
Aide: Lieutenant Alexander Stiller
Aide: Lieutenant Colonel Charles R. Codman
Orderly: Sergeant George Meeks
Chief of Staff: Brigadier General Hobart R. Gay
Deputy Chief of Staff (Operations): Colonel Paul D. Harkins
Secretary, General Staff: Major G. R. Pfann
Assistant Chief of Staff G-1: Colonel Frederick S. Matthews
Assistant Chief of Staff G-1 (Casualties and Replacements): Lieutenant Colonel
    Coy Eklund
Assistant Chief of Staff G-2: Colonel Oscar W. Koch
Assistant Chief of Staff G-2 (Assistant): Lieutenant Colonel Robert S. Allen
Assistant Chief of Staff G-2 (Air) Executive Officer: Colonel Harold M. Forde
Assistant Chief of Staff G-2 (Air) Liaison: Major Frank Pajerski
Assistant Chief of Staff G-3 (Operations): Colonel Halley G. Maddox
Assistant Chief of Staff G-4 (Logistics): Colonel Walter J. Muller
Assistant Chief of Staff G-5: Colonel Nicholas W. Campanole
Adjutant General: Colonel Robert E. Cummings
Antiaircraft Artillery: Colonel Frederick R. Chamberlain
Artillery: Colonel E. T. Williams
Chaplain: Colonel James H. O'Neil
Chemical Warfare: Colonel Edward C. Wallington
Chief Liaison Officer: Colonel Brenton G. Wallace
Engineers: Colonel John F. Conklin
Medical: Colonel Thomas D. Hurley
Ordnance: Colonel T. H. Nixon
Personal Physician: Colonel Charles B. Odom
Personal Secretary: Joseph D. Rosevich
Quartermaster: Colonel Everett Busch
Signals: Colonel Elton F. Hammond
Signals Security Officer: Major Charles W. Flint
ULTRA Representatives: Lieutenant Colonet Melvin C. Helfers, Captain George C. Church

Notes

Owing to the reorganization of World War II material at the National Archives and Records Administration in College Park, Maryland, the source citations in many recent works have become outdated. For example, the Foreign Military Studies collection, containing the interrogations of German senior officers, used to be held in RG 319 but is now in RG 549.3 (Records of the Foreign Military Studies Program and Related Records 1941–67). Because box numbers may change as well, I do not cite them for material at College Park. In citing archival sources in this work I have relied on the 2007 edition of *Citing Records in the National Archives of the United States.*

Abbreviations

AAR	after-action report
ACSDB	Ardennes Campaign Simulation Data Base
CARL	Combined Arms Research Library, Fort Leavenworth, Kans.
CG	commanding general
CMH	Center of Military History, Washington, D.C.
CofS	chief of staff
CSI	Combat Studies Institute, Fort Leavenworth, Kans.
DDEL	Dwight D. Eisenhower Presidential Library and Museum, Abilene, Kans.
DEFE	class list designation for the Public Record Office
ETHINT	European Theater Historical Interrogations
GPO	Government Printing Office
HMSO	Her Majesty's Stationery Office
KTB	*Kriegstagebuch* (War Diary)
LAC	Library and Archives Canada, Ottawa, Ontario
LC	Library of Congress, Washington, D.C.
NARA II	National Archives and Records Administration, College Park, Md.
NSA	National Security Agency
RG	Record Group
RMCC	Royal Military College of Canada, Kingston, Ontario
SAMS	School of Advanced Military Studies
SCAEF	Supreme Commander, Allied Expeditionary Force
SITREP	Situation Report
SRH	Special Research History
USACGSC	United States Army Command and General Staff College, Fort Leavenworth, Kans.

USAFHRA   United States Air Force Historical Research Agency, Maxwell Air
           Force Base, Ala.
USAHEC   United States Army Heritage and Education Center, Carlisle
           Barracks, Pa.

Studying Patton

1. Peter Mansoor, *The G.I. Offensive in Europe: The Triumph of American Infantry Divisions, 1944–1945* (Lawrence: University Press of Kansas, 1999), 216.

2. See John Nelson Rickard, *Patton at Bay: The Lorraine Campaign, September to December 1944* (Westport, Conn.: Praeger, 1999).

3. War Department, FM 100–5, *Field Service Regulations, Operations*, June 15, 1944, p. 3, USAHEC; War Department, FM 100–15, *Larger Units*, paragraphs 127–28; Colonel Raymond O. Ford, "Groups of Armies," *Military Review* 25, no. 11 (February 1946): 3–6. Army group headquarters was considered the link between army and theater, just as corps headquarters was the link between division and army.

4. Edward N. Luttwak, "The Operational Level of War," *International Security* 5, no. 3 (winter 1980–1981): 62. There are many definitions of the operational level of war. Keith Bonn, for example, defined the term *operational* as those actions "taken to conduct a campaign, usually at the corps (sometimes divisional) through army group levels." Keith E. Bonn, *When the Odds Were Even: The Vosges Mountains Campaign, October 1944–January 1945* (Novato, Calif.: Presidio Press, 1994), 235. In his 1871 work *Uber Strategie*, Helmuth von Moltke used the term *operations* almost exclusively to describe the movement of troops to a point for a decisive battle. Citino has even suggested that the transitional phase between tactics and operations is the pursuit because it "turns a victorious battle into a victorious campaign." Robert M. Citino, *Quest for Decisive Victory: From Stalemate to Blitzkrieg in Europe, 1899–1940* (Lawrence: University Press of Kansas, 2002), xii–xiii.

5. Roland G. Ruppenthal, *U.S. Army in World War II: Logistical Support of the Armies*, vol. 2, *September 1944–May 1945* (Washington, D.C.: CMH, 1987), 6, 503 (cited hereafter as *Logistical Support*). Martin van Creveld observed that Allied success in 1944 was due as much to the "disregard for the preconceived logistics plans as to their implementation." Martin van Creveld, *Supplying War: Logistics from Wallenstein to Patton* (Cambridge: Cambridge University Press, 2004), 236.

6. Bill McAndrew, "Operational Art and the Northwest European Theatre of War," *Canadian Defence Quarterly* 21, no. 3 (December 1991): 20; Luttwak, "The Operational Level of War," 62; Roger H. Nye, *The Patton Mind: The Professional Development of an Extraordinary Leader* (Garden City, N.Y.: Avery Publishing, 1993), 57.

7. For a good brief discussion, see John A. English, *Marching through Chaos: The Descent of Armies in Theory and Practice* (Westport, Conn.: Praeger, 1996), 55–56.

8. He added that it was the "art of posting troops upon the battlefield according to the accidents of the ground, of bringing them into action." Antoine Henri de Jomini, *The Art of War* (London: Greenhill Books, 1992), 69. It was only in the 1982 edition of FM 100–5 that the operational level of war and the corresponding concept of operational maneuver were introduced.

9. I say this because British theorist Brigadier Richard Simpkin was correct when he stated that *operational* had taken on a new meaning "divorced from [the] organizational level." Richard Simpkin, *Race to the Swift: Thoughts on Twenty-First Century Warfare* (London: Brassey's, 1985), 23–24.

10. *Wehrmacht* doctrine also held that the operational level began at the army level. Karl-Heinz Frieser, *The Blitzkrieg Legend: The 1940 Campaign in the West* (Annapolis, Md.: Naval Institute Press, 2005), 6.

11. This is called "operational art" today. See John Kiszley, "Thinking about the Operational Level," *RUSI Journal* (December 2005): 39–40. When one tests this observation on the British side, one quickly discovers that it does not hold up in the command environment of Twenty-First Army Group. Sir Brian Horrocks recalled that Montgomery selected XXX Corps to lead the advance into Belgium and decided on the number of divisions it should have under its command. This implies that Sir Miles Dempsey, commander of British Second Army, had little freedom to make such decisions on his own. Sir Brian Horrocks, *Corps Commander* (New York: Charles Scribner's Sons, 1977), 30–31.

12. Stephen Ashley Hart, *Montgomery and "Colossal Cracks": The 21st Army Group in Northwest Europe, 1944–45* (Westport, Conn.: Praeger, 2000), 12–13. Although the Germans preached the doctrine of decisive battles of annihilation (campaigns of annihilation may be a better term), this almost never happened, and they were forced to conduct further operations to win the campaign. Bruce Condell and David T. Zabecki, eds., *On the German Art of War: Truppenführung* (Boulder, Colo.: Lynne Rienner, 2001), 3.

13. FM 100–5, p. 34. At the time, *command* was defined by the U.S. Army as the authority that an individual "lawfully exercised over subordinates by virtue of rank or assignment." For a good discussion of the American philosophy of command up to World War II, see Harold R. Winton, *Corps Commanders of the Bulge: Six American Generals and Victory in the Ardennes* (Lawrence: University Press of Kansas, 2007), chap. 2.

14. Martin van Creveld, *Command in War* (Cambridge, Mass.: Harvard University Press, 1985), 6.

15. Roger A. Beaumont, "Command Method: A Gap in the Historiography," *Naval War College Review* 31, no. 3 (winter 1979): 61, 64, 68.

16. George S. Patton Jr., *War as I Knew It* (New York: Bantam, 1980), 273; Omar N. Bradley, *A Soldier's Story* (New York: Henry Holt, 1951), 358; Bradley's commentary on World War II, as recorded by Chester Hansen, Omar Bradley Papers, 16-b s-o, USAHEC, Carlisle Barracks, Pa.; Martin Blumenson, ed., *The Patton Papers*, 2 vols. (Boston: Houghton Mifflin, 1972, 1974), 2:203.

17. The basis for this categorization of responsibilities and means of influence is John A. English's *Patton's Peers: The Forgotten Allied Army Commanders of the Western Front, 1944–1945* (Mechanicsburg, Pa.: Stackpole Books, 2009), xiv–xviii. I have, however, made amendments for my purposes. It should be pointed out that American doctrine identified only three principal means of influence: committing reserves, coordinating additional fire support, and coordinating combat aviation. FM 100–5, p. 98.

18. The section on the estimate was actually shorter than that found in the 1941

edition, but there was little change in the essentials. War Department, FM 100–5, *Field Service Regulations: Operations, 1941*, p. 25; FM 100–5 (1944), pp. 35–36.

19. War Department, FM 101–5, *Staff Officers' Field Manual: The Staff and Combat Orders*, August 19, 1940, p. 128, USAHEC. The British army prepared written estimates. Lucien K. Truscott Jr. believed that the British staff procedures were very good and wrote, "I was always impressed with the care taken to insure that a final paper represented accurately the considered views of the committee, [and] the careful selection of words to express exact shades of meaning." Lucien K. Truscott Jr., *Command Missions: A Personal Story* (Novato, Calif.: Presidio Press, 1990), 32.

20. Roger Cirillo to author, February 2, 2008. In British practice, full estimates were produced only when needed, but the Americans required systematic reports. The American army produced a daily Periodic Report, and the consequent requirement to fill in all the blanks invariably meant, according to one ULTRA representative, that "people tend to read them that way." Interview with Adolph G. Rosengarten Jr., December 22, 1947, Forrest C. Pogue Interviews, USAHEC.

21. I have taken this directly from Mansoor's *G.I. Offensive in Europe*, 3, but I excluded his assertion that the definition includes material resources. I see nothing in the Allied thinking at this point to suggest that saving resources was inherent in the decision-making process. To the contrary, expending massive amounts of material was (and still is) seen as a worthwhile price to pay for saving lives. One definition of *combat effectiveness* is "the probability of success in combat operations," but this offers little to the analysis of historical battles. Philip Hayward, "The Measurement of Combat Effectiveness," *Operations Research* 16, no. 2 (March 1968): 316.

22. Allan R. Millett and Williamson Murray, eds., *Military Effectiveness*, vol. 3, *The Second World War* (Boston: Allen & Unwin, 1988), 37. See FM 3–0, *Operations*, February 2008, pp. 4-1, 4-2, for a modern definition.

23. Condell and Zabecki, *On the German Art of War*, 18; Martin van Creveld, *Fighting Power: German and U.S. Army Performance, 1939–1945* (Westport, Conn.: Greenwood Press, 1982), 3.

24. *Generalmajor* Walter Denkert, commander of *3rd PGD*, reflected that errors naturally arose in the *Kampfwert* classification because it was dependent on the personal conception of the division commander. Moreover, the *Kampfwert* of individual branches within the division could be different. MS #B-465 (Denkert), "Commitment of 3 Panzer Grenadier Division in the Ardennes Offensive," April 1947, p. 12, RG 549.3 (Records of the Foreign Military Studies Program and Related Records 1941–67), NARA II; Hugh M. Cole, *U.S. Army in World War II: The Lorraine Campaign* (Washington, D.C.,: CMH, 1984), 576 (cited hereafter as *Lorraine*).

25. Hayward, "The Measurement of Combat Effectiveness," 316.

1. Origin of the Ardennes Counteroffensive

1. Martin Blumenson, *U.S. Army in World War II: Breakout and Pursuit* (Washington, D.C.: CMH, 1989), 234 (cited hereafter as *Breakout and Pursuit*); ETHINT 66 (Bayerlein), "Pz Lehr Div (Jan–28 July 44)," August 7–9, 1945, p. 49, RG 549.3, NARA II. Bayerlein recalled that "at least 70 percent of my troops

were out of action—dead, wounded, crazed or numbed. All my forward tanks were knocked out." Quoted in Chester Wilmot, *The Struggle for Europe* (London: Collins, 1952), 391.

2. Quoted in Blumenson, *Breakout and Pursuit*, 323.

3. Ibid., 457; Hitler quoted in Forrest C. Pogue, *U.S. Army in World War II: The Supreme Command* (Washington, D.C.: CMH, 1989), 207 (cited hereafter as *Supreme Command*); Carlo D'Este, *Decision in Normandy* (New York: E. P. Dutton, 1983), 415.

4. Ralph Bennett has convincingly argued that the Allied commanders knew of Hitler's intentions "in time for them to take steps to counter it." Ralph Bennett, *Ultra in the West: The Normandy Campaign of 1944–1945* (London: Hutchinson, 1979), 113; D'Este, *Decision in Normandy*, 418–19. Mark Reardon has argued that ULTRA gave no specific warning. Mark J. Reardon, *Victory at Mortain: Stopping Hitler's Panzer Counteroffensive* (Lawrence: University Press of Kansas, 2002), 178. See also F. H. Hinsley, *British Intelligence in the Second World War: Its Influence on Strategy and Operations*, vol. 3, pt. 2 (London: HMSO, 1988), 238.

5. Gerhard L. Weinberg, *Germany, Hitler and World War II: Essays in Modern German and World History* (Cambridge: Cambridge University Press, 1995), 274–86; David K. Yelton, "Ein Volk Steht Auf": The German Volkssturm and Nazi Strategy, 1944–45," *Journal of Military History* 64, no. 4 (October 2000): 1061.

6. ETHINT 50 (Jodl), "Planning the Ardennes Offensive," July 26, 1945, p. 5, RG 549.3, NARA II; Walter Warlimont, *Inside Hitler's Headquarters, 1939–1945* (Novato, Calif.: Presidio Press, 1990), 457.

7. Pogue, *Supreme Command*, 359n3.

8. Quoted in Charles B. MacDonald, *The Battle of the Bulge* (London: Weidenfeld & Nicolson, 1984), 11.

9. On September 3 Hitler issued the following orders with respect to hitting Patton from the south: "On the left flank, Army Group G will assemble a mobile force forward of the Vosges, to attack the deep eastern flank of the enemy . . . by mobile operations against the southern flank of XII American Corps. Later, its main task will be to deliver a concentrated attack against the deep eastern flank and rear positions of the Americans." H. R. Trevor-Roper, ed., *Blitzkrieg to Defeat: Hitler's War Directives, 1939–1945* (New York: Holt, Rinehart & Winston, 1964), 191.

10. Charles V. P. von Luttichau, MS #R-12, "The Ardennes Offensive: Planning and Preparations," chap. 2, "The Framework for Operation WACHT AM RHEIN," August 1953, pp. 51–52, CMH; DEFE 3/315, HP 8826 (Z), December 7, 1944, reel 53, microfilm collection, Massey Library, RMCC.

11. ETHINT 50, pp. 16–17; Eddy Bauer, *Der Panzerkrieg: Die Wichtigsten Panzeroperationen des Zweiten Weltkrieges in Europa und Afrika*, vol. 2, *Der Zusammenbruch des Dritten Reiches* (Bonn: Verlag, 1965), 2.

12. Adam Tooze, *The Wages of Destruction: The Making and Breaking of the Nazi Economy* (New York: Allen Lane, 2006), xxiv, 396–425.

13. Quoted in Helmut Heiber and David M. Glantz, eds., *Hitler and His Generals: Military Conferences 1942–1945* (New York: Enigma Books, 2002), 92–93. At one time Hitler had voiced considerable respect for the United States because of the similarities between its racial policies and his own. Adolf Hitler, *Mein Kampf*

(London: Hurst & Blackett, 1933), 174; Gerhard L. Weinberg, ed., *Hitler's Second Book: The Unpublished Sequel to Mein Kampf* (New York: Enigma Books, 2003), 107, 109.

14. The other plans prepared by the General Staff included Operation HOL-LAND, a single thrust from the Venlo area with the objective of Antwerp; Operation LIÈGE-AACHEN, a pincer effort from northern Luxembourg and the Aachen area; and Operation ALSACE, an envelopment to close on Vesoul. Hugh M. Cole, *U.S. Army in World War II: The Ardennes: Battle of the Bulge* (Washington, D.C.: CMH, 1988), 20 (cited hereafter as *Ardennes*).

15. Quoted in MacDonald, *Battle of the Bulge*, 35; Cole, *Ardennes*, 26.

16. Rundstedt's concept, embodied in PLAN MARTIN, was to attack on a narrow twenty-five-mile front with the *Fifth* and *Sixth Panzer Armees* between Simmerath and Bleialf. A secondary thrust, heavy in armor, from the Roermond sector would meet the main thrust near Liège. Model's plan, *HERBSTNEBEL* (Autumn Fog), rejected a pincer movement and instead advocated a single powerful thrust on a forty-mile front between the Hürtgen Forest and Lützkampen, with the *Seventh Armee* and a sizable armored component making up a second wave. In late October, Model incorporated most of Rundstedt's ideas into his own plan. Cole, *Ardennes*, 25–27.

17. Russell F. Weigley, *The Age of Battles: The Quest for Decisive Warfare from Breitenfeld to Waterloo* (Bloomington: Indiana University Press, 1991), 193.

18. Luttichau, MS #R-12, chap. 2, p. 9; John S. D. Eisenhower, *The Bitter Woods* (New York: G. P. Putnam, 1969), 115.

19. Cole, *Ardennes*, 43.

20. Ibid., 42–43.

21. Ibid., 42.

22. *Heeresgruppe B* Operational Order cited in Jean Paul Pallud, *The Battle of the Bulge: Then and Now* (London: After the Battle, 1999), 32.

23. Roger Cirillo, *The U.S. Army Campaigns of World War II: Ardennes–Alsace* (Washington, D.C.: CMH, 2004), 11 (cited hereafter as *Ardennes–Alsace*); Percy Ernst Schramm, ed., *Kriegstagebuch des Oberkommandos der Wehrmacht*, vol. 4, *1944–1945* (Frankfurt am Main: Bernard & Graefe, 1963), 442.

24. Trevor N. Dupuy, *Hitler's Last Gamble: The Battle of the Bulge, December 1944–January 1945* (New York: HarperCollins, 1994), 12; *Generaloberst* Kurt Student, Commander Army Group H and C-in-C Paratroops, Special Interrogation Report, p. 5, MG 31G21, vol. 5, "German Commanders," LAC.

25. James J. Weingartner, *Hitler's Guard: Inside the Führer's Personal SS Force* (New York: Berkley Books, 1990), 158–59.

26. Hinsley, *British Intelligence*, 432; Bennett, *Ultra in the West*, 175; Danny S. Parker, *The Battle of the Bulge: Hitler's Ardennes Offensive, 1944–1945* (Conshohocken, Pa.: Combined Books, 1991), 39; Colonel Basil J. Hobar, "The Ardennes 1944: Intelligence Failure or Deception Success?" *Military Intelligence* 10, no. 4 (October–December 1984): 12. SHAEF does not seem to have been fooled by the German link of *Gruppe von Manteuffel* with *Fifteenth Armee*. G-2 observed, "For some unknown reason Fifth Pz Army now seems to be using this title." SHAEF G-2 Digest #188, December 11, 1944, SHAEF Selected Records, 1943–45, accession 60–14, box 3, DDEL.

2. The Opposing Armies in December 1944

1. SHAEF/17422/Ops(A), Subject: Numerical Superiority for Offensive Operations, December 13, 1944, RG 331, entry 58, G-3 War Diary, December 1944, NARA II; SHAEF Diary, book XII, June 22, 1944, p. 1416; Hinsley, *British Intelligence*, 367. Ending the war by the end of 1944 had been the key objective of the First Quebec Conference in August 1943. John Ehrman, *Grand Strategy*, vol. 6, *October 1944–August 1945* (London: HMSO, 1956), xii. The JIC assessments may have been influenced by this.

2. John Nelson Rickard, "Allied Superiority, Operational Tempo and the Defeat of the German Army in the West," Seventy Years On: New Perspectives on the Second World War, University of Calgary, September 2, 2009. German operations included the following: (1) counterattack on D-Day by *21st PD*; (2) counterattack by *17th SS PGD* at Carentan; (3) *II SS Panzerkorps'* counterattack at the Odon; (4) *Panzer Lehr's* counterattack along the Vire River; (5) *II SS Panzerkorps'* counterattack at Verrières Ridge; (6) Operation LÜTTICH at Mortain; (7) *Fifth Panzer Armee's* counterattack against Patton in Lorraine; (8) counterattack against Veghel during MARKET GARDEN; (9) *XLVII Panzerkorps'* counterattack in the Peel Marshes; and (10) the Ardennes counteroffensive.

3. Patton also attracted *VAK 404* and two panzer brigades. Luttichau, MS #R-12, "The Ardennes Offensive: Planning and Preparations," August 1953, chap. 3, pp. 4–5, CMH.

4. U.S. Army Concepts Analysis Agency, "The Ardennes Campaign Simulation Data Base (ACSDB), Final Report," vol. 1 (Fairfax, Va.: Data Memory Systems, February 7, 1990), II-G-4–9. The ACSDB is a computerized database using dBASE IV data management software to manipulate the data. Colonel Trevor N. Dupuy was the brain behind the research, but Hugh M. Cole and Charles B. MacDonald consulted on the project. The ACSDB has limitations, but it has been used here because of the tremendous amount of primary research in German sources.

5. Ibid.; ETHINT 21 (Fritz Kraemer), "Sixth Pz Army (16 Nov–4 Jan 45)," August 14–15, 1945, pp. 3–4, RG 549.3, NARA II. ULTRA also suggested that this battalion may have had four Panthers, either for its own use or on the same train. DEFE 3/315, HP 8981 (ZZ), December 9, 1944, reel 54, microfilm collection, Massey Library, RMCC.

6. Hubert Meyer, *The 12th SS: The History of the Hitler Youth Panzer Division* (Mechanicsburg, Pa.: Stackpole Books, 2005), 227–29; Pallud, *Battle of the Bulge*, 23. Kraas indicated that the reconnaissance battalion was weak, with only one rifle company; the panzer regiment had only one battalion of *Panzerjäger IV, Jagdpanther*, Panzer IV, and Panthers. The artillery was good but suffered from a deplorable vehicle situation.

7. MS #P-065a (Reinhardt), "The Volksgrenadier Division and the Volkssturm," September 22, 1950, p. 13, RG 549.3, NARA II; Larry T. Balsamo, "Germany's Armed Forces in the Second World War: Manpower, Armaments, and Supply," *History Teacher* 24, no. 3 (May 1991): 274.

8. Strengths for the *3rd FJD* and the *12th* and *277th VGDs* are from ACSDB, II-G-4–9; DEFE 3/315, HP 8971 (ZZ), December 9, 1944, reel 53. For the artillery

strength of the *VGDs*, see MS #P-065a, p. 13; Gerhard Martin, *Letzter Lorbeer: Fallschirmpioniere in der Ardennenschlacht, 1944/1945: Im Rahmen der 5. Fallschirmjägerdivision* (Coburg: Nation Europa Verlag, 2002), 55; George Forty, *The Reich's Last Gamble: The Ardennes Offensive, December 1944* (London: Cassell, 2000), 97; W. J. K. Davies, *German Army Handbook, 1939–1945* (London: Ian Allen , 1973), 48. Albert Seaton suggests the divisions possessed thirty-two guns. Albert Seaton, *The German Army, 1933–1945* (London: Weidenfeld & Nicolson, 1982), 241.

9. ACSDB, II-G-4–9; DEFE 3/315, HP 8971, December 9, 1944; MS #B-092 (Kashner), "Ardennes, 16 Dec–25 Jan 45," September 8, 1950, p. 1, RG 549.3, NARA II.

10. ACSDB, II-G-4–9; ETHINT 21, pp. 3–4.

11. DEFE 3/313, HP 8464 (ZZZZ), December 3, 1944; ACSDB, II-G-4–9, reel 54.

12. Helmut Ritgen, *The Western Front, 1944: Memoirs of a Panzer Lehr Officer* (Winnipeg: J. J. Fedorowicz, 1995), 259; Walter J. Spielberger, *The Spielberger German Armor and Military Vehicle Series*, vol. 1, *Panther and Its Variants* (Atglen, Pa.: Schiffer Military History, 1993), 169. Only one battalion of PGR 901 was equipped with armored self-propelled weapons, and *Panzer Artillerie Regiment 130* was armored in name only. It lost its guns in Lorraine and consisted of the light *III Abteilung* (heavy field howitzer) with two batteries. The supply troops "were in even worse shape." See also MS #A-940 (Lüttwitz), "XXXXVII Panzer Corps in the Battle of the Ardennes," June 13, 1950, p. 2, RG 549.3, NARA II.

13. MS #A-940, p. 2; ACSDB, II-G-4–9; DEFE 3/315, HP 8971 (ZZ), December 9, 1944. Here is one example where ULTRA and the ACSDB do not match up. The ACSDB calculated the strength at 9,951.

14. ACSDB, II-G-4–9; MS #A-873 (Waldenburg), "Commitment of the 116th Panzer Division in the Ardennes 1944–1945," December 16, 1945, p. 4, RG 549.3, NARA II; Heinz Günther Guderian, *From Normandy to the Ruhr: With the 116th Panzer Division in World War II* (Bedford, Pa.: Aberjona Press, 2001), 291. The division was short 432 trucks, 32 tractors of all sizes, 111 *Maultier* tracked transports, and 50 percent of the required artillery prime movers.

15. ACSDB, II-G-4–9; MS #B-024 (Bäder), "Ardennes Campaign (16 December 1944 to 25 January 1945)," May 30, 1946, pp. 2–3, RG 549.3, NARA II.

16. ACSDB, II-G-4–9.

17. MS #B-447 (Brandenberger), "Questions for the 7 Armee," May 14, 1946, p. 38, RG 549.3, NARA II.

18. ETHINT 64 (Heilmann), "Evaluation of 5 FS Div (Dec 44)," March 1, 1946, in Donald S. Detwiler with Charles B. Burdick and Jürgen Rohwer, eds., *World War II German Military Studies*, 24 vols. (New York: Garland Publishing, 1979), vol. 3, pt. 2. The ACSDB (II-G-4–9) gives a divisional strength of 13,500. According to Brandenberger, the division had upward of 20,000 men. MS #A-934 (Brandenberger), "Questions and Answers on the Ardennes Campaign and Later Operations of 19 Army," December 22, 1945, p. 13, RG 549.3, NARA II. He also claimed that it had a weak lower command element, "very little artillery and not nearly enough motor vehicles." Detwiler et al., *World War II German Military Studies*, vol. 12. Roland Gaul, *The Battle of the Bulge in Luxembourg: The Southern Flank December 1944–January 1945*, vol. 1, *The Germans* (Atglen, Pa.: Schiffer Military History, 1995), 39; MS #A-932 (Gersdorff), "Item No. 8, Evaluation and Equipment of Units Attached

to 7 Army in Ardennes Offensive," n.d., p. 1, RG 549.3, NARA II. This division had two replacement training battalions of 1,000 men each, but they lacked vehicular transport. In postwar interrogations, Gersdorff, Brandenberger's former chief of staff, stated that the greatest deficiency in *5th FJD* was leadership. When Manteuffel read this, he wrote in the margin, "I disagree." ETHINT 54 (Gersdorff), "Seventh Army in the Ardennes Offensive," November 26, 1945, RG 549.3, NARA II; MS #A-934, p. 3.

19. ACSDB, II-G-4–9; Gaul, *Battle of the Bulge in Luxembourg*, 1:35–36; DEFE 3/315, HP 8971, December 9, 1944. According to *Oberstleutnant* Drawe, commander of *VGR 915*, the artillery troops knew little of tactics and technical matters. As late as December 10, 1944, they were confusing orders to adjust the aiming device and physically moving the guns forward. Brandenberger stated that the division did not have the prescribed number of self-propelled guns, and *Seventh Armee* gave it a considerably less mobile *StuG* battalion. MS #A-934, p. 3.

20. MS #A-930 (Sensfuss), "212th Volksgrenadier Division (Ardennes)," April 10, 1946, p. 2, RG 549.3, NARA II; ACSDB, II-G-4–9; DEFE 3/315, HP 8971, December 9, 1944.

21. Divisional strengths as calculated by the ACSDB were as follows: *79th VGD*, 10,132; *3rd PGD*, 11,442; *15th PGD*, 10,988; *167th VGD*, 11,050; *246th VGD*, 8,958; *9th PD*, 12, 889; *11th PD*, 10,157; *FBB*, 7,000; *FGB*, 6,270.

22. Alan F. Wilt, *War from the Top: German and British Military Decision Making during World War II* (Bloomington: Indiana University Press, 1990), 276; Pallud, *Battle of the Bulge*, 31; ACSDB, II-G-4–9. Another source calculated the initial start strength as 330,320. This study tabulated the total based on twenty-five divisions, the *FBB*, the *FGB*, and *Panzer Brigade 150*. Although divisional strengths were derived from the ACSDB, there are differences. U.S. Army Concepts Analysis Agency, Tactical Analysis Division Study Report CAA-SR-95–8, Ardennes Campaign Simulation (ARCAS), 1995, D-7. The ration strength is in debate. Bennett states that *Heeresgruppe B*'s ration strength on January 1 was 882,560, with the following breakdown: *Fifteenth Armee*, 205,193; *Sixth Panzer Armee*, 319,031; *Fifth Panzer Armee*, 187,769; *Seventh Armee*, 170,567. Bennett, *Ultra in the West*, 194.

23. MS #B-286 (Zanssen), "Ardennes 16 December 1944–25 January 1945," April 14, 1946, p. 2, RG 549.3, NARA II. Each *Werfer* had six barrels.

24. MS #B-311 (Tholholte), "Army Group B Artillery, Ardennes," September 1946, p. 2, RG 549.3, NARA II.

25. Operations Support Division, U.S. Army Concepts Analysis Agency, Technical Paper CAA-TP-96–1, Simulation Enhancements from Ardennes Campaign Analysis (SEACA), October 1996, 3–13. Wilt offers 3,409 pieces in *War from the Top*, 276. Pallud argues that there were 685 nondivisional guns in *Sixth Panzer Armee*, 596 in *Fifth Panzer Armee*, and 381 in *Seventh Armee*. Pallud, *Battle of the Bulge*, 45, 52, 55. See also Parker, *Battle of the Bulge*, 249, and Martin, *Letzter Lorbeer*, 55, for calculation.

26. There were 10,078 guns of all types on the Eastern and Southern Fronts combined. OKH/Stab Gen. Art. Beim Gen. St. d. H. *KTB* Anlagen #830 and #860, as referenced in Cole, *Lorraine*, 534.

27. Cole, *Ardennes*, 652; MacDonald, *Battle of the Bulge*, 82. *General der Panzertruppen* Horst Stumpff also stated that *Heeresgruppe B* had 1,800 tanks from Aachen

to Trier. ETHINT 61 (Horst Stumpff), "Tank Maintenance in the Ardennes Offensive," August 11, 1945, p. 2, RG 549.3, NARA II. Cole stated that 250 Tigers fought in the Bulge, and MacDonald stated 150, but it is apparent that no more than 76 were committed in *Schwere SS-Panzer Abteilung 501, Schwere Panzer Abteilung 560,* and *Schwere (Funklenk) Panzer Abteilung 301.* To appreciate the difference between TO&E and operational status, see Michael Reynolds, *The Devil's Adjutant: Jochen Peiper, Panzer Leader* (New York: Sarpedon, 1995), 69, and Parker, *Battle of the Bulge,* 234–35.

28. MS #A-862 (Percy E. Schramm), "The Preparations for the German Offensive in the Ardennes (Sep to 16 Dec 1944)," pp. 199–200, USAHEC; Parker, *Battle of the Bulge,* 234–39; Dupuy, *Hitler's Last Gamble,* 18. Pallud cites 1,034 panzers and *StuGs* in *Battle of the Bulge,* 22. Ronald D. Fricker Jr. posits that the Germans had 747 tanks (he does not differentiate between tanks proper and assault guns), 2,161 armored personnel carriers, and 5,130 pieces of artillery in "Attrition Models of the Ardennes Campaign," *Naval Research Logistics* 45, no. 1 (February 1998): 9. One must be careful when using modeling/operational research data. Fricker (ibid., 3), for example, stated that the front was restored to pre–December 16 positions on January 16, but this was merely the linkup at Houffalize. Two more weeks were required to push the Germans back to the Siegfried Line. Manteuffel told B. H. Liddell Hart he had 800 tanks. B. H. Liddell Hart, *The Other Side of the Hill: Germany's Generals, Their Rise and Fall with Their Own Account of Military Events, 1939–1945* (London: Cassell, 1948), 289. Another (ARCAS, D-5) study states 825. Estimates of the actual number of tanks deployed by *Sixth Panzer Armee* vary. Dietrich stated that he had 500 tanks at the start, but 100 were nonoperational because of mechanical failings. ETHINT 15 (Dietrich), "Sixth Pz Army in the Ardennes Offensive," August 8–9, 1945, p. 3, RG 549.3, NARA II. See also Charles V. P. von Luttichau, "Armor in the Ardennes Offensive," 1952, CMH.

29. ETHINT 61, p. 1.

30. Albert Speer suggested that to free up 17,500 metric tons (4.49 million gallons) of fuel for the offensive (equivalent to two and a half days of production), they had to begin holding back fuel from the army groups on November 10. Albert Speer, *Inside the Third Reich* (New York: Macmillan, 1970), 406. Speer was quoting Jodl's diary; Cole, *Ardennes,* 68. Jodl's diary for December 8, 1944, states that 7,150 cubic meters of fuel was available, 6,000 was on the way, and 2,400 would be coming from the east. Warlimont, *Inside Hitler's Headquarters,* 485. Jodl noted that some fuel was held back "on principle" because "otherwise, the commanders would have been too extravagant with it. This was Keitel's idea." ETHINT 50, p. 12, RG 549.3, NARA II. Exactly what a VS represented is difficult to determine. One source stated that it was equivalent to only thirty miles. General Board, United States Forces, European Theater of Operations, Study No. 1, "Strategy of the Campaign in Western Europe 1944–1945," p. 64, CARL. This is based on a statement from General Siegfried Westphal on June 12, 1945.

31. MS #A-862, p. 206; MS #A-938 (Lüttwitz), "Correction Sheet to the German Copy of MS #A-938: 'XLVII Panzer Corps—Ardennes, General Questions,'" December 1, 1952, p. 3, RG 549.3, NARA II; MS #B-447, p. 42; Cole, *Ardennes,* 73.

32. MS #B-311, p. 7; Colonel A. G. Cole, "German Artillery Concentrations in

World War II," *Journal of the Royal Artillery* 75, no. 3 (July 1948): 198. According to *General der Artillerie* Graf Ralp von Oriola, the scale for each German artillery battery during the Bulge was as follows:

	Rounds per day	
	Light Field Howitzer	Heavy Field Howitzer
Quiet days	16	4
Fighting days	32	8

See also Major General J. B. A. Bailey, *Field Artillery and Firepower* (Annapolis, Md.: Naval Institute Press, 2004), 321n115. Speer indicated that he set up an ad hoc system with Model to keep *Heeresgruppe B* supplied with improvised armaments, but he never explained what that meant. Speer, *Inside the Third Reich*, 417.

33. Cole, *Ardennes*, 665; MS #B-393 (Richard Metz), "The Use of Artillery in the Ardennes Offensive 1944 by the 5 Armored Army," end of June 1945, p. 46, RG 549.3, NARA II.

34. MS #B-447, p. 32–33. Brandenberger added that up to the beginning of the offensive he had "received half a non-mobile bridging column; also supplies subsequently brought up were inadequate and consequently useless inasmuch as value. These columns were brought to our disposal as non-mobile units, and the Army did not have the means at hand for rendering [them] . . . mobile." MS #B-172a (Brandenberger), "My Attitude to the Report of Lieutenant General Wirtz," August 24, 1946, p. 1, RG 549.3, NARA II.

35. MS #B-172b (Manteuffel), "Requested Expression of Opinion on the Report Written by Major-General Wirtz, Dated 24 August 1946," August 31, 1946, p. 1, RG 549.3, NARA II.

36. Cole, *Ardennes*, 86, 660. The German air order of battle on December 16, 1944, consisted of the following: jet aircraft, 40; level bombers, 55; ground attack aircraft, 390; single-engine fighters, 1,770; twin-engine fighters, 140; reconnaissance aircraft, 65. This totaled 2,460, but only 1,376 were ever operational at any one time. Wesley F. Craven and James L. Cate, eds., *The Army Air Forces in World War II*, vol. 3, *Europe: Argument to VE Day, January 1944 to May 1945* (Chicago: University of Chicago Press, 1958), 673. Adolf Galland, the C-in-C of the Fighter Command, reflected that the *Luftwaffe* fighter arm had been consciously horded and reequipped and trained for a decisive encounter with the Allied bomber force over the skies of the Reich. Adolf Galland, *The First and the Last: The German Fighter Force in World War II* (London: Methuen, 1955), 316–17; Cajus Bekker, *The Luftwaffe War Diaries* (Garden City, N.Y.: Doubleday, 1969), 533. On November 20 sixteen of the eighteen fighter groups (minus the 300th and 301st) assigned to the defense of the Reich were transferred to the west.

37. Creveld, *Fighting Power*, 56; Kent Roberts Greenfield, Robert R. Palmer, and Bell I. Wiley, *U.S. Army in World War II: The Organization of Ground Combat Troops* (Washington, D.C.: Historical Division, 1947), 351 (cited hereafter as *Organization of Ground Combat Troops*). On December 1 Twelfth Army Group's divisional slice was about 27,000. Ruppenthal, *Logistical Support*, 289.

38. Combined Intelligence Committee, "Estimate of the Enemy Situation,

Europe, January 22, 1945," p. 8; Charles B. MacDonald, *U.S. Army in World War II: The Last Offensive* (Washington, D.C.: CMH, 1973), 8 (cited hereafter as *Last Offensive*); Creveld, *Fighting Power*, 45.

39. ETHINT 45 (Manteuffel), "Fifth Pz Army (11 Sept 44–Jan 45)," June 21, 1945, p. 13; ETHINT 46 (Manteuffel), "Fifth Pz Army (Nov 44–Jan 45)," October 29–31, 1945, p. 4, RG 549.3, NARA II.

40. Matthew Cooper, *The German Army, 1933–1945: Its Political and Military Failure* (New York: Bonanza Books, 1984), 487.

41. Edward A. Shils and Morris Janowitz, "Cohesion and Disintegration in the Wehrmacht in World War II," *Public Opinion Quarterly* 12, no. 2 (summer 1948): 281; W. Victor Madej, "Effectiveness and Cohesion of German Ground Forces in World War II," *Journal of Political and Military Sociology* 6, no. 2 (1978): 234; Omer Bartov, "The Conduct of War: Soldiers and the Barbarization of Warfare," *Journal of Modern History* 64, Supplement (December 1992): S32, S45; M. I. Gurfein and Morris Janowitz, "Trends in Wehrmacht Morale," *Public Opinion Quarterly* 10, no. 1 (spring 1946): 78. See also Jürgen E. Forster, "The Dynamics of Volksgemeinschaft: The Effectiveness of the German Military Establishment in the Second World War," in Millett and Murray, *Military Effectiveness*, 3:212.

42. MS #B-235 (Carl Wagener), "Commitment of the 5th Panzer Army in the Ardennes Winter Offensive 1944–45," December 20, 1945, p. 48, RG 549.3, NARA II. Bayerlein offered some insight from the perspective of a commander. Clearly fatigued by years of fighting, he admitted that he tried to persuade himself that he was going to succeed, "so as to give my orders and measures the necessary force although I was really convinced that the offensive would fail." P. A. Spayd, *Bayerlein: From Afrikakorps to Panzer Lehr* (Atglen, Pa.: Schiffer Military History, 2003), 192.

43. Robert S. Rush, "A Different Perspective: Cohesion, Morale, and Operational Effectiveness in the German Army, Fall 1944," *Armed Forces and Society* 25, no. 3 (spring 1999): 478; Ritgen, *Western Front*, 59; ETHINT 45; Gaul, *Battle of the Bulge in Luxembourg*, 1:35–36; Detwiler et al., *World War II German Military Studies*, 12:65; Liddell Hart, *Other Side of the Hill*, 290. There appeared to be little defeatist talk even as late as mid-December. Marlis G. Steinert, *Hitler's War and the Germans: Public Mood and Attitude during the Second World War* (Athens: Ohio University Press, 1977), 282–83.

44. Twelfth Army Group, Situation 1200 hours, December 15, 1944, Twelfth Army Group outline maps, 1:1,000,000, World War II military situation maps, http://www.TheHistoricalArchive.Com; Ruppenthal, *Logistical Support*, 302. This map does not indicate the location of the 75th Infantry Division.

45. J. A. Whiteley, memorandum for General O'Hare, December 15, 1944, appendix 10 to General Board, United States Forces, European Theater, Study No. 3, "Reinforcement System and Reinforcement Procedures in the European Theater of Operations," microfilm collection, Massey Library, RMCC; Twelfth Army Group Report of Operations (Final After Action Report), vol. 1, Summary, p. 11, CARL; Cole, *Lorraine*, 594. The 17,581 figure is roughly in line with Chester Hansen's comment that the army group reported shortages of 7,000 per army. Chester Hansen Diary, December 16, 1944, USAHEC. The planning assumption, based on experience up to September 1944, was 78.3 percent infantry (70 percent riflemen). Ruppenthal,

Logistical Support, 316. In Lorraine, Patton noted that 92 percent of his casualties occurred in the rifle companies. Blumenson, *Patton Papers*, 2:586.

46. Bradley's TO&E cutting edge was probably somewhere around 120,000 infantry soldiers (22 divisions times 5,184, plus the armored infantry of the armored divisions), but when losses are subtracted, Bradley's cutting-edge infantry strength was likely just over 90,000. The infantry and tank components of the 1944 triangular armored division equaled only 5,190, giving Twelfth Army Group's eight armored divisions a cutting edge of 41,520.

47. Ruppenthal, *Logistical Support*, 507.

48. Compiled from Parker, *Battle of the Bulge*, 304–5.

49. Cole, *Ardennes*, 659; Cole, *Lorraine*, 591.

50. Henry L. Stimson and McGeorge Bundy, *On Active Service in Peace and War* (London: Hutchinson, n.d.), 234; Maurice Matloff, "The 90-Division Gamble," in *Command Decisions*, ed. Kent Roberts Greenfield (Washington, D.C.: CMH, 1960), 381; MacDonald, *Last Offensive*, 14.

51. MacDonald, *Last Offensive*, 7.

52. Ehrman, *Grand Strategy*, 6:xi; Ruppenthal, *Logistical Support*, 6, 135, 137–39, 236.

53. Dwight D. Eisenhower, *Crusade in Europe* (Garden City, N.Y.: Doubleday, 1948), 337, 340; emphasis added.

54. John Kennedy Ohl, *Supplying the Troops: General Somervell and American Logistics in World War II* (De Kalb: Northern Illinois University Press, 1994), 236; Twelfth Army Group Summary, 24.

55. Army Ground Forces—that is, combat engineer and signals troops and all ground units in the combat zones, including close support services—peaked at 2.7 million. Greenfield et al., *Organization of Ground Combat Troops*, 194, 290.

56. David M. Glantz and Jonathan M. House, *When Titans Clashed: How the Red Army Stopped Hitler* (Lawrence: University Press of Kansas, 1995), 307; Burkhart Müller-Hillebrand, *Das Heer: 1933–1945* (Frankfurt am Main: E. S. Mittler & Sohn, 1969), 2:248–286; Madej, "Effectiveness and Cohesion of German Ground Forces," 240; Gerhard L. Weinberg, *A World at Arms: A Global History of World War II* (Cambridge: Cambridge University Press, 1994), 264.

57. Quoted in Matloff, "The 90-Division Gamble," 374.

58. Greenfield et al., *Organization of Ground Combat Troops*, 190; Mansoor, *G.I. Offensive in Europe*, 250. The crisis in the Ardennes produced significant results. By April 1945 the reported actual strengths for all U.S. divisions worldwide were 99 percent of authorized strength.

59. 21 Army Group, "Operation MARKET GARDEN 17–26 September 1944," p. 6, CARL. For British figures, see Major L. F. Ellis, *Victory in the West*, vol. 1, *The Battle of Normandy* (London: HMSO, 1962), 535.

60. Shelby L. Stanton, *World War II Order of Battle* (New York: Galahad, 1991), 29–30; General Board, United States Forces, European Theater, Study No. 15, "Organization, Equipment, and Tactical Employment of the Infantry Division," p. 9, USAHEC. An armored field artillery battalion had eighteen 105mm guns.

61. Christopher R. Gabel, *Seek, Strike and Destroy: U.S. Army Tank Destroyer Doctrine in World War II*, Leavenworth Papers No. 12 (Fort Leavenworth, Kans.: CSI,

1985), 63; John L. S. Daley, "From Theory to Practice: Tanks, Doctrine, and the U.S. Army, 1916–1940" (PhD diss., Kent State University, 1993).

62. Ruppenthal, *Logistical Support*, 317; Cole, *Lorraine*, 592; Robert R. Palmer, Bell I. Wiley and William R. Keast, *U.S. Army in World War II: The Procurement and Training of Ground Combat Troops* (Washington, D.C.: CMH, 1948), 172, 217, 227, 229 (cited hereafter as *Procurement and Training*).

63. Cole, *Lorraine*, 595; Patton Diary (annotated transcript), December 16, 1944, George S. Patton Papers, box 3, Manuscript Division, LC; Brigadier General Fred Wharton Rankin, *Medical Department United States Army in World War II, Clinical Series, Internal Medicine in World War II*, vol. 1, *Activities of Medical Consultants* (Washington, D.C.: Office of the Surgeon General, Department of the Army, 1962), 327–29.

64. Colonel James N. Peale Jr., Third Battalion, 101st Infantry Regiment, U.S. Army, in the Ardennes Campaign, December 1944 and January 1945, April 13, 1958, John Toland Papers, box 34, LC; S. L. A. Marshall, *The Soldier's Load and the Mobility of a Nation* (Quantico, Va.: Marine Corps Association, 1950), 97. The U.S. Army suffered from quality issues even before the replacements dried up. The official historians noted that the army, and the infantry in particular, received the poorest quality manpower. The air force, navy, marines, airborne, and technical services took the cream of the crop in terms of intelligence. Palmer et al., *Procurement and Training*, 3. The implication, of course, is that intelligent, physically superior men fight better.

65. Blumenson, *Patton Papers*, 2:176, 317, 521, 526, 614; Patton Diary, September 27, 1944; Paul D. Harkins, *When the Third Cracked Europe: The Story of Patton's Incredible Army* (Harrisburg, Pa.: Army Times Publishing, 1969), 16.

66. D. K. R. Crosswell, *Beetle: The Life of General Walter Bedell Smith* (Lexington: University Press of Kentucky, 2010), 772; Allan R. Millett, "The United States Armed Forces in the Second World War," in Millett and Murray, *Military Effectiveness*, 3:76.

67. W. K. Hancock and M. M. Gowing, *British War Economy* (London: HMSO, 1949), 336; MacDonald, *Last Offensive*, 5. The German and U.S. armies were not equal in combat power in December 1944. The 1941 German army was more comparable to the 1944 U.S. Army. John Desch, "The 1941 German Army/The 1944–45 U.S. Army: A Comparative Analysis of Two Forces in Their Primes," *Command Magazine* 18 (September/October 1992):554–63.

68. James J. Carafano, *After D-Day: Operation Cobra and the Normandy Breakout* (Boulder, Colo.: Lynne Rienner, 2000), 260–61.

3. Onslaught

1. Robert W. Coakley and Richard M. Leighton, *U.S. Army in World War II: Global Logistics and Strategy, 1943–1945* (Washington, D.C.: CMH, 1968), 813; Cole, *Ardennes*, 56; Alfred D. Chandler Jr., ed., *The Papers of Dwight David Eisenhower: The War Years* (Baltimore: Johns Hopkins University Press, 1970), 4:2417 (cited hereafter as *Eisenhower Papers*).

2. Eisenhower, *Crusade in Europe*, 341; Major General Kenneth Strong, *Intelligence at the Top: The Recollections of an Intelligence Officer* (London: Cassell, 1968),

211; SHAEF Weekly Intelligence Summary No. 36, November 26, 1944, SHAEF Selected Records, 1943–1945, accession 69–14, box 10, DDEL. Weekly Intelligence Summary No. 38 shows two SS PDs north and two south of Cologne.

3. Bennett, *Ultra in the West*, 172; Strong, *Intelligence at the Top*, 212; L. F. Ellis, *Victory in the West*, vol. 2, *The Defeat of Germany* (London: HMSO, 1968), 170–71; SHAEF Weekly Intelligence Summary No. 34, November 12, 1944, SHAEF Selected Records, 1943–1945, accession 69–14, box 10, DDEL. Strong did not address the probability of the Germans capturing American fuel in the summaries. He later said that they probably had enough fuel for immediate operations but would have needed to capture American dumps to go further. Strong, *Intelligence at the Top*, 212.

4. War Department, FM 100–5, *Field Service Regulations, Operations*, June 15, 1944, p. 26, USAHEC; War Department, FM 101–5, *Staff Officer's Field Manual: The Staff and Combat Orders*, August 19, 1940, appendix II, "Terrain Appreciation," USAHEC.

5. SHAEF Weekly Intelligence Summary No. 38, December 10, 1944, SHAEF Selected Records, 1943–1945, accession 69–14, box 10, DDEL; Pogue, *Supreme Command*, 364; Harry C. Butcher, *My Three Years with Eisenhower* (New York: Simon & Schuster, 1946), 714. This was the appreciation of the G-2 Division in the War Department as well. It fixated on the Germans' ability to withdraw their armored divisions into local reserves to commit them to sharp, brief encounters against American penetrations. Minutes, meeting of the General Council, December 4, 1944, p. 11, USAHEC. On December 6 a POW indicated that the SS divisions in reserve, supported by the *Luftwaffe*, would execute such a counterattack when the Americans crossed the Roer. SHAEF G-2 *Digest* #189, December 12, 1944, SHAEF Selected Records, accession 69–14, box 6, DDEL.

6. Pogue, *Supreme Command*, 36; Forrest C. Pogue, "The Ardennes Campaign: The Impact of Intelligence," remarks to the National Security Agency Communications Analysis Association, December 16, 1980, p. 31.

7. Bradley to Montgomery, December 3, 1944, Bradley Papers, USAHEC; Chandler, *Eisenhower Papers*, 4:2328–32; Stephen E. Ambrose, *The Supreme Commander: The War Years of General Dwight D. Eisenhower* (Garden City, N.Y.: Doubleday, 1970), 552. While traveling through the area on his way to meet Montgomery at Maastricht on December 7, Eisenhower observed that the relative weakness of American forces there might invite a "nasty little Kasserine." Even Marshall had questioned the weakness in the area during a trip to the front on October 11. MacDonald, *Battle of the Bulge*, 73; Forrest C. Pogue, *George C. Marshall: Organizer of Victory* (New York: Viking, 1973), 484.

8. However, Strong also stated that the wireless telegraph silence ordered for all SS formations did not necessarily indicate an imminent counteroffensive. RUBY/SH 173, December 13, 1944, in Hinsley, *British Intelligence*, 436; Strong, *Intelligence at the Top*, 212. SHAEF *Digest* #191 (December 14) makes no such observation. Eisenhower had no choice but to admit later that Strong had definitely highlighted the possibility of an attack through the Ardennes. Bedell Smith claimed that Eisenhower clearly understood that the German High Command "might attempt a desperate gamble," but such phraseology implies an all-out counteroffensive. Walter Bedell Smith, *Eisenhower's Six Great Decisions: Europe 1944–1945* (New York: Longmans,

Green, 1956), 91. In 1947 Bedell Smith declared, "We thought it would come in the Ardennes or near Strasbourg." Interview with Lieutenant General Walter Bedell Smith, May 8, 1947, Pogue Interviews, USAHEC.

9. Eisenhower, *Crusade in Europe*, 340.

10. On December 12 he was in London to explain his strategy to Churchill and the British Chiefs of Staff. Eisenhower talked of establishing a general reserve, but when the Chief of the Imperial General Staff Sir Alan F. Brooke pressed him on where he would, or could, locate it, General Sir Frank Simpson, director of military operations at the War Office, recalled that Eisenhower was "clearly not sure about that." Nigel Hamilton, *Monty: The Field Marshal, 1944–1976* (London: Hamish Hamilton, 1986), 172–73.

11. Eisenhower repeated this reasoning to Marshall on January 10, 1945. Chandler, *Eisenhower Papers*, 4:2341, 2417, 2445.

12. Twelfth Army Group Weekly Intelligence Summary No. 18, December 12, 1944, CARL; Pogue, *Supreme Command*, 369n29; Crosswell, *Beetle*, 798. Sibert's document was in fact tainted. He signed it, but Major Ralph Ingersoll, a journalist before the war and a terrain specialist in Twelfth Army Group's Plans Section, wrote sections of it, at Sibert's request, to impart a measure of success to Bradley's November offensives that was not actually perceivable on the ground. Ingersoll, an intense Anglophobe, put his journalistic spin on the report to "sell" Bradley's accomplishments during the fall. Gerald Astor, *A Blood-Dimmed Tide: The Battle of the Bulge by the Men Who Fought It* (New York: Donald I. Fine, 1992), 75–76; Pogue, "The Ardennes Campaign," 31. Ingersoll also worked on deception and served as a liaison officer.

13. Twelfth Army Group Weekly Intelligence Summary No. 18. Of the 361 missions flown by 67th Group, 242 were successful, despite ten totally nonoperational days between November 17 and December 16. Craven and Cate, *Army Air Forces in World War II*, 673–81.

14. Strong's map showed only five—the *18th, 26th, 36th, 326th,* and *352nd VGDs.* Sibert's map showed the *18th, 26th, 212th, 277th, 326th,* and *352nd VGDs.*

15. FM 100–5, June 1944, p. 62.

16. Twelfth Army Group G-2 Periodic Report No. 165, annex 2 and 3, November 17, 1944, RG 407, entry 427, 99/12–2.1 Dec 1944–Jan 1945 to 99/12–2.1 Mar 1945, NARA II; Milan Vego, "Clausewitz's Schwerpunkt: Mistranslated from German—Misunderstood in English," *Military Review* 87, no. 1 (January–February 2007): 103.

17. Bradley conceded that although the buildup he could physically account for opposite Middleton was much heavier than Rundstedt required for security there, "we were too much addicted to the anticipation of counterattack on the Roer to credit the enemy with more fanciful or ambitious intentions." Bradley, *Soldier's Story*, 441, 447–48, 455; SHAEF Weekly Intelligence Summary No. 38.

18. Karl Tholholte, "A German Reflects upon Artillery," *Field Artillery Journal* 35, no. 12 (December 1945): 714.

19. Albert Seaton has argued that the Germans never achieved the kinds of concentrations on the Eastern Front that the Allies achieved in the west. Albert Seaton, *The Russo-German War, 1941–1945* (New York: Praeger, 1970), 75, 82. The heaviest fire occurred in *Sixth Panzer Armee's* area. *Generalleutnant der Waffen-SS* Walter

Staudinger, *Sixth Panzer Armee's* artillery commander, indicated that thirty minutes of preparatory fire had been planned, but ammunition shortages created pauses. ETHINT 62 (Staudinger), "Sixth Pz Army Artillery in the Ardennes Offensive," August 11, 1945, pp. 1–2, RG 549.3, NARA II. The War Diary of Supreme Commander West indicated ten minutes at the most. It may be that *Sixth Panzer Armee's* artillery program lasted for a short duration and division artilleries continued the action at the tactical level.

20. Forty, *Reich's Last Gamble*, 104–5; Cirillo, *Ardennes–Alsace*, 17; Pogue, *Supreme Command*, 372–73. V Corps sent its first message to First Army at 1244 and received information from the 99th Infantry Division at 1350.

21. On December 13 Gerow launched a two-pronged assault—the 78th Infantry Division in the north, and the 2nd Infantry Division, assisted by a regiment of the 99th Infantry Division, in the south. By December 16 the 78th Infantry Division had suffered almost 1,000 casualties. In the south the 2nd Infantry Division had managed to advance to Wahlerscheid.

22. Numerous U.S. Army records use Regimental Combat Team (RCT), but I use the correct doctrinal term, CT, throughout unless RCT is specifically stated. A CT usually included a direct support (D/S) artillery battalion. If a regiment was cross-attached, it would not bring its artillery along.

23. Cole, *Ardennes*, 89. The 3rd Battalion, 395th Infantry, was supported by the 196th FA Battalion, 62nd Armored FA Battalion, and 893rd Tank Destroyer Battalion.

24. MS #B-447.

25. DEFE 3/318, HP 9612 (ZZZ), December 16, 1944, reel 54, microfiche collection, Massey Library, RMCC.

26. 4th Infantry Division AAR, RG 407, entry 427, 304–0.3, NARA II; MS #A-930 (Sensfuss), "212th Volksgrenadier Division (Ardennes)," April 10, 1946, p. 4, RG 549.3, NARA II. Brandenberger indicated the division had only five assault guns in MS #B-447. Cole indicated four in *Ardennes*, 240.

27. 9th Armored Division AAR, December 1944, RG 407, entry 427, 609–33.4, NARA II.

28. Cole, *Ardennes*, 216.

29. *I SS Panzerkorps* committed two engineering companies from the *1st SS PD* to clear the minefield.

30. 106th Infantry Division AAR, December 1944, RG 407, entry 427, 3106–0.3, NARA II.

31. Russell F. Weigley, *Eisenhower's Lieutenants: The Campaigns of France and Germany, 1944–1945* (Bloomington: Indiana University Press, 1981), 450.

32. William Richardson and Seymour Freidin, eds., *The Fatal Decisions* (London: Michael Joseph, 1956), 235. As *Generalmajor* Richard Metz, *Fifth Panzer Armee's* senior artilleryman, declared, Manteuffel decided on a silent infiltration under darkness "without artillery preparation, but with all artillery and smoke shell mortars ready to fire . . . the opening fire to occur only after an order from the front line." MS #B-393, p.14. Metz stated that the only artillery fire allowed prior to 0600 was "against firing, already known enemy batteries." The 28th Infantry Division AAR suggests that heavy artillery concentrations did not begin falling along its front until after 0700. Manteuffel strongly opposed Hitler's initial plan to unleash the artillery at

0730, three and a half hours before the actual ground assault started, stating that it would only "wake the Americans" and give them time to respond. Liddell Hart, *Other Side of the Hill*, 291.

33. MS #A-873 (Waldenburg), "Commitment of the 116th Panzer Division in the Ardennes 1944–1945," December 16, 1945, RG 549.3, NARA II; J. E. Kaufmann and R. M. Jurga, *Fortress Europe: European Fortifications of World War II* (Conshohocken, Pa.: Combined Books, 1999), 74–75; Charles B. MacDonald, *U.S. Army in World War II: The Siegfried Line Campaign* (Washington, D.C.: CMH, 1990), 31, 34 (cited hereafter as *Siegfried Line*); Guderian, *From Normandy to the Ruhr*, 305; Cole, *Ardennes*, 153.

34. *Panzer Lehr* engineers had no dozers. They had to construct two bridges just north of Gemünd to get across the Our. Just north of Gemünd, an additional water obstacle ran northeast from the Our. *Lehr* had to bridge this one first before bridging the Our. Ritgen, *Western Front*, 262; MS #A-873, p. 5.

35. Ralf Tiemann, *The Leibstandarte IV/2* (Winnipeg: J. J. Fedorowicz, 1998), 33–34; ETHINT 10 (Peiper), "1 SS Pz Regt (11–24 Dec 44)," September 7, 1945, p. 14, RG 549.3, NARA II; James Lucas, *Kommando: German Special Forces of World War II* (Toronto: Stoddart, 1985), 131; DEFE 3/318, HP 9588 (ZZZZZ), December 16, 1944, reel 54, RMCC. According to one historian, the delay imposed at Losheimergraben may have been decisive. Stephen M. Rusiecki, *The Key to the Bulge: The Battle for Losheimergraben* (Westport, Conn.: Praeger, 1996).

36. 106th Infantry Division AAR, December 1944, p. 2; Frank J. Price, *Troy H. Middleton: A Biography* (Baton Rouge: Louisiana State University Press, 1974), 216; Cole, *Ardennes*, 161.

37. David W. Hogan Jr., *A Command Post at War: First Army Headquarters in Europe, 1944–1945* (Washington, D.C.: CMH, 2000), 209; William Sylvan Diary, December 16, 1944, USAHEC. The signal for the formations to go on alert was sent apparently at or shortly after 1100. Charles B. MacDonald stated that Gerow did not call until the early afternoon. MacDonald, *Battle of the Bulge*, 180, 181; Mansoor, *G.I. Offensive in Europe*, 223.

38. Chandler, *Eisenhower Papers*, 4:2173.

39. Although Strong suggested the meeting commenced at 1400, other authors place it in the early evening. Strong, *Intelligence at the Top*, 156.

40. Bradley, *Soldier's Story*, 449; Strong, *Intelligence at the Top*, 212; John T. Greenwood, ed., *Normandy to Victory: The War Diary of General Courtney H. Hodges and the First U.S. Army* (Lexington: University Press of Kentucky, 2008), 213. The calculation of seven hours is derived from Strong's admittance, Sylvan's statement, and the probable timing of the meeting with Eisenhower and Bradley in the late afternoon. First Army would have reported to Twelfth Army Group headquarters, which in turn would have reported to SHAEF.

41. Carlo D'Este, *Eisenhower: A Soldier's Life* (New York: Henry Holt, 2002), 640.

42. Major General Troy H. Middleton, commander of VIII Corps, later stated that as early as 1000 he had received word that elements of sixteen different divisions had been identified. His biographer stated that Middleton "communicated his understanding of this fact to Bradley early in the day." Price, *Middleton*, 215. However, it seems highly unlikely that such a clear operational picture could have emerged at

corps headquarters so early, given that communication to subordinate units was so poor. Royce L. Thompson, *American Intelligence on the German Counteroffensive, 1 November–15 December 1944* (Washington, D.C.: CMH, 1949), pt. 2, p. 240.

43. Eisenhower, *Crusade in Europe*, 342; Chester Hansen Diary, December 16, 1944. The standard version is that Bedell Smith told Bradley, "You've been wishing for a counterattack. Now it looks as though you've got it." D. K. R. Crosswell, *The Chief of Staff: The Military Career of General Walter Bedell Smith* (Westport, Conn.: Greenwood Press, 1991), 282.

44. Eisenhower, *Crusade in Europe*, 342; Chandler, *Eisenhower Papers*, 4:2373. Stephen E. Ambrose's declaration that Eisenhower was as "surprised as everyone else" does not hold up under scrutiny. Ambrose, *Supreme Commander*, 553. Charles B. MacDonald suggested that Eisenhower received a September 4 MAGIC intercept in which Hitler told Baron Hiroshi Oshima at the *Wolfschanze* that he was planning a large-scale offensive in the west after the beginning of November. Oshima reported this to Tokyo, where MAGIC intercepted it and sent it to Washington. MacDonald, *Battle of the Bulge*, 25, 186.

45. Condell and Zabecki, *On the German Art of War*, 89.

46. ETHINT 50, pp. 7–8; Charles B. MacDonald, "The Neglected Ardennes," *Military Review* 43, no. 4 (April 1963): 90; Cole, *Ardennes*, 270–71. The operation was Model's idea, but he wanted to use the *Fallschirmjäger* much closer to the line of departure in the Krinkelt area. See Steven H. Newton, *Hitler's Commander: Field Marshal Walter Model, Hitler's Favorite General* (New York: Da Capo Books, 2006), 334.

47. Quoted in Parker, *Battle of the Bulge*, 83.

48. ETHINT 54 (Gersdorff), "Seventh Army in the Ardennes Offensive," November 26, 1945, p. 2; Richardson and Freidin, *Fatal Decisions*, 231. For a breakdown of the engagement between the *212th VGD* and the 4th Infantry Division, see Trevor N. Dupuy, *Numbers, Predictions and War: Using History to Evaluate Combat Factors and Predict the Outcome of Battles* (Indianapolis: Bobbs-Merrill, 1979), 66.

49. Alistair Horne, *To Lose a Battle: France 1940* (London: Macmillan, 1969), 180–84, 197–98; Robert A. Doughty, *The Breaking Point: Sedan and the Fall of France, 1940* (New York: Archon Books, 1990), 65.

4. Enter Patton

1. Cole, *Lorraine*, 24–25; Third Army AAR, vol. 2, Staff Section Reports, G-4, 6–7, Digital Archives, CARL; Ruppenthal, *Logistical Support*, 193; Ambrose, *Supreme Commander*, 508–9; Pogue, *Supreme Command*, 253.

2. Major Bradford J. Swedo, *XIX Tactical Air Command and ULTRA: Patton's Force Enhancers in the 1944 Campaign in France*, Cadre Paper No. 10 (Maxwell Air Force Base, Ala.: Air University Press, 2001), 106; Air Commodore Peter Dye, "To What Extent Were Logistics Shortages Responsible for Patton's Culmination on the Meuse in 1944?" *Air Force Journal of Logistics* 23, no. 2 (summer 1999): 30–32.

3. MacDonald, *Siegfried Line*, 10; Ruppenthal, *Logistical Support*, 8–10; Anthony Kemp, *The Unknown Battle: Metz 1944* (London: Frederick Warne, 1981), 228. Major General James M. Gavin did not favor Eisenhower's broad-front strategy and thought it "overwhelmingly clear" that Patton should have been given all

the resources he needed in early September to drive a deep wedge into Germany. Air Marshal Sir Arthur Tedder believed that if all the MARKET GARDEN fuel had been given to "poor Georgie Patton," Third Army could have advanced to the Rhine. James M. Gavin, *On to Berlin: Battles of an Airborne Commander, 1943–1946* (New York: Viking Press, 1978), 202–3; interview with Lord Tedder, February 13, 1947, Pogue Interviews, USAHEC. Air Marshal Sir Arthur Coningham also thought that Patton, not Montgomery, should have been Eisenhower's main effort. Interview with Air Marshal Sir Arthur Coningham, February 14, 1947; interview with Group Captain T. P. Gleave, January 9, 1947, USAHEC. B. H. Liddell Hart also thought that Patton could have penetrated deep into Germany, but a discussion of the logistical factors is lacking. B. H. Liddell Hart, *History of the Second World War* (New York: Putnam, 1970), 567. For a discussion of why Patton could not have reached the Rhine, see Dennis Showalter, "The Southern Option: The Path to Victory in 1944?" *Military Chronicles* 1, no. 1 (May–June 2005): 59.

4. Patton, *War as I Knew It*, 174; David N. Spires, *Patton's Air Force: Forging a Legendary Air-Ground Team* (Washington, D.C.: Smithsonian Institution Press, 2002), 174.

5. Blumenson, *Patton Papers*, 2:589.

6. Quoted in Eisenhower, *Bitter Woods*, 215. Strong's account gives a conflicting impression of Bradley. On the one hand, Bradley's skepticism is clearly evident, but on the other hand, Strong stated that Bradley reacted quickly, had a plan to use the two armored divisions, and "asked to be excused while he telephoned instructions for their use." Strong, *Intelligence at the Top*, 216.

7. Patton Diary, December 16, 1944; DEFE 3/318, HP 9559, 1618Z, December 16, 1944 (ZZ), reel 54. Proof that Third Army received the message lies in the addressee list at the top of the ULTRA message. ZE was the code for Third Army. All further references to Third Army and ULTRA are based on the ZE code being present on the messages cited. The artillery fire was referenced in Third Army G-2 Intelligence Summary (ISUM) No. 410 2400A, December 15, 1944, RG 407, entry 427, NARA II. ISUMs were factual reports sent by coded telegraph at least twice a day to higher and lateral headquarters. They did not contain analyses of information.

8. Research and Evaluation Division, Armored School, "The Defense of St. Vith, Belgium 17–23 December 1944: An Historical Example of Armor in the Defense," John Toland Papers, box 38, LC; MacDonald, *Siegfried Line*, 566; George S. Patton Jr., "Notes on Bastogne Operation," January 16, 1945, RG 407, entry 427, 103–0.5, NARA II; CCA/10th Armored Division AAR, December 1944, p. 4, RG 407, entry 427, 610-CCA-2, NARA II. The 10th Armored Division was withdrawn from the line on December 6.

9. Patton Diary, December 16, 1944; Blumenson, *Patton Papers*, 2:595; Bradley, *Soldier's Story*, 465.

10. Blumenson, *Patton Papers*, 2:573.

11. Jerry D. Morelock, *Generals of the Ardennes: American Leadership in the Battle of the Bulge* (Washington, D.C.: GPO, 1994), 71.

12. Bradley, *Soldier's Story*, 464; Lord Tedder, *With Prejudice: The War Memoirs of Marshal of the Royal Air Force Lord Tedder* (London: Cassell, 1966), 625. For a

full discussion of this subject, see John Nelson Rickard, "Eisenhower, Bradley and the Calculated Risk in the Ardennes, December 1944," *Global War Studies* 8, no. 1 (2011).

13. CCA and CCB AAR, 10th Armored Division, December, 1944, RG 407, entry 427, 610-CCB-0.3, NARA II. Major General Robert W. Hasbrouck's 7th Armored Division was alerted to move south at 1730. Research and Evaluation Division, Armored School, "Defense of St. Vith."

14. Lieutenant Colonel Dean A. Nowowiejski, "Concepts of Information Warfare in Practice: General George S. Patton and the Third Army Information Service, August–December, 1944" (SAMS, USACGSC, 1995), 18.

15. Oscar W. Koch, G-2: *Intelligence for Patton* (Philadelphia: Whitmore, 1971), 165; Brigadier General Robert W. Williams, "Patton Knew the Secret, Moving Information: The Third Imperative," *Army* 25, no. 4 (April 1975): 18. He dedicated significant assets to the 6th Cavalry Group until December 1, when the group was assigned combat duty in Lorraine. As a corps commander in Tunisia, Patton did not like the fact that Phantom could bypass him, report to higher headquarters, and possibly prompt directives from higher headquarters to him based on information he was not aware of. Koch, *Intelligence for Patton*, 16.

16. Major Kevin Dougherty, "Our MI Heritage, Oscar Koch: An Unsung Hero behind Patton's Victories," *Military Intelligence Professional Bulletin* 28, no. 1 (April–June 2002): 66. For flattering assessments of Koch's effectiveness, see Weigley, *Eisenhower's Lieutenants*, 390; John M. Vermillion, "The Pillars of Generalship," *Parameters* 17, no. 2 (summer 1987): 8; H. Essame, *Patton: A Study in Command* (New York: Charles Scribner's Sons, 1974), 122.

17. Helfers received ULTRA directly from Hut 3 at the Government Code and Cypher School, Bletchley Park, four times a day, and he signed for each message. SRH-006, "Synthesis of Experiences in the Use of Ultra Intelligence by U.S. Army Field Commands in the European Theatre of Operations," Studies in Cryptology, NSA, pp. 12–13, RG 457 (Records of the National Security Agency), NARA II. Paul Harkins called him "Captain John J. Helfers of the super-secret 'Black Market' or SIS, Signal Intelligence Service." Harkins, *When the Third Cracked Europe*, 39.

18. Swedo, *XIX Tactical Air Command*, 15, 19; SRH-108 (Major Warrack Wallace), "Report on Assignment with Third United States Army, August 15–September 18, 1944." Helfers concurred in "My Personal Experience with High Level Intelligence," p. 10. Both the Wallace and Helfers documents are in the Melvin C. Helfers Papers, A1974.5, box 1, folder 1, Citadel Archives and Museum, Charleston, S.C. Harold C. Deutsch, "Commanding Generals and the Uses of Intelligence," *Intelligence and National Security* 3, no. 3 (1988): 230. Those officers in Third Army who were ULTRA recipients and had been indoctrinated in its use included Gay; Harkins; Colonel Halley G. Maddox, the G-3; Colonel Harold M. Forde, G-2 executive officer; Colonel Robert S. Allen, assistant G-2; Major Charles W. Flint, Third Army's signals security officer; Weyland; his chief of staff, Colonel Roger Browne; and Major Harry M. Grove, the ULTRA representative at XIX TAC. Captain George C. Church, memorandum for Colonel Taylor: Ultra and the Third Army, May 28, 1945, p. 1, in SRH-023–026, "Reports by U.S. Army Ultra Representatives with

Army Field Commands in the European Theater of Operations," RG 457, NARA II. See also Harry M. Grove, "ULTRA and Its Use by XIX Tactical Air Command," May 30, 1945, in SRH-023, ibid., pt. 2. Thomas R. Waring, "Officer Spreads Word about World War II–Winning Secret," *News & Courier/ Saturday Evening Post*, October 2, 1983.

19. Koch, *Intelligence for Patton*, 54; Fred Ayer Jr., *Before the Colors Fade: Portrait of a Soldier: George S. Patton, Jr.* (Boston: Houghton Mifflin, 1964), 164.

20. Koch, *Intelligence for Patton*, 81, 84; Hinsley, *British Intelligence*, 423; Craven and Cate, *Army Air Forces in World War II*, 675, 678.

21. First Army was not pleased to discover the existence of the OSS detachment. Anthony Cave Brown, ed., *The Secret War Report of the OSS* (New York: Berkely, 1976), 516; "A Study of Operations of G-2 (Intelligence Branch) in the 12th Army Group," July 1, 1945, p. 36; Lyman B. Kirkpatrick, "Combat Intelligence: A Comparative Evaluation," *Studies in Intelligence* 5, no. 4 (fall 1960): 49.

22. SRH-006, pp. 12–13.

23. Harold R. Winton could not ascertain the reason why Koch modeled the German activity in the Eifel differently from Dickson, but he concluded that VIII Corps and First Army made "a subtle but inaccurate inferential leap" in concluding that the Germans were mimicking the American practice of resting tired divisions there. Winton, *Corps Commanders of the Bulge*, 82.

24. Swedo, *XIX Tactical Air Command*, 18; Captain George C. Church, SRH-108, "Reports by US Army ULTRA Representatives in the European Theater of Operations," May 21, 1945, p. 4, RG 457, NARA II. Church joined Third Army in March 1945.

25. Raymond H. Burros, "U.S. Corps-Level Intelligence in World War II: A Quantitative Study of Identification, Strength, and Location," December 15, 1959, p. 3, Combat Operations Research Group, CORG-R-81, USAHEC.

26. Koch, *Intelligence for Patton*, 85–87.

27. Quoted in Robert S. Allen, *Lucky Forward: The History of Patton's Third U.S. Army* (New York: Vanguard Press, 1947), 213. Koch's recollection of Periodic Report No. 165 was slightly different from Allen's. Koch stated the German divisions constituted a strategic reserve "for either piecemeal or coordinated counteroffensive employment." Koch, *Intelligence for Patton*, 82. Koch's estimates about German intentions in the Ardennes were more accurate than those of other G-2s at the army or army group level. Deutsch, "Commanding Generals and the Uses of Intelligence," 249; Michael E. Bigelow, "Big Business: Intelligence in Patton's Third Army," *Military Intelligence* 18, no. 2 (April–June 1992): 35.

28. Blumenson, *Patton Papers*, 2:582; Greenwood, *Normandy to Victory*, 192.

29. Craven and Cate, *Army Air Forces in World War II*, 675, 678, 680; Spires, *Patton's Air Force*, 189; SRH-042, Signal Intelligence Service, Headquarters Third U.S. Army, "Third Army Radio Intelligence History in Campaign in Western Europe," p. A-5, RG 407, NARA II.

30. DEFE 3/314, HP 8707 (ZZZ), 1201Z, December 6, 1944, reel 51, RMCC.

31. Koch, *Intelligence for Patton*, 85–88; Allen, *Lucky Forward*, 167, 214. MacDonald stated that Koch expressed this in Third Army G-2 Periodic Report Nos. 186, 188, December 13–14, 1944. MacDonald, *Battle of the Bulge*, 69.

32. Koch, *Intelligence for Patton*, 87; FM 101–5, p. 8. Patton apparently anticipated some type of contingency operation on December 12, declaring, "I decided
definitely to place the 6th Armored and the 26th Division in the III Corps near Saarbruecken, because if the enemy attacked the VIII Corps of the First Army, as was
probable, I could use the III Corps to help by attacking straight north, west of the
Moselle River." Patton, *War as I Knew It*, 177.

33. Charles R. Codman, *Drive* (Boston: Little, Brown, 1957), 229; Harkins, *When
the Third Cracked Europe*, 39. Brenton G. Wallace stated that they first heard about
the attack on December 16 when a Third Army liaison officer at First Army reported
it, but he gave no time. Brenton G. Wallace, *Patton and His Third Army* (Harrisburg,
Pa.: Military Service Publishing, 1946), 142.

34. Codman, *Drive*, 229; Colonel Robert S. Allen Journal, December 16, 1944,
Robert S. Allen Collection, box 1, General George Patton Museum Archives, Fort
Knox, Ky.; Third Army G-2 ISUM No. 411, 0900A, December 16, 1944, NARA II.
ISUM No. 412 was not released until 1800 hours. Moreover, there is little evidence
of such radio intercepts by non-ULTRA sources. SRH-042, p. 43.

35. Patton, *War as I Knew It*, 179. Stanley P. Hirshson suggested that Patton heard
of the attack "innocently enough" when Bradley called. Stanley P. Hirshson, *General
Patton: A Soldier's Life* (New York: HarperCollins, 2002), 570. Blumenson made the
same mistake; see *Patton Papers*, 2:595.

36. Third Army G-2 ISUM No. 412, 1800A, December 16, 1944, NARA II.

37. Craven and Cate, *Army Air Forces in World War II*, 676.

38. Wilson A. Heefner, *Patton's Bulldog: The Life and Service of General Walton H. Walker* (Shippensburg, Pa.: White Mane Books, 2001), 109; Third Army G-2
ISUM No. 413, 2400A, December 16, 1944, RG 407, entry 427, 208-7.2 Dec 44
to 208-7.2 Jan 45, NARA II; Allen Journal, December 16, 1944. Patton could have
phoned Middleton directly, but since VIII Corps still belonged to Hodges at this
time, protocol probably made it easier for Walker to contact his neighbor than for
Patton to bypass an army peer.

39. Blumenson, *Patton Papers*, 2:596.

40. 4th Armored Division AAR, December 1944, RG 407, entry 427, 604–33.4,
NARA II; Albin F. Irzyk, *He Rode up Front for Patton* (Raleigh, N.C.: Pentland Press,
1996), 234–35; Patton Diary, December 17, 1944; Patton, *War as I Knew It*, 180. The
G-3 SITREP No. 554 (172400A–180600A, RG 407, entry 427, NARA II) indicated
that 4th Armored "continued advance in Eastern portion of corps zone." Eddy did
note in his diary that Patton phoned and ordered him to "go right ahead with present
plans and to be expecting a German attack on our front in the near future." Manton
S. Eddy War Log, December 17, 1944, U.S. Army Infantry School, National Infantry
Museum, Fort Benning, Ga.

41. Blumenson, *Patton Papers*, 2:595; Third Army G-2 ISUM No. 415, 1800A,
December 17, 1944; Patton Diary, December 17, 1944; Third Army G-2 Work Map,
Situation as of 0300, December 17, 1944.

42. DEFE, HP 9631 (ZZZZ), 0755Z, and HP 9642 (ZZZZ), 1351Z, December 17, 1944, reel 54; Major General Otto P. Weyland, "Diary, July 29, 44–May 18,
45," December 17, 1944, Weyland Papers, USAFHRA; Allen Journal, December 17,
1944.

43. Heefner, *Patton's Bulldog*, 109; Patton, *War as I Knew It*, 180. This might reflect some rewriting of the Patton diary by his wife Beatrice or by Harkins to make him look a bit more prescient. Other sources that state Patton met with Millikin on December 17 include Martin Blumenson, *Patton: The Man behind the Legend, 1885–1945* (New York: William Morrow, 1985), 256, and Winton, *Corps Commanders of the Bulge*, 188.

44. III Corps AAR, December 1944, p. 6, RG 407, entry 427, 303–0.3, NARA II.

45. MacDonald, *Battle of the Bulge*, 261; Colonel Charles W. Parker Jr. and Colonel William J. Thompson, *Conqueror: The Story of Ninth Army, 1944–1945* (Nashville: Battery Press, 1980), 117. Simpson would later offer the 2nd Armored Division without permission from Bradley.

46. Greenwood, *Normandy to Victory*, 215; Hogan, *Command Post at War*, 212; English, *Patton's Peers*, 121–22.

47. D. K. R. Crosswell, *The Chief of Staff: The Military Career of General Walter Bedell Smith* (Westport, Conn.: Greenwood, 1991), 282; Chester Hansen Diary, December 17, 1944; Bradley, *Soldier's Story*, 466.

48. Bennett, *Ultra in the West*, 194. MacDonald argued that Eisenhower and Bradley "could hardly have been unaware that that meant the Fifth and Sixth Panzer Armies." MacDonald, *Battle of the Bulge*, 186.

49. Hansen Diary, December 17, 1944.

50. Greenwood, *Normandy to Victory*, 218.

51. Hobart R. Gay Diary, December 18, 1944, Special Collections, U.S. Military Academy Library, West Point, N.Y.

52. Hansen Diary, December 18, 1944; DEFE 3/318, HP 9723 (ZZZZZ), 0819Z, December 18, 1944; DEFE 3/318, HP 9714 (ZZZZZ), 0451Z, December 18, 1944; DEFE 3/318, HP 9707 (ZZZZZ), 0126Z, December 18, 1944; DEFE 3/318, HP 9709 (ZZZZ), 0328Z, December 18, 1944, reel 53.

53. DEFE 3/318, HP 9714 (ZZZZZ), 0451Z, HP 9723 (ZZZZZ), 0819Z, and HP 9778, 2337Z, December 18, 1944.

54. DEFE 3/318, HP 9703 (ZZ), 0030Z, and HP 9720 (ZZZZ), 0727Z, December 18, 1944.

55. DEFE 3/318, HP 9721 (ZZZZZ), 0739Z, December 18, 1944; Third Army G-2 ISUM No. 417, 0900A, December 18, 1944. The report of the paratroop drop between 2000 and 2200 the previous day comes from Joseph C. Fitzharris, ed., *Patton's Fighting Bridge Builders: Company C, 1303rd Engineer General Service Regiment* (College Station: Texas A&M University Press, 2007), 78. See also Wallace, *Patton and His Third Army*, 143.

56. Bradley, *Soldier's Story*, 469; Blumenson, *Patton Papers*, 2:596.

57. CCA/10th Armored Division AAR, December 1944, RG 407, entry 427, 610-CCA-0.3, NARA II.

58. VIII Corps AAR, December 1944, p. 12, RG 407, Entry 427, 208-0.3, NARA II.

59. Chandler, *Eisenhower Papers*, 4:2178. Morelock argues that Patton, not Bradley, suggested the ninety-degree turn of Third Army into the Bulge. Morelock, *Generals of the Ardennes*, 124.

60. Patton, "Notes on Bastogne Operation"; Blumenson, *Patton Papers*, 2:597. A short time later on December 18 Maddox called Gay to confirm that Gay

understood what Patton wanted. Then Bradley called Gay, asking if a CC from Gaffey's division could move that night. Gay said yes. Bradley then asked Patton to call at 2000. Right after this Gay issued a warning order to Gaffey. Gay Diary, December 18, 1944.

61. Bradley, *Soldier's Story*, 469. Chester Hansen recorded this exact phrase by Bradley, but for the Verdun meeting on the nineteenth, not the eighteenth. Hansen Diary, December 19, 1944.

62. Hamilton, *Monty*, 189.

63. Hansen Diary, December 18, 1944.

64. Blumenson, *Patton Papers*, 2:597; Gay Diary, December 18, 1944. The actual time of this conversation is in question. Patton noted at the time that it was 2000. Patton, "Notes on Bastogne Operation." However, 2300 has also been cited. Blumenson, *Patton Papers*, 2:597; Patton, *War as I Knew It*, 180.

65. Quoted in Hamilton, *Monty*, 193; Hansen Diary, December 18, 1944.

66. Blumenson, *Patton Papers*, 2:597–98.

5. The Verdun Conference

1. Eddy War Log, December 19, 1944; Patton, "Notes on Bastogne Operation." Blumenson stated that Patton met with Eddy and Millikin around 0700 hours, but Eddy's diary suggests that he first saw Patton at the 0800 meeting. Blumenson, *Patton Papers*, 2:598.

2. Wallace, *Patton and His Third Army*, 148–49; George Dyer, *XII Corps: Spearhead of Patton's Third Army* (Baton Rouge: Military Press of Louisiana, 1947), 284.

3. VIII Corps AAR, December 1944, p. 15; Eddy War Log, December 19, 1944. Patton, however, apparently told Eddy to place a combat command of Gaffey's division in a central reserve location in the rear to strike in any direction. Wallace, *Patton and His Third Army*, 149–50.

4. SHAEF G-2 Weekly Intelligence Summary No. 40, p. 994, SHAEF Selected Records, 1943–1945, accession 69–14, box 10, DDEL.

5. Third Army G-2, Preliminary Study of the Terrain, December 19, 1944, Koch Papers, USAHEC; emphasis added.

6. DEFE 3/318, HP 9670 (ZZZ), 2008Z, December 17, 1944, reel 53. A POW stated that the *21st PD* CP was at Wissembourg. Third Army G-2 ISUM No. 409, 1800A, December 15, 1944.

7. See the order of battle map accompanying G-2 Periodic Report No. 190, December 18, 1944, in Third Army AAR, vol. 2, Staff Section Reports, G-2 Section, pp. 120–21, USAHEC; Cole, *Lorraine*, 607.

8. XX Corps, "The Capture of the Saar–Moselle Triangle and Trier 15 December 1944–12 March 1945: An Operational Report," RG 407, entry 427, 220–0.3.0 to 220–0.23, NARA II.

9. DEFE 3/318, HP 9633 (ZZ), 0854Z, December 17, 1944.

10. DEFE 3/318, HP 9719 (ZZZZ), 0714Z, December 18, 1944; DEFE 3/318, HP 9706 (ZZZZZ), 0302Z, December 18, 1944; DEFE 3/319, HP 9801 (ZZZ), 0614Z, December 19, 1944; DEFE 3/318, HP 9720 0727Z, December 18, 1944.

11. DEFE 3/318, HP 9626 (ZZZ), 0445Z, December 17; DEFE 3/318, HP 9734

(ZZ), 1121Z, December 18; DEFE 3/318, HP 9656 (ZZZZ), 1557Z, December 17; DEFE 3/319, HP 9795 (ZZZZ), 0441Z, December 19, 1944.

12. Patton Diary, December 19, 1944; Harkins, *When the Third Cracked Europe*, 42. The code names for the other routes are not known.

13. Patton, *War as I Knew It*, 181.

14. Dupuy, *Hitler's Last Gamble*, 12–13.

15. Allen Journal, December 19, 1944.

16. Hamilton, *Monty*, 200; Strong, *Intelligence at the Top*, 219, 221; Major General Sir Francis de Guingand, *Operation Victory* (London: Hodder & Stoughton, 1947), 425–27. Guingand makes no mention of the Verdun meeting in this work or in his subsequent *Generals at War* (London: Hodder & Stoughton, 1964).

17. Eisenhower, *Crusade in Europe*, 351.

18. Montgomery Diary, December 17–19, 1944, Papers of Field Marshal Montgomery of Alamein, Imperial War Museum, London.

19. Stephen E. Ambrose, "A Fateful Friendship," *American Heritage* 20, no. 3 (April 1969): 97; Chandler, *Eisenhower Papers*, 1:400. Eisenhower told Harry Butcher that "Patton, I think comes closest to meeting every requirement made on a commander." But Eisenhower's judgment looked awful when one considers that he also told Butcher, "Just after him [Patton] I would, at present rate Fredendall." Eisenhower soon had to relieve Fredendall for virtually every leadership shortcoming possible in Tunisia.

20. Chandler, *Eisenhower Papers*, 2:938–39, 1353, 1387–88. General A. G. L. McNaughton, commander of the First Canadian Army, recalled that Eisenhower "spoke particularly of the landings behind the enemy and of the 'end runs' round the right flank; also of his satisfaction that the U.S. Army had been the first into Messina." McNaughton, memorandum of conversation with General Eisenhower at AFHQ, August 31, 1943, McNaughton Papers, MG30 E133, vol. 250, PA 1-3-14-2, War Diary, Appendix G, LAC.

21. Chandler, *Eisenhower Papers*, 2:939, 1349–41. Eisenhower told Patton, "No letter that I have been called upon to write in my military career has caused me the mental anguish of this one, not only because of my long and deep personal friendship for you but because of my admiration for your military qualities; but I assure you that conduct such as described in the accompanying report will *not* be tolerated in this theater no matter who the offender may be." For the best account of the slapping episodes, see Carlo D'Este, *Bitter Victory: The Battle for Sicily, 1943* (New York: E. P. Dutton, 1988), 484–86.

22. Chandler, *Eisenhower Papers*, 2:1353, 3:1594; quoted in Ambrose, *Supreme Commander*, 229; Stimson and Bundy, *On Active Service*, 274.

23. Eisenhower to Marshall, August 27, 1943; Eisenhower to Marshall, September 6, 1943; Eisenhower to Walter Campbell Sweeney, December 28, 1943, in Chandler, *Eisenhower Papers*, 2:1388, 1357, 3:1630. Eisenhower wanted to use Patton like Hitler used Model—as a rover to be thrown into bad situations. During the debacle at Anzio, Eisenhower told Marshall, "If the troops in that beachhead need a lift and no one else is available Patton is the man that can give it to them." Chandler, *Eisenhower Papers*, 3:1731. Eisenhower offered Patton to Alexander for a month, but Mark Clark apparently did not want Patton in Italy. Admiral Sir John Cunningham, commander of the combined Allied fleet, lamented, "It's a thousand pities we did not

let Patton do the job." Carlo D'Este, *Fatal Decision: Anzio and the Battle for Rome, 1943* (New York: HarperCollins, 1991), 268.

24. Chandler, *Eisenhower Papers*, 3:1439, 1473, 1572, 1606. He informed Patton on September 30, 1943, "I told him [Marshall] that you were the best assault man we had. Will let you know if I hear anything about it." Eisenhower also considered Patton to be the best man to plan ANVIL. His "reputation as an assault commander, which is respected by the enemy, would serve to increase the value of the threat." Eisenhower thought Patton should stay in the Mediterranean and Hodges should command Third Army. SHAEF Diary, book X, pp. A991–2, Cables Eisenhower, United States Army in World War II, The European Theater of Operations, The Supreme Command, 2–3.7 CB 8, CMH.

25. Charles B. Odom, *General George S. Patton and Eisenhower* (New Orleans: Word Picture Productions, 1985), 5, 17; Blumenson, *Patton Papers*, 2:480.

26. Strong, *Intelligence at the Top*, 161; Eisenhower, *Crusade in Europe*, 350; Chandler, *Eisenhower Papers*, 4:2177.

27. DEFE 3/319, HP 9790 (ZZZZZ), 0257Z, December 19, 1944; Bennett, *Ultra in the West*, 210.

28. Chester Hansen Diary, December 17, 1944; General Omar N. Bradley and Air Effects Committee, 12th Army Group, "Effect of Air Power on Military Operations: Western Europe," July 1945, p. 155, USAFHRA.

29. SRH-049, "Technical Signal Intelligence Transmitted Directly to G-2, 12th Army Group, European Theater of Operations from August 14, 1944 to May 1945," n.d.; SRH-006, p. 19. Signal Security Detachment D provided analytical support to the signal radio intelligence companies at the army group and field army levels. John Patrick Finnegan, *Military Intelligence* (Washington, D.C.: CMH, 1998), 90.

30. Bradley, *Soldier's Story*, 455; SHAEF G-2 Weekly Intelligence Summary No. 39, December 17, 1944, SHAEF Selected Records, 1943–1945, accession 69–14, box 10, DDEL; Twelfth Army Group G-2 Weekly Intelligence Summary No. 18, December 9, 1944, p. 2, RG 407, entry 427, NARA II. MI 14 agreed that relieving pressure was an objective of the attack, but against the Ruhr, not the Saar. Hinsley, *British Intelligence*, 440. SHAEF Weekly Intelligence Summary No. 40, pp. 989–90, for December 24 highlighted the importance of this region.

31. Third Army AAR, vol. 2, G-2 Annexes, p. 121; Eisenhower's confirmatory direction to commanders on December 20 is in Chandler, *Eisenhower Papers*, 4:2364; DEFE 3/319, HP 9791 and HP 9801 (ZZZ), 0614Z, December 19, 1944.

32. Eisenhower, *Crusade in Europe*, 350. XXX Corps consisted of Guards Armored Division; the 43rd, 51st Highland, and 53rd Divisions; and three independent armored brigades. The corps assembled in the Louvain–St. Trond–Gembloux area. Hamilton, *Monty*, 196–98.

33. Gay Diary, December 18, 1944.

34. War Department, FM 100–10, *Field Service Regulations, Administration*, November 15, 1943, p. 7, USAHEC; Ruppenthal, *Logistical Support*, 19, 39; SHAEF G-2 Weekly Intelligence Summary No. 40, p. 37.

35. Patton, *War as I Knew It*, 181; Blumenson, *Patton Papers*, 2:599. Both were heavily edited, and the validity of certain entries has been questioned. Harkins helped Patton's wife, Beatrice, edit *War as I Knew It*, and the possibility of subtle tinkering

382	Notes to Pages 106–7

cannot be ignored. As for *The Patton Papers*, it remains an excellent source, but one historian has accurately pointed out that two copies of Patton's wartime diary exist—a manuscript and a typescript copy. The typescript contains several revisions. Important differences have been discovered, for instance, with regard to Patton's role in Operation COBRA in July 1944. See Ulick Hallinan, "From Operation Cobra to the Liberation of Paris: American Offensive Operations in Northern France, 25 July–25 August 1944" (PhD diss., Temple University, 1988), 131–40. For the present work, I relied on the typescript copy, keeping in mind its limitations. Those works that cite December 22 include Cole, *Ardennes*, 487; Codman, *Drive*, 232; Reminiscences of General Paul D. Harkins, April 28, 1974, pp. 28–30, USAHEC; Peter Elstob, *Hitler's Last Offensive* (London: Secker & Warburg, 1971), 215; and Weigley, *Eisenhower's Lieutenants*, 500. Ladislas Farago cited December 22 but later stated that Patton had assured Eisenhower he could be in action in the north within twenty-two hours. Ladislas Farago, *Patton: Ordeal and Triumph* (New York: Ivan Obolensky, 1964), 677, 690. There are also instances of historians changing their dates. Charles B. MacDonald stated in 1969 that it was the twenty-second, yet in 1984 he said the twenty-first. Moreover, he engaged in some creative math, suggesting that Patton's intention to attack on December 22 represented forty-eight hours from the time he said it at the Verdun meeting. The Verdun meeting commenced at 1100, so forty-eight hours would have meant an attack date of December 21, not December 22. Charles B. MacDonald, *The Mighty Endeavor: American Armed Forces in the European Theater in World War II* (New York: Oxford University Press, 1969), 382; MacDonald, *Battle of the Bulge*, 420.

36. Bradley, *Soldier's Story*, 472; Eisenhower, *Bitter Woods*, 257; notes of meeting held in Supreme Commander's Office SHAEF (Main) at 10.00 hours, December 20, 1944. SHAEF Diary, CMH. Strong also indicated that Patton replied "forty-eight hours." Strong, *Intelligence at the Top*, 221. Bradley stated in his memoirs that he asked Patton when he could attack, not Eisenhower.

37. Chandler, *Eisenhower Papers*, 4:2179. Eisenhower reflected, "We estimated that Patton could begin a three-division attack by the morning of December 23, possibly by the twenty-second." Eisenhower, *Crusade in Europe*, 351. Tedder recalled that Patton was to organize a major counter blow "for 23 or 24 December." Tedder, *With Prejudice*, 626. Clearly, these statements were based on Eisenhower's direction and not on what Patton actually said. However, Patton later declared: "I stated it [Third Army] could attack with III Corps on the 23rd of December." Patton, "Notes on Bastogne Operation." Major General David T. Zabecki argues for December 23 as well in "Third Army Counterattack, December 1944: Myths, Facts, and the Military Decision Making Process" (loaned to the author by Zabecki).

38. Several historians cite December 21, including Carlo D'Este, *Patton: A Genius for War* (New York: HarperCollins, 1995), 681; David Eisenhower, *Eisenhower at War, 1943–1945* (New York: Random House, 1986), 569; Ian V. Hogg, *The Biography of George S. Patton* (New York: Gallery Press, 1982), 128; Astor, *A Blood-Dimmed Tide*, 232; Eisenhower, *Bitter Woods*, 257; Geoffrey Perret, *Eisenhower* (New York: Random House, 2000), 329; and Dupuy, *Hitler's Last Gamble*, 141.

39. Codman, *Drive*, 232; Kay Summersby, *Eisenhower Was My Boss* (New York: Prentice-Hall, 1948), 202; Bradley, *Soldier's Story*, 472; Senior Officer's Debriefing

Program, conversation between General Paul D. Harkins and Major Jacob B. Couch Jr., USAHEC.

40. Eisenhower, *Crusade in Europe*, 351–52. Ironically, he gave almost the exact advice to Lieutenant General Lloyd R. Fredendall, commander of U.S. II Corps, in Tunisia. Chandler, *Eisenhower Papers*, 2:952.

41. Eisenhower, *Eisenhower at War*, 569–70; Morelock, *Generals of the Ardennes*, 124; Eisenhower, *Crusade in Europe*, 352; Patton Diary, December 19, 1944; Jeffrey J. Clarke and Robert R. Smith, *U.S. Army in World War II: Riviera to the Rhine* (Washington, D.C.: CMH, 1993), 491; Bonn, *When the Odds Were Even*, 140–41. For an overview of the Eisenhower-Devers relationship and its impact on strategy and operations in the fall of 1944, see John A. English's excellent recent study, *Patton's Peers*, 164–65, 180.

42. FM 100–10, p. 13; Chandler, *Eisenhower Papers*, 4:2222–23. Eisenhower demonstrated some difficulty adjusting to such a wide span of control. From the moment he assumed the duties of C-in-C of Ground Forces from Montgomery on September 1, his directives lacked precision and a clear thought process. Dominick Graham and Shelford Bidwell, *Coalitions, Politicians and Generals: Some Aspects of Command in Two World Wars* (London: Brassey's, 1993), 239, 291.

43. Chandler, *Eisenhower Papers*, 4:2364.

44. Eisenhower, *Bitter Woods*, 257; Patton Diary, December 19, 1944.

6. The Ninety-Degree Turn

1. 35th Infantry Division AAR, December 1944, RG 407, entry 427, 335–0.3; 6th Armored Division AAR, December 1944, RG 407, entry 427, 606–0.3, NARA II.

2. Colonel William N. Taylor to Brigadier General James A. Norell, December 8, 1960, Correspondence Relating to Cole's *Ardennes*, RG-407, entry 427, NARA II. The 4th Armored Division operated in XII Corps' zone but remained under XV Corps command. Cole, *Lorraine*, 534n23.

3. The 3rd Battalion/101st Infantry Regiment was isolating a sector of Fort Jean d'Arc. Elements of the division began shuttling to Metz on December 10, while the entire 328th Infantry continued to push east to cross the German frontier before it was relieved by the 347th Infantry/87th Infantry Division. Cole, *Lorraine*, 539.

4. Third Army AAR, vol. 2, Provost Marshal, p. 16; Fifteenth Army Historians, "The Intervention of the Third Army: III Corps in the Attack, 22 December–28 December 1944," p. 6, CMH.

5. Patton, "Notes on Bastogne Operation"; Headquarters, Third United States Army, Operational Directive (Confirmation of Fragmentary Orders), December 20, 1944, RG 407, NARA II.

6. Blumenson, *Patton Papers*, 2:597.

7. III Corps AAR, December 1944, p. 14. Harold Winton stated that the reasons for the change were unclear, but Patton and Bradley had "presumably" discussed it earlier at Verdun. Winton, *Corps Commanders of the Bulge*, 188. Millikin stayed at Eagle TAC long enough to see Bradley upon his return from Verdun.

8. MacDonald, *Last Offensive*, 15; Cole, *Ardennes*, 487.

9. Eddy War Log, December 18, 1944; Major Donald E. Vandergriff, "Before

There Was Digitization: How MG J. S. Wood's 4th Armored Division Stormed across France without Written Orders," *Armor* 109, no. 5 (September–October 2000): 24–25. The footprint of the division trains was 1,300 yards by 1,300 yards, or three-quarters of a square mile. War Department, FM 17–55, *Armored Force Field Manual: Trains and Trains Headquarters Company Armored Division*, September 29, 1942, pp. 8, 19, USAHEC.

10. 4th Armored Division AAR, December 1944, p. 2, RG 407, entry 427, 604–33.4, NARA II; FM 17–55; Irzyk, *He Rode up Front for Patton*, 237; Major Peter S. Kindsvatter, "An Appreciation for Moving the Heavy Corps: The First Step in Learning the Art of Operational Maneuver" (SAMS, USACGSC, 1986), p. 8. The 37th Tank Battalion crossed the IP at 0830. 37th Tank Battalion AAR, December 1944, p. 4, CARL. The columns would have gone no faster than the slowest vehicle, the M4 Sherman, which could travel at roughly seventeen miles per hour, but the prescribed speed was actually eight miles per hour. FM 17–55, p. 19.

11. 80th Reconnaissance Troop AAR, December 1944; 318th Infantry Regiment AAR, December 1944, p. 4, RG 407, entry 427, 380-INF (318)-0.2, NARA II. At 2300 on December 17 two truck companies moved from Toul to Puttelange, the assembly area of McBride's 80th Infantry Division, approximately seven miles southwest of Sarreguemines. At 0100 on December 18 another truck company departed Pont-à-Mousson for Puttelange. The first unit to move was the 80th Reconnaissance Troop, which departed Etting at 0530 on December 19 and arrived in Luxembourg City at 0700 the next day, covering seventy-two miles on route C in less than fifteen hours. The division AAR was unclear as to exactly how it moved. It stated that the division moved from St. Avold to Sarre-Union in two shuttles on December 18–19, but this was a movement of some thirty miles in the wrong direction.

12. FM 10–35, *Quartermaster Truck Companies*, July 1945, pp. 39–40, USAHEC. For distances of less than 150 miles, it was considered better to march an infantry division by rail and motor rather than simply by rail. FM 100–5, p. 84. However, there is no evidence that Patton's infantry divisions were moved by rail.

13. 80th Infantry Division AAR, December 1944, p. 4, RG 407, entry 427, 380-0.3, NARA II. The 12th Armored Division officially assumed McBride's area by 1700 hours on December 19.

14. 702nd Tank Battalion AAR, December 1944, CARL.

15. James N. Peale Jr., "Third Battalion, 101st Infantry Regiment, U.S. Army, in the Ardennes Campaign, December 1944 and January 1945," John Toland Papers, box 34, LC; 26th Infantry Division AAR, December 1944, p. 3.

16. 319th Infantry Regiment AAR, December 1944, RG 407, entry 427, 380–INF (319)–0.2, NARA II; Wyatt E. Barnes, "A Rifleman's Story," *World War II* (2004): 66. Doctrine dictated that "when contact with the enemy is probable tactical considerations govern march dispositions." FM 100–5, p. 72.

17. Major Gregory V. Morton, "Field Artillery Support for III Corps Attack, 18–26 December 1944" (master's thesis, Fort Leavenworth, Kansas, 1985).

18. Third Army G-3 Operations Diary, entry for December 19, 1944, RG 407, entry 427, 103–0.3.0 to 103–0.21, NARA II.

19. Ibid.; Third Army G-2 Work Map, Situation as of 0300A, December 19, 1944, RG 407, entry 427, NARA II; Twelfth Army Group, Situation 1200 hours, December

19, 1944, Twelfth Army Group Outline Maps, 1:1,000,000, World War II Military Situation Maps, http://www.TheHistoricalArchive.com; 35th Infantry Division AAR, December 1944, p. 9.

20. Eddy War Log, December 19, 1944. Patton had done something like this in Sicily, establishing a provisional corps under Major General Geoffrey Keyes, and in Normandy he had placed Leonard T. Gerow in charge of a provisional corps south of Falaise.

21. Koch indicated it was either late on the nineteenth or early on the twentieth. Koch, *Intelligence for Patton*, 106; Cole, *Ardennes*, 309.

22. Third U.S. Army G-2 Work Map, Situation as of 0300A, December 20, 1944; Blumenson, *Patton Papers*, 2:602; Price, *Middleton*, 262; Troy H. Middleton to Major General John H. Stokes Jr., October 22, 1956, Correspondence Relating to Cole's *Ardennes*, NARA II; Patton to Middleton, April 25, 1945, *Golden Acorn News* 2, no. 35 (May 8, 1945); Middleton interview with John Toland, n.d., box 36, Toland Papers, LC; John C. McManus, *Alamo in the Ardennes: The Untold Story of the American Soldiers Who Made the Defense of Bastogne Possible* (New York: John A. Wiley & Sons, 2007), 253.

23. Blumenson, *Patton Papers*, 2:602; Fifteenth Army Historians, "Intervention," 34; Senior Officer's Oral History Program, Project 81-G, Hobart Gay interviewed by Willard L. Wallace, 1981, USAHEC.

24. Gay Diary, December 20, 1944; Eddy War Log, December 20, 1944.

25. Canine quoted in Dyer, *XII Corps*, 286.

26. Cole, *Ardennes*, 489–90; 5th Infantry Division AAR, December 1944, RG 427, 305–3 to 305–3.2, NARA II.

27. Ruppenthal, *Logistical Support*, 183–84; Third Army AAR, vol. 2, Staff Section Reports, G-4 Section, p. 37.

28. Third Army AAR, vol. 2, G-4 Section, pp. 37, 41; War Department, FM 100–10, p. 7. Bradley sent his chief combat liaison officer, Colonel Karl L. Bendetsen, to Third Army to assist with the movement north. Bendetsen attended the 0800 December 19 staff meeting and was told by Patton to get a freight train "by all means, fair or foul." Reminiscences of Karl L. Bendetsen, October 24, 1972, pp. 129–30, Oral History Collection, Harry S. Truman Library, Independence, Mo.

29. Third Army AAR, vol. 2, G-4 Section, p. 40.

30. Ibid.; Fifteenth Army Historians, "Intervention," 6.

31. Captain L. B. Clark and First Lieutenant William J. Dunkerley, interview with Brigadier General Holmes E. Dager and Lieutenant Colonel Clay Olbon, "Relief of Bastogne," 4th Armored Division Combat Interviews, January 9, 1945. Only one ASP partially served XII, XX, and III Corps in the last third of December. XII Corps was served by two depots and two railheads, which necessitated longer hauls. By the end of December, however, Depot 38 was fully stocked. XII Corps AAR, December 1944, p. 35, RG 407, Entry 427, 212–0.3, NARA II. Supplying armored divisions was somewhat different from supplying infantry divisions. The 4th Armored Division, for example, had no organic QM company to break down supplies to the division's subunits. As a result, the division G-4 established a division control point, and it was commanded by the division QM to provide a provisional breakdown ability. Lieutenant Colonel Herbert F. Krucker, "Quartermaster Supply of an Armored

Division in Combat," *Military Review* 25, no. 7 (October 1945): 62–63. The division control point had an attached QM truck company (fifty trucks).

32. Third Army AAR, 1:173.

33. War Department, FM 100–10, pp. 81–82.

34. Lieutenant General Edward T. Williams to John Toland, January 13, 1958, Toland Papers, box 36, LC; Allen Journal, December 22, 1944. There were some premature bursts of proximity fuses in dense cloud cover, but only with the early fuses.

35. War Department, FM 11–22, *Signal Operations in the Corps and Army*, January 1945, pp. 56–57; Fifteenth Army Historians, "Intervention," 10. Apparently, the problem was eased somewhat by using the existing facilities of Twelfth Army Group and the *Postes Telephones Telegraphes* system. This was a doctrinal issue. Because of the extent of the signals system required in an army, "particular emphasis must be placed on existing commercial facilities." FM 11–22, p. 51.

36. Otto P. Weyland Diary, December 17 and 19, 1944, USAFHRA; Spires, *Patton's Air Force*, 194; Headquarters Third Army, G-3 Operations Diary, entry for December 19, 1944.

37. Third Army AAR, 1:174.

38. Ibid., 169. Another source stated that Third Army moved 11,800 vehicles on these routes on December 18 alone. Fifteenth Army Historians, "Intervention," 9. XII Corps claimed that it moved more than 11,000 vehicles and 80,000 men between December 19 and 23. XII Corps AAR, December 1944, p. 36.

39. Blumenson, *Patton Papers*, 2:602–3; Patton, "Notes on Bastogne Operation"; Ruppenthal, *Logistical Support*, 184; Stephen Biddle, *Military Power: Explaining Victory and Defeat in Modern Battle* (Princeton, N.J.: Princeton University Press, 2004), 267n59. Patton later stated that those wishing to learn how to move an army "should study this operation as set forth in meticulous detail in the 'After Action Operations Report' of the Third Army. Patton, *War as I Knew It*, 187.

40. Kindsvatter, "Appreciation for Moving the Heavy Corps," 13; Weigley, *Eisenhower's Lieutenants*, 500; Hogan, *Command Post at War*, 213; First United States Army Report of Operations, August 1, 1944–February 22, 1945. The 10th Armored Division, moved by Third Army into VIII Corps' sector on December 17, reduces First Army's total claim of vehicles moved.

41. Pogue interview with Lieutenant General Walter Bedell Smith, May 8, 1947. For the background of this decision, see Bradley, *Soldier's Story*, 476; Crosswell, *Chief of Staff*, 284–87.

42. Blumenson, *Patton Papers*, 2:601; Patton, *War as I Knew It*, 185; interview with Brigadier General Holmes Dager and Colonel Clay Olbon, January 7, 1945, 4th Armored Division Combat Interviews, RG 94, NARA II; Delk M. Oden, "The 4th Armored Division in the Relief of Bastogne," *Military Review* 27, no. 10 (January 1948): 40; Narrative Summary of Operations of 4th Armored Division in the Relief of Bastogne, December 22–29, 4th Armored Division Combat Interviews, p. 1; VIII Corps AAR, December 1944, p. 20.

43. Blumenson, *Patton Papers*, 2:602; Cole, *Ardennes*, 457; Third Army G-3 Operations Diary, entries for December 19–20, 1944, RG 407, entry 427, 103–0.3.0 to 103–0.21, NARA II; G-3 Periodic SITREPs, entries for December 19–20, 1944, entry 427, NARA II. The 4th Armored Division AAR had little to offer. It merely stated that

CCB went in to "learn their situation and render support if necessary." RG 407, entry 427, 604–33.4, NARA II.

44. Dager interview, January 7, 1945.

45. Albin F. Irzyk, "4th Armored Division Spearhead at Bastogne," *World War II* (November 1999): 74. Dager declared that it was never actually committed, which in point of fact, was correct. The VIII Corps AAR made no mention of any orders being issued to send a task force into Bastogne.

46. Cole, *Ardennes*, 514.

47. Baum quoted in Astor, *A Blood-Dimmed Tide*, 231. CCB/10th Armored Division's AAR stated that it made contact with Dager's column at Vaux-les-Rosières and that Dager then withdrew to Léglise at 1500. This does not mean that Roberts had elements that far southwest. Only Team O'Hara could have made contact with Ezell. CCB/10th Armored Division AAR, December 1944, RG 407, entry 427, 610–CCB–0.3, NARA II.

48. Irzyk, "Spearhead at Bastogne," 37; Blumenson, *Patton Papers*, 2:601; Patton, *War as I Knew It*, 185. Cole stated that Gaffey ordered the task force out. Cole, *Ardennes*, 514. The Narrative Summary (p. 1) stated that VIII Corps ordered it out. Irzyk, *He Rode up Front for Patton*, 241–42.

49. MacDonald, *Battle of the Bulge*, 504–5. See also Weigley, *Eisenhower's Lieutenants*, 520; Parker, *Battle of the Bulge*, 143; Elstob, *Hitler's Last Offensive*, 288; Fifteenth Army Historians, "Intervention," 16.

50. Baum quoted in Astor, *A Blood-Dimmed Tide*, 231. Oden believed that Dager should have conducted a more aggressive reconnaissance to the north and northeast to detect enemy intentions. It may have speeded up the relief by two days. Oden, "4th Armored in Relief of Bastogne," 44.

51. See the color map depicting *Lehr*'s movements for December 20 in Spayd, *Bayerlein*, 290.

52. 28th Infantry Division AAR, December 1944, p. 6, RG 407, entry 427, 328–0.3, NARA II.

7. Third Army Attacks, December 22–23

1. Patton, *War as I Knew It*, 188.

2. Diary of Air Vice Marshal Robb, December 21, 1944, quoted in Hamilton, *Monty*, 223; notes of meeting held in Supreme Commander's Office SHAEF (Main), 1000 hours, December 21, 1944.

3. Chandler, *Eisenhower Papers*, 4:2374–75.

4. Hansen Diary, December 20, 1944.

5. Twelfth Army Group, Situation 1200 hours, December 21, 1944, Twelfth Army Group Outline Maps, 1:1,000,000, World War II Military Situation Maps, http://www.TheHistoricalArchive.com.

6. Third U.S. Army G-2 Work Map, Situation as of 0300A, December 20, 1944, RG 407, entry 427, NARA II.

7. Third U.S. Army G-2 Work Map, Situation as of 0300A, December 21, 1944. This map also showed that the *36th* VGD had moved to a new location. DEFE 3/319, HP 9927, December 20, 1944, cited in Hinsley, *British Intelligence*, 445.

8. War Department, FM 100–5, *Field Service Regulations, Operations,* June 15, 1944, pp. 111–12, USAHEC.

9. Allen Journal, December 20, 1944; Rickard, *Patton at Bay,* 101–2.

10. Koch, *Intelligence for Patton,* 104–5; Third Army AAR, vol. 1, p. 174; Periodic Report, December 20, Third Army AAR, vol. 2, G-2 Section, p. 122.

11. FM 100–5, p. 26.

12. Bradley's instructions to Patton were issued "for your information and guidance." Third Army was to immediately launch a counteroffensive against the southern flank "from general area" Luxembourg–Arlon "in the direction of St. Vith." Twelfth Army Group instructions, December 22, 1944, Annex No. 1, Twelfth Army Group Directives, Twelfth Army Group Final Report of Operations, CARL.

13. Interview with James Polk, Senior Officers Debriefing Program, Polk Papers, USAHEC; Headquarters, Third United States Army, Operational Directive, December 21, 1944, RG 407, NARA II.

14. Headquarters Third Army, G-3 Operations Diary, December 19, 1944; War Department, FM 100–15, *Field Service Regulations for Larger Units* (Washington, D.C.: GPO, 1942), para. 173.

15. Quoted in Winton, *Corps Commanders of the Bulge,* 46.

16. Harold R. Winton, "The Education of Two Generals: Leonard T. Gerow and John Millikin" (paper presented at the Society for Military History annual conference, Madison, Wis., April 4–7, 2002), 34. After the Bulge, Millikin would be relieved of command by Hodges for command failings at Remagen. William C. Westmoreland, chief of staff of the 9th Infantry Division at the time, later wrote, "So irresolute was the III Corps commander, so lacking in confidence, that I feared for the safety of the bridgehead." William C. Westmoreland, *A Soldier Reports* (Garden City, N.Y.: Doubleday, 1976), 25.

17. Wade H. Haislip, "Corps Command in World War II," *Military Review* 70, no. 5 (May 1990): 22; Winton, *Corps Commanders of the Bulge,* 7–8; Matthew B. Ridgway, *Soldier: The Memoirs of Matthew B. Ridgway* (New York: Harper & Brothers, 1956), 18. The level of corps command had given both Marshall and General Leslie J. McNair, commander of U.S. Army Ground Forces, the greatest anxiety during the 1941 Louisiana maneuvers. Recalling his World War I experience, Marshall stated, "I saw the unfortunate results of corps command by individuals who had never commanded divisions in actual operations." He subsequently insisted that a commander had to possess a "sound basic knowledge of divisional requirements and operations" before moving up to take over a corps. Larry I. Bland, ed., *The Papers of George Catlett Marshall,* 5 vols. (Baltimore: Johns Hopkins University Press, 1981–2003), 2:632.

18. Third Army, G-3 Operations Diary, December 19, 1944; Colonel H. C. Mewshaw, ACofS, G-3, Memorandum for Record, 1345 hours, December 21, 1944, RG 407, entry 427, 203–3.2, III Corps, NARA II.

19. Letter of Instruction No. 3, May 20, 1944, quoted in Charles M. Province, *The Unknown Patton* (New York: Bonanza Books, 1983), 235; Ernest N. Harmon, *Combat Commander: Autobiography of a Soldier* (Englewood Cliffs, N.J.: Prentice-Hall, 1970), 123. According to Martin van Creveld, Patton declared that American commanders did not understand *Auftragstaktik* (mission tactics), but Creveld's evidence

is faulty. He cited *The Patton Papers*, but there is no mention of it there. Creveld, *Fighting Power*, 37; Blumenson, *Patton Papers*, 2:486.

20. Mewshaw, Memorandum for Record, 1345 hours, December 21, 1944; Winton, *Corps Commanders of the Bulge*, 217.

21. Michael D. Doubler observed that these types of attacks "supported by massed firepower were common in Europe and usually got the job done." Michael D. Doubler, *Closing with the Enemy: How GIs Fought the War in Europe, 1944–1945* (Lawrence: University Press of Kansas, 1994), 232.

22. FM 100–5, p. 117; FM 101–5, pp. 131–32.

23. Bruce C. Clarke, "Principles of the Employment of Armor," Armored School, Fort Knox, Ky., April 12, 1948, John S. Wood Papers, box 1, file "Incoming Correspondence, Brig-Gen. Bruce C. Clarke," Bird Library, Syracuse University, Syracuse, N.Y.

24. Headquarters III Corps AAR, December 1944, p. 8.

25. VIII Corps ISUM No. 302, December 20, 1944, RG 407, NARA II; III Corps AAR, p. 7; Twelfth Army Group, Situation 1200 hours, December 20, 1944, Twelfth Army Group Outline Maps; Colonel J. H. Phillips, Memorandum for Record, December 21, 1944, RG 407, entry 427, 203–3.2, III Corps, NARA II; SRH-042, p. A-5; Third Army AAR, vol. 2, G-2 Section, p. 122.

26. III Corps, Operations Directive No. 1, December 23, 1944, RG 407, NARA II.

27. III Corps Field Order No. 1, 1500, December 21, 1944, RG 407, NARA II.

28. War Department, FM 100–20, *Field Service Regulation, Command and Employment of Air Power*, July 1943, pp. 10–11, USAHEC; Colonel William R. Carter, "Air Power in the Battle of the Bulge: A Theater Campaign Perspective," *Airpower Journal* 3, no. 4 (winter 1989): 28. Ninth Air Force developed its air plan on request from Bradley, who focused on attacking German armored elements, isolating the Ardennes–Eifel region from rail support, harassing road traffic inside and outside the Bulge, and eliminating supply facilities immediately beyond the Ardennes. Spires, *Patton's Air Force*, 194.

29. Spires, *Patton's Air Force*, 196; Third Army AAR, vol. 1, p. 175.

30. Morton, "Field Artillery Support for III Corps Attack," 1. Patton declared there were 108 battalions of division, corps, and army artillery, totaling some 1,296 guns of 105mm or bigger. Blumenson, *Patton Papers*, 2:604. Patton later stated that there were 88 battalions, totaling 1,056 guns of 105mm or bigger, for the December 22 attack. Patton, *War as I Knew It*, 189. Robert S. Allen cites 108 as the total number of Third Army artillery battalions on December 26. Allen, *Lucky Forward*, 253. This number seems reasonable when compared against Third Army's Troop List No. 17 for December 27.

31. War Department, FM 6–20, *Field Service Regulations, Field Artillery Tactical Employment*, February 1944, p. 40, USAHEC.

32. Millikin wanted to focus on the Arlon–Bastogne route, while Middleton favored pushing on both. Fifteenth Army Historians, "Intervention," 30.

33. Ibid., 16; Albin F. Irzyk to author, March 21, 2004; Letter of Instruction No. 3, quoted in Province, *Unknown Patton*, 232. MacDonald stated that CCB did not reach Burnon until nightfall. MacDonald, *Battle of the Bulge*, 519.

34. III Corps ISUM No. 22, 212400A to 221200A, and ISUM No. 23, 221200A to 112400A, December 22, 1944, RG 407, NARA II. One study suggested that the

historical record "is full of cases of attacks being stalled by very small opposing forces, because the attackers thought they were meeting heavy resistance rather than because that heavy resistance really existed." Leonard Wainstein, "Rates of Advance in Infantry Division Attacks in the Normandy–Northern France and Siegfried Line Campaigns" (Weapons Systems Evaluation Group, December 1973), 40.

35. Letter of Instruction No. 3, quoted in Province, *Unknown Patton*, 228.

36. Lieutenant General Willard S. Paul to General James A. Norell, May 23, 1960, Hugh M. Cole Papers, correspondence relating to official history, NARA II. Paul was not happy over the lack of coverage of his division in the official history.

37. Fifteenth Army Historians, "Intervention," 12; Willard S. Paul to Colonel Mewshaw, Century 3, December 22, 1944, RG 407, entry 427, 203–3.2, III Corps, NARA II.

38. Henry G. Phillips, *The Making of a Professional: Manton S. Eddy, USA* (Westport, Conn.: Greenwood, 2000), 172; Eddy War Log, September 22, 1944.

39. III Corps ISUM No. 22, 2400A December 21 to 1200A December 22, 1944, RG 407, entry 427, NARA II. It should also be pointed out that LXXXV *Armeekorps* reported early on December 22 that it was battling guerrillas in Ettelbruck. DEFE 3/320, BT 92 (ZZ), 1541Z, December 22, 1944, reel 55. The role of the resistance movements during the Bulge should be explored further.

40. Fifteenth Army Historians, "Intervention," chap. 1, p. 5; MS #A-934, p. 12; MS #A-876 (Brandenberger), "Ardennes Offensive of Seventh Army (16 Dec 1944–25 Jan 1945)," in Detwiler et al., *World War II German Military Studies*, vol. 12, pt. 5, p. 30. Lüttwitz and Manteuffel appreciated that American forces were coming up near Bastogne. *Panzer Lehr* reported that it expected the 4th Armored Division and 96th (probably meaning 26th) Infantry Division in the St. Hubert area. DEFE 3/320, BT 127 (ZZ), 2324Z, December 22, 1944, reel 55.

41. DEFE 3/322, BT 656 (ZZ), 1414Z, December 29, 1944, reel 56.

42. SCAEF to Twelfth Army Group and Sixth Army Group, S-71781, 2243A, December 20, 1944; MS #P-038 (Albert Praun), "German Radio Intelligence," 1950, p. 82, CMH; Major Laurie G. Moe Buckout, "Signal Security in the Ardennes Offensive: 1944–1945" (master's thesis, Fort Leavenworth, 1997), 81; Wilmot, *Struggle for Europe*, 599; Bennett, *Ultra in the West*, 197.

43. Colonel J. H. Phillips, Chief of Staff, Memorandum for Record, December 22, 1944, RG 407, entry 427, 203–3.2, NARA II; Fifteenth Army Historians, "Intervention," chap. 1, p. 25; III Corps message to VIII Corps, received 1500, December 22, 1944, VIII Corps G-3 File, RG 407, NARA II.

44. Conference with General Patton—attended by General Gaffey and General Millikin, December 22, 1944, RG 407, entry 427, 203–3.2, III Corps G-3 File, NARA II; Cole, *Ardennes*, 525; Blumenson, *Patton Papers*, 2:604.

45. SLU SHAEF to Lieutenant Colonel Gore-Browne, MI 807 (Immediate), 1640, December 20, 1944, OLSU Flimsies, SB-SH (SHA), 1/10/44–31/12/44, for SCU ZETA (ZZ), 1250Z, December 21, 1944, HW/20/457, Public Record Office, Kew, England.

46. Eddy War Log, December 21, 1944.

47. CCA/10th Armored Division AAR, December 1944, p. 9, RG 407, entry 427, 610-CCA-0.3, NARA II.

48. Bradley, *Soldier's Story*, 101; Omar N. Bradley and Clay Blair, *A General's Life*

(New York: Simon & Schuster, 1983), 136; Blumenson, *Patton Papers*, 2:559, 560, 591; Patton, *War as I Knew It*, 170; Rickard, *Patton at Bay*, 186–87, 220; Patton Diary, December 16, 1944. Cole also concluded that Eddy was a conservative commander. Cole, *Ardennes*, 495. Eddy's biographer argued that Eddy was "not a chronic worrier. His diary shows repeatedly that the man had learned to pace himself and could turn off 'battle' when [the] day was done." Phillips, *Making of a Professional*, 176.

49. Major General S. Leroy Irwin Diary, December 20, 1944, RG 407, entry 427, Combat Interviews, NARA II.

50. Cole, *Ardennes*, 491; XII Corps Operational Directive No. 57, December 22, 1944, RG 407, entry 427, NARA II. It is important to note that these written orders only confirmed the verbal orders issued the day before. CCA/10th Armored Division was on one-minute alert to counterattack east or southeast on division order. AAR, December 1944, p. 9.

51. 4th Infantry Division AAR, December 1944, Section III—Intelligence, p. 9, RG 407, entry 427, 304–0.3, NARA II; Eddy War Log, December 22, 1944; DEFE 3/320, BT 85 (ZZZZ), 1249Z, December 22, 1944, reel 55. XX Corps generated an enormous smoke screen in the Saar Valley from Dillingen to Saarlautern to cover further withdrawals of the 90th Infantry Division, but the Germans identified empty pontoons crossing to the east bank and loaded pontoons returning to the west bank. However, *LXXX Armeekorps* was aware early in the morning that American reinforcements were probably moving up to Waldbillig because of the substantial noise made by U.S. vehicles. DEFE 3/320, BT 75 (ZZ), 0917Z, December 22; BT 127 (ZZ), 2324Z, December 22, 1944, reel 55.

52. Blumenson, *Patton Papers*, 2:609.

53. MS #A-876, p. 32; Blumenson, *Patton Papers*, 2:604.

54. MS #A-876, p. 33.

55. MS #B-783 (Riedel), "Seventh Army Artillery (18 Dec 44–31 Jan 45)," 1948, p. 3; MS #B-030 (Kniess), "The Ardennes (16 Dec 44–12 Jan 45)," p. 7; RG 549.3, NARA II.

56. George S. Patton Jr., "Tactical Use of Separate Tank Battalions," April 15, 1944, Patton Papers, box 2–4, LC.

57. Irzyk, *He Rode up Front for Patton*, 246; Irzyk to author, June 30, 2003; III Corps G-3 Journal, December 22, 1944. Brandenberger rejected night attacks because of the troops' lack of training and their unfamiliarity with the terrain. MS #B-447.

58. ETHINT 54 (Gersdorff), "Seventh Army in the Ardennes Offensive," November 26, 1945, p. 2, RG 549.3, NARA II.

59. DEFE 3/320, BT 171 (ZZ), 1692Z, December 23, 1944, reel 54; ETHINT 40 (Kniess), "LXXXV Inf Corps (Nov–26 December 1944)"; DEFE 3/320, BT 131 (ZZ), 2352Z, December 22, 1944, reel 54; MS #B-172a, p. 2. Brandenberger also claimed that up to December 22, the division had sustained very few casualties. MS #A-876, pp. 30, 65.

60. The boundary between *LIII* and *LXXXV Armeekorps* was Moetsch–Bettingen–Roth–Heiderscheid–Grevels. DEFE 3/320, BT 87 (ZZZZ), 1349Z, December 22, 1944, reel 54.

61. MS #A-876, p. 69.

62. DEFE 3/320, BT 137 (ZZZZ), 0449Z, December 23, and DEFE 3/320, BT 207 (ZZZ), 0346Z, December 24, 1944, reel 54; Captain L. B. Clark, interview with Captain Stedman Seay, Assistant G-3, 4th Armored, "Relief of Bastogne," January 4, 1945, 4th Armored Division Combat Interviews.

63. Seay interview, January 4, 1945; Nat Frankel and Larry Smith, *Patton's Best: An Informed History of the 4th Armored Division* (New York: David McKay, 1978), 99. Captain Stedman Seay, the division assistant G-3, said there was an initial counterattack at 0910. Baum, however, said the cavalry troop took losses at Chaumont as early as 0500. T/Sergeant C. J. Angulo, interview with Captain Baum, Battalion S-3, 10th Armored Infantry, assisted by Major Cohen, executive officer of the battalion, "Relief of Bastogne," January 8, 1945, 4th Armored Division Combat Interviews.

64. III Corps G-3 Journal, December 23, 1944; Cole, *Ardennes*, 526.

65. III Corps ISUM No. 25, 231200–232400, December 1944; ETHINT 34 (Heinz Kokott), "Breakthrough to Bastogne," November 29, 1945, pp. 2–3, RG 549.3, NARA II.

66. Baum interview, January 8, 1945; ETHINT 34, p. 2. MacDonald argued that they were from *Panzerjäger Abteilung 653*, which had somehow been diverted to the Ardennes from Italy. MacDonald, *Battle of the Bulge*, 521. However, this cannot be confirmed.

67. Captain L. B. Clark, interview with Captain B. P. Ezell, executive officer, January 7, 1945, p. 3, 4th Armored Division Combat Interviews.

68. Bruce C. Clarke, memorandum, John S. Wood Papers, box 1, file "Incoming Correspondence, Brig-Gen. Bruce C. Clarke."

69. Albin F. Irzyk to the author, March 21, 2004; Irzyk, *He Rode up Front for Patton*, 248; Baum interview, January 8, 1945.

70. Irzyk to author, March 21, 2004.

71. Captain L. B. Clark, material to be added to 4th Armored Division, December interviews. Another source suggested it did not happen because of the need for greater reinforcement of the assault into the center of the town.

72. Baum interview, January 8, 1945.

73. Headquarters III Corps AAR, December 1944; Baum interview, January 8, 1945.

74. Clark, material to be added to 4th Armored Division, December interviews; Irzyk, *He Rode up Front for Patton*, 250.

75. Ezell interview, January 7, 1945; interview with Brigadier General Holmes E. Dager and Colonel Clay Olbon, January 7, 1945, p. 4; Irzyk, *He Rode up Front for Patton*, 253; Cole, *Ardennes*, 521–22. Brandenberger stated that the next day Kahler declared the FGB incapable of commitment, and it was not employed until January 8, 1945. MS #A-934, p. 16.

76. Ritgen, *Western Front*, 275; III Corps ISUM No. 23, 221200A to 222400A, December 23, 1944. Clearly, some of the reported tanks had to have been assault guns. Fifteenth Army Historians, "Intervention," 15n17.

77. Baum interview, January 8, 1945; Dager and Olbon interview, January 7, 1945.

78. Craven and Cate, *Army Air Forces in World War II*, 689. *Luftwaffe* orders expected good weather on December 23: "All forces to be made ready to engage successfully

in possible air battle on grand scale." The greatest danger to the ground forces was from four-engine bombers. "All formations therefore ruthlessly to attack these exclusively." DEFE 3/320, BT 150, 0848Z, December 23, 1944, reel 54.

79. Irzyk, *He Rode up Front for Patton*, 253; Spires, *Patton's Air Force*, 199.

80. Baum interview, January 8, 1945. Frankel actually blamed Patton for overcontrol. "I am convinced," Frankel declared, "that, had Wood still been in power, the whole Chaumont incident would have been radically different and radically easier." Frankel and Smith, *Patton's Best*, 98.

8. A Rendezvous with Eagles, December 24–26

1. Interview with Lieutenant Colonel Hal C. Pattison, executive officer, CCA, 4th Armored Division, at CP, Preish, January 13, 1945, 4th Armored Division Combat Interviews. Delk M. Oden stated that the bridge was not completed until 1700, at which point his task force passed through the bridgehead. Oden, "4th Armored Division in Relief of Bastogne," 42.

2. Pattison interview; Eisenhower, *Bitter Woods*, 340.

3. 735th Tank Battalion AAR, December 1944, CARL. Cole suggested that it was natural for green troops to want the "comforting presence of friendly tanks or guns." Cole, *Ardennes*, 523; 328th Infantry Regiment, Frag Order No. 27, cited in Fifteenth Army Historians, "Intervention," chap. 1, p. 28; Headquarters, 26th Infantry Division, memorandum, December 20, 1944, RG 407, entry 427, 326–0.3, NARA II; Allen Journal, December 19, 1944.

4. Cole, *Ardennes*, 522; III Corps Chief of Staff, memorandum for record of Millikin's conversation with Paul at 26 Infantry Division CP, 1645, December 23, 1944, III Corps G-3 Files.

5. Fifteenth Army Historians, "Intervention," chap. 2, p. 6.

6. Cole, *Ardennes*, 493. Eddy War Log, December 23, 1944; Allen Journal, December 23, 1944. Cole also stated that the 10th Infantry's attack on December 23 was not supported by divisional guns.

7. Eisenhower, *Bitter Woods*, 335; Third Army AAR, vol. 1, Operations, August 1, 1944–May 9, 1945, p. 175, USAHEC; Situation 1200 hours, December 22, 1944, Twelfth Army Group Outline Maps, 1:1,000,000, World War II Military Situation Maps, http://www.TheHistoricalArchive.com.

8. DEFE 3/320, BT 87 (ZZZZ), 1349Z, December 22; BT 115 (ZZZZ), 2114Z, December 22; BT 116 (ZZZ), 2118Z, December 22, 1944, reel 55. The boundary between *LIII* and *LXXXV Armeekorps* was to be Moetsch–Roth–Heiderscheid–Grevels. The screen ran from Bizory–Marvie–Lutrebois–Assenois–Villeroux–Magerotte–Amberloup.

9. Allen Journal, December 23, 1944. Patton apparently received captured orders on December 22 suggesting that the Germans intended to move west beyond Arlon, turn south, and attack Luxembourg City from the west. Patton, *War as I Knew It*, 189. Walker's XX Corps zone was vulnerable. ULTRA intercepted a *Heeresgruppe B* report of 0013 December 23 highlighting Third Army's withdrawal from the Saarlautern bridgehead. All the pillboxes in the Dillingen and Roden sectors were in German hands. DEFE 3/320, BT 218 (ZZ), 0732Z, December 24, 1944, reel 55.

10. Pattison said Warnach was cleared by 1300; Oden said 1715. Oden, "4th Armored in Relief of Bastogne," 42. Cole offered noon in *Ardennes*, 530.

11. Abrams declared, "In the 4th Armd Div, the commitment of CCR means that the division has committed its reserve; it is not used, as CCR of the 6th Armd Div occasionally is, as a combat command with one of the letter commands in the reserve role." Captain L. B. Clark, interview with Lieutenant Colonel Creighton W. Abrams, commanding officer, 37th Tank Battalion, "Relief of Bastogne Pocket," January 5, 1945, 4th Armored Division Combat Interviews. The 4th Armored Division had only two large maneuver elements on a wide frontage, and Patton certainly did not care for the armored division organization by this stage of the war. Shortly after the end of hostilities, he prepared a report arguing for a triangular armored division with three equally balanced combat commands. Bruce C. Clarke commented on Patton's report and declared that a triangular armored division was faulty: "There is no magic in organizing by threes. Any organization so organized must of necessity have limited battlefield endurance. The two combat command organization is basically a square organization and as such permits all units to be rotated in and out of the front for necessary periods of rehabilitation. The triangular organization does not permit this because almost immediately after the battle starts all three units are committed and there is no chance for rotation of units." Memorandum to Major General Cook, A CofS, Plans, "Comments on Report of General Patton," November 16, 1945, John S. Wood Papers, box 1.

12. Cole, *Ardennes*, 530; Jim Newman, "Battle of the Bulge: Beaufort Man Helped Halt Last German Offensive," *Beaufort Gazette*, December 24, 2000, D. Leach was also strafed by four P-47s from XIX TAC.

13. Patton, *War as I Knew It*, 191; SRH-042, p. 43. Major Goswin Wahl, commander of *FJR 13*, indicated that his regiment had serious radio communications deficiencies due to the loss of equipment and had to rely heavily on messengers. Gaul, *Battle of the Bulge in Luxembourg*, 1:41.

14. Frankel and Smith, *Patton's Best*, 97; Albin F. Irzyk, letter to author, June 30, 2003.

15. DEFE 3/320, BT 208 (ZZZZZ), 04212Z, December 24, 1944, reel 54.

16. Fifteenth Army Historians, "Intervention," chap. 6, p. 1.

17. III Corps Operations Directive No. 2 (Confirmation of Fragmentary Orders), December 24, 1944.

18. Cole, *Ardennes*, 532. This seems to have been effected on December 23, when III Corps directed Paul to assume responsibility for the Rambrouch–Koetschette–Arsdorf road. III Corps Operations Directive No. 1 (Confirmation of Fragmentary Orders), December 23, 1944.

19. Patton, *War as I Knew It*, 191; Winton, *Corps Commanders of the Bulge*, 223; Cole, *Ardennes*, 552. The 37th Tank Battalion received orders to move to the division's left flank at 1230. 37th Tank Battalion AAR, December 1944, p. 5, CARL.

20. Fifteenth Army Historians, "Intervention," chap. 5, pp. 1–2; Oden, "4th Armored in Relief of Bastogne," 42. Colonel Harry W. Johnston, chief of staff of 9th Armored Division, argued that the battle proved that the organic infantry element in the armored division was "woefully inadequate." The leadership of the 10th Armored Division felt the same way, especially if combat commands were operating in teams. Quoted in 9th Armored Division AAR, December 1944, p. 18; CCB/10th Armored

Division AAR, December 1944, p. 21. See also comments in Fifteenth Army Historians, "Intervention," 5:3.

21. The 109th Infantry had been attached to CCA/9th Armored Division at 1930 on December 20.

22. Eddy War Log, December 23 and 24, 1944; 5th Infantry Division AAR, December 1944, p. 11; Winton, *Corps Commanders of the Bulge*, 244. The XII Corps G-2 estimated that there was one infantry and one armored division in reserve behind *LXXX Armeekorps*. Cole, *Ardennes*, 495.

23. MS #A-930, p. 5.

24. Allen Journal, December 24, 1944.

25. D'Este, *Eisenhower*, 654; Patton Diary, December 24, 1944.

26. ETHINT 47, p. 8; Magna E. Bauer, MS #R-15, "Key Dates during the Ardennes Offensive 1944, Part I" (Washington, D.C.: CMH, April 1952), 6; Charles Messenger, *The Last Prussian: A Biography of Field Marshal Gerd von Rundstedt, 1875–1953* (London: Brassey's, 1991), 210; ETHINT 45, pp. 10, 13; MS #A-940, 1950, p. 9.

27. Charles V. P. von Luttichau, MS #R-11, "Key Dates during the Ardennes Offensive, Part II" (Washington, D.C.: CMH, April 1952), 140; MS #B-151a (Manteuffel), "Fifth Panzer Army (Ardennes Offensive)," RG 549.3, NARA II. Manteuffel told Jodl that although the *schwerpunkt* was now *Fifth Panzer Armee*, owing to Dietrich's failure to advance, neither the *OKW* reserves nor divisions from Dietrich's army had been transferred south. He asked Jodl for permission to switch *Fifth Panzer Armee*'s line of operations to the "smaller" solution—a sharp swing to the north with the army's left flank on the Meuse. Manteuffel also expressed concern for the safety of his southern flank.

28. *OB West KTB*, December 24, 1944, Anlagen 1691, cited in MS #R-11, pt. 2, p. 148; H. A. Jacobsen, and Jürgen Rowher, eds., *Decisive Battles of World War II: The German View* (New York: G. P. Putnam, 1965), 409; Cole, *Ardennes*, 475, 564. Manteuffel reflected, "In the hope that we might still get additional fuel and renew the attack to the north, I decided to reduce Bastogne, which assumed added importance when it became apparent that we were going to fight east of the Meuse River." ETHINT 46, p. 8. Clearly, however, he did not make this decision on his own.

29. Special Interrogation Report—Lüttwitz, LH 15/15/148/4, Liddell Hart Center for Military Archives, King's College, London; Jacobsen and Rowher, *Decisive Battles of World War II*, 409; MS #A-940, p. 9; MS #B-393, pp. 30–32. In the afternoon of December 24 Metz and his staff moved to Gives to assist Kokott in the Bastogne fight. This made personal communication with Manteuffel more difficult, but a good field wire link existed between Kokott's division and Lüttwitz and Krüger.

30. Gaffey, "Disposition of Final Objective," December 25, 1944, G-3 Journal, 4th Armored Division, RG 407, entry 427, 604–33.4, NARA II.

31. Fifteenth Army Historians, "Intervention," chap. 5, pp. 7–8; 37th Tank Battalion AAR, December 1944, p. 6.

32. III Corps G-3 message of phone conversation with Third Army G-3, 0845, December 25, 1944; Patton Diary, December 25, 1944; Fifteenth Army Historians, "Intervention," chap. 6, p. 6.

33. Fifteenth Army Historians, "Intervention," chap. 6, p. 7.

34. The argument is that the 80th's attacks prevented the *79th* VGD from deploying farther west as planned. Fifteenth Army Historians, "Intervention," chap. 3, p. 7.

35. Ibid., 5; 80th Infantry Division AAR, December 1944, p. 6.

36. Eddy War Log, December 25, 1944. However, the 4th Infantry Division observed that by the end of the day "it was felt that our over-all position had been greatly strengthened." 4th Infantry Division AAR, December 1944.

37. III Corps Chief of Staff, memorandum for the record of conversation with Third Army G-3, 1045, December 25, 1944, RG 407, entry 427, NARA II; Gay Diary, December 24, 1944; Fifteenth Army Historians, "Intervention," chap. 5, p. 1.

38. Patton Diary, December 26 and 27, 1944; notes of meeting held in Supreme Commander's office, December 26, 1944.

39. Spires, *Patton's Air Force*, 207; Weyland Diary, December 26, 1944.

40. ETHINT 44 (Heinz Kokott), "Breakthrough to Bastogne," November 29, 1945, pp. 3–5, RG 549.3, NARA II.

41. Senior Officers Debriefing Program, Hal Pattison conversations with Colonel James P. Bergen, February 25, 1977, USAHEC; Patton Diary, December 26, 1944. However, another account argues that Abrams made the decision on his own. Indeed, Pattison declared that Abrams did not inform Blanchard. Lewis Sorely, *Thunderbolt: From the Battle of the Bulge and Beyond: General Creighton Abrams and the Army of His Times* (New York: Simon & Schuster, 1992), 77.

42. Robert M. Parker Jr., "Recollections of the Second World War," World War II Veterans Survey, 4th Armored Division, USAHEC; Captain L. B. Clark, interview with Abrams, January 5, 1945, 4th Armored Division Combat Interviews; Patton Diary, December 26, 1944; III Corps G-3 Journal, December 26, 1944.

43. 37th Tank Battalion AAR, December 1944, p. 8.

44. ETHINT 44, p. 5; MS #B-393, p. 33.

45. Patton Diary, December 26, 1944.

46. Morton, "Field Artillery Support for III Corps Attack," 66–67.

9. Patton's Alternative Lines of Action

1. Headquarters Twelfth Army Group, Letter of Instruction No. 11, December 25, 1944, Twelfth Army Group Final Report of Operations, Annex No. 1: Twelfth Army Group Directives, CARL.

2. Maxwell Taylor, *Swords and Plowshares* (New York: W. W. Norton, 1972), 102. The Screaming Eagles also received some 400 replacements on December 27, but S. L. A. Marshall argued, "We were in no shape to move . . . I could not understand either Patton's issuing the order or General Taylor accepting the order." Reminiscences of Brigadier General S. L. A. Marshall, pt. 1, 1974, pp. 13–14, USAHEC.

3. CCA closed at 0600; CCB closed at 0730; and Division Artillery closed at 0800, followed by CCR. 6th Armored Division AAR, December 1944, p. 21, RG 407, entry 427, 606–0.3, NARA II.

4. Amendment No. 1, December 26, to Operational Directive dated December 21, Third Army AAR, vol. 1; III Corps AAR, December 1944, p. 13, RG 407, entry 427, NARA II; Headquarters Third Army, Troop Assignment No. A-80, December 27, 1944, RG 407, entry 427, NARA II.

5. Headquarters Third Army, G-3 Historical Subsection, Third Army Operations, December 1944–March 1945: A Brief Summary, January 16, 1946, RG 407, entry 427, 103–0.3.0, NARA II; Allen, *Lucky Forward*, 253–54; Patton, *War as I Knew It*, 193–95. The staff appreciation was signed by Harkins, Maddox, and Koch.

6. Patton, *War as I Knew It*, 196. Patton's frustration at Eisenhower's delay in giving him these divisions was apparent: "Why in hell SHAEF was doing this," Patton grumbled on December 26, "is beyond me. They should be attacking." Patton Diary, December 27, 1944.

7. DEFE 3/322, BT 502 (ZZZZ), 2039Z, December 27, 1944, reel 54. The screen traversed Rochefort–Wavreville–Bure–Hatrival–Vesqueville–Moircy–Remagne before linking with the *FBB*.

8. Ritgen, *Western Front*, 275.

9. Colonel Ralph M. Mitchell, *The 101st Airborne Division's Defense of Bastogne* (Fort Leavenworth, Kans.: CSI, USACGSC, 1986), 43.

10. Twelfth Army Group Weekly Intelligence Summary No. 20, for week ending December 24, 1944, p. 2, RG 407, entry 427, 99/12–2.1 Apr 1945 to 99/12–2.6 Jan 1945, NARA II.

11. Third Army G-2 Work Map, Situation as of 2400A, December 26, 1944, RG 407, entry 427, NARA II. Koch's map also shows an unidentified division just south of Trier.

12. Twelfth Army Group, Situation 1200 hours, December 26, 1944, Twelfth Army Group Outline Maps, 1:1,000,000, World War II Military Situation Maps, http://www.TheHistoricalArchive.com; Weekly Intelligence Summary No. 20. XX Corps stated that *11th PD*, "celebrated for its ability to appear without warning in the sector where it was least expected," was moved north of Trier after mid-December in anticipation of its use in the Ardennes. "The Capture of the Saar–Moselle Triangle and Trier." For a detailed route of the division at the time, see Peter Schmitz, Klaus-Jürgen Thies, Günter Wehmann, and Christian Zweng, *Die deutschen Divisionen 1939–1945*, vol. 3, *Die Divisionen 11–16* (Osnabrück: Biblio Verlag, 1996), 18, 281.

13. Peter Schmitz, Klaus-Jürgen Thies, Günter Wehmann, and Christian Zweng, *Die deutschen Divisionen 1939–1945*, vol. 4, *Die Divisionen 17–25* (Osnabrück: Biblio Verlag, 2000), 631; SRH-042, pp. A-8, A-11. The *11th PD* was supposed to move to the Bitburg area to be rebuilt and form part of the OKW reserve. Schramm, *Kriegstagebuch des Oberkommandos der Wehrmacht*, 447.

14. Parker and Thompson, *Conqueror*, 117.

15. Air Marshal Robb Diary, "Notes of Meeting Held in Chief of Staff's Office," December 26, 1944; Bradley, *Soldier's Story*, 480–81; Montgomery Diary, December 23, 1944. Bradley later reflected that the "arrogant and egotistical" field marshal "began by lecturing and scolding me like a school boy." Montgomery told Bradley he had received a "real 'bloody nose'" and that it was useless trying to pretend because it was a "proper defeat." Montgomery concluded: "Bradley entirely agreed with all I said. Poor chap; he is such a decent fellow and the whole thing is a bitter pill for him. But he is man enough to admit it, and he did." Bradley and Blair, *A General's Life*, 369; Hamilton, *Monty*, 247–48. As far as Montgomery was concerned, Bradley had handed him a "proper 'dog's' breakfast" when the change in command occurred on December 20.

16. Patton was completely incensed: "I feel that this is disgusting and might

remove the valor of our army and the confidence of our people. It will have tremendous political implications. . . . If ordered to fall back, I think I will ask to be relieved."
Blumenson, *Patton Papers*, 2:606; Patton Diary, December 25, 1944.

17. Hamilton, *Monty*, 248; Montgomery Diary, December 26, 1944. In fact, by
December 28 Montgomery believed the German offensive was being completely
held, but he still wanted the enemy to expend more effort "and then hit him a large
blow on the rebound." Montgomery Diary, December 28, 1944.

18. Bradley to Hodges, December 26, 1944, RG 331, entry 199, Headquarters
Twelfth Army Group, 371.3 vol. III to vol. VI, NARA II. Eisenhower was not satisfied
with Devers and instructed "Pink" Bull on December 26 to go see him and give him
a withdrawal line to the Vosges north of Colmar. Eisenhower declared, "It will be a
disappointment giving up ground, but this area is not where I told DEVERS to put
his weight." Robb Diary, "Notes of Meeting Held in Supreme Commander's Office,"
December 26, 1944.

19. Blumenson, *Patton Papers*, 2:607; Third Army G-2 ISUM No. 444, RG 407,
entry 427, NARA II; Cole, *Ardennes*, 606. Patton felt that "with our entry into Bastogne, the German was licked, and that it was not necessary to hold a reserve, but to
attack with everything we had." Patton, *War as I Knew It*, 196.

20. Headquarters Twelfth Army Group, G-2 Periodic Report No. 205, 2300A, De-
cember 27, 1944, RG 407, entry 427, 99/12–2.1 Dec 44–Jan 45 to 99/12–2.1 Mar 45,
NARA II; DEFE 3/321, BT 479 (ZZZZ), 1656Z, December 27, 1944, reel 55. UL-
TRA revealed the German fear of an attack between Diekirch and the mouth of the
Our River late on December 28. DEFE 3/322, BT 605, 2234Z, December 28, 1944.
Koch also identified heavy vehicular traffic moving north three to five miles east of
Merzig. Third Army G-2 ISUM No. 444 up to 0900A, December 27, 1944, RG 407,
entry 427, NARA II.

21. Eddy War Log, December 26, 1944.

22. Patton Diary, December 26, 1944; Irwin Diary, December 27 and 28, 1944.
ULTRA confirmed that the withdrawal across the Sauer had been ordered. DEFE
3/322, BT 584, 1805Z, December 28, 1944.

23. DEFE 3/322, BT 504 (ZZZ), 2056Z, December 27, 1944.

24. Koch, *Intelligence for Patton*, 107; Third Army AAR, 1:180–81.

25. Colonel James McCormack Jr., Chief, Movement Branch, G-4, memorandum for General Moses, Future Operations—1945, January 2, 1945, RG 331, entry
199, 371.3 vols. 3–6, NARA II. See Headquarters Twelfth Army Group (drafter: Colonel H. H. D. Heiberg), Attack on Köln, January 12, 1945, Study on Future Operations, RG 407, entry ML-209, NARA II. This study contains a map showing Third
Army advancing on Bonn, just south of Cologne. Bradley later stated that he had
wanted to break straight through to Bonn. Bradley, *Soldier's Story*, 495.

26. Twelfth Army Group Weekly Intelligence Summary No. 20, Annex No. 2,
Terrain of the Eifel Summary, p. 1.

27. Winton, *Corps Commanders of the Bulge*, 208. The idea that the terrain
would not facilitate the move is well established. See Major Francis M. Cain III, "The
Ardennes—1944: An Analysis of the Operational Defense" (SAMS, USACGSC, 1986),
p. 26. Brooke noted in his diary on January 5 that Montgomery was confident that
he and Bradley could handle the western end of the salient, "but that the base of the

salient would present a more difficult problem." Alex Danchev and Daniel Todman, eds., *War Diaries, 1939–1945: Field Marshal Lord Alanbrooke* (London: Weidenfeld & Nicolson, 2001), 643. Jodl anticipated the main counterattack from the north side of the salient: "Personally, I expected it a little farther east—from the Aachen side—driving south from Elsenborn." ETHINT 50, p. 23.

28. Headquarters Twelfth Army Group, Estimate of the Situation, December 28, 1944 (drafter: Colonel H. H. D. Heiberg), RG 407, ML-209, NARA II. Heiberg was chief of the Plans Branch (G-3).

29. Bradley and Blair, *A General's Life*, 370. Danny S. Parker's view that Bradley proposed to attack the shoulders to trap the entire German army simply does not withstand scrutiny. Parker, *Battle of the Bulge*, 209.

30. Interview with Brigadier E. T. Williams, May 30–31, 1947, Pogue Interviews, USAHEC. Williams's reflection could only have been based on seeing Patton at the Verdun meeting, but his attendance there was unlikely.

31. George F. Hofmann, *The Super Sixth: History of the 6th Armored Division in World War II and Its Post-War Association* (Nashville: Battery Press, n.d.), 273–74; Patton Diary, December 26, 1944. Another version of this thought is as follows: "I believed then that this movement of the 6th Armored Division was premature. I should have waited longer and would then have found that it was better to engage it on the left flank, because the corridor north from Diekirch, which was my favorite line of attack, was supposed to be too narrow for armor. From later observation I think this was a mistake and that armor could have gone up the corridor. One never knows." Patton, *War as I Knew It*, 195. Patton probably meant the right flank, not the left, because Grow's division was initially employed in the Bastogne area. Grow assumed responsibility for the western sector of XII Corps at 0900 on December 27. At that hour CCB relieved the 109th CT, the remnant of the 28th Infantry Division.

32. See Third Army G-2 ISUM Nos. 444 to 453.

33. MacDonald, *Siegfried Line*, 57–60. A terrain analysis employing Google Earth clearly demonstrates that once Third Army crossed the Prüem River and passed through the village of Irrel, the terrain became a legitimate corridor for a divisional advance with two roads converging on Bitburg.

34. Ibid., 99–115. MacDonald argued elsewhere that it was worth the risk for the Americans to maneuver through the Ardennes–Eifel terrain, "however inhospitable," if the Germans lacked the mobile forces to seriously impede progress. MacDonald, "Neglected Ardennes," 91. In early February 1945 Grow's 6th Armored Division crossed the Our between Karlborn and Dahnen, leading one observer to conclude that armor could effectively operate in challenging terrain and cross a river in bad weather. Major Elbridge L. Brubaker et al., "The Deliberate River Crossing: The 6th Armored at the Our River," *Armor* 59, no. 4 (July–August 1950): 39.

35. Twelfth Army Group Weekly Intelligence Summary No. 22, for week ending January 9, 1945, Annex No. 5, "Enemy Use of Road Routes into the Salient," RG 407, entry 427, 99/12–2.1 to 99/12–2.6, NARA II.

36. Eddy War Log, December 26, 1944. What influence Eddy had is unknown, but he clearly "felt better tonight about the tactical situation than I have for some time. This may be our chance to end the war west of the Rhine." Ibid. There seemed

to be some confusion about boundaries. The G-3 4th Infantry Division spoke to Canine: "There is an acute boundary problem for the 4th Inf Div. The Regiments are basing their plans on the Div boundary given to them by Gen Eddy rather than the one submitted to them by XII Corps G-3. Gen Canine said that our G-3 probably misunderstood and that G-3 would straighten it out. 4th Inf Div G-3 stated that because of the time limit for plans to be submitted for the coming operation, the plans that they will submit will only be map studies. Gen Canine said that XII Corps could do the coordinating from these map studies and that they would be sufficient." Telephone conversation, General Canine and G-3 4th Infantry Division, C/S Section 26 1345 Dec 44, XII Corps, RG 407, entry 427, NARA II.

37. Irwin Diary, December 26 and 27, 1944; Eddy War Log, December 27, 1944.

38. At the end of day, XII Corps possessed 321 Shermans with either 75mm or 76mm guns, operational within six hours. XII Corps Tank Status Report as of 2200, December 26, 1944; XII Corps Operational Directive No. 58, 1130, December 25, 1944; XII Corps Operational Directive No. 59, December 26, 1944, RG 407, entry 427, NARA II. Division commanders were to submit their plans for all these elements by 1800 on December 26.

39. Eddy War Log, December 28, 1944; XII Corps Operational Directive No. 60, 1200, December 28, 1944; Gay Diary, December 28, 1944; Patton Diary, December 28, 1944. Eddy scheduled another meeting with Anderson the next day "so that we can have a better idea of what we want to do and shall be able to discuss in more detail this plan."

40. DEFE 3/320, BT 191 (ZZZ), 2202Z, December 23, 1944, reel 54; Patton Diary, December 28, 1944; Operational History of the Ninth Air Force, book 1, Battle of the Ardennes, December 1, 1944–January 26, 1945, 2:4. See the map in Craven and Cate, *Army Air Forces in World War II*, 691. It is unclear whether Patton's total of five divisions was for XII Corps's operation alone or included XX Corps' participation.

41. Chief of Staff Journal, Headquarters XII Corps, December 27, 1944, RG 407, entry 427, NARA II.

42. Eddy War Log, December 29, 1944.

43. Patton, *War as I Knew It*, 329.

44. Robb Diary, "Notes of Meeting Held in Chief of Staff's Office," December 26, 1944; Bradley and Blair, *A General's Life*, 367.

45. FM 100–5, pp. 99–100.

46. Reminiscences of General Otto P. Weyland, June 1960, pp. 24–25, Aviation Project, Oral History Research Office, Columbia University, New York. Cole outlines the military problem posed by Patton's concept in *Ardennes*, 611. *Generalmajor* Carl Wagener, Manteuffel's chief of staff, expressed this concept as follows: "Had the Allies allowed the attacker to reach the Maas or the crossing of the Maas, then simultaneously attacked with their strong forces, then they would have caused the destruction of the whole Army Group 'B.'" MS #A-963 (Wagener), "Main Reasons for the Failure of the Ardennes-Offensive," December 1945, p. 14, RG 549.3, NARA II.

47. Dupuy, *Hitler's Last Gamble*, 210. Dupuy, however, chose to avoid serious discussion of the military problem posed by such a line of action.

48. Patton, *War as I Knew It*, 332.

49. Allen Journal, August 13, 1944.

10. Path to Attrition, December 27–29

1. Guderian, *From Normandy to the Ruhr*, 340. See also Newton, *Hitler's Commander*, 342–43; Bauer, MS #R-15, "Key Dates during the Ardennes Offensive," pt. 1, pp. 7–8, 39.

2. MS #A-858 (Percy E. Schramm), "The Course of Events of the German Offensive in the Ardennes, 16 Dec 44 to 14 Jan 45," in Detwiler et al., *World War II German Military Studies*, vol. 10, pt. 4, p. 8; Heinz Guderian, *Panzer Leader* (London: Michael Joseph, 1952), 384; ETHINT 39 (Guderian), "Employment of Panzer Forces on the Western Front," August 16, 1945, p. 7; Warlimont, *Inside Hitler's Headquarters*, 490; Reinhard Gehlen, *The Gehlen Memoirs*, trans. David Irving (London: Collins, 1972), 116. Rundstedt added the following appreciation to Model's estimate during the evening of December 26: "Any transport of troops and supplies during the present weather is just about impossible, since our Luftwaffe does not have sufficient impact on the superiority of the enemy, in spite of strong deployment . . . the impression remains that the battles of 26 December reached a certain climax and that if the weather stays as it is, a supply and provision crisis can develop." Rundstedt quoted in Guderian, *From Normandy to the Ruhr*, 340; Siegfried Westphal, *The German Army in the West* (London: Cassell, 1951), 185.

3. MS #R-11, pt. 2, p. 132, 136, 154; DEFE 3/322, BT 504 (ZZZ), 2056Z, December 27, and BT 598 (ZZZ), 2153Z, December 28, 1944, reel 56; MS #B-151a, p. 253; MS #B-235, p. 30.

4. MS #R-11, pt. 2, p. 141.

5. MS #B-151a, p. 212; MS #R-11, pt. 2, p. 155; ETHINT 45, p. 13. He stated that "this withdrawal was necessary because the enemy forces which were attacking against the line Mande–St. Étienne–Tillet–St. Hubert were being reinforced continually." Rundstedt seemed to be thinking generally the same thing. See ETHINT 47, p. 9.

6. Cole, *Ardennes*, 614.

7. MS #A-940, p. 11, RG 549.3, NARA II. Another German source states that a *Korps Gruppe* was a tactical grouping of two to three understrength divisions. MS #B-779 (Rudolf Lehmann), "I SS Panzer Corps (15 December 1944–25 January 1945)," p. 39, RG 549.3, NARA II.

8. DEFE 3/322, BT 628 (ZZ), 0358Z, December 29, 1944, reel 56.

9. *OB West* KTB (text), December 27, Anlagen 1762–64, 1770, in MS #R-11, pt. 2, p. 141; Cole, *Ardennes*, 614. The reference to Patton does not appear in either Luttichau's or Bauer's study of key dates.

10. CCA, 4th Armored Division Field Order No. 4, December 27, 1944, in Lieutenant Colonel Robert R. Summers et al., "Armor at Bastogne," research report prepared by Committee 4, Officer's Advanced Course, Armored School, 1948–1949, Fort Knox, Ky., May 1949, pp. 226–27. The *Fallschirmjägers* flushed from Sainlez withdrew east and struck the 1st Battalion/318th CT in the rear, just as it cleared Livarchamps. Cole stated that CCA engaged *FJR 15*. Cole, *Ardennes*, 607. However, "Armor at Bastogne," 155, cites *FJR 14*. Numerous companies of the *13th* and *15th FJRs* were identified opposite the right flank of the 35th Infantry Division. III Corps ISUM No. 33, 1200A–2400A, December 27, 1944. The lack of

identification of *FJR 14* companies suggests that this regiment was farther west, opposite Gaffey.

11. The three task forces were TF Collins, built around the 60th Armored Infantry Battalion; TF Karsteter, built around the 19th Tank Battalion, reinforced; and TF Brownfield, built around the 811th Tank Destroyer Battalion. Clearly, reconnaissance was doing its job. See Summers et al., "Armor at Bastogne," 160. Cole states that "no one knew where the enemy might be found or in what strength." Cole, *Ardennes*, 615.

12. DEFE 3/322, BT 502 (ZZZZ), 2039Z, December 27, 1944, reel 56.

13. MS #B-592 (Remer), "The Fuehrer-Begleit-Brigade (The Brigade under the Command of Remer) in the Ardennes Offensive (16 Dec 44 to 26 Jan 45)," May 11, 1947, in Detwiler et al., *World War II German Military Studies*, vol. 12, pt. 5, p. 20; Helmut Spaeter, *The History of the Panzerkorps "Großdeutschland*," trans. David Johnston (Winnipeg: J. J. Fedorowicz, 1995), 2:481–82. Cole states that advance elements did not arrive until the morning of December 28. Cole, *Ardennes*, 614. The bulk of the antiaircraft artillery assets were also deployed around Tronle. Remer apparently launched some type of spoiling attack at 1800 from Chenogne against CCA/9th Armored Division, but to no avail. MS #R-11, p. 158.

14. Cole, *Ardennes*, 616; Third Army G-2 ISUM No. 445 (to 271800A), RG 407, entry 427, NARA II.

15. 35th Infantry Division AAR, December 1944, p. 10; 26th Infantry Division AAR, December 1944, p. 7.

16. MS # B-783, p. 6.

17. MS #R-11, pp. 178–79; MS #B-032 (Bodenstein), "Report of My Activities during the Americans' Campaign on the West Front, Ardennes, 16 Dec 44–25 Jan 45," April 17, 1946, p. 5; 26th Infantry Division AAR, December 1944, p. 4; Spaeter, *History of Panzerkorps*, 482.

18. MS #R-11, p. 180.

19. MS #B-521 (Werner Kolb), "The Ardennes-Offensive in the Sector of the 9 Volks Gren Div (25 Dec 1944 until 25 Jan 1945)," pp. 5, 14–15, RG 549.3, NARA II; MS #A-876, vol. 1 (*General der Panzertruppen* Erich Brandenberger), "Ardennes Offensive of Seventh Army (16 Dec 1944–25 Jan 1945)," in Detwiler et al., *World War II German Military Studies*, vol. 12, pt. 5, p. 74; Cole, *Ardennes*, 547; Twelfth Army Group G-2 Periodic Report No. 206, 1800, December 28, 1944, RG 407, entry 427, 99/12–2.1 Dec 1944–Jan 1945 to 99/12–2.1 Mar 1945, NARA II. Trevor N. Dupuy stated that by December 27 about 70 percent of *9th VGD* had arrived. Dupuy, *Hitler's Last Gamble*, 287.

20. MS #B-070 (Hummel), "Report on the Defense by the 79 Volks Gren Div of the Sauer Bridgehead at Baunscheid and the Retreat to the West Wall during the Period from 30 Dec 44–31 Jan 45," p. 1, RG 549.3, NARA II.

21. Ibid., 3; Cole, *Ardennes*, 539; MS #B-070 (*Oberst* Kurt Hummel), "79th Volks Grenadier Division (30 Dec 1944–31 Jan 1945)," p. 2; Guderian, *From Normandy to the Ruhr*, 341; MS #R-11, p. 158.

22. Bradley and Blair, *A General's Life*, 372; Hansen Diary, December 28, 1944.

23. Leonard Rapport and Arthur Northwood Jr., *Rendezvous with Destiny: A History of the 101st Airborne Division* (Washington, D.C.: Infantry Journal Press, 1948), 595.

24. Only four of thirteen C-47s of the 440th Troop Carrier Group survived German antiaircraft fire. Cole, *Ardennes*, 609.

25. Patton Diary, December 27, 1944; III Corps AAR, December 1944, p. 15; DEFE 3/322, BT 504 (ZZZ), 2103Z, December 27, 1944, reel 56. Tronle was the CP of the *FBB*.

26. Patton Diary, December 27, 1944.

27. Weyland Diary, December 28, 1944; MS #B-592, pp. 21–22; ETHINT 46, p. 8; ETHINT 42 (Heinrich von Lüttwitz), "The Breakthrough to Bastogne," November 1, 1945, p. 2; MS #C-002 (*Generalmajor* Walter Denkert), "3 Pz Gren Division (from 28 Dec 44 to 25 Jan 45)," n.d., p. 2, RG 549.3, NARA II. Denkert states that he met with Model and Manteuffel at Mont-le-Ban the night of December 27–28.

28. The division AAR states that the 134th CT moved to Warnach during the early morning of December 28, and its 3rd Battalion immediately went into action. 35th Infantry Division AAR, December 1944, p. 11.

29. Cole, *Ardennes*, 609; 134th Infantry Regiment AAR, December 1944, RG 407, entry 427, 335-INF(134)-0.3, NARA II. It is unclear who gave the orders.

30. Telegram, *OB West* to Army Group B, 2020, December 29, 1944, in Bauer, MS #R-15, p. 62; ibid., 10, 60; MS #R-11, p. 158; Tiemann, *Leibstandarte*, 126.

31. Montgomery Diary, December 28, 1944.

32. Eisenhower to Montgomery, December 29, 1944, in Chandler, *Eisenhower Papers*, 4:2383. Montgomery told Eisenhower that all operations north of the Moselle should be under a single commander to achieve that goal. Hamilton, *Monty*, 261; Eisenhower, *Crusade in Europe*, 360.

33. Hamilton, *Monty*, 262n1; M401, 1940 hours, December 28, 1944, Montgomery Papers. It is unclear what potential action of Bradley's Montgomery considered unsound.

34. Eisenhower to Devers, 1024A, December 28, 1944, S-72681, RG 331, entry 58, G-3 War Diary, NARA II.

35. It had made a forced overland march from Barneville and Rennes, France, to concentrate and prepare for battle in the Soissone–Laon–Sissone area, northeast of Reims. On December 25 Middleton designated Kilburn commander of the VIII Corps Meuse River sector (from Givet to Verdun) until relieved by the 17th Airborne Division at a time mutually agreeable to the division commanders concerned. At 1200 on December 27 command of the VIII Corps Meuse River sector was formally relinquished to the 17th Airborne Division. At 0230 the division issued Field Order No. 3, directing a march from assembly areas west of the Meuse via Charleville–Sedan–Carignan and Jamoigne to the vicinity of Neufchâteau, Belgium. Rear echelon division headquarters remained at Rethel, France.

36. J. Ted Hartman, *Tank Driver: With the 11th Armored Division from the Battle of the Bulge to VE Day* (Bloomington: Indiana University Press, 2003), 54; Gay Diary, December 29, 1944.

37. Cole, *Ardennes*, 612; Gay Diary, December 28, 1944; interviews with Lieutenant General Walter Bedell Smith, May 8, 1947, Major General J. F. M. Whiteley, December 18, 1946, and Colonel James Gault, February 13, 1947, Pogue Interviews, USAHEC. Montgomery regularly called him during the Bulge to express his views, and although Whiteley was not particularly enraptured by the field marshal, he was

probably influenced by him. Carlo D'Este has argued that this was further proof that Bradley's role during the Bulge was irrelevant. D'Este, *Eisenhower*, 659. However, Bradley had selected corridor A as well. John S. D. Eisenhower's comment that Patton placed the SHAEF reserve on the west to cover the LC into Bastogne misses the subtleties of the scheme of maneuver issues at the time. Eisenhower, *Bitter Woods*, 409.

38. "Copy of Instructions Handed to Comdr VIII Corps. 26.12.44" (handwritten), RG 331, entry 29, 370–46 to 370–61, NARA II. This note has "53BB" in the top right-hand corner and a G-3 minute.

39. Brigadier A. Franklin Kibler, memorandum for Brigadier H. G. Maddox, December 26, 1944, RG 331, entry 199, Headquarters Twelfth Army Group, 371.3 vols. 3–6, NARA II; Robb Diary, "Notes of Meeting Held in Chief of Staff's Office," and "Notes of Meeting Held in Supreme Commander's Office," December 26, 1944. Whiteley intended to tell the 11th Armored Division how to support the British 29th Armored Brigade along the Meuse River.

40. Third Army Operational Directive, December 28, 1944, RG 407, entry 427, NARA II.

41. The VIII Corps AAR (p. 30) states that Third Army issued the attack date of December 30 early on December 29.

42. Colonel Paul D. Harkins, Deputy Chief of Staff, December 28, 1944, RG 407, entry 427, 203–3.2 27 Dec to 31 Dec 44, NARA II. Gay implies that Harkins was dispatched *before* Third Army received word that the SHAEF reserve had been released to it. Gay Diary, December 28, 1944.

43. Gay Diary, December 29, 1944. Cole stated that Middleton convinced both Patton and Bradley. Cole, *Ardennes*, 615; Rickard, *Patton at Bay*, 87, 100.

44. III Corps AAR, December 1944, pp. 15–16; Colonel J. H. Phillips, CofS, Memorandum for Record, December 29, 1944, RG 407, entry 427, 203–3.2 27 Dec to 31 Dec 44, NARA II.

45. Patton Diary, December 29, 1944. Gaffey also received fourteen new Shermans with the long 76mm gun. Irzyk's 8th Tank Battalion received seven new-model Shermans with a long-barreled, high-velocity gun on December 28; this was the M4A3E8, soon designated by the tankers as the "Easy 8." The 4th Armored Division had lost 50 Shermans and 263 killed, 909 wounded, and 53 missing in action. During the same period it received 1,636 replacements. III Corps AAR, December 1944, p. 14; Irzyk, *He Rode up Front for Patton*, 265; 4th Armored Division AAR, December 1944, p. 3.

46. 6th Armored Division AAR, December 1944, RG 407, entry 427, 606–0.3, NARA II; Patton Diary, December 28, 1944; III Corps AAR, December 1944, pp. 16, 18.

47. Robb quoted in Hamilton, *Monty*, 269; Crosswell, *Beetle*, 825; J. F. C. Fuller, *Armored Warfare: An Annotated Edition of Lectures on F.S.R. III (Operations between Mechanized Forces)* (Harrisburg, Pa.: Military Service Publishing, 1955), 97, 183; Jomini, *Art of War*, 186.

48. Conversely, Simpson noted that Montgomery always gave "clear and definite orders what I had to do." Quoted in Hamilton, *Monty*, 254. Montgomery recognized this weakness in Eisenhower as well, noting that he had had no orders from him since December 20.

49. Blumenson felt that Middleton suffered from the conflicting leadership styles of Bradley and Patton in Normandy. Blumenson, *Breakout and Pursuit*, 357–58, 378–79; John J. McGrath, *Crossing the Line of Departure: Battle Command on the Move, a Historical Perspective* (Fort Leavenworth, Kans.: Combat Studies Institute Press, 2007), 108; Gay Diary, December 29, 1944.

50. Gay Diary, December 29, 1944.

51. VIII Corps AAR, December 1944, p. 30.

52. Blumenson, *Patton Papers*, 2:531, 609.

53. Patton Diary, December 27, 1944. Harold Winton properly stresses the fact that Houffalize was a driving factor in their decision making. Winton, *Corps Commanders of the Bulge*, 237.

54. Montgomery Diary, December 28, 1944.

55. Eisenhower added: "The presence of your British 30th Corps, not yet employed, gives you great flexibility." Chandler, *Eisenhower Papers*, 4:2384.

56. Headquarters VIII Corps, Field Order No. 12, 1400, December 29, 1944, RG 407, entry 427, 208–7.2 1 Dec 44 to 208–7.2 Jan 45, NARA II.

57. VIII Corps Field Order No. 12; FM 100–5, p. 103.

58. Hal D. Steward, *Thunderbolt: The History of the Eleventh Armored Division* (Nashville: Battery Press, 1981), 26; War Department, TM 20–205, *Dictionary of United States Army Terms*, 1944, USAHEC.

59. Gay Diary, December 29, 1944.

60. See John J. Mearsheimer, "Why the Soviets Can't Win Quickly in Central Europe," *International Security* 7, no. 1 (summer 1982): 16–17, and "Assessing the Conventional Balance: The 3:1 Rule and Its Critics," *International Security* 13, no. 4 (spring 1999): 54–89. The British official historian, Brigadier General James E. Edmonds, traced the origin of the concept to the Franco-Prussian War. *Military Operations, France and Belgium, 1917*, vol. 2 (London: HMSO, 1948), 386. For a discussion of required ratios in excess of 3:1, see Shelford Bidwell and Dominick Graham, *Fire-Power: British Army Weapons and Theories of War, 1904–1945* (London: George Allen & Unwin, 1982), 284.

61. Colonel Trevor N. Dupuy, "Combat Data and the 3:1 Rule," *International Security* 14, no. 1 (summer 1989): 196; Dupuy, *Numbers, Predictions and War*, 13; Joshua M. Epstein, "Dynamic Analysis and the Conventional Balance in Europe," *International Security* 12, no. 4 (spring 1988): 155; Joshua M. Epstein, "The 3:1 Rule, the Adaptive Dynamic Model, and the Future of Security Studies," *International Security* 13, no. 4 (spring 1989): 90–127.

62. B. H. Liddell Hart, "The Ratio of Troops to Space," *Military Review* 40, no. 1 (April 1960): 8–9.

63. F. O. Miksche, *Blitzkrieg* (London: Faber & Faber, 1941), 29–30.

64. FM 100–5, pp. 110, 114–15, 118. It has been argued that American infantry consistently required overwhelming volumes of artillery fire on frontline units and air strikes on reserves unless they enjoy a local superiority approaching 4:1. Millett and Murray, *Military Effectiveness*, 61; Weigley, *Eisenhower's Lieutenants*, 416.

65. Quoted in Hamilton, *Monty*, 269.

66. *Fifth Panzer Armee* reported during the evening of December 29 that LVIII *Panzerkorps* had assumed responsibility for *2nd PD*'s sector at the tip of the Bulge.

2nd PD was ordered to withdraw behind the river L'Homme, if compelled to do so, but to hold its bridgehead at all costs. The *9th PD* reported at 0008 on December 30 that it was holding a defensive line between Forrieres and Hargimont. The bridgeheads at Forrieres and Jemelle were to be held. DEFE 3/322, BT 616, December 29; DEFE 3/322, BT 736 (ZZZZ), 1317Z, December 30; DEFE 3/323, BT 763 (ZZZZ), 1804Z, December 30, 1944. Also at 0008, *9th PD* requested *Jagdkorps II* to attack Allied supply depots near Rochefort and Marche. DEFE 3/322, BT 737 (ZZZZ), 1419Z, December 30, 1944, reel 56.

67. Koch, *Intelligence for Patton,* 107; Third Army G-2 ISUM No. 451, 1800A, December 29, 1944; Third Army G-2 ISUM No. 447, 0900A, December 28, 1944, ibid.

68. DEFE 3/322, BT 591 (ZZZZ), 2004Z, December 28, 1944, reel 56.

69. Third Army G-2 ISUM No. 450, 0900A, December 29, 1944; MS #A-978 (Denkert), "Commitment of the 3 Pz Gren Div during the Ardennes Offensive," January 1946, p. 4, RG 549.3, NARA II; Third Army G-2 Work Map, Situation as of 0300A, December 30, 1944; Third Army G-2 ISUM No. 453, 0900A, December 30, 1944; Twelfth Army Group, Situation 1200 hours, December 29, 1944, Twelfth Army Group Outline Maps, 1:1,000,000, World War II Military Situation Maps, http://www.TheHistoricalArchive.com.

70. Third Army G-2 ISUM No. 451, 1800A, December 29, 1944. The last elements of the division could not depart until 1200 on December 29. Tiemann, *Leibstandarte,* 127–29. *Obersturmbannführer* Joachim Peiper contacted Heilmann at the *5th FJD* CP to get oriented to the front line, but no clear picture was possible. According to Michael Reynolds, Peiper appears to have played no part in the fighting at this stage, possibly because of a mental and physical breakdown. Reynolds, *Devil's Adjutant,* 246–49.

71. Third Army G–2 ISUM No. 451, 1800, December 29, 1944. In his memoirs Koch used the phrase "most dangerous" to describe the threat to the Bastogne corridor at this time. Koch, *Intelligence for Patton,* 107. The term *most dangerous line of action* was in use in 1944 but was not generally part of the estimate of the situation. For a good discussion, see Colonel Hollis L. Muller, *Technique of Modern Arms* (Harrisburg, Pa.: Military Service Publishing, 1940).

72. ULTRA had already revealed such bombing intentions early on December 28 and again early on December 29. DEFE 3/322, BT 526 (ZZZZ), 0013Z, and BT 641 (ZZZZ), 0658Z, December 29, 1944, reel 56. This must have been the source of Sibert's assessment during the meeting to which Gay was invited. Moreover, III Corps apparently alerted 4th Armored Division on December 28 to be prepared to receive a division-plus counterattack. Clarke, *Combat History of the 4th Armored Division,* cited in Summers et al., "Armor at Bastogne," 166. There is no mention of this, however, in the III Corps AAR. Gay Diary, December 29, 1944. Maddox and Harkins were also present. Third Army G-3 Operations Diary, entry for December 29, 1944.

73. Patton Diary, December 29, 1944.

74. Low-priority messages were often passed along for after-the-fact fleshing out of orders of battle and general situational awareness. Various other reasons could explain this omission. The lines of the Special Communications Units (SCUs) at Hut 3 could have been overloaded, the SCUs in question might have been moving, or there may have been a fear of compromising superior headquarters. David O'Keefe,

e-mails to author, August 26 and September 7, 2010. The intention to use the *167th VGD* and *3rd PGD* is found in DEFE 3/322, BT 578, December 28, and BT 674 (Z), 1741Z, December 29, 1944, reel 56; Hinsley, *British Intelligence*, 450. Bennett suggests that these divisions made an attack against Bastogne prior to December 29, but this is inaccurate. Bennett, *Ultra in the West*, 202.

75. Before D-Day Marshall had given Eisenhower explicit directions to protect the source of ULTRA at all costs. Marshall to Eisenhower, March 15, 1944, SRH-026, RG 457, NARA II; F. W. Winterbotham, *The Ultra Secret* (London: Harper & Row, 1974), 88–89.

76. The other capabilities included delaying and withdrawing to successive defensive positions exploiting the Ourthe River, reinforcing his front with major elements of three infantry divisions, and counterattacking utilizing reinforcements. VIII Corps G-2 Estimate No. 13, December 29, 1944, RG 407, entry 427, 208–7.2 1 Dec 44 to 208–7.2 Jan 45, NARA II. Reeves's listing of the *36th Infantry Division* and *25th PGD* made little sense. Both were in Lorraine. The *9th* and *79th VGDs* were identified opposite III and XII Corps. There is evidence that during the evening of December 29 the *FBB*, attached to the *3rd PGD*, was counterattacking in the area just south of Senonchamps. DEFE 3/322, BT 744 (ZZ), 1512Z, December 30, 1944, reel 56.

77. Steward, *Thunderbolt*, 27; Third Army G-2 Periodic Report No. 203, December 31, 1944, p. 5, RG 407, entry 427, 208–7.2 Jan 45 to 208–7.2 Feb 45, NARA II; 87th Infantry Division, Intelligence Annex to Field Order No. 4, December 29, 1944, RG 407, entry 427, 208–7.2 Dec 44 to 208–7.2 Jan 45, NARA II; Headquarters VIII Corps, Intelligence Annex No. 1 to accompany Field Order No. 12, December 29, 1944, RG 407, entry 427, 208–7.1 1 December 44 to 208–7.2 January 1945, NARA II. Cole argued that American intelligence "had practically no knowledge of any German units except those immediately in contact." Cole, *Ardennes*, 614. Bennett argued that from December 27 onward, the tactical usefulness of ULTRA declined. Bennett, *Ultra in the West*, 201.

78. *OB West* KTB 1784–1828. That Manteuffel believed it was possible to achieve a victory east of the Meuse is reflected in a *Fifth Panzer Armee* report received by the *Luftwaffe* at 0023 on December 29, stating that Third Army's attempts to broaden the gap into Bastogne had been unsuccessful. This same report also stated that *Seventh Armee* was making good progress against Allied penetrations south of Harlange. Richardson and Freidin, *Fatal Decisions*, 250–51; Cole, *Ardennes*, 619; DEFE 3/322, BT 738 (ZZ), 1433Z, December 30, 1944, reel 56.

79. Blumenson, *Patton Papers*, 2:608.

11. Slugging Match, December 30–31

1. MS #C-002, pp. 3–6; Third Army G-2 Periodic Report No. 203, p. 2, RG 407, entry 427, 208–7.2 1 Dec 44 to 208–7.2 Jan 45, NARA II; VIII Corps SITREP No. 549, 1245, December 30, 1944, ibid.

2. The *FBB* artillery battalion moved into the valley southeast of Rechrival. Spaeter, *History of Panzerkorps*, 2:485; MS #B-592, p. 28.

3. Cole, *Ardennes*, 622. The 345th CT appears to have cleared Moircy by 1300. VIII Corps AAR, December 1944, p. 31.

4. Third Army G-2 Periodic Report No. 203, p. 5.

5. TF White consisted of 63rd AIB minus A Company, plus A Company/42nd Tank Battalion; TF Blue consisted of 42nd Tank Battalion minus A Company, A Company/63rd AIB, and B Company/602nd Tank Destroyer Battalion. Post Combat Interviews Regarding the 11th Armored Division, http://www.11tharmoreddivision .com; Cole, *Ardennes*, 621; interview with Major Carl Sheely and executive officer Captain Clarence A. Rechter, 63rd AIB, 11th Armored Division, Battalion CP, Buret, Belgium, January 25, 1945.

6. VIII Corps SITREP No. 550, 1800, December 30, 1944.

7. Third Army G-2 ISUM No. 454, 1800A, December 30, 1944.

8. Ralf Tiemann stated that the *Leibstandarte kampfgruppen* crossed the LD at 0625. Tiemann, *Leibstandarte*, 127. Koch stated 0500 in G-2 ISUM No. 454, 1800A, December 30, 1944.

9. Third Army G-2 Periodic Report No. 203, p. 6; Ritgen, *Western Front*, 278.

10. Cole estimated its strength at 8,000, which would have been 80 percent of a *volksgrenadier* TO&E. Cole, *Ardennes*, 623; MS #B-041 (Hoecker), "Report on the Participation of the 167 Volks Gren Div, the 59 Div and the Corps Group Hoecker in the Ardennes Campaigns," November 9, 1946, p. 5, RG 549.3, NARA II.

11. Summers et al., "Armor at Bastogne," 169–71. The 35th Infantry Division informed III Corps at 0945 that Baade had called Gaffey, seeking assistance. III Corps G-3 files, NARA II. It seems that two regiments of the *167th* VGD attacked, but little information is available.

12. MS #B-041, p. 7, RG 549.3, NARA II; Cole, *Ardennes*, 626. Only XIX TAC flew during December 29–30, carrying out some 949 sorties in the Echternach, Bastogne, and Arlon areas during those two days. Craven and Cate, *Army Air Forces in World War II*, 698–99.

13. 134th Infantry Regiment AAR, December 1944, p. 4, RG 407, entry 427, 335-INF (134)-0.3, NARA II; Tiemann, *Leibstandarte*, 128.

14. Tiemann, *Leibstandarte*, 131; Cole, *Ardennes*, 621, 625.

15. CG LUCKY (Colonel Wright) to CG CENTURY (G-3), 1410, December 30, 1944, RG 407, entry 427, 203–3.2 27 Dec to 31 Dec 44, III Corps, NARA II. Maddox instructed III Corps to send someone to Baade's CP to get the report. Major H. J. McAlister, the corps assistant G-3, made the journey and produced a memorandum of the visit.

16. 35th Infantry Division AAR, December 1944, p. 11; 4th Armored Division G-3 telephone call to III Corps G-3, 1515, December 30, 1944.

17. Third Army G-2 ISUM Nos. 453, 454, and 455 up to 2400A, December 30, 1944.

18. Patton Diary, December 30, 1944.

19. Gay Diary, December 30, 1944.

20. Blumenson, *Patton Papers*, 2:609–10; Winton, *Corps Commanders of the Bulge*, 229. Patton indicated he had no idea of the impending German attack in a letter the next day to his wife. Later he declared it "very fortuitous . . . because had we not hit the flank of the Germans, they might have again closed the corridor into Bastogne." Patton, *War as I Knew It*, 197.

21. Patton, "Notes on Bastogne Operation." He drove into Bastogne during the height

of the battle to decorate McAuliffe and the commander of the 502nd PIR. "They were delighted," recalled Patton, "and wanted me to drive slowly so the soldiers could see me." Patton Diary, December 30, 1944. This suggests he did not fear German attacks.

22. McBride "felt that it might be better to push troops through a hole that they now have rather than trying in a new place." Eddy War Log, December 30, 1944.

23. Gay Diary, December 30, 1944. *LXXXII Armeekorps* of *First Armee* expected a significant change in the Saarlautern bridgehead as a trigger to a full-scale attack. It also reported that the increased activity opposite the Orscholz switch line might signify an attack. DEFE 3/323, BT 859, 2314Z, December 31, 1944, reel 56.

24. III Corps, Annex No. 2 to Field Order No. 2, Intelligence Annex, 1100, December 30, 1944, RG 407, entry 427, 203–3.2 27 Dec 1944 to 203–3.2 31 Dec 1944, NARA II.

25. DEFE 3/322, BT 752 (ZZZZZ), 1642Z, December 30, 1944, reel 57.

26. 11th Armored Division AAR, December 1944, RG 407, entry 427, 208–7.2 Dec 44 to 208–7.2 Jan 45, NARA II.

27. The combat command received verbal instructions to move at 2300 on December 30. Headquarters, 11th Armored Division, Field Order No. 5, 0100, December 31, 1944, RG 407, entry 427, 208–7.2 1 Dec 44 to 208–7.2 Jan 45, NARA II; MS #B-592, p. 28.

28. III Corps, Field Order No. 2, 1100, December 30, 1944, RG 407, entry 427, 203–3.2 27 Dec 1944 to 203–3.2 31 Dec 1944, NARA II; III Corps AAR, December 1944, p. 18; Cole, *Ardennes*, 628.

29. Millikin to Gaffey, 2200, December 30, 1944, RG 407, entry 427, 203–3.2 27 Dec 1944 to 203–3.2 31 Dec 1944, NARA II.

30. Hofmann, *Super Sixth*, 275–77. Hofmann implied that the 11th Armored Division had been redirected from its original assignment to advance immediately left of 6th Armored Division out of the Bastogne Pocket to meet the threat of *XLVII Panzerkorps'* attack on December 30. The last part is inaccurate, but the first part matches with Middleton's desire not to send the 11th Armored Division into the pocket.

31. Ibid., 277.

32. The trains commander, Colonel Droste, reported he could not get forward because he was blocked by friendly units and the icy conditions. Colonel J. H. Phillips, Memorandum for Record, December 31, 1944, RG 407, entry 427, 203–3.2 31 Dec 44 to 5 Jan 45, III Corps, NARA II.

33. 6th Armored Division AAR, December 1944, p. 24; Major T. J. Sharpe, Assistant G-3, Memorandum for Record, December 30, 1944, RG 407, entry 427, 203–3.2 27 Dec to 31 Dec 44, III Corps, NARA II; Millikin to Grow, 1640 hours, December 30, 1944, ibid.

34. Third Army G-3 SITREP No. 606, 2400A December 30 to 0600A December 31, 1944.

35. MS #B-592, p. 29.

36. 11th Armored Division Field Order No. 5; Steward, *Thunderbolt*, 30. TF Blue led, and TF White followed 1,000 yards behind. Verbal orders were issued to attack north between CCR and CCB at 1230. Middleton reported a coordinated attack was scheduled for 1215, but this did not occur. VIII Corps G-3 SITREP No. 553, 1215, December 31, 1944.

37. III Corps AAR, December 1944, p. 18; 35th Infantry Division AAR, December 1944, p. 12; Cole, *Ardennes*, 629. Indeed, *Fifth Panzer Armee* reported that Third Army was strong in artillery. DEFE 3/323, BT 884 (ZZ), 0618Z, January 1, 1945, reel 57. See also Michael Reynolds, *Men of Steel: 1st SS Panzer Corps: The Ardennes and Eastern Front 1944–1945* (New York: Sarpedon, 1999), 153.

38. Cole, *Ardennes*, 635. During the evening *FJR 14* was subordinated to *PGR 1*. DEFE 3/324, BT 1011 (ZZ), 1603Z, January 2, 1945, reel 57.

39. Phillips, Memorandum for Record, December 31, 1944; Cole, *Ardennes*, 641.

40. CCB/10th Armored Division AAR, December 1944, pp. 4, 19, RG 407, entry 427, 610-CCB-0.3, NARA II; Hofmann, *Super Sixth*, 277.

41. Hofmann, *Super Sixth*, 275–77; Grow to Millikin, 1325 hours, December 31, 1944, RG 407, entry 427, 203–3.2 31 Dec 44 to 5 Jan 45, III Corps, NARA II.

42. *Battle Book: A Combat History of Headquarters and Headquarters Battery, Division Artillery 6th Armored Division* (1945), http://www.super6th.org/divarty /Artillery.htm.

43. Phillips, Memorandum for Record, December 31, 1944. Grow reported that CCB was now closing up but would have to refuel, and "it is estimated that it will be daylight tomorrow before enough of CCB can be ready to get them started." Grow to Millikin, 1325 hours, December 31, 1944.

44. Phillips, Memorandum for Record, December 31 1944. Grow stated that Fickett "would be of no help to him on his left flank because he was convinced that Fickett was not equipped to do the job. . . . He also asked what the 101st was going to do." Millikin replied that Taylor was not under his command but that he was to stay in his present positions for now. Millikin to Grow, 1640 hours, December 30, 1944, RG 407, entry 427, 203–3.2 27 Dec to 31 Dec 44, III Corps, NARA II.

45. CG CENTURY (Mewshaw) to CG BAMBOO (Major Brogan, G-3), 2335, December 31, 1944, RG 407, entry 427, 203–3.2 31 Dec 44 to 5 Jan 45, III Corps, NARA II.

46. III Corps AAR, December 1944, p. 19; Blumenson, *Patton Papers*, 2:610.

47. VIII Corps issued the orders at 0230 on December 30. 9th Armored Division AAR, December 1944, RG 407, entry 427, 609–33.4, NARA II.

48. Third Army AAR, pp. 187, 196.

49. The nearest supply points for 155mm gun, 8-inch howitzer, and 4.5-inch gun ammunition were at Verdun and Etain. III Corps AAR, December 1944, p. 14. Third Army's ammunition supply as a whole was well supported by the railhead at Audunle-Roman. When Third Army reoriented its logistical footprint north, it abolished the practice of serving units directly from railheads; however, because of the volume of issues at Point No. 38 at Mamer, III Corps, which was using huge amounts of ammunition, was now served directly from the railhead at Athus. Mamer continued to support XII Corps, while Point No. 39 at Mellier served VIII Corps. Third Army AAR, vol. 1, pp. 196, 204–5, 213. The strength of Third Army did not include 25,336 men supplied to the AdSec or 2,271 French and 2,344 miscellaneous troops.

50. Third Army G-2 Periodic Report No. 203, pp. 1–5. The German *First Armee* reported this at 0016 December 30. DEFE 3/323, BT 782 (ZZZZ), 2214Z, December 30, 1944, reel 58. ULTRA had earlier revealed that the rehabilitation of the

division was proceeding according to schedule. All convalescents were ordered to field units. DEFE 3/323, BT 755 (ZZ), 1903Z, December 30, 1944, reel 56. *Colonel-General* Johannes Blaskowitz declared on December 28 that it "is in good condition at the moment." Heiber and Glantz, *Hitler and His Generals*, 543. Sibert also agreed that the *11th PD* had not been identified in any portion of the salient, but it remained a candidate for commitment anywhere in the west. Twelfth Army Group G-2 Periodic Report No. 208, 2300, December 30, 1944.

51. *II SS Panzerkorps* contained the *2nd*, *9th*, and *12th SS PDs* and the *560th VGD*. DEFE 3/322, BT 745 (ZZZZ), 1546Z, December 30, and BT 869 (ZZZZ), 2333Z, December 31, 1944, reel 56. Sometimes ULTRA was simply out of date and of no use to Patton. One example is a message sent at 2054 on December 31 indicating that *1st SS PD*, as of 1130 on December 30, intended to "thrust south of Bastogne . . . to [the] west." This was more than twenty-four hours out of date and explains why neither Third Army's nor Twelfth Army Group's code was on it. DEFE 3/323, BT 850 (ZZ), 2054Z, December 31, 1944, reel 56.

52. Third Army AAR, vol. 1, p. 187.

53. Ibid.; Third Army G-2 Periodic Report No. 203, pp. 1–7. Even the Germans appreciated the lack of pressure to the north. *II SS Panzerkorps* reported at 0008 on December 31 that it was unclear whether the enemy was regrouping or intending to attack and that the Allies were digging in on the whole front. DEFE 3/323, BT 813, 1255Z, December 31, 1944. See also BT 819 (ZZZ), 1419Z, December 31, reel 58, for the same lack of offensive intentions.

54. Chandler, *Eisenhower Papers*, 4:2389; Greenwood, *Normandy to Victory*, 244. It has been argued that Patton only now recognized that he could not maneuver until the Germans in front of him were destroyed. Winton, *Corps Commanders of the Bulge*, 230–31.

12. Culmination, January 1–4

1. Chandler, *Eisenhower Papers*, 4:2209, 2391.

2. Kibler (signed Bradley) to Third Army, December 31, 1944, RG 331, entry 199, 371.3 vols. 3–6, NARA II. Bletchley Park sent a message a little over an hour later declaring that the order of battle of the German *First Armee* in Lorraine "needs careful watching" because several divisions were "apparently not repeat not in line." DEFE 3/323, BT 844, 1938Z, December 31, 1944, reel 57.

3. MS #A-858, pp. 5–6.

4. Bonn, *When the Odds Were Even*, 181; Jeffrey J. Clarke, *U.S. Army in World War II: Riviera to the Rhine* (Washington, D.C.: CMH, 1994), 494; MS #A-862, pp. 67–68.

5. Pallud, *Battle of the Bulge*, 481.

6. DEFE 3/324, BT 1015 (ZZZZ), 1625Z, and BT 1026 (ZZZ), 1817Z, January 2, 1945; DEFE 3/324, BT 1084 (ZZ), 0907Z, January 3, 1945, reel 57; MS #B-393, p. 38.

7. The *12th* and *9th SS PDs* had been ordered to Bastogne on December 30 and 31, respectively. Cole, *Ardennes*, 631. At 0014 that day the *9th SS PD* was still in the Grandmenil area. DEFE 3/323, BT 896 (ZZZZ), 1242Z, January 1, 1945, reel 57.

At this time the *II SS Panzerkorps* had the *2nd, 9th,* and *12th SS PDs* and the *560th VGD.*

8. MS #B-779, p. 40. ULTRA indicated that *I SS Panzerkorps* assumed control at 0001. DEFE 3/323, BT 923 (ZZZZZ), 1714Z, January 1, 1945, reel 57. The new boundary with XLVII *Panzerkorps* was apparently Sprimont–Morhet, but this does not match up with map X of Cole's history.

9. Only 43 percent of tonnage capacity was roadworthy. Ritgen, *Western Front,* 282; MS #B-286 (Leo Zanssen), "Ardennes 16 Dec 1944 to 25 January 1945," p. 3, RG 549.3, NARA II.

10. Meyer, *12th SS,* 332.

11. MS #C-002, p. 11; MS #B-592, p. 30; 11th Armored Division AAR, January 1945.

12. VIII Corps AAR, January 1945, p. 3, RG 407, entry 427, 208–0.3, NARA II.

13. Price, *Middleton,* 268; Gay Diary, January 1, 1945. Eisenhower ordered this. SHAEF Main to Twelfth Army Group, 17 Airborne Division, 1609A, January 1, 1945, S-73266. Divisions assigned to SHAEF reserve were under command of the Fifteenth Army. See SHAEF Main, signed SCAEF, to CG, Fifteenth Army, 1613A, January 1, 1945, S-73267, RG 331, entry 58, SHAEF G-3 War Diaries, 1943–1945, NARA II; VIII Corps AAR, January 1945, p. 4; Blumenson, *Patton Papers,* 2:612; Patton Diary, January 1, 1945.

14. Colonel J. H. Phillips, Memorandum for Record, January 1, 1945, RG 407, entry 427, 203–3.2 31 Dec 44 to 5 Jan 45, III Corps, NARA II; Patton, "Notes on Bastogne Operation," 7. III Corps' Operational Directive No. 1, issued on January 1, declared that 6th Armored was to "make plans for encirclement of enemy in direction Bras . . . in conjunction with 26th Inf Div." III Corps G-3 files.

15. Heavy tank and vehicular movement was reported northeast of Lutremange to Lutrebois between 0400 and 0700. Third Army G-2 ISUM No. 460, 1800, January 1, 1945.

16. Lieutenant Colonel Renfroe to Colonel H. C. Mewshaw, 0925 hours, January 1, 1945, and Colonel H. C. Mewshaw to Lieutenant Colonel Renfroe, 1220 hours, January 1, 1945, RG 407, entry 427, 203–3.2 31 Dec 44 to 5 Jan 45, III Corps, NARA II. At 1030 the division sent III Corps an emergency request for armored assistance. Colonel J. H. Phillips, Memorandum to CG, January 1, 1945, ibid. However, the III Corps AAR clearly stated that Baade had the 654th Tank Destroyer Battalion. 35th Infantry Division AAR, January 1945, pp. 1–2, RG 407, entry 427, 335–0.3, NARA II; III Corps AAR, December 1944, p. 25.

17. Eisenhower to Marshall, January 1, 1945, in Chandler, *Eisenhower Papers,* 4:2391.

18. Patton, *War as I Knew It,* 202; Blumenson, *Patton Papers,* 2:612; SRH-042, p. 44.

19. Spires, *Patton's Air Force,* 215; Gay Diary, January 1, 1945; Galland, *The First and the Last,* 319; Weyland Diary, January 1, 1945. German losses were perhaps 300 fighter pilots.

20. Planning apparently started on December 30. MS #R-15, p. 63; MS #A-858, pp. 4, 6; MS #R-11, pt. 2, p. 171.

21. Allan R. Millett, Williamson Murray, and Kenneth H. Watman, "The

Effectiveness of Military Organizations," *International Security* 11, no. 1 (summer 1986): 70.

22. Devers to Eisenhower, 1620A, December 31, 1944, BX22119; Devers to Eisenhower, 1935A, December 31, 1944, B-22132; Devers to Eisenhower, 2047A, December 31, 1944, BX-22149, RG 331, entry 58, G–3 War Diary, NARA II.

23. SHAEF meeting, January 1, 1945, RG 331, entry 58, G–3 War Diary, NARA II. Eisenhower to Devers, 1906A, January 1, 1945, S-73308. Eisenhower informed all his army group commanders the next day that any formations placed in SHAEF reserve would receive high priority in replacements and equipment. Eisenhower to army group commanders, 2003A, January 2, 1945, S-73437, RG 331, entry 58, G–3 War Diary, NARA II; minutes of SHAEF meetings, January 3, 1945; Pogue, *Supreme Command*, 398–402.

24. On December 31 Eddy visited Blakeley and asked whether he had a plan to cross the river. Blakeley replied he did not, because he was waiting on boundaries from corps. Two patrols had crossed during the night and reported that the banks were very steep. Eddy War Log, December 31, 1944, and January 1, 1945.

25. Blumenson, *Patton Papers*, 2:610–11; Gay Diary, January 1, 1945.

26. III Corps AAR, January 1945, p. 4, RG 407, entry 427, 303–0.3, NARA II.

27. MS #C-002, pp. 12–13.

28. VIII Corps AAR, January 1945, p. 4. Remer noted that his battalions were now down to 150 men and declared, "In order to save blood, the heavy weapons . . . became the mainstay of the defensive battle." MS #592, p. 32.

29. DEFE 3/324, BT 1110 (ZZ), pt. 2, 1618Z, and BT 1126 (ZZZZ), 1709Z, January 3, 1945, reel 57.

30. Cole, *Ardennes*, 632; III Corps ISUM No. 44, 2400A January 1 to 1200A January 2.

31. 6th Armored Division AAR, January 1944, p. 3, RG 407, entry 427, 606–0.3, NARA II; Meyer, *12th SS*, 336.

32. MS #A-876, p. 79.

33. MS #R-15, p. 61; MacDonald, *Last Offensive*, 28. The date set by Model for the attack is uncertain. Both Cole and MacDonald cite January 4. Cole, *Ardennes*, 632; MacDonald, *Last Offensive*, 34. The problem arises from Priess's postwar comment that he told Model the attack could not take place before January 4. Priess also said he requested a delay until January 5 but was refused by Manteuffel. MS #A-877 (Priess), "Commitment of the I SS Panzer Corps during the Ardennes Offensive (16 Dec 1944–25 Jan 1945)," pp. 51, 53, RG 549.3, NARA II. *Oberst* Rudolf Lehmann, *I SS Panzerkorps* chief of staff, supported Priess's comment. MS #B-779 (Rudolf Lehmann), "The I SS Panzer Corps during the Ardennes Offensive," p. 44. Hubert Meyer, however, stated that Priess requested a postponement until January 4, implying that the original date was January 3. Meyer, *12th SS*, 336; Reynolds, *Men of Steel*, 174n11. MS #R-11, pt. 2, p. 163, said January 3. The message traffic, ISUMs at both army and corps levels, and AARs all cite major attacks on January 3 against III Corps.

34. Eddy War Log, January 2, 1945; Gay Diary, January 2, 1945.

35. XII Corps Field Order No. 13, 1900, January 3, 1945, RG 407, entry 427, 212–0.3, NARA II. Radio silence was to be maintained during the preliminary stages of the move.

36. Hamilton, *Monty*, 285, 288.

37. Twelfth Army Group Weekly Intelligence Summary No. 21, for week ending January 2, 1945, RG 407, entry 427, 99/12–2.1 Apr 45 to 99/12–2.6 Jan 45, NARA II. On January 1 ULTRA located *11th PD* at Badem, northeast of Bitburg. The next day the division was located at Contwig under conditions of radio silence. DEFE 3/323, BT 874, 0136Z, January 1, 1945, and DEFE 3/324, BT 1044 (ZZZZZ), 2131Z, January 2, 1945, reel 57.

38. Patton Diary, January 2, 1945.

39. Greenwood, *Normandy to Victory*, 247. Twelfth Army Group seems to have been under the impression that VII Corps was still assembling in attack positions and would launch its coordinated attack on January 4. Twelfth Army Group G-3 Report Nos. 212 and 213, January 3 and 4, 1945.

40. Gay Diary, January 3, 1945. According to Blumenson, Middleton called at 1700. Blumenson, *Patton Papers*, 2:612; Third Army G-2 ISUM No. 465, 0900A, January 3, 1945.

41. Gay Diary, January 3, 1945.

42. MS #C-002, p. 16; MS #B-592, p. 32.

43. Cole, *Ardennes*, 647.

44. Rapport and Northwood, *Rendezvous with Destiny*, 617. The VIII Corps AAR (January 1945, p. 5) stated that a single regiment took part. Meyer stated that Model pressed for continuation of the attack, but Stadler convinced him that a night attack would be better. Meyer, *12th SS*, 337–38.

45. III Corps ISUM No. 44, January 2, 1945, p. 2; Third Army G-2 ISUM No. 465, 0900A, January 3, 1945.

46. III Corps ISUM No. 46, 2400A January 2 to 1200A January 3, 1945; Third Army G-2 ISUM No. 466, 1800A, and ISUM No. 467, 2400A, January 3, 1945.

47. MS #B-151a, pp. 217–18; MS #A-940, pp. 9–10; MS #A-858, p. 16; MS #R-15, pp. 65–66. *OB West* informed *Heeresgruppe G* of the intended transfer of *XXXIX Panzerkorps* on January 2.

48. Third Army G-3 SITREP No. 623, 0600A to 1200A, January 4, 1945; VIII Corps AAR, January 1945, p. 5.

49. 17th Airborne Division, G-3 Summary of Operations, February 2, 1945, RG 407, entry 427, 317–3, NARA II; MS #C-002, p. 17.

50. Price, *Middleton*, 272. Weigley answered Miley's question: the Germans were still capable of dealing "harshly with even the best American units entering combat for the first time." Weigley, *Eisenhower's Lieutenants*, 559.

51. William M. Miley, "17th Airborne Division in the Bulge," January 19, 1945, RG 407, entry 427, Combat Interviews, NARA II; Third Army G-2 ISUM No. 464, 2400A, January 2, 1945. Edward G. Miller argued that Koch contributed to Miley's difficulties by providing inaccurate assessments of the enemy. Edward G. Miller, *Nothing Less than Full Victory: Americans at War in Europe, 1944–1945* (Annapolis, Md.: Naval Institute Press, 2007), 186. This does not square with the record.

52. Patton, "Notes on Bastogne Operation," 8; Blumenson, *Patton Papers*, 2:615. During the first three days of action the division apparently suffered almost 1,000 casualties per day. Don R. Pay, *Thunder from Heaven: Story of the 17th Airborne Division 1943–1945* (1947; reprint, Nashville: Battery Press, 1980), 21.

53. Blumenson, *Patton Papers*, 2:615; Patton, "Notes on Bastogne Operation," 7. Despite his experience, Patton also noted, "How men live, much less fight," in such extreme weather conditions "is a marvel to me."

54. Colonel J. H. Phillips, Memorandum for Record, January 4, 1945, RG 407, entry 427, 203–3.2 31 Dec 44 to 5 Jan 45, III Corps, NARA II; Memorandum for Record (of conversation with commanders, 6th and 4th Armored Divisions and 35th Infantry Division), January 4, 1945, RG 407, entry 427, 203–3.2 31 Dec 44 to 5 Jan 45, III Corps, NARA II; 4th Armored Division AAR, January 1945, p. 4, RG 407, entry 427, 604–33.4, NARA II.

55. Third Army G-2 ISUM No. 479, 2400A, January 4, 1945; MS #R-11, p. 164.

56. 35th Infantry Division AAR, January 1945, p. 4; MS # B-521, p. 23; 26th Infantry Division AAR, January 1945, p. 1, RG 407, entry 427, 326–0.3, NARA II.

57. MS #R-15, p. 67; Spaeter, *History of Panzerkorps*, 2:488–89.

58. Twelfth Army Group G-2 Periodic Report No. 212, 2300A, January 3, 1945; Blumenson, *Patton Papers*, 2:615.

59. MS #B-506 (Triepel), "LVIII Panzer Corps Ardennes Offensive, 1 November 1944 to 1 February 1945," April 25, 1947, p. 6, RG 549.3, NARA II.

60. Price, *Middleton*, 272.

61. Danchev and Todman, *War Diaries*, 642.

62. Montgomery Diary, January 4, 1945.

63. Bradley, *A Soldier's Story*, 377.

64. Hansen Diary, January 4, 1945.

13. The Harlange Pocket, January 5–8

1. Blumenson, *Patton Papers*, 2:615; Gay Diary, January 5, 1945.

2. See Third Army G-2 ISUM Nos. 471–473, January 5, 1945; III Corps G-2 ISUM No. 50, 042400A to 051200A, January 1945.

3. Colonel J. H. Phillips, Memorandum for Record (conversation with Grow), January 5, 1945, RG 407, entry 427, 203–3.2 5 Jan to 11 Jan 45, III Corps, NARA II.

4. Third Army G-2 ISUM No. 473, 2400A, January 5, 1945; 6th Armored Division AAR, January 1945, p. 5.

5. Colonel J. H. Phillips to Middleton, "III–VIII Corps Boundary," January 4, 1945, and Colonel Cyrus H. Searcy to Millikin, January 4, 1945, RG 407, entry 427, 208–7.2 Jan 44 to 208–7.2 Feb 45, NARA II.

6. Colonel J. H. Phillips, Memorandum for Record (conversation with Baade), January 5, 1945, RG 407, entry 427, 203–3.2 5 Jan to 11 Jan 45, III Corps, NARA II; 35th Infantry Division AAR, January 1945, p. 4; Blumenson, *Patton Papers*, 2:615. The *1st SS PD* line on January 5 ran from approximately two miles east of Remonfosse to Villers-la-Bonne-Eau. DEFE 3/325, BT 1429 (ZZZZ), 1351Z, January 6, 1945, reel 58.

7. Patton Diary, January 5, 1945; SHAEF Main, signed SCAEF, to Twelfth Army Group, ComZ, 94th Infantry Division, 2004A, January 5, 1945, S-73840, RG 331, entry 58, SHAEF G-3 War Diaries, 1943–1945, NARA II.

8. Paul Braim, *The Will to Win: The Life of General James A. Van Fleet* (Annapolis, Md.: Naval Institute Press, 2001), 124.

9. III Corps AAR, January 1945, p. 7; 90th Infantry Division AAR, December 1944, RG 407, entry 427, 390–0.3, NARA II.

10. Patton Diary, January 5, 1945.

11. III Corps Operational Directive No. 2, January 5, 1945.

12. Colonel J. H. Phillips, Memorandum for Record, January 6, 1945, RG 407, entry 427, 203–3.2 5 Jan to 11 Jan 45, III Corps, NARA II; 6th Armored Division AAR, January 1945, p. 5; Hofmann, *Super Sixth*, 297; 35th Infantry Division AAR, January 1945, p. 5.

13. Patton Diary, January 6, 1945.

14. 80th Infantry Division G-2 AAR, January, 1945, p. 2, RG 407, entry 407, 380–0.3, NARA II. The regiment captured more than 100 POWs.

15. MS #A-876, p. 81.

16. 90th Infantry Division AAR, January 1945, p. 2.

17. Patton, "Notes on Bastogne Operation," 8; Patton Diary, January 6, 1945.

18. III Corps G-2 ISUM Nos. 54–57, January 7 and 8, 1945.

19. DEFE 3/328, BT 2020 (ZZ), 0016Z, January 12, 1945, reel 58. Apparently, *Fallschirmjäger Flak Abteilung 5* had been brought forward and resubordinated to the division, based on an order from Model. DEFE 3/327, BT 1849 (ZZ), 1554Z, January 10, 1945, reel 57.

20. Hofmann, *Super Sixth*, 296.

21. MS #B-032, p. 8, RG 549.3, NARA II; MS #A-876, p. 82. See also DEFE 3/326, BT 1645, 1455Z, January 8, 1945, reel 57.

22. MS #A-876, p. 82; 80th Infantry Division AAR, January 1945, p. 3.

23. 87th Infantry Division G-2 Periodic Report No. 20, 0001 to 2400, January 8, 1945, RG 407, entry 427, 208–7.2 Dec 44 to 208–7.2 Jan 45, NARA II.

24. MS #C-002, pp. 1, 22; Miley, "17th Airborne in the Bulge," January 19, 1945, Combat Interviews.

25. Blumenson, *Patton Papers*, 2:619; Patton Diary, January 7, 1945; Headquarters 11th Armored Division, G-3 Periodic Report No. 11, 1200, January 6, 1945, RG 407, entry 427, 208–7.2 1 Dec 44 to 208–7.2 Jan 45, NARA II.

26. Patton, "Notes on Bastogne Operation," 8.

27. Gay Diary, January 6 and 7, 1945; Twelfth Army Group G-2 Periodic Report Nos. 214 and 215, 2300A, January 5 and 6, 1945; Allen Journal, January 6, 1945.

28. Patton, "Notes on Bastogne Operation," 8; Patton Diary, January 7, 1945; DEFE 3/325, BT 1438 (ZZZZ), 1528Z, January 6, 1945; DEFE 3/326, BT 1564 (ZZZZ), 1734Z, January 7, 1945, reel 57; Third Army G-2 Work Map, Situation as of 0300, January 8, 1945.

29. 90th Infantry Division AAR, January 1945, p. 5; III Corps Field Order No. 3, January 7, 1945. See Annex 3, Troop List, for the attachment of the 735th Tank Battalion to Baade and Paul.

30. Third Army Operational Directive, January 8, 1945.

31. MS #C-020 (Percy E. Schramm), "The German Wehrmacht in the Last Days of the War (1 Jan–7 May 1945)," 1948, p. 94, RG 549.3, NARA II; Patton Diary, January 8, 1945.

32. VIII Corps Field Order No. 2, 1200A, January 8, 1945, RG 407, entry 427, 208–7.2 1 Dec 44 to 208–7.2 Jan 45, NARA II.

33. 101st Airborne Division G-3 Periodic Report No. 20, 1300, January 8, 1945, RG 407, entry 427, 208–7.2 1 Dec 44 to 208–7.2 Jan 45, NARA II.

34. Gay Diary, January 8, 1945.

35. Blumenson, *Patton Papers*, 2:620; Patton, "Notes on Bastogne Operation," 9; Patton Diary, January 8, 1945. The 94th Infantry Division (minus the 302nd CT) closed in XX Corps' zone at 1900 January 8.

36. III Corps AAR, January 1945, pp. 5, 8.

14. No Risk, No Reward, January 9–25

1. Blumenson, *Patton Papers*, 2:619; 17th Airborne Division AAR, January 1945, p. 3, RG 407, entry 427, 317–3, NARA II; Miley, "17th Airborne Division in the Bulge"; VIII Corps AAR, January 1945, p. 9, RG 407, entry 427, 208–3.2, NARA II; Third Army G-3 SITREP No. 643, 0900–1200, January 9, 1945. Kibler reported the same thing. Twelfth Army Group G-3 Report No. 218, 2300, January 9, 1945, RG 407, entry 427, 99/12–3.1, NARA II.

2. Gay Diary, January 9, 1945.

3. VIII Corps AAR, January 1945, p. 8; Twelfth Army Group Weekly Intelligence Summary No. 22, for week ending January 9, p. 1, RG 407, 99/12–2.1 Apr 1945 to 99/12–2.6 Jan 1945, NARA II.

4. Rapport and Northwood, *Rendezvous with Destiny*, 635–36; VIII Corps AAR, January 1945, p. 8.

5. 35th Infantry Division AAR, January 1945, p. 6, RG 407, entry 427, 335–0.3; 26th Infantry Division AAR, January 1945, p. 2, RG 407, entry 427, 326–0.3, NARA II.

6. MS #A-876, p. 83; DEFE 3/327, BT 1858, 1647Z, January 10, 1945, and DEFE 3/327, BT 1875, 1933Z, January 10, 1945, reel 57; Twelfth Army Group Weekly Intelligence Summary No. 22, p. 26; 90th Infantry Division AAR, January 1945, p. 10.

7. Henry G. Cole, *General William E. Depuy: Preparing the Army for Modern War* (Lexington: University Press of Kentucky, 2008), 58–60; 90th Infantry Division AAR, January 1945, p. 10. Exactly how much fire was received is unknown, but III Corps determined that German firing positions in the Harlange Pocket dropped off dramatically between 1600 January 8 and 1200 the next day. It went from nine or ten firing positions to only three or four north of Wiltz. III Corps ISUM No. 58, 082400A to 091200A January 1945.

8. Millikin, Notes on Today's Activities, January 9, 1945, and Millikin, Memorandum of Telephone Conversation with LUCKY 6, at 1940, January 9, 1945, RG 407, entry 427, 5 Jan to 11 Jan 45, III Corps, NARA II; III Corps AAR, January 1945, p. 8.

9. 4th Armored Division AAR, January 1945, p. 1.

10. 35th Infantry Division AAR, January 1945, p. 6.

11. Millikin, Memorandum of Telephone Conversation with LUCKY 5, at 1010, January 10, 1945, RG 407, entry 427, 5 Jan to 11 Jan 45, III Corps, NARA II; CSI Report No. 5, Conversations with General J. Lawton Collins, 1983, USACGSC.

12. Patton Diary, January 10, 1945; Spires, *Patton's Air Force*, 223.

13. Patton wanted XIX TAC to destroy an unspecified bridge over the Saar.

Weyland Diary, January 9, 1945; Gay Diary, January 9, 10, 1945; Twelfth Army Group Weekly Intelligence Summary No. 22, p. 20; Twelfth Army Group, Situation 1200 hours, January 10, 1945, Twelfth Army Group Outline Maps, 1:1,000,000, World War II Military Situation Maps, http://www.TheHistoricalArchive.com.

14. Gay Diary, January 10, 1945.

15. 17th Airborne Division AAR, January 1945, p. 4.

16. Gay Diary, January 10, 1945; Rapport and Northwood, *Rendezvous with Destiny*, 642–43. Winton stated that Taylor had no armor to support his gains, but CCB/10th Armored Division was attached to the division. Winton, *Corp Commanders of the Bulge*, 318. CCB/4th Armored Division was attached as well, but it was relieved during the day and closed southeast of Bastogne at 1845. VIII Corps AAR, January 1945, pp. 8–9.

17. Blumenson, *Patton Papers*, 2:621.

18. Ibid., 621–22; Patton, "Notes on Bastogne Operation," 9; Eddy War Log, January 10, 1945; Gay Diary, January 11, 1945.

19. Eddy War Log, January 7 and 9, 1945; XII Corps Operational Directive No. 65, 1800, January 10, 1945.

20. Patton Diary, January 10, 1945; Blumenson, *Patton Papers*, 2:621–22; Patton, "Notes on Bastogne Operation," 9; DEFE 3/327, BT 1867 (ZZZ), 1734, January 10, 1945; DEFE 3/327, BT 1875 (ZZ), 1933, January 10, 1945, reel 57.

21. 90th Infantry Division AAR, January 1945, p. 10; John Colby, *War from the Ground Up: The 90th Division in WW II* (Austin, Tex.: Nortex Press, 1991), 365–70; 26th Infantry Division AAR, January 1945, p. 2; Lieutenant Colonel Albert J. McWade to John Toland, September 26, 1957, Toland Papers, box 34, LC, reel 57.

22. DEFE 3/327. BT 1933 (ZZZ), 0801, January 11, 1945, reel 57.

23. Tiemann, *Leibstandarte*, 153; DEFE 3/329, BT 2367 (ZZ), 0904Z, and BT 2340 (ZZ), 0119Z, January 15, 1945, reel 58.

24. 90th Infantry Division AAR, January 1945; MS #B-023 (Heilmann), "5th Fallschirmjager Division (1 Dec 1944–12 Jan 1945)," pp. 49, 52. Trevor N. Dupuy argued that from January 9 to 11, the 90th Infantry Division had a combat effectiveness value of 1.1 to the *5th FJD's* 0.90 at Harlange. This was "more of a tribute" to Heilmann's division than to Van Fleet's. Dupuy, *Hitler's Last Gamble*, 500.

25. Patton Diary, January 11, 1945.

26. DEFE 3/327, BT 1990 (ZZ), 2042, January 11, 1945; DEFE 3/327, BT 1975, 11724Z, and BT 1990, 2042Z, January 11, 1945, reel 57.

27. 11th Armored Division AAR, January 1945.

28. MS #B-049 (Bayerlein), "Ardennes—Panzer Lehr Division: Description of Combat Operations from 12 to 20 January 1945 (Withdrawal from the Ardennes)," August 8, 1950, p. 2, RG 549.3, NARA II; Spaeter, *History of Panzerkorps*, 2:489; DEFE 3/327, BT 1903 (ZZZZ), 2128, January 10, 1945, reel 57.

29. 17th Airborne Division AAR, January 1945, p. 4.

30. Phillips, memorandum of 26th Infantry Division telephonic report to III Corps, 1330, January 13, 1945, III Corps G-3 files.

31. MS # B-235, p. 36, RG 549.3, NARA II; DEFE 3/329, BT 2344 (ZZ), 0138, January 15, 1945, reel 58.

32. Earl F. Ziemke, *Stalingrad to Berlin: The German Defeat in the East* (New York: Military Heritage Press, 1985), 421.

33. Tiemann, *Leibstandarte*, 153; Meyer, *12th SS*, 2:353; DEFE 3/328, BT 2035 (ZZ), 0144, January 12, 1945, reel 57; Heiber and Glantz, *Hitler and His Generals*, 597.

34. Bradley, *Soldier's Story*, 495; Gay Diary, January 12, 1945; Patton Diary, January 11, 1945; Blumenson, *Patton Papers*, 2:624; Patton, "Notes on Bastogne Operation," 10; SHAEF Main, signed SCAEF, to Twelfth Army Group, Sixth Army Group, Fifteenth Army, ComZ, 2020A, January 10, 1945, S-74482, and 2021A, January 10, 1945, S-74483, RG 331, entry 58, SHAEF G-3 War Diaries, 1943–1945, NARA II.

35. Gay Diary, January 12, 1945.

36. VIII Corps AAR, January 1945, p. 11.

37. DEFE 3/329, BT 2359 (ZZZ), 0555, January 15, 1945, reel 58; Eddy War Log, January 12, 1945.

38. G-3 Operations Diary, entry for January 15, 1945.

39. Spaeter, *History of Panzerkorps*, 491.

40. III Corps AAR, January 1945, p. 14. CCB/10th Armored Division was released from VIII Corps' control at 1200 but was still with the 101st Airborne Division the next day.

41. MS #A-945 (Bayerlein), "Additional Questions—Ardennes Offensive: Description of Operations from 11 to 20 January 1944 in Area of Houffalize," February 23, 1946, p. 2, RG 549.3, NARA II; Spayd, *Bayerlein*, 191; Blumenson, *Patton Papers*, 2:615.

42. Twelfth Army Group Weekly Intelligence Summary No. 23, for week ending January 16, 1945, p. 2, RG 407, entry 427, 99/12–2.6 Jan 1945 to 99/12–2.6 Feb 1945, NARA II.

43. Patton Diary, January 17, 1945.

44. Gay Diary, January 15, 1945. Gay had proposed this very plan to Patton the day before.

45. Winton, *Corps Commanders of the Bulge*, 329.

46. MS #A-876, p. 89; MacDonald, *Last Offensive*, 48; Eddy War Log, January 12 and 15, 1945; Gay Diary, January 17, 1945.

47. Eddy War Log, January 17, 1945; 87th Infantry Division Field Order No. 12, 1600A, January 17, 1945, RG 407, entry 427, 208–7.2 Dec 44 to 208–7.2 Jan 45, NARA II; XII Corps Operational Directive No. 68, 1300, January 16, 1945, RG 407, entry 427, 103–2.6–1-3.2.10, NARA II.

48. XII Corps Operational Directive No. 68, January 16, 1945; Third Army AAR, vol. 2, Artillery, p. 20.

49. Eddy War Log, January 16, 1945.

50. 80th Infantry Division AAR, January 1945, p. 5.

51. 5th Infantry Division AAR, January 1945, p. 3. XII Corps stated that the 2nd CT crossed in a column of battalions. XII Corps AAR, January 1945, p. 14.

52. 4th Infantry Division AAR, January 1945, pp. 14–15, RG 407, entry 427, 304–0.3, NARA II.

53. Eddy War Log, January 18, 1945.

54. Allen Journal, January 23, 1945.

55. MS #B-417 (Wietersheim), "The 11 Panzer-Division in the Rhineland Part III (from 20 Dec 44 to 10 Feb 45)," February 7, 1947, pp. 2–5, RG 549.3, NARA II.

56. Ritgen, *Western Front*, 292.

57. XII Corps AAR, January 1945, p. 28; Eddy War Log, January 20, 22, 1945.

58. Colonel William B. Reed, ed., *Condensed Analysis of the Ninth Air Force in the European Theater of Operations* (1946; reprint, Washington, D.C.: Office of Air Force History, 1984), 43.

59. Allen Journal, January 23, 1945.

60. XII Corps Operational Directive No. 72, January 23, 1945.

61. XII Corps AAR, January 1945, p. 29.

62. MS #A-940, 17, RG 549.3, NARA II; MS #B-032 (Bodenstein), "Report of My Activities during the Americans' Campaign on the West Front, Ardennes 16 Dec 44–25 Jan 45," April 17, 1946, p. 9, RG 549.3, NARA II; Chandler, *Eisenhower Papers*, 4:2439.

15. Assessment

1. Blumenson, *Patton Papers*, 2:625.

2. John Toland interview with Maxwell Taylor, June 11, 1957; Paul quoted in Phillips, *Making of a Professional*, 172; Senior Officer's Debriefing Program, conversations between Van Fleet and Colonel Bruce H. Williams, January 20, 1973, USAHEC.

3. Hansen Diary, December 24, 1944; Weyland quoted in Colonel Alfred F. Hurley and Major Robert C. Ehrhart, eds., *Air Power and Warfare*, Proceedings of the 8th Military History Symposium, U.S. Air Force Academy, October 18–20, 1978 (Washington, D.C.: Office of Air Force History, 1979), 190–192; James K. Graff to John Toland, February 28, 1957, Toland Papers, box 35, Manuscript Division, LC.

4. Cole, *Lorraine Campaign*, 15.

5. War Department, FM 100–5, p. 25.

6. Blumenson, *Patton Papers*, 2:559, 616; FM 100–15, pp. 56–65.

7. Blumenson, *Patton: Man behind the Legend*, 246; Winton, *Corps Commanders of the Bulge*, 187–88; English, *Patton's Peers*, 248–49.

8. Rickard, *Patton at Bay*, 104.

9. Patton relieved Major General John S. Wood, commander of the 4th Armored Division in Lorraine, for fatigue. Hodges sacked ten subordinates. Daniel P. Bolger, "Zero Defects: Command Climate in First U.S. Army, 1944–1945," *Military Review* 71, no. 5 (May 1991): 64; Robert H. Berlin, "United States Army World War II Corps Commanders: A Composite Biography," *Journal of Military History* 53, no. 2 (April 1989): 163–66.

10. Patton Diary, January 21, 1945.

11. Ibid., January 17, 1945.

12. Millett, "United States Armed Forces in the Second World War," 67. Ladislas Farago was simply wrong to suggest that Patton could make war as he liked in the Ardennes. Farago, *Patton*, 681.

13. John Strawson, *The Battle for the Ardennes* (London: Batsford, 1972), 174.

14. FM 100–5, p. 24.

15. Senior Officer's Debriefing Program, Conversations between General Paul D. Harkins and Major Jacob B. Couch Jr., USAHEC; Blumenson, *Patton Papers*, 2:588; MacDonald, *Last Offensive*, 15.

16. Patton, *War as I Knew It*, 203. This passage does not appear in either *The Patton Papers* or Patton's typescript diary. It could have been a postwar addition by Patton or Harkins, in which case it can be considered an ex post facto excuse.

17. Doubler, *Closing with the Enemy*, 287.

18. Carl von Clausewitz, *On War*, ed. Michael Howard and Peter Paret (Princeton, N.J.: Princeton University Press, 1984), 190–91.

19. Blumenson, *Patton Papers*, 2:505; Patton Diary, December 27, 1944, and January 26, 1945; Clausewitz, *On War*, 190–91; Bedell Smith quoted in D'Este, *Eisenhower*, 671; MacDonald, *Last Offensive*, 18. As Blumenson concluded, Patton's "relatively junior status" prevented him from exercising the command and control necessary to execute the concept of encirclement. Martin Blumenson, "Bradley-Patton: World War II's 'Odd Couple,'" *Army* 35, no. 12 (December 1985): 64. See Roman J. Jarymowycz, *Tank Tactics: From Normandy to Lorraine* (Boulder, Colo.: Lynne Rienner, 2001), 305, for a similar perspective.

20. MacDonald, *Last Offensive*, 24.

21. During the Tennessee maneuvers Patton pushed his 2nd Armored Division, nicknamed "Hell on Wheels," 200 miles in twenty-four hours. Donald E. Houston, *Hell on Wheels: The 2nd Armored Division* (San Rafael, Calif.: Presidio, 1977), 69; Christopher R. Gabel, *The US Army GHQ Maneuvers of 1941* (Washington, D.C.: CMH, 1991), 52, 108, 110; ETHINT 39.

22. Christopher R. Gabel, *The Lorraine Campaign: An Overview* (Fort Leavenworth, Kans.: CSI, 1985), 36.

23. Dominick Graham and Shelford Bidwell have argued that "American generals, whatever their text books might advise, indulged in the Western Front practice of attacking on as wide a front as possible, for as long as possible, in search of tactical rewards." Graham and Bidwell, *Coalitions, Politicians and Generals*, 287.

24. Blumenson, *Patton Papers*, 2:531, 562, 616; Patton Diary, January 24, 1945.

25. Price, *Middleton*, 391; General J. Lawton Collins, "Elements of Command," August 30, 1971, CARL.

26. General Board, Study No. 1, "Strategy of the Campaign in Western Europe, 1944–1945," 73.

27. Leonard Wainstein, "Rates of Advance in Infantry Division Attacks in the Normandy–Northern France and Siegfried Line Campaigns," Institute for Defense Analyses, Program Analysis Division, December 1973, p. 11.

28. MacDonald, *Siegfried Line*, 616.

29. Roger A. Beaumont, "Assessing Operational Impact: A Problem in Military Analysis," *Military Affairs* 46, no. 3 (October 1982): 132–33. The official history gives total American casualties as 75,482, with 8,407 killed, 47,170 wounded, and 20,905 missing, but Forrest C. Pogue stated that this was a "hasty compilation prepared for General Eisenhower during the action." Total U.S. casualties for Ardennes–Alsace were estimated at 104,944. Pogue, *Supreme Command*, 396, 402; MacDonald, *Battle of the Bulge*, 618. Both George Forty and Danny S. Parker suggest the figure of 81,834. Forty, *Reich's Last Gamble*, 10; Parker, *Battle of the Bulge*, 293; Twelfth Army Group G-3 Reports No. 200, December 22, 1944, to No. 223, January 14, 1945.

30. Patton, "Notes on Bastogne Operation," 11.

31. Cole, *Lorraine*, 593. In terms of nonbattle casualties, during the Bulge, Third

Army had the highest incidence of trench foot, and First Army was close behind. Patton considered this a command responsibility. Rankin, *Medical Department United States Army in World War II*, 327–29. Third Army suffered from a shortage of cold-weather clothing and footgear during the worst of the winter weather.

32. General Board, "Strategy of the Campaign in Western Europe," 73. Bauer suggested between 81,413 and 95,030. MS #60 (Bauer), "The Cost of the Ardennes Offensive," 1955, p. 10, CMH. In one place Schramm suggested that German casualties were 12,652 dead, 38,600 wounded, and 30,582 missing, for a total of 81,834. In another place he offered 98,024. MS #A-858, p. 20; MS #C-020 (Schramm), "History of the Armed Forces," p. 108. Parker favored the 100,000 range. Parker, *Battle of the Bulge*, 293.

33. Hornst Boog, Gerhard Krebs, and Detlef Vogel, *Germany and the Second World War*, vol. 7, *The Strategic Air War in Europe and the War in the West and East Asia, 1943–1944/45* (Oxford: Oxford University Press, 2006), 694; Hrowe H. Saunders, *Die Wacht am Rhein: Hitlers letzte Schlacht in den Ardennen, 1944/45* (Berg am See: Kurt Vowinckel-Verlag, 1984), 270; Martin, *Letzter Lorbeer*, 272; Werner Haupt, *Das Ende Im Westen 1945: Bildchronik vom Kampf in Westdeutschland* (Dorheim: Podzun-Verlag, 1972), 40. Hermann Jung offers two sets of calculations: an OKH report indicated 10,749 killed, 34,225 wounded, and 22,487 missing; OKW reported 12,652 killed, 38,600 wounded, and 30,582 missing. Karl-Heinz Frieser believes the OKW figures are more complex because they included losses well behind the front, most likely the result of Allied air interdiction. Hermann Jung, *Die Ardennen-Offensive 1944/45* (Gottingen: Musterschmidt, 1971), 195; Karl-Heinz Frieser, e-mail to Roger Cirillo, November 9, 2010. Using data generated from the ACSDB, Dupuy calculated American casualties from December 16 to January 16 as 62,439 and German casualties as 74,459. Dupuy, *Hitler's Last Gamble*, 469–71.

34. Typically, Patton declared, "We believe that these figures are low." Patton, "Notes on Bastogne Operation," 12.

35. Dupuy, *Numbers, Predictions and War*, 62; Trevor N. Dupuy, "Mythos or Verity? The Quantified Judgment Model and German Combat Effectiveness," *Military Affairs* 50, no. 4 (October 1986): 204–10. My findings appear to be supported by one operational research study that concluded that the individual effectiveness of the Americans and the British was better than that of the Germans. C-Y Hung et al., "Fitting Lanchester's Square Law to the Ardennes Campaign," *Journal of the Operational Research Society* 56 (2005): 944.

36. General Board, Study No. 15, "Organization, Equipment, and Tactical Employment of the Infantry Division," 14.

37. Ridgway declared in 1943 that the airborne divisions "must not be employed against organized defenses manned by first class troops. It has not enough power." Extract from letter of July 26, 1943, to C-in-C Allied Forces (through CG, Seventh Army), Subject: "Analysis of Methods of Employment of 82nd Airborne Division, Northwest African Theatre, Summer of 1943," Ridgway Papers, Citadel Archives, Charleston, South Carolina.

38. Even Patton himself, prone to exaggeration at times, declared that the air force overstated its claims by "at least 50% but they do scare the Huns." Blumenson, *Patton Papers*, 2:607; Ellis, *Victory in the West*, 192; Carter, "Air Power in the Battle of the Bulge," 22.

39. Headquarters, III Corps AAR, December 1944, p. 21; Thoholte, "A German Reflects upon Artillery," 714. Cole, however, stated that this was "far too high." Cole, *Ardennes*, 659. *Heeresgruppe B*'s day report for December 31 noted that the transportation and supply situation was heavily strained due to heavy attacks in Dusseldorf, Neunkirchen, and Koblenz. During the evening Model submitted a report stating that the Allied air force was systematically destroying all traffic centers and that the supply situation in the Eifel was verging on dangerous. DEFE 3/323, BT 942 (ZZ), 2153Z, January 1, 1945; DEFE 3/323, BT 1104 (ZZ), 1522Z, January 3, 1945, reel 57.

40. Cole, *Ardennes*, 659; John Sloan Brown, "The Wehrmacht Mythos Revisited: A Challenge for Colonel Trevor N. Dupuy," *Military Affairs* 51, no. 3 (July 1987): 146. It has been argued elsewhere that the Ardennes campaign was direct, not indirect, fire combat. This is logical, considering the capabilities and limitations of infantry and armor, but not when discussing the capabilities and missions of artillery. Hung et al., "Fitting Lanchester's Square Law," 943. Patton made the following observation at the infantry division conference on November 20, 1945: "The infantry component of the division, which is 65.9% of the total personnel, inflicts on the enemy by means of small arms, automatic weapons, mortars and hand grenades approximately 37% of the casualties. In order to inflict 37% of the casualties the infantry sustains 92% of the total casualties in the division. The artillery, which comprises 15% of the division, inflicts on the enemy 47% of the total casualties for which it pays but 2%. However, we have to qualify this statement because in practically all divisional operations the division is supported by a large amount of corps and army artillery." General Board, "Organization, Equipment, and Tactical Employment of the Infantry Division," appendix 15, Conference on the Infantry Division, November 20, 1945, p. 2. Patton's percentages are open to interpretation. Cole stated that U.S. records on the causes of combat deaths and wounds were "woefully inadequate and German records for this period do not exist." Third Army estimated that between August 1 and November 31, 27 to 30 percent of its casualties were the result of gunshot wounds, and 50 to 60 percent were from artillery, mortars, bombs, and mines. Cole conceded that the number of artillery rounds required to kill a single enemy soldier was probably very high. Cole, *Ardennes*, 656, 659.

41. General Board, Study No. 61, "Study of Field Artillery Operations," p. 106. Hodges declared in no uncertain terms that infantry, armor, and airpower were all "seriously handicapped by the weather and terrain. Through all, however—day and night, good weather and bad—the flexibility and power of our modern artillery was applied unceasingly." Lieutenant Colonel Joseph R. Reeves, "Artillery in the Ardennes," *Field Artillery Journal* 36, no. 3 (March 1946): 138.

42. This was possible even though Eisenhower told General Thomas Handy at the War Department on December 19 that, "despite drastic action here, our infantry replacement situation is critical." Chandler, *Eisenhower Papers*, 4:2360. Replacements and returns to duty (RTDs) were usually subcategories of "Reinforcements" under the U.S. Army system. ACSDB, p. II-A-50. On December 25 Eisenhower informed Bradley that replacements for Third Army between December 24 and 31 would equal 12,309. Of the total number of basic-trained infantry, 1,971 were from other uncommitted divisions. Forty percent of the total were retrained personnel in the theater. The breakdown of scheduled replacements per day for Third Army was as follows: December 24, 1,521; December 25, 995; December 26, 907; December 27,

2,350; December 28, 1,366; December 29, 3,647; December 30, 1,273; and December 31, 250. SHAEF Main from Smith (signed Eisenhower) to Twelfth Army Group, 1742A, December 25, 1944, S-72409, RG 331, entry 58, G-3 War Diary, December 1944, NARA II. During the same time frame, Eisenhower was allocating 17,474 replacements to Montgomery to rebuild the First and Ninth Armies; of these, 2,200 were coming directly from the 69th Infantry Division. SHAEF Main from Smith (signed Eisenhower) to EXFOR TAC, Personal for Field Marshal Montgomery, 1742A, December 25, 1944, S-72408, ibid. Replacements arrived directly from the United States by ship and were flown into airfields at Nancy, Toul, and Etain from Marseille. Many had no rifles. See SHAEF Main (signed SCAEF) to Twelfth Army Group, ComZ, 2000A, December 24, 1944, S-72344, ibid.

43. ACSDB, p. II-G-4–9. This figure is for replacements received for the *entire* month. MS #A-858, pp. 21–22; Cole, *Ardennes*, 615; Headquarters Third Army, Annex No. 1 to G-2 Periodic Report No. 203, Tactical IPW Report No. 134 from 291600A to 301600A Dec 1944, RG 407, entry 427, 208–7.2 Jan 44 to 208–7.2 Feb 45, NARA II; Spaeter, *History of Panzerkorps*, 2:486.

44. The priority, however, was interesting: 35th, 90th, and 95th Infantry Divisions; 6th Armored Division; 4th Armored Division; and 80th, 5th, and 26th Infantry Divisions. Fifty-three percent of the 13,187 replacements reported by the army went to XII Corps, and 18 percent went to a single division, the 80th. Gay Diary, December 25, 1944. Patton was informed on December 26 that the 94th Infantry Division was assigned to his army. It was assembling near Longwy but could be committed only on Bradley's approval. Gay Diary, December 26, 1944. On December 27, 400 replacements were sent forward to Gaffey and Taylor. Third Army's G-1 was also trying to send the 48th Replacement Battalion forward to III Corps on December 27. See Major H. H. Chase, Memorandum for Record, December 27, 1944, RG 407, entry 427, 203–3.2 23 Dec to 27 Dec 44, NARA II.

45. Twelfth Army Group G-2 Periodic Report No. 206, 1800, December 28, 1944, p. 2, RG 407, entry 427, 99/12–2.1 Dec 1944–Jan 1945 to 99/12–2.1 Mar 1945, NARA II. See SRH-015, Notes on German Fuel Position by G-2 SHAEF, January 31, 1945, for an assessment of the impact of the fuel shortage on German operations based on ULTRA material.

46. Condell and Zabecki, *On the German Art of War*, 90; MS #B-151a, pp. 216–17; R. L. Dinardo and Austin Bay, "Horse-Drawn Transport in the German Army," *Journal of Contemporary History* 23, no. 1 (1988): 135. ULTRA intercepted a message from Goering early on December 27 stating that all motor transport not required for the conduct of the immediate battle was to be immobilized. DEFE 3/321, BT 452 (ZZ), 0359Z, December 27, 1944, reel 56. That was because the fuel shortage crippled proper movement and assembly. "Applied Air Power and the Ardennes Offensive, December 1944–January 1945, a Report Prepared by Office of the Director of Intelligence, United States Strategic Air Forces in Europe," Sidney H. Negrotto Papers, USAHEC. *Heeresgruppe B* allocated 300 cubic meters of fuel to *Fifth Panzer Armee*, but it had to be brought forward from Bozen to a fuel dump at Bayern, more than 150 miles from Trier. DEFE 3/324, BT 1201 (ZZ), 1334Z, January 4, 1945, reel 57.

47. Boog et al., *Germany and the Second World War*, 694.

48. David Belchem, *All in the Day's March* (London: Collins, 1978), 251.

49. Boog et al., *Germany and the Second World War*, 693.

50. MS #B-444 (*Oberst* Werner Wagner), "276 Volks-Grenadier Division (21 January–16 March 1945)," p. 4, RG 549.3, NARA II; Combined Intelligence Committee, "Estimate of the Enemy Situation—Europe," January 22, 1945, p. 9; Cole, *Ardennes*, 674; Eisenhower, *Crusade in Europe*, 358.

51. Omar N. Bradley, "On Leadership," *Parameters* 11, no. 3 (September 1981): 2–7; Blumenson, *Patton Papers*, 2:610; Chandler, *Eisenhower Papers*, 4:2368.

52. Clausewitz, *On War*, 190–91.

Selected Bibliography

Unpublished Sources

Center of Military History, U.S. Army, Washington, D.C.
Bauer, Magna E. MS #R-15, "Key Dates during the Ardennes Offensive 1944, Part I." April 1952.
————. MS #R-60, "The Cost of the Ardennes Offensive." May 1955.
Devers, Jacob L. Diary.
First United States Army Combat Operations Data, Europe, 1944–1945.
First United States Army Report of Operations, August 2, 1944–February 22, 1945.
Luttichau, Charles V. P. von. "Armor in the Ardennes Offensive." 1952.
————. MS #R-8, "The Ardennes Offensive: Progressive Build-up and Operations, 11–19 December 1944." November 1952.
————. MS #R-11, "Key Dates during the Ardennes Offensive, Part II." April 1952.
————. MS #R-12, "The Ardennes Offensive: Planning and Preparations." August 1953.

Citadel Archives, Charleston, South Carolina
Helfers, Melvin C. Papers.

Combined Arms Research Library (Digital Archives), Fort Leavenworth, Kansas
Headquarters, European Theater of Operations. Standard Operating Procedures No. 50. "Road Traffic Regulation and Control on the Continent." October 7, 1944.
Summers, Lieutenant Colonel Robert R., et al. "Armor at Bastogne." Research report prepared by Committee 4, Officer's Advanced Course, Armored School, 1948–1949, Fort Knox, May 1949.
Twelfth Army Group Report of Operations (Final After Action Report). Vol. 1: Summary.
Twelfth Army Group Final Report of Operations. Annex No. 1: Twelfth Army Group Directives.
U.S. Army, Headquarters, European Theater of Command. "Movement of XII Corps Artillery." Army Ground Forces Report No. 509, APO 887, January 3, 1945.

Dwight D. Eisenhower Library, Abilene, Kansas
Bedell Smith, Walter. Papers.
Butcher, Harry C. Diary.
SHAEF G-2 Digests.
SHAEF G-2 Weekly Intelligence Summaries.

General George Patton Museum, Fort Knox, Kentucky
Allen, Robert S. Papers.

Imperial War Museum, London
Papers of Field Marshal Montgomery of Alamein.

Library of Congress, Washington, D.C.
Patton, George S., Jr. Papers.
Toland, John. Papers.

Massey Library, Royal Military College of Canada, Kingston, Ontario
ULTRA messages (microfilm collection).

National Archives and Records Administration II, College Park, Maryland
RG 94
    4th Armored Division Combat Interviews (Ardennes).
RG 319 (Records of the Army Staff)
    Correspondence relating to the official history, *The Ardennes: Battle of the Bulge.*
RG 331
    SHAEF G-3 War Diary.
RG 407 (Records of the Adjutant General's Office)
    American regiment, division, corps, and army after-action reports; SHAEF Weekly
       Intelligence Summaries for December 1944; Twelfth Army Group Weekly Intelli-
       gence Summaries for December 1944 and January 1945; George S. Patton, "Notes
       on Bastogne Operation," January 16, 1945.
    Irwin, Stafford Leroy. Diary (December 20–28, 1944).
RG 457 (Records of the National Security Agency)
    Box 31: Lieutenant Colonel Harry L. Dull Jr. *Addendum to USAWC Military Re-*
    search Program Paper: The Ultra Study, "The Battle of the Bulge."
    SRH-006, Synthesis of Experiences in the Use of Ultra Intelligence by U.S. Army-
    Field Commands in the European Theater of Operations.
RG 549.3 (Records of the Foreign Military Studies Program and Related Records
    1941–67)

Public Record Office, Kew, England (National Archives)
ULTRA, HW 20/457, Parts 1 and 2.

U.S. Air Force Historical Research Agency, Maxwell Air Force Base, Alabama
Army Air Forces Evaluation Board in the European Theater of Operations. "The Ef-
    fectiveness of Third Phase Tactical Air Operations in the European Theater, 5
    May 1944–8 May 1945." A1175.
Bradley, General Omar N., and Air Effects Committee, 12th Army Group. "Effect of
    Air Power on Military Operations: Western Europe." July 1945.
Operational History of the Ninth Air Force. Book I: Battle of the Ardennes, Dec 1,
    1944–Jan 26, 1945.
Weyland, Otto P. Diary.

U.S. Army Heritage and Education Center, Carlisle Barracks, Pennsylvania
Abrams, Creighton. Papers.
Bradley, Omar N. Papers.
Dager, Holmes E. Papers.
Gay, Hobart R. Papers.
General Board United States Forces, European Theater. Study No. 1, "Strategy of the Campaign in Western Europe, 1944–1945."
———. Study No. 3, "Reinforcement System and Reinforcement Procedures in the European Theater of Operations."
———. Study No. 15, "Organization, Equipment, and Tactical Employment of the Infantry Division."
———. Study No. 54, "The Tactical Air Force in the European Theater of Operations."
Grow, Robert W. Papers.
Hansen, Chester. Diary.
Harkins, Paul D. Papers.
Hodges, Courtney. Papers.
Koch, Oscar W. Papers.
MacDonald, Charles B. Papers.
Maddox, Halley. Papers.
Miley, William. Papers.
Muller, Walter J. Papers.
Negrotto, Sidney H. Papers.
Observer Board (ETO), U.S. Army, Army Ground Forces. *Reports of the AGF.*
Polk, James K. Papers.
Ridgway, Matthew B. Diary.
Third U.S. Army After Action Report. Vol. 1: Operations, August 1, 1944–May 9, 1945.
Third U.S. Army After Action Report. Vol. 2: Staff Section Reports.
Van Fleet, James A. Papers.
War Department. FM 6–20, *Field Service Regulations, Field Artillery Tactical Employment.* February 1944.
———. FM 11–22, *Field Service Regulations, Signal Operations in the Corps and Army.* January 1945.
———. FM 17–100, *Field Service Regulations, Armored Command Field Manual, The Armored Division.* 1944.
———. FM 21–30, *Basic Field Manual, Conventional Signs, Military Symbols, and Abbreviations.* October 1943.
———. FM 100–5, *Field Service Regulations: Operations.* May 22, 1941.
———. FM 100–5, *Field Service Regulations: Operations 1944.* June 15, 1944.
———. FM 100–10, *Field Service Regulations, Administration.* November 15, 1943.
———. FM 100–15, *Field Service Regulations: Larger Units.* June 29, 1942.
———. FM 100–20, *Field Service Regulations, Command and Employment of Air Power.* July 1943.
———. FM 101–10, *Staff Officers' Field Manual: Organization, Technical and Logistical Data.* June 15, 1941.
———. FM 101–15, *Field Service Regulations, Staff Officers' Field Manual: Traffic Circulation and Control.* January 1943.

————. TM 30–506, *German-English Military Dictionary.* May 20, 1944.

U.S. Army Infantry School, National Infantry Museum, Fort Benning, Georgia
Eddy, Manton S. War Log. "Activities of General Eddy."

U.S. Military Academy Library (Special Collections), West Point, New York
Bradley, Omar N. Papers.
Gay, Hobart R. Diary.

Published Sources

Primary

Bland, Larry I., ed. *The Papers of George Catlett Marshall.* 5 vols. Baltimore: Johns Hopkins University Press, 1981–2003.

Blumenson, Martin, ed. *The Patton Papers.* 2 vols. Boston: Houghton Mifflin, 1972, 1974.

Chandler, Alfred D., Jr., ed. *The Papers of Dwight D. Eisenhower: The War Years.* Vols. 3 and 4. Baltimore: Johns Hopkins University Press, 1970.

Detwiler, Donald S., with Charles B. Burdick and Jürgen Rohwer, eds. *World War II German Military Studies.* 24 vols. New York: Garland Publishing, 1979.

Ferrell, Robert H., ed. *The Eisenhower Diaries.* New York: W. W. Norton, 1981.

Greenwood, John T., ed. *Normandy to Victory: The War Diary of General Courtney H. Hodges and the First U.S. Army.* Lexington: University Press of Kentucky, 2008.

Heiber, Helmut, and David M. Glantz, eds. *Hitler and His Generals: Military Conferences 1942–1945.* New York: Enigma Books, 2002.

Mehner, Kurt, et al. *Die Geheimen Tagesberichte der Deutschen Wehrmachtführung im Zweiten Weltkrieg 1939–1945.* Vol. 2, *1. September 1944–31. December 1944.* Osnabrück: Biblio Verlag, 1984.

Schramm, Percy Ernst, ed. *Kriegstagebuch des Oberkommandos der Wehrmacht.* Vol. 4, *1944–1945.* Frankfurt am Main: Bernard & Graefe, 1963.

Memoirs

Allen, Robert S. *Lucky Forward: The History of Patton's Third U.S. Army.* New York: Vanguard Press, 1947.

Belchem, David. *All in the Day's March.* London: Collins, 1978.

Bradley, Omar N. *A Soldier's Story.* New York: Henry Holt, 1951.

Bradley, Omar N., and Clay Blair. *A General's Life.* New York: Simon & Schuster, 1983.

Butcher, Harry C. *My Three Years with Eisenhower.* New York: Simon & Schuster, 1946.

Codman, Charles R. *Drive.* Boston: Little, Brown, 1957.

Collins, J. Lawton. *Lightning Joe: An Autobiography.* Baton Rouge: Louisiana State University Press, 1979.

Doolittle, General James H. *I Could Never Be So Lucky Again.* New York: Bantam, 1991.

Egger, Bruce E., and Lee MacMillan Otts. *G Company's War: Two Personal Accounts of the Campaigns in Northwest Europe, 1944–1945.* Edited by Paul Roley. Tuscaloosa: University of Alabama Press, 1992.

Eisenhower, Dwight D. *Crusade in Europe.* Garden City, N.Y.: Doubleday, 1948.

Felix, Charles Reis. *Crossing the Sauer: A Third Army Memoir.* Springfield, N.J.: Burford, 2002.

Frankel, Nat, and Larry Smith. *Patton's Best: An Informal History of the 4th Armored Division.* New York: David McKay, 1978.

Garrison, Gene. *Unless Victory Comes: Combat with a Machine Gunner in Patton's Third Army.* Havertown, Pa.: Casemate, 2004.

Gavin, James M. *On to Berlin: Battles of an Airborne Commander, 1943–1946.* New York: Viking Press, 1978.

Gehlen, Reinhard. *The Gehlen Memoirs.* Translated by David Irving. London: Collins, 1972.

Guderian, Heinz. *Panzer Leader.* London: Michael Joseph, 1952.

Harkins, Paul D. *When the Third Cracked Europe: The Story of Patton's Incredible Army.* Harrisburg, Pa.: Army Times Publishing, 1969.

Harmon, Ernest N. *Combat Commander: Autobiography of a Soldier.* Englewood Cliffs, N.J.: Prentice-Hall, 1970.

Hartman, J. Ted. *Tank Driver: With the 11th Armored from the Bulge to VE Day.* Bloomington: Indiana University Press, 2003.

Horrocks, Sir Brian. *Corps Commander.* New York: Charles Scribner's Sons, 1977.

Irzyk, Albin F. *Gasoline to Patton: A Different War.* Oaklan, Ore.: Elderberry Press, 2008.

———. *He Rode up Front for Patton.* Raleigh, N.C.: Pentland Press, 1996.

Koch, Oscar W. *G-2: Intelligence for Patton.* Philadelphia: Whitmore, 1971.

Koyen, Kenneth. *The Fourth Armored Division: From the Beach to Bavaria.* Cleveland: Dillon/Liederbach, 1974.

Luciano, Eugene W. *Our Blood and His Guts! Memoirs of One of General Patton's Combat Soldiers.* Chapel Hill, N.C.: Professional Press, 1995.

Luck, Hans von. *Panzer Commander: The Memoirs of Colonel Hans von Luck.* New York: Praeger, 1989.

Manstein, Erich von. *Lost Victories.* Chicago: Regnery, 1958.

Mayhall, Colonel Van R. *Cranking up a Fine War: A Louisiana Soldier from Boot Camp to General's Aide.* Austin, Tex.: Byren Press, 1999.

Mellenthin, F. W. von. *Panzer Battles: A Study of the Employment of Armor in the Second World War.* Norman: University of Oklahoma Press, 1955.

Montgomery, B. L. *The Memoirs of Field Marshal Montgomery of Alamein.* London: Collins, 1958.

Patton, George S., Jr. *War as I Knew It.* New York: Bantam, 1980.

Richardson, William, and Seymour Freidin, eds. *The Fatal Decisions.* London: Michael Joseph, 1956.

Ridgway, Matthew B. *Soldier: The Memoirs of Matthew B. Ridgway.* New York: Harper & Brothers, 1956.

Ritgen, Helmut. *The Western Front, 1944: Memoirs of a Panzer Lehr Officer.* Winnipeg: J. J. Fedorowicz, 1995.

Smith, C. Cabanne. *My War Years, 1940–1946: Service on General Patton's Third Army Staff*. Houston: Tex Source, 1989.

Speer, Albert. *Inside the Third Reich*. New York: Macmillan, 1970.

Stahlberg, Alexander. *Bounden Duty: The Memoirs of a German Officer 1932–1945*. London: Brassey's, 1990.

Strong, Major General Kenneth. *Intelligence at the Top: The Recollections of an Intelligence Officer*. London: Cassell, 1968.

Summersby, Kay. *Eisenhower Was My Boss*. New York: Prentice-Hall, 1948.

Taylor, Maxwell. *Swords and Plowshares*. New York: W. W. Norton, 1972.

Tedder, Lord. *With Prejudice: The War Memoirs of Marshal of the Royal Air Force Lord Tedder*. London: Cassell, 1966.

Truscott, Lucien K., Jr. *Command Missions: A Personal Story*. Novato, Calif.: Presidio Press, 1990.

Wallace, Brenton G. *Patton and His Third Army*. Harrisburg, Pa.: Military Service Publishing, 1946.

Warlimont, Walter. *Inside Hitler's Headquarters, 1939–1945*. Novato, Calif.: Presidio Press, 1990.

Westmoreland, William C. *A Soldier Reports*. Garden City, N.Y.: Doubleday, 1976.

Whitman, George P. *Memoirs of a Rifle Company Commander in Patton's Third U.S. Army*. West Topsham, Vt.: Gibby Press, 1993.

Secondary Sources

Works on the Bulge

Astor, Gerald. *A Blood-Dimmed Tide: The Battle of the Bulge by the Men Who Fought It*. New York: Donald I. Fine, 1992.

Cain, Major Francis, III. "The Ardennes—1944: An Analysis of the Operational Defense." School of Advanced Military Studies, U.S. Army Command and General Staff College, Fort Leavenworth, Kans., 1986.

Cirillo, Roger. *The U.S. Army Campaigns of World War II: Ardennes–Alsace*. Washington, D.C.: Center of Military History, 2004.

Claflin, Lieutenant Colonel R. C. "The Operational Art as Practiced by General George Patton, Jr. during the Battle of the Bulge." Naval War College, Newport, R.I., 1994.

Cole, Hugh M. *U.S. Army in World War II: The Ardennes: Battle of the Bulge*. Washington, D.C.: Center of Military History, 1988.

Connell, J. Mark. *Ardennes: Battle of the Bulge*. London: Brassey's, 2003.

Crookenden, Napier. *Battle of the Bulge 1944*. New York: Scribner's, 1980.

Dupuy, Trevor N. *Hitler's Last Gamble: The Battle of the Bulge, December 1944–January 1945*. New York: HarperCollins, 1994.

Dworschak, Thomas W. *Hitler's Watch on the Rhine: The Battle of the Bulge*. Arlington, Va.: Institute of Land Warfare, 1992.

Eisenhower, John S. D. *The Bitter Woods*. New York: G. P. Putnam, 1969.

Elstob, Peter. *Hitler's Last Offensive*. London: Secker & Warburg, 1971.

Forty, George. *The Reich's Last Gamble: The Ardennes Offensive, December 1944*. London: Cassell, 2000.

Gaul, Roland. *The Battle of the Bulge in Luxembourg: The Southern Flank December 1944–January 1945*. 2 vols. Atglen, Pa.: Schiffer Military History, 1995.

Jung, Hermann. *Die Ardennen-Offensive 1944/45*. Gottingen: Musterschmidt, 1971.

Kennedy, Major James L. "The Failure of German Logistics during the Ardennes Offensive of 1944." School of Advanced Military Studies, U.S. Army Command and General Staff College, Fort Leavenworth, Kans., 2000.

Kindsvatter, Major Peter S. "An Appreciation for Moving the Heavy Corps: The First Step in Learning the Art of Operational Maneuver." School of Advanced Military Studies, U.S. Army Command and General Staff College, Fort Leavenworth, Kans., 1986.

MacDonald, Charles B. *The Battle of the Bulge*. London: Weidenfeld & Nicolson, 1984.

Marshall, S. L. A. *Bastogne: The First Eight Days*. Washington, D.C.: Infantry Journal Press, 1946.

Merriam, Robert E. *The Battle of the Ardennes*. London: Souvenir Press, 1958.

Moe Buckout, Major Laurie G. "Signal Security in the Ardennes Offensive: 1944–1945." School of Advanced Military Studies, U.S. Army Command and General Staff College, Fort Leavenworth, Kans., 1997.

Morelock, Jerry D. *Generals of the Ardennes: American Leadership in the Battle of the Bulge*. Washington, D.C.: Government Printing Office, 1994.

Morton, Major Gregory V. "Field Artillery Support for III Corps Attack, 18–26 December 1944." School of Advanced Military Studies, U.S. Army Command and General Staff College, Fort Leavenworth, Kans., 1985.

Nobécourt, Jacques. *Hitler's Last Gamble: The Battle for the Ardennes*. London: Chatto & Windus, 1967.

Operations Support Division, U.S. Army Concepts Analysis Agency. *Simulation Enhancements from Ardennes Campaign (SEACA)*. October 1996.

Pallud, Jean Paul. *The Battle of the Bulge: Then and Now*. London: After the Battle, 1999.

Parker, Danny S. *Battle of the Bulge: Hitler's Ardennes Offensive, 1944–1945*. Conshohocken, Pa.: Combined Books, 1991.

Phillips, Robert H. *To Save Bastogne*. New York: Stein & Day, 1983.

Pimlott, John. *Battle of the Bulge*. New York: Gallery Books, 1990.

Rosenbaum, Lieutenant Colonel Michael D. "The Battle of the Bulge: Intelligence Lessons for the Army after Next." U.S. Army War College, Carlisle Barracks, Pa., 1999.

Saunders, Hrowe. *Die Wacht am Rhein: Hitlers letzte Schlacht in den Ardennen 1944/45*. Berg am See: Kurt Vowinckel-Verlag, 1984.

Strawson, John. *The Battle for the Ardennes*. London: Batsford, 1972.

Thaden, Major Russell H. "Intelligence Preparation of the Battlefield and Predictive Intelligence." School of Advanced Military Studies, U.S. Army Command and General Staff College, Fort Leavenworth, Kans., 1986.

Toland, John. *Battle: The Story of the Bulge*. New York: Random House, 1959.

U.S. Army Concepts Analysis Agency. "The Ardennes Campaign Simulation Data Base (ACSDB), Final Report." Vol. 1. Fairfax, Va.: Data Memory Systems, February 7, 1990.

———. Ardennes Campaign Simulation (ARCAS), Study Report CAA-SR-95–8. December 1995.

Winton, Harold R. *Corps Commanders of the Bulge: Six American Generals and Victory in the Ardennes*. Lawrence: University Press of Kansas, 2007.

Zabecki, Major General David T. "Third Army Counterattack, December 1944: Myths, Facts, and the Military Decision-Making Process." Manuscript, courtesy of Major General Zabecki.

Unit Histories

Battle Book: A Combat History of Headquarters and Headquarters Battery, Division Artillery 6th Armored Division. 1945.

Colby, John. *War from the Ground Up: The 90th Division in WW II.* Austin, Tex.: Nortex Press, 1991.

Craig, Berry. *The Legacy of the 4th Armored Division.* Paducah, Ky.: Turner Publishing Company, 1990.

Dupuy, Colonel R. Ernest. *St. Vith: Lion in the Way.* Washington, D.C.: Infantry Journal Press, 1949.

Dyer, George. *XII Corps: Spearhead of Patton's Third Army.* Baton Rouge: Military Press of Louisiana, 1947.

80th "Blue Ridge" Infantry Division. Paducah, Ky.: Turner Publishing Company, 1991.

The Fifth Infantry Division in the ETO. Nashville: Battery Press, 1997.

Fitzharris, Joseph C., ed. *Patton's Fighting Bridge Builders: Company C, 1303rd Engineer General Service Regiment.* College Station: Texas A&M University Press, 2007.

Fox, Donald M. *Patton's Vanguard: The United States Army's Fourth Armored Division.* Jefferson, N.C.: McFarland & Company, 2003.

Grow, Robert W. *From Brest to Bastogne: The Story of the Sixth Armored Division.* Paris: Stars and Stripes, 1945.

Guderian, Heinz Günther. *From Normandy to the Ruhr: With the 116th Panzer Division in World War II.* Bedford, Pa.: Aberjona Press, 2001.

Hofmann, George F. *The Super Sixth: History of the 6th Armored Division in World War II and Its Post-War Association.* Nashville: Battery Press, n.d.

Hogan, David W., Jr. *A Command Post at War: First Army Headquarters in Europe, 1943–1945.* Washington, D.C.: Center of Military History, 2000.

Hogg, Ian V. *German Order of Battle 1944.* London: Greenhill Books, 1994.

Lentz, Brigadier General John M. *XII Corps Artillery in Combat.* Regensburg, Germany: U.S. Army, 1945.

Martin, Gerhard. *Letzter Lorbeer: Fallschirmpioniere in der Ardennenschlacht, 1944–1945: Im Rahmen der 5. Fallschirmjägerdivision.* Coburg: Nation Europa Verlag, 2002.

Meyer, Hubert. *The 12th SS: The History of the Hitler Youth Panzer Division.* Mechanicsburg, Pa.: Stackpole Books, 2005.

Mitchell, Colonel Ralph M. *The 101st Airborne Division's Defense of Bastogne.* Fort Leavenworth, Kans.: Combat Studies Institute, 1986.

Nafziger, George F. *The German Order of Battle: Waffen SS and Other Units.* Conshohocken, Pa.: Combined Books, 2001.

Nichols, Lester M. *Impact: The Battle Story of the Tenth Armored Division.* Nashville: Battery Press, 2000.

Parker, Colonel Charles W., Jr., and Colonel William J. Thompson. *Conqueror: The Story of Ninth Army, 1944–1945.* Nashville: Battery Press, 1980.

Pay, Don R. *Thunder from Heaven: Story of the 17th Airborne Division, 1943–1945.* Nashville: Battery Press, 1980.

Presenting . . . the 35th Infantry Division in World War II, 1941–1945. Nashville: Battery Press, 1988.

Province, Charles M. *Patton's Third Army: A Daily Combat Diary.* New York: Hippocrene Books, 1992.

Quarrie, Bruce. *The Ardennes Offensive, V Panzer Armee: Central Sector.* Oxford: Osprey, 2000.

Rapport, Leonard, and Arthur Northwood Jr. *Rendezvous with Destiny: A History of the 101st Airborne Division.* Washington, D.C.: Infantry Journal Press, 1948.

Reagan, Bruce W., et al. *An Odyssey with Patton: A Revised History of the 150th Engineer Combat Battalion, XII Corps, Third Army, Europe, 1944–1945.* Bennington, Vt.: Merriam Press, 2000.

Reynolds, Michael. *The Devil's Adjutant: Jochen Peiper, Panzer Leader.* New York: Sarpedon, 1995.

——. *Men of Steel, 1st SS Panzer Corps: The Ardennes and Eastern Front 1944–1945.* New York: Sarpedon, 1999.

——. *Sons of the Reich: II SS Panzer Corps, Normandy, Arnhem, Ardennes, Eastern Front.* New York: Sarpedon, 2002.

Schmitz, Peter, Klaus-Jürgen Thies, Günter Wehmann, and Christian Zweng. *Die deutschen Divisionen 1939–1945. III: Die Divisionen 11–16.* Osnabrück: Biblio Verlag, 1996.

——. *Die deutschen Divisionen 1939–1945. IV: Die Divisionen 17–25.* Osnabrück: Biblio Verlag, 2000.

Shapiro, Milton. *Tank Command: Patton's 4th Armored Division.* New York: David McKay, 1979.

Spaeter, Helmut. *The History of Panzerkorps "Großdeutschland."* Vol. 2. Translated by David Johnston. Winnipeg: J. J. Fedorowicz, 1995.

Steward, Hal D. *Thunderbolt: The History of the Eleventh Armored Division.* Nashville: Battery Press, 1981.

Tiemann, Ralf. *Chronicle of the 7. Panzer-Kompanie I. SS-Panzer Division "Leibstandarte."* Atglen, Pa.: Schiffer Military History, 1998.

——. *The Leibstandarte IV/2.* Winnipeg: J. J. Fedorowicz, 1998.

General Secondary Sources

Adams, John A. *The Battle for Western Europe, Fall 1944: An Operational Assessment.* Bloomington: Indiana University Press, 2010.

Ambrose, Stephen E. *The Supreme Commander: The War Years of General Dwight D. Eisenhower.* Garden City, N.Y.: Doubleday, 1970.

Baily, Charles M. *Feint Praise: American Tanks and Tank Destroyers during World War II.* Hamden, Conn.: Archon Books, 1983.

Bauer, Eddy. *Der Panzerkrieg: Die Wichtigsten Panzeroperationen des Zweiten Weltkrieges in Europa und Afrika. II: Der Zusammenbruch des Dritten Reiches.* Bonn: Verlag, 1965.

Bennett, Ralph. *Ultra in the West: The Normandy Campaign of 1944–1945.* London: Hutchinson, 1979.

Bidwell, Shelford, and Dominick Graham. *Fire-Power: British Army Weapons and Theories of War, 1904–1945.* London: George Allen & Unwin, 1982.

Blumenson, Martin. *Patton: The Man behind the Legend 1885–1945*. New York: William Morrow, 1985.

———. *U.S. Army in World War II: Breakout and Pursuit*. Washington, D.C.: Center of Military History, 1989.

Bonn, Keith. *When the Odds Were Even: The Vosges Mountains Campaign, October 1944–January 1945*. Novato, Calif.: Presidio Press, 1994.

Boog, Hornst, Gerhard Krebs, and Detlef Vogel. *Germany and the Second World War*. Vol. 7, *The Strategic Air War in Europe and the War in the West and East Asia, 1943–1944/45*. Oxford: Oxford University Press, 2006.

Braim, Paul. *The Will to Win: The Life of General James A. Van Fleet*. Annapolis, Md.: Naval Institute Press, 2001.

Brown, Anthony C., ed. *The Secret War Report of the OSS*. New York: Berkeley, 1976.

Brownlow, Donald G. *Panzer Baron: The Military Exploits of General Hasso von Manteuffel*. North Quincy, Mass.: Christopher Publishing House, 1975.

Burros, Raymond H. "U.S. Corps-Level Intelligence in World War II: A Quantitative Study of Identification, Strength, and Location." Combat Operations Research Group, CORG-R-81, December 15, 1959.

Carafano, James J. *After D-Day: Operation Cobra and the Normandy Breakout*. Boulder, Colo.: Lynne Rienner, 2000.

Carver, Field Marshal Lord. *The Apostles of Mobility*. London: Weidenfeld & Nicolson, 1979.

Clausewitz, Carl von. *On War*. Edited by Michael Howard and Peter Paret. Princeton, N.J.: Princeton University Press, 1984.

Coakley, Robert W., and Richard M. Leighton. *U.S. Army in World War II: Global Logistics and Strategy, 1943–1945*. Washington, D.C.: Center of Military History, 1968.

Cole, Henry G. *General William E. Depuy: Preparing the Army for Modern War*. Lexington: University Press of Kentucky, 2008.

Cole, Hugh M. *U.S. Army in World War II: The Lorraine Campaign*. Washington, D.C.: Center of Military History, 1984.

Colley, David P. *Decision at Strasbourg: Ike's Strategic Mistake to Halt the Sixth Army Group at the Rhine in 1944*. Annapolis, Md.: Naval Institute Press, 2008.

Condell, Bruce, and David T. Zabecki, eds. *On the German Art of War: Truppenführung*. Boulder, Colo.: Lynne Rienner, 2001.

Cooper, Matthew. *The German Army 1933–1945: Its Political and Military Failure*. New York: Bonanza Books, 1984.

Craven, Wesley F., and James L. Cate, eds. *The Army Air Forces in World War II*. Vol. 3, *Europe: Argument to VE Day, January 1944 to May 1945*. Chicago: University of Chicago Press, 1958.

Creveld, Martin van. *Command in War*. Cambridge, Mass.: Harvard University Press, 1985.

———. *Fighting Power: German and U.S. Army Performance, 1939–1945*. Westport, Conn.: Greenwood Press, 1982.

———. *Supplying War: Logistics from Wallenstein to Patton*. Cambridge: Cambridge University Press, 2004.

Crosswell, D. K. R. *Beetle: The Life of General Walter Bedell Smith*. Lexington: University Press of Kentucky, 2010.

————. *The Chief of Staff: The Military Career of General Walter Bedell Smith.* Westport, Conn: Greenwood, 1991.

Danchev, Alex, and Daniel Todman, eds. *War Diaries, 1939–1945: Field Marshal Lord Alanbrooke.* London: Weidenfeld & Nicolson, 2001.

Davies, W. J. K. *German Army Handbook, 1939–1945.* London: Ian Allan, 1973.

D'Este, Carlo. *Decision in Normandy.* New York: E. P. Dutton, 1983.

————. *Eisenhower: A Soldier's Life.* New York: Henry Holt, 2002.

————. *Patton: A Genius for War.* New York: HarperCollins, 1995.

Dixon, Norman F. *On the Psychology of Military Incompetence.* London: Jonathan Cape, 1976.

Doubler, Michael D. *Closing with the Enemy: How GIs Fought the War in Europe, 1944–1945.* Lawrence: University Press of Kansas, 1994.

Doughty, Robert A. *The Breaking Point: Sedan and the Fall of France, 1940.* New York: Archon Books, 1990.

Dupuy, Trevor N. *Numbers, Predictions and War.* Indianapolis: Bobbs-Merrill, 1979.

Ehrman, John. *Grand Strategy.* Vol. 6, *October 1944–August 1945.* London: Her Majesty's Stationery Office, 1956.

Eisenhower, David. *Eisenhower at War, 1943–1945.* New York: Random House, 1986.

Ellis, John. *Brute Force: Allied Strategy and Tactics in the Second World War.* London: Andre Deutsch, 1990.

Ellis, L. F. *Victory in the West.* Vol. 2, *The Defeat of Germany.* London: Her Majesty's Stationery Office, 1968.

English, John A. *Marching through Chaos: The Descent of Armies in Theory and Practice.* Westport, Conn.: Praeger, 1996.

————. *Patton's Peers: The Forgotten Allied Field Army Commanders of the Western Front 1944–1945.* Mechanicsburg, Pa.: Stackpole Books, 2009.

————. *A Perspective on Infantry.* New York: Praeger, 1981.

Essame, H. *Patton: A Study in Command.* New York: Charles Scribner's Sons, 1974.

Farago, Ladislas. *Patton: Ordeal and Triumph.* New York: Ivan Obolensky, 1964.

Finnegan, John Patrick. *Military Intelligence.* Washington, D.C.: Center of Military History, 1998.

Flowers, Major Jack D. "Patton, Third Army and Operational Maneuver." School of Advanced Military Studies, U.S. Army Command and General Staff College, Fort Leavenworth, Kans., 1998.

Forty, George. *The Armies of George S. Patton.* London: Arms & Armour Press, 1996.

————. *Patton's Third Army at War.* New York: Charles Scribner's Sons, 1979.

Friedli, Lukas. *Die Panzer Instandsetzungder Wehrmacht.* Winnipeg: J.J. Fedorowicz, 2002.

Frieser, Karl-Heinz. *The Blitzkrieg Legend: The 1940 Campaign in the West.* Annapolis, Md.: Naval Institute Press, 2005.

Fuller, J. F. C. *Armored Warfare: An Annotated Edition of Lectures on F.S.R. III (Operations between Mechanized Forces).* Harrisburg, Pa.: Military Service Publishing, 1955.

Gabel, Christopher R. *Seek, Strike and Destroy: U.S. Army Tank Destroyer Doctrine in World War II.* Leavenworth Papers No. 12. Combat Studies Institute, Fort Leavenworth, Kans., 1985.

Galland, Adolf. *The First and the Last: The German Fighter Force in World War II.* London: Methuen, 1955.

Gawne, Jonathan. *Ghosts of the ETO: American Tactical Deception Units in the European Theater 1944–1945.* Havertown, Pa.: Casemate, 2002.

Geyer, Michael. "German Strategy in the Age of Machine Warfare, 1914–1945." In Peter Paret, ed., *Makers of Modern Strategy from Machiavelli to the Nuclear Age.* Princeton, N.J.: Princeton University Press, 1986.

Glantz, David M. *Soviet Operational Art: In Pursuit of Deep Battle.* London: Frank Cass, 1991.

Greenfield, Kent Roberts, Robert R. Palmer, and Bell I. Wiley. *U.S. Army in World War II: The Organization of Ground Combat Troops.* Washington, D.C.: Historical Division, 1947.

Hallinan, Ulick. "From Operation Cobra to the Liberation of Paris: American Offensive Operations in Northern France, 25 July–25 August 1944." PhD diss., Temple University, 1988.

Hallion, Richard P. *Strike from the Sky: The History of Battlefield Air Attack, 1911–1945.* Washington, D.C.: Smithsonian Institution Press, 1989.

Hamilton, Nigel. *Monty: The Field Marshal 1944–1976.* London: Hamish Hamilton, 1986.

Hastings, Max. *Armageddon: The Battle for Germany, 1944–1945.* New York: Alfred A. Knopf, 2004.

Haupt, Werner. *Das Ende Im Westen 1945: Bildchronik vom Kampf in Westdeutschland.* Dorheim: Podzun-Verlag, 1972.

Heefner, Wilson A. *Patton's Bulldog: The Life and Service of General Walton H. Walker.* Shippensburg, Pa.: White Mane Books, 2001.

Hill, Major James R. "A Comparative Analysis of the Military Leadership Styles of George C. Marshall and Dwight D. Eisenhower." School of Advanced Military Studies, U.S. Army Command and General Staff College, Fort Leavenworth, Kans., 2008.

Hinsley, F. H. *British Intelligence in the Second World War: Its Influence on Strategy and Operations.* Vol. 3, pt. 2. London: Her Majesty's Stationery Office, 1988.

Hirshson, Stanley P. *General Patton: A Soldier's Life.* New York: HarperCollins, 2002.

Hofmann, George F. *Cold War Casualty: The Court Martial of Major-General Robert Grow.* Kent, Ohio: Kent State University Press, 1993.

Horne, Alistair. *To Lose a Battle: France 1940.* London: Macmillan, 1969.

Hughes, Thomas A. *Overlord: General Pete Quesada and the Triumph of Tactical Air Power in World War II.* New York: Free Press, 1995.

Ingersoll, Ralph. *The Battle Is the Payoff.* New York: Harcourt, Brace, 1943.

———. *Top Secret.* New York: Harcourt, Brace, 1946.

Irving, David. *The War Between the Generals.* New York: Congdon & Lattes, 1981.

Jacobsen, H. A., and Jürgen Rowher, eds. *Decisive Battles of World War II: The German View.* New York: G. P. Putnam, 1965.

James, D. Clayton. *A Time for Giants: Politics of the American High Command in World War II.* New York: Franklin Watts, 1987.

Jomini, Antoine Henri de. *The Art of War.* London: Greenhill Books, 1992.

Kemp, Anthony. *The Unknown Battle: Metz 1944.* London: Frederick Warne, 1981.

Kennett, Lee. *G.I.: The American Soldier in World War II.* New York: Charles Scribner's Sons, 1987.

Kingseed, Cole C. *Old Glory Stories: American Combat Leadership in World War II.* Annapolis, Md.: Naval Institute Press, 2006.

Kroener, Bernhard R., et al. *Germany and the Second World War.* Vol. 5, *Organization and Mobilization of the German Sphere of Power,* pt. 1, *Wartime Administration, Economy, and Manpower Resources 1939–1941.* Oxford: Oxford University Press, 2000.

Kursietis, Andrus J. *The Wehrmacht at War, 1939–1945: The Units and Commanders of the German Ground Forces during World War II.* Soesterberg, Netherlands: Aspekt, 1999.

Lande, D. A. *I Was with Patton: First Person Accounts of WWII in George S. Patton's Command.* St. Paul, Minn.: Motor Books International, 2001.

Lewin, Ronald. *Ultra Goes to War.* New York: McGraw-Hill, 1978.

Liddell Hart, B. H. *History of the Second World War.* New York: Putnam, 1970.

———. *The Other Side of the Hill: Germany's Generals, Their Rise and Fall with Their Own Account of Military Events, 1939–1945.* London: Cassell, 1948.

Lucas, James, and Matthew Cooper. *Panzergrenadiers.* London: Macdonald & Janes, 1977.

MacDonald, Charles B. *The Mighty Endeavor: American Armed Forces in the European Theater in World War II.* New York: Oxford University Press, 1969.

———. *U.S. Army in World War II: The Last Offensive.* Washington, D.C.: Center of Military History, 1973.

———. *U.S. Army in World War II: The Siegfried Line Campaign.* Washington, D.C.: Center of Military History, 1990.

Mansoor, Peter. *The G.I. Offensive in Europe: The Triumph of American Infantry Divisions, 1944–1945.* Lawrence: University Press of Kansas, 1999.

Matloff, Maurice. "The 90-Division Gamble." In Kent Roberts Greenfield, ed., *Command Decisions.* Washington, D.C.: Center of Military History, 1960.

McGrath, John J. *Crossing the Line of Departure: Battle Command on the Move, a Historical Perspective.* Fort Leavenworth, Kans.: Combat Studies Institute Press, 2007.

McManus, John C. *Alamo in the Ardennes: The Untold Story of the American Soldiers Who Made the Defense of Bastogne Possible.* New York: John A. Wiley & Sons, 2007.

Mellenthin, F. W. von. *German Generals of World War II as I Saw Them.* Norman: Oklahoma University Press, 1977.

Messenger, Charles. *Hitler's Gladiator: The Life and Times of Oberstgruppenführer and Panzergeneral der Waffen SS Sepp Dietrich.* London: Brassey's, 1988.

———. *The Last Prussian: A Biography of Field Marshal Gerd von Rundstedt, 1875–1953.* London: Brassey's, 1991.

Miksche, F. O. *Blitzkrieg.* London: Faber & Faber, 1941.

Miller, Edward G. *Nothing Less than Full Victory: Americans at War in Europe, 1944–1945.* Annapolis, Md.: Naval Institute Press, 2007.

Miller, Robert. *Division Commander: A Biography of Major General Norman D. Cota.* Spartanburg, S.C.: Reprint Company, 1989.

Millett, Allan R., and Williamson Murray, eds. *Military Effectiveness.* Vol. 3, *The Second World War.* Boston: Allen & Unwin, 1988.

Model, Hansgeorg, and Dermot Bradley. *Generalfeldmarschall Walter Model (1891–1945): Dokumentation eines Soldatenlebens.* Osnabrück: Biblio Verlag, 1991.

Muller, Colonel Hollis L. *Technique of Modern Arms.* Harrisburg, Pa.: Military Service Publishing, 1940.

Murray, Williamson, and Allan R. Millett. *A War to Be Won: Refighting the Second World War.* Cambridge, Mass.: Belknap Press of Harvard University Press, 2000.

Newton, Steven H. *Hitler's Commander: Field Marshal Walter Model, Hitler's Favorite General.* New York: Da Capo Books, 2006.

Nowowiejski, Lieutenant Colonel Dean A. "Concepts of Information Warfare in Practice: General George S. Patton and the Third Army Information Service, August–December, 1944." School of Advanced Military Studies, U.S. Army Command and General Staff College, Fort Leavenworth, Kans., 1995.

Nye, Roger H. *The Patton Mind: The Professional Development of an Extraordinary Leader.* Garden City, N.Y.: Avery Publishing, 1993.

Odom, Charles B. *General George S. Patton and Eisenhower.* New Orleans: Word Picture Productions, 1985.

Ohl, John Kennedy. *Supplying the Troops: General Somervell and American Logistics in World War II.* De Kalb: Northern Illinois University Press, 1994.

Overy, Richard. *Why the Allies Won.* London: Jonathan Cape, 1995.

Palmer, Robert R., Bell I. Wiley, and William R. Keast. *U.S. Army in World War II: The Procurement and Training of Ground Combat Troops.* Washington, D.C.: Center of Military History, 1948.

Perret, Geoffrey. *There's a War to Be Won: The United States Army in World War II.* New York: Random House, 1991.

Phillips, Henry G. *The Making of a Professional: Manton S. Eddy, USA.* Westport, Conn.: Greenwood, 2000.

Pogue, Forrest C. "General of the Army Omar N. Bradley." In Field Marshal Sir Michael Carver, ed., *The War Lords: Military Commanders of the Twentieth Century.* Boston: Little, Brown, 1976.

———. *U.S. Army in World War II: The Supreme Command.* Washington, D.C.: Center of Military History, 1989.

Price, Frank J. *Troy H. Middleton: A Biography.* Baton Rouge: Louisiana State University Press, 1974.

Province, Charles M. *The Unknown Patton.* New York: Bonanza Books, 1983.

Puryear, Edgar F. *Nineteen Stars.* Novato, Calif.: Presidio Press, 1971.

Rankin, Brigadier General Fred Wharton. *Medical Department United States Army in World War II. Clinical Series, Internal Medicine in World War II.* Vol. 1, *Activities of Medical Consultants.* Washington, D.C.: Office of the Surgeon General, Department of the Army, 1962.

Rickard, John Nelson. *Patton at Bay: The Lorraine Campaign, September to December 1944.* Westport, Conn.: Praeger, 1999.

Ruppenthal, Roland G. *U.S. Army in World War II: Logistical Support of the Armies.*

Vol. 2, *September 1944–May 1945*. Washington, D.C.: Center of Military History, 1987.

Sanderson, Major Jeffrey R. "General George S. Patton, Jr.: Master of Operational Battle Command. What Lasting Battle Command Lessons Can We Learn from Him?" School of Advanced Military Studies, U.S. Army Command and General Staff College, Fort Leavenworth, Kans., 1997.

Scheibert, Horst. *Kampf und Untergang Der Deutschen Panzertruppe, 1939–1945*. Dorheim: Podzun-Verlag, 1994.

Schwien, Colonel Edwin E. *Combat Intelligence: Its Acquisition and Transmission*. Washington, D.C.: Infantry Journal Press, 1936.

Simpkin, Richard. *Race to the Swift: Thoughts on Twenty-First Century Warfare*. London: Brassey's, 1985.

Sixsmith, E. K. G. *Eisenhower as Military Commander*. New York: Stein & Day, 1972.

Sorely, Lewis. *Thunderbolt: From the Battle of the Bulge to Vietnam and Beyond: General Creighton Abrams and the Army of His Times*. New York: Simon & Schuster, 1992.

Spayd, P. A. *Bayerlein: From Afrikakorps to Panzer Lehr*. Atglen, Pa.: Schiffer Military History, 2003.

Spielberger, Walter J. *The Spielberger German Armor and Military Vehicle Series. I: Panther and Its Variants*. Atglen, Pa.: Schiffer Military History, 1993.

———. *The Spielberger German Armor and Military Vehicle Series. IV: Panzer IV and Its Variants*. Atglen, Pa.: Schiffer Military History, 1993.

Spires, David N. *Patton's Air Force: Forging a Legendary Air-Ground Team*. Washington, D.C.: Smithsonian Institution Press, 2002.

Stanton, Shelby L. *World War II Order of Battle*. New York: Galahad, 1991.

Stimson, Henry L., and McGeorge Bundy. *On Active Service in Peace and War*. London: Hutchinson, n.d.

Stouffer, Samuel A., et al. *Studies in Social Psychology in World War II*. Vol. 2, *The American Soldier: Combat and Its Aftermath*. Princeton, N.J.: Princeton University Press, 1949.

Strawson, John. *Hitler's Battles for Europe*. New York: Charles Scribner's Sons, 1971.

Swedo, Major Bradford J. *XIX Tactical Air Command and ULTRA: Patton's Force Enhancers in the 1944 Campaign in France*. Cadre Paper No. 10. Maxwell Air Force Base, Ala.: Air University Press, 2001.

Trevor-Roper, H. R. *Blitzkrieg to Defeat: Hitler's War Directives 1939–1945*. New York: Holt, Rinehart & Winston, 1964.

Wade, Lieutenant Colonel Gary. "World War II Division Commanders." CSI Report No. 7, Fort Leavenworth, Kans.

Wallach, Jehuda L. *The Dogma of the Battle of Annihilation: The Theories of Clausewitz and Schlieffen and Their Impact on the German Conduct of Two World Wars*. Westport, Conn.: Greenwood Press, 1986.

Weeks, John. *Men against Tanks: A History of Anti-Tank Warfare*. London: David & Charles, 1975.

Weigley, Russell F. *Eisenhower's Lieutenants: The Campaigns of France and Germany, 1944–1945*. Bloomington: Indiana University Press, 1981.

Whiting, Charles. *Patton*. New York: Ballantine, 1970.

Wilmot, Chester. *The Struggle for Europe*. London: Collins, 1952.

Zabecki, David T., ed. *Chief of Staff: The Principal Officers behind History's Greatest Commanders*. Vol. 2, *World War II to Korea and Vietnam*. Annapolis, Md.: Naval Institute Press, 2008.

Articles

Ambrose, Stephen E. "A Fateful Friendship." *American Heritage* 20, no. 3 (April 1969): 41–41, 97–103.

Barnes, Wyatt E. "A Rifleman's Story." *World War II* (2004): 66–71.

Beaumont, Roger A. "Assessing Operational Impact: A Problem in Military Analysis." *Military Affairs* 46, no. 3 (October 1982): 132–33.

———. "Command Method: A Gap in the Historiography." *Naval War College Review* 31, no. 3 (winter 1979): 61–74.

Berlin, Robert H. "United States Army World War II Corps Commanders: A Composite Biography." *Journal of Military History* 53, no. 2 (April 1989): 147–68.

Bigelow, Michael E. "Big Business: Intelligence in Patton's Third Army." *Military Intelligence* 18, no. 2 (April–June 1992): 31–36.

Blumenson, Martin. "Bradley-Patton: World War II's 'Odd Couple.'" *Army* 35, no. 12 (December 1985): 56–64.

———. "General of the Army Omar N. Bradley, 1893–1981." *Army* 31, no. 5 (May 1981): 16–19.

———. "Patton and Montgomery: Alike or Different?" *Army* 22, no. 6 (June 1972): 16–22.

Bolger, Daniel P. "Zero Defects: Command Climate in First U.S. Army, 1944–1945." *Military Review* 71, no. 5 (May 1991): 61–73.

Bradley, Omar N. "On Leadership." *Parameters* 11, no. 3 (September 1981): 2–7.

Brubaker, Major Elbridge L., et al. "The Deliberate River Crossing: The 6th Armored at the Our River." *Armor* 59, no. 4 (July–August 1950): 34–39.

Carr, Caleb. "The American Rommel." *Military History Quarterly* 4, no. 4 (summer 1992): 76–85.

Carter, Colonel William R. "Air Power in the Battle of the Bulge: A Theater Campaign Perspective." *Airpower Journal* 3, no. 4 (winter 1989): 10–33.

Crandall, William F. "Eisenhower the Strategist: The Battle of the Bulge and the Censure of Joe McCarthy." *Presidential Studies Quarterly* 17, no. 3 (summer 1987): 487–501.

Daley, John. "Patton versus the 'Motor Maniacs': An Inter-War Defense of Horse Cavalry." *Armor* 106, no. 2 (March–April 1997): 12–14.

Deutsch, Harold C. "Commanding Generals and the Uses of Intelligence." *Intelligence and National Security* 3, no. 3 (1988): 194–260.

Dietrich, Steve E. "The Professional Reading of General George S. Patton, Jr." *Journal of Military History* 53, no. 4 (October 1989): 387–418.

Dinardo, R. L., and Austin Bay. "Horse-Drawn Transport in the German Army." *Journal of Contemporary History* 23, no. 1 (1988): 135.

Dougherty, Major Kevin. "Our MI Heritage: Oscar Koch: An Unsung Hero behind Patton's Victories." *Military Intelligence Professional Bulletin* 28, no. 1 (April–June 2002): 64–66.

Dupuy, Trevor N. "Combat Data and the 3:1 Rule." *International Security* 14, no. 1 (summer 1989): 195–201.

———. "Mythos or Verity? The Quantified Judgment Model and German Combat Effectiveness." *Military Affairs* 50, no. 4 (October 1986): 204–10.

Epstein, Joshua M. "The 3:1 Rule, the Adaptive Dynamic Model, and the Future of Security Studies." *International Security* 13, no. 4 (spring 1989): 90–127.

Ford, Colonel Raymond O. "Groups of Armies." *Military Review* 25, no. 11 (February 1946): 3–6.

Fricker, Ronald D., Jr. "Attrition Models of the Ardennes Campaign." *Naval Research Logistics* 45, no. 1 (February 1998): 1–21.

Ganz, A. Harding. "Patton's Relief of General Wood." *Journal of Military History* 53, no. 3 (July 1989): 257–73.

Gavin, James M. "Two Fighting Generals: Patton and MacArthur." *Army* 15, no. 4 (April 1965): 32–38.

"G.I. General: From the Notebook of a Member of the 12th Army Group Headquarters." *Infantry Journal* 63, no. 10 (October 1948): 5–9.

Grow, Robert W. "Mounted Combat: Lessons from the European Theater." *Cavalry Journal* 54, (November–December 1945): 35–36.

Haislip, Wade H. "Corps Command in World War II." *Military Review* 70, no. 5 (May 1990): 22–32.

Hammond, Colonel Elton F. "Signals for Patton." *Signals* 2, no. 1 (September–October 1947): 5–11.

Hayward, Philip. "The Measurement of Combat Effectiveness." *Operations Research* 16, no. 2 (March 1968): 316.

Hobar, Colonel Basil J. "The Ardennes 1944: Intelligence Failure or Deception Success?" *Military Intelligence* 10, no. 4 (October–December 1984): 12.

Hofmann, George F. "Armor History and Operations in 1944: The 6th Armored Division Experience in the European Theater of Operations: A Study in Leadership Development and Education." *Armor* 103, no. 5 (September–October 1994): 6–11.

Hung, C-Y, et al. "Fitting Lanchester's Square Law to the Ardennes Campaign." *Journal of the Operational Research Society* 56 (2005): 942–46.

Irzyk, Albin F. "Bastogne: A Fascinating Obscure Vignette." *Armor* 95, no. 2 (March–April 1986): 24–31.

———. "4th Armored Division Spearhead at Bastogne." *World War II* (November 1999): 34–40, 88, 90.

———. "The Name Enough Division." *Armor* 96, no. 4 (July–August 1987): 8–12.

Johnson, Frank S. "The Battle of the Bulge Foreshadowed." *Military Review* 75, no. 1 (December 1994–January 1995): 110–12.

Jordan, Lieutenant Colonel Thomas M. "Battle Command: Bradley and Ridgway in the Battle of the Bulge." *Military Review* 80, no. 2 (March–April 2000): 95–98.

Kingseed, Major Cole C. "The Falaise-Argentan Encirclement: Operationally Brilliant, Tactically Flawed." *Military Review* 64, no. 12 (December 1984): 2–11.

Kirkpatrick, Lyman B. "Combat Intelligence: A Comparative Evaluation." *Studies in Intelligence* 5, no. 4 (fall 1960): 45–51.

Krucker, Herbert F. "Quartermaster Supply in an Armored Division in Combat." *Military Review* 25, no. 7 (October 1945): 62–63.

Leach, Colonel James H. (Ret). "A Tanker—A Soldier." *Armor* 89, no. 5 (September–October 1980): 3.

Liddell Hart, B. H. "The Ratio of Troops to Space." *Military Review* 40, no. 1 (April 1960): 3–14.

Luttwak, Edward N. "The Operational Level of War." *International Security* 5, no. 3 (winter 1980–1981): 61–79.

MacDonald, Charles B. "The Neglected Ardennes." *Military Review* 43, no. 4 (April 1963): 74–91.

Madej, W. Victor. "Effectiveness and Cohesion of German Ground Forces in World War II." *Journal of Political and Military Sociology* 6, no. 2 (1978): 233–34.

McAndrew, Bill. "Operational Art and the Northwest European Theatre of War, 1944." *Canadian Defence Quarterly* 21, no. 3 (December 1991): 19–26.

McLain, Raymond S. "One of the Greatest: A Study in Leadership." Edited by Albert N. Garland. *Military Review* 49 (December 1969): 18–25.

———. "They Had Charisma: Marshall, Bradley, Patton, Eisenhower." *Army* 21 (May 1971): 26–31.

Mearsheimer, John J. "Assessing the Conventional Balance: The 3:1 Rule and Its Critics." *International Security* 13, no. 4 (spring 1999): 54–89.

———. "Why the Soviets Can't Win Quickly in Central Europe." *International Security* 7, no. 1 (summer 1982): 16–17.

Munch, Paul G. "Patton's Staff and the Battle of the Bulge." *Military Review* 70, no. 5 (May 1990): 46–54.

Nye, Roger H. "Whence Patton's Military Genius?" *Parameters* 21, no. 4 (1991–1992): 60–73.

Oden, Delk M. "The 4th Armored Division in the Relief of Bastogne." *Military Review* 27, no. 10 (January 1948): 39–44.

O'Keeffe, Captain Elbert B. "Artillery Was the Answer." *Infantry Journal* 56, no. 6 (June 1945): 25.

Pogue, Forrest C. "The Ardennes Campaign: The Impact of Intelligence." Remarks to the National Security Agency Communications Analysis Association, December 16, 1980.

Polk, General James K. "Patton: 'You Might as Well Die a Hero.'" *Army* 25, no. 12 (December 1975): 39–44.

Pratt, Fletcher. "The Tactician of the West." *Infantry Journal* 61–62 (December 1947): 4–14, (January 1948): 52–59, (February 1948): 19–25.

Reeves, Lieutenant Colonel Joseph R. "Artillery in the Ardennes." *Field Artillery Journal* 36, no. 3 (March 1946): 138–84.

Rickard, John Nelson. "Eisenhower, Bradley and the Calculated Risk in the Ardennes, December 1944." *Global War Studies* 8, no. 1 (2011).

Rosengarten, Adolph G., Jr. "The Bulge: A Glimpse of Combat Intelligence." *Military Review* 41, no. 6 (June 1961): 29–33.

Rush, Robert S. "A Different Perspective: Cohesion, Morale, and Operational Effectiveness in the German Army, Fall 1944." *Armed Forces and Society* 25, no. 3 (spring 1999): 477–508.

Showalter, Dennis. "The Southern Option: A Path to Victory in 1944?" *Military Chronicles* 1, no. 1 (May–June 2005): 44–59.

Strobridge, Truman R. "Old Blood and Guts and the Desert Fox." *Military Review* 64, no. 6 (June 1984): 33–48.

Tholholte, Karl. "A German Reflects upon Artillery." *Field Artillery Journal* 35, no. 12 (December 1945): 709–15.

Vagts, Alfred. "Battle and Other Combatants Casualties in the Second World War: I." *Journal of Politics* 7, no. 3 (August 1945): 256–94.

Vandergriff, Major Donald E. "Before There Was Digitization: How MG J. S. Wood's 4th Armored Division Stormed across France without Written Orders." *Armor* 109, no. 5 (September–October 2000): 20–27.

Vermillion, John. "The Pillars of Generalship." *Parameters* 17, no. 2 (summer 1987): 2–17.

Weintraub, Stanley. "Patton's Last Christmas." *MHQ: The Quarterly Journal of Military History* 19, no. 2 (winter 2007): 7–15.

Williams, Brigadier General Robert W. "Moving Information: The Third Army Imperative." *Army* 25, no. 4 (April 1975): 17–21.

Winton, Harold R. "The Education of Two Generals: Leonard T. Gerow and John Millikin." Paper presented at the Society for Military History annual conference, April 4–7, 2002, Madison, Wisc.

Woolley, William J. "Patton and the Concept of Mechanized Warfare." *Parameters* 15, no. 3 (1985): 71–79.

Maps

GSGS 4042. Sheet No. 6, Map 9, The Ardennes, June 1944.

12th Army Group Outline Maps, 1:1,000,000, World War II Military Situation Maps, http://www.TheHistoricalArchive.com.

Index of Military Units

January 1–4, 243–47, 249, 251–
58, 259, 260
boundary shift with Sixth Army
Group, 108
boundary with First Army in the
Ardennes, 131
Bradley's long-range plans following
the collapse of the Harlange
Pocket, 288
Bradley's orders to Patton for a
counteroffensive in the Ardennes,
388n12
capability after Bastogne, 181–83
casualties in the Ardennes
campaign, 314–17
casualties in the Lorraine campaign,
315
causes of combat death, 423n40
chief opponent in the Ardennes, 28
classes of supply, 125
commander of, 2
deployment on December 19 in
Lorraine, 113–15
deployment on December 21, 129
Eisenhower's operational plans
following the relief of Bastogne,
212–13, 215
Eisenhower's response to the rapid
redeployment of, 137
estimates of German strength
opposite, 45, 97, 253
First Armee opponent in Lorraine,
89
G-2 section, 79
German forces facing following the
relief of Bastogne, 183–90
Harlange Pocket operations,
261–74, 275–81, 282, 284–85,
286–87
Hitler attacks in September, 1944,
15–16
infantry shortage in, 43–44
inflation of enemy losses, 316
January 9 offensive, 275–80
linkup with First Army at
Houffalize, 290–91

Lorraine offensive, 26, 73–75, 290,
312, 313
Luftwaffe raids on, 128, 150
Operation COBRA, 13–14
Operation LÜTTICH, 14
operations on January 13–16,
288–89
order of battle following Bastogne,
182
order of battle on December 21, 130
order of battle on December 22, 146
order of battle on December 29, 220
Patton on the redeployment of,
129–30
Patton's army plan of January 1,
248–49
Patton's concept of operations in the
Ardennes, 138, 140–41
Patton's December 21 orders for,
141
Patton's estimate on December 29,
219–24
Patton's intelligence-gathering,
77–83
Patton's operational plans following
the relief of Bastogne, 208–9,
213–17
Patton's operational technique,
308–13
Patton's tentative plan for attack by,
120–21
Patton's time estimate for an
attack into the Ardennes, 106–7,
382n37
prisoners of war processed by, 321
problems with signal security, 154
rail net, 125–26
redeployment of III Corps, 117–20
redeployment of logistical support,
124, 125–26, 127
redeployment of signals
communication, 128
redeployment of XII Corps, 123,
125, 311
redeployment ordered by Patton,
115, 117

General Index

Aachen, 16, 17–18
Abrams, Lt. Col. Creighton, 174, 177, 394n11
ABWEHRSCHLACHT IM WESTEN, 23
airborne divisions, Ridgway on the employment of, 422n37
airpower
  Allied tactical air assets on December 22, 147, 150
  American doctrine of priorities in, 147
  of the United States Army, 46
  See also Luftwaffe; XIX Tactical Air Command
Albert Canal, 22
Allen, Maj. Gen. Leven C., 70, 75, 83, 86, 87, 93, 117, 126, 138, 168, 270, 298
Allen, Col. Robert S., 82, 100
Allied commanders
  effect of logistical considerations on, 3
  grand tactics and, 4–5
  levels of command, 2–3
  operational level approaches and, 3–4
Ambrose, Stephen E., 373n44
American commanders
  estimate process, 7–8
  measures of combat effectiveness, 8
Anderson, Maj. Gen. Samuel E., 196, 197
Antwerp, 18, 20, 22
ANVIL, 381n24
Ardennes counteroffensive
  American estimates of the likelihood of, 55–60

casualties in, 314–17
frontage of the VIII Corps on the eve of, 55
German attack plan, 19, 21–23
German casualties, 422n32, 422n33
German code name for, 23
German estimates of American strength, 21
German operations launched in, 1
German preparations, 23
Hitler's strategic intent, 18, 20
initial attacks of *Heeresgruppe B*, 60–72, 371–72n32
literature on Patton's leadership during, 9
origin of, 15–17
Patton's early intelligence on, 79–83
Patton's first General Staff meeting on, 94–95
preliminary moves by American forces, 83–93
significance of, 1
weakness of German contingency planning, 23–24
Ardennes terrain
  features of, 20
  Field Manual 100–5 on, 56
  Koch's assessment of, 95–99
  road net, 20–21, 95–96
  Twelfth Army Group long-term campaign planning and, 190–93
armored divisions
  composition in the United States Army, 49
  organic infantry element, 394n20
  triangular, 394n11
armored personnel carriers, 27
armor wedge, 145

Irzyk, Maj. Albin *(cont.)*
on the fighting qualities of the 5th
FJD, 169
night attacks on December 22–23, 158
on the redeployment north, 118
Task Force Ezell and, 132
on the use of reconnaissance in tank
warfare, 161–62

Jacques, Lt. Col. George, 177
Jodl, Alfred, 15, 16, 17, 70–71,
364n30, 398–99n27
Johnston, Col. Harry W., 394n20
Joint Intelligence Committee (JIC), 25
Jomini, Antoine-Henri de, 4, 215, 356n8
Jones, Maj. Gen. Alan, 66
Juin, Alphonse, 248
"Jumbos," 154

Kahler, Hans-Joachim, 152, 207
Kampfwert classification, 358n24
Kampkraft, 8
Kasserine Pass, 109
Kean, Maj. Gen. William B., 87
Keitel, Wilhelm, 15
Keyes, Maj. Gen. Geoffrey, 385n20
Kibler, Brig. Gen. A. Franklin, 69,
212, 241
Kilburn, Brig. Gen. Charles S.
Bastogne corridor operations,
December 30, 226, 227, 233, 236
Bastogne corridor operations,
January 1–4, 243, 246, 254
commander of the VIII Corps
Meuse River sector, 403n35
Harlange Pocket operations, 269–
70, 286
movement of the 11th Armored
Division to Neufchâteau, 211
operations on January 13, 289
Patton's handling of, 307
VIII Corps attack on December 30
and, 218–19, 224
King Tiger tanks, 26
Kinnard, Lt. Col. Harry W. O., 133
Kittel, Friedrich, 30

Kluge, Günther von, 14
Kneiss, Baptist, 64, 158
Koch, Col. Oscar W.
accuracy of estimates about German
intentions in the Ardennes,
376n27
assessment of forces opposing the
Third Army, 97
assessment of German forces
following the relief of Bastogne,
184, 185, 187
on the Bastogne corridor actions,
229, 239
the decision to hold Bastogne and,
121, 122
enemy capabilities identified on
December 20, 140
intelligence estimate for XII Corps
on January 8, 270
intelligence estimate for XX Corps
on January 10, 281
intelligence estimate of German
capability prior to the Ardennes,
80–83
intelligence estimate of German
withdrawal from the Harlange
Pocket, 270
intelligence estimate on December
29, 221, 406n71
intelligence estimate on December
30, 221, 223
intelligence estimates for January 2
and 3, 254, 255
Edward Miller on, 414n51
on Patton's views of command
intelligence, 77, 78–79
Periodic Report No. 165, 376n27
study of the Ardennes terrain, 95–96
at the Verdun conference, 104, 105
work map for December 20, 138
work map for December 24, 174
work map for December 28, 189–90
Kokott, Heinz, 28, 159, 161, 176–78, 319
Kolb, Werner, 207
Königstiger II, 26
Kraas, Hugo, 26, 27, 242, 250, 255

Kraemer, Fritz, 28
Krüger, Walter, 29, 67, 259, 287

Lammerding, Heinz, 28
Last Offensive, The (MacDonald), 9
Lattre de Tassigny, Jean de, 2, 3
Lauchert, Meinrad von, 28, 67
Lauer, Maj. Gen. Walter E., 65
Leach, Capt. James, 169
leadership
  Field Manual 100–5 on, 5
  by Patton, 303–4, 305
Leonard, Maj. Gen. John W., 64, 121
logistical system, of the United States
  Army, 47
Lorraine offensive, 26, 49–50, 73–75,
  92
Losheim Gap, 65, 66, 71, 86
Low Ardennes, 20
Lucht, Walter, 30, 66
Lutes, Maj. Gen. LeRoy, 59
Luttwak, Edward, 3–4
Lüttwitz, Heinrich Freiherr von
  attacks on Bastogne, 174
  commander of the *XLVI*
    Panzerkorps, 28
  estimate on December 28, 209
  on the German Army withdrawal to
    the West Wall, 300–301
  on the German fuel supplies, 38
  initial attacks in the Ardennes, 67
  situation on December 24, 172
  situation on December 27, 202
Luxembourg City, 91

M4 Sherman tanks, 384n10
MacDonald, Charles B., 9, 309, 310,
  311, 373n44, 381–82n35
Maddox, Col. Halley G., 99, 100, 120,
  212, 228–29, 275
Mäder, Hellmuth, 206–7
MAGIC, 373n44
Manteuffel, Hasso Eccard von
  attack on Third Army in September,
    1944, 16
  Bastogne corridor actions, 251

belief in possible victory east of the
  Meuse, 407n78
combat power reorganization,
  December 31–January 2, 241–42
decision to reduce Bastogne,
  395n28
on the diminished capacity of the
  German Army, 320
estimate of December 25, 200
estimate of December 28, 209
estimate of December 29, 224–25
on German morale, 41
Harlange Pocket actions, 268
informed of the Ardennes
  counteroffensive plan, 17
initial attacks in the Ardennes, 66–
  67, 371–72n32
Kokott's attacks on Bastogne and,
  176–77
massing of forces for attack on
  Patton at Bastogne, 225
orders withdrawal from the Bastogne
  sector, 255
on the Organization Todt, 39
planned attacks in the Ardennes
  counteroffensive, 22
praise for Brandenberger's efforts,
  72
on the quality of replacements, 40
response to the relief of Bastogne,
  201–2
situation on December 24, 172–73
strength of the *Fifth Panzer Armee*
  in late 1944, 28–30
withdrawal from the Bastogne
  corridor, 258
March, Peyton C., 142
Marne, Battle of, 21
Marshall, Gen. George C., 47–48,
  102, 103, 241, 388n17, 407n75
Marshall, Samuel Lyman Atwood,
  50–51, 396n2
Martelange, 151
McAlister, Maj. H. J., 408n15
McAuliffe, Brig. Gen. Anthony C.,
  133, 135, 408–9n21

Tiger tanks, 364n27
Todt, Fritz, 39
Tolbukhin, Polkovnik, 23
Tolsdorff, Theodor, 250, 251
trench foot, 421–22n31
triangular divisions, 48, 394n11
Triepel, Gerhard, 268
truck companies, 120, 126
Truscott, Lucien K., Jr., 358n19
turning movements, 198

ULTRA
Bennett on the decline of tactical
usefulness in, 407n77
code for the Third Army, 374n7
on German movements on
December 28, 208
Lt. Col. Helfers and, 375n17
intelligence on German anticipation
of Allied resistance, 99
intelligence on German fuel
shortage, 424n46
intelligence on German
movements, January 10, 283–84
intelligence on German
movements, January 18, 298
intelligence on German transition
to the defensive in the Ardennes,
189
intelligence on the initial German
moves in the Ardennes, 85–86,
87, 88–89
intelligence prior to the Ardennes
counteroffensive, 81
intelligence provided at the Verdun
conference, 103–4
Koch's use of, 80
on the location of the 11th PD,
January 1, 414n37
Marshall orders Eisenhower to
protect the source of, 407n75
Operation LÜTTICH and, 14
out of date messages, 411n51
Patton's estimate on December 29
and, 223–24
in Patton's intelligence-gathering, 78

Patton's request for Gaffey to retain
access to, 155
recipients in Third Army, 375n18

V1 rocket, 34, 61
V2 rocket, 34
Vandenberg, Maj. Gen. Hoyt S., 75,
147
Van Fleet, Maj. Gen. James A.
arrival in the Bastogne corridor,
265–66
Harlange Pocket operations, 271,
284–85, 287
operations on January 15, 290
Patton's leadership and, 304
preparation for 90th Infantry
Division's attack on January 6,
267
Venlo, 16
Verdun conference, 100–101, 103–9
Vergeltungswaffe (Revenge Weapon
No. 1), 34
Viebig, Wilhelm, 27
Volksartilleriekorps (VAKs), 34, 35,
250
Volksgrenadier Divisions, 27, 32, 35
volksgrenadiers, 40
Volkswerferbrigaden (VWBs), 34, 35,
250

Wadehn, Walther, 27
Wagener, Carl, 41, 173, 201, 401n46
Wahl, Goswin, 394n13
Wainright, Jonathan M., 142
Waldenburg, Siegfried von, 29–30,
67
Walker, Maj. Gen. Walton H., 83, 86,
92, 97, 113, 120, 232, 300
Wallace, Col. Brenton G., 94–95,
377n33
Wallace, Maj. Warrack, 78
War as I Knew It (Patton), 86, 106,
170, 309, 381–82n35
Ward, Maj. Gen. Orlando, 144
Warnach, 166
Weber, Alois, 207